RESCUED FROM THE NATION

BUDDHISM AND MODERNITY

A series edited by Donald S. Lopez Jr.

Recent Books in the Series

Grains of Gold: Tales of a Cosmopolitan Traveler by Gendun Chopel, translated by Thupten Jinpa and Donald S. Lopez Jr. (2014)

Religious Bodies Politic: Rituals of Sovereignty in Buryat Buddhism by Anya Bernstein (2013)

The Birth of Insight: Meditation, Modern Buddhism, and the Burmese Monk Ledi Sayadaw by Erik Braun (2013)

From Stone to Flesh: A Short History of the Buddha by Donald S. Lopez Jr. (2013)

The Museum on the Roof of the World: Art, Politics, and the Representation of Tibet by Clare E. Harris (2012)

RESCUED FROM THE NATION

Anagarika Dharmapala and the Buddhist World

STEVEN KEMPER

THE UNIVERSITY OF CHICAGO PRESS

CHICAGO AND LONDON

STEVEN KEMPER is the Charles A. Dana Professor of Anthropology at Bates College and the author of *The Presence of the Past* and *Buying and Believing*, the latter also published by the University of Chicago Press.

The University of Chicago Press, Chicago 60637
The University of Chicago Press, Ltd., London
© 2015 by The University of Chicago
All rights reserved. Published 2015.
Printed in the United States of America

24 23 22 21 20 19 18 17 16 15   1 2 3 4 5

ISBN-13: 978-0-226-19907-8 (cloth)
ISBN-13: 978-0-226-19910-8 (e-book)
DOI: 10.7208/chicago/9780226199108.001.0001

Library of Congress Cataloging-in-Publication Data

Kemper, Steven, 1944– author.
    Rescued from the nation : Anagarika Dharmapala and the Buddhist world / Steven Kemper.
        pages cm — (Buddhism and modernity)
    Includes bibliographical references and index.
    ISBN 978-0-226-19907-8 (cloth : alkaline paper) — ISBN 0-226-19907-X (cloth : alkaline paper) — ISBN 978-0-226-19910-8 (e-book) — ISBN 0-226-19910-X (e-book)
    1. Dharmapala, Anagarika, 1864–1933. 2. Buddhist monks—Sri Lanka—Biography.
I. Title. II. Series: Buddhism and modernity.
    BQ950.H37K46 2015
    294.3092—dc23
    [B]
                                                                2014028190

⊗ This paper meets the requirements of ANSI/NISO Z39.48-1992 (Permanence of Paper).

For Anne, Jordan and Baylor, Miles and Max,
Shannon and Scott, and Jessica and Inacio

CONTENTS

PREFACE

I am indebted to many people, but I want to acknowledge an institution straightaway. I can say it simply. Bates College has made my scholarly life possible. I am appreciative of the endless forms that support has taken. I also owe thanks for the support of the Dana Foundation and the Freeman Foundation, which made several of my research trips to South Asia, Japan, and London possible.

Several decades ago I played a small part in hiring John Strong at Bates. My support was not meant to be self-serving, but there is a lot to be said for having a Buddhologist among Buddhologists at arm's reach, willing to hear my questions and investigate. His responses did a lot more than provide answers. They educated me.

I have also been the beneficiary of the kindness of Dennis McGilvray, John Rogers, Frank Reynolds, Richard Jaffe, Danny Danforth, Michael Aung-Thwin, Val Daniel, and Ian Copeland, who read the manuscript and tried to steer me right. Anne Blackburn, Sarah Strong, Gananath Obeyesekere, H. L. Seneviratne, Prasenajit Duara, and Alan Trevithick gave me invaluable advice along the way. Alan made me aware of notebooks residing at the Dharmapala library in Sarnath, and that was no small gift. In Tokyo Yuko Eguchi guided me through the Diet Library and Gakushuin University. Her translations of Japanese texts give the impression that I know more of Japan than I do, and I appreciate both the illusion making and the great kindness she and her family showed me in both Japan and this country. Soon after I arrived, Ishii Kosei took me out to dinner, shared his knowledge of Dharmapala, and then out of the blue gave me photocopies of Japanese sources on Dharmapala. Another gift I did not deserve.

After I finished the manuscript, I came across two articles on Dharmapala and found the authors, Michael Roberts and Stephen Prothero, saying

ix

things that I had concluded myself. My first reaction to both discoveries was to cite the author and leave it at that. My second thought was to leave the order of discovery as it had happened as evidence that there might be something to the assertions I make in this book. In any case, I want to recognize my two colleagues for what I take to be insights and acknowledge them both.

Sylvia Hawks has provided a lifetime of secretarial skill essential to the making of books, and I am deeply appreciative. At Sarnath Noel Salmond produced an annotated bibliography to Dharmapala's notebooks, which has helped everyone who has used it. It made my life easier. So did the resident bhikkhu Kahawatte Siri Sumedha, who made the Dharmapala library available to me. George Tanabe and Michael Aung-Thwin gave me wise counsel in Hawaii, as did Kikyu Tanaka, Yuichiro Tanaka, and Kosaku Yoshino in Tokyo. I have presented parts of the argument at seminars at Boston University, the University of Hawaii, the University of Pennsylvania, the National University of Singapore, Columbia University, and the Second China-India International Cultural Forum in New Delhi, and I have learned from each of those occasions. Finally, I thank Banagalla Upatissa, who hosted me in Japan and Sri Lanka, fed me, swept me along with him into the presidential compound in Colombo, made it possible for me to make images of Dharmapala's diaries, and introduced me to Ven. Siri Sumedha, who graciously allowed me to make images of the notebooks.

I did not intend for this book to be an intervention, and I do not know whether anyone will read it as such. I undertook the project because of my sense that Dharmapala had to be more than a reformer and ethnic chauvinist. Portraying the man in full will antagonize people who want to hold on to the bowdlerized Dharmapala. It would be gratifying if the Dharmapala who emerges in these pages had some effect on the degraded relationships of Sri Lanka's peoples. Whether that happens or not, I am encouraged by the Sinhalas, Tamils, and Muslims who helped me. Their kindness makes it possible to contemplate a future where academic work has some influence on prejudice and misunderstanding.

In rereading these pages, I am struck by how often the pronoun "I" appears, when my intention has been to make others more visible, not my relationship to them. Blame the logic of exposition. William Carlos Williams's aphorism—"No ideas but in things"—speaks as much to anthropologists as poets, but access to things depends on people. My thanks to everyone who cleared the way.

World Renunciation in
a Nineteenth-Century World

At the center of this book lies a historical moment—the late nineteenth and early twentieth centuries—marked by the efflorescence of new forms of universalism, the upswing of European and New World nationalisms, and early signs of nationalist movements in colonies held by European powers. In this context, human beings were pulled in opposite directions—away from local sources of identity by the forces of universalism and toward nearby ones shaped by the nationalist imagination. Consider Rabindranath Tagore's career as a poet committed to universalist values, Asian solidarity, and cultural exchange. When he won the Nobel Prize for Literature in 1913, little of his poetry had been translated into English, but non-Bengali readers knew him as a poet of soaring idealism and properly Indian thoughts about the unity of humankind. Three years later, on his way to the United States, he stopped in Japan and was greeted as more than a hero. He was an Asian hero and likely a man who recognized the need for national identity and reform. Some twenty thousand people met him when he arrived at Tokyo Station. While in Japan he gave several speeches excoriating the evils of nationalism and then sailed on to the United States. On his way home, he stopped again in Japan and was greeted by two people.[1] An age when some Asians were beginning to think of broader forms of community was equally an age when other Asians had a hard time even making sense of the idea. In 1879 Edwin Arnold's *The Light of Asia* gained a worldwide following for its retelling of the Buddha's life as an epic poem. Translated into Japanese, *The Light of Asia* became *The Sun Rises.*[2]

---

1. Rustom Bharucha, *Another Asia: Rabindranath Tagore and Okakura Tenshin* (Oxford: Oxford University Press, 2006), 7.

2. To be more precise, in the 1920s Japanese Buddhists composed a hymn based on *The Light of Asia*, the title of which translates as " the sun rises" or " sunrise comes." Judith Snod-

What Kant meant by universalism is the proposition that a human being's highest obligation belongs to humankind as such.[3] When an actor must
make a choice, Kant argued, he should favor the universal over the local.
The absolutism of Kant's definition duly noted, there are less absolute ways
of thinking about universalism, as well as a large number of historical examples of universalizing movements. To the extent that they incorporated
individuals categorized as "outsiders" and recategorized them as "insiders,"
the world's twenty-odd civilizations qualify as universalizing, as do the religions that spread over great stretches of the world—Islam, Christianity, and
Buddhism. I will use the expressions "universalist" or "universalizing" to
refer to a social movement that transcends local identities and incorporates
different kinds of people in the same project, settling for inclusion that falls
short of the Kantian extreme.

My interest in universalism derives from its being nationalism's binary opposite. As one particularism among many, nationalism rests on an
identity defined as commensurate with other identities, and that identity
does not appear as such without the existence of an encompassing universalism in the form of "the total ground that constitutes the differences as
differences."[4] Universalisms come in various forms, but two are pertinent
here—the religious and the civilizational—and their allure derives from
their kinship to our common humanity, rationality, and the very possibility
of seeing others in ourselves (or as ourselves or in lieu of ourselves). Most
universalisms benefit from a good press, the more so when compared to the
inferiority and danger of the particularisms, giving force to the notion that
particularity corrupts the universal. But any survey of real-world universalisms exposes their own corruptions. Its appeals as trope or value duly noted,
"civilization," once unpacked, turned out to be European civilization, another particularism dressed up as a universal. The same could be said of modernity or socialism. Putting aside the allure of the universal, I will use the
expression without worrying about definitional issues, assuming only that
universalisms are social movements that transcend local identities.

In what follows I want to pursue the historical realization of a universalizing movement in the life of a Buddhist reformer whose life has seldom

3. Immanuel Kant, "Towards Perpetual Peace," especially 105–8, and "The Metaphysics of
Morals," 132–6, in *Kant's Political Writings*, ed. Hans Reiss (Cambridge: Cambridge University
Press, 1970).

4. Ernesto Laclau, "Universalism, Particularism, and the Question of Identity," *October* 61
(1992): 84.

been associated with bringing together different sorts of people. Anagarika Dharmapala (1864–1933) was a spokesman for reviving Sinhala (Sri Lanka's dominant ethnic group) pride and reforming the island's traditional religion, Buddhism. For Sinhala Buddhists, he has become the figure that countered the effects of three hundred years of colonial domination and missionary effort. During his lifetime his uncompromising temperament made him his share of enemies, but his beatification began before he died in 1933. When his ashes were brought back to Colombo, they were carried in a miniature casket raised above the head of a senior monk, leading a procession of many thousands, itself made up of smaller processions of Buddhists from across the island.[5] The procession led from the Fort Railway Station to Maha Bodhi headquarters—a journey of some two miles—the procession itself stretching half that distance. Cries of "sadha, sadhu, saaa" were raised as the procession advanced. The late president Ranasinghe Premadasa remembered attending as a student, having been asked to "come bare-footed to participate in the function as a mark of respect."[6] These are gestures usually reserved for the Buddhist monkhood, membership in which requires the president of Sri Lanka or the king of Thailand to show respect to the youngest initiate.

Dharmapala's status has grown over the years. His birthday is remembered with celebrations across the island. There were six processions on that occasion reaching Colombo by 1964; by 1979 the island had twelve statues of Dharmapala; and nowadays there are several streets named after him in Colombo and others in Anuradhapura, Galle, Matara, and Kandy.[7] Speeches given at Dharmapala's birthday celebration at Maha Bodhi Society headquarters—the organization he founded in 1891—suggest why people take him seriously. In 1986 Hedigalle Pannatissa said "that there would be no Sinhala Buddhists today if not for the Anagarika . . . and that Buddhism in this country would survive only if the Maha Bodhi Society survives."[8] He was followed by Akuretiye Amarawansa, who described Anagarika as a *bodhisatta* (a person who strives to become an enlightened being, such as

5. "The Late Ven. Dhammapala," *Ceylon Daily News*, May 15, 1933.

6. A. S. Fernando, " Anagarika Dedicated His Life to Serve Entire Mankind," *Sunday Observer*, June 2, 1991.

7. "Six Processions for Dharmapala Meeting Today," *Ceylon Observer*, September 13, 1964; "Anagarika Dharmapala Remembered," *Ceylon Daily News*, September 29, 1979; Kahawatte Siri Sumedha, *Anagarika Dharmapala: A Glorious Life Dedicated to the Cause of Buddhism* (Varanasi: Maha Bodhi Society of India, 1999), 36.

8. "Anagarika Would Doubt Sincerity of Those Who Praise Him," *Ceylon Daily News*, September 19, 1986.

the Lord Buddha). The Indian high commissioner summed it up, saying that Dharmapala was

> a Jeffersonian persona of the East . . . scholar, nationalist, first a lay Buddhist preacher, then a Buddhist monk, a founding father of Sinhala education . . . [and] nationalist journalism . . . who singlehandedly restored a sense of dignity and self-respect to the people of Sri Lanka about their own past and gave them confidence about the future.

The high commissioner's words of appreciation have not kept others from trying to rescue Dharmapala from misunderstanding and neglect. Gunadasa Amerasekera's *Dharmapala Marksvadida?* (Was Dharmapala a Marxist?) sets the record straight. Even half a century after his death

> the masses and scholars have no clear idea of the services rendered by him. There are several reasons for this. . . . Every political party in this country has ignored and tried to forget him. . . . Sri Lankans influenced by colonial practices and their descendants brought to the public a view of Dharmapala that suited their purposes. . . . The historians who rose from the colonial class added no small injury to Dharmapala. . . . Lankan historians have completely forgotten him.[9]

In popular accounts, he more often appears as a transformative figure become a saint.[10]

Dharmapala's mythologized status in the Sinhala public sphere makes him a figure not to be criticized. In a paper read at the International Center for Ethnic Studies in Colombo in 1998, Michael Roberts drew on the early diaries to suggest that Dharmapala "continuously battled with his sexual urges which came into serious conflict with his goal."[11] In the hubbub that followed, a member of Parliament delivered a speech calling for an investigation into Roberts's "smear campaign."[12] The MP had served as vice chancellor of Sri Jayewardenepura University and did not question Roberts's research. What he questioned was why the article "with many negative references to the Anagarika" appeared in a state-owned newspaper

---

9. Gunadasa Amerasekera, *Dharmapala Marksvadida?* (Colombo: M. D. Gunasena, 1980), 2. Amerasekera's target is the Catholic historian G. C. Mendis.

10. "Dharmapala and the National Identity," *Divaina*, September 17, 1993.

11. "Dharmapala Battled His Sexual Urges," *Sunday Observer*, September 20, 1998.

12. "MP Seeks Probe over Defamation of Anagarika," *Sunday Times*, October 4, 1998.

and "whether the Sri Lankan identity and Sinhala culture had become bad words to the Lake House [the newspaper's publisher] hierarchy." In the 1920s Lake House regularly pummeled Dharmapala. In the 1990s a member of Parliament wanted Lake House investigated for an article that treated him as a human being.

Amerasekera's anxieties about Dharmapala's being neglected duly noted, no one writes about modern Sri Lanka without writing about Dharmapala, and his historical contributions are more likely to be overstated than undervalued. He was, according to K. M. de Silva, among the first to advocate *svaraj*, or national independence, seeing full well the political potential of the Buddhist resurgence.[13] Others make Dharmapala function as a placeholder, an ancestor to invoke, recall, and invent for the sake of explaining contemporary events:

> Michael Roberts has said that Wijeweera [the leader of the 1971 insurrection in Sri Lanka] is a progeny of Anagarika Dharmapala. Gamini Keerawelle has asserted that the JVP [Wijeweera's political party] is a continuation of the political tendency initiated by Dharmapala and John de Silva.[14]

Richard Gombrich and Gananath Obeyesekere associate his name with a new way of practicing an old religion, Protestant Buddhism, arguing that the hybridized values and practices associated with Dharmapala (and his mentor, the Theosophist Henry Steel Olcott) shaped the expansion of bourgeois values as they spread through villages and provincial towns during the first half of the twentieth century.[15] S. J. Tambiah and H. L. Seneviratne look upon his career as giving shape to the virulent nature of contemporary Sri Lankan politics.[16] Tambiah points out that Dharmapala's journalism joined Buddhism to Sinhala ethnic identity and constructed that identity as a racial one. Seneviratne writes that he gave rise to a tradition of Dharmapalite monks, linking those monks in turn to the estrangement among Sinhalas, Tamils, and Muslims that now motivates the island's politics.

---

13. K. M. de Silva, *A History of Sri Lanka* (Delhi: Oxford University Press, 1981), 377.

14. C. A. Chandraprema, "The J.V.P. and Gunadasa Amarasekera: Two Sinhala Buddhist Tendencies," *Lanka Guardian* 11 (1988): 15 and 24 at 15.

15. Richard Gombrich and Gananath Obeyesekere, *Buddhism Transformed: Religious Change in Sri Lanka* (Princeton, NJ: Princeton University Press, 1988), 207–18.

16. See, for instance, S. J. Tambiah, *Buddhism Betrayed: Religion, Politics, and Violence in Sri Lanka* (Chicago: University of Chicago Press, 1992), 131; and H. L. Seneviratne, *The Work of Kings: The New Buddhism in Sri Lanka* (Chicago: University of Chicago Press, 1999).

Much is overlooked in these accounts. Even though Dharmapala was the leading figure in the emergence of Sinhala nationalism, he spent most of his life living outside Lanka. He lived the great majority of his adult years in Calcutta and London. The man who took the title *anagarika* (homeless) purchased, worried over, and lived in a number of residences.[17] But it is equally true that he was frequently away from whatever place he was then calling home. He traveled around the world in 1889, 1896, 1902, 1913, and 1925–6; visited Japan on four occasions; and made tours of Akyab (1892), Shanghai (1894), Siam (1894), north India (1899 and 1923), London (1904), Hawaii (1913), China, Korea, and Borobudur (1913). In 1925 and 1926 he toured Europe and the United States, before spending considerable time in London, where he established the first Buddhist temple in Europe. In these contexts he associated himself with clerics, Theosophists, scholars, and a steady stream of well-to-do Westerners, usually female and interested in Asian spirituality. Nor did his days end in Lanka. When he returned from Europe at the end of his life, he settled not in Colombo but in North India near a temple he built to celebrate the place where the Buddha preached his first sermon. To the extent that he spent most of his life away from the island, he was homeless in a sense of the word not usually intended.

Between the time he found a place to live in Calcutta in 1892 and his final move to Sarnath in 1931, he returned to Sri Lanka some twenty-five times. (Because the text that follows does not proceed chronologically, readers may want to consult Appendix 2 to get a sense of Dharmapala's life as it unfolded.) A number of visits were brief sojourns (a visit home on his way to somewhere else), most lasted for a few months, and three kept him in the island for about a year. On those visits he established and managed schools, hospitals, and seminaries and made tours through the villages of Sri Lanka in an oxcart or lorry that he had rebuilt to serve as a camping car. He established a school just outside Colombo to teach volunteers the skills of self-reflection and missionary work. He gave a series of fiery speeches. He campaigned against beef eating. He purchased land and started a rubber estate and weaving school in Hiniduma, his father's native place. The newspaper he established in 1906, the *Sinhala Bauddhaya*, spoke directly to readers about these projects (as opposed to the more cosmopolitan content of the journals he published abroad). He wrote a regular column for the *Bauddhaya*, Karunu Denagatuyutu (Things you should know), addressing

---

17. In 1930 Dharmapala transferred eleven pieces of property to the Anagarika Dharmapala Trust. Sinha Ratnatunga, *They Turned the Tide: The 100 Year History of the Maha Bodhi Society of Sri Lanka* (Colombo: Government Press, 1991), 134.

readers in a way that was by turns inspirational, informative, and hectoring. Even though the great majority of those articles were written in Calcutta or London, most addressed his Sinhala readers about local affairs and conveyed his insistence that Buddhists live up to his standards.

Dharmapala's universalizing mission depended on the historical moment. Steamships and trains made traveling long distances practical, the printing press allowed him to distribute his ideas widely, and an international postal system allowed him to do so quickly.[18] Wherever he happened to be residing, he was able to send forth not only the weekly *Sinhala Bauddhaya* articles, regular contributions to the *Journal of the Maha Bodhi Society and the United Buddhist World*, and the English-language newspaper he established in 1911 but also a prolific stream of letters to supporters, newspaper editors, and colonial officials. He lived a life of few possessions. He wore his robes and underclothes until they were tattered. He cut his own hair. His eyeglasses broke, and he decided not to replace them. His one indulgence was fountain pens, which he purchased frequently and gave away just as often. When the typewriter became available, he became an early adopter. Before he constructed his camping car, he made preaching tours of the villages of Lanka, traveling by oxcart. The cart had uses beyond transport. At night he mounted a gramophone and magic lantern on it and projected images on a bedsheet of sacred places in India, Burma, Japan, and other parts of the island of Sri Lanka, talking to people about his travels to Buddhist places as well as Europe and America.[19] After the show, he slept in the cart.

In India Dharmapala pursued projects with enthusiasm at least equal to that of his work at home—recovering the place in North India where the Buddha had his enlightenment, building a temple at the place where he preached his first sermon and another temple in Calcutta, establishing a movement to restore the *sasana* (the Buddha's teaching and its institutional context) to India. In these contexts, he associated with elite Bengalis who were intellectually drawn to Buddhism and congenial to Dharmapala because of their common ties to the Theosophical Society. His challenge was convincing Bengalis who had no intention of becoming Buddhists to

---

18. Mark Frost, "'Wider Opportunities': Religious Revival, Nationalist Awakening and the Global Dimension in Colombo, 1870–1920," *Modern Asian Studies* 36 (2002): 937–67.

19. "Anagarika Dharmapala," *Journal of the Maha Bodhi Society and the United Buddhist World* 14 (1906): 126. At the end of his 1892 diary, Dharmapala made a list of "magic lantern slides" he showed in village settings. The majority show the Bodh Gaya temple, but he also screened images of Hindu ascetics, a funeral pyre, Indian convicts, a Bengali wedding ceremony, an Indian *darbar* (council), the Jain temple in Calcutta, and Lord Elgin and his suite.

support a specifically Buddhist cause. The moment was favorable to Bengalis taking an interest in a religion not their own, but it was only a moment. In Calcutta he established the *Journal of the Maha Bodhi Society and the United Buddhist World*, the title announcing his hopes for drawing Buddhists into a pan-Asian community linked to supporters in Europe and America (Calcutta itself was not home to any Buddhist community except for a small number of Arakanese and Chinese). The journal was almost entirely his own operation—he wrote many of the articles, solicited and edited the others. He used it for his purposes: shaping Buddhist opinion worldwide, publicizing his views, criticizing his enemies, publishing articles by Western scholars on the array of Buddhisms next to news of the British Empire and marriages in his own family. In a similar way, the Maha Bodhi Society was his society, he its only full-time worker and the person who made ends meet.

The worldwide reach of the Maha Bodhi Society gave him a vehicle to pursue the great cause of his life, putting the weight of the world's Buddhists behind recovering Bodh Gaya, the place in North India where the Lord Buddha attained enlightenment. The sense of having lost a precious resource made the struggle poignant, and he sought redress in modern contexts—British colonial administrative and legal systems, newspapers, lectures he gave on his travels, and the salons of well-to-do people he met in the West. In the Bodh Gaya case Buddhists took the offensive, putting a group of Saivite world renouncers on notice that Buddhists would no longer tolerate the old accommodation. Despite British sympathy for the Buddhist cause, the legal issue was straightforward. The Saivites held a deed to the place. The struggle spilled outside the courtroom, serving to define two religious communities, Hindu and Buddhist. In other parts of India a set of interlinked, continent-wide Hindu pilgrimage sites have served not only to rally a religious community to a cause. Such struggles have allowed Indians of different kinds to see themselves as Hindus, insisting that a sacred space now in the hands of a cruel and demonic other must be returned to its rightful owners.[20] The struggle for Bodh Gaya had wider implications, inserting non-Indian Buddhists into Indian affairs. That intervention was still more consequential because it came at a time of diplomatic tension among Britain, China, and Japan.

Returning Buddhist attention to Bodh Gaya was poetic because it was the place from which Buddhism had begun and spread across Asia. But now

---

20. Sheldon Pollock, "Ramayana and Political Imagination in India," *Journal of Asian Studies* 52, no. 2 (1993): 261–97.

that place belonged to the Hindu other. The initial diffusion of Buddhism across Asia began some two hundred years BCE and ran to the thirteenth century CE or so, creating the landscape of Asia before the colonial period. Benedict Anderson speaks of the effects of certain religions—Christianity and Islam are his chief examples—as universalisms that played similar roles around the world. He calls them "great transcontinental sodalities," linking people in far-flung places in communities that were held together by a script language offering access to the highest truths, sacred sites and kings who ruled by divine warrant, and a sense of temporality that merged history and cosmology.[21] The diffusion of Buddhism meant that since early in the Common Era there had been a community of Buddhists—their considerable differences duly noted—spanning South and East Asia. These communities were more notional than administrative, but displacing these identities from people's minds, Anderson says, was essential to making space for the nineteenth-century rise of the nation-state.[22]

For reasons that are more historical than philosophical, nationalism complicated Dharmapala's universalizing project. As Lanka's leading nationalist campaigned to create a united Buddhist world, he needed to gain the cooperation of people themselves energized and reshaped by nationalist feelings. His challenges included not only nationalism but also the proliferation of other universalisms. To make a united Buddhist world Dharmapala had to engage with the British imperium, Theosophy, Christianity, and Western civilization. Each interacted with Dharmapala's own universalizing project, but I will concentrate on Theosophy and the British Empire in successive chapters, not ignoring Christianity and Western civilization altogether, but seeing both in their relationship to Theosophy and empire. My goal is to lay out the interaction of these contrary forces. Seeing Dharmapala only in a Sri Lankan context has led to his life's being misconstrued

---

21. Benedict Anderson, *Imagined Communities: Reflections on the Origin and Spread of Nationalism* (London: Verso, 1983), 40.

22. Gombrich has argued against calling the premodern Buddhist world a social formation, even a notional one. His view is that Buddhism's lack of interest in civilizational matters and disregard for exclusive allegiance meant that there was no Buddhist world save what little coherence the monkhood as a transcontinental institution provided. "The Buddhist Way," in *The World of Buddhism*, ed. Heinz Bechert and Richard Gombrich (London: Thames and Hudson, 1984), 9–14. An account of Buddhism that neither hypostatizes the tradition nor reduces it to what the Buddha taught can be found in Frank E. Reynolds and Charles Hallisey, "Buddhism," in *Encyclopedia of Religion*, ed. Lindsay Jones, 2nd ed. (Detroit: Thomson/Gale, 2005), 1087–1101. I prefer to think of early Buddhism as a social formation held together by civilizational practices, such as the importance of Asokan kingship, as well as traffic in relics, ordination traditions, monks, texts, and artistic forms.

by scholars and nationalists alike. But the antidote is not assuming that locating Dharmapala outside of Sri Lanka allows us access to his universalism. The antidote involves recognizing that he negotiated a variety of universalisms and particularisms both in Sri Lanka and beyond. Understanding Dharmapala outside of Sri Lanka does not give us a different Dharmapala. It simply gives us more Dharmapala.

When the nation-state became a worldwide phenomenon in the nineteenth century, new nations developed against the background of these universalisms. The spread of the national idea was modular and reiterative, emergent nations imitating the older ones, dividing the landscape into relatively smaller social units, typically bound together by a common language and the idea that citizens shared a common identity, usually ethnic or religious. Anderson's argument to the contrary, the rise of nationalism did not altogether displace these older forms of community.[23] It simply complicated them. Since the First World War, for instance, universalism called people to identities and practices that made distinctions among nation-states ("We [the citizens of Japan or Turkey, to cite well-known cases] are now civilized and deserve equality with Western nations") or that functioned both beyond and within the nation-state ("We are reformed Hindus, brothers and sisters to our coreligionists in India, but equally much Indonesians"). The immediate issue is how a Buddhism of universal aspirations was joined to the Buddhism of national identity. Did any Buddhist ever say, "We are Sinhala patriots, but also future members of an united Buddhist world"?

Practical problems beset the activist who assumes the role of nationalist at home and universalist abroad. One arises in respect to dealing with other kinds of people. "What distinguishes the civilizational idea from nationalism," Prasenjit Duara writes, "is its appeal to a higher transcendent source of value and authority, capable of encompassing the Other."[24] The same definition works as well for "religion," assuming a distinction between what the word "transcendent" references in each instance. In the case of religion, the transcendent source "transcends" in the sense of emanating from, and resonating with, the ultimate conditions of existence. A civilization, by contrast, makes its claim to value and authority on a more worldly basis, transcendent in another sense and residing in this world, not the other. China offered outlying communities access to prestigious forms

23. I have made this argument more fully in *The Presence of the Past: Chronicles, Politics, and Culture in Sinhala Life* (Ithaca, NY: Cornell University Press, 1991).

24. "The Discourse of Civilization and Decolonization," *Journal of World History* 15 (2004): 2.

of value and identity with the adoption of Han practices for everyday behavior, ranging from ancestor veneration to eating with chopsticks. Buddhism provides an example of a religious universalism, spread by offering non-Buddhist communities access to practices of value and authority through venerating the founder, his teachings, and the monks who embodied his example. There is no reason why these two forms of universalist practice cannot be joined (or utilized by Western colonial regimes). The British colonial model came to combine both, legitimating rule over faraway societies in terms of a civilizational project that promised peace, protection of property rights, and religious freedom. As the nineteenth century went on, that project was joined to a religious one (in the form of the Christian faiths then being proselytized in the colonies).

The conflict between universalism and nationalism produced a clear winner. The nationalisms do not need to be named because they have given us the landscape of a world made of nation-states and revolutionary movements still struggling to forge their own. The nineteenth-century universalisms do not rush to mind, but there has been a full complement of examples—Esperanto, Baha'ism, vegetarianism, universal international arbitration, Theosophy, antivivisectionism, animal-rights campaigns, as well as other movements that worked against the grain of both nationalism and other localisms. The list has a quixotic quality, exacerbated by the decline of these movements' fortunes over the last century. If I add international labor, Marxist, socialist, anti-imperial and anarchist movements, the list of universalizing movements suddenly profits from including movements with larger influence joined to the same high ideals. What recommends all of these projects from the whimsical to the deadly earnest is neither politics nor its absence but their common commitment to reason, human dignity, social reform, and hope.[25] A disproportionate number emerged in the late nineteenth century.

Universalism has been further reshaped by another development, the rise of "world religions," and this notion has had effects on both the nation-state and processes that operate beyond it.[26] There were "religions of the

25. See Martha Nussbaum, "Kant and Cosmopolitanism," in *Perpetual Peace: Essays on Kant's Cosmopolitan Ideal*, ed. James Bohman and Matthias Lutz-Bachmann (Cambridge: MIT Press, 1997), 27.

26. In its original form, the expression appeared in German, referring to Christianity as the "uniquely universal" religion of Christ. As the taxonomic and pluralistic expression "world religions" developed, this Christian-monopolistic use of the term persisted. Tomoko Masuzawa, *The Invention of World Religions; or, How European Universalism Was Preserved in the Language of Pluralism* (Chicago: University of Chicago Press, 2005), 23.

world"—in the sense of great transcontinental sodalities—long before there were "world religions" according to Tomoko Masuzawa's definition. Her focus falls on "world religions" as a discursive formation by which religions were made commensurate. Because the commentators were typically Christians, they took their own religion as the paradigm, organizing (and often inventing) their knowledge of other traditions on a Christian matrix. A world religion naturally has a dogma or coherent set of beliefs. Its adherents bring an exclusive orientation to that religion. It is organized around sacred places and pilgrimage. But comparison itself had effects on both the study of religion and the missionary enterprise:

> One of the most consequential effects of this discourse is that it spiritualizes what are material practices and turns them into expressions of something timeless and suprahistorical, which is to say, it depoliticizes them.[27]

The Buddhism Dharmapala carried to India, other parts of Asia, and the West, was a world religion in just this sense. It was Buddhism spiritualized. That said, the depoliticizing effects of the "world religion" idiom hardly applied to his work at home. When he approached the Buddhism of his own people, he took it as anything but timeless. In the nineteenth century it had been driven to ruin by Christian missionaries and colonial domination, and the religion he struggled for in Lanka was a Buddhism remade politically and economically.

The commensuration of Asian religions had real-world advantages. Having Buddhism defined as a world religion and Southern Buddhism (which he came to represent) defined as distinct from Northern (embodied in the persons of several Japanese monks and laymen) got him invited to the World's Parliament of Religions—even though Theosophy was not. The occasion put a relatively young and underprepared layman in a position of equality with venerable figures. Many—Dharmapala, the Japanese Buddhist delegation, and Swami Vivekananda—would continue to encounter one another after the parliament. Commensuration produced a formal equality that was not realized in practice. The parliament's organizers were explicit about their motives:

> As any wise missionary in Bombay or Madras would be glad to gather beneath the shelter of his roof the scholarly and sincere representatives

27. Masuzawa, *Invention of World Religions*, 20.

of the Hindu religions, so Christian America invites to the shelter of her hospitable roof . . . the spiritual leaders of mankind . . . though light has no fellowship with darkness, light does have fellowship with twilight . . . and those who have the full light of the Cross should bear brotherly hearts toward all who grope in a dimmer illumination.[28]

As Masuzawa has argued, the parliament was the most spectacular expression of the comparative project applied to religion, preserving Western advantage in a language of pluralism.

Dharmapala learned a lot of what he knew about Buddhism from texts, most of which were written in English and the work of Western scholars.[29] From those texts he acquired a sense of Buddhism's structural congruence with Western religions. He read Ernest Eitel and learned that one European thought that Buddhist morality was second only to Christian;[30] he traveled to the Parliament of Religions with a copy of *The Light of Asia*, which provided him an account of the Buddha as a human being (Diary, August 3, 1893).[31] Arnold's treatment of the Buddha's greatness gave Dharmapala hope that he could engage Westerners from a position of equality. Even before he read *The Light of Asia*, he had read Arnold's *Return to India*, which described the ruination to which Bodh Gaya had fallen. In Western contexts he found a cause, representing Buddhism to the world at large and renew-

28. Walter R. Houghton, ed., *Neely's History of the Parliament of Religions and Religious Congresses at the World's Columbian Exposition* (Chicago: F. T. Neely, 1893), 28.

29. Gombrich writes that Dharmapala was perhaps the first Buddhist to learn meditation from a text. *Theravada Buddhism: A Social History from Ancient Benares to Modern Colombo* (London: Routledge, 1988), 189. It is true that he learned how to embody the *chela* role (the student of a Tibetan *mahatma*) from reading Blavatsky's "Chelas and Lay Chelas" (*Theosophist*, July 1882), and how to be a vegetarian from reading a vegetarian cookbook (Diary, August 12, 1925). Meditation, as it happened, he learned in person during the annual convention of the Theosophical Society in Adyar. As his diaries have it, "Woke at 3 a.m. & sat for a while in meditation. . . . Bro. S. Ramasamier of Chela fame came in the evening. . . . Ramasamier showed me how to sit in 'Siddhasana.' I saw at Mihintale two years ago a marble statue of the Buddha sitting in this posture. You sit in such a way as to shut the passages of the anus and the penis" (January 2, 1891). At the same meeting he "had a few instructions on Dhyana Bhavana from my Burmese friend" (January 9, 1891). The manual on dhyana meditation—to which Gombrich refers—he did not locate until 1893. So if we are to make any claim here, we might say that Dharmapala was the first Buddhist to learn meditation from Theosophists.

30. Ernest Eitel, *Buddhism: Its Historical, Theoretical and Popular Aspects* (London: Trübner, 1873), 64.

31. Edwin Arnold, *The Light of Asia; or, The Great Renunciation: The Life and Teaching of Gautama, Prince of India and Founder of Buddhism* (New York: A. L. Burt, 1879); The Diaries of Anagarika Dharmapala, typescript, 36 vols., Maha Bodhi Society, Colombo, Sri Lanka, hereafter cited parenthetically as "Diary" followed by specific dates. For more information about the form and content of the Diaries, see appendix 1.

ing it in the land where it originated. Every world religion had a sacred
center; Bodh Gaya was the Buddhist Mecca, but it belonged to a community
of Saivite renouncers. Returning the place to Buddhists would return Buddhism to India. The Buddhism Dharmapala wanted to install there would
be a universalized Buddhism. It would be neither sectarian nor national, its
universality enabled by remaining undefined.

The "world religioning" of Bodh Gaya had another effect, allowing
Dharmapala to ignore the fact that Bodh Gaya had functioned historically
as part of a set of political and economic formations. The place was embedded in those relationships when the Buddhists held it, and it came to be
embedded in a new set of relationships as Buddhists disappeared from India.
When the Tibetan Dharmasvamin reached Bodh Gaya in the thirteenth century, he found the shrine in disrepair and only a few monks living there.
The Buddhist presence soon disappeared altogether, and between 1590 and
1690 Saivite monks of the Dasanami order established a *math* (monastery)
at the place. In 1727 a Mughal prince gave the Saivites a deed to the temple
and its environs, and their rights from that point on were confirmed by the
kind of evidence—property rights established by a written document—that
the British thought counted. When Dharmapala first visited in 1891, the
place had been reembedded in a set of colonial political and economic arrangements, and in that formation the Saivites' rights were hard to deny.
The strangeness of the arrangement—the central place in the history of
Buddhism now controlled by Hindus—and the sympathy shown him by
Englishmen from Arnold to Lord Curzon made him downplay the Saivites'
legal advantages. Even the archeological office reconstruction of the place in
1883 gave him further reason for hope. The British knew the importance of
the place, and they would surely restore it to its rightful owners.

IMPERIAL CITIZENSHIP

Comparing one religion to another had benefits for religious actors as well
as scholars. For one thing, emphasizing a religion's spiritual content made it
available for missionizing. Even though Dharmapala was less of a missionary than he might have been, he characterized his work as missionizing,
and his plan was to station Buddhist monks in the temples he established.
He converted only two people in his lifetime, and when he spoke of returning Buddhism to India, he usually had in mind recovering Bodh Gaya, not
growing the number of Indian Buddhists. In the West he spoke of conversion as irrelevant to his mission. He understood Buddhism as an energetic,
expansive religion, but the mission consisted in *Dhammadana* (the gift of

Dhamma), putting the Buddha's teachings on offer, making them present in new parts of the world, not conversion itself.[32] From his perspective, what motivated both spreading the Dhamma and recovering Bodh Gaya derived from a sense that Buddhism was a "spiritual" tradition, ready to be carried to new places and logically the only tradition to belong at Bodh Gaya.

India's connection to a Buddhist past aside, the subcontinent was part of an empire, and that empire allowed Dharmapala to pursue his campaign in English and in tandem with Indian and British scholars, civil servants, and citizens of the Raj sympathetic to the religion.[33] Having a place in the empire gave him the possibility of claiming "a language (if not a status) of citizenship on the very virtue of its denial, [foregrounding] the imperial aegis as the basis for delineating universal ideals of citizenship."[34] The same double game—leveraging the rights of imperial subjects to conclusions the masters of empire would not countenance but that followed logically from those they would consider—was even more the case for Dharmapala when he moved to London in 1926 to share the Dhamma with the British. At its grandest, carrying Buddhism to the British put him in roles both civic and religious. He would carry Buddhism into the heart of the empire and show the British the kind of compassion they had not shown Buddhists and other people in the colonies. He imagined effects at a distance—having understood the Buddha's compassion, English Buddhists would no longer tolerate the brutal treatment of Buddhists in Lanka.

Sukanya Banerjee has argued that in Dharmapala's time the way elite Indians saw themselves as citizens of the empire was soon overwhelmed by the rise of Indian nationalism. To make the case, she investigates two autobiographical accounts, Surendranath Banerjea's *Nation in the Making* and Cornelia Sorabji's *India Calling*. Banerjea and Sorabji's memoirs articulated the universalist ideal of citizenship, moving their positions as

---

32. His disdain for conversion derived from his encounter with Christian teachers in the missionary schools he attended as a boy. There was a second constraint that must have occurred to him. A layperson such as himself could not administer the Three Refuges to anyone, and thus he could not convert anyone. Olcott traveled in the West with a heterodox, if official, warrant in the form of a certificate from Hikkaduve Sumangala and other leading monks, which authorized him to "register interested people" as Buddhists. C. V. Agarwal, *The Buddhist and Theosophical Movements, 1873–2001* (Calcutta: Maha Bodhi Society of India, 2001). Olcott's document, dated February 2, 1884, is reprinted as the endpaper of the book.

33. Philip Almond provides a persuasive account of the affinity between Buddhism and the Victorian imagination in *The British Discovery of Buddhism* (Cambridge: Cambridge University Press, 1988).

34. Sukanya Banerjee, *Becoming Imperial Citizens: Indians in Late-Victorian Empire* (Durham, NC: Duke University Press, 2010), 17.

subjects toward citizenship as a rights-bearing category. The moderate Bengali legislator framed citizenship in a parliamentary idiom, just as India's first female attorney (and the first Indian woman to study law at Oxford) spoke of vocational choice in a professional one. When Sorabji found her path to becoming an attorney blocked, she invoked her status as a citizen of the empire. However much both visions of imperial citizenship were supplanted by nationalist citizenship, Banerjee argues that more modest aspirations such as inclusion in the Indian civil service marked the beginning of nationalist political development. Her conclusion is pertinent. It was empire, "rather than a pre-existing prototype of the nation that generated a consciousness of the formal equality of citizenship."[35] The British set in motion contradictory aspirations—inclusion in the empire as equals and construction of colonies as prospective nation-states free from British domination.

If the British were able to make plausible a vision of equality and inclusion, they were equally good at inflicting prejudice and petty insult on the subjects of the empire who were most interested in citizenship and equality. Dharmapala's travels were regularly unsettled by confrontations with supercilious British civilians, civil servants, drunken soldiers, and unthinking travelers who treated him as a curiosity or inferior. Almost all of these incidents happened in India, many on trains or at train stations, or more generally as he traveled, converting impromptu opportunities for temporary solidarity and equality into moments of humiliation. There is no doubt that these incidents wounded him: in his diaries and notebooks he periodically wrote out lists of these encounters, always noting the severity of his response, which included throwing a Englishman's liquor bottle from a moving train on one occasion and pushing a person out of a compartment while the train stood in the station on another. The imperium was uneven and uncoordinated, its brutalities emerging irregularly from assumptions about the relationship of colonizers and colonized. Doris Lessing recalls the preposterousness of it all: "How very careless, how lazy, how indifferent the British Empire was, how lightly it took on vast countries and millions of people."[36] The counterpoint to lightness was those moments when the British encountered the people of their colonies—often well-to-do and traveling on trains or steamers—and misused them.

Banerjee argues that Dadabhai Naoroji's political critique, *Poverty and*

35. *Becoming Imperial Citizens*, 17.
36. Doris Lessing, *Walking in the Shade: Volume Two of My Autobiography, 1949–1962* (New York: HarperCollins, 1997), 209.

Un-British Rule in India, reveals another side of the paradox implicit in Dharmapala's project, that "the universal ideal of citizenship . . . chooses the particularized category of the nation-state to announce its universality."[37] Naoroji had a language to encompass both empire and its constituent parts. Conceiving of the empire as the body politic, Naoroji envisioned the body constituted of colonies, held together by the principles of classical political economy. In *Poverty and Un-British Rule in India*, he argued that Britain was draining India's wealth and thus bleeding it to death, moving repeatedly between the blood that sustained the body politic and the capital that sustained its economy. Banerjee points out that Naoroji was not hostile to the English presence in India. He endorsed it, and wanted that presence increased, urging the English to consider India their home, their interests brought into alignment with India's.[38] What he railed against were English people who behaved as "strangers" and "invaders."

The affinity between Naoroji and Dharmapala goes beyond their common response to British condescension. Both saw themselves as imperial citizens, Naoroji using the discourse of political economy to argue that draining the wealth of India was bad not only for the colony but also for the metropole. The exploitation of India had simultaneous effects in both places, threatening the metropole's financial position, its citizens' well-being, and the moral claims implicit in British identity—thus the title of Naoroji's book. What made the poverty of India a threat to the economic health of England was simply that the empire was a corporate entity. Prosperity, he argued, was key to the empire's health, and it depended on British sympathy for, and fellow feeling with, Indians. Dharmapala, by contrast, made his case for the body imperial by speaking in Buddhist terms, arguing for British sympathy as the foundation of Britain's own moral progress. Political economy, professionalism, bureaucracy, and travel from one part of the empire to another all carry the signs of rational modernity. Each context offers distinct rhetorical advantages for making claims to citizenship. South Asians fought for citizenship in many ways, and two South Asians—Gandhi and Dharmapala—found ways to use asceticism to assert the universalist ideal of citizenship.

In 1913 Dharmapala visited parts of China then under Japanese occupation. From Tientsin, he wrote to His Majesty George V, identifying himself as a Buddhist missionary "born in Ceylon, of Sinhala parents, working for the welfare of all Buddhists in Asia, especially Ceylon, and trying to

---

37. *Becoming Imperial Citizens*, 193.
38. *Becoming Imperial Citizens*, 53.

resuscitate Buddhism in India." In the balance of the letter, he developed themes familiar from his public addresses as well as articles in the *Journal of the Maha Bodhi Society* and the *Sinhala Bauddhaya*: The "Government pass[es] such laws as are prejudicial to the progress of the people," destroying local education in favor of vernacular schools, drawing tax revenue from the liquor trade that profits only the British officials, helping British colonials while the "sons of the soil" are treated as "aborigines and savages." The legislation of Governor Sir West Ridgeway's administration took land from villagers and left them "wandering as vagrants." The government takes revenue from the people but does not give: "There are no technical schools, no industrial schools, no agricultural schools, no weaving schools, and this after 100 years of British rule!" His arguments were well meant if not always politically astute. He concluded with a reference to the proper use of colonial possessions: "Japan is showing what a civilized nation could accomplish in colonies. Formosa and Korea are instances," making the case for the leading Asian example of "civilization."[39]

Once Dharmapala is removed from the national context, "civilization" comes into view as a central idea in understanding his life's work. Where Buddhism distinguished Sinhalas from Christians—British and Sri Lankan alike—civilization gave Buddhists a claim to equality with the British. Civilization united the metropole and the colony and made them commensurate. The British had their civilization, and Sinhala Buddhists had theirs, even if now fallen into disrepair.

Dharmapala portrayed the imperium by tying everything together in the person of the king:

> The Sinhalese are a loyal people and they are absolutely loyal to your Majesty. But it is not to be expected that the Sinhalese will see in every Englishman in Ceylon the personality of the King, and this is what every white man that hails from a British colony or from Great Britain expects from the native Sinhalese.[40]

In quick order, Dharmapala moved from the body politic as worldwide political and economic formation, an array of colonies being sucked dry by taxation and land appropriation without reciprocity, to the colony in terms of either education or sympathy. Leaving the imperial formation behind,

---

39. British National Archives, CO/54/768/33250, September 24, 1913.
40. Ibid., CO/54/768/33250, 1913.

he reduced colonial relations to three persons—the king, Sinhalas, and the Englishmen they see in lieu of the king. Looking upon the king, those subjects feel absolute loyalty. They simply cannot feel the same affection for the local official who thinks he is king. Those officials have insulted Sinhalas by taking them for savages, denying the kind of education that they most need (and that the West—Dharmapala is thinking of America and Japan—can provide), and corrupting them with the arrack shops that supply the empire with tax revenue, while leaving the locals destitute.

Dealing with the monarchy, Dharmapala spoke as subject, not citizen. He insisted on his loyalty, which he demonstrated by conferring face to face with colonial officials, offering unsolicited advice by mail, sending the secretary of state for the colonies a copy of his booklet *The Arya Dharma*, and lending the empire financial support—buying war bonds during the First World War, donating his own money to the war effort, adding substantial amounts of Maha Bodhi funds, and making donations of cloth for flood relief. Just as often he approached the colonial state with a petition, writing to an array of British officials, from local administrators to the governor in Lanka, local magistrates to the viceroy in India, and the secretary of state for the colonies and King George back in England. While in Calcutta he wrote to colonial officials about the 1915 riots in Lanka, sending three petitions to Whitehall and asking for an independent commission to look into the incident. The administrative cover page to the letter in the Colonial Office lays out a bureaucrat's response to his petition: "This scoundrel is suspected of being more responsible for the riots than anybody else."[41] Whatever influence Dharmapala exerted on the riots, it was indirect because he had left the island a year earlier.

When he spoke to Sinhala audiences, he was usually contemptuous of the British, but his official letters were courteous and expressed loyalty to the empire. Colonial officials misread his intentions, he insisted, in the same way they had misread the character of the 1915 riots:

The riots in Ceylon had no political bearing. It was religious. But the causes have not been traced as yet, why such a loyal people as the Sinhalese have been after a hundred years of settled government, that they should throughout the Island rise against only a particular community should be soberly inquired into.[42]

41. Ibid., CO/54/791/39771, August 28, 1915.
42. Ibid., CO/54/791/35095, July 30, 1915.

In 1915 British officials had suspicions about his connections to Germans and Japanese (and in one case to the Russians). Dharmapala saw those relationships as religious—he had written to a Russian official trying to locate a Buryat lama. As he traveled to places such as Japan, he met the usual collection of foreigners with social causes, usually associated with religion. British intelligence gathering on him was unreliable, but it discovered that he met the Indian revolutionary figure Mohammed Barakatullah in Japan. Dharmapala was fully aware of, and put off by, Barakatullah's efforts to spread Islam in Japan. But his reaction to the man derived from his feeling that Islam was "unsuited to civilized people," not Barakatullah's revolutionary aspirations.[43]

Dharmapala had little feel for the ways his associations (not to mention his writings in the *Sinhala Bauddhaya* and his speeches) might be construed. He assumed that British suspicions about his loyalty were brought on by an article he wrote in the *Sinhala Bauddhaya* questioning the chastity of British women (Sarnath Notebook no. 23, Diary for 1918).[44] He did not use the word *citizen*, but he identified with the empire, making reference in World War I to "our losses in the Dardanelles, " putting the figure at "87,650 up to August 21, 1915" (Sarnath Notebook no. 53). Being part of the empire was only one rationale for his presumption. His condemnation of British rule was moral, motivated by a practice independent of both subjecthood and citizenship. He thought his asceticism and high aspirations gave him grounds for criticism, and his status as a world renouncer allowed him to criticize not just bureaucrats and British rule but everyone (Sarnath Notebook no. 53, September 6, 1915):

> My comfort is the Buddha, His Dhamma, and the Holy Ones. The British in Ceylon resent criticism, they do not want that we should criticize them. Since 1896 I am criticized, the Sinhalese resented my criticism and attacked me. The Christians have been always against me. The Cey-

---

43. "Islam in Japan," *Journal of the Maha Bodhi Society* 19 (1911): 28–30, at 29.

44. "1900 June at Chittagong. I had written an article for the Bauddhaya condemning the habits of the European women. This gave offense to the European community. This was before the war. The whole European community rose up in arms, and the Govt of Ceylon prosecuted the printer of the paper and he was sentenced to 3 months imprisonment. My mother advised me not to return to Ceylon for 2 years." The Notebooks of Anagarika Dharmapala, manuscript, 58 vols., Dharmapala Museum, Sarnath, India. Hereafter cited parenthetically as Sarnath Notebook followed by notebook number. For more information about the form and content of the Notebooks, see appendix 1.

lon papers have attacked me, Burmese, Arakanese. Siamese, Japanese, Bangalese [sic] have followed suit. The bureaucrats are angry. They wish to see me hanged.[45]

He could have mentioned more targets—his own family, all of his associates, and the Buddhist monkhood.

In a town near Kandy he offered a rationale for criticizing the British Crown that followed the logic of citizenship. He had seen a working-class European in the audience when he preached earlier that day, and the man stopped him at the train station, insisting that he should not criticize the British. He responded that he was the loyal opposition, trying to do for Sinhalas what Lloyd George had done for the Welsh.[46] His diaries paraphrase that same sentiment throughout the first two decades of the twentieth century (which was the period when his loyalty was most at issue). As he wrote the attorney general in Lanka,

> True that I criticize in my articles the officials; but my loyalty to the British Throne is as solid as rock and I have invariably expressed sentiments of loyalty to the King. But I love my religion and Sinhalese Race, and my happiness depends on their welfare.[47]

His defense follows from the nature of the empire, a corporate entity constituted of component parts, each with the right to object. He made a bolder claim. In making the Lloyd George analogy, he put Lanka and Wales on the

45. The meaning of Dharmapala's reference to "the Holy Ones" is unclear. At first glance, the referent is obvious—the Buddhist monkhood—but he avoids using "*sangha*," the expression that conventionally follows the other two parts of the Triple Refuge. He might be referring to the Theosophical mahatmas, Buddhist adepts residing in the Himalayas, but I suspect he is overcoding the Buddhist monastic role in Theosophical terms.

46. Dharmapala's critic turned out to be a kinsman of Lloyd George, a connection that led to a friendship between a Welsh train conductor and a Buddhist ascetic. The two always greeted one another in later years when they ran into one another on the Kandy line.

47. In Ananda Guruge, ed., *Return to Righteousness: A Collection of Speeches, Essays and Letters of the Anagarika Dharmapala* (1965; repr., Colombo: Ministry of Cultural Affairs, 1991), 59. When Dharmapala inaugurated Buddhist temples in Calcutta and Sarnath, he invited the most senior British officials and used the occasion to invoke his devotion to the Crown. But he also did so on occasions where his expressions of loyalty were hardly required by the event. He established his short-lived newspaper the *Ceylon Nation* in 1911, for example, to commemorate the coronation of King George V. The paper was intended as a vehicle for Sinhalese Buddhists to express their grievances to British authorities. "The Ceylon Nation," *Journal of the Maha Bodhi Society*, 10 (1912): 30.

same plane, arguing that a man from a Crown colony had as much right to political critique and strong language as a politician born to a country in the United Kingdom.

Dharmapala justified his criticism further by invoking his love for not only the monarchy but also the British people. Those expressions came to the fore after his internment in 1915, when he turned his attention to spreading the Dhamma in Europe and America. Looking back, he wrote that "the idea was put in my mind" long before, in 1886 (Diary, October 7, 1925). There are real-time references as early as 1891 (Diary, May 8). The statements of conciliation are also early. In 1894, he wrote in his diary that the thought had come to him to be gentle to all—"There is no use in abusing the Government." But as time went on, he moved back and forth between affection and abuse, the abuse predominating. By 1913 his brother was appealing to readers of the *Journal of the Maha Bodhi Society* for funds to build a hostel or house "in the heart of the Empire," where a Buddhist Society could popularize Buddhism and allow a sympathetic bond of union between Sinhala and advanced thinkers in England.[48] That same year Dharmapala wrote in his diary that England would be his next project (August 22, 1913). By the 1920s his plans for a Buddhist mission in London became more serious, and he turned his mind fully to the project, responding to being interned and a string of failed projects elsewhere. Whatever affection he expressed for the British people earlier, he now fixed his attention on them as an exercise in loving those who had mistreated him. He would humanize them through the power of Dhamma (Sarnath Notebook no. 27, Diary for 1918).

In London he developed another argument for reciprocity in the empire. Internment in Calcutta kept him confined to the city limits for eighteen months, leading him to compare himself recovering from internment and the people of Europe then recovering from war: "May all Europe realize Peace! My individual suffering is nothing compared to the sufferings of millions wounded in the battlefield" (Sarnath Notebook no. 105, June 12, 1917). Even though he had received the "greatest share" of the unjust punishment given Sinhalas after the 1915 riots, he wrote of having "no ill will against his persecutors" (Sarnath Notebook no. 40). As he tried to set up a center for the Dhamma in London, many landlords sent him away because of his

48. C. A. Hewavitarne, "An Appeal," *Journal of the Maha Bodhi Society*, September 21, 1913, 197. Hewavitarne notes that spreading the Dhamma in England would draw "Ceylon closer to the heart of the Empire."

plans to use a house for institutional purposes or because he was Asian. He found a suitable place, but before he installed monks there, he returned home and sailed on to India. His plans outraced his circumstances: he envisioned young Englishmen marrying Sinhala women to become preachers of the Dhamma to the people of England. He could imagine such matches occurring in England (and not in the colonies) because English people are civilized at home. South Asia attracted a lower class of Englishman, he thought, but even when a civilized person went out to India, the place itself made him become cruel and rapacious. The colonies almost insisted on it. The metropole was a venue for thoughtful exchange and even marriage between people from different parts of the empire. But the imperial system was not only interlocked, it was transitive; making English people in London appreciate the Dhamma would have effects in Asia.

The Delhi durbar of 1911 inspired its own attempt to picture the empire as an articulated and interactive entity. A district judge from Trichinopoly compared the relationship of metropole and colony to marriage:

Today, amid scenes of enthusiasm unparalleled in the history of the world the marriage conceived nearly 25 years ago by the great poet Disraeli has finally been consummated and England's King was publicly proclaimed India to be England's help meet in this great Imperial work.[49]

From that great day onward, the judge concluded, after one hundred years of striving for the welfare and prosperity of India, "the people of both countries will be welded in one, and Indians and Englishmen alike will be citizens of one common Empire."[50] Once settled in London, Dharmapala contemplated the work of imperial citizenship in a less bodily and more abstract way. Those good citizens of the metropole would exercise their influence over British officials and civilians who ran wild in India and Lanka. The model was Dhamma study and intellectual exchange, English people humanized by exposure to the Dhamma, in turn restraining their peers who had no knowledge of compassion because they knew nothing of Buddhism.

49. E. L. R. Thornton, "God Save the King," *Hindu*, quoted in "A Notable Speech," *Journal of the Maha Bodhi Society* 20 (1912): 22–3, at 23.

50. It was only with the coming of the British Commonwealth that the British began to think that the status of imperial subject was inadequate to the complexity of people in the Commonwealth. To that extent, Dharmapala's lifetime spanned the same period when the interaction of universalism and particularism came to the fore, and the structure of the empire played a part in producing the category "citizen."

Abdullah Laroui has spoken of class as sometimes enabling nationalism, however much class at first seems to be antithetical to it.[51] For two hundred years, class and nationalism competed for the heart of the historical subject. In Dharmapala's case, class considerations shaped his thinking about proper behavior, and assertions usually attributed to his being a Protestant Buddhist make more sense as deriving from his sense of class identity. Once joined together, high birth and Buddhist belief, he thought, had a synergistic force, giving his well-to-do equals in London the tools to discipline their less refined compatriots in South Asia. Whatever loyalty the empire inspired, that patriotism had a higher expression that could be realized in the empire properly reformed:

> I think of the future greatness of the English and I therefore wish to make them learn Dhamma. [?] The Anglo-Indian bureaucrats in India & Ceylon are not the best representatives of the British people. (Diary, September 27, 1927)

Buddhist universalism, to be sure, meant more to Dharmapala than the universalism of empire, but both universalisms were motivated by a class factor, itself tied to civilization. The Buddhists with whom Dharmapala associated—his immediate supporters, his family, and members of the Maha Bodhi Society at home and abroad—were in his judgment civilized people. So were the English people he encountered in London. The lower-class behavior of both colonial officials and Sinhala villagers owed to their lack of civilization. Class functioned in contradictory ways in Dharmapala's life, linking him to like kinds of people across the empire while putting him in a position of responsibility at home to people not of his class. That responsibility underlay the national project.

UNIVERSALISM AND OTHER LOCAL FORCES

Universalism takes its force from its opposites—localism, nationalism, particularism, and so on. The conventional response to their interaction is to conclude that the unfolding of the nineteenth and twentieth centuries saw the particularisms prevail over the universalisms. The historical record supplies persuasive examples—Banerjee's elite Indians seeing themselves as imperial citizens, feelings displaced by the onrushing force of Ben-

---

51. *The Crisis of the Arab Intellectual: Traditionalism or Historicism?*, trans. Diarmid Cammel (Berkeley: University of California Press, 1976), 153–77.

gali nationalism and then swept away by a larger, Indian nationalism. Even without encountering more particularistic forces, universalist movements confront their own self-contradictions because of the nature of things—they are framed from a particular point of view and constructed in local form. The most notorious example is French universalism, although American universalism has its own illusions. In a postmetaphysical world, it is hard to make a decisive argument for any set of values having universal warrant. But universalisms do not live in the world of truth claims; they live in a world of historical forces. However deep the French commitment to spreading a universal religion—in this case Catholicism—the revolution by all rights should have ended it. Instead the French carried on with the civilizing mission in the form of Enlightenment values.

French universalism has been motivated by the idea that the French language is simply better than other languages. It deserves special treatment because it offers the world not only its famous clarity but unique access to universal values. Naomi Schor recalls a fax from President Jacques Chirac she found one day in her departmental mailbox, addressed to her as a teacher of French:

> To call oneself Francophone is ultimately to combat a major risk for humanity: linguistic and therefore cultural uniformity. . . . The question is: why should French of all languages lead the campaign against linguistic globalization? . . . First, French is essentially suited to express a full range of human attributes; it is "A language reputed for its capacities to synthesize reality, reflect ideas, feelings, emotions." Second, and inevitably, French is the language of the universal: "Every language has its genius. The one we [Francophones] share predisposes to a certain vision of the relationships between men and communities. A vision that inspires the values of solidarity, fraternity: a sense of the universal."[52]

The immediate threat to French linguistic universalism was the worldwide spread of the English language. Worrying over the loss to humanity in English "linguistic and cultural uniformity," Chirac found no irony in hoping for the success of its French equivalent.

When he began the Maha Bodhi Society, Dharmapala made a commitment to include all varieties of Buddhism in the cause. As he put it in the first issue of his journal, "The society representing Buddhism in general . . . shall preserve absolute neutrality with respect to doctrines and dogmas

---

52. "The Crisis of French Universalism," *Yale French Studies* 100 (2001): 45n4.

taught by sections and sects among Buddhists."[53] Recovering Bodh Gaya, he thought, would provide a unifying focus for Buddhist communities across Asia, however disparate. Drawing Buddhist communities—some national, some sectarian—into a unified movement was originally Henry Steel Olcott's idea, and respect for Olcott provided motivation for Dharmapala's openness to other varieties of Buddhism. Having accompanied the Theosophical leader to Japan in 1889, Dharmapala had seen the antipodes of the Buddhist world before he saw Bodh Gaya, and he knew just how different Japanese Buddhism was from his own, the more so because of the sectarian differences among Buddhists in Japan. Olcott wanted all Buddhist leaders to agree to points of doctrine and thus produced an appendix to his *Buddhist Catechism*, offering fourteen propositions to which Buddhists could agree. The fourteen points are followed by the signatures of ranking monks of Japan, Burma, Lanka, Chittagong, which Olcott personally solicited by traveling to meet each group, often coercing agreement after the application of force majeure.[54] Where Olcott wanted unity among different kinds of Buddhists, Dharmapala wanted only neutrality at Bodh Gaya. He was also committed to doctrinal neutrality in the *Journal of the Maha Bodhi Society*, which published articles on Mahayana and Tibetan Buddhism.

For Olcott, pursuing doctrinal unity was joined to a commitment to brotherhood. Against a colonial background, Olcott's reputation as a Civil War hero, man of science, and Westerner sympathetic to Buddhism made him welcome from Lanka to Japan. Those virtues also made his insistence on Buddhist universalism at least tolerable to the Japanese. Olcott's antiracist views and genuine affection for Asians gave doctrinal universalism an existential character. He was a likable man, and his values made him more so. Dharmapala did not share his hopes for world brotherhood, speaking of the "consolidation of the Buddhist nations" when he represented Buddhism to non-Buddhists more often than when he dealt directly with Buddhists.[55] But the symmetry of the two journals they founded—*The Theosophist or Universal Brotherhood* and the *Journal of the Maha Bodhi Society and the United Buddhist World*—was not accidental.[56] If brotherhood was not an

53. *Journal of the Maha Bodhi Society* 1, no. 1 (1892): 1–2.

54. Olcott, *Old Diary Leaves: The True Story of the Theosophical Society*, 6 vols. (Adyar: Theosophical Publishing House, 1895–1935), 2:301.

55. "Diary Leaves of the Buddhist Representative to the World's Parliament of Religions," in *The Maha Bodhi Centenary Volume, 1891–1991*, ed. M. Wipulasara (Calcutta: Maha Bodhi Society, 1991), 72–5, at 73.

56. The principles, rules, and bylaws of the society itself showed the dual commitment, as did the society's name, The Theosophical Society, or Universal Brotherhood. The first principle

end in itself, Dharmapala saw some connection between his efforts to rally forces for Sinhala reform and a universalist project: "And what is the cry of my own race, is it not the cry of all humanity—all the world over?"[57] And he saw the connection between the shrine at Bodh Gaya and Buddhist universalism: "I took up the larger work of universal Buddhism in January 1891 at the holy spot under the shade of the Bodhi tree" (Diary, February 18, 1930). What drew none of his energy was promoting doctrinal agreement relative to a universalized Buddhism, valuing the "united Buddhist world" only as a force useful in recovering Bodh Gaya. The phrase disappeared without explanation from the journal's masthead in 1924.

The oxymoronic qualities of universalist programs duly noted, the situatedness of all human lives poses further complexities. Dharmapala's commitment to include all varieties of Buddhism in promoting the Buddhist cause did not keep him from assuming that the Maha Bodhi Society would play the lead role in recovering Bodh Gaya and spreading Buddhism. He had established his journal toward that end, and he wrangled an invitation to the World's Parliament of Religions in 1893 as the representative of Southern Buddhism, a considerable achievement for a man of twenty-nine, especially as he was not a member of the group that traditionally spoke for Buddhism, the Buddhist monkhood. In his opening remarks, he conveyed greetings to the delegates of Asia's 475 million Buddhists, ignoring the Japanese monks seated nearby who had traveled to Chicago to represent Buddhism in its Japanese form. Had their English been better, they would have resented his preemptory words. Beyond his claim to speak not just for Sinhala Buddhism or Southern Buddhism but for Buddhism as such, Dharmapala faced challenges, however he understood the Buddhism he represented. Olcott understood that his success at producing consensus—in particular the agreement to the principles at the end of the *Buddhist Catechism*—owed in part to his not being a Buddhist at all.[58]

What motivated Chirac's anxiety for French universalism was a contending universalism in American form—arrogant, successful, and indiffer-

was "The Theosophical Society is formed upon the basis of a Universal Brotherhood of Humanity." *Theosophist* 1 (1880): 179–80, at 179.

57. "What Is Buddhism?," *Journal of the Maha Bodhi Society* 36 (1928): 502–12, at 510.

58. *Old Diary Leaves*, 2:301. Olcott was a Buddhist, but a white Buddhist, and embodying those two identities allowed him to slip out of one identity and into the other. David Karunaratne's account of Dharmapala, for instance, critiques Olcott's universalism, arguing that Sinhalas doubted his "Buddhist sincerity because he married the daughter of a Christian father and looked after Christian children. He became a Buddhist but he treated all religions as one religion. Therefore it is well-known that Colonel Olcott was not sufficiently Buddhist." *Anagarika Dharmapala* (Colombo: M. D. Gunasena, 1965), 66–7.

ent to the virtues of French language and civilization. Dharmapala's work as a Buddhist reformer was constrained by the effect of as many universalisms as one is likely to encounter in a single life. In chapters 4 and 5 I concentrate on two of those universalisms, the British imperium and Theosophy.[59] Neither had anything resembling the historical depth of Buddhism, yet they enjoyed important advantages. Both aspired to universality, and both pursued universalizing goals. The traditional word for Buddhism as a social formation, *Buddhasasana*, may not have begun as a universalizing project. The Buddha's teachings were understood as applicable to the human condition as such, and the spread of Buddhism across Asia must have had some connection to his universalizing logic. But Buddhism saw itself as a come-and-see thing, available to the curious but not requiring its propagation for doctrinal reasons. Even if it had missionizing ambitions and saw its reach extending at least across Asia, the Buddhasasana was constrained by the travel and communication technologies of the premodern world. Olcott and Dharmapala, by contrast, lived in the age of steamships, railways, and automobiles as well as telegraphy, typewriters, telephony, and a global postal system. Olcott traveled some forty-three thousand miles in 1890, and Dharmapala made five world tours, one time making a trip from India to Hawaii merely to felicitate his patron Mary Foster.[60] Even in old age Dharmapala's mother made seven pilgrimages from Colombo to Bodh Gaya.

Dharmapala founded and managed the Maha Bodhi Society. In 1916 he informally adopted a young Sinhala boy Mallika Hewavitarne had brought to Calcutta to be educated, assist him, and eventually manage the Maha Bodhi Society. Devapriya Valisinha took over for him after he received higher ordination in 1931, but until that point, Dharmapala comprised the Maha Bodhi Society as a working organization.[61] He edited the journal, and he made all decisions relating to establishing branches of the society, building new establishments at Calcutta and Sarnath, and pursuing the Bodh Gaya cause. When he moved to Calcutta, the headquarters of the Maha

59. Dharmapala's universalism followed logically from his commitment to the mahatmas, whose renunciation and spiritual advancement led them to transcend nation, ethnicity, and other social identities. "They are, then a very small number of highly intelligent men belonging not to any one nation but to the world as a whole." Anagarika Dharmapala, "The Great White Brotherhood," *Journal of the Maha Bodhi Society* 18 (1910): 362–3, at 363.

60. "General Report of the Sixteenth Convention and Anniversary of the Theosophical Society," supplement, *Theosophist* 13 (1892): 1–42, at 2.

61. "Past General Secretaries after Anagarika Dharmapala," in Wipulasara, *Maha Bodhi Centenary Volume*, 56–7.

Bodhi Society moved to Calcutta. He started the journal with money he had raised for supporting four monks at Bodh Gaya; when they abandoned their posts, he simply moved on to the next project, feeling free to reallocate funds as he saw fit. He made the Maha Bodhi Society the choke point that controlled access to Bodh Gaya or at least the platform for a Buddhist presence at the place, and his imperious personality made that centrality even less appealing to other Buddhist leaders. As much as he constituted the Maha Bodhi Society, it is also possible to say that his family constituted it. The society was the family charity. His mother led pilgrimages, his father's gave financial support, and his brothers did a variety of things—serving on the board, endowing a publication series, negotiating for relics in India, and overseeing the construction of his projects abroad.

Dharmapala drifted away from the Burmese members of the Maha Bodhi Society over his accusations that the Burmese wanted to pursue the Buddhist cause on their own. Some Thai princes showed interest when Dharmapala first visited Bangkok in 1894, but by 1902 the Thai king was complaining to British officials of his importuning them. There were already Buddhists in Calcutta—ethnic Maghs from Chittagong who had their own temple and their own monk—and they joined forces with Dharmapala on a few occasions.[62] After a promising beginning, he showed little interest in including this community of Indian Buddhists in his efforts to recover Bodh Gaya. Nor did he develop any relationship with the Chinese community in Calcutta. He lost the support of the Japanese, who had been more than welcoming on his first two visits to Japan. By 1902 they began to ignore him altogether. When Sister Nivedita brought a Japanese Buddhist to Bodh Gaya to strike a deal with the mahant, the party arrived at a time when Dharmapala was out of town. In 1905 a British military officer and a group of Tibetans and Bengalis established the Buddhist Shrine Restoration Society to make another end run around the Maha Bodhi Society. By the 1920s, the Lanka Dharmadutha Sabha and the International Buddhist Brotherhood began to duplicate the Maha Bodhi Society's mission and shared members with it.

---

62. These Arakanese Buddhists celebrated Vesak early on with the Maha Bodhi Society, Maha Bodhi Society events were sometimes held at their vihara, and the Arakanese helped Dharmapala rent his quarters at 2 Creek Road (Diary, December 13, 1917). The two groups also enjoyed the patronage of the same elite Bengalis. Hemendu B. Chowdhury, *Jagajjyoti Kripasaran Mahathera 125 Birth Anniversary Volume* (Calcutta: Bauddha Dharmankur Sabha, 1990). Why there was not more solidarity between the two groups is unclear, although differences of class are hard to overlook. Dharmapala had misgivings about Kripasaran, whom he described as ""illiterate but respected" (Sarnath Notebook no. 23).

These initiatives represented only a few of the divisions that beset uniting the Buddhist world. Not a few of them were products of Dharmapala's efforts to create that world.

However central to his goals a united Buddhist world may have been, Dharmapala's relationship to Buddhism was itself scarcely unitary.[63] It is more to the point to speak of his Buddhisms.[64] Leaving aside the Protestant Buddhism that Obeyesekere and Gombrich attribute to him, Dharmapala presented a distinctive Buddhism for every constituency. In village settings, correspondence with colonial officials, and the pages of the *Sinhala Bauddhaya*, he understood Buddhism as emerging from a political tradition that colonialism had disrupted. That Buddhism was dominated by civilizational elements, now brought low by political and economic domination. The idea that organized the Buddhism he preached at home was reform. In Calcutta the Buddhism he advocated had no political content because Dharmapala emphasized the spiritual tradition characteristic of a world religion. Under these circumstances the Buddhism he proposed was a "world religion," defined by its civilizational affinity with Hinduism. Both early and late, he argued that there was no difference between Buddhism and Hinduism.[65] In 1923 he gave a speech at the annual meeting of the Hindu Maha Sabha that went one step further, insisting that Buddhists were Hindus.[66] His thinking was shaped by Vivekananda's thinking, and early on he borrowed Vivekananda's statement that "Hinduism cannot live without Buddhism, Buddhism cannot live without Hinduism" as the epigraph of the *Journal of the Maha Bodhi Society*. In an Indian context, he insisted on Buddhism's vigor and missionary impulse, again responding to Vivekananda's views and the broader perception that India's historical downfall derived from Buddhist passivity and quietism.

63. I have discovered after the fact that I have been thinking about Dharmapala's several Buddhisms in a way that parallels Anne Blackburn's approach to Hikkaduve Sumangala. I thank her for articulating the point better than I could. *Locations of Buddhism: Colonialism and Modernity in Sri Lanka* (Chicago: University of Chicago Press, 2010).

64. In 1897 Dharmapala responded to an article by a Protestant minister who dismissed Buddhism by saying that it was "one thing in Ceylon, quite another in Tibet, and still another in China and Japan." Dharmapala's response was to insist that all Buddhists shared the same basic beliefs, while admitting everyday differences in Buddhist practice. "Is There More Than One Buddhism?," *Open Court* 2 (1897): 82.

65. Dharmapala gave his first lecture, "Buddhism in Its Relationship to Hinduism," in Calcutta at the Albert Hall on October 25, 1891.

66. "The Hindu Maha Sabha," *Amrita Bazar Patrika*, reprinted in *Journal of the Maha Bodhi Society* 31 (1923): 354–6.

In Western settings Dharmapala presented a Westernized Buddhism. He traveled with a Bible, which he employed as a reference tool. His education in a variety of missionary schools had given him knowledge of Christianity at least equal to what he knew of Buddhism before he turned his mind to his own religion. He used his knowledge of both religions to argue for their similarity. At the World's Parliament of Religions he set Buddhism apart from other religions and then brought it into congruence with Christianity: "[Buddha] taught that sin, sorrow, and deliverance . . . are the inevitable results of his own acts (Karma). He thus applied the inexorable law of cause and effect to the soul. What a man sows he must reap."[67] In both his diaries and speeches to audiences at home, he was contemptuous of Christianity, but he also saw Buddhism looming behind Christianity:

> People in America call themselves Methodists, Presbyterians, etc. They are followers of Wesley, Luther, Calvin, and other personalities, but not Jesus. If they had followed the teachings of Christ they would have then been Buddhists. (Diary, August 25, 1897)

This was scarcely his conception of Christianity in Lanka, nor was his saying in Calcutta that Hinduism and Buddhism were one something he brought up when he went home. He wrote in his diary that Christianity needed reform, suggesting that the Old Testament be dropped from the text altogether (Diary, August 12, 1919). When he settled in London, he had more evolved views of what a Western Buddhism would look like, deciding that it would need more emphasis on compassion, in keeping with the New Testament, and less asceticism.

The central Buddhism in his life was of course his own, and it differed substantially from what might be called the regional Buddhisms of India, England, and Sri Lanka. Those Buddhisms had elements of equality, but there was nothing egalitarian about his own Buddhism.[68] What drew him to Theosophy was what defined his own Buddhism—idealism and commitment to asceticism far in excess of anything he could expect from Western Theosophists or Buddhist monks in his own society. He was equally com-

67. "Buddhism and Christianity," in Houghton, *Neely's History*, 803.

68. Part of Gombrich's rationale for saying that Dharmapala practiced a "Protestant Buddhism" is based on an argument for religious egalitarianism: "Dharmapala accepted the Western Protestant view of religion as one and the same for everybody." *Theravada Buddhism: A Social History from Ancient Benares to Modern Colombo* (London: Routledge, 1988), 192.

mitted to the Theosophical masters, or mahatmas (advanced seekers whose orientation was Buddhist and who had shared their wisdom with Blavatsky first in person when she visited them and later in astral letters with which they communicated with her). At various points Dharmapala called this Buddhism *sabba nuta yana, bodhiyana,* or the path of *samma sambodhi* (Sarnath Notebook no. 53). The most instructive expression he used for his own Buddhism was *uttari manussa dhamma*—the moral code of the spiritually advanced man. Sometimes he referred to it as the "sacred science of the uttari manussa dhamma," and what he had in mind was the science of *dhyana* meditation that leads to increasing elevated states of consciousness and ultimately to nirvana (which Sinhala monks believe is not possible in the present age).[69] It was his celibacy, dietary restraint, and meditative practice that produced his own spiritual growth. It also set him apart from other Buddhists.

Don Carolis Hewavitarne, Dharmapala's father, pointed his son toward the bodhisattva path (Diary, August 14, 1925).[70] He told his son to try to become a Buddha (Diary, November 30, 1930). Dharmapala remembered that the best part of his childhood was spent alone in his father's garden (Sarnath Notebook no. 53). "I liked solitude," he wrote elsewhere. He improvised ritual offerings in the garden and suggested preoccupations that continued through his life:

> I liked the company of ascetics. I used to bathe twice a day, and was very clean, and kept everything neat and tidy. Sweeping the floor, cleaning the furniture was my hobby, and I liked flowers. Evil companionship I abhorred. Cruelty to animals, and their destruction I abhorred. . . . I had no reverence for people because of their wealth and position. I wished to follow the Bodhisat life of self-sacrifice. I was very susceptible to unjust criticism. The simple life I liked. The life of King Sirisanghabo was to me a great incentive to adopt the life of ascetic renunciation. (Sarnath Notebook no. 4)

69. "The Maha Bodhi Society," *Ceylon Daily News*, December 29, 1926.

70. Don Carolis put great confidence in astrology, and when he examined his son's horoscope, Dharmapala noted that "within my hearing he said that my stars were bad and that I could therefore make no progress in my studies. This was balm to me" ("My Autobiography," Sarnath Notebook no. 53). In a later passage he writes of his father, "He did not care to have me follow him to learn his business, and he had a clerk who did all correspondence." I suspect Don Carolis discovered that his son was a *hatara kendra paluvima kenek,* having a horoscope that destines a man to become either a king or a beggar. In the local context what recommends a life of renunciation is the practical impossibility of becoming a king and the undesirability of becoming a beggar.

By 1889 he was rising at 2 a.m. to meditate. In 1891 he vowed to take only one meal a day (monks take two) (Diary, August 12, 1891). He writes in one of his notebooks:

> In the early days of the MBS [Maha Bodhi Society] many were the days that I had not an anna for expenses. I did not have the means to buy kerosene oil for the night. I have gone without food and to satisfy my hunger I have swallowed the chewed betel. There was no sacrifice I was not prepared to go through. My motto was "Victory or death, the motto of Prince Siddhartha." (Sarnath Notebook no. 101)

There was another paradigm for Dharmapala's unceasing expectations of himself, the "Holy Ones" living in the Himalayas. In 1897 he planned a trip to Tibet to encounter the two mahatmas with a Buddhist orientation, a prospect that so terrified his father that he gave his son a meditation retreat in Colombo to keep him home (Sarnath Notebook no. 101).

Dharmapala's lifelong commitment to the Himalayan masters and Blavatsky is either forgotten in accounts of his life or disregarded after Dharmapala broke with Olcott in the late 1890s. Nationalist writers need to protect the purity of his views by showing him pulling away from Theosophy—attacking first Olcott, then the Buddhist Theosophical Society in Colombo—and it is true that Dharmapala had a public falling out with Olcott and the Colombo Theosophists. When Annie Besant took over the society, he became estranged from Indian Theosophy too. But their estrangement can be overstated—having broken away from the Theosophical Society, he started paying dues again in 1913 and lent Besant considerable sums of money (despite her refusing his request for a loan). He lent much larger sums of money to the Colombo Theosophists in the 1920s. More to the point, Dharmapala maintained his affinity for the mahatmas and Blavatsky until the end of his diary keeping in 1930. Throughout the 1920s, his daily entries often begin with an injunction from Master Koot Hoomi: "The only refuge for him who aspires to true perfection is the Buddha alone." Koot Hoomi's aphorism was given in an astral letter transmitted to A. P. Sinnett and conveyed to Dharmapala by Blavatsky. It can be read in two ways: as a statement of his commitment to the Buddha or of the intervention of the "Holy Ones." If the appeal of the aphorism depended on its Buddhist references, why invoke the authority of a mahatma to warrant the Buddha's being the only refuge? The ambiguity of the statement is a fair characterization of Dharmapala's own Buddhism: he sought perfection and looked to the Buddha and Koot Hoomi for it.

One gets a better sense of the late nineteenth-century world by noting how many figures he encountered pursuing their own universalisms—Colonel Olcott and Madame Blavatsky, Lord Elgin, Lord Curzon, Prince Kropotkin, Swami Vivekananda, Sister Nivedita, and Okakura Kakuzo. Their projects suffered from their own contradictions. The Theosophists were undone in a variety of ways. Their universalist project appealed to other well-born people and had little reach beyond them. The Theosophical commitment to spiritualism did not sit comfortably with its scientism. The British imperial system was another universalism, its political and economic interests justified by reference to the self-proclaimed virtues of colonial rule—peace, the rule of law, the protection of private property, and perhaps most fundamentally, the encouragement of liberty.[71] If the empire was the first imperial formation since antiquity to promote liberty, the attempt to export British freedom was contradicted by the very nature of imperialism. As P. J. Marshall put it in his inaugural lecture as professor of imperial history at King's College, the British were a "free though conquering people."[72] The larger point is that most of Dharmapala's encounters with other ideological movements—from Curzon to Olcott, Vivekananda, and Okakura—brought one universalizing project into contact with another. To say that the universalisms were destined to yield to nationalism is to get it only half right. The failure of the universalisms was guaranteed by intrinsic problems—self-contradiction, the impracticality of their totalizing aspirations, and economic and political isolation—sufficient to undermine any movement.

RESCUING DHARMAPALA FROM THE NATION

A world has been lost by either treating Dharmapala's life abroad as a sidebar to his life at home or ignoring it altogether, and that loss entails more than the sheer volume of his career spent away from the island. The narrow focus creates a teleological understanding of his life as leading to the major events in subsequent Sri Lankan history. Without attending to his life abroad, we lose track of the role he and other Buddhists played in the historical moment because universalism and nationalism were interactive, not to say kindred, movements. By not considering the effects of travel between Calcutta and Colombo and onward to Japan and the West, we lose the exis-

---

71. Jack P. Greene, ed., *Exclusionary Empire: English Liberty Overseas, 1600–1900* (Cambridge: Cambridge University Press, 2010), 2–8.

72. *A Free Though Conquering People: Eighteenth-Century Britain and Its Empire* (London: Ashgate, 2003).

tential effects on him of moving among different worlds and what Stanley Cavell calls the "returned familiar." These foreign experiences influenced his views on empire and social class, which in turn shaped his ideas about reform at home. We distort the character of his nationalism and the way ideas about class and civilization shaped him because of the way he embodied these identities abroad. We fail to notice three of the four Buddhisms I've suggested—the Buddhism he pursued in India, the Buddhism he preached to Westerners, and his own Buddhism, organized around meditation, asceticism, and abiding regard for the two Buddhist mahatmas. He practiced that Buddhism wherever he went, and he tried to propagate it at home by establishing the Ethico-Psychological College in 1898 to educate people to become the kind of Buddhist he was, with an emphasis on meditation and missionary work. That part of his life—even though it was centered on his own country—has been overwhelmed by the attention given to Protestant Buddhism and his role in constructing a nationalist movement.[73]

The most ubiquitous form of political community in the modern world, the nation has been drawn irresistibly to historical accounts of its own origins. As Prasenjit Duara notes, both before the "nation" becomes the nation-state and after, it creates a force field, attracting historical writings to it, calibrating the historical task to the life of the nation, and producing accounts that are incomplete, exclusionary, and teleological. National identities are unstable not simply because they call forth competing claims from other ethnic communities living in the same colony or territory. They are also unstable because "all good nationalisms contain a transnational vision." Duara's examples are pan-Africanism, pan-Asianism, pan-Europeanism, pan-Islamism, Shiism, and Judaism.[74] In the persons of Vivekananda and Okakura, Dharmapala encountered the pan-Asian side of both Indian and Japanese nationalisms, giving the three of them parallel motivations for conflict over Bodh Gaya. For Vivekananda and Okakura, a legitimate place at Bodh Gaya resonated with both pan-Asian and nationalist causes. But for Dharmapala, the struggle at Bodh Gaya—which continued for four decades as opposed to Vivekananda and Okakura's week-long

73. Gombrich and Obeyesekere, *Buddhism Transformed.* Gombrich and Obeyesekere characterize Kitsiri Malalgoda, *Buddhism in Sinhalese Society, 1750–1900* (Berkeley: University of California Press, 1976), as itself a history of Protestant Buddhism, 6. Malalgoda applies the Protestant Buddhism notion to circumstances that predate Olcott's arrival, characterizing the Buddhist resistance more as an indigenous response to Christian missionizing than a product of Theosophical intervention, 246.

74. *Rescuing History from the Nation: Questioning Narratives of Modern China* (Chicago: University of Chicago Press, 1995), 7–16, at 13.

foray—had no motivations of a nationalist kind.[75] His struggle for Bodh
Gaya was pan-Asian; at moments, it reached beyond Asia. He called that
campaign simply Buddhist.

While he never thought of making a specifically Sinhala claim on Bodh
Gaya, Dharmapala argued that regaining control over the place was essential for the well-being of his people. The nationalist side of his transnational
vision was simply that the energy necessary for spreading Buddhism and
recovering its sacred places was also essential for reinvigorating the Sinhala
nation. When Buddhism first became a pan-Asian force, he thought, it had
been vital because it had been a missionizing religion. It could regain that
initiative, throwing off colonial domination by relaunching this transnational project. He saw the local advantages of a grand enterprise; the leading
figures in reforming the nation—D. B. Jayatilaka, W. A. de Silva, D. C. Senanayake, F. R. Senanayake, and other leaders of the temperance and Buddhist
movements more generally—did not agree. The considerable Sinhala support Dharmapala enjoyed when he first began to litigate for Bodh Gaya fell
away after he lost the 1895 case, and in the years following he never enjoyed
any appreciable amount of domestic support for his missionizing abroad.
What popular support he gathered came from villagers, and they had little
to give him. Instead he relied on his father and Mary Foster, the Hawaiian
Theosophist who became his chief supporter after the death of his father.[76]
Other nationalists may have been less "militant" than Dharmapala, but
they had a steady focus on the nation, and he did not. They also had little
sympathy for the self-disciplining character of his local work. Even the most
overtly Buddhist of the other nationalists of the time, D. B. Jayatilaka, kept
his distance. In view of the Whiggish character of most accounts of Dharmapala's Sinhala nationalism, it is therapeutic to be reminded that there was
once a Sri Lankan nationalism.[77]

75. When he visited in the fifth century, Faxian saw three monasteries at Bodh Gaya, one
of which was the Sinhala monastery. In the seventh century Xuanzang found only the Sinhala
monastery, and he says the monks there were studying the "Great Vehicle." Li Rongxi, The
Life of Hsuan-Tsang: The Tripitaka-Master of the Great Tzu En Monastery (Beijing: Chinese
Buddhist Association, 1993). When the Tibetan Dharmasvamin visited just before the place was
abandoned by Buddhists, one of the last remaining monks at Bodh Gaya was Sinhala. But it is
unclear whether "Sinhala" carries an ethnic referent or an ideological one, as in the Buddhism
spread from the island to Burma and Thailand in medieval times.

76. Frank J. Karpiel, "Theosophy, Culture, and Politics in Honolulu, 1890–1920," Hawaiian
Journal of History 30 (1996): 177–89.

77. For all of its emphasis on fostering Buddhism and Sinhala causes, Dharmapala's newspaper, the Bauddhaya, gave editorial support to both Ponnambalam Ramanathan in the first
legislative council election, and E. W. Perera, a Catholic, who led the Lankan delegation in talks
in London about independence. Ratnatunga, They Turned the Tide, 94.

Scholars sometimes assert that the central role as a Buddhist nationalist that is currently ascribed to Dharmapala is the product of Ananda Guruge's 1965 *Return to Righteousness*. On this view, Dharmapala's prominence was a product of a government publication that celebrated his role in reviving the spirit of the Sinhala people. Anyone who has read newspaper accounts of the enshrinement of his remains in Colombo will dismiss that idea. Long before his death he was a national figure and lightning rod for public feelings regarding religion and nation.[78] In the cause of showing how he turned monks into activists, Seneviratne provides an example of his public presence in the 1940s:

> Hendiyagala [Silaratana, one of Seneviratne's Dharmapalite monks] held a Dharmapala commemoration meeting in 1945. A large color portrait of Dharmapala was carried around the villages of his [rural development] activity. This was consciously done "to give an idea of Dharmapala to our children."[79]

Guruge may have provided a convenient compendium of Dharmapala's words and accomplishments, but his popular appropriation began long before its publication.

Where Guruge's book had its effect was not so much on the Buddhist public as on scholars who have relied on the book's treatment of Dharmapala. It is not surprising that he comes across as a patriot in a government publication. What is surprising is that scholars have approached Dharmapala only in terms of Guruge.[80] We can do better by looking at the evidence. Before 1911 and after his internment in Calcutta ended, Dharmapala did not spend any appreciable amount of time in Sri Lanka. He did not want to die there, and he did not want his ashes returned to his homeland after his death. Approaching the island for the first time after the British allowed

78. A newspaper account describing Dharmapala as a curious blend of the prophet Jeremiah and Jonathan Swift suggests why Buddhists and non-Buddhists found him hard to ignore. "A Colombo Diary," *Ceylon Daily News*, January 13, 1927.

79. *The Work of Kings*, 96–117, at 103, quoting Hendiyagala Silaratana, *Vinnanaya* (Kuliyapitiya: Sastrodaya Press, n.d.), 289, 310.

80. Not looking for evidence beyond Guruge has led to inferences that have no warrant. Consider Gombrich's saying that Dharmapala left Colombo because his political activities had attracted official attention. *Theravada Buddhism*, 188. In 1892 he left for Calcutta to continue his campaign for Bodh Gaya, not because his militancy had gotten him into trouble with colonial officials. Trouble came some two decades later. After he returned to Calcutta in 1914, his mother wrote him that he should not come home because she had heard rumors of official displeasure. But he was not "exiled" in 1915. Ibid.

him to return to Lanka, he wrote, "All good thoughts vanish when one arrives in Ceylon. Today it is occupied by an accused [*sic*] people who do more evil than good. Liquor, opium etc. are found in abundance, the trade is in the hands of aliens" (Diary, April 18, 1921). In 1930 his thoughts had moved to death and rebirth: "What a blessing to be born in India. Ceylon is the country of Chandalas" (Diary, July 22, 1930).[81] At the very least we need to begin with a more nuanced view of the man's complexities and contradictions. Removed from the nationalist context, we can see him clearly and return him to that context in a defensible way.

The conventional reading of Dharmapala's deathbed wish—"May I be born twenty-five times to preach the Dhamma in India"—stresses his commitment to Buddhism. And noting that reference is fair enough, but there is something unsettling about a nationalist's projecting himself deep into the samsaric future in a place other than home. It is also instructive to cite another aspiration, his wanting to be reborn to a "righteous Brahmin family" in India (Diary, November 17, 1930). The deeper one looks into Dharmapala's diaries, the more curious the whole thing becomes. The obvious way to account for his investment in India is to attribute his deciding to spend his last days abroad to his estrangement from family and friends. His hypercritical way of dealing with others had cumulative effects on many people, and scandal played another part in driving him away. Perhaps it is fitting for a man who lived as a solitary renouncer to die alone, be cremated in India, and request his ashes be interred in a sacred place. Rather than reading the wish for twenty-five futures in India as a hyperbolic religious wish and nothing else, I think that the Indian reference derives from his conception of himself as a world renouncer, solitary and homeless. Long before scandal and estrangement, he expressed similar wishes—while in Japan he wished for rebirth there, and during a visit to Switzerland rebirth there—but there is no reference in the diaries to his wanting to be reborn in Lanka. Once he put two destinies in one aspiration: "I shall be born in Japan to save India" (Diary, July 14, 1913). When he was desperate to raise money for the London vihara, he contemplated dying in still another place, threatening "to lay his bones in London" if followers did not contribute.[82]

I do not mean to reduce the question of Dharmapala's self-understanding

81. Dharmapala's comment links his people to low birth by making a literary reference to low status that I suspect he learned from the *Mahavamsa*.

82. A Sincere Buddhist, "Mr. Dharmapala and His Work," *Ceylon Daily News*, December 9, 1926.

to deathbed wishes or his diaries. Nor do I mean to be churlish to my colleagues, but they have misused him as much as the nationalists. Let me focus on two cases, both of which illustrate what happens when Dharmapala's career is used as an opening exercise in the rise of a nationalist struggle and party to an evolving national subjectivity. K. M. de Silva writes that Dharmapala saw the political potential inherent in the revival of Buddhism and was among the first to advocate svaraj.[83] The word is more generally associated with Gandhi and his struggle for Indian independence, and that is likely where Dharmapala got the notion. Gandhi used the neologism to mean self-rule in two senses, discipline over the self and political independence.[84] When Dharmapala used the expression in his diaries, he too emphasized that political change depended first on individual moral reform. To this extent, de Silva is right: Dharmapala invoked self-rule, but he did so in reference to moral reform, saying that home rule under the aegis of the British Empire would come only after Sinhalas had reformed themselves. I doubt that most scholars who speak of his politics would think that his political aspirations began with Lankans practicing self-discipline. Nor would they assume that svaraj for Dharmapala meant home rule, as opposed to independence pure and simple.

De Silva characterizes Dharmapala's career as an effort "to make an ideological link between religion and political nationalism."[85] The project failed, de Silva concludes, because other nationalists rejected his leadership,

83. *A History of Sri Lanka*, 377. In a chapter on the nationalist movement in the early twentieth century, de Silva suggests that the failure of the nationalist movement to influence "the formal political activities of the elite at this time" was due to Dharmapala's "being out of the island for considerable amounts of time." "The Reform and Nationalist Movements in the Early Twentieth Century," in *University of Ceylon History of Ceylon*, vol. 3 (Colombo: Colombo Apothecaries, 1973), 384. De Silva finds another source of the failure of nationalist movement in Dharmapala's failure to act on "clearly defined political objectives" because he had so many other interests. I would say that these other interests need to be understood in the context of personal reform preceding social reform. De Silva's assertion that Dharmapala was the "most militant" of the nationalists needs more substantive reconsideration. It implies that Dharmapala, advocating svaraj, fell out with other nationalists because he was more radical than they were. His language was more radical, but the change he advocated understood svaraj as personal reform, and his political goals were much the same as other nationalists. What separated Dharmapala from his colleagues is what separated Gandhi from Nehru—his politics were driven by a spiritual agenda not shared by others.

84. The diaries track Dharmapala's relationship with Gandhi over several decades with comments on Gandhi's political strategies, public presence, and minimal knowledge of Buddhism and temporizing support for the Bodh Gaya cause. On one occasion Gandhi spoke on Buddhism at the temple Dharmapala built in Calcutta.

85. *A History of Sri Lanka*, 378.

and without that solidarity the nationalists could not turn the discontent and enthusiasm he provoked into "a political force of real significance." The man who emerges from the diaries, notebooks, journals, periodicals, and correspondence was more of an ascetic than a political leader. But the fact is that the nationalist narrative begs for a militant leader, and Dharmapala's speeches were nothing if not militant. The question is how much of a leader he wanted to be. If scholars can make him that political leader, they can attribute the failure of nationalism to secondary causes: he was away from the island, or he spread his energy across many projects that were not political, or he was hard to like. The British misreading of his intentions— suspecting him of sedition—itself facilitates the nationalist appropriation of Dharmapala. That for which the colonial government reviled him nationalists honor him.

No one has made as much of Dharmapala's influence as Gananath Obeyesekere, and he has discovered that influence in a variety of contexts. Dharmapala gave "all Buddhists a sense of self-respect." He gave educated village intellectuals something more profound—he politicized them. He gave them "a way of life and a new identity." With independence this class of people became the leadership of village Sri Lanka. They harnessed the village vote in the 1956 election that brought S. W. R. D. Bandaranayake to power. But his influence on village life does not stop there:

> This was also the stratum that led the 1971 insurrection in Ceylon. The ascetic dedication, rigid Puritanism, and organizational skills of the 1971 rebels, and their nationalist adaptation of Marxism, reflect at least partly the heritage of Anagarika Dharmapala.[86]

I do not intend to dispute this genealogy of influence except to note the overreaching. Obeyesekere puts Dharmapala to still other ends, seeing him as the source of a Protestant Buddhism, which then becomes a precondition for an evolving national subjectivity. Sri Lanka had a nationalist movement, but it was tepid and neither confrontational nor violent, making it tempting to look for its sources in cultural movements—temperance campaigns, riots against other ethnic groups, and Buddhism as remade by Dharmapala.

---

86. Gananath Obeyesekere, "Personal Identity and Cultural Crisis: The Case of Anagarika Dharmapala of Sri Lanka," in *The Biographical Process: Studies in the History and Psychology of Religion*, ed. Frank E. Reynolds and Donald Capps (The Hague: Mouton, 1976), 221–52, at 244.

I hate to drag Kitsiri Malalgoda's account of religious controversies between Christians and Buddhists, the rise of low-country monastic fraternities, and their subsequent segmentation into this matter, but Malalgoda linked all of these events to Protestant Buddhism in a way that illustrates the narrative compulsions of both the nation and Protestant Buddhism.[87]

Obeyesekere used the expression to emphasize that the changes Olcott and Dharmapala brought to Buddhism were Protestant in two ways. They were borrowed from Protestant missionaries who dominated many coastal settings in the island, and they were a protest against Christian domination of the public sphere.[88] Malalgoda's reading of Obeyesekere's argument adds a third feature of Protestant Buddhism, itself derived from the logic of Protestantism—that laypeople became involved in religious leadership, displacing monks who historically played that role alone. Over the years, Obeyesekere himself packed more and more into the expression.[89] By 1975, he talked more of Puritan values and this-worldly asceticism; by 1988 Gombrich and Obeyesekere produced a book chapter on Protestant Buddhism, associating it with a polemical style, fundamentalism, the idea that Buddhism was a philosophy, not a religion, and dependent on a battery of English-language concepts.[90] The emphasis on Protestantism led Obeyesekere to conclude that Dharmapala's Buddhism was influenced by the Protestant emphasis on individual responsibility, and Obeyesekere passed the baton to Gombrich, who carried it onward.

Gombrich and Obeyesekere deduced even more changes in Sinhala Buddhism from the historical development of Protestantism. Protestant influence brought both religious individualism and egalitarianism to the practice of Buddhism in Sri Lanka. The Protestant rejects priests and saints, and in a Buddhist context individualism means denying the intermediary role of the monkhood.[91] Gombrich and Obeyesekere linked that individualism to still

---

87. *Buddhism in Sinhalese Society,* 246, 260–2.

88. "Religious Symbolism and Political Change in Ceylon," 58–78.

89. As John Holt points out, Protestant Buddhism in its first iteration, that is, Obeyesekere's "Religious Symbolism and Political Change in Ceylon," *Modern Ceylon Studies* 1 (1970): 43–63, represented a protest against Christianity, and in Gombrich and Obeyesekere's 1988 *Buddhism Transformed,* it became a protest against traditional Buddhism. Holt, "Protestant Buddhism?," *Religious Studies Review* 17, no. 4 (1991): 309.

90. Obeyesekere, "On Buddhist Identity in Sri Lanka," in *Ethnic Identity: Creation, Conflict, and Accommodation,* ed. Lola Romanucci-Ross and George A. De Vos, 3rd ed. (Walnut Creek, CA: Altamira, 1993), 222–47, originally published in Gombrich and Obeyesekere, *Buddhism Transformed,* 202–40.

91. *Buddhism Transformed,* 215–6.

more social change: the laicization of Buddhism made the religion "one and the same for everybody."[92] The facts speak otherwise. Dharmapala had no interest in undermining the role of the monkhood, not at home and not in missionizing Buddhism abroad. He wanted rather to reform the monkhood. For that matter, he believed in the role of religious intermediaries, putting the monkhood and brahmacaryas such as him in the position to lead others because of their asceticism. Focusing on this-worldly Protestantism rather than his interest in the occult, meditation, and the otherworld leads Obeyesekere and Gombrich to mistake what Dharmapala intended. The man who followed the *uttari manussa dhamma* was anything but egalitarian in matters of his spiritual development and everyday conduct.[93] He did not believe in the "priesthood of all believers."

With the exception of Harischandra Valisinha, Dharmapala had little success in attracting others to take on the anagarika role.[94] The five anagarikas he ordained in 1897 soon faded away. He had thought of establishing a brahmacarya order as early as 1891, and in the 1920s he returned to his hopes for a Brahmacarya Samagama (Diary, May 29 and July 22, 1920, February 5, 1921). The language is itself instructive of the way he thought of himself and his plans for the Anagarika Order, the vocabulary to which he reverted in 1925.[95] He stipulated that the order would wear "the orange coloured robe: but not sewn in the Bhikkhu fashion." More suggestive of his own self-conception was his attitude toward laymen, brahmacarya, and monks. The Four Noble Truths and the Noble Eightfold Path apply to both roles, but he added:

> Of the four holy stages, Anagami, Sakadagami and Sotapatti are for Upasakas and Brahmacharis [men observing celibacy]. No householder can be an Anagami. The tradition is that Arhats do not exist to-day. We

92. *Theravada Buddhism,* 192.

93. At the Paris Congress of Orientalists in 1897, Dharmapala told his audience: "Buddhism has two aspects—one for the simpleminded, the other for the philosopher. . . . Worship was intended for the simple people." (Diary, September 14, 1897).

94. Harischandra adopted the robes of a tapasa when he took on the brahmacarya role on January 1, 1898. Praneeth Abhayasundere, *Brahmachari Walisinghe Harischandra* (Colombo: Department of Cultural Affairs, 2000), 35. Dharmapala said Harischandra was "the only individual who follows my ideas." Ibid., 20. Harischandra called himself an anagarika, and the only other anagarika was Devapriya. He did not exactly choose that role, having been brought up by Dharmapala to follow him as leader of the Maha Bodhi Society.

95. "Why Not Establish an Anagarika Order of Brothers?," *Journal of the Maha Bodhi Society* 33 (1925): 181–2.

may try and attain the fruits of holiness of Sotapatti, Sakadagami, and Anagami.[96]

In other words, he believed in the possibility of enlightenment in a way that Sinhala monks did not.[97] He sought it for himself—thus the dhyana meditation—and to that extent did not see himself as a householder: "no householder can be an Anagami." He did not see it being realized in this lifetime but made it a realistic goal. Once he said nirvana was achievable in seven lifetimes.

Even if we separate Dharmapala's Buddhism from "Protestant" Buddhism, emphasizing religion itself causes us to overlook the class prejudices that weighed on his instructions to Sinhala villagers (and his behavior on Indian trains). Instead of suggesting that Dharmapala—his family only one generation removed from their village origins—was ill at ease in Colombo, his own remarks suggest that he was considerably more uncomfortable in village settings.[98] I can make the case for his feelings about both class and village life with a single example and flesh out the account later:

> There was a kind of haughtiness inherent in me which made me think low of wealth and rank. . . . If my class made [me] wear silk outside, I wore my silk cloth as an undershirt. But I loved the poor. I wish to show my sympathy by feeling myself poor, and make them feel I was like them. New clothes, silk dresses I abhorred. (Sarnath Notebook no. 53)

He did not replace worn clothes very often, and his robes were cotton, but he wore silk underclothes throughout his life. He did not identify with the generality of human beings and did not want to live in the world they inhabited because that was the realm of samsara.

Gombrich and Obeyesekere say that nowadays Protestant Buddhism "exerts sway over larger areas of the nation." They also project Protestant Buddhism backward in time, writing that Malalgoda "accepted [this term] for his masterly account of the movement's origins."[99] The thrust of Malalgoda's analysis ends long before Dharmapala's life although he concludes

96. Ibid., 181.
97. Bhikkhu Devamitta Dhammapala, "Reminiscences of My Early Life," *Journal of the Maha Bodhi Society* 41 (1933): 151–62, at 155.
98. Gombrich, *Theravada Buddhism*, 186.
99. *Buddhism Transformed*, 8, 6.

with a short chapter entitled "Protest Consolidated," mentioning Protestant Buddhism for the first time on page 246 of a 262-page book, then suggesting that there were signs of Protestant Buddhism even before Olcott's arrival in 1880.[100] Whatever salience Protestant Buddhism has for understanding the efforts of Olcott and Dharmapala to reform the religion after 1880, pushing the idea backward in time more than a hundred years follows from the temptation to tie all things to a theoretical idea with a provocative name. Agglomerating events ranging from the politics of the Kandyan kingdom, caste assertion, and monastic segmentation to Protestant Buddhism is overtly teleological, the nation-to-be looming on the narrative horizon.

The argument for Dharmapala's life marking the beginning of the growing laicization of Buddhist life serves a narrative that centers on the growth of lay domination in the life of Buddhism and the nation. In place of this formulation, I want to start with simple matters. He wore ochre robes, not white, because he was an ascetic who pursued social reform, not a social reformer who practiced asceticism.[101] In that color choice rest several implications. He thought he was entitled to lead Buddhist affairs not because he was a pious layman but because he was a world renouncer and considerably more ascetic than the monks he knew. But for a childhood disability at age four—sometimes he says a nanny dropped him, but more often he speaks of a paralytic stroke, and once he wrote that he became lame by "running about" (Diary, January 31, 1919)—he would have become a monk and not invented a role that made him neither a monk nor a layperson but an ascetic without a community.[102] He wore white robes to the World's Parliament of Religions, but by 1895 he began to wear the color of South Asian renunciation. The switch is symptomatic of his sense of himself not as a pious layman but a brahmacarya, a word that he used in a variety of ways to describe himself—"brahmacharya" of the bodhisattva path, world wanderer,

100. *Buddhism in Sinhalese Society, 1750–1900*, 246.

101. Gombrich has him in white robes. *Theravada Buddhism*, 190. On July 12, 1892, Dharmapala was sent to Darjeeling by Hikkaduve Sumangala to present a relic and leaves from the Bodh Gaya bo tree to Tibetan lamas. At a procession, Dharmapala rode "on a dark bay horse, dressed in the orange colored garment of the order of Upasakas." F. H. Muller, "Meeting at Darjeeling," supplement, *Theosophist* 13 (1892): lxxxvii–lxxxviii, at lxxxvii. I'd call that foray a trial and locate the decisive change as coming in 1895.

102. "In my 4th year, my left [crossed out] right leg was permanently injured and I could not [crossed out] which debarred me from entering the order of Bhikkhus. Had not this defect been a hindrance I would have become a Bhikkhu. Some bad karma I might have done in the past or it might have been due to neglect of my nurse." (Sarnath Notebook no. 4). Elsewhere he speaks of his right leg in particular—"But for my lameness in my right leg I would have joined the order" (Diary, January 31, 1919)—or attributes the injury to a "paralytic stroke" (Diary, September 17, 1926).

pilgrim, and "Brahmacharya Anagarika Dharmapala." He followed a course other Buddhists did not follow. Speaking at Town Hall in New York City in 1925 he made this distinction:

> Popular Buddhism is what the Western Pali scholars have so far been able to expound. The real psychology of Buddhism is too abstruse for the masses to apprehend, and only very few have the desire even among the yellow robed fraternity in Buddhist lands to enter into the penetralia of Paramartha Dharma wherein is to be found the secrets of mystic development.[103]

He was a world renouncer, not an everyman in a simulacrum of national dress.

Accounts of Dharmapala's life sometimes characterize him as an activist and reformer who invented the anagarika role to allow him to act in the world while also practicing asceticism. Most say something about the name emphasizing the activist role—Dharmapala was the "protector of Buddhism" and thus an activist first and foremost.[104] I hope to show that his asceticism was foundational and his activism secondary. All he reveals of how he decided on the name Dharmapala is that he was attracted to its Aryan virtue. On his trip to Adyar in 1884 he noted that "the sight of the Brahmans made an impression on my mind as to make me follow the Aryan customs" (Sarnath Notebook no. 101). A few pages later, still writing about his life, he made an analogy:

> However unselfish I may be there are bad people who take advantage of my goodness. Khantivada tapasa was innocent as a babe but the King who confronted him was like a demon. Dhammapala Bodhisat was ordered to be killed by the King. The earthquake does not recognize good from bad. All are killed.[105]

Another precedent may have been the medieval Dharmapala, the author of the *mahatika* to Buddhaghosa's *Visuddhimagga*, and a monk associated

---

103. "Message of the Buddha," in Wipulasara, *Maha Bodhi Centenary Volume*, 76–83, at 81.

104. See, for instance, Torkel Brekke, *Makers of Modern Indian Religion in the Late Nineteenth Century* (Oxford: Oxford University Press, 2002), 68.

105. Dharmapala made another reference to Khantivada in his diary: "I do no harm to anybody but there are many who work agst: me. Khantivada was patience personified, but his holy body was hacked to death by a cruel king" (January 4, 1927).

with esoteric knowledge, trance states, and spiritual attainments.[106] None of these speculations settles the matter, but we get closer to Dharmapala's self-understanding by following his own words, and those words speak more of spiritual progress than "protecting the Dhamma."

With the exception of Tessa Bartholomeusz, no one has paid much attention to the way Dharmapala understood his renunciation. She does so for other purposes, interpreting the recent history of female renunciation in the island by arguing that he thought of renunciation in three ways. Each of those ways derives from a stage of his life—the pious layman, the brahmacarya, and the *samanera* (monastic initiate) who will one day received ordination as a bhikkhu.[107] Stressing the liminal qualities of the way he understood brahmacarya, she says that he invented a way of staying active in the world while following moral precepts that laypeople do not follow. She takes the brahmacarya role as evidence of Dharmapala's "re-inventing" a way of being a pious layman by blurring the distinction between laity and monkhood. Here she is led astray by the Protestant Buddhism notion, causing her to emphasize the wrong side of the brahmacarya or anagarika role, the interface between the role of a layman and a brahmacarya. The emphasis belongs on the interface between the role of a brahmacarya and a monk. He was a liminal figure well enough, but he occupied the far side of the limen at the interface of two forms of renunciation. He did not choose the yellow robes casually; he wore them to distinguish himself from the pious layman.

In "What a Bhikkhu Is Expected to Do," Dharmapala made the distinc-

---

106. L. S. Cousins, "Aspects of Esoteric Southern Buddhism," in *Indian Insights: Buddhism, Brahmanism and Bhakti: Papers from the Annual Spalding Symposium on Indian Religion*, ed. Peter Connolly and Sue Hamilton (London: Luzac Oriental, 1997), 185–207. The society in Lanka distributed five thousand copies of the "Dhammapala Jataka" to Theosophical Schools. C. P. Goonewardene, "Report on the Buddhist Work of the Theosophical Soc'y," supplement, *Theosophist* 10 (1889), 20–3 at 22. The "Dhammapala Jataka" itself appeared in *Theosophist* 10 (1888): 100–5. The story centers on a young boy of the Dhammapala lineage who is reported to have died under tragic circumstances. His family is completely nonplussed by the news, responding that they know the boy has not died because no Dhammapala dies young. Their lineage is so righteous that they invariably enjoy long lives. What might have recommended the story of Dhammapala to Dharmapala is the conventional closing in which the Buddha says, "And the characters of this story are we ourselves; the Brahman Dhammapala is now King Suddhodana, the preacher is Sari Putra . . . and the Prince Dhammapala is I Myself" (105). The story and the five thousand books both speak of Dhammapala, unlike Dharmapala's own spelling. Although it was not consistent, the journal itself referred to him as Dhammapala (when he was going by Dharmapala). See, for example, "Brother Dhammapala," supplement, *Theosophist* 10 (1889), cxix.

107. *Women under the Bo Tree: Buddhist Nuns in Sri Lanka* (Cambridge: Cambridge University Press, 1899), 55–6.

tion that "the lesser duties are called the abhi sama carika and the greater duties adi brahma cariya," but he then used the story of Sariputta, who the *Samantapasadika* says violated one of the lesser duties of a monk by entering a trance state for seven days without having swept the place before he sat down to meditate. "The Blessed One," Dharmapala concluded, "emphasized that the bhikkhu who fails to observe the minor duties of *abhi sama carika vattam* shall never fulfill the larger duties of *addi brahma cariyam*." The higher duties are more important but depend on the lower duties, leading him to say, "The Blessed One was very explicit in his condemnation of the slothful Bhikkhu who lives on the charity of others and avoid[s] the duties of the Brahmachari" (Sarnath Notebook no. 4).[108] He is writing about the monkhood, but he is thinking of himself, the brahmacarya who is committed to lower duties such as cleanliness and higher ones such as celibacy and meditation, both carried out with the unceasing energy that marked the Buddha's life.

From his boyhood Dharmapala saw himself becoming a monk (and he came back to that aspiration throughout his life). He was comfortable in his solitude and committed to self-discipline. He sought out the company of monks. His disabled leg caused him to believe that he was unqualified to be a full-fledged monk. But as a young man he sought lower ordination as a samanera. The first time came when he planned to ask Hikkaduve Sumangala to ordain him as a samanera under the bo tree at Bodh Gaya (Diary, February 8, 1899).[109] His diaries do not explain why that ordination did not happen, but he mentions that in 1906 bhikkhu Devamitta offered to make him a samanera. "Then my work was unfinished. Today everything is finished" (Diary, December 30, 1930).[110] He was initiated as a samanera at Bodh Gaya in 1931 and given higher ordination early in 1933. From the time of his renunciation in 1895 he was a monastic manqué—more ascetic than the monkhood and seeking a goal that was impossible for a pious layman and unrealistic for Buddhist monks of his time, his own enlightenment.[111]

108. Dharmapala gave a title to this account of bhikkhu life and signed it, and eventually published it.

109. Bartholomeusz does not speak of Dharmapala's disability or his early interest in becoming a monk. She mentions the episode when he sought ordination in 1899 and his taking ordination in the 1930s (*Women under the Bo Tree*, 55–6) but attributes no significance to either.

110. When he received ordination in 1933, he took the name Dhammapala. The transition from "Dharmapala" to "Dhammapala" reflects his recognition that the Pali form of his name was more appropriate.

111. I read that diary entry in 1930 as saying that being a samanera in 1906 would have impeded his sasana work, even if the thrust of the comment falls on 1930 when he was ready to

His insistence on his activism notwithstanding, Seneviratne quotes Dhar-mapala telling monks not to abandon the *paramartha dhamma* for social service.[112] That distinction confounds the claim that he was a "champion of Protestant Buddhism."[113]

Gombrich and Obeyesekere mention a religious wish that Dharmapala made—*Gautama namin budu vemva* (May I become enlightened / May I become a Buddha Gautama / May I become the Buddha Gautama).[114] That aspiration pinpoints the center of his self-understanding and life's work. They suggest that that the assertion is triply ambiguous—the conventional wish is for enlightenment (bodhi or budu); the two presumptuous aspirations are "May I become the Buddha" and "May I become a Buddha." This is a puzzle with a solution. He sometimes expressed his wish to become a bodhisattva, but in other places he was explicit about the higher aspiration:

> My life will be given birth after birth to Humanity. I will practice param-itas. I will save the world. I will take *vivarana* [a warrant] from the com-ing Buddha. (Diary, April 1, 1897)[115]

His identification with the Buddha did not end with a warrant that set him on his own path to Buddhahood; he wrote in his diary, "I have given up the Arhat path and have taken the Sama Sambodhi path" (January 11, 1904). He tied his robes to mimic the way the Buddha tied his in lithographs (Diary, December 30, 1895). He measured his public life against a forty-five-year standard, the length of the Lord Buddha's ministry (Diary, July 17, 1905).[116]

---

step aside from involvement in the world. Whether he became a samanera in 1906 or remained a brahmacarya, the key was celibacy for both his spiritual development and social reform.

112. *The Work of Kings*, 110n40.

113. Bartholomeusz, *Women under the Bo Tree*, 55.

114. *Buddhism Transformed*, 312.

115. The Pali tradition assumes that there were twenty-five previous Buddhas in the infinite past. When the historical Buddha met the previous Buddha countless lifetimes before his incarnation as Gautama, he made a vow to become a Buddha. The *vivarana* functions as a warrant, given by the incumbent Buddha, that the vow will be realized. See I. B. Horner, *Bud-dhavamsa* (London: Pali Text Society, 1975); and Jan Nattier, "The Meanings of the Maitreya Myth: A Typological Analysis," in *Maitreya, the Future Buddha*, ed. Alan Sponberg and Helen Hardacre (Cambridge: Cambridge University Press, 1988), 23–47. Arhats do not receive a war-rant, but the texts equivocate on this point. Even when an arhat achieves nirvana in a flash, he has seen the Buddha in a previous life. Otherwise he would not have known the Dhamma. See Peter Masefield, *Divine Revelation in Pali Buddhism* (London: Allen and Unwin, 1995). I think it is fair to say that Dharmapala knew only the tradition that has only future Buddhas meeting and receiving a warrant from the Buddha.

116. Before his public career reached that forty-five-year point, Dharmapala worried that his health problems would keep him from matching that figure, noting, "If I live 18 years more,

His own intentions aside, he was born to the role. His parents set him on that path. When he asked them for permission to become a lifelong brahmacarya, he did so by letter. His father replied by letter, "Dear Son, you had better become a Buddha."[117]

Obeyesekere misconstrues Dharmapala's relationship with his parents, and whatever one wants to make of his Freudian reading of his behavior, that reading needs to begin with getting the domestic facts right. He argues that Dharmapala loved his mother but despised his father.[118] His frequent wishing his parents well notwithstanding, his diaries reveal that he was alienated from both of them. Obeyesekere says that his father tried to insinuate him into the Colombo elite and wanted him to enter business. Quoting the passage where his father advises him to aspire to become a Buddha, he misses clues that one can find even in Guruge's book. Dharmapala's father did not want him to enter business, and Dharmapala did not flee to India to avoid the Oedipal conflict with him. He left the island and spent his life in India trying to recover Bodh Gaya. For the record, Dharmapala did not take on the burden of celibacy to accommodate the homosexuality Obeyesekere attributed to him.[119] The conflicts that drove his life did not derive from Freudian forces, whatever their form. They derived from his seeking the highest spiritual goals—enlightenment, bodhisattva status, Buddhahood—in a world where he was involved with other people, linking them together in new ways, reforming, and admonishing them.

Sorting out the facts accomplishes more than setting the record straight. Understanding the man's identity goes to the issue of what Buddhist nationalists had to work with when they appropriated him. I have no quarrel with Seneviratne's saying that a lineage of Dharmapalite monks invoked him to justify their activism, although he presents almost no evidence that Dharmapala himself had their activism in mind. What he wanted from monks was for them to engage their traditional obligations more energetically and spread the Dhamma abroad. The key is his celibacy. His sexual orientation was heterosexual, and mastering his sexual desire bedeviled him through-

---

I would have worked 45 years" (Diary, December 20, 1917). By 1930 he was writing that he had lived the life of an anagarika for forty-five years (Diary, September 26, 1930). He also made calculations relative to how old his reincarnated self would be at the Buddha Jayanti, assuming he were to die presently: "If I die in 1932, I will be 15 in 1956" (Diary, May 11, 1930).

117. Lakshman Jayawardana, ed., *Mage Jivita Kathava* (Colombo: Dayawansa Jayakody, 2000), chapter 10.

118. "Personal Identity and Cultural Crisis," 230–1.

119. "Personal Identity and Cultural Crisis," 231. Obeyesekere says that Dharmapala was at least "latently" homosexual because of his close identification with his mother. He was not close to his mother and struggled with heterosexual urges virtually to the end of his life.

out his life. Celibacy was central to his life's work because he was a South Asian who wanted to make spiritual progress. It had nothing to do with his adoring his mother or harboring Oedipal feelings toward his father. It had to do with his aspiration to follow the Buddha's example. His "this-worldly asceticism" was not a product of his Protestant values. It was a product of his wanting to achieve nirvana. Had he not had a damaged leg, he would have joined the monkhood. Even his "service to Humanity" had no obvious connection to Protestantism, but it has one to Theosophy. Helping others had to do with his wanting to imitate the Buddha's course, which consisted in forty-five years of sharing the truth with other seekers. His struggle to recover Bodh Gaya was not motivated by worldly purposes alone. It was motivated by his identifying with the Buddha and following his course toward enlightenment.

During Dharmapala's lifetime, the *Journal of the Maha Bodhi Society* published a number of articles by distinguished Buddhologists—from von Glasenapp and Sylvain Levy to B. C. Law, Nalinaksha Dutt, and Fyodor Stcherbatsky—and he was appreciative of the role Western scholarship played in making the Dhamma known around the world. He valued the many scholars who were personally sympathetic to Buddhism, but he insisted that they could not themselves understand the Dhamma. They were not celibate, and not practicing celibacy kept them from fully understanding the teachings. By contrast he was celibate and therefore capable of knowing things Western scholars could not. He had parallel reservations about Buddhist laypeople working for the welfare of the sasana. As he wrote to his assistant Devapriya, himself an *anagarika brahmacarya*, "If you don't like to be a 'brahmacharya' enter the order of monks. You must be a monk or a brahmacharya to do sasana work. As a householder you can't do any work for the sasana."[120] So much for the argument that Dharmapala intended the laicization of Buddhism.

In thinking about his social projects, it is essential to begin with the solitary and otherworldly direction of Dharmapala's life and to think of him as a man who was first a religious seeker and second a social reformer.[121] When he entered the Buddhist monkhood late in life, he did not follow the local convention of attaching the name of his birthplace to his monastic

120. "Writing to Devapriya with Fatherly Love," in Ananda W. P. Guruge, ed., *Dharmapala Lipi (Anagarika Dharmapala ge Sinhala Lipi Sangrahayaki)* (Colombo: Government Press, 1965), 415.

121. In Gombrich's account, "By devoting his life to Buddhism Dharmapala meant not merely, in fact not primarily, seeking his own salvation, but promoting the Sasana, and indeed the general welfare of Buddhists as he saw it." *Theravada Buddhism*, 190.

name. He replaced the village name with Devamitta (sent by the gods).[122]
He did not so much invent a new Buddhist role for laymen as adapt an
overdetermined South Asian role to his own life circumstances. Trying to
recover Bodh Gaya, he acted not as a nationalist, universalizer, pious layman, or social reformer. He imitated the life of the Buddha, who vowed not
to leave the *padmasana* (the place where he sat as he attained nirvana) until
he achieved enlightenment. Dharmapala's vow promised that he would not
leave the spot until he had returned it to Buddhist control. His vow had social implications, to be sure, but the place where he made it and the way it
resonated with the Buddha's own vow indicates his motivation to become
a Buddha. Paying attention to his sense of himself as a world renouncer
avoids using him for the sake of either the nation or Protestant Buddhism.
It avoids dividing his life into irreconcilable parts, nationalist at home and
universalist abroad. It avoids teleology. What allowed him to move easily
and often between contexts was that he was a world renouncer at home and
abroad, keeping distance from the roles he embodied in both places. His
thinking of himself as such made it easy for him to imagine being reborn in
India, Japan, Switzerland, or England.

122. That choice can be interpreted in numerous ways—as evidence of his seeing himself
without connection to any one place in Sri Lanka, disdain for Sri Lanka, an expression of his
universalism, his sense of mission, or a reference to the monk Devamitta who was going to give
him ordination in 1906.

CHAPTER ONE

Dharmapala as Theosophist

Who will be the agent between the world and the Masters?
—Anagarika Dharmapala, at Madame Blavatsky's death

Dharmapala was much more deeply influenced by Theosophy than scholarly accounts have allowed. Neglecting those Theosophical influences derives from the allure of a national subjectivity—specifically Buddhist and Sinhala—as a tool for interpreting postcolonial Sri Lanka. Such accounts reduce Theosophy to a vehicle for Buddhist reform or limit Theosophy's influence on Dharmapala's life to the period between 1891 and 1905, when he left Theosophy behind and became a Buddhist pure and simple. Often they mark the turn at the point when Blavatsky told him to fix his mind on learning Pali or when he fell out with Olcott. For many of the Sinhala Buddhists who joined the Theosophical Society after Olcott's arrival, what recommended Theosophy was the society's Western associations and willingness to help the Buddhist cause. For Dharmapala, Theosophy was quite a lot more. He learned how to embody the brahmacarya role by reading Sinnett's *Occult World*.[1] The mahatmas (advanced spiritual beings) gave him a compelling example of selfless service. Right up to the end of his diary keeping, he continued to invoke the mahatmas who watched over humanity from their Himalayan retreats. They provided him with examples that advanced spiritual states were possible, and they modeled the service to humankind that he pursued throughout his life.

Theosophy served as an instrument for his own high aspirations and

1. "My Impressions in Europe and America," *Journal of the Maha Bodhi Society* 34 (1926): 266–78, at 278.

idealism: the content remained largely Buddhist, but the notion that one could aspire to higher states of consciousness came from the mahatmas, who had themselves achieved those states. In contrast with the low spiritual aspirations of local monks, the mahatmas gave him a paradigm for his perfectionism. Theosophy gave him a rationale for carrying Buddhism to the West.[2] Theosophy taught him that doing so was an act of the highest wisdom (parama vijnana). Summing up his life just before his death, he focused on people who had shaped his career; two were his parents and two Theosophists:

> Sadhu! Sadhu! Buddhists of Japan, China, Tibet, Siam, Cambodia, Ceylon & Burma are dead. The germ of Bodhi was impregnated in my heart by my father. The germ of renunciation was impregnated by my Mother, and the Devas induced Mrs. Mary Foster of Honolulu to help me. The path of perfection was shown to me by Mme. Blavatsky in my 21st year. (Diary, December 20, 1930)

Even someone as peripheral to his life as C. F. Powell played a part.[3] When they worked together at Theosophical headquarters, Dharmapala found a real-world example of service to humanity and realized that he could do it himself.

Giving proper balance to Buddhism and Theosophy in Dharmapala's life confronts challenges unlike comparable analytical tasks—sorting out, let's say, the ways Gandhi was influenced by Christianity although never ceasing to think of himself as a Hindu. What makes the present task complicated derives from the same virtues that made Theosophy successful as a social movement. Two of those virtues reinforce one another. Theosophy thought about itself as something other than a religion. It was rationalistic and scientific. Its self-description emphasized that the group was devoted to discussion and exploration. Joining the group did not entail abandoning the religion the new Theosophist had practiced previously. Membership in a Theosophical society was additive, and the society exercised authority that was softer than soft. The group that Olcott established in Colombo got the

2. Jayawardana, Mage Jivita Kathava, 29.

3. Like Olcott, Powell was a Civil War veteran who came to Colombo in 1889 as a volunteer for Buddhist work. He died shortly thereafter. Curuppumullage Jinarajadasa, ed., The Golden Book of the Theosophical Society: A Brief History of the Society's Growth from 1875–1925 (Adyar: Theosophical Publishing House, 1925), 95.

name Buddhist Theosophical Society. The specifically Theosophical content was negligible, but the group retained the name long after Olcott died
and any need remained for reliance on Theosophy.

Leela Gandhi characterizes Theosophy as an "affective community" in
which people of one sort mixed freely with others in the spirit of equality and solidarity. In her account imperialism did not itself foster human
solidarity, but the imperial condition—in places as diverse as London and
Calcutta—gave rise to cosmopolitanism, which had an elective affinity for
intercultural friendship. That cosmopolitanism produced "affective communities," each marked by belonging without uniformity. Those communities provided an alternative to self-identical communities where an
actor encounters others in "relation to himself, perpetually repeated."[4] The
emphasis on equality and solidarity duly noted, the situation among Theosophists was more complicated. The movement produced its own variety of self-identical communities. In Burma there were three Theosophical
societies—a Buddhist one for Burmese, a Hindu one for Indians, and one
made up of Europeans and "half-castes," specifically occupying themselves
with the study of mesmerism.[5] Members of the Philadelphia Theosophical
Society requested permission to form a branch to admit only Germans to
membership, leading to the establishment of Die Deutsche Theosophische
Gesellschaft.[6] Whether bringing members of different sorts into one circle of
inquiry or providing separate Theosophical venues for self-identical groups
of people, Theosophy offered its members the invidious pleasures of inves-
tigating traditional religious truths at a depth that ordinary Hindus, Buddhists, and Christians did not know.

A second virtue was more semiotic than organizational. Blavatsky began
by appropriating ancient Egyptian categories and practices, but she hit her
stride after turning her attention to South Asia, a turn that was initiated by
the putative trip she made to Tibet to learn the "ancient wisdom" from a
group of adepts who lived in ashrams scattered across the Himalayas. These
mahatmas made up what Blavatsky called a Great White Brotherhood, and
their wisdom could be found in diminished form in all religions. At full
strength, that wisdom was delivered in letters that Blavatsky and others
received from the mahatmas. The language was English or French; the concepts were Hindu or Buddhist. Shifting between registers gave Theosophical

---

4. Leela Gandhi, *Affective Communities: Anticolonial Thought, Fin-de-Siècle Radicalism,
and the Politics of Friendship* (Durham, NC: Duke University Press), 24–5.

5. "Burma Revisited," *Theosophist* 12 (1891): 323–32, at 323.

6. "Annual Report," *Theosophist* 13 (1892): 1–34, at 18.

talk a kind of transidiomaticity that it shared with South Asian figures such as Vivekananda, Aurobindo, and Mahatma Gandhi. Transidiomatic South Asian talk spread to people as diverse as Rudyard Kipling, James Joyce, and Robert J. Oppenheimer.[7] As this discourse traveled from its first occupational niche, it mutated, and its rhetorical force was transformed. When J. Robert Oppenheimer said the first nuclear explosion reminded him of a passage from the *Bhagavad Gita*—"Now I am become Death, the destroyer of worlds"—he put the Hindu text to new purposes, acquiring new meanings and losing old ones. What was originally a discourse framed in a particular register could speak to new audiences without having to "posit the particular medium of communication as a coherent foundation," bypassing the necessity for a "more conscious or full-fledged translation." In this context, Theosophical discourse profited from an advantage it did not earn—it borrowed the authority of older ones without continually having to provide context and explication, and that authority enabled it to become "a material phenomenon with corresponding effects within social networks of power."[8]

Blavatsky was no South Asian, but she outstripped her Indian peers by the volume and audacity of her appropriations, taking Sanskrit expressions and fitting them to her own purposes. Her teachings took their rhetorical force from head-to-head exchanges she had with the Tibetan adepts she had met in the Himalayas, although the first conversation came when an exceptionally tall Indian prince—whom she immediately recognized as her "Protector"—approached her in Hyde Park and told her that she had great work to do for humankind. If she accepted, he told her, she would have to spend years in Tibet learning the knowledge to be transmitted.[9] The knowledge that ended up in *Isis Unveiled* derived from some one hundred books on the occult and cited some fourteen hundred works in various languages.[10] To her followers, what the mahatmas told her was explicated by scholarly citations; to the cynical, what the mahatmas told her came directly from those sources. In this context Hindu and Buddhist religious terms had already entered a transidiomatic environment before Blavatsky appropriated them— the index to *Isis Unveiled* runs from *akasa* and *arhat* to *yama* and *yuga*, but there are hundreds of terms in between. That vocabulary in hand, she managed to create a world of intimacy, brotherhood, spiritual growth, and hu-

7. Srinivas Aravamudan, *Guru English: South Asian Religion in a Cosmopolitan Language* (Princeton, NJ: Princeton University Press, 2006), 6–10.

8. Aravamudan, *Guru English*, 6.

9. Howard Murphet, *When Daylight Comes: A Biography of Helena Petrovna Blavatsky* (Wheaton, IL: Theosophical Publishing House, 1975), 31.

10. Aravamudan, *Guru English*, 107.

manitarian purpose, and that world naturally meshed with Western knowledge of South Asian religion that was de facto authoritative. Texts were
everywhere—not Sanskrit or Pali but English and German—and the messages themselves appeared in either book or letter form, their allure coming from their having been communicated to Blavatsky directly. She alone
had actually encountered a mahatma, and she controlled access to them.

Gombrich and Obeyesekere find theoretical leverage in a notion that
parallels Srinivas Aravamudan's "transidiomaticity." When Sinhalas today
say that Buddhism is not itself a "religion," they "overcode" other religions.
By claiming that Buddhism is a philosophy and not a religion, they gain a familiar advantage: "If Buddhism is not a religion like Christianity, Hinduism,
or Islam, that leaves open the possibility that it moves on a higher plane of
generality, a more exalted plane."[11] Buddhists gain another advantage in the
bargain, subsuming mere religions under their wing. Gombrich and Obeyesekere write that Buddhism may have learned this trick from Theosophy.
The present chapter confirms their speculation by tracing the Buddhist "not
a religion" argument to Theosophy. There are other discourses and practices that modern Buddhism owes to Theosophy. The additive nature and
transidiomatic diction of Theosophy allowed Dharmapala to move casually
between subject positions that could be Buddhist, Theosophist, or both.[12] To
the extent that Dharmapala was a Buddhist universalist, he was so because
he was first a Theosophical universalist.

In Japan, Bodh Gaya, Calcutta, and the West, Dharmapala negotiated
forces well beyond his control and encountered people who spoke different
languages and entertained different objectives even as they cooperated with
him. He made his own decision about renouncing the world, invented a role
for himself, and made, broke, and remade a relationship with the Theosophical Society on his own terms. All of these turns engaged issues of identity
and difference, universalism and particularism by way of Dharmapala's own
self-understanding, and after the fact, he could see just how fateful was the
decision to push his Buddhist identity to the fore:

> Had I remained in the T.S. [Theosophical Society] I don't know what I
> would have been today. I would have studied Theosophical literature and

---

11. *Buddhism Transformed*, 222.

12. The relevant circuits of influence were more complicated than the overcoding argument
allows. In Dharmapala's time some Western scholars called Buddhism a philosophy, treating it
as something less than a religion. Lacking a god, it failed to qualify as a religion. Dharmapala
took the absence of a god figure as a virtue that made Buddhism appropriate for a world in
which science reigned.

become half Vedantin, half Buddhist, or become a chela and [line buried in crease of page] . . . and work in the Theosophical Society carrying out the wishes of the Theosophical leaders, or become the general Secretary of the Buddhist Section. I would have had a larger field to work with friends all over the Theosophical world. But my impulse and wisdom carried me towards the Path of Samma sambodhi. (Sarnath Notebook no. 53)

The problem here is that after his turn back to Buddhism, he continued to speak regularly in a Theosophical idiom and hold to a set of Theosophical practices. Phrases such as "samma sambodhi" resonate with both Buddhism and Theosophy.[13]

Scholars have found Theosophical influence in a variety of modernist contexts, from W. B. Yeats to linguistic theory, from James Joyce to abstract art.[14] Gauri Visvanathan argues that Annie Besant's conversion to Theosophy from socialism and atheism "prepares the ground for the emergence of the relational model of the commonwealth," replacing rule by force with the idea that the empire realized the Theosophical notion of universal brotherhood.[15] Laurie Sears finds more unlikely effects. In her account Javanese shadow puppetry was less a long-standing indigenous tradition than a tradition remade under Theosophical inspiration. *Wayang* under Theosophical interpretation had other applications. It became a way of imagining a nation that transcended Java and incorporated the rest of Indonesia.[16] Joy Dixon has shown how Theosophy informed fin-de-siècle feminism in both Britain and India.[17] There is little news in asserting that a religious movement committed to universal brotherhood would appeal to other social formations, but the connections embody the spirit of an extraordinary historical moment.

The conventional treatment of Dharmapala's Theosophy suffers from two misreadings. The first—that he gave up his commitment to Theosophy

13. H. P. Blavatsky, *The Secret Doctrine*, vol. 6 (London: Theosophical Publishers, 1971), 475.

14. See Katherine Mullin, "Typhoid Turnips and Crooked Cucumbers," *Modernism/modernity* 8 (2001): 77–97; and Christopher M. Hutton and John E. Joseph, "Back to Blavatsky: The Impact of Theosophy on Modern Linguistics,' *Language and Communication* 18 (1998): 181–204.

15. *Outside the Fold: Conversion, Modernity, and Belief* (Princeton, NJ: Princeton University Press, 1998), 186–8.

16. "Intellectuals, Theosophy, and Failed Narratives of the Nation in Late Colonial Java," in *A Companion to Postcolonial Studies*, ed. Henry Schwarz and Sangeeta Ray (London: Blackwell, 2000), 333–57.

17. "Sexology and the Occult: Sexuality and Subjectivity in Theosophy's New Age," *Journal of the History of Sexuality* 7, no. 3 (1997): 409–33.

sometime between 1891 and 1905—simply ignores the facts. It is true that
he sometimes said things that support the two-part model. Usually he attributed the transition to Blavatsky's counsel, but sometimes he took the
arrival at Bodh Gaya as critical, as when he noted, "I came to India first
because I was a Theosophist, and I came to Buddha Gaya as a Buddhist"
(Memorandum to Diary of 1919). In other places he attributed the break to
Olcott's disrespect for the relic that he had given him. In any case, what he
abandoned was the Theosophical Society; he did not abandon Theosophy as
a philosophy of spiritual advancement but held on to a belief in the mahatmas, dhyana meditation, and Blavatsky's teachings till the end of his life.
His alienation was alienation not from Blavatsky's Theosophical Society
but from Annie Besant's. She took Theosophy in a Hinduized direction, but
Dharmapala never left the Blavatsky's Theosophy. Besant's Theosophy left
him. To complicate things, he was reconciled with Besant in 1911 and re-
joined the Indian Theosophical Society in 1913, even while railing against
her betrayal of the society's commitment to Buddhism.

The second misreading is more consequential. It bears on Obeyesekere's
argument that Dharmapala invented a "Protestant Buddhism," leading to a
contemporary Buddhism in Sri Lanka shaped by Protestant characteristics—
internalization, rationalization, and the elevation of the laity, or laicization.[18] As productive as the idea has been for Obeyesekere as well as other
scholars working on Buddhist modernity, Dharmapala's life was more influenced by the exposed hand of Theosophy than the hidden hand of Protestantism. Olcott led him toward a universalism of the "affective community" variety. Seeking a united Buddhist world held together by "general
principles of belief universally recognized by the entire Buddhist world,"
Olcott traveled across Asia for the sake of Buddhist unity.[19] Where Olcott
called his journal *The Theosophist or Universal Brotherhood*, Dharmapala
called his the *Journal of the Maha Bodhi Society and the United Buddhist
World*. But Theosophy, as Olcott told Sinhala Buddhists, was quite a lot
more than Buddhism:

> You see . . . gentlemen that the Theosophical Society is not a Buddhist,
> any more than it is a Parsee, a Hindu, a Jain, a Jew, or a Christian Pro-

18. Obeyesekere's first formulation of Dharmapala's role in creating a "Protestant"
Buddhism came in "Religious Symbolism and Political Change in Ceylon," *Modern Ceylon
Studies* 1, (1970): 43–63, and was reprinted in Obeyesekere, Frank Reynolds, and Bardwell L.
Smith, *The Two Wheels of Dhamma: Essay on the Theravada Tradition in India and Ceylon*
(Chambersburg, PA: American Academy of Religion, 1972), 58–78.

19. Olcott, "An United Buddhist World," *Theosophist* 13 (1892): 239–43, at 239.

paganda. If it were, then there would no room in its membership for any but Buddhists, whereas, here before your very eyes, you see that its Hindu and Parsee fellows are thoroughly devoted to its interests. The salutation of brotherhood has smoothed all the common asperities that keep man and man asunder, and a responsive thrill from every heart attests the tie of common humanity that links us all together beneath our varied complexions, costumes, and creeds.[20]

Local Buddhists had little interest in what Leela Gandhi calls a "cobelonging of non-identical singularities."[21] They had great interest in Olcott's hostility to Christianity.

Dharmapala had scant interest in brotherhood that transcended Buddhism, and even his interest in building a Buddhist world did not seek that unity as an end in itself. He wanted Buddhist unity for one purpose: recovering a site of importance to all Buddhists, Bodh Gaya. But his belief in the mahatmas made him a universalist in another sense that transcended Buddhism. Like the mahatmas, who work for the good of all humanity, Dharmapala pledged himself to the same cause:

[Blavatsky] gave me the key to open the door of my spiritual nature and Col. Olcott taught me to work forgetting myself. I left home, parents, Govt: service and everything for the sake of this blessed life. . . . My aspirations are towards the highest goal of perfection to become Buddha and save Humanity, and this I will do. (Diary, March 10, 1897)

One could say that he became a Buddhist working to save humanity by way of a Theosophical intervention or that his being a Buddhist led him to a Theosophy that confirmed what he believed and reinvigorated his childhood religion. The less segmentary way of putting it is to say that he devoted his life to universalizing goals that were transidiomatic and overcoded.

DHARMAPALA BECOMES A THEOSOPHIST

There were signs of Dharmapala's future early in his childhood, and they pointed to a life of religious seeking. His childhood was difficult. His father moved him so frequently that he had attended eight institutions before he

---

20. "Theosophy and Buddhism," in *A Collection of Lectures on Theosophy and Archaic Religions, Delivered in India and Ceylon* (Madras: A. Theyaga Rajier, 1883), 27.
21. *Affective Communities*, 27.

finished secondary school. His diaries never speak of his playing with other children, and he had a distant relationship with his brothers and sisters, first because he was the eldest and later because of his temperament. Instead he writes of playing by himself in his father's garden and enjoying the beauty of the place: "The best part of my youth was spent in my father's garden house at Kotahena from 1874–1876. . . . The garden was a paradise . . . [an] expanse of ever green garden, mainly lawn, the best in Colombo" (Sarnath Notebook no. 53). Finding a sapling of the bo tree that grew there, Dharmapala guarded it with bricks and offered lights to it; his "father would say this is 'Kaputu bo' [crow's bo tree] and I must not worship it" (Sarnath Notebook no. 4).

Over the forty-four-year interval he kept a diary, he frequently referred to his "dear" father and his "beloved" mother, but being fostered out from age four to ten put emotional as well as physical distance between him and his parents:

> From my tender age up I was being brought up in my uncle's home. I was used to strict discipline. Whatever my aunt gave I had to sit silently. I did not receive the tender affection which a boy of four should receive from his mother. (Sarnath Notebook no. 4)[22]

He had more grievances toward his mother than his father:

> My mother's attitude towards me was strange. I prayed for her happiness many thousand times in 1901. I went to her with great expectations; but I found a cold heart; and she forced me by her expressions to leave her home. Why should this have happened. Miss Holmes [Josephine Holmes, American socialite and Theosophist] thinks it was the work of the angels of light; they did not want that I should be tied down to a home life; and nobody could have forced me out except mother and she was influenced to make me get out!! Today I am without father, mother, brothers, leaving my share to go to the devil; with one supreme idea in my mind to be pure and righteous and to spread the Dhamma to all English speaking people. (Diary, August 16, 1902)

Dharmapala's attitude toward his father was marked by the same sense of rejection:

---

22. His uncle S. P. D. Gunawardana "had wealth . . . influence, and was most social. . . . My uncle was a redoubtable person fearless, daring and a leader of men, and I bathed in his magnetism." "My Early Associations," Sarnath Notebook no. 4.

I have not seen my father since last Monday. The fact that there is no attachment to me neither could I show my attention to the people at home. Never did I receive kindness at their hands. When I was a little boy I was brought up by my uncle; then I was put into School as a boarder, someway or other I was away from home. In 1885 renounced home. I see now that my residence with my parents since last December had no good results. Several times I suggested to set apart Gunter House for religious work. My father loves money more than me. (Diary, March 19, 1898)

His independence had several sources—one of them was the lack of affection he felt from the mother who fostered him out and a father who had "no attachment to [him]." His father also introduced him to the idea of renunciation, initiating him as a brahmacarya at age nine.[23] The vow lasted only for a day, but the pattern was set. The father who—according to his son at least—felt no attachment to his son guided him to practice nonattachment.

When he returned to his parents' home after his stay with his uncle, Dharmapala spent considerable amounts of time alone—in their garden where the snakes glided about openly, knowing that they would not be harmed—and began to envision a life of service, discipline, and sacrifice:

In . . . School I was fearless, daring, and had a kind of aristocratic hauteur, and did not care anybody [sic]. At home I had the same spirit, and what I wanted I got. I was stubborn [crossed out] resolute, and could not bear any kind of intolerance. I had no love for worldly things. I loved simplicity, solitude, and any form of helping the poor, even to the extent of giving everything I had. . . . [My mother] used to preach to me the doctrine of impermanency weekly, and my father exhorted me to practice humility. He used to tell me "do not depend on worldly wealth." Well then if everything is to end in change I thought I shall not want this worldly wealth. From my 10th year the ethic of "other-worldliness" and the beauty of saintliness became impregnated in my mind. (Sarnath Notebook no. 4)

The "aristocratic hauteur" Dharmapala saw in himself and the otherworldliness his father urged on him gave shape to his withdrawal from the household life, strengthening both his innerliness and personal reserve. Attending Christian schools provided discipline in another form:

23. Dharmapala, "Reminiscences of My Early Life."

In my 12th year began the strict discipline of the Christian Boarding
School. It was horrid, unnatural, fit for a criminal bible and prayer all
day long. The Christian teachers knew only so much and nothing more.
But I was cheerful. I did not submit to the discipline where the mind was
concerned. I read the Bible and also books of my own religion. I did not
pray. I sang the glory of the Buddha's greatness, and prayer was to me the
characteristics [sic] of the coward. (Sarnath Notebook no. 4)

Sending the boy to Christian schools was his father's effort to do the best
for his son, not an act of cruelty. Don Carolis had the idea that his eldest
son was out of the ordinary.[24] His horoscope said as much. It did not bode
well for success in worldly endeavors, and he noted that "my father therefore gave me liberty of action."[25] He did quite a lot more. He told the boy
to aspire to Buddhahood and provided a monthly stipend as he pursued the
bodhisattva path (Diary, August 12, 1925). The life that the boy envisioned,
in other words, became the life that the man lived.

  During his childhood Dharmapala had another inspiration when he saw
an apparition:

I do not know whether the sight I witnessed, when [I] was a little boy,
was a phantasm; but I do remember very well the time. The house was
vacant. It was noon. I climbed the stairs alone and reached the steps
wherefrom I could see three men dressed in silken robes of a green colour with tribal decorations, all glittering, sleeping on the bare floor. One
raised his head, and I greatly frightened ran down. Whether it was a hal-
lucination or a phantasm, I have no idea. The picture has *never* left my
mind. (Sarnath Notebook no. 23)

  24. At some point around 1907 the family began using "Hewavitarne" in place of "Hewavitarana" as their surname, and I will follow the later spelling.
  25. Don Carolis was a close friend of C. Don Bastian, who produced several plays of Shake-
speare and edited the first Sinhala language newspaper. "My father had great faith in him,"
Dharmapala noted, "and whatever advice he gave, my father promptly carried out. He advised
my father to put me in the Notarial line, and I was articled as a clerk under Proctor & Notary
Mr. W. P. Ranasinha. After a few months he suggested that I should be trained for Govt. Service
and accordingly I was apprenticed as a clerk in the Department of Public Instruction" ("C. Don
Bastian," Sarnath Notebook no. 4). Brekke argues that his father attempted to keep Dharmapala
from making his first trip to Adyar because of "the young man's lack of interest in worldly
affairs" (*Makers of Modern Indian Religion*, 72). The opposite is the case. Don Carolis guided
Dharmapala toward a life of renunciation and service, in part because he thought the boy had no
head for business. Dharmapala writes, "I don't know why he did not put me into business. He
employed a clerk to help him in his furniture business" (Sarnath Notebook no. 23).

The three men in silken robes foreground the Tibetan adepts who enter his life later. He never made that connection explicit, but that uncanny experience prepared him for what was to come. He learned a life of discipline from his father; he received more discipline (of a Christian variety) in school and learned to resist with his own resolve. And he had direct experience of another world that was the object of that discipline.

Dharmapala came upon Shelley's *Queen Mab* in his uncle's library, and it became his favorite poem. The affinity between a Buddhist reformer and an English poem is not obvious, but part of its appeal came from Queen Mab's rebellion against orthodoxy, Christianity, and the social order. The poem's hope for human perfectibility spoke to his own spiritual goals, as did its invocation of individual destiny against the backdrop of social degradation: "I have never ceased to love its lyric indignation against the tyrannies and injustices that man heaps on himself and its passion for individual freedom," he wrote.[26] A Sinhala account of his feeling for the poem reveals still more:

> I never had desire [*asava*] for cruelty and injustice which the normal man carries on his back. The ordinary man never believed that by his perseverance that he could go to higher planes spiritually. But this poem gave the paradigm [*siddhantaya*].[27]

The poem resonates with the encounter with the three phantasms, his own sense of having no ordinary destiny, and his father's plan that he should aspire to a role beyond the borders of his historical moment and social class. Dharmapala later wrote that the poem should be placed in the hands of young men (Diary, October 9, 1909), and he reread it as late as age fifty-five, returning to the tortured romance of self and society (Diary, October 19, 1919).

Dharmapala's solitude had other motivations. As an adult he had suspicions about other people's intentions, and many relationships came and went. His own understanding of the failure of many relationships was linked to his own idealism:

> It is perhaps due to my past Karma that prevents me from associating with people who are not upright. I expect strict uprightness from people,

---

26. Sri Chandra Sen, "The Ven'ble Sri Devamitta Dhammapala," *Journal of the Maha Bodhi Society* 41 (1933): 330.
27. Jayawardana, *Mage Jivita Kathava*, 28.

and when I find a so-called friend showing signs of dishonesty I leave him. This has been my characteristic since my boy-hood. (Diary, May 8, 1927)

His solitude extended to his spiritual life. Early on he received two messages from one of the Himalayan adepts, Master Koot Hoomi, relayed to him by Blavatsky. Those communications came in 1884 and 1886, followed by forty years with no sign of recognition from the mahatmas. By Dharmapala's reasoning, changes in the organization of the Theosophical Society itself broke the relationship to the mahatmas: "Even the Masters left the Theosophical Society because they found none to take HPB's [Blavatsky's] place" (Diary, May 8, 1927).

In January 1884 Dharmapala attended the annual Theosophical meetings in Adyar and accepted the principles of chelaship. It was his first trip abroad. Once home he began to live the life of a *chela* (student) "and exerted daily to get the blessings of the Masters, to work for Humanity, and to follow the example of the *Bodhisatva*."[28] In November 1885 he took the next step, renouncing the worldly life. He had no clear idea of what that career would entail, but it would not include marriage or close relations with his family:

> [I wrote] a letter to my beloved father, expressing my resolve to be a Brahmachari and solicited his permission. This letter I handed to my mother requesting her to deliver it [to] my father. I was then staying at the T.S. headquarters at 61, Maliban Street. When I saw my mother next time, she expressed her deep satisfaction and blessed me. . . . My dear father simply said, "You are the eldest in the family, and your brothers are all young, and if you leave me who will take care of them?" I answered and said, "Dear father each one has his own Karma, and their Karma will take care of them." In this wise the parting took place.[29]

Everyone has his own karma, and karma, not family, takes care of people. Recognizing that he had been fostered out and felt unwelcome in his par-

---

28. "To the Beloved Mahatmas Who Loved Our Lord," October 4, 1919, Sarnath Notebook no. 50. This is one of a handful of entries in the Sarnath notebooks that is titled and signed, in this case by "Thine obedient Lanoo, Dharmapala Hevavitarana." Some of these entries, such as "My Early Associations" "My Persecution," summarize one particular aspect of Dharmapala's life. This entry is framed as part of a conversation that began with his first letter to the mahatmas in 1884. The expression "Lanoo" served as a textual salutation, which Blavatsky used to address a chela.

29. "To the Beloved Mahatmas Who Loved Our Lord."

ent's house when he returned suggests the name he chose for himself: "anagarika" (homeless) was as much about his self-understanding as the act of renunciation.[30]

A childhood accident shaped his life's trajectory. Dharmapala explained how his leg was injured in several ways, running from karma to a paralytic stroke to the inattention of a nursemaid:

> In my 4th year my left [crossed out] right leg was permanently injured, and I could not [crossed out]. which debarred me from entering the order of Bhikkhus [Buddhist monks]. Had not this defect been a hindrance I would have become a Bhikkhu. Some bad karma I might have done in the past or it might have been due to neglect of my nurse. I was irreverent to all except the holy. I liked the real ascetic Bhikkhus. (Sarnath Notebook no. 4)

His diaries make references in other places to his wanting to become a Buddhist monk, but he led a full-time religious life outside the monkhood, and that meant a religious life that had no Buddhist precedent.[31] But it had a Theosophical precedent. In what I take to be a mature characterization of his self-understanding, Dharmapala spoke of his life course in terms that capture the transidiomatic character of his renunciation—"brahmacariya of the bodhisattva path" (Diary, December 17, 1917).

He learned cleanliness from one of his teachers: "I was greatly influenced by my Sinhalese teacher, a man of immaculate habits and a strict

30. Consider the theme of family abandonment in contrast to the kindness of a distant stranger, Mary Foster, the patron he met in Honolulu in 1893. He refers to her as his "Foster" mother decades before his own mother died, but here she plays the part of his "Foster" father: "My beloved father supported me and left me a legacy for my maintenance. Mary Foster has taken the place of my beloved father. I owe my life since my father's death to her absolutely. I was the eldest in the family of 4 brothers and one sister. The legacy left to me by my father, my younger brothers [had] not yet been given to me. Two brothers are dead and gone. My surviving youngest brother is absolutely indifferent to my welfare. They have done me great injustice and have committed a sin in not paying the legacy left by my father for doing meritorious deeds." "My Early Associations," Sarnath Notebook no. 4.

31. Gombrich and Obeyesekere suggest that there was a South Asian paradigm in the life of a *naisthika brahmacharin*, a Hindu boy who forsakes the householder stage of life to remain celibate and devoted to study. *Buddhism Transformed*, 217. The point is plausible, but there are no signs that Dharmapala made that connection. There was a Theosophical paradigm that he both understood and embodied. He would become a chela, the rejiggered category Blavatsky invented for a young Theosophical devotee who apprentices himself to a guru. Dharmapala had a real life example to follow, Damodar Mavalankar, who came to Sri Lanka with Blavatsky and Olcott in 1880. Mavalankar also served as an inspiration for Dharmapala's wanting to visit Tibet and find the mahatmas.

disciplinarian. He was a bachelor. I learnt lessons of cleanliness from him. He was known as Harmanis Gurunanse" ("My Early Associations," Sarnath Notebook no. 4). He adds,

> In my early boyhood I was a constant attendant of the Roman Catholic Church attached to St. Mary's School. . . . On feast days of the Catholics it was my habit to take [a] basketful of flowers to the Church. Continuous attendance daily made me quiet at home [and] in the monastery. The fathers knew me as a Buddhist. My most beloved father taught me Pali gathas as a protection from evil. He was a calligraphist and he wrote the gatha on a palm leaf for me and asked that I commit into memory which I did. He was very devout and was in the habit of reciting the adoration gatha whenever he was riding in the carriage with me. He never showed that he loved me. To me he appeared rather strict. I feared him because he insisted that I should study, which was abhorrent to me. I did not like to be tied down to a place. The garden was to me an arcadia. I loved to roam about. . . . I never could take, even when I was twelve years old, the Bible seriously. To pray to God I abhorred. It meant cowardice.

Absent a psychological interpretation, his references to discipline, cowardice, and the synergy between abandonment and world renunciation still leap off the page.

As a boy Dharmapala frequented the temple of the orator Migettuvatte Gunananda, who "was thundering week after week by his denunciations against the Catholic faith." Migettuvatte told his listeners about the founding of the Theosophical Society "for the study of religion" and that the two principal members were themselves Buddhists; Dharmapala recalled that "the very utterance made a profound impression in my mind." He was still more impressed when Migettuvatte "commenced to issue a pamphlet about the doings of the T.S. and about Tibetan Mahatmas. I became more and more interested" (Sarnath Notebook no. 4). As Dharmapala was becoming more interested in Theosophy, the two leading Theosophists were becoming more interested in Asia, settling in Bombay in 1879.

> It was in 1878 when the late Miggettuwatta Priest first announced at a bana preaching in the Pahala pansala that a TS had been formed in America. In 1878 I read the first number of the Theosophist. Since then devotedly I followed the path of the Theosophist. In 1883 Nov I sent my application but it was refused as I was young. Then I sent a letter to the

"Unknown Brother," c/o HPB having read Sinnett's Occult World. In 1884 Jany: I joined the TS along with Peter D'Abrew L. Ed: Silva. Walking, talking eating etc. I knew only one thing:—"Mahatma." (Diary, September 21, 1905)

For the rest of his life, he remained committed to that mahatma, Koot Hoomi, the adept most closely associated with Buddhism.

A year or so later Dharmapala had an experience that bore directly on his views about sexuality and asceticism:[32]

In my 17th year, my mother lost her youngest infant daughter suddenly. She became frantic, for a work [sic; week?] she refused to come out of the room and refrained from taking food. I went and accosted her and said "Mother what is the meaning of this. Get up and wash yourself." She woke up from her dream. This suffering of my mother made us to think of the misery of bringing forth children, and the future results of having sexual contact with a woman. I said to myself "I shall not be the cause of giving pain to a woman." From that day I avoided the company of woman, and in November 1883 I took the vow of chastity and pledged to observe the precept of Brahmacariya. In Jany 1884 I joined the TS and Col. Olcott initiated me, and I was accepted as a Chela by the Master KH. Mme Blavatsky addressed me as "Chela" and "Lanoo." (Diary, October 18, 1930)

This passage emphasizes his trying to snap his mother out of her depression or at least to keep herself clean, but it moves off in a different direction. He will avoid sex to avoid giving pain. The conclusion is such a logical jump that it is tempting to suppose that by the time of his infant sister's death in 1881 or 1882 he had already been influenced by reading the *Theosophist* and its accounts of the Tibetan mahatmas and their celibacy.

The first link in the chain that joined Dharmapala to the Theosophical movement reached back to the public debate between Migettuvatte and a group of local Christians.[33] The Panadura *vadaya* (controversy or debate) came as the last of several exchanges marked by vituperation from both

---

32. Jayawardana, *Mage Jivita Kathava*, 27, tells the story with more emphasis on Dharmapala's displeasure at his mother's coming undone with grief.

33. "A Letter of Venerable Dhammapala," *Journal of the Maha Bodhi Society* 41 (1933): 388–90, at 388.

parties as Buddhists began to resist the hegemony of Christianity in the local public sphere.[34] Following the Panadura debate, these encounters were reported in the *Ceylon Times* and later published with revisions made by the two parties, along with an introduction and annotations by an American Methodist minister with spiritualist interests. When Olcott read Reverend Peebles's account, he made contact with Migettuvatte, sending him a copy of *Isis Unveiled* and a Theosophical pamphlet.[35] What is pertinent here is that first contact between Theosophists and Buddhists was motivated by interests that were as much political as ideological—Olcott saw a chance to come to the aid of Buddhists trying to defend their territory; Migettuvatte saw a foreigner willing to help.

Migettuvatte was attracted to Olcott because of his hostility to Christian missionizing, not his interest in universal human spirituality. But the monk was interested enough to publish a pamphlet discussing the Tibetan mahatmas, and Dharmapala thus acquired some of his knowledge of the mahatmas in a pamphlet with a Buddhist imprimatur: "Then the priest commenced to issue a pamphlet about the doings of the T.S. and about Tibetan Mahatmas. I became more and more interested" (Sarnath Notebook no. 4). He could not get enough of the latest Theosophical intelligence about the mahatmas, and the order of events is itself instructive:

> In 1883 I read A. P. Sinnett's Occult World and a copy of the Theosophist of August 1882 on the "Chelas." I read [obscure] the article and decided to become a chela of the Masters. I addressed a letter to the "Unknown Brother" and sent it to HPB's address at Adyar. I gave up eating meat & fish and vowed to lead the Chela's life. (Sarnath Notebook no. 4)[36]

In the *Theosophist* he read Sinnett and Blavatsky on "Chelas and Lay Chelas," and he read them before he read *The Light of Asia* and *India Revisited*. None of his early influences were scholarly, and none were canonical texts, and of what he read, Theosophy predominated.

34. R. F. Young and G. P. V. Somaratna, *Vain Debates: The Buddhist-Christian Controversies of Nineteenth-Century Ceylon* (Vienna: Sammlung De Nobili, 1996).

35. Ria Kloppenberg, "A Buddhist-Christian Encounter in Sri Lanka: The Panadura Vada," in *Religion: Empirical Studies*, ed. Steven. J. Sutcliffe (Aldershot: Ashgate, 2004), 179–91.

36. Between 1882 and 1892 Dharmapala began to read more Buddhist texts: "Dharmapradipaka, Visuddhi Magga, Mahavamsa, Attanagaluvamsa, Mihinda prasna, Meyyartha [obscure] dipaniya, Sumanta Kuta vannane, Satipathana Sutta, Light of Asia, Theosophist, Occult World, Esoteric Buddhism, Isis Revealed, Buddhist Suttas, Col. Olcott's Lectures, Voice of the Silence, Grimalot's Sept [sic] Suttas Path" (Sarnath Notebook no. 51).

When he withdrew from the world in November 1883, he did so as a Theosophist.

> The July No: Theosophist of 1882 containing the article "Chelas & Lay Chelas" fell into my hands in Novr: 1883 when I decided to follow the Path of Chelaship, and I wrote a letter to HPB & to the "Unknown Mahatma." In Jany: 1884 Col. Olcott initiated me. In Decr: 1884 HPB took me to Adyar. In Oct:, 1885 I left home. (Diary, August 12, 1925)

To say that he renounced the world as a Theosophist is not to say that he was a Theosophist before he was a Buddhist. But by his late teens, he was reading Theosophy, and the cognitive interests he found there—the mahatma Koot Hoomi, Blavatsky, mediation, and Tibet—laid out the path his Buddhism would follow. He recalled:

> It was in 1885 that I desired to visit Tibet and I was very serious to come across any one who could tell me about Dhyana Yogis. I heard that Thero Doratiyawa was practicing Dhyana—I sincerely believed in the existence of the Himalayan adepts. To work for them was to me a great privilege, and I was assured by Col: Olcott that the Masters had accepted me as a Chela. In 1885 I received a presentation copy of the Voice of Silence from H.P.B. with the words—"Lanoo"—In the hope that he will be the light that has begun to shine on him. (Memorandum to Diary for 1919)

From that point onward, he spoke of the voice that Blavatsky celebrated in *Voice of Silence* as a source of counsel.

After he had finished his schooling at Saint Thomas College in 1883, he spent eight months reading books borrowed from the Pettah library, which provided him with the general knowledge he craved. His father did not like his idling in the library, but Dharmapala thought he was preparing himself: "I did reading, thinking, educating myself in the highest knowledge [*parama vijnana*]. I considered taking the message of Buddhism to the Western world was a *parama vijnana*."[37] His father had his own goals, to apprentice his son to a local proctor and to guide his son to a job in a government office. In 1883 Catholics attacked Buddhists, bringing Olcott back to Colombo,

---

37. Jayawardana, *Mage Jivita Kathava*, 29 and 32. *The Theosophist* published a journal or a pamphlet also titled *Parama Vijnana Vadaya*. By the end of his life Dharmapala came to recognize the heterodoxy of this particular overcoding: "'Parama Vignana' is not in the Pali Doctrine. To say that Vigana is Parama is against the paticca samuppada doctrine" (Diary, June 19, 1930).

and he admitted Dharmapala to the Theosophical Society in January 1884 (Diary, February 17, 1920). He announced his intention to carry Buddhism to the Western world—inspired by the Theosophical universalism implicit in the "brotherhood of mankind" trope—as opposed to joining together the Buddhist countries of Asia. It is hard to miss the echoes in his characterization of his Buddhist work as a *parama vijnana*, a staple of Theosophical discourse or in his plan to carry Buddhism to the West the same way Olcott brought Theosophy to Asia.

While clerking in the Department of Public Instruction from 1884 to 1886, Dharmapala got more involved with the Theosophical Society. When he passed the government clerical examination, his father again asked him—also via letter—to take the job offered in the Department of Public Instruction, saying that he would match the salary to underwrite works of charity. Dharmapala declined the job and his father's support for charity: "I loved Humanity more and to be a servant of another servant to me meant degradation. My friends thought I did a foolish act in rejecting Govt. service, but to me it meant freedom."[38] He described himself as committed to *lokottara* culture, an expression for the otherworld with both Buddhist and Theosophical referents. One of the many appeals of the Theosophical Society was its insistence on the possibility of becoming an arhat in this world.[39] Such was not the conventional belief of Sinhala Buddhists of the time, who assumed that it was no longer possible to achieve nirvana in this lifetime, but only after numberless lifetimes of perfecting one's moral virtues.[40] He looked at the monkhood's diminished expectations as symptomatic of their spiritual decline. They had settled for less; he would not. His own high expectations led him to Theosophy, and his exposure to it provided a script—meditation, Tibet, adepts, advanced spiritual states—for those expectations. He did not expect liberation in short order, and to that extent his views were no different from the Sinhala monkhood. He simply thought that the struggle for liberation ought to begin at once and with appropriate intensity.

38. "To the Beloved Mahatmas Who Loved Our Lord."

39. Agarwal, *The Buddhist and Theosophical Movements*, 35–6. Theosophy offered only the possibility. A fledging Theosophical Society in Boulder, Colorado "very soon dissolved because it had been organized by individuals under a misapprehension, they supposing that becoming members of the Society was the next step to becoming adepts. "Annual Report," *Theosophist* 13 (1892): 1–34, at 18.

40. The disparity between the low expectations of most Buddhist bhikkhus and the hopes of lay Buddhists to achieve "Nirvana Now" lived on past Dharmapala's death. See Steven Kemper, "Buddhism without Bhikkhus: The Sri Lanka Vinaya Vardana Society," in *Religion and the Legitimation of Power in Sri Lanka*, ed. Bardwell Smith (Chambersburg, PA: Anima, 1974), 212–35.

Blavatsky played the oracular role in the Theosophical Society and Olcott the administrative. He said that Theosophy aspired to "direct as distinguished from a revealed knowledge of God."[41] Its objectives were twofold, "to know something of man and his powers, [and] to discover the best means to benefit humanity—physically, morally, spiritually."[42] Once Olcott reached India, he established levels of membership for each objective, giving priority to those fellows who entered the Esoteric Section—"freed from all exacting obligations to country, society, and family, [they] must adopt a life of strict celibacy":

> A man may be a most zealous, useful, and respected Fellow, and yet be a patriot, a public official, and a husband. Our highest section is composed of men who have retired from active life to spend their remaining days in seclusion, study, and spiritual perfection. You have your married priests, and your sanyasis and yogis. So we have our visible, active men, seen in the world, mixed up in its concerns, and a part of it; and we have our unseen, but none the less active, adepts . . . who benefit mankind without their hand being ever so much as suspected.[43]

Olcott got down to his own case: "Though I am ostensibly President of the Theosophical Society, yet I am less than the least of these Emancipated Ones." In joining the Esoteric Section, Dharmapala put himself beyond "country, society, and family," a constraint that did not stop him from reforming Sinhala Buddhist society and having a say in the family business. But it also provided a charter for his renunciation and service to humanity.

Dharmapala's journey to meet the Emancipated Ones began when he attended his first Theosophical convention at Adyar in December 1884. His own chronology of those days shows him being pulled in two directions—he began his account with his work, quickly turning to his yearning for solitude:

> In 1884 February I joined the T.S. [and] in February I was in office; but my soul yearned after peace. In 1886 I severed from the bustling world; in 1887 working for Humanity, in 1888 ditto, 1889 in Japan, in 1890 working for humanity, in 1891 in Japan. Suffering Humanity wants rest.

41. "The Theosophical Society and Its Aims," in *A Collection of Lectures on Theosophy and Archaic Religions* (Madras: Theyaga Rajier, 1883), 3.
42. Olcott, "The Theosophical Society and Its Aims," 8.
43. Olcott, "The Theosophical Society and Its Aims," 10–11.

Prayer to a god won't relieve the man from the miseries of Existence, rites and ceremonies won [sic] do. Purity of life *is* needed. This night at 12 for the first time in my life I experienced that "Peace which passesth [sic] all understanding." How peaceful it was. (Diary, February 17, 1891)[44]

The entry for the previous day speaks of a dream of "spirited horses and a turtle of extraordinary size. . . . What does this mean?" And the entry for the day after has him saying that the individual who yearns after peace and rest can have it by following the Noble Eightfold Path for seven years, noting that it took the Buddha six years of "deep research and an unswerving life of purity." Blavatsky used the seven-year figure for the time required for a chela to become an adept, claiming that she had lived that long in Tibet.

Koot Hoomi was Blavatsky's favorite mahatma, and he became Dharmapala's favorite, sending him two astral messages.[45] As with Olcott, Sinnett, and other Theosophists fortunate enough to receive communications, his messages came in the form of letters. Koot Hoomi communicated with Blavatsky, and in time she presented the chela with another letter, not written by the mahatma but in her own handwriting, transcribing what the mahatma had told her. The process was implausible enough to force Blavatsky to defend it, the more so because messages "were tinged throughout with the very obvious peculiarities of her own inimitable style, and are sometimes interspersed with remarks definitely emanating from her own mind."[46] She explained to Sinnett that "these letters are not written but impressed, or precipitated, and then all mistakes corrected. . . . I have to think it over, to photograph every word and sentence carefully in my brain, before it can be repeated for precipitation. . . . For the present it is all I can tell you."[47] Later she provided a fuller account, saying that "the Masters have been pleased to permit the veil to be drawn aside a little more, and the modus operandi can thus be explained now more fully to the outsider."

44. Dharmapala took the phrase about peace from Philippians 4:7, his Christian education furnishing another source for his transidiomatic diction.

45. Another expression of the theme of abandonment and solitude that I suggested earlier came at the end of Dharmapala's life when he felt his struggles in India had received no support from other Buddhists, blurring the distinction between the long silence from Koot Hoomi and the absence of Buddhist support: "The Master took compassion on him [?] in 1884 & 1886. Since 40 years there is no sign of recognition. Is there no one in any Buddhist country who could come to help me?" (Diary, May 8, 1927).

46. Boris De Zirkoff, ed., *H. P. Blavatsky: Collected Writings, 1883* (Los Angeles: Philosophical Research Society, 1950), xii.

47. A. P. Sinnett, *Occult World* (London: Trübner, 1881), 143–4.

The work of writing these letters in question is carried on by a sort of psychological telegraphy; the Mahatmas very rarely write their letters in the ordinary way. An electro-magnetic connection, so to say, exists on the psychological plane between a Mahatma and his chelas, one of whom acts as his amanuensis. When the Master wants a letter to be written in this way, he draws the attention of the chela, whom he selects for the task, by causing an astral bell to be rung near him.[48]

Even with her own hand giving shape to the way the message was relayed to the world, Blavatsky had explanations—the mahatmas were working through her, and the process was a mystery she herself did not fully understand.

The Great White Brotherhood was made up of adepts who practiced a variety of religions, but Master Koot Hoomi and Master Moriya were Buddhists, so their communications held special interest for both Blavatsky and Dharmapala. When he was making his third American tour in 1902–3, he noticed an advertisement for a lecture he was to give, identifying him as a pupil of Blavatsky. He wanted nothing of it, writing, "This is incorrect. I was pupil of the Master 'K.H.' Through H.P.B. I sent the letter to the Mahatma K.H. She called me 'Lanoo, Brother Dharmapala'" (Diary, March 9, 1903). An aphorism from Koot Hoomi that Dharmapala inserted regularly at the top of the daily entries in his diary of the 1920s metonymized the relationship between Buddhism and Theosophy: "The only refuge for him who aspires to true perfection is Buddha alone, Master K.H." Blavatsky had told him that the message had come to her from Koot Hoomi, and it reinforced her more mundane advice to turn his mind to learning Pali.[49] Blavatsky and Koot Hoomi's insistence on the Buddha alone notwithstanding, he remained committed to both Blavatsky and Koot Hoomi, and his ties to Theosophy ran through Buddhism, as his ties to Buddhism ran through Theosophy:

Reading "Blavatsky Letters." She sacrificed everything for the Master. The Master KH gave our Buddha's teachings to the West through Sinnett, and Master M gave occult teachings through HPB. Theosophy at first was nothing but Mesmerism, Spiritualism, Crystal gazing and Kab-

48. "Precipitation," Theosophist 5 (1883–4): 64.

49. Ellawala Nandiswara, "The Life & Times of a National Hero," Ceylon Daily News, September 17, 1965.

bala. The early volumes of the Theosophist are evidence thereto. Master
KH through Sinnett opened the door of the "Occult World." Since then
the world came to know of the existence of the Adepts beyond Himalayas. (Diary, January 17, 1926)

Like Blavatsky, Dharmapala's knowledge of the occult and Buddhism came
from texts, but he conceptualized its transmission along human lines of descent, one guru passing that knowledge on to his chela.[50]

Blavatsky described Damodar Mavalankar as her one "full success."
Hundreds of aspirants were called to Tibet, she said. Damodar actually tried
to go, and she thought that he was destined to become a mahatma himself.[51]
Olcott loved him for his energy and his obedience—in contrast to Dharmapala's disobedience.

> Among other real helpers whom we had found in India, there was poor,
> slender, fragile Damodar Mavalankar, who had thrown himself heart and
> soul into the work with a devotion which could not be surpassed. Frail
> as a girl though he was, he could sit at his table writing, sometimes all
> night, unless I caught him at it and drove him to bed. No child was ever
> more obedient to a parent, no foster-son more utterly selfless in his love
> to a foster-mother, than he to H.P.B. . . . When a lad, brought near to
> death by fever and tossing in delirium, he had had a vision of a benignant
> sage, who came and took his hand and told him he should not die but
> should live for useful work. After meeting H.P.B., his interior vision
> gradually opened, and in him whom we know as Master K.H., Damodar
> saw revealed the visitor of his youthful crisis. That sealed his devotion
> to our cause, and his discipleship to H.P.B. (Sarnath Notebook no. 53)[52]

Dharmapala knew of Damodar, having met him in 1880 when he came to
Lanka as part of the Theosophical party, and he took pride in Blavatsky's
calling him the "Ceylon Damodar."[53]

---

50. Dharmapala never gave up on the idea that Blavatsky served as intermediary for Koot
Hoomi. "How wonderful that she should have met the Master in flesh," he marveled in his
diary (April 23, 1924).

51. Basil Crump, "A Theosophical Criticism of Mrs. Cleather's Books," *Journal of the
Maha Bodhi Society* 31, no. 12 (1923): 480. Crump adds that the mahatmas referred to Blavatsky
as "Our Brother," and "Our direct agent," two expressions borrowed from other registers.

52. *Old Diary Leaves*, 2:212.

53. *Old Diary Leaves*, 2:292. Olcott remembered that Damodar identified so thoroughly
with the Theosophists that he became a Buddhist himself and drove other members of his
family out of the Theosophical Society and provoked them to attack Olcott back in Bombay.

Damodar remained a devotee of Master Koot Hoomi and an enthusiastic worker for the society until 1885. Having taken the vows of a sannyasin
and practicing various austerities—"regulating his diet, devoting specified
hours to meditation, cultivating a spirit of perfect unselfishness, and working night and day . . . on the duties [Olcott] gave him in the Society"—he
resided at Theosophical headquarters in Adyar and traveled with Olcott on
trips through India.[54] According to Olcott, he was enjoying "rapid psychical
development," making nightly astral visits to the master's ashram in the
Himalayas. Koot Hoomi responded to those visits by sending astral emis-
saries to Dharmapala and Olcott camping near Lahore. On another occasion, while staying with the maharajah of Kashmir in his summer place
in Jammu, Damodar made an astral visit that lasted sixty hours; described
as "frail" and "girlish" before, he returned "robust, tough, and wiry, bold
and energetic."[55] While Olcott was away in Burma, Damodar left Adyar for
Tibet and was never seen again.[56]

The lure of Tibet transcended the Theosophical Society. Sarat Chandra Das made several trips there, bringing back texts for the Buddhist Text
Society and intelligence for the government of India. In Calcutta the Zen
monk Ekai Kawaguchi won Das's support and made two trips to Tibet and
four to Nepal. In 1887 the Sinhala monk Ilukwatte Medhankara made plans
to visit Bodh Gaya with Dharmapala, but he also cherished the idea of going
to Tibet to meet the masters.[57] After Damodar's disappearance Dharmapala
met a Burmese monk at Bodh Gaya who told him that he intended to make
the trip because the Burmese believed that there were three arhats living in
Tibet (Diary, February 25, 1891). Olcott attributed the interest in mahatmas
to the popularity of his own journal and proposed an alternative to the life-
threatening trek across the Himalayas:

> Western curiosity, piqued by our Theosophical literature, has been in ac-
> tive quest of the Mahatma in Tibet and its Borderland, but has not found
> him. . . . Many a postulant for spiritual knowledge, despairing of meeting
> with a Guru near by, has undertaken the fearful foot journey to the Hi-

54. *Old Diary Leaves*, 3:15.
55. *Old Diary Leaves*, 3:30.
56. *Old Diary Leaves*, 3:142.
57. *Old Diary Leaves*, 3:208. As Olcott says, "Almost alone among the monks, he believed
in the Masters, and his strongest desire was to go to Tibet in search of them" (208). Had he not
died young, Ilukwatte would likely have played a larger role in Dharmapala's life. I take Olcott's
remark that Ilukwatte was "almost alone among the monks" in believing in the masters as an
indication of how little influence Theosophical belief had on most Sinhala Buddhist monks.

malayas in search of one; often braving the extremes of physical misery
under the spur of hope. . . . If they had only known their own Shastras,
they might have spared themselves the painful quest by so purifying
their minds and heart by self-mastery as to draw the Guru to their own
doorstep.[58]

Dharmapala applied himself to mastering the self by giving up meat and
fish, reducing the quantity of food he ate, and practicing meditation and
celibacy, confident that service to humanity would itself reduce selfishness.

Dharmapala was certain the mahatmas were living in the Himalayas,
the evidence lying in the very sophistication of their communications, and
his reasoning makes clear how much he wanted to believe:

> It cannot be believed that there is no Hermit in Tibet who had attained
> the Dhyanas. During the Buddha era or in a non-Buddhist era for there
> could be panna abigannalabis [seekers who had attained five stages of
> wisdom]. These great beings should exist there. The letters sent to Mr.
> Sinnett are from two Buddhist hermits. Any other man from another re-
> ligion would not be able to write letters of that nature.[59]

He knew that both Master Moriya and Koot Hoomi were trying to revive
the sasana in India (Diary, May 9, 1924).[60] In 1897 he began discussing his
own desire to visit Tibet (Sarnath Notebook no. 101). Traveling home from
America that year, he stopped in Paris to attend the Congress of Orientalists. There he announced to the delegates his intention to visit Tibet "in
search after truth."[61] Eventually he recognized that his disability made the
trek thoroughly impractical, writing in his diary that "in the next life I hope
to be born physically strong to climb the Himalayas and to study the sacred
science" (May 9, 1924).

As a young man, Dharmapala was serious enough about the trek to
cause his father to make him an offer—call off the trip in return for a medi-

---

58. "The Mahatma Quest," *Theosophist* 16 (1894): 173–80, at 173 and 180. Olcott never
mentions any Theosophist who made the trek other than Damodar.

59. Guruge, *Dharmapala Lipi*, 358.

60. Restoring the *sasana* to India looks to be a perfectly Buddhist motivation, depending on
whether Buddhism traditionally was a missionary religion in a form that resembles the modern
practice.

61. Anagarika Dharmapala, "European Explorers of Tibet," *Journal of the Maha Bodhi
Society* 7 (1899): 115. Lord Reay, Sir Alfred Lyall, and Sir Charles Elliot were in the audience,
and Elliot promised to write the commissioner of Darjeeling to afford Dharmapala facilities for
the trip.

tation retreat in Colombo (Sarnath Notebook no. 101). By the time he was gifted the meditation hall, he had discovered two meditation manuals in out-of-the-way places in the Kandyan highlands. He found both in 1890, having learned some years before of the existence of *vidarsana* monks at Hanguranketa. On a lecture tour with his Theosophical colleague Bowles Daly, Dharmapala stopped at the monastery of Doratiyawa and discovered the text he sought in the temple library (Sarnath Notebook no. 23). The second text he found in a temple in Teldeniya while on another lecture tour. In this case, he could not borrow the manuscript immediately but had D. B. Jayatilaka arrange for copying the text, which Dharmapala then carried to London, where it was translated by T. W. Rhys Davids.[62] He kept both manuscripts with him and constructed meditational exercises from them, focusing his attention on dhyana meditation, which had esoteric goals not shared by the *vipassana* meditation that came to dominate local practice.

When he began diary entries with Koot Hoomi's aphorism "The only refuge for him who aspires to true perfection is Buddha alone, Master K.H.," he referenced both Theosophy and Buddhism. The same ambiguity appears in Theosophical statements that he drew on for the sake of imagining what was at stake in the activist side of his life. He cited the mahatma letters as a warrant for returning Buddhism to India:

> There was a time, when from sea to sea from the mountains and deserts of the north to the grand woods and downs of Ceylon there was but one faith one rallying cry—to save Humanity from the miseries of ignorance in the name of him who taught first the solidearity [*sic*] of all man. (October 29, 1930)

Saving "Humanity from the miseries of ignorance" was an equally Buddhist and Theosophical goal but framed in an idiom specifically Theosophical. Even at the end of his life Dharmapala saw returning Buddhism to India as motivated by the mahatmas: "The two Masters wished the Religion of the Lord Buddha to be reestablished in India. Subba row and his clique conspired against the scheme" (September 24, 1930).[63] Subba row was the least of his problems. With Blavatsky's death most Theosophists turned toward

---

62. Rhys Davids called that translation *The Yogavachara's Manual* (London, 1896). It was later published by the Pali Text Society as *Manual of a Mystic* (London: Pali Text Society, 1916).

63. Both Rhys Davids and Max Muller warned Dharmapala away from Theosophy, Muller insisting, "If you want your work to be successful, you must make it quite clear that you have nothing in common with the Mahatmas." "Words of Advice," *Journal of the Maha Bodhi Society* 4 (1895), 18.

Hinduism, and under Annie Besant's hand Theosophy had no interest in Buddhism and even less in missionizing it.

IN THE THEOSOPHICAL SOCIETY AND OUT

After he finished his day's work at the Department of Public Instruction copying documents, Dharmapala went to the Theosophical Society office and did chores for C. P. Gunawardana. He slept in the office, lying on a bench and using a coir mat as a pillow with the idea that the rough surface would keep him from sleeping (Sarnath Notebook no. 53). Once he gave up government service, he found other ways to serve and suffer. Despite his commitment to Blavatsky, who he said "influenced me and my spiritual life more than any other" (Sarnath Notebook no. 53), he had little contact with her after he joined the society because she left India after the Coulomb affair in 1884.[64] In 1888 Dharmapala and Charles Leadbeater started the *Buddhist*, the journal of the Buddhist Theosophical Society. They were steady companions, working and residing together at Theosophical headquarters on Maliban Street.[65] From 1886 until 1890 Dharmapala served as general manager and assistant general secretary of the Buddhist Theosophical Society in Colombo and manager of its newspaper, the *Sarasavi Sandarasa*.[66]

When Olcott was in the island, Dharmapala traveled with him by oxcart on village tours, where Olcott lectured and Dharmapala translated into Sinhala. Olcott was in and out of the island during the time. His travels were prodigious—one year he traveled 43,000 miles and 47,000 the next—and he visited Lanka regularly, some three times more than any other part of the Theosophical world.[67] He was a man always in motion, and his restlessness

---

64. That influence did not lapse: "For 39 years I have lived the life directed by HPB," Dharmapala later observed ("Birthday Musings," Sarnath Notebook no. 53). In the last days of his life, he continued to make notes on her *Secret Doctrines* ("Tit Bits," Sarnath Notebook no. 32). The Coulombs were Blavatsky's live-in assistants who accused her of faking the delivery of astral messages.

65. Dharmapala claims that he once saved Leadbeater's life: "In 1889 there was a scandal. [Leadbeater] kidnapped Jinarajadasa and had the boy concealed. Jinarajadasa's father came rushing upstairs with a loaded revolver to shoot Leadbeater. It was about 7 pm. I was just coming out of the Shrine room, and I asked him what is the matter. He said, 'I am come to shoot Leadbeater for having robbed my boy.' I reasoned and calmed him" (Diary, February 17, 1919).

66. Karunaratne, *Anagarika Dharmapala*, 50.

67. "General Report of the Sixteenth Convention and Anniversary of the Theosophical Society," *Theosophist* 13 (1892): 1–56, at 2, and supplement, *Theosophist* (1892), lviii. Olcott visited Lanka almost regularly. L. A. Wickremeratne, "Annie Besant, Theosophism and Buddhist Nationalism in Sri Lanka," *Ceylon Journal of the Historical and Social Sciences* 6 (1976): 63. In the chronology at the end of Howard Murphet's biography of Olcott, *Hammer on the*

The Late Ven. Anagarika Dharmapala on a Preaching Tour in Ceylon.

1. Dharmapala on preaching tour in camping car, Sri Lanka.

must have set an example for Dharmapala, who himself was "always on wing."[68] Although a vegetarian, Olcott had no personal interest in asceticism, and traveling by oxcart along unpaved roads and pathways was the only way to get where he was going.[69] For Dharmapala the oxcart provided ascetic practice as much as transportation. Sleeping in the oxcart—and later, when auto travel developed in Sri Lanka, in the lorry that served as his camping car—kept Dharmapala from lodging with local families, which in turn allowed him to maintain both solitude and distance.

Dharmapala read widely during those first years in the society, while also following Blavatsky's direction to turn his mind to learning Pali. He

Mountain: The Life of Henry Steel Olcott (1832–1907) (Wheaton, IL: Theosophical Publishing House, 1972), 328–36, I count thirty-four visits, some of them brief.

68. The expression comes from an account of his work in "The Maha Bodhi Society Appeals for Help in the Indian Famine," *Open Court* 2 (1897): 490.

69. *Theosophist* 11 (1890): lxxiii–lxxix. Olcott avoided meat for medical reasons (to combat gout), not ascetic ones, and he had "no sympathy for undiscriminating fanatics" with regard to diet. *Old Diary Leaves*, 2:439–40.

says that his knowledge of Buddhism during the first days of his work in the society was limited to the Satipatthana Sutta—"philosophical study of the Dhamma was then impossible having no printed texts" ("Notes on the Muslim Period," Sarnath Notebook no. 6). With no formal instruction in the language, he simply began reading—first the Dhamma Pradipika and then the first fascicule of the *Visuddhimagga*, the text enabling him to learn Pali by reading Pali (Sarnath Notebook no. 23). The *Visuddhimagga*, he thought, was the book all Buddhist monks must understand ("What a Bhikkhu Is Expected to Do," Sarnath Notebook no. 4). That said, most of the texts he read were English-language books:

> Theosophical literature was my love. No book on Buddhism had been published except the Light of Asia. Col. Olcott's Buddhist Catechism was the only Buddhist exegesis. [obscure] time Sinnett's Occult World and Esoteric Buddhism I devoured. The journal Theosophist I read thoroughly. My Buddhist studies began after I met Mg Hpo Mhyin in Rangoon. He was a mine of information. He had a splendid library, and my stay with him in April 1891 was supremely beneficial to me. I read the "Sacred Books of the East" volumes and gathered information. I perused the P.T.S. publications and discovered the explanation given about the Sukara Maddavam in the Udana P.T.S. During my stay in Calcutta . . . I visited the B.A.S. Library daily and gathered information. At Buddha Gaya in Feby I read Dutt's History of India. I read Elliot's History of the Muhammedan Period and discovered the fact that Buddhism was destroyed by Muhammedan invaders. (Sarnath Notebook no. 4)

He moved among books and periodicals, works of Buddhist doctrine, Theosophy, and history. The center of his life was Buddhism, but a Buddhism inflected by the cognitive interests of Theosophy in mysticism, the esoteric, and intensive striving.

Olcott meant the Theosophical Society to provide a vehicle for study and research, and belonging did not prevent a member's working for his own religion. Olcott encouraged it. Dharmapala acted on that premise, starting the Maha Bodhi Society as a vehicle for Buddhist work alongside his work for Theosophy. In its first headquarters in Calcutta, the Maha Bodhi Society shared space with Theosophical Society. He moved between a Maha Bodhi activity here and a Theosophical activity there; when he attended the World's Parliament of Religions, he attended a Theosophical conference beforehand. But he could recount his work with the society as a linear narrative:

2. Buddhist Theosophical Society, Colombo, 1889. Seated on ground: far left, Dharmapala; two places to right, Don Carolis; two places further right, C. P. Gunawardana. Seated on chairs, from left: two Japanese monks, Ven. Heyiyantuduve Devamitta, Hikkaduve, Olcott, a third Japanese monk, and, extreme right, A. P. Dharmagunawardene. Standing: Charles Leadbeater, center.

> I joined the TS January 1884. In 1886 I worked with Col. Olcott & CW Leadbeater. From 1886 to 1889 with CWL and also with Charles Francis Powell, in 1890 with Dr. Bowles Daly. From 1884 to 1904 I was in the Theosophical Society. In 1905 I resigned. From 1905 to 1910 I was at loggerheads with Mrs. Besant and the CTS. In 1911 reconciled. In 1914 rejoined the TS. Since 1915 active [work?] in my sympathy with Mrs. Besant gave her Rs. 500 in 1917. (Sarnath Notebook no. 23)

He undertook some of his most important Maha Bodhi projects in the interval from 1884 to 1905, when he resigned from the Theosophical Society. His estrangement from Theosophy is often noted, his reconciliation in 1911 ignored.

From the beginning Olcott and Dharmapala had a teacher-student relationship. As long as Dharmapala assumed the student role, the relationship continued, but he became uncomfortable in that role after their visit to Japan. Olcott had an affectionate relationship with him, and he left government service to work for Olcott. He could not leave his post without a medical excuse. Peter de Abrew gave a bribe, and a medical waiver was produced. Dr. Rockwood insisted on a medical problem, not simply a letter of excuse, and he created one by applying a poultice to Dharmapala's chest. The blister that resulted was painful: "The whole night I kept crying on account of the excruciating pain. . . . H.S.O. came and comforted me and spoke words of encouragement, saying that the Mahatmas want heroes not cowards" ("To the Beloved Mahatmas Who Loved Our Lord," Sarnath Notebook no. 50). The affection continued, Olcott expecting him to remain as obedient as Damodar, but Dharmapala was not inclined to obedience. As he said of his work in the colonial bureaucracy, he was not happy being a servant of a servant. Olcott opposed Dharmapala's trip to the World's Parliament, and he became much more independent afterward.

They fell out for a variety of reasons, the most common explanation fixing on relics. As an outsider and rationalist, Olcott had no feel for relic veneration and dismissed the notion that the relic of the Buddha's tooth, venerated at the Dalada Maligawa in Kandy, was even a human tooth.[70] Dharmapala was committed to relic veneration: he presented the Koreans with a relic, having carried it on his person for thirteen years (Diary, August 20, 1913); he spoke of bequeathing the Foster Seminary in Kandy to the Temple of the Tooth (Diary, March 25, 1926); and he wanted his own ashes distributed to various Buddhist sites on the model of the Buddha's remains (Diary, April 30, 1926).[71] Accounts that invoke relics as the source of their breakup are complicated by their sometimes looking to one incident and sometimes to another. Olcott had received several relics. The first was a relic of Sivali arhat given first to Leadbeater that Olcott came to possess, but it was a second relic, the tooth relic, that produced the crisis. On a visit to Adyar, Dharmapala found the relic being exhibited and took offense: "I rebuked him for his rudeness in exposing the replica of the Tooth Relic and for using harsh words. He got angry, and thus came the separation in 1905" (Sarnath Notebook no. 58). Another incident followed remarks Olcott made about the relic. Hikkaduve reacted strongly, expressing his disappointment in Olcott's calling Buddhists "bigoted and ignorant" for believing in the authenticity of the tooth.[72] Olcott's words seem to have offended Dharmapala more than his treatment of the relics themselves.

Whatever role relic veneration played in Olcott's alienation from Dharmapala, there were signs of conflict long before 1905. In 1887 Olcott told

70. The tooth looks quite a lot like a large animal's incisor, leading Blavatsky to say that, of course, it was the Buddha's tooth, simply one that came from one of the Buddha's previous lives when he was incarnated as a tiger. *Old Diary Leaves*, 2:186–7. It is easy to see why others were charmed by Blavatsky's mythopoetic virtues.

71. During Dharmapala's stay in Kandy, the tooth relic was placed in the outer hall of the Temple of the Tooth to receive adoration. Dharmapala had a thoroughly un-Protestant response to the prospect: "My karma does not allow me to approach the Relic. On the 7th day I shall try to approach the Holy Presence" (Diary, January 1, 1925).

72. "High Priest Sumangala and the Theosophical Society," *Journal of the Maha Bodhi Society*, 14 (1906): 57–8, at 58.

him not to make the pilgrimage to Bodh Gaya with Ilukwatte Medhankara, and he complied. Olcott had reservations when Dharmapala established the *Journal of the Maha Bodhi Society*, fearing that it was not well-edited and could not compete with "the most serious organs of learned Societies."[73] When Dharmapala got himself invited to the Parliament of Religions, Olcott urged him not to go.[74] In the early days at Bodh Gaya, Olcott supported his plans for the place, both men believing that the mahant would sell the Maha Bodhi temple. Later when the Tikari Raj land became available, Olcott agreed—at least initially—that Buddhists should be allowed to own their most sacred place, and Olcott sailed to Burma to raise support to buy Bodh Gaya.[75] He made himself a party to the dispute, negotiating with the mahant, meeting with the collector, and attending the police inquiry into the assault on the meditating monks in February 1893. Olcott was alarmed by the attack and arranged for quarters in Gaya for the monks to be resettled but from that point pulled away from Bodh Gaya.[76] He wrote to Dharmapala that his hopes for Bodh Gaya were a chimera (Sarnath Notebook no. 23), and elsewhere Dharmapala says that he had told him to abandon Bodh Gaya altogether.[77] Olcott urged him to restore Sarnath instead (Diary, June 23, 1930). A year later when Olcott accompanied Annie Besant on her lecture tour of North India, he took her to Sarnath but ignored Bodh Gaya.

Contrary to Olcott's wishes, Dharmapala did not abandon his campaign to gain control of Bodh Gaya, keeping to the vow he had made on his first day there. In February 1895 the Calcutta High Court granted the mahant's appeal of the lower-court decision calling for punishment for the attack on the Bodh Gaya monks. At some point in 1896 Olcott and Besant advised Dharmapala not to buy land at Bodh Gaya.[78] That same year, when Olcott returned to the island to inspect Buddhist schools, he attended a meeting of the Maha Bodhi Society and resigned his position as honorary general adviser because "Mr. Dharmapala did not seem disposed to take my advice when given."[79] Dharmapala wrote in his diary that "I became self reliant after Col. Olcott had deserted me in May 1896," the month of Olcott's res-

73. Olcott, "The Buddhist Revival," *Theosophist* 13 (1892): 576.

74. Elsewhere Dharmapala writes that Olcott "loved me like a father. But a change came after my appearance at the Parl. of Religions. He was displeased as he did not find his name mentioned." "Visits to America," Sarnath Notebook no. 101.

75. *Old Diary Leaves*, 5:32–3.

76. *Old Diary Leaves*, 5:7–11.

77. Guruge, *Dharmapala Lipi*, 57.

78. Sarath Amunugama, "A Sinhalese Buddhist 'Babu': Anagarika Dharmapala (1864–1933) and the Bengal Connection," *Social Science Information* 30, no. 3 (1991): 567.

79. *Old Diary Leaves*, 6:16.

ignation (Diary, November 24, 1926), and that although the final breach did
not come until 1905, "since 1898 he became selfish" (Diary, February 17,
1920). Olcott felt that Dharmapala was the selfish one. Their falling out
aside, Dharmapala continued to attend Theosophical conventions, noting
that there had been no discord at the 1898 convention and that he was welcome at Adyar until 1904.

The following year Olcott launched a broadside against Dharmapala that
marked the public dissolution of their relationship. In the wake of the Calcutta High Court's decision that ended hopes of recovering the Maha Bodhi
temple, other Sinhala Buddhists began to complain not so much about the
cost of litigation but the disparity between the amount of contributions received and the amount Dharmapala had paid his attorneys. Contributions
for his other projects ebbed away, and he began to publicly criticize the Buddhist public—they had forsaken him, and they did not care about the great
cause. Losing Bodh Gaya left him bitter and judgmental, and he said things
sure to antagonize all constituencies. Prospects for Buddhism in Lanka were
gloomy, he told Sinhalas, while things looked better for the growth of Buddhism in India. The fact of the matter was that his chief supporters in the
Calcutta Theosophical Society had gone over to the dark side, abandoning
the Buddhism of Blavatsky for the Hinduism of Besant. Olcott rushed in,
defending the unsteady relationship between the Theosophists and the Buddhists. He said that even in Blavatsky's day, most Theosophists had not become Buddhists, although the twenty Theosophists who accompanied him
to the island in 1880 had done just that. In helping others to understand their
own religions better, Olcott acted as a Theosophist. But he also continued
to help his "avowed" religion, Buddhism.[80]

Olcott went after Dharmapala in an article in the Theosophist, looking
back on a twenty-year friendship:

> I do not want to say a harsh word to Dharmapala, but I am duty bound
> to defend the Sinhalese from his unjust aspersions and to tell the truth.
> Dharmapala has been in intimate relations with me from the time
> when, as a very young man, he threw up his clerkship in a Government
> office at Colombo, to devote himself to Buddhistic propaganda, and for

80. In the wake of the success of The Buddhist Catechism, which had gone through some
forty editions by this time, Olcott published a Shinshu catechism, welcomed a Vashisthvaitha
catechism, and envisioned a Zoroastrian catechism and a Muslim catechism. At the same time
a Tamil Hindu produced "A Catechism of the Arya Dhamma of Gotama Buddha," Theosophist
13 (1892): 55–68.

many years he followed my advice. Scores of times he has been held up by us as a model of an unselfish, devoted young man, a second Damodar. But since his visit to America, to attend the Exposition, he has not seemed willing to listen to the advice of his elders, but has put forth various schemes which they were obliged to regard as impracticable, if not utopian. Among them, was his "Ethico-Psychological College"—a title bad enough to strangle it at its birth. This embryonic college was opened without pupils or teaching staff, with a big and showy procession, a great tom-toming and trumpet-blowing, a sensational telegraphing to the papers, and after that came reaction and silence. Our dear young man, finding himself saddled with a thing that he could not manage, wrote me that I ought now to retire from the Theosophical Society and come and live there: in other words, pull his very hot chestnuts out of the fire!

He acknowledged Dharmapala's "philanthropic . . . intentions, perfect integrity, and unselfish zeal." His problems were willfulness and an lack of business sense. His having turned on Besant and his other well-wishers, he added, revealed his "juvenile critical incapacity."[81]

Taking responsibility for consenting to Dharmapala's bringing litigation against the mahant, Olcott noted that even with excellent legal representation he had failed to deliver Bodh Gaya. The result was "many Buddhists, showing bitter feelings against Dharmapala because of the heavy cost of the now famous suit." On the witness stand, Dharmapala "made almost as bad a figure as was possible," becoming confused, losing his memory, and alienating his supporters.[82] Olcott concluded by pointing out that public suspicion about the casual way he shifted his contributors' funds from one project, recovering Bodh Gaya, to others, establishing the Ethico-Psychological College and the Sanghamitta convent, had no basis. Dharmapala was as honest as could be; he simply lacked business sense and discretion. Olcott's private thoughts reveal neither nuance nor sympathy. Writing Leadbeater, he called him a "spoilt suckling," as "vain to a degree and more kinds of an ass . . . than are enumerated by Linnaeus in his classification of the varieties in the family of *Equus Asinus*."[83]

81. "The 'Wail' of Dharmapala," supplement, *Theosophist* 20, no. 7 (1899): xxviii–xxx, at xxviii–xxix.

82. "The 'Wail' of Dharmapala," xxix–xxx. Olcott had not been present in the courtroom.

83. Olcott to Leadbeater, November 9, 1902, Olcott correspondence, Theosophical Society Archives, Adyar, India, quoted in Prothero, *The White Buddhist: The Asian Odyssey of Henry Steel Olcott* (Bloomington: Indiana University Press, 1996), 217n30.

As Dharmapala became increasingly disturbed by the Theosophical Society's emphasis on Hinduism that followed Blavatsky's death, he wrote that his Pali studies "gave [him] insight into Buddhism & [his] interest in Theosophical bunkum declined. It was dry hash" (Sarnath Notebook no. 101). The Theosophists soon broke into two groups—the Blavatsky Association and the Besantine party. When he traveled in the West, he had more encounters with Blavatsky Theosophists than with the Besantine party, but he tried to avoid getting involved in Theosophical sectarianism. As he wrote in a notebook, he reconciled with the Calcutta Theosophical Society in 1911. By contrast his relationship with Colombo Theosophists did not warm until the 1920s. Reconciled with Besant, he made a further gesture in 1915:

> Seeing a carriage I presumed that it was Mrs. Besant's, and that she had come to the TS [Theosophical Society] Hall. I found out that she was there and I went to the TS, and sat in the bench for some time. She was inside the room with doors closed. When the members came out I asked her to visit the MBS quarters. She came and I took her upstairs & showed the Shrine Room. She worshipped the Image of the Lord. I asked her to send me photos of HPB, HSO [Olcott] & herself. She suggested that I should hang Norendro Babu's picture. (Diary, October 7, 1915)

Soon he had new hopes: "Mrs. Besant the good mother has arrived in Calcutta. She is staying at the TS. I went to see her. I offered my services to her. May she be a mother to me henceforth" (Diary, February 1, 1916).

Dharmapala lent Besant money in 1916, grousing that she had refused him a loan earlier: "In 1900 when I wanted a loan from Mrs. Besant of Rs. 600/- she declined to advance it, and last year I gave her for her use Rs. 500/-" (Diary, December 23, 1917). By 1920 he thought his relationship with the society was entirely rehabilitated: "I believe I am one of the oldest members of the Theosophical Society, and one of the few surviving members among those who met [Blavatsky] in 1880" (Diary, May 18, 1920). By then he had come to see Besant against the background of Blavatsky and the mahatmas:

> Received letter from Mrs. Besant that she is coming to attend the ceremony on the 26. Tears rushed down my eyes when writing to her, and I thought of dear HPB & the Masters. The former was instrumental in bringing me to Madras in 1881 Decr. In those days the Masters were to me everything. Pali studies opened my eyes to know of the infinite nature of the Tathagato. (Diary, November 14, 1920)

What motivated his reconciliation with Theosophists in Calcutta is hard to rationalize because he received less and less support from them as time passed. The steady point in his life as a Theosophist was Koot Hoomi, who exemplified his aspirations for spiritual growth.

Dharmapala's relations with Theosophists in Colombo had begun to sour when he argued for removing the word "Theosophical" from the Buddhist Theosophical Society in 1897–8. By 1905 he declared that no Buddhist could be a Theosophist. But he remained entangled with Theosophy and Theosophists for decades, a continuity usually overlooked by focusing on his life in Sri Lanka alone. When Olcott established the Buddhist Theosophical Society in Colombo, D. B. Jayatilaka became a member, serving as principal first of Dharmaraja College in Kandy and later of Ananda College in Colombo. He founded the Young Men's Buddhist Association and led the temperance movement, giving him a base of influence parallel to, and separate from, the Maha Bodhi Society. When the Hewavitarne family went to court to recover the Rajagiriya school from local Theosophists, Jayatilaka became a defendant in the case.[84] By 1906 Dharmapala saw that he had other Buddhist enemies: "Jayatilaka, Mirando, Wickramaratna, H. S. Perera & W. A. de Silva are in league and are conspiring to destroy me" (Diary, April 20, 1906). It is unclear whether the "one stupid Buddhist" mentioned in a later passage from the diary is Jayatilaka, but hostility between Dharmapala and the Colombo Theosophists had a personal basis as much as an ideological one:

> Since last September I have been trying to make the local Theosophists see the danger [because of the heterodox views of the *Buddhist Catechism*]; they pooh-poohed me. The high priest remained indifferent, and the foolish Theosophists circulated 80,000 copies of the two Supplements agst me personally. . . . One stupid Buddhist will cause distruction [*sic*] to thousands. (Diary, May 25, 1906)

A libel case followed in 1909, and he wrote that he was prepared to pay the damages discussed by Jayatilaka (Diary, July 27, 1909).

When the Colombo Theosophists needed money in 1906, they mortgaged Ananda College to Adyar. As strained as Dharmapala's relations were with the Colombo Theosophists, he shared an interest in Ananda College and by the 1920s was making common cause with them to avoid Adyar's taking control of what had begun as a local enterprise:

84. Nandadeva Wijesekera, *Sir D. B. Jayatilaka* (Colombo: n.p., 1973), 29–30.

> They [the Adyar Theosophists] lent Rs. 34000 . . . and the latter was paid
> intense [sic] on the amount @ 4% for 24 years Rs. 32640/-. I must be
> ready to lend Rs. 34000 to the Colombo Theosophical Society to redeem
> the mortgage. (Diary, December 17, 1930)

He lent Rs. 5,000/- in 1928 without a promissory note and never recovered
that money (Diary, June 3 and September 28, 1930). Those loans were not
prompted by new affection for Jayatilaka, who, Dharmapala claimed, mis-
managed Buddhist schools and failed to pay the arrears of salaries of "starving teachers" while wasting his time at political meetings (Diary, November 13, 1930). He thought Jayatilaka "had abandoned his coreligionists and is
now a government man. He will betray his coreligionists and hand over the
Buddhist Schools to Govt" (Diary, September 27, 1930). In the small world
of Buddhist reformers, Dharmapala saw his need for support from Colombo
Theosophists. By 1930 he was able to imagine merging the publishing efforts of Theosophical Society and the Maha Bodhi Society: "Big commercial
concerns are amalgamated. Why not the Sandaresa & the S. Bauddhaya, the
Buddhist Press & the Maha Bodhi Press[?] stet . . . A United Buddhist Press
is needed." A paragraph later, he imagined complete consolidation: "wrote
out my dying suggestions to Arthur Silva about the amalgamation of the TS
and MBS" (Diary, December 17, 1930).

THEOSOPHICAL BUDDHISM

When the Theosophical party reached the island in 1880, they came with
the intention of becoming Buddhists, and all twenty members of the party
did so. The Sinhala elite knew that Olcott was a man who would stand
up to the missionaries and help them in their efforts to revive Buddhism,
carrying forward Migettuvatte's efforts. Olcott had already declared himself
a Buddhist in New York City, and Buddhism was his "avowed" religion.[85]
In other words, they came with a specifically Buddhist mission, and local
Buddhists understood their mission in specifically Buddhist ways. Such
specificity ran counter to standard practice of the society. Most members
of the party were Bombay Hindus and Zoroastrians; henceforth they would
be Buddhists in addition to whatever other involvements they might have

---

85. One does not become a Buddhist by self-declaration, and Olcott and Blavatsky were
doing something unprecedented. Dharmapala took his own liberties with Buddhist tradition. Because he was not a bhikkhu, he had no authority to convert, but he did so in the case of Charles
Strauss in 1893 and Marie Canavarro in 1897.

as Theosophists. Exactly how Zoroastrians and Hindus understood their conversion is another question, as is the complicated relationship between their birth religions, Theosophy, and Buddhism.

At least a few local Buddhists were interested in phenomenalism. It was Migettuvatte who had received Olcott's mailing with *Isis Unveiled* as well as Theosophical literature, and he had pieces of both translated into Sinhala, printed in pamphlet form, and circulated.[86] He had seen an early demonstration of Olcott's producing phenomena, and other monks wanted to follow suit:

> The monks, who had read Megittuwatte's excerpts from H.P.B.'s books, pressed her to exhibit her powers, and young Wijeratne, on hearing about the handkerchief phenomenon on board ship, asked her to repeat it for him. So she did, and again for a Mr. Dias; each time obliterating her own embroidered name and causing theirs to replace it. . . . The excitement, of course, rose to fever heat and culminated when she made some fairy bells ring out sharp in the air, near the ceiling and out on the verandah.[87]

Dharmapala noticed interest among some laypeople in phenomenalism, observing that "in my youth many elderly persons testified to the remarkable things that [Blavatsky] had done."[88] There were other signs of local predispositions to Theosophy. Like many Sinhalas, Don Carolis Hewavitarne took astrology seriously, and he was interested in the interpretation of dreams. Others were impressed—for reasons both practical and intellectual—by the mesmeric healing Olcott demonstrated as he traveled about the island.

The Theosophical Society planned to solicit interest from South Asians by employing a two-part strategy, using curiosity about phenomenalism performed by newly arrived Western members to draw interest from South Asians:

> When the natives see that an interest is taken by the English, and even some high officials in India, in their ancestral science and philosophies, they will themselves take openly to their study. And when they come to realize that the old "divine" phenomenon were not miracles, but scien-

86. Bhikshu Sangharakshita, "Anagarika Dharmapala: A Biographical Sketch," in *Maha Bodhi Society of India Diamond Jubilee Souvenir, 1891–1951*, 18–20.

87. *Old Diary Leaves*, 2:159–60. Blavatsky is mentioned in Migettuvatte's testimony on phenomenalism in the second edition of *Isis Unveiled*.

88. *Asia*, September 1927, reprinted in Guruge, *Return to Righteousness*, 675–96 at 687.

tific effects, superstition will abate. . . . The present tendency of education is to make them materialistic and root out spirituality. With a
proper understanding of what their ancestors mean by their writings and
teachings, education would become a blessing.[89]

The scheme is nothing if not clever: use ancient "phenomenalism" now
understood scientifically to return South Asians to their own traditions,
drawing them away from superstition, and converting education from a self-
estranging practice to a reformative one. In such contexts practices such as
phenomenalism were as transidiomatic as "guru English."

Olcott did not begin to practice mesmeric healing until his third visit
in 1882, when his public demonstrations drew still more people to him.[90]
He explained his ability to heal by passing his hands over the body of the
distressed person in terms of the local belief in *budu ras*, which he over-
wrote as "auras," explaining that such auras extended eighteen inches beyond the periphery of the human body. He shared an interest in budu ras
with Hikkaduve. Olcott traveled upriver in Burma to see colored emana-
tions from a Buddhist relic mound, and Hikkaduve saw similar effects at a
stupa in Badulla on the Buddha's birthday.[91] In this context it is hard not to
understand the Maha Bodhi flag, the "universal" symbol of Buddhism, in
a light that has Theosophical references. The flag was designed by members of the Colombo Theosophical Society, and it displays the six colors
that hovered around the Buddha's body (budu ras). Olcott did not design the
flag—Buddhist Theosophists did that—but Olcott was confident that the
mahatmas themselves had influenced the design.[92] Olcott's contributions
to the flag continue to be a point of contention in Sri Lanka, but the flag's
Theosophical motivations are altogether forgotten.

Once Olcott began corresponding, Migettuvatte got his letters translated into Sinhala and distributed them to his own followers. He also began
to lecture his supporters "regarding the manifold advantages that the Bud-

89. *Occult World* (1881; repr., London: Theosophical Publishing House, 1984), 119–20.

90. *Old Diary Leaves*, 2:374, 378, 381, 429, and 436–9. Olcott started to do mesmeric healing on that trip inadvertently, but he also had a strategic motive, having heard that local Roman
Catholics were establishing a healing shrine near Kelaniya. He regarded his command of *siddhi*
(extraordinary abilities) as a matter of science. He came to see mesmeric healing as an act of
compassion, performing numerous acts of healing in India, including at the home of Sir Jotendro
Nath Tagore. Murphet, *Hammer on the Mountain*, 157–65.

91. *Old Diary Leaves*, 4:1887–92, 520; Olcott, "The Buddha Rays at Badulla," *Theosophist*
11, no. 125 (1890): ci–cii.

92. *Old Diary Leaves*, 3:188 and 4:492.

dhists were to receive by the acquisition of Colonel Olcott and Mme. Blavatsky into their fold." He assured them that "the Mahatmas" were "devoted followers of Gautama Buddha."[93] A week or so after they had arrived at Galle, Olcott and Blavatsky received *pan sil* (the five precepts) from Bulatgama Sumanatissa, and they "were formally acknowledged as Buddhists," despite the fact that they "had previously declared [themselves] Buddhists long before, in America, privately and publicly. So that this was but a formal confirmation of [their] previous professions."[94] The self-conversion is itself indicative of their heterodox relationship to Buddhism.

> Our Buddhism was that of the Master-Adept Gautama Buddha, which was identically the Wisdom Religion of the Aryan Upanishads, and the soul of all the ancient world-faiths. Our Buddhism was, in a word, a philosophy, not a creed.[95]

Local Buddhists assumed that Olcott and Blavatsky were accepting a creed, their creed.

The party's warmth of feeling was reciprocated by their hosts. Blavatsky was moved into the background, and Olcott's affability made friendship easy.[96] The Buddhists were likely to have assumed the metaphysical discussions Olcott mounted with Buddhist monks were the questions of a new Buddhist trying to learn more about his avowed religion; for Olcott they were occasions for looking for points of contact between his highly imagined interpretation of Buddhist esotericism and the views of scholarly monks such as Hikkaduve, Dodanduve Piyaratana, and Vaskaduve Subhuti. Before the party arrived in 1880, Olcott had corresponded with Dodanduve Piyaratana, telling him that the Theosophical Society was predicated "on the basis of a Brotherhood of Humanity" and assuring him that "it is also a league of religions against the common enemy—Christianity."[97] He announced that he would be coming to India in a few months and added that

---

93. *Old Diary Leaves*, 4:520; Olcott, "The Buddha Rays at Badulla," ci–cii.

94. *Old Diary Leaves*, 2:167–8.

95. *Old Diary Leaves*, 2:168–9.

96. As Murphet writes, "Apart from the lectures, there were long discussions with priests on Buddhist metaphysics, in some of which H.P.B. was allowed to play a part, despite the handicap of being a woman. She often illustrated her points, and enlivened the proceedings, with flashes of her psychic powers," *Hammer on the Mountain*, 137.

97. Ananda Guruge, *From the Living Fountains of Buddhism: Sri Lankan Support to Pioneering Western Orientalists* (Colombo: Ministry of Cultural Affairs, 1984), 338–44, at 340.

"it is important to see you and the holy and learned ministers of the true faith. . . . I know nothing, having no means of observation. I ought or might feel called upon to make a public profession and enter the fold."[98]

In establishing the Theosophical Society in New York, Blavatsky continued to play the intellectual role that she had developed in Europe. Her views about universal brotherhood came from that same oracular source. Her Great White Brotherhood was a community of adepts whose rigorous training and absolute purity gave them supernatural powers. Heading the brotherhood was the Lord of the World, who

> came originally from Venus with several helpers and now inhabits the body of a sixteen-year old boy. In descending order of authority, his helpers are the Buddha, the Mahachohan, Manu and Maitreya. . . . Other Masters include Jesus, a "Syrian" who rather confusingly has responsibility for all religions, not merely Christianity; the Hungarian Prince Rakoczi—also known as the Comte de Saint Germain—who presides over Magic and whose previous incarnations included both Roger and Francis Bacon; Hilarion, a handsome Greek in charge of Science; Serapis . . . and the Venetian Master. . . . Much lower down the hierarchy is Master Dwaj Khool, who does celestial odd jobs. In addition, the Brotherhood of Masters includes all great religious leaders and occult teachers of the past. Buddha, Confucius, Solomon, Lao Tzu, Boehme, Roger Bacon, Francis Bacon, Cagliostro, Mesmer, Abraham, Moses and Plato are all members. Below them . . . are the arhats . . . and their disciples, known as chelas.[99]

The exuberant architecture of the occult world, its cosmopolitanism across space and time, and its genius for seeing the this of that and the that of this gave Blavatsky's vision a wondrous plausibility that must have been part of its appeal to considerable numbers of people. It was a world that appealed to Olcott, who regarded chance as "a word void of sense" and thought that

98. *From the Living Fountains*, 343. In a later letter to Ven. Piyaratana, Olcott declared that Piyaratana was wrong in addressing him as a medical doctor. He was only "an ignorant student of the occult sciences in which [he] include[d] Mesmerism or Animal Magnetism" (347).

99. Peter Washington, *Madame Blavatsky's Baboon* (New York: Schocken Books, 1993), 34–5. Manu's assistant is Master Moriya, who was Blavatsky's original visitor. He had been incarnated as a Rajput prince and lives in a secluded Tibetan valley. Maitreya's assistant is Master Koot Hoomi, a Kashmiri Brahman with blue eyes, and as Washington says, "Having attended the University of Leipzig, he spends much time meditating and is well qualified to look after the vast occult Museum in underground chambers near his home, which is located in the same valley as Master Moriya's." Washington, *Blavatsky's Baboon*, 35.

"all men whose minds lie open to the spiritual intelligence . . . are born Theosophists."[100]

From their mountain ashrams the brotherhood worked for the good of humanity, acting through human agents to counteract malign powers known as the Dark Forces. Those agents were chelas, and the young Dharmapala began by resolving to study the occult sciences as a way to learn more of the Himalayan Brotherhood and to serve Koot Hoomi, who himself served the Buddha. Blavatsky told him to turn his attention to studying Pali, and he would find all he sought there, advice usually taken to mean to devote himself to Buddhism. But on at least two occasions he wrote that her instructions were for him to study Pali and to serve humanity. In one notebook entry he wrote:

> HPB studied the philosophy of Buddhism and became a Buddhist and paved the way for Buddhism by her writings—She did not tell me to study Theosophy but advised me to study Pali and work for Humanity. (Sarnath Notebook no. 43)

The mahatmas also "serve Humanity," that last word appearing in Theosophical literature with a capital *H*. Dharmapala's first encounters with "Humanity" came during those early days when he was consuming a steady diet of Theosophical literature.[101] When he recounted the short version of Blavatsky's instructions to him, he has her saying, "Study Pali wherein you shall find all you seek." In the long version, published in *Asia* magazine, he remembered her as saying, "It will be much wiser for you to dedicate your life to the service of humanity. And, first of all, learn Pali, the sacred language of the Buddha."[102]

The ambiguity of Blavatsky's advice may owe to either her transidiomatic instructions or Dharmapala's way of remembering her advice. He went on in the same passage to conflate Buddhism and Theosophy even more:

---

100. *Old Diary Leaves*, 6:136, and "The Buddhist Apostle in England," *Indian Mirror*, October 12, 1899.

101. The following passage imbricates both Buddhism and Theosophy, but Theosophy dominates (and Buddhist arhats do not make utterances): "The train started at 9.30. Had good sleep. In the train I had a curious dream. An Arhat struggling and uttered the word . . . *Sudahat*. The letters were the initials of a sentence. Many interpreted it differently; but Priest Devananda, who is noted as a clever priest, interpreted it as a Arhat who crys [sic] to save Humanity—or in the words of the Voice of Silence 'Can there be bliss when all that lives must suffer? . . . I cry to save the world'" (Diary, November 17–18, 1891).

102. *Asia*, September 1927.

H. S. Olcott came to Ceylon to work for Buddhism and started the Bud-
dhist national Fund in 1881. There was no Theosophy then. It was all
Buddhism. A good Theosophist can't be a Mohammedan. He can't be a
Hindu, he can't be a Christian. He can only be a Buddhist.

There are several puzzles in this passage, but I assume that he is claiming
that—because Buddhism is the clearest window on the ancient wisdom that
is Theosophy—Buddhism is the only religion that allows one to understand
Theosophy. When his relationship with the society—both with Olcott and
the branch in Colombo—soured in 1905, he wrote a series of articles that
made it clear that a Buddhist could not be a member of the Theosophical Society.[103] The salient point is not the flip-flop, first excluding everyone who
was not a Buddhist from Theosophy, then denying that a Buddhist could be
a Theosophist. There are two other points here: he saw Theosophy only in
relationship to Buddhism, ignoring the society's attempt to comprehend the
wisdom of all religions, and his grievances in 1905 were aimed at the Theosophical Society in Colombo, less so at Theosophy as an ideology.

UNIVERSALISMS

Blavatsky was more of a universalist than Olcott. She wanted discussion
of all religions, Christianity included. Responding to a question regarding
advertisements that would be accepted by the *Theosophist*—are advertisements for freethinking literature acceptable, and what about anti-Christian
advertisements?—she wrote,

> I, as an Editor, will never permit Christ to be attacked personally, no more
> than Buddha. But I must insist upon being allowed to remain entirely
> impartial in the *dissection* as in the praise of all and every religion the
> world over, without pandering to people's personal emotional prejudices.
> This will never do in a *Universal* Brotherhood [emphasis in original].[104]

The commitment to gathering together all human beings in the Theosophical Society was essential to Blavatsky, but the vocabulary itself was incho-

103. "Can a Buddhist Be a Member of the Theosophical Society," *Journal of the Maha Bodhi Society* 14 (1906): 42–4; and "The Parting of the Ways," *Journal of the Maha Bodhi Society*
14 (1906): 117–24. The first article carries Dharmapala's byline.
        104. "H.P.B. and Freethought," in De Zirkoff, *H. P. Blavatsky: Collected Writings, 1883*,
122–25, at 123.

ate. Olcott was more focused on creating a brotherhood of all human beings than bringing Christian doctrine into the Theosophical fold. Sojourning
in India meant dealing with others who were "racially" different. Settled
in Bombay, they began to develop the notion of universal brotherhood—
"wherein all good and pure men of every race shall recognize each other as
the equal effects (upon this planet) of the one Un-create, universal, Infinite
and Everlasting Cause."[105]

They found India unprepared for their message. They tried to join forces
with the Arya Samaj, oblivious to the fact that Dayananda Saraswati was
not the universalist they were. Nor was the Indian elite ready:

> When the founders of the Society landed at Bombay in 1879, they did
> not find even half a dozen Indians ready to receive their idea of an Uni-
> versal Brotherhood, and not even the idea of an Indian Brotherhood. . . .
> The Theosophists were not only to be brothers among themselves, but
> also brothers to all men with whom the world brought them in contact.
> Theosophists in India, therefore, began to look about them to see if they
> could not ameliorate the lot of their fellows.[106]

The founders soldiered on, continuing "studying occult science" as the society's chief aim, but now addressing two new objectives. One was a formulation of universal brotherhood and the other the study of Oriental literature
and philosophy.[107]

The society's motto said nothing about Buddhism or the Asian religions
that furnished most of its ideology. It read, "There is no religion higher
than Truth," and because truth can be found in all religions, the society's
work was to draw together people of all religions in its investigation of the
esoteric truths accessible in those religions, even if now obscure. The message of inclusion and equality appealed to South Asians accustomed to the
condescension, hierarchy, and racist attitudes of the British Raj, on the rise
after the events of 1857, when Indian troops rebelled against British officers,
raising the prospect of a oncoming struggle for independence. That appeal
transcended the ideological charms of Theosophy itself. Olcott had no anti-
imperial motives in his work in India and regarded the Theosophical Society as nonpolitical. The founders brought two other people with them to
India, a Mr. Wimbergh and a Miss Bates, and Blavatsky innocently thought

105. Murphet, *Hammer on the Mountain*, 96–7.
106. *Indian Mirror*, November 21, 1889.
107. Murphet, *Hammer on the Mountain*, 96–7.

that because they were "respectable" English people, their presence would reduce government suspicion about their motives as non-Britons working in India.[108] Olcott was more than apolitical, and, his feelings about brotherhood aside, he was hesitant to pursue social change in India. He was even unwilling to see *panchama* (*Dalit*) Indians gathered into the Buddhist fold until doctrinal evidence—the first-century CE Buddhist poet Asvaghosa came to the rescue—could be produced to show that they were not converting to a new religion but reverting to their ancient faith, Buddhism.[109]

Even a short time in India led Olcott to recognize the invidious attitudes of British officials:

> To us who know the Hindus, it is hardly credible how little is known of this side of their character [i.e., their intelligence] by their official superiors. . . . How could they possibly expect to be on terms of good understanding with high-caste men (i.e. gentlemen) whom they treat in official intercourse with unconcealed disdain, commonly classifying them as "niggers," without caring at all whether it comes to the insulted gentlemen's ears or not? It is inexpressibly sad to me to see this awful waste of good opportunity to bind the Indian empire to the British throne with silken bands of love.[110]

The equation of gentlemanly behavior with high caste reveals Olcott's own prejudice—he preached equality while treating his servants with something less—but to his credit, he became more committed to the idea of brotherhood as he spent more time in India.[111] By 1898 he was arguing that it was the first objective of the society.[112]

In 1897 a Thai monk living in Colombo wrote to Olcott urging him to concern himself with the disorder and corruption that had befallen the local monkhood. A member of the royal family with considerable knowledge of the world, Jinavaravamsa was no ordinary monk. He attributed Lankan dis-

---

108. *Old Diary Leaves*, 2:109–10. Olcott writes that he and Blavatsky were suspected of being Russian agents. *Old Diary Leaves*, 2:228–31 and 245–8.

109. *Old Diary Leaves*, 6:345–7 and 397.

110. *Old Diary Leaves*, 4:260.

111. Alan Trevithick points out the class complications of everyday life for Olcott and Blavatsky once they set up house in India. Their concern for universal brotherhood and equality did not prevent them from hiring Indian servants. "The Theosophical Society and Its Subaltern Acolytes (1880–1986)," *Marburg Journal of Religion* 13 (2008), http://www.uni-marburg.de /fbo3/ivk/mjr/pdfs/2008/articles/trevithick2008.pdf.

112. *Indian Mirror*, October 12, 1889.

array to the British government's giving control over substantial amounts of monastic lands to the incumbents of temples. The incumbents of the two Kandyan orders of the Siyam Nikaya said the same thing, complaining to Olcott of the disobedience of their own subordinates. Without a proper Buddhist king, monks who controlled sources of wealth were able to defy monastic authority, leading to what Olcott called "an atmosphere of personal bickering, childish sectarian squabbles, ignorance of the world about them, and incapacity to fit themselves to the ideals which the Lord Buddha had depicted for the government of his Sangha."[113] Jinavaravamsa proposed addressing the corruption problem as it had been handled in traditional times, first unifying the monkhood, then reforming it by royal decree.[114] But the Prince Priest had a transnational vision that no one ever dreamed of—first unify the Sinhala *sangha*, join it to the Burmese *sangha*, and then ally both with the Thai *sangha* under the authority of the Thai king. The last Buddhist king would surely welcome that mandate.

On his way to Europe, King Chulalongkorn stopped in the island, and Jinavaravamsa and Olcott used his visit as an occasion to solicit his support. Things went terribly wrong in Kandy when the king was denied the right to hold the tooth relic. Although others had been given that privilege in the recent past—including Christians—a Kandyan aristocrat denied the king access, who went away in a huff. He agreed to consider the union of the monkhoods, which Anne Blackburn calls "the Lankan proposal," linking it to Hikkaduve. The proposal had a lot to do with Olcott and Jinavaravamsa.[115] Later Jinavaravamsa attended the annual meetings in Adyar. He asked not to speak because of his status as a samanera, giving Olcott a letter to read to the group:

If Theosophy is the medium through which negotiation for the peace between all men proceeds . . . I am heart and soul with it. . . . If Theosophy would undertake, in addition to the work of bringing men together into one Universal Brotherhood, the duty of leading men by example and practice . . . so that they might be either true Christians or Hindus, or Buddhists, etc, whatever be their religion, and not hypocrites as they

113. *Old Diary Leaves*, 6:154–5.

114. See S. J. Tambiah, *World Conqueror and World Renouncer: A Study of Buddhism and Polity in Thailand against a Historical Background* (Cambridge: Cambridge University Press, 1976).

115. Blackburn, *Locations of Buddhism*, 167–86.

now appear to be, it would be conferring the greatest of all boons of the century. . . . Personally . . . I think that all the elements necessary for the basis of a Universal religion are found in Buddhism.[116]

The careful language suggests the monk's earlier life as a diplomat—he saw the advantage of working with the Theosophists, but he would not join their movement.

Once the proposal for union reached Bangkok, the Council of Elders of the Thai monkhood discussed the issue for some three hours, rejecting the proposal on the grounds that Sri Lanka "is a separate country and the various Lanka people and factions were hostile to one another."[117] One Thai prince noted another problem: the island was a British colony. Jinavaravamsa and Olcott kept at it, sailing to Burma in 1899 with Annie Besant. In Rangoon Besant and Olcott gave a number of lectures before Olcott and Jinavaravamsa traveled upriver to Mandalay to meet the ranking Buddhist monks of Burma on the topic of education and "the union of the Buddhists of Burma, Ceylon, and Siam in one great religious fraternity under the patronage of H.M. the King of Siam."[118] In view of Jinavaravamsa's initiating the proposal, his recruiting Olcott to the cause, and their carrying on with the project after the idea lapsed in Lanka, I would give the Prince Priest majority ownership of the proposal—whatever the interest of high-ranking Sinhala monks—and note the transnational character of the Theosophical Society's involvement and the connection to unity. At the very least, there was a Theosophical subtext in this case.

Olcott's efforts to unify the monkhood make an instructive contrast with Dharmapala's disinterest in unifying either monks or laypeople. The diaries do not speak of his motivations, but several circumstances constrained him. One was his caste. His father was Goyigama and his mother Durava, but what brought them together was their social class, their origins in the Southern Province, the timber business, and their piety.[119] His complicated origins could have been a motive for seeking unity among monks of different castes, but it could equally well have furnished reason

---

116. "An Open Letter," *Theosophist* 19 (1898): 291–4, at 291–2. Jinavaravamsa called the Theosophical Society by a name that suggests his own interests, "The Universal Brotherhood Working Samagama" (Diary, March 1, 1906).

117. Blackburn, *Locations of Buddhism*, 184.

118. "The Burmese Visit of Mrs. Besant and the President," *Theosophist* 20 (1899): xxi.

119. Michael Roberts, "Himself and Project. A Serial Autobiography. Our Journey with a Zealot, Anagarika Dharmapala," *Social Analysis* 44, no. 1 (2000): 116.

to avoid the caste issue altogether. He mentioned caste sporadically in the diaries, and he had his own prejudices, but he never mentioned his mother's caste. His disinterest in caste reform might also have derived from his being considerably more knowledgeable of Sinhala society than Olcott, and thus more realistic. Since Dharmapala's time, the monkhood has grown to more than thirty communities. A final motivation, needless to say, was his assumption that recovering Bodh Gaya was more important than monastic reform.

Universal brotherhood came to Olcott in both Theosophical and Buddhist form. He wrote that the visit of the master to Blavatsky in 1881 had a bearing on bringing the idea to the fore in the Theosophical Society.[120] Doing so had structural implications for the society, for as soon as brotherhood became more prominent, Olcott decided to create an Esoteric Section as the highest level of membership in the society. He directed his own energies toward worldly projects, and the initiatives often had a Buddhist purpose—the *Buddhist Catechism* and the Buddhist flag were vehicles for exoteric ends, most important, establishing Buddhist doctrine common to all Buddhist countries so that there might be more social unity. Dharmapala pursued his share of worldly projects in the Buddhist cause. His 1892 trip to meet the chief lama of Sikkim was prompted by a desire to bring Buddhists together—at least for the sake of recovering Bodh Gaya—and at this early point in his career Dharmapala wrote glowingly of opening the way for brotherly intercourse.[121] His trips to Burma and Japan can be read in the same light. Late in his life Dharmapala gave a talk arguing that "Buddhism is not racial or national, but international" (Diary, December 8, 1925). He urged Buddhists to forgive Gandhi because Theosophy teaches the equality of all religions.[122] He also took pleasure in knowing that the Vidyodaya *pirivena*, which his family had established, educated monks of all *Nikayas* and served laypeople of castes other than the dominant Goyigama.[123]

120. *Old Diary Leaves*, 2:294. "Keeping the occultism more in the background" changed the very nature of the society.

121. "Dharmapala's Work," supplement, *Theosophist* 13 (1892): lxxxviii–lxxxix, at lxxxix.

122. *Sinhala Bauddhaya*, May 23, 1925, quoted in Guruge, *Dharmapala Lipi*, 302. In that same month Gandhi had made comments at the Dharmarajika vihara in Calcutta—drawing no distinction between Buddhist and Hindu teachings and asserting that the Buddha was not an atheist—which must have given Buddhists pause. "Mahatma Gandhi on Buddhism," *Bengalee*, June 1925, excerpted in Wipulasara, *Maha Bodhi Centenary Volume*, 222–4.

123. Guruge, *Dharmapala Lipi*, 66.

Dharmapala did not make much of the universal brotherhood idea that lay at the center of Olcott's plans. It is true that he called his publication the *Journal of the Maha Bodhi Society and the United Buddhist World.*[124] The last message Olcott received from the mahatmas, and the only one he received directly (as opposed to receiving their messages via Blavatsky), called for the Society to work for unity:

> Cease from such turmoil and strife, and from causing such disturbance in the Unity of Brotherhood, and thus weakening its strength; but instead work together in harmony, to fit yourselves to be useful instruments to aid us, instead of impeding our work. . . . Hold together in brotherly love, since you are part of the Great Universal Self.[125]

Dharmapala understood the "United Buddhist World" not as an end in itself but as a constituency that would enable him to make Bodh Gaya Buddhist once again. After many trips around the Buddhist world, he left behind no bureaucratic structure to sustain whatever unity he had created, and in contrast with Olcott's interest in human solidarity and equality, he was satisfied with "brotherly intercourse."

The Theosophical practice that interested Dharmapala centered on the mahatmas, and Koot Hoomi in particular authorized a set of associated practices—dhyana meditation, celibacy, vegetarianism, and what he calls variously *lokottara* (otherworldly) culture, *uttari manussa dhamma* (the morality of the higher man), and *parama vijnana* (highest insight). Following practices associated with Koot Hoomi gave him the moral authority to separate himself from all the important communities in his life. It allowed him to critique Western scholars (who he thought could not understand Dhamma because they did not practice asceticism), Sinhala monks (whose lack of discipline and commitment drew his fire), and the local elite, including his own family (who he thought were Europeanized "elephants"). Koot Hoomi provided him with a paradigm for his own isolation because, even as he complained that others had abandoned him—and he did so with great frequency—their indifference to him allowed him to see his life as a matter of suffering. Koot Hoomi gave him a cause, serving humanity, and pursuing it gave meaning to both his wandering and his solitude.

In his own understanding, Dharmapala lived alone. He chose the name

---

124. Olcott, "An United Buddhist World," 239–40, and "Correspondence," *Journal of the Maha Bodhi Society* 13 (1892): 513.

125. "A Recent Conversation with the Mahatmas," *Theosophist* 18 (1907): 388.

Anagarika (homeless) for a reason: "The world was my home. . . . The Buddhists were all against me" (Diary, April 10, 1926). Yet despite the universalism implied by saying that the world was his home, he spent forty years
living in Calcutta, and he owned a number of residences there. He owned
at least a share of several homes in Sri Lanka, most important his family's
home on Aloe Avenue and the house he purchased in Kandy to use as a
seminary for training missionary monks, but the homelessness and solitude
of his own self-understanding trumped everyday reality. He employed servants. On an average day, he saw visitors and acquaintances who joined him
for breakfast, took a stroll with him or went for a ride at the end of the day,
and frequently he had people living with him. In Calcutta Devapriya lived
with him for several decades.[126] Failing to make the trek to the Himalayas,
Dharmapala found solitude among others, and that solitude was the foundation of his identity: "Buddha has no friends in India. Neither do I," he wrote,
and "Helpless, neglected, abandoned by all, I am struggling on" (Diaries,
April 1 and September 30, 1918, from Sarnath Notebook no. 27, "Diaries
1915–1919"). The practical source of his isolation was of his own doing. He
was hypercritical. He understood criticism as both a public responsibility
and privilege he had earned by way of his asceticism and philanthropy:

> Bro. Wickramaratna has gone to the High Priest to find fault against
> me for using the work [sic] "Anagarika." All this opposition agst me
> simply because I want to maintain the sublimity of the Dharma. Every-
> where opposition. The Dharma will protect me. My father writes a letter
> which is enough to drive a fool mad; in the same tone did King Suddhod-
> hana utter of [sic] words of reprobation to the Supreme Buddha (Diary
> March 10, 1898).

The life of the arhat, fully realized, makes one enlightened. The life of the
Bodhisat makes one a Buddha. Dharmapala had his gaze fixed on the latter.

RENOUNCER IN THE WORLD

Dharmapala described himself variously as a chela, a brahmacarya of the
bodhisattva path, and an anagarika, all of these roles entailing celibacy. Renunciation required discipline in several contexts, but celibacy posed the

---

126. Dharmapala's mother brought the young boy to Calcutta with the idea that Dharmapala would educate him there and that the boy would take over the Maha Bodhi Society after
his death. He did so, serving as general manager of the Maha Bodhi Society until 1968.

great challenge.[127] His commitment to celibacy was regularly tested abroad, especially on his trips to Japan, where he was in close contact with hotel personnel, and the United States, where relations between men and women were considerably more casual than in Sri Lanka. Throughout his adult life he wrote of being troubled by lustful thoughts (referring to them as *kama chanda nivarana* and *kama bahu dukkha*, "nighttime aberrations" and "physical weakness"). In Colombo he had a tempestuous relationship with Madame Marie de Souza Canavarro. She appeared in Colombo to work at the Sanghamitta Convent after a ceremony in New York City by which Dharmapala made her an *upasika* (pious Buddhist laywoman).[128] The diary reveals Canavarro pressed Dharmapala for a closer relationship:

> "Better to embrace a *red-hot* iron ball than embrace a woman." I will remain pure. The Upasika wrote a loving letter offering me the "highest sacrifice." I read it thrice, then burnt it; and to my surprise I found a bit of a remnant left. In it were the words "I cannot permit . . . the act. It will pass away," this was strange. I will be burnt to death; I prefer, but let me remain pure. "Oh, let all go, only O Lord let me save that blessed life." Buddha saved me. May I become *Buddha*. I showed my power to the Upasika. I will shake the foundation of the world. I had a rainwater bath. (Diary, November 23, 1898; emphasis in original)

Receiving no encouragement from him, Canavarro stormed off to Calcutta.[129]

Once Dharmapala thought he had broken his brahmacarya vow, and he returned to the incident from time to time. It is not clear exactly what occurred, but it involved a Japanese woman who gave him a massage in a Japanese hotel.[130] Summing up his life, he returned to the incident:

127. The diaries show Dharmapala on occasion eating chicken, eggs, fish, and mutton. I suspect that he understood vegetarianism to mean eating no beef whatsoever and avoiding other animal products as much as possible. I think that his relative laxness with regard to diet derived from thinking that celibacy alone was decisive to spiritual progress and a South Asian sense that meat eating meant beef eating in particular.

128. As a Theosophist, and a friend of Marquis, the leader of the Hawaiian Society, Canavarro might have been one of the party that met Dharmapala shipboard in Honolulu. Frank Karpiel, "Theosophy, Culture, and Politics in Honolulu, 1890–1920," *Hawaiian Journal of History* 30 (1996): 183.

129. Canavarro later contracted a "spiritual" marriage with another Theosophist, Myron Phelps.

130. "In Japan May 1902—the two months I spent in Tokio was bad for me. Kama thoughts sprang up but I submitted. In New York in Decr 1903—Kama thoughts came but I vanquished them. Although I was asked by women to submit to their passions yet I did not yield to them. Nevertheless just as a pure white cloth is stained with dirt, I too became stained with Kama

In 1886 March made the Renunciation. Lead [sic] a purifying life of spirituality till 1902 May. Since 1902 May the Brahmachari life was made
impure. I allowed women to touch my body. Since 1902 May sensual-
izing tendencies began to influence me. Impure associations in 1903—at
San Francisco, Green Acre, Boston, and New York. In 1904 the effects of
1903 were visible. (Diary, September 17, 1904)

He said he formed "an attachment to a woman in the USA," remembering events that occurred twenty years earlier (Diary, October 8, 1925). The
woman was Gudrun Friis Holm, a Danish American Theosophist he met
at a chautauqua while on tour in 1904. She worked as a physician in the
United States, and she too gave him a massage. The treatment had made
him feel better, but it "awakened sensations which go to show the truth
of the Great Law of Dependent Origination. . . . How easy to go under the
clutches of Mara. . . . In the evening Miss Holm treated me and put me to
sleep. She is very kind" (Diary, August 6, 1903).

It is hard to know what to make of a celibate renouncer contemplating
a life with a woman while pursuing the bodhisat life. His first reference
to the idea followed something Honganji officials suggested when he was
considering staying on in Japan and working as a missionary. If he planned
to stay for ten years, his hosts advised him, he should take a companion.
He wrote that he had the perfect candidate, a Miss Otake, who had been
kind to him and wanted to work for Buddhism (Diary, June 27, 1902). He
vowed to "keep her in the place of my younger sister," which is to say he
planned to pursue religious work with her and live platonically. Whatever
one makes of his even contemplating female companionship needs to begin
with one certitude—that his diaries show no signs that he ever imagined
breaking his commitment to celibacy. He mentioned Miss Otake twice in
the diaries, but Holm was a more serious matter. With her he remained in
contact for more than twenty years, and as late as 1908 he held onto hopes
that she would join him in India. They corresponded as late as 1926 (Diary,
November 10, 1926). When he convalesced in Switzerland that summer, he
made plans to visit her in Denmark.

Chautauquas were nondenominational camps committed to lectures,
study, and companionship in the cause of promoting human growth, and
they often had their own universalizing programs. Dharmapala spent time

---

thoughts. Association is everything. Good and saintly people purify your company. *Women drag
you down* [underscoring in original]. Avoid the contact of women and you are so far safe" (Diary,
November 20, 1907).

3. Dharmapala on world tour, Eliot, Maine, 1901. Seated on chair, Sarah Farmer, his
hostess at Green Acre. Standing, left, Mirza Abu'l Fadl.

at several, including one at Green Acre in Eliot, Maine, as did Swami Vive-
kananda, Jacob Riis, Annie Besant, Clarence Darrow, Booker T. Washington,
Paul Carus, Countess Canavarro, W. E. B. DuBois, and Mirza Abu'l Fadl.[131]
The spirit was cosmopolitan and high minded, devoted to religious argu-
ment, although there was a lot more Theosophy in the air than Buddhism.
The founder of Green Acre was Sarah Farmer, who had attended the World's
Parliament of Religions, and Farmer's frequent visitor there was Sara Bull,
who entertained Dharmapala in Cambridge and provided much of Vive-

131. Anne Gordon Perry et al., *Green Acre on the Piscataquis* (Wilmette, IL: Baha'i Publishing Trust, 2005), 121–32.

kananda's support in the United States. In a letter of 1902 Vivekananda told Sara Bull his views of marriage:

> A race must first cultivate a great respect for motherhood, through the sanctification and inviolability of marriage, before it can attain to the ideal of perfect chastity. The Roman Catholic and the Hindus, holding marriage sacred and inviolate, have produced great chaste men and women of great power. . . . As you have come to see that the glory of life is chastity, so my eyes also have been opened to the necessity of great sanctification for the vast majority in order that a few lifelong chaste powers may be produced.[132]

Theosophy shared Vivekananda's ideas about "spiritual marriage" as the formula that would allow both human growth and traditional companionship.

Shortly after Vivekananda's letter to Sara Bull, Dharmapala met Holm at Green Acre, although his diaries are not forthcoming about what transpired between them. He spoke of her as his "spiritual companion," who would work with him in India. The textual context comes from the stream of articles that appeared in the *Theosophist* of the time, raising questions about traditional marriage and imagining alternatives such as spiritual marriage. When Dharmapala reached the US West Coast after his visit to Japan in 1902, he had an invitation to stay at the home of Josephine Holmes in Los Angeles. That visit exposed him directly to a spiritual marriage:[133]

> Miss Josephine Holmes of Los Angeles is now the spiritual wife of Arthur Steele. How hard it is for man and woman to live together for any length of time in a pure condition. Contact produces sensation. Sensation produce selfish desires. Self-desires—clinging, produces existence of sex desires etc. (Diary, January 21, 1904)

Keeping company with well-to-do Americans with surprising ideas about marriage spoke to Dharmapala's commitment to celibacy, providing a transidiomatic rationale for what he knew all along, that spiritual development requires sexual restraint; a "man and woman living together" required more restraint and produced more progress.

---

132. *The Complete Works of Swami Vivekananda*, (Calcutta: Advaita Ashrama, 1977), 5:180.

133. Blavatsky herself provided Dharmapala an earlier real-life example. He believed that "HPB had three husbands, yet she was sexually a virgin" (Diary, June 3, 1926).

There are some thirty references to Holm in the diaries, most of them referring to her as "Amara." She first presented herself to Dharmapala in a way that put him in mind of Mara, the women who tempted the Buddha just before enlightenment. "When 'Amara' offered me her body," he wrote, "I told her that I shall not bring shame on her, but asked her to be my eternal companion" (Diary, March 7, 1904).[134] The articles that appeared over the late nineteenth and early twentieth century in the *Theosophist* address the tension between animal passions and spiritual growth in the context of marriage, reconfiguring the relationship between husband and wife. Several of the articles considered abstinence in marriage in the context of the historical moment. G. N. Chakravarti's article reflected on the example of Rukhmabai, the Hindu wife who refused to live with her husband, and praised her abstinence in a time when "marriage has degenerated into a contract for physical happiness."[135]

Another article made the argument for the married person's having higher spiritual power than a world renouncer, as long as his marriage is "spiritual":

> A celibate [renouncer] who has no temptation and who has no one to care for but himself, has undoubtedly superior advantages for meditation and study. . . . A [married] man who is surrounded by [temptations] is every day and every hour under the necessity of exercising his will-power to resist their surging violence. . . . When he rises up to a higher state in his next incarnation, his will-power will be more developed, and he will be in the possession of the password, which is CONTINENCE.[136]

When he was a volunteer for the Theosophical Society, Dharmapala saw those articles, and he later heard similar talk at chautauquas about the power of spiritual marriage. Sexual restraint in marriage has a Hindu warrant, but he came to it under Theosophical auspices.

Dharmapala's struggles with sexual urges continued into old age. He thought about sexuality in ways that moved un-self-consciously between

134. At one point he says that he had "saved Amara from Mara," (Diary, January 13, 1904). The privative *A* denies the force of the morpheme that follows, Mara (evil, in this case, evil in the form of sexual desire).

135. Gyanendra N. Chakravarti, "Hindu Marriage," *Theosophist* 10 (1888): 53–8 at 56. See Paul B. Courtright, "Sati, Sacrifice, and Marriage: The Modernity of Tradition," in *From the Margins of Hindu Marriage: Essays on Gender, Religion, and Culture*, ed. Lindsey Harlan and Courtright (Oxford: Oxford University Press, 1995), 184–203.

136. An American Buddhist, "Chastity," *Theosophist* 5 (1884): 161–2.

mahatmas and Mara. In Buddhist logic, self-abnegation was its own reward
and moved him along the path that led to bodhisat status and nirvana. But
Theosophy offered a chela something more. In return for a life of celibacy,
dietary discipline, and indifference to luxury, he could expect the mahatmas' assistance in pursuing humanitarian projects. He was a member of a
brotherhood that included advanced human beings in service to humankind, but only if they disciplined their sexual instincts:

> When mother in 1902 March used unmotherly language, I kept cool and
> left the place. Conscientiously and with strenuous energy I exerted to
> be pure. Since the affections began with Amara these sudden Kama im-
> pulses come to me. In August last we pledged ourselves to each other to
> be eternal companions. May I keep myself pure and teach her purity as
> well? In Feby 1894 when I was talking to Prince Bhanuransi in his own
> palace in Bangkok I heard the voice say "My son, in your purity lies your
> strength"—that was ten years ago. In the secrecy of my chamber I have
> tried to be pure. Practicing the Paramitas, as an Anagarika since 1886 I
> have lived the Bodhisat life. Wealth, worldly decoration, sense pleasures
> and amusements I have not had since my 19th year. Having sacrificed
> everything I gave up my life to the Mahatmas as they were followers of
> the Buddha. When Mrs. Besant began to preach of Krishna the Mahatma
> idea underwent change (Diary, March 23, 1904)

The "pure" life that he wanted to pursue had its own transidiomatic sources.
His thinking that he could live as renouncer while accompanied by a
spiritual companion was not his own innovation. Nor was it a way for him
to devote his life as a layman to the Buddhist cause. Marriage as a spiritual
discipline had Theosophical sources, but it reminded the society's South
Asian members of the spiritual greatness of their ancient ancestors.[137] Dharmapala had enough affection for Gudrun Holm to envision her coming to
India to work with him: "I told Gudrun that I shall expect her later on.
She said she will come. She is good and generous, and I will treat her as
my sister" (Diary, January 13, 1904). He imagined something on the order
of the relationship between Maud Gonne and W. B. Yeats.[138] As had Cana-

---

137. Gyanendra N. Chakravarti, letter to the editor, *Theosophist* 10 (1889): 510–1, at 510.

138. Long after the relationship with Gudrun Holm had lapsed, Dharmapala looked to a
mahatma letter to explicate spiritual marriage: "Letter 19 is strangely applicable in the present
situation. Know that where a truly spiritual love seeks to consolidate itself doubly by a pure
permanent union of the two, in its earthly sense, it commits no sin, no crime. On such a union
angels may well smile. It is beautifully expressed; but is it sound? Since 29th April, physical

varro, Holm initiated the relationship: "I told her that it is wrong for me to give pain to another & treated her as a sister," Dharmapala wrote (Diary, March 7, 1904). The pain harks back to his mother's pain when she lost an infant daughter and the vow he made when he was seventeen: "I shall not be the cause of giving pain to a woman." In the United States Holm was involved in medical studies, moved from coast to coast, and after serving as the Maha Bodhi Society representative in San Francisco until the 1920s, eventually returned to Denmark to practice holistic medicine. Although they corresponded for several years, she never joined him in India, and he never visited her in Denmark.

My intuition is that his involvement with Otake, Holm, and, much later, Vera Wickremasinghe needs to be seen in that light—the imaginings of a man who considered several life courses, rejected most of them, and soldiered on, looking for ways to achieve spiritual growth in Japan, the United States, and England, where he was freer than he would have been at home. His encounter with "spiritual marriage" takes the same form as his contemplating staying in Japan and working as a Shinshu missionary. Whatever conclusion one reaches, Dharmapala's interest in spiritual companionship complicates his role as either a brahmacarya or a Protestant Buddhist. But it fits nicely with the turn-of-the-century world he inhabited.

When he was troubled by the contradictions of renunciation and life in this world, he called on the mahatmas for guidance.[139] They provided him with a link between his life as a Buddhist and Theosophist, and Koot Hoomi was central to that linkage. That seamlessness marks much of his writing—he begins with the Buddha and then without benefit of a logical transition moves on, writing suddenly about the mahatmas. Before he realized that the mahant was not going to sell the Maha Bodhi temple, Dharmapala invoked the Buddha's blessing on the mahant:

> The divine Lord conquered the world by the fulfillment of the Paramitas
> ten and for the last five days I invoked his powerful Name that I should

---

weakness is expressing itself in my mind. I hope it will soon vanish. Where there is phasso there is Vedana & Vedana is Dukkha" (Diary, June 3, 1929). Yeats proposed to Maud Gonne four times, and she refused him each time. Eventually she consented to a "spiritual marriage." See Susan Johnston Graf, *W. B. Yeats, Twentieth-Century Magus* (York Beach, ME: Samuel Weiser, 2000).

139. The mahatmas struggled with the incongruity between karma and their own intervention in human affairs. "Since every one of us is the creator and producer of the causes that lead to such or some other results, we have to reap what we have sown. Our chelas are helped but when they are innocent of the causes that lead them into trouble; when such causes are generated by foreign, outside influences." A. T. Barker, trans. and ed., *The Mahatma Letters to A. P. Sinnett from the Mahatmas M. & K.H.* (Pasadena, CA: Theosophical University Press, 1926), 310.

succeed in His work. I invoked his blessings on the Mahant more than a thousand times so that he may give the plot of land and that his heart may be changed. How true the words of the blessed *Master*, H.P.B.'s Gun—*"You have still to learn that so long as there are Three Men worthy of our Lords blessing in the Theosophical Society—it can never be destroyed."* Ah! How difficult to realize even for those who are trying to lead the Life the truth of the utterances of the *Masters*. The devoted followers of Gautama Buddha . . . This is the 17th day since I put my foot on Gaya. Great works require time for their accomplishment. Self sacrifice is the secret of success. The divine Teacher, Bhagavan was the embodiment of absolute self sacrifice, we his humble and devoted followers, if we are to succeed in His work, should lovingly and faithfully imitate *His Great Example*. Brother Bhikhari and I went to meet the Mahant. The land was at last given. . . . The Voice speaks in solitude. (Diary, August 17, 1891; emphasis in original)

Throughout the last full decade of his life and the terminus of his diary keeping, Dharmapala was as much a Theosophist as ever, but he was also as much a Buddhist. His life had been marked by the patronage of Theosophical women—Blavatsky, Besant, and Foster, Countess Wachmeister, Canavarro, Holmes, Sara Bull, Alma Senda, Mabel Eaton, Iona Davey, and Alice Cleather. In the 1920s only a few remained. He could not mistake Besant for a Buddhist, but his relationship with Mary Foster was another thing altogether. He framed that relationship in a Buddhist way:

"Brahmachari of the Bodhisatva Path"—That shall be my future appellation. There is none other except the Dharma to look up to. Strict adherence to Dharma has been my principle. The Dharma protects me. The Dharma brought me in contact with Mrs. Foster. (Diary, December 13, 1917)

Foster was a Theosophist when she went down to Honolulu harbor to meet him upon returning home from the World's Parliament of Religions.[140] And in spite of the predominance of his role as a representative of Buddhism on that occasion, days earlier he had spoken as a Theosophist at the Theosophi-

140. Mary Foster's last letter to Dharmapala closes with "May it please the Great All that we may meet again." Nalinaksha Dutt, "The Maha Bodhi Society, Its History and Influence," in *Maha Bodhi Society of India Diamond Jubilee Souvenir 1891–1951*, ed. Suniti Kumar Chatterjee, (Calcutta: Maha Bodhi Society, 1951), 133.

cal preliminary conference he attended.[141] Late in life he came to understand that Foster had also given financial support to at least two Hindu gurus.[142]

The mahatmas stood behind several of Dharmapala's projects, but most of all they called him to India, where Koot Hoomi wanted him to reestablish the sasana:

> Got up at 5. The Sinnett letters from KH brought me in touch with the Himalayan Brother-hood. In 1884 I was absorbed in KH. In 1924 I am again thinking of the Masters. The two Adepts are trying to revive the Sasana. How they love each other. M says of KH. "My brother, the light of my soul." In this life I have not succeeded, but in the next life I hope to be born physically strong to climb the Himalayas and to study the sacred science. (Diary, May 9, 1924)

He had recognized this mandate decades earlier. "The two Masters wished the Religion of the Lord Buddha to be reestablished in India," he wrote. "Subba Row and his clique conspired against the scheme" (Diary, September 24, 1930). The problem was the chelas: "The Mahatmas Letters are full of inspiration, and yet every one who became a Chela went wrong. The TS under Mrs. Besant is a Christianized necromancy" (Diary, August 14, 1924). At the end of his diary keeping, he was still fixed on the decline of his fellow chelas:

> Out of the millions upon millions born in India only the *two Adepts M & KH* are followers of the Lord Buddha. All their disciples who became Buddhist at first later on became Apostates. . . . Damodar, Babajee, Paddhah, Bhavani Shanker, Ananda, Nivaran, Balai Ch. Malik, Leadbeater, Hartmann, Brown were known as "Chelas & lay Chelas." They all went wrong. (Diary, November 17, 1930)

In the 1920s he purchased new copies of the *Mahatma Letters* and *The Light of Asia* and reread the *Secret Doctrine* and *Mahatma Letters*, making diary entries as his reading proceeded (Diary, April 17, 1924, and March 12,

141. Dharmapala spoke at the Congress of Theosophists before the parliament, and that address is even less noticed than Annie Besant's solicitous behavior toward Dharmapala in London, and their crossing the Atlantic together had a Theosophical motivation. At the congress he spoke of "Theosophy as the underlying truth of all the world's scriptures." "Congress of Theosophists," in Houghton, *Neely's History*, 926–8, at 926.

142. Namely, Yogananda and Abhedananda Swami (Diary, November 23 and December 9, 1925).

1926). "The two Brothers," he said at one point, "tried to help the Western world and failed" (Diary, August 20, 1924). Reading the letters again reminded him of his long struggle with celibacy: "Today an evil thought came to my mind, 'When shall I leave this place,' 'Be reasonable' were the words I heard. That was 41 years ago and am still struggling to be passionless" (Diary, August 12, 1925). An earlier entry summarized his high aspirations:

> Reading "Mahatma Letters." They are very interesting. This incarnated body of mine to reach the summit of Samadhi failed for certain reasons. . . . I built a Vihara, a Dharmasala, and so on but failed to acquire the transcedent [sic] powers. The *abhijynas*, due to want of a *Kalyana Mitra*. (Diary, June 10, 1924; emphasis in original)

He does not say just who might have served as his *kalyana mitra* (friend who leads one on the right path). Gudrun Holm's name comes to mind, and it if was her, Dharmapala reveals his rationale for spiritual marriage. It helps a man achieve "transcendent powers."

Dharmapala's engagement with the masters was more than interior monologue. He gave a public lecture entitled "Mahatmas and Buddhism" in 1924 (Diary, August 15, 1924).[143] When he lectured at Town Hall in New York City in 1925, he characterized his talk as his attempt to deliver "the Message as it is the result of 40 years' experimental studies," and the reference to experimental studies is a reference to Theosophy.[144] Preparing to give that lecture, he met a Miss Chamberlain, who pressed a ten-dollar bill on him. Not wanting to take her money, he bought her a copy of the *Mahatma Letters* with the money (Diary, December 10, 1925). Most of all he used the *Journal of the Maha Bodhi Society* to engage publicly with the masters. Some of the articles were not written by Dharmapala, but he remained managing editor through 1925, and many of the articles reflect not broad Buddhist interests but his own distinctive concerns. And they all follow the same logic, arguing that the Theosophical Society forgot its values when Blavatsky left:

> It is evident that the T.S. no longer represents H. P. Blavatsky's work, and that the Masters have long since abandoned it to its fate. . . . There are still clean-minded altruistic people in the T.S. who desire that the pure

---

143. I believe that this talk was a lecture he gave at the Dharmarajika Vihara, Calcutta.

144. Diary, November 28, 1925. The next sentence in that day's entry reads "Got copy of Mahatma Letters from Bro. Wadia."

Trans-Himalayan teachings should be revived. But it would seem as if
no real scholars and mystics are left in it, but only dabblers in psychism
who mislead many.[145]

The problem lay not in Theosophy, but the anti-Buddhist turn the movement had taken.

After Dharmapala gave up his membership in the Theosophical Society
in 1905, the *Journal of the Maha Bodhi Society* ignored Theosophy for a
time. When he published articles in the journal, they were accounts of the
Maha Bodhi temple or Sarnath, denunciations of Buddhist apathy, or calls
for monks and brahmacaryas to propagate Buddhism in non-Buddhist countries.[146] As the years passed, there appeared articles under his name that
suggest more Theosophy than Buddhism. In 1914 he argued that Buddhism
had an esoteric aspect, and in 1925 he made the same argument in another
form.[147] In the first article he wrote that the Buddha laid out the teaching in two parts, the *uttari manussa dhamma* for monks and the *manussa
dhamma* for laypeople. The line between the two moralities is hard and
fast. A monk will be dismissed from the monkhood should he even exhibit
his phenomenal powers (*iddhi*) to laypeople. But acquiring those powers is
what the monk seeks. Likewise the Buddha preached two kinds of truth,
one kind for monks and the other for laypeople. By the end of the article
he shifted his attention to his own life course: "This is the Uttari manussa
dhamma which is supra-normal and only confined to the Brahmacharis,
who have renounced the fetters of lay life."[148] In the later article he describes the brahmacarya's path, keyed this time not to the ten *iddhi* but
jhanic states as Buddhaghosa explicated them in the *Visuddhimagga*. In the
Buddhist tradition, the expression "brahmachari" represents "the spiritual
or holy life that monks follow." He uses it to represent the life course of a
renouncer who observes the uttari manussa dhamma.

Although Dharmapala does not speak of the mahatmas in these two ar-

145. "Buddhism and Theosophy," *Journal of the Maha Bodhi Society* 30 (1922): 209–15,
at 214.

146. See, for instance, "The Spread of the Buddha's Arya Dhamma in Western Lands,"
Journal of the Maha Bodhi Society 17 (1909): 1–4; "Propagation of the Religion of Righteousness
in other Lands," *Journal of the Maha Bodhi Society* 24 (1916): 233–7; "The Apathy of Modern
Buddhists," *Journal of the Maha Bodhi Society* 27 (1919): 105–9; and "The Duty of Bhikkhus
and Laymen," *Journal of the Maha Bodhi Society* 27 (1919): 115–7.

147. "Buddhism in Relation to the Supra-Normal," *Journal of the Maha Bodhi Society* 22
(1914): 211–5; and "The Mystic Element in Buddha Dhamma," *Journal of the Maha Bodhi Society* 33 (1925): 641–4.

148. "Buddhism in Relation to the Supra-Normal," 215.

ticles, he struggled with the Theosophical side of his worldview. Using the
expression "brahmachari" allowed him to explain his own religious course,
because he was not a bhikkhu but a brahmacarya, living out his commitment to the uttari manussa dhamma.[149] Another set of articles appeared in
the 1920s, and they spoke directly to Theosophy, Blavatsky, and the mahatmas. Some appeared without attribution, some were written by Theosophists such as Basil Crump and S. Haldar of the Blavatsky party. One continuing article on "The Bodhi-Dharma or Wisdom Religion" began with its
author, Alice Leighton Cleather, saying that Dharmapala had asked her to
contribute the series.[150] All of these articles convey his understandings even
absent his name.[151] They reach much the same conclusion:

> Theosophy has become a misnomer, for the word was originally Greek
> for Divine Wisdom. But the Sanskrit name for the Wisdom—Religion is
> Bodhidharma which is understood throughout the East. It is that archaic
> doctrine, Esoteric Buddhism, of which the Trans-Himalayan Masters are
> the custodians for the human race.[152]

That the Adyar Theosophical Society had lost its way did not diminish the
virtues of the Himalayan Brotherhood and their chelas, still working for the
good of humanity because of their love for the Lord Buddha.

In the early 1920s, a flurry of articles appeared in the *Journal of the Maha
Bodhi Society* concerned with issues of peculiar interest to Dharmapala—

149. "Animal Slaughter in Buddhism," *Journal of the Maha Bodhi Society* 6 (1897): 52. The
focus on vegetarianism aside, Dharmapala concluded by writing that he wanted to restore the
"Uttari Manussa Dhamma, the divine science of Mind." "Divine science" is Blavatsky's expression. *Isis Unveiled: Collected Writings, 1877*, rev. and corr. ed., 2 vols. (Wheaton, IL: Theosophical Publishing House, 1972), 1:25. I suspect that Dharmapala got the idea of there being
two Buddhisms—one popular and the other secret philosophy—from Blavatsky, *Isis Unveiled*,
2:587–640, especially p. 607.

150. "Buddhism and Theosophy," 30 (1922): 209–15; Alice Leighton Cleather, "The
Bodhi-Dharma or Wisdom Religion," 30 (1922): 215–23, 30 (1922): 244–68, 30 (1922): 291–99,
30 (1922): 322–34, 30 (1922): 387–95, 30 (1922): 402–5, and 30 (1922): 462–72; "An Abominable
Falsehood," 31 (1923): 42–44; Basil Crump, "A Theosophical Criticism of Mrs. Cleather's
Books," 41 (1923): 474–81; Basil Crump, "The Trans-Himalayan Masters on the Buddha," 32
(1924): 195–203, 32 (1924): 234–9, and 32 (1924): 300–7; "Notes and News," 32 (1924): 419–24;
Iona Davey, "The Blavatsky Association," 32 (1924): 464–67; "Theosophy and Buddhism," 33
(1925): 619–21.

151. Basil Crump says that Cleather wrote "The Bodhi-Dharma or Wisdom Religion" for
Dharmapala, adding that Dharmapala also asked her to "found a branch of the Esoteric School
[of Theosophy] at Sarnath." "What the Founders of the Theosophical Society Did for Buddhism," *Journal of the Maha Bodhi Society* 50 (1942): 83–7, at 86.

152. "Buddhism and Theosophy," 214–5.

the life of an anagarika. Only one appeared under his name, and it made no reference to Theosophy.[153] I suspect he wrote several of these articles and encouraged articles from supporters about issues of particular interest to a man who by then had been an anagarika for some forty years. Devapriya was a fledgling anagarika, Harischandra Valisinha assumed the role, and other men—Anagarika Govinda and a latter-day Anagarika Dhammapala—followed suit in subsequent years. But practically speaking, Dharmapala was the sole token of the type. Decades after his public falling out with the Buddhist Theosophical Society, and Besant, the pages of the *Journal of the Maha Bodhi Society* show so many of his cognitive interests—in the uttari manussa dhamma, esoteric Buddhism, the brahmacarya life—that it is plain that he was exercising editorial control when not writing the articles.

A pair of articles that appeared in 1922 will make the point.[154] The first begins by saying, "The sacred science of transcendentalism in Buddhism is called 'Uttarimanussa dhamma'" and adds that the Buddha intended this pathway to arhatship for brahmacaryas and bhikkhus, but that the brahmacarya must become a bhikkhu "to lead the holy life in completeness." The writer gives a summary history of the Theosophical Society, quotes a message from the Maha Chohan (the mahatma who was the guru of Koot Hoomi), saying that the Theosophical Society should perish before restricting the occult life to the few while ignoring the many. He urges Westerners to take up the study of Abhidhamma. A Burmese U Kyaw Dun responded to this article by critiquing it as a Buddhist. The monastic law prohibits monks from showing laypeople the powers they have acquired by following the uttari manussa dhamma, but the higher form of the Buddha's teaching is open to laypeople to follow.[155] It is thus a monkly privilege in the end and requires the layperson who pursues it to eventually join the monkhood for the realization of that knowledge. Against this backdrop Dharmapala's own life course—following the uttari manussa dhamma as a brahmacarya for most of his days and ending his life as a monk—acquires new meaning as his growing spiritual accomplishments moved him from one role to another.

153. "The Mystic Element in Buddha Dhamma," *Journal of the Maha Bodhi Society*, 33 (1925): 641–4.

154. "The Esoteric Doctrine in Buddhism,' *Journal of the Maha Bodhi Society*, 30: (1922): 195–200; and U Kyaw Dun, "'The Esoteric Doctrine in Buddhism,'" 30 (1922): 409–14. The 1922 table of contents attributes both articles to U Kyaw Dun K.S.M. It seems unlikely he wrote the first piece because he critiques it in the second.

155. Peter Masefield argues that during the Nikaya period the criterion for spiritual accomplishment was whether one were a *savaka*—that is, someone who had entered the path, beginning with sotapanna status—never whether one was a monk or a layperson. Laymen could become savakas. *Divine Revelation in Pali Buddhism*, chapter 1.

Dharmapala did not need to redefine terms or locate new ones because the language that Theosophy and Buddhism shared was already transidiomatic—he needed only to reidentify himself. The world renouncer who claimed both identities emphasized the Buddhist part of his identity in public contexts but spoke in his diaries of his regard for Blavatsky, Master Koot Hoomi, and the uttari manussa dhamma. He had every reason to discard his membership in the Theosophical Society—his alienation from Olcott, his growing suspicion of Jiddu Krishnamurti, whom the Theosophical Society began to promote as a messiah figure, and the practice of Theosophists in India claiming to be arhats, as well as his troubles with Theosophists in Colombo. In urging the Colombo Theosophists to drop "Buddhist" from their group's name, Dharmapala tried to redescribe others against their will. By contrast it was easy to discard his own Theosophical identity—his rejoining the Society in 1914 aside—and to hold onto his old vocabulary, its Buddhist meanings now foregrounded. Those expressions were, after all, ones Blavatsky had taken from Buddhism in the first place.

The irony was that the one Theosophical notion that he cared most about was furnished by the mahatmas, and the Himalayan adept notion was simply not transidiomatic with Buddhism. That expression did not derive from Buddhist texts or tradition, and it makes little sense introduced into a Buddhist context. He never ceased to admire Blavatsky, even after he reread the *Secret Doctrine* and suspected her of plagiarism. He never ceased to talk about his regard for Koot Hoomi, calling himself long after 1905 a "chela of the Masters." I doubt that he spoke of the masters before Sinhala audiences, but he wrote about the uttari manussa dhamma for English readers, whether Sinhala, Asian, or Western. In his diaries he steered away from the expression "mahatma," preferring the equivalent but less markedly Theosophical and Hindu "Masters." But it was his continuing regard for them, the uttari manussa dhamma, and the brahmacarya life that made his Buddhism more complicated than Theravada and anything but Protestant.

CHAPTER TWO

Buddhists in Japan

Without Japan, Asia is a funeral house.[1]
—Anagarika Dharmapala

At the beginning of his career Dharmapala made a number of trips overseas in rapid succession. He traveled to Japan with Olcott in 1889 and
to India with two Japanese in 1891, and in 1893 he sailed to the World's Parliament of Religions, returning home by way of Japan and Southeast Asia.
It is tempting to begin with the 1893 trip and take up his public life with an
extraordinary moment in the nineteenth-century encounter of universalism
and the world's religions. The World's Parliament of Religions represented
more than a spectacle—although it was that—bringing together religious
leaders who ranged from Japanese Buddhists, Swami Vivekananda, and Confucianists to Protestant ministers and patriarchs of the Greek and Russian
Orthodox churches all dressed in clerical clothes. It gave participants a platform to present their universalizing programs and a common register that
put all of those programs on a par. The 1889 trip had its own epic moments,
but Olcott was the hero and Dharmapala his acolyte.[2] The trip belonged to
Olcott; he was the Buddhist reformer the Japanese sought, and the younger
man's presence was ignored in newspaper accounts of Olcott's activities.[3]
What made Dharmapala entirely invisible was being hospitalized for the
first half of their four-month visit. Once recovered, he tried himself out in

1. Guruge, *Dharmapala Lipi*, 52, and Diary, June 27, 1925.
2. Dharmapala had traveled overseas as early as 1884, if we count his attendance at the
annual conventions of the Theosophical Society in South India as overseas. He attended those
meetings as a Theosophist, and those trips were not intended to build a united Buddhist world.
3. Kazushige Yamakawa, "Dharmapala and Japan: His First and Second Visits," *Journal of
Pali and Buddhist Studies* 14 (2000): 46.

preparation for the serious work to follow. In the bargain, he came to appreciate the Buddhist world as it had developed across Asia, the great variety of Buddhisms, and Japan's success in fending off colonial powers and developing itself.

The first of Dharmapala's four visits to Japan was the one campaign that Olcott and Dharmapala waged together to unify what they took to be the dominant traditions of Buddhist thought and practice—the Northern school represented by Japan and the Southern tradition centered in Sri Lanka.[4] Some Japanese had knowledge of India at the time of Dharmapala's first three trips (1889, 1893, and 1902), and some of those viewed it as a promised land, tied to Japan by Buddhism and Bodh Gaya. For Dharmapala Japan was a Buddhist nation that could serve as a model of Asian civilization preserved and development achieved. In time his optimism faded, and the Japanese changed as well, coming to regard India by the time of his last visit in 1913 less as sacred land and more as a society oppressed by colonial power.[5] Before visiting Japan, Olcott and Dharmapala knew that including Japan in an united Buddhist world was going to require first creating some sort of unity among the eight sects that dominated Japanese Buddhism. They arrived at a favorable moment, but the moment soon passed. When Dharmapala returned to Japan in 1893 and 1902, he encountered a Japan that had changed, with little interest in India, the Maha Bodhi Society, or Olcott's plans for a united Buddhist world. Dharmapala scaled back his plans to gain Japanese support for reclaiming Bodh Gaya.

If the first trip had Dharmapala serving as Olcott's assistant or lying flat on his back in the hospital with rheumatism, the second had him arriving with newly acquired powers. He returned to Japan immediately after his appearance at the World's Parliament of Religions, where he had held his own. Commentators said that he and Swami Vivekananda were the stars of the occasion. Dharmapala edited a journal with readers scattered around the world; he had sympathizers in Lanka, Calcutta, and the United States; and he brought direct experience of conditions at Bodh Gaya to Japan. When he reached Tokyo with Professor Tanaka, he was met at the station by a few

4. What we now call Theravada was identified with a geographical reference. The present-day term—despite being an ancient expression—only came into currency as an alternative to Southern Buddhism or Hinayana in 1907. Todd Leroy Perriera, "Whence Theravada: The Modern Genealogy of an Ancient Term," in *How Theravada Is Theravada? Exploring Buddhist Identities*, ed. Peter Skilling et al. (Chiang Mai, Thailand: Silkworm Books, 2012), 550.

5. Yukiko Sumi Barnett, "India in Asia: Okawa Shumei's Pan-Asian Thought and His Idea of India in Early Twentieth-Century Japan," *Journal of the Oxford University History Society* 1 (2004): 1–13.

laymen and one hundred young priests (Diary, October 31, 1893). He had
not yet taken on the ochre robes of full renunciation, which he adopted two
years later.[6] He had begun his practice of rising at 2 a.m. to practice meditation in 1891.[7] He had contemplated trying to live on one meal a day (Diary,
August 12, 1891). Above all he had concluded that his chances of recovering
Bodh Gaya would depend on his "purity of mind," which is to say, his celibacy. In that regard Japan was going to present challenges.

Dharmapala came to raise funds for his struggle at Bodh Gaya, moving
around Japan by train, meeting people and giving lectures along the way. His
considerable respect for Japan aside, many practices challenged him—he
was invested in the trope of Japanese civilization, but he could not reconcile
sake drinking with civilized behavior. By his second trip he felt self-assured
enough to rebuke a Buddhist monk who drank liquor, telling him he was a
bad example of the pure life and showing him the relic he carried only under
protest (Diary, November 3, 1893). He fretted over the way the Japanese
practiced Buddhism: "They have made Buddhism to suit their own taste
and convenience" (Diary, November 16, 1893). At the same time, he began
to experience disheartening results. He gave a talk on Bodh Gaya and India,
appealing to his audience to restore the sacred site, but no support followed.
A few days later he displayed the Buddha image from Bodh Gaya that he carried on his travels to a minister of the imperial household, concluding that
the crown prince would be the savior of India (Diary, November 22, 1893).
Before he left Japan, he discovered that his supporters were trying to make
money by making casts of the image he brought with him. What they saw
as resourcefulness, he saw as simony.

For many Japanese, India was a mythical place, and when Dharmapala
recounted the present-day destitution of Bodh Gaya—as he did at home
and in the West—he had an additional task, making his Japanese listeners appreciate that India was both a real place and a land that deserved to
be treated by all Buddhists as sacred (Diary, November 22, 1893). He took
advantage of his own association with India and indirectly with the figure of the historical Sakyamuni. Richard Jaffe has shown how the travels
of Japanese monks to India and Lanka—even before Dharmapala reached

6. To judge from the photograph that Tanaka Chigaku had taken of their visit to Nichiren's
shrine, Dharmapala wore white robes at least one time on his 1902 visit to Japan. My guess is
that reverting to white was Dharmapala's attempt to respond to Japanese sensibilities. *Graphic
Biography of Chigaku Tanaka* (Tokyo: Kokuchukai, 1961), 23.

7. He began after his first visit to Bodh Gaya (Diary, March 6, 1891).

Japan—contributed to local interest in the Buddha as a historical figure and India as the place where Buddhism began.[8] Dharmapala was often taken as an Indian, and in Japan he regularly spoke for India and assumed the subject position of an Indian.[9] Recovering Bodh Gaya was of course an Indian issue, and it must have been hard for the Japanese to make a distinction between India and Lanka. Dharmapala failed to raise any substantial amount of support on this trip, but at the Tentokuji temple in Tokyo he was given a wooden image of the Buddha that he would use to establish a foothold for Buddhism at Bodh Gaya. Until 1910 the image also served as a placeholder for Japan's interest in the place.

His 1889 visit to Japan had given Dharmapala firsthand experience of Japan's economic development. He knew the Japanese had means to support the Bodh Gaya cause at a level impossible to imagine for Sinhalas, Thais, or Burmese, not to mention his supporters in India, England, and the United States, who were well off but few and far between. More to the point, Japan was an Asian country that had developed economically without losing its traditional way of life. Although the Japanese occupied the farthest reach of the Buddhist world, they showed signs of being interested in giving help to other Asians. After all, Toki Horyu had spoken at the parliament of the work the Maha Bodhi Society was doing at Bodh Gaya and indicated his hope to combine Northern and Southern Buddhism.[10] Dharmapala first came to Bodh Gaya in 1891 in the company of two Japanese who had been studying in Colombo.[11] From the time he reached Bodh Gaya, Dharmapala brought a lot of Japanese support with him. He had the help of Sir Edwin Arnold, who made two tours of Japan in 1889 and 1892 trying to raise support for Dharmapala's project, and Dharmapala corresponded regularly with

8. "Seeking Sakyamuni: Travel and the Reconstruction of Japanese Buddhism," *Journal of Japanese Studies* 30, no. 1 (2004): 65–96.

9. He said, for example, "Right now three hundred millions of lives in India are in a diseased state. . . . Though I am from India, I'm still claiming that my country is sick. I'm insulting my ancestors, I'm speaking ill of my brothers. Please sympathize with me for my regrets and resentments toward my country." "Japan and India," *Chuo Koron* 17, no. 6 (June 1902). The article is a translation into Japanese of Dharmapala's talk at Koyokan Hall in Suraga. On other occasions in Japan, Dharmapala identified himself as Sri Lankan, usually in the cause of emphasizing the oppressed condition of Sinhala Buddhists.

10. "Buddhism in Japan," in *The World's Parliament of Religions: An Illustrated and Popular Story of the World's First Parliament of Religions*, 2 vols., ed. John Henry Barrows (Chicago: Parliament, 1893), 1:544.

11. Richard Jaffe suggests that Kozen Gunaratana could be considered a cofounder of the Maha Bodhi Society, but he was absent from the founding of the first two branches at Colombo and Calcutta. "Seeking Sakyamuni," 86.

4. Japanese Buddha Image at Bodh Gaya.

his Japanese supporters, apprising them of the state of the struggle at Bodh Gaya. His third visit to Japan began in May 1902 on his way to a longer visit (August 1902–December 1904) to the United States, raising funds for educational projects he was trying to get moving in India. He gave speeches emphasizing Japan's obligations to India, giving the Japanese more reason to assume he was Indian.

He wanted Japanese businessmen to make India prosperous, and he envisioned doing business himself in Japan:

> Wrote to father about the work I intend doing in Japan; viz to open trade communications with Japan and to export Japanese goods to Ceylon. . . . What I wish to do is to earn money by legitimate commercial dealings and to spend all that money on religion, to propagate the Dhamma. My father has spent for me all these 16 years and now I must earn and show him that I am also concerned in his welfare. (Diary, May 13, 1902)

His visits made him aware of the sophistication of Japanese manufacturing, but seeing that the Japanese were not going to simply throw in with the Maha Bodhi Society made him contemplate earning the money the Japanese would not be contributing to his cause. When the Hewavitarne family went into the matchbox business, they made use of his connections to the Japanese match industry. Although making furniture was its main business, the family firm began to import rickshaws from Japan. By 1906 Dharmapala had set up a program to send Sinhala men to Tokyo to be trained in Japanese industrial practices. The first of those students, U. B. Dolapilla, returned in 1911 and began teaching at the weaving school Dharmapala had established near Colombo. On his 1913 trip he added a new element to his hopes for a Lanka-Japan trading company. He contemplated sending a Japanese carpenter, mason, lacquer man, and landscape gardener to Colombo to demonstrate Japanese skills and teach them to Sinhala youths (Diary, June 4, 1913).

The first two visits to Japan did not test Dharmapala's renunciation. When he took a room at Nishimura's Hotel in Kobe on his third visit, everything changed:

> A public hotel is not the place for a Brahmachari life. From 5 A.M. till late after midnight it is all sensual, women exhibiting their natural weaknesses. At 11 P.M. accidentally I happened to go to the privy and there was a woman! When I think of the many pitfalls that surround me I am afraid. Already the degenerating signs of passions I begin to see. They must be crushed; but they cannot be crushed if I am to live around women. . . . Today's experiences began at 6 A.M. The maid came seven times when I was alone between 6 & 11 A.M. Another came at 12 A.M. bringing milk; and she showed me her breasts. They touched my body. Naturally the passions were aroused. . . . Thinking of the Higher Life and trying to calm the excitement, but the constant association with young

women these few days is killing me. *With them no man is safe* [emphasis in original]. (Diary, May 5, 1902)

Amid the swirl of temptations, he held on to the South Asian strategy for leading the pure life:

> In 1898 No. a woman touched my body when I fell ill. The sensations were terrific, the whole body was excited, and it was a revolution; but I kept my thoughts concentrated on the Holy One. There was no cure of the neuralgia; but only experienced a sensual change. No passionate thoughts arose; because the mind was attuned to a higher idea. But the sensation is injurious to spiritual progress.
>
> According to the Vinaya Rules, I am debarred from entering the Upasampada order; but I can be a samanera. At times sensual thoughts trouble me; and Mara is suggesting evil ideas. After keeping myself pure for so many years, is it proper that I should degenerate? . . . But there is the Dhamma and there is Nirvana. May the Dhamma protect me and lead me to discover the Path to Nirvana for the good of the World! (Diary, May 4, 1902)

Without ordination he could still aim for nirvana, as long as he maintained his celibacy. Being celibate removed him from the social order and allowed him to act for the good of all, ignoring gender and nationality as well as religion. Rejecting a woman's advances, he pointed to a universalizing moral: "A sudden impulse seized me and tears began flowing from my eye. Pledged my life for Humanity" (Diary, September 14, 1891).

The third trip was the occasion for Dharmapala's encounter with Tanaka Chigaku, the founder of a Nichirenist movement that eventually came to be known as Kokuchukai.[12] His fourth visit was in fact two visits, laying over in Japan on his way to and from Honolulu where he went to felicitate Mary Foster. If some Japanese were willing to entertain the notion that their Buddhism should move in a universalizing direction when he arrived in 1889, by 1913 the moment had given way to national feeling. Early on he followed Olcott's program. "The future work of union between Southern & Northern Buddhism is full of consequences, and the future spread of Bud-

---

12. Edwin B. Lee, "Nichiren and Nationalism: The Religious Patriotism of Tanaka Chigaku," *Monumenta Nipponica* 30, no. 1 (1975): 19–35. Tanaka did not establish Kokuchukai until 1914, the last and most successful of a series of religious movements he had established.

dhism rests upon that," he observed (November 7, 1893). By the third visit he had asked Noguchi Zenshiro "whether it was expedient for me to join the W[estern] Honganji" (Diary, May 3, 1902). Noguchi told him that it was good to get their sympathy but that he (Dharmapala) "should not become a Sectarian."[13]

As he abandoned hopes for recruiting Japanese for the Maha Bodhi Society, he tried to save something of the relationship. He looked at Japan's militarization with quaint innocence:

> At Yokosika. Mr. Sato and others were rather inclined that I should see the Dockyard. . . . What a unique sight it will be if the battle ships when not engaged in wars, should be used as ships of peace in spreading the Wisdom of the Tathagato? (Diary, June 23, 1902)

When he left Japan after that third visit, he wrote that the Buddhist Young Men's Association, Educational Society, Economical Society, and Tokyo Chamber of Commerce had given dinners for him, but "the Buddhist priests were indifferent" (Diary, July 1, 1902). On the fourth trip new forces arose. The Japanese government complied with a British request and put him under surveillance.[14] He met the Indian revolutionary Mohammed Barakatullah several times on that trip—unaware of his revolutionary activities in Japan—and dined with Daetetsu Suzuki and other Buddhist scholars, advising them that a society "should be organized to Japanise the Europeans who visit Japan" (Diary, July 11, 1913).[15]

Three years earlier in Calcutta Dharmapala had met Count Otani, who controlled Higashi Honganji. Otani told him that if Indians wished to make progress, they must follow the Buddha. But he gave no sign of support. The

---

13. He took the advice and did not become a member of Western Honganji. But later that month he told a representative of Honganji of his interest in becoming a Shinshu missionary (Diary, May 27, 1902). Honganji the sectarian movement (known as Jodo Shinshu) needs to be distinguished from Honganji the headquarters temples of the movement. Minor L. Rogers and Ann T. Rogers, "The Honganji: Guardian of the State (1868–1945)," *Japanese Journal of Religious Studies* 17, no. 1 (1990): 3–28. I will refer to the sect as Jodo Shinshu and the headquarters temple as Honganji, eastern and western, and speak specifically of the two branches as the context requires.

14. Grant Goodman, "Dharmapala in Japan, 1913" *Japan Forum* 5, no. 2 (1993): 195–202.

15. Barakatullah moved to Japan in 1909 as instructor of Urdu at the School of Foreign Languages and used anti-British feeling in Japan to establish a center for revolutionary work among Indians living there. Arun Coomer Bose, *Indian Revolutionaries Abroad, 1905–1922: In the Background of International Developments* (Patna: Bharati Bhawan, 1971), 66–71.

Maha Bodhi's account of that meeting announced Dharmapala's plans to send Indian Buddhist missionaries to Japan, but it also provided an accounting of where his project stood twenty years after his first trip:

> The Count in his talk with the Anagarika made it very clear that the Japanese Buddhists had no idea of Indian Buddhism, and there is very little hope of the Japanese ever helping the Indian propaganda. The first thing to be done is to educate the Japanese Buddhists about India, for the majority of them believe that India is in heaven. The only way to educate the people of Japan is by means of lectures delivered by an Indian Buddhist Missionary.[16]

The count had visited many of the Buddhist sites in Northern India on his 1910 trip, but seeing Bodh Gaya produced no interest in throwing in with Dharmapala or helping the Maha Bodhi Society.

Dharmapala was approached by Japanese to make overtly anti-Western comments on that final trip to Japan, and he was an old hand at that. Now he would do so for the sake of specifically Japanese interests. In Osaka he gave a talk sponsored by the newspaper *Asahi Shimbun*, making the case for Japan's obligations to other Asians on the basis of their common origins:

> The Aryans of India, whose representative I am, are glad that their ancient Aryan civilization had been preserved by the sons of the thrice favored land. To the great Aryanised family, whose home is India, numbering about 800 millions, belong the Japanese, Koreans, Mongolians, Chinese, Siamese, Cambodians, Burmese, Tibetans, Sinhalese. This great Asiatic brotherhood under the leadership of Japan can again regain their lost place in the world's history.[17]

Those were sentiments that the Japanese were certain to like, and on his way home from Japan—touring parts of China and Korea under Japanese control—Dharmapala gave a talk in Dairen that must have also pleased. He told audiences in East Asia that the threat to the world was not yellow peril but white, and that the Japanese were a unique people because they had never been subjected to colonial domination.

The Japanese managed Dharmapala's travels in Korea and China, and

---

16. "Count Otani," *Journal of the Maha Bodhi Society* 18 (1910): 379–80.

17. "Japan's Duty to the World," *Journal of the Maha Bodhi Society* 21 (1913): 177–82, at 181.

he saw what his hosts wanted him to see and met people they wanted him to meet. In the days before he left, he visited the secretary to the Ministry of Foreign Affairs (Diary, August 10, 1913), and when his steamer arrived at Pusan, he was met by priests of the various sects—which presumably were Japanese—and the editor of the newspaper *Shozen Jiho* (Diary, August 18, 1913). He visited a Korean village, saying to himself that he was glad the Japanese had taken Korea and recalling his wish of 1889 "that Japan should civilize Korea. . . . My wish is fulfilled. . . . I hope they will civilize the whole world by [their] superior morality" (Diary, August 19, 1913). He gave a public lecture and went to visit the oldest Japanese resident of Korea, who had arrived in Pusan forty-six years earlier (Diary, August 19, 1913). He took the train to Seoul, where he was greeted by Japanese and Korean priests. When he visited a Buddhist temple outside the city, he learned that the Korean emperor some three hundred years earlier had discovered the great influence of Buddhism and forbade priests from entering Seoul in order to suppress the religion. "Buddhism declined," he concluded, "and Korean civilization went down" (Diary, August 21, 1913).

He had a similar experience in China because his onward ticket left him only a few days to visit. Again he stayed at Japanese hotels, seeing a Chinese temple and meeting a Chinese newspaper editor with interpretation provided by a Mr. Yokoyama (Diary, August 24, 1913). In China he made more public appearances than in Korea, lecturing at Dairen at the Mantetsu Reading Club, directing his remarks to a Japanese audience and invoking Japan's obligations to stem the tide of Western influence, by going "all over Asia and propagat[ing] the gospel of Man. You are each a kind of Missionary."[18] In Shanghai he met American missionaries, who asked him to give a lecture, although they were concerned enough to ask him to submit his remarks to them before he spoke (Diary, September 16, 1913). He explained the principles of Buddhism to an audience that was likely full of Christians, forgoing comments about white peril and Christianity. The title of his talk notwithstanding, it emphasized a life of self-discipline and civilized behavior, not social activism.

> Mind is the chief factor in human progress. . . . Let the mind be so trained in the gospel of selfless activity that it will be master of the senses, of evil passions and selfish desires. This is the Gospel of Buddha.[19]

18. "The Danger of 'White Peril.'"
19. "The Social Gospel of the Buddha," speech at International Institute of Shanghai, September 18, 1913, published in *Journal of the Maha Bodhi Society* 21 (1913): 221–4.

5. Dharmapala (front right) with local Buddhist monks, China, 1913.

What he thought the Japanese were doing, civilizing the less developed parts of Asia, is what he thought he could do—bring civilization to Sinhala villages and India.

On one occasion he spoke of beginning a long-term project in Japan and becoming a naturalized Japanese citizen (Diary, July 11, 1913). It is easy to see the attraction. Japan was not Britain. It was Buddhist, industrialized, and civilized. What could be wrong with Japan's "promoting the prosperity of the Koreans" (Diary, August 21, 1913) or bringing progress to Manchuria (Diary, August 24, 1913)? Japanese economic expansionism had a religious side, and Dharmapala was as committed as the Japanese to venture capitalism, industrialization, and foreign trade. Honganji was building temples overseas in areas under Japanese control or in Japanese communities, and he took their efforts as compatible with his. The polite guest, he criticized the Japanese in only one regard. Besides the Japanese monk he chided (Diary, November 3, 1893), he criticized laymen at a meeting to discuss Buddhist problems where sake was served.[20] What he did not attempt in Japan was propagate Theravada Buddhism or Theosophy or reform Japanese institutions. He made no plans for finding ways for the Buddhist sects to act in unison. He spoke at first of "purifying" Japanese Buddhism, but soon gave up that idea. His goal, narrowly conceived, was to gather Japanese support for his campaign to recover Bodh Gaya; more broadly, he wanted to drag the Japanese onto the world stage, urging them to spread civilization across Asia.

BUDDHISM AS DHARMAPALA FOUND IT IN JAPAN

Japanese Buddhists had good reason for seeking out Olcott. They had been motivated by external pressures on the religion and its officiants since long before the Meiji Restoration in 1868. For some 250 years Buddhist temples had maintained the social order of the Tokugawa authorities, conducting rituals—usually associated with death—that upheld the proper order between family, community, and government. In a period of cultural and economic isolation Buddhism's universalizing potential gave way to its potential for supporting that political order. The position of Buddhism during the time has been characterized as privileged but defensive, comfortable but regulated. That privilege was itself a target. Rejecting Buddhism, Martin Collcutt writes, ran throughout Tokugawa intellectual history. He adds that it is arguable whether the regulated comfort Buddhist monks enjoyed led to "clerical laxity and spiritual torpor."[21] But such were the charges raised against Buddhism, and even before Meiji, temples had been razed or amalgamated with Shinto shrines and monks defrocked.

In the late Tokugawa period the threat to Buddhism came from Japanese intellectuals who wanted to suppress both Confucianism and Buddhism in

---

20. *Hansei-kai zasshi*, January 1894.

21. "Buddhism: The Threat of Eradication," in *Japan in Transition: From Tokugawa to Meiji*, ed. Marius B. Jensen and Gilbert Rozman (Princeton, NJ: Princeton University Press, 1986), 144.

favor of Shinto, *kami* worship, and "national learning." Hirata Atsutane, to
cite an extreme case, condemned the contamination of Shinto by Buddhism
and made contempt for India a central part of his nativist program. He made
outrageous arguments about Indians, calling them "vulgar" and "yellow-
black" or dirt colored. Indians followed repulsive practices such as spreading cow dung on floors and anointing themselves with oils because "in the
stifling heat all the people of this nation naturally stink."[22] He abused the
Buddha—who he said Indians believed had been born from the right side of
his mother's belly—observing that "he probably was, like the viper he is."
The parables of the Buddha were simply fanciful stories, as was the idea
that there is a Pure Land, that is, India in heavenly form, where the Lord
Buddha resided. Atsutane concluded that there was no place where such a
"country" is found. If there is a paradise on earth, it is Japan, and certainly
not India. The one thing that he could say for Indians is that they had the
good sense to abandon Buddhism. The sects Atsutane found most offensive
were Jodo Shinshu and Nichiren, and those were the two sects that became
involved with Dharmapala's activities in Japan.

Buddhism in Japan suffered further blows after the coming of Westerners, and it suffered from Western knowledge itself. Christian missionaries
insisted that Buddhism was "unscientific" and "anti-modern." The monks
were indolent and unlearned. They took advantage of laypeople and kept
Japan from realizing its potential as a modern country. By the late 1860s a
movement to suppress Buddhism began to inflict renewed devastation on
monks and temples—temples were burned, statues destroyed, and lands
appropriated. The severity of the suppression can be seen in the number of
temples razed in prefectures where local officials took government policy—
itself ambiguous and open to interpretation—most seriously. In Satsume
some forty-five temples and halls were eliminated.[23] In Toyama prefecture,
of 1,639 temples 7 survived.[24] The first Japanese census measured the decline more generally, estimating that there were 465,049 Buddhist temples
in Japan in 1871. By 1876 that number had been reduced to 71,962.[25] The
Buddhist temples and monks who survived continued to provide rituals
linked to death, grave sites, and ancestors, but they could hardly ignore anti-
Buddhist feeling.

---

22. James Ketelaar, *Of Heretics and Martyrs in Meiji Japan: Buddhism and Its Persecution*
(Princeton, NJ: Princeton University Press, 1990), 313.

23. Ketelaar, *Of Heretics and Martyrs in Meiji Japan*, 65.

24. Hiroko Kawanami, "Japanese Nationalism and the Universal *Dharma*," in *Buddhism
and Politics in Twentieth-Century Asia*, ed. Ian Harris (London: Pinter, 1999), 120n1.

25. Collcutt, "Buddhism: The Threat of Eradication," 162.

The promulgation of a new ceremonial structure, the Unity of Rite and Rule (*saisei itchi*), in early Meiji had its own influence on Buddhism. It served as

> an ideological tool to create, articulate, and manifest an "alliance" extending from the myriad deities through the figure of the Emperor and the mediation of his ministers "even unto the least persons under heaven." . . . It served, in other words to insert the Emperor into the political realm and simultaneously to elevate "the people" as full participants in the drama of nation-building.[26]

Putting the emperor at the center of this ceremonial structure made it possible in turn to construct the people of the place as coparceners in the nation. The Meiji Restoration separated Shinto and Buddhism, keeping each in a distinct space, and constrained both by tying the two religious systems to government. These two government initiatives, *shimbutsu bunri* (the separation of Shinto deities, *kami*, and Buddhas) and *haibutsu kishaku* (eradication of Buddhism) meant that Buddhism faced a crisis of more than transition.[27] The issue was not so much whether Buddhism was a national institution or a universal one but whether Buddhism deserved to continue to remain a Japanese institution whatever form it took.

For Buddhism the imposition of government control and the appropriation of land had effects that depended on how each sect made its living. Older monasteries that had held large amounts of land under the Tokugawa system were threatened. Temples such as Rinzai Zen temples that depended on feudal lords (*daimyo*) as their patrons suffered. Sects that engaged in esoteric rituals (*kito*)—Tendai, Shingon, and Soto Zen—were undone. The sect that suffered least was Jodo Shinshu. It quickly recovered its losses during the first decades of Meiji rule. Its livelihood came from popular support, and that support kept coming.[28] Higashi (Eastern) and Nishi (Western) Honganji, the headquarters temples of Jodo Shinshu Buddhism, were wealthy, powerful institutions, legitimating their independence by lending money to the Meiji government, an act that represented more than a gesture when the government was nearly destitute. Honganji took reverence for the emperor

26. Ketelaar, *Of Heretics and Martyrs in Meiji Japan*, 89.

27. See Allan G. Grapard, "Japan's Ignored Cultural Revolution: The Separation of Shinto and Buddhist Divinities in Meiji (*shimbutsu bunri*) and a Case Study: Tonomine," *History of Religions* 23, no. 3 (1984): 240–65.

28. Collcutt, "Buddhism: The Threat of Eradication," 163.

as a principle as fundamental as respect for *kami* (spirits) and the propagation of heavenly reason.[29] But the very division of Jodo Shin Buddhism into
these two branches had been a Tokugawa strategy to counterbalance the
massive strength of Honganji.[30] The division lingered on even as Honganji
rebuilt its strength.

After early Meiji suppression, Buddhists fought back by trying to put their
own house in order and drawing closer to the state. While closing ranks with
the state, Buddhists tried the opposite approach to the state, invoking the notion of freedom of religion. Buddhist sects sought to achieve a degree of unity
that institutional Buddhism had not known. On his way to Japan Dharmapala learned from his companion Noguchi's reading of a Japanese newspaper
that the chief abbots of the Buddhist sects were joining forces to establish a
Buddhist university (Diary, February 7–8, 1889). This attempt at unification
went back to the Tokugawa period when Buddhist intellectuals sought to
make sense of the proliferation of sects and subsects. The two Honganjis took
the lead in trying to create unity among the sects. The monks who later participated in the World's Parliament of Religions in 1893—Shimaji Mokurai,
Ashitsu Jitsunen, Shaku Soen, and Toki Horyu—tried to find doctrinal unity
by compiling their five-volume *Essentials of the Buddhist Sects*.[31] Buddhists,
usually affiliated with Honganji, also began to bring Western scholarly skills
to the study of their own religion, thinking that philological and historical
knowledge would enable them to compete with Christian missionaries. And
a small number of monks—including Shaku Unsho, who was motivated by
deep feeling for both the Theravada tradition and the historical Buddha—
initiated a movement to institute *Vinaya* (the monastic law).[32] Well before
Dharmapala initiated his career as a world reformer, Shaku Unsho had sent
his student Kozen to Colombo to study Pali with Hikkaduve Sumangala.

Since the medieval period, the monkhood had been divided into eight

---

29. Rogers and Rogers, "The Honganji: Guardian of the State," 13.

30. Richard Jaffe, *Neither Monk nor Layman: Clerical Marriage in Modern Japanese Buddhism* (Princeton, NJ: Princeton University Press, 2001), 36–7.

31. Ketelaar, *Of Heretics and Martyrs in Meiji Japan*, 197–207. Published under the authority of the Transsectarian Cooperative, the five volumes do not represent as much of an attempt
to find common ground as do the fourteen principles that Olcott attached to his *Buddhist
Catechism*. Chapters were written by representatives of the several denominations, and the
introduction created a measure of unity by recounting Sakyamuni's life.

32. Richard Jaffe, "Seeking Sakyamuni: Travel and the Reconstruction of Japanese Buddhism," *Journal of Japanese Studies* 30, no. 1 (2004): 65–96. Shaku Unsho was an ascetic
Shingon reformer who met Edwin Arnold in Tokyo and resolved to purchase Bodh Gaya. Kozen
was the monk who traveled with Dharmapala to Bodh Gaya in 1889. Tsunemitsu Konen, *Meiji
no Bukkyo-sha* (Buddhists in the Meiji Period) (Tokyo: Shunju-sha, 1968), 87.

sects—a number fixed by the state—with substantial differences of belief and practice. The state acted to preserve these divisions, keeping the Buddhist establishment weak by prohibiting transectarian organizations. A person who supported one temple was obliged to continue to do so, and shifting allegiances did not happen. From the early Meiji period onward, Buddhists turned their minds toward rationalizing sectarianism or arguing for new arrangements that would unify their cause. Buddhist modernizers seeking to concoct a new understanding of Buddhism looked back to Gyonen (1240–1322), who had written about the same problem and argued that the sects of his time were not evidence of degeneration but particularization.[33] By 1868 the two branches of Jodo Shin Buddhism took the unprecedented step of trying to forge a common Buddhism by establishing the Alliance of United Sects for Ethical Standards (*Shoshu Dotoku Kaimei*) and seeking to create the unity of the Law of the Sovereign and the Law of the Buddha, an initiative reflecting the hegemony of the two Honganjis.

Olcott's first visit happened to coincide with Christian missionaries conducting their own debate about sectarianism.[34] By early 1889, an argument developed between "Sigma" and a Dr. Eby in the correspondence section of the leading English-language paper of the day.[35] Sigma pointed out that Eby's contention that all Christians, even if divided into sects, are "spiritually" united in Christ "is true neither in theory or practice." Sigma commiserated with Japanese Christians pondering the meaning of biblical verses such as "That they may be one, even as we" when the proliferation of Christian missions in Japan made it hard for the Japanese to locate that oneness. Sigma denounced sectarianism as a perversion of Christianity. By early March he wrote of the Protestant missionaries' failed efforts to create unity: "Again, I ask, what keeps the Methodists out of the Union Church in Japan?"[36] Sectarianism, whether Christian or Buddhist, functioned in the moment as an obstacle to true belief, each religion critiquing the other for lacking unity. From the Buddhist perspective, Christian missionary efforts—even if the Christians were disunited—were threatening because of their own sense of disunity.

---

33. Ketelaar, *Of Heretics and Martyrs in Meiji Japan*, 182.

34. An April 2, 1887, article in the *Japan Weekly Mail* spoke of "the strange spectacle of national churches," emphasizing the Japanese case and drawing the contrast with the "the tendency to union, now everywhere observable in Presbyterian countries," citing the American Mission joining the Mission of the United Presbyterian Church of Scotland, and then these two groups joining the Dutch, having a common theological hall in Tsukiji, Tokyo.

35. "The Church 'Official Recognition,'" *Japan Weekly Mail*, February 9, 1889, 131–2.

36. "Christianity versus Sectarianism," *Japan Weekly Mail*, March 9, 1889, 237–8.

Olcott had fought the centripetal effects of caste politics in Lanka among Buddhist monks who would not cooperate with one another. He came to Japan with hopes not so much for the unification of the Buddhist sects as a unified movement for overseas work emerging from the sects. He could not move toward a united Buddhist world without first forging some solidarity among the Japanese sects. Doing so required haranguing the very people he needed:

> [Olcott] has publicly warned them on several recent occasions [that revival of our national religion] will depend entirely upon the coming forward of a number of earnest, unselfish, persevering, and courageous men, to unite, without distinction of sect, for the vigorous promotion of the pure religion taught by Sakya Muni.[37]

By 1894 the Buddhist periodical *Tsuzoku* began to argue for a universal Buddhism, and it aimed to present this universal Buddhism in language that ordinary people could understand, making it universalist in a second way.

Of the Japanese Buddhists who spoke at the World's Parliament of Religions, it was Noguchi Zenshiro—the emissary who had come to Colombo to fetch Olcott—who took on the sectarian issue most directly. By its nature the occasion invited comments that found the universal in the particular, and Noguchi framed his remarks in inclusive terms: "Each sect and religion," he said, "as its ultimate object aims to attain truth." The only hope for reducing the profusion resided in the fact that truth is one, and the passing of time would bring not only convergence among religions but between "faith and reason, religion and science." Noguchi's vision of convergence was not simply sentimental, inclusive, or eventualist. It rested on self-interest, for convergence required that the leading role in achieving it be played by Japanese Buddhists. He argued: "If the thousands of religions do continue to develop and reach the state of full development there will be no more any distinction between them," concluding, "This is the end at which we aim and to which we believe that we know the shortest way."[38] The "we" in this conclusion are Japanese Buddhists such as himself, willing to transcend Buddhist sectarianism and seek truth in a new Buddhism (*shin bukkyo*).

As the Japanese delegation steamed home from the parliament, Christians on board found a real-life example of what they thought was Buddhist

---

37. "Colonel Olcott in Japan," *Japan Weekly Mail*, March 16, 1889, 262.
38. "Would Win Converts to Buddhism," in Houghton, *Neely's History*, 157.

hypocrisy, with its own connection to sectarianism. Put off by the way Japanese Buddhists had made much of the "brotherhood of man" at the parliament, Christians seized on the death of a Japanese traveler to undermine their presumption. The Reverend B. C. Haworth provided this account of the man's last hours:

> One of the Japanese passengers in the steerage was sick unto death. When the ship's surgeon found that the end was near . . . he sent for the Rev. Shaku Soyen, requesting his presence at the bed of death. . . . He had many questions to ask in regard to the name, circumstances, and so on of the patient. Among these questions was one to this effect:—"Do you think he belongs to the labouring class?" The surgeon replied that as nearly as he could judge from appearances he was a labouring man. . . . Through the interpreter, the reverend gentleman sent back the reply that he did not think it worth while to go.

The account speaks of class, not sectarianism, but that was the problem. Each was tied to the other. The interpreter who asked Shaku Soen to come to the dying man's bedside reported that he gave another reason for not attending his countryman: "There are so many religions in Japan, and he did not know to which religion the patient belonged!"[39]

Whether Shaku Soen's concerns were class, doctrine, or sectarianism, the Japanese found themselves in a world where divisions that separated some people and united others were beginning to matter in new ways. In the context of the reformative moment, sectarianism was a small part of what had to be addressed. From a Japanese point of view, drawing the sects together cleared the way for a stronger Buddhism at home. The World's Parliament of Religions represented for them a different effort to spread a cosmopolitan Buddhism that hardly existed in Japan.[40] Olcott had the same thing in mind, hoping that he could return Buddhists to the "pure religion taught by Sakya Muni." But unifying Japanese Buddhist sects came first, just as it had in Lanka. When he left for Japan, the *Theosophist* put it this way: "As he began his Ceylon work by convening . . . Priests of the Siam

39. "Mr. Shaku Soyen and the Brotherhood of Man," *Japan Weekly Mail*, March 3, 1894, 276.

40. Ketelaar makes the useful distinction among three forms of unity, which he says Japanese Buddhists sought: transsectarian, transnational, and cosmopolitan. *Of Heretics and Martyrs*, 177. The writing of Buddhist "histories for drawing together the Buddhists of Asia"— transnational Buddhism in Ketelaar's terms—"discursively produced a cosmopolitan Buddhism which could not be constrained within Asia because the logic of Buddhism's spread across Asia was already universalizing or cosmopolitan."

and Amarapura sects, so he hopes to call a similar one of the forty sects into which Japanese Buddhism is said to be divided."[41]

After Dharmapala's convalescence Olcott and Dharmapala were taken to the parade ground of a Buddhist school affiliated with Honganji. Dharmapala was surprised to see the exercises of a group of military cadets. They had come for the sake of building a united Buddhist world, and he found the pairing of religious and constitutional reform a "curious coincidence" (Diary, February 11–12, 1889). Of course the timing was not coincidental, and he overlooked the larger coincidence—they had been asked to visit Japan at the moment when the relationship between Buddhism and the state was being formalized and tightened, perhaps the least promising moment for the visitors to move Buddhism in an universalizing direction. What else Olcott and Dharmapala knew about the troubled history of Buddhism during the Tokugawa and early Meiji eras is not clear. Olcott says simply that before he met Noguchi he "had none of his present familiarity with his nation."[42] He recognized the rising force of Christian missionizing in Japan, and Olcott had heard Noguchi suggest in his address to the Theosophical conference in Adyar that the first step in reforming Buddhism was "the unification of all Buddhists, no matter what sect they are, nor of what country."[43] As they approached Kobe harbor, what they knew of Buddhist sectarianism in Japan and the shifting relationship between the state and Buddhism was what they had learned from Noguchi.

OLCOTT IN JAPAN

The Japanese were drawn to Olcott because of his fame as a Westerner who had reformed Buddhist life in a faraway part of Asia. They sent Noguchi to fetch Olcott, and he appeared unannounced—as the story has it—at the Colombo office of the Theosophical Society in 1888. Having lodged with the Hewavitarne family in Colombo during his stay, Noguchi asked Dharmapala to join Olcott on the trip. Those encounters duly noted, the inaugural moment in the construction of a Buddhist world was preceded by considerable correspondence between South Asian Buddhists and Japan that Dharmapala initiated. Noguchi had written to Olcott several times

41. "The President in Ceylon," supplement, *Theosophist*, 10 (February 1889): xxxvii–xxxix, at xxxvii.

42. *Old Diary Leaves*, 4:93.

43. *Old Diary Leaves*, 4:88.

before meeting Olcott at the Theosophical Society convention in November 1888. Behind Noguchi stood Hirai Kanezo (or Kinzo), the headmaster of an English-language school in Kyoto, and Sano Masamichi, a Jodo Shinshu priest. They established an organization in Kyoto, collected funds to bring Olcott to Japan, and sent several letters of invitation. When no reply appeared, they sent Noguchi to deliver the invitation in person.[44]

Before Noguchi reached Colombo, Dharmapala had begun to correspond with other Japanese Buddhists. He first got the idea of visiting Japan by reading an article in the *Fortnightly Review* in 1887.[45] That account of Japan led him to write Akamatsu at Honganji, having come across Akamatsu's and Sano Masamichi's names in the article.[46] Both were scholarly monks with some knowledge of English. He had also sent Olcott's *Buddhist Catechism* to Japan, and that small booklet led to further correspondence with Noguchi prior to his arrival in Colombo. Another series of letters put him in touch with the students of Nishi Honganji, who in 1886 had established a society for temperance and monastic reform (*Hanseikai*) that published the journal *Hansei zasshi* in the same cause. Before Dharmapala visited Japan, he began publishing articles in *Hansei zasshi* (and *Chuo koron*, the newspaper that replaced it).[47] By 1894 he had shared his views with Japanese readers on issues ranging from temperance, the recently designed Buddhist flag, Christianized names such as his birth name, and Olcott's upcoming visit.

Those letters voiced concerns that Dharmapala knew the members of Hanseikai shared. He began with two examples of the behavior that abusing

44. I rely on Noguchi's account, "The Way That Dharmapala Who Has Passed Away Recently, Came to Japan," *Contemporary Buddhism* 106 (1933): 77.

45. Jayawardana, *Mage Jivita Kathava*, 45.

46. In his diaries Dharmapala says that Takakusu Junjiro was his first correspondent in Japan and "therefore my first friend since the time when he was a student at the Bunga Kurio" (May 10, 1902). Takakusu was the scholar and reformer associated with Nishi Honganji, and through him Dharmapala came to know Sakurai Gicho, who was the founding editor of *Young East*, the English-language journal established in 1925 to promote pan-Asian Buddhist solidarity. Judith Snodgrass, "Performing Modernity." Dharmapala was likely to have known of Akamatsu in another way because he had sent one of the two Japanese students to Colombo to learn Pali or Sanskrit. "The President in Ceylon," xxxvii. The two students lived at the Theosophical Society headquarters, where Dharmapala himself worked and lived.

47. Yamakawa, "Dharmapala and Japan," 45. Before he arrived, Dharmapala had published four articles in *Hansei zasshi*. He kept corresponding with the journal during his visit, and articles by him or about him continued sporadically through his second visit to Japan after the World's Parliament of Religions. The last piece appeared January 1894 (9, no. 1) and concerned his dinner with a chief monk at Koishikawa Dentsuin. During his first visit, he also witnessed an evening of "high revelry, drinking & C [?] Dancing" with priests and laypeople in Kyoto that left a lasting impression (Diary, April 17, 1889).

alcohol produced.[48] The first was the ancient Indian king Ajatasatru, who killed his father in a drunken rage; the second was another drunken king who ordered his son killed to provide meat for the dinner table. "These are all results from drinking 'crazy water,'" he wrote. "Once a human being drinks alcohol, he loses his mind. . . . Ah, brothers and sisters, have you ever heard of any person who is drunk and does good things at the same time?" He concluded with the connection between alcohol and Christianity:

> I respect the Buddha's prohibitions and teach them to other people. In places where these rules are enforced, it is rare to see people who commit crimes, the society is healthy, and people live in peace. . . . In New York there are more than nine thousand liquor stores. In London, there are infinite numbers. . . . Christians are not ashamed of their drinking habit—in one hand, they have a bible, in the other hand, they hold a bottle of brandy. Fellow Buddhist brothers and sisters, please do not be deceived by Christians. . . . Please be proud of your land, your art, and your highly intelligent people.

Before he reached Japan, he had a constituency who shared his values. The problem was that they were young and few in number and lacked resources.[49]

Dharmapala told *Hansei zasshi* of the work of the Japanese monk Kozen Gunaratana, then studying Pali in Colombo.[50] He had been sent by his teacher Shaku Unsho Daiyo, himself a Shingon priest. Another Japanese priest, Shaku Soen—with whom Dharmapala had a continuing relationship in Lanka, India, Japan, and the United States—was a prominent Zen monk, which is to say that Japanese interest in South Asia transcended Jodo Shinshu. But Noguchi came to Colombo as a representative of people affiliated with Honganji, and in Japan Dharmapala spent most of his time in Honganji contexts. Doing so did not keep him from interacting with monks of other sects, both in Japan and South Asia. But those connections were personal and episodic, unlike the steady connection to Honganji that overshadowed

---

48. "Temperance," *Hansei-zasshi*, March 1888.

49. Although it began as a movement advocating temperance among Buddhist students, Hanseikai influenced a variety of new Buddhist movements. Notto Thelle, *Buddhism and Christianity in Japan: From Conflict to Dialogue, 1854–1899* (Honolulu: University of Hawaii Press, 1987), 199–202. In Dharmapala's time it had some four hundred members. By 1895 the movement had enrolled twenty thousand members (200).

50. The other student, Tokuzawa Chiezo, came to study Sanskrit with Pandit Batuwantudawe, and Dharmapala says little of him even though he must have encountered both students in Colombo and traveled to Bodh Gaya with them.

his personal connections to monks of other sects.[51] He did not speak of Honganji hegemony as a problem, but he must have recognized limits on his actions.

Hirai Kanezo—who later went with Noguchi to translate for the Japanese priests at the Parliament of Religions—sent Noguchi to Colombo to invite Olcott to visit Japan in 1889.[52] A leading member of the Young Men's Buddhist Committee, Hirai made a living as the headmaster of Oriental Hall in Kyoto.[53] After his letters to Olcott brought no response, he began to feel pressure from the organization to make his visit happen. His fellow members had given funds to Hirai, and they were impatient with the delay. Hirai's earlier recommendation had gotten Noguchi a teaching job at a local school, and when Hirai asked Noguchi to make the trip by steamer, he also asked Noguchi to pay his own way. When he finally reached Theosophical Society headquarters in Colombo, Noguchi learned from Dharmapala that Olcott had left the island and was pursuing the Theosophical cause in London. Until he returned to Adyar—where the Theosophical Society in India had moved its headquarters from Bombay—Dharmapala provided Noguchi with a room at his parents' house, and Noguchi toured the island, meeting Shaku Kozen and a Jodo Shinshu priest, Kichiren Norihiko, who was studying Sanskrit with Pandit Batuwantudawe.

Noguchi caught up with Olcott at the Theosophical meetings in Adyar, where he addressed the delegates as a humble petitioner:

> We, Japanese Buddhists, now ask you to lend us this worker of social miracles, this defender of religion, this teacher of tolerance, for a little time, so that he may do for the religion of my country what he and his colleagues have done for the religion of India.[54]

51. Jaffe mentions in passing another complication: the Zen and Shingon monks represented two primarily monastic denominations as opposed to Jodo Shin Honganji, a nonmonastic sect. "Seeking Sakyamuni," 80.

52. "The Way That Dharmapala Came to Japan," 77–82. Before he became a teacher at a school owned by the Otani group of the Ibaraki branch of Honganji, Noguchi was a storyteller, whose task was to relate light stories of historical events at Oriental Hall (78). Elsewhere Noguchi described himself as a Buddhist who belonged to no sect. "Would Win Converts to Buddhism," 156. On his third trip to Japan Dharmapala learned that Noguchi had become a Unitarian (Diary, May 1, 1902).

53. Noguchi Zenshiro, "The Way That Dharmapala Came to Japan," 77–82.

54. *Old Diary Leaves*, 4:85–6. Noguchi spoke in Japanese as a prepared English translation was read to his audience. My guess is that by "the religion of India" he meant that of both India and Lanka, the Japanese blurring the distinction in the same way Dharmapala did in his interactions with them.

After giving an account of the Japanese Buddhist sects, their beliefs, and their demoralized condition, Noguchi laid out plans for reform:

> The first important step we must make is the unification of all Bud-
> dhists, no matter what sect they are, nor of what country. . . . The second
> step is to make every priest and layman educated. . . . The third step is
> to reconvert the Japanese to Buddhism. The fourth step is to encour-
> age the Japanese to take all that is good from Europe, and to reject all
> the bad (85).

Hirai and Sano had organized a branch of the Theosophical Society in Kyoto, evidence that reforming Japanese religion was compatible with the interests of Theosophy. He concluded by urging the delegates—most of whom were not Buddhists but Hindus and Zoroastrians—to work "mutually for the ad-vancement of our ancient religions" (86).

Olcott accepted the invitation late in December 1888, and by February 1889 the party had arrived in Kobe.[55] Aboard ship Dharmapala had come down with a painful case of rheumatism that continued for two months. Just after arriving, Olcott was taken to Kyoto, where he addressed a crowd of six hundred Japanese priests at the Chion-in temple. If Olcott's Theosophi-cal Buddhism had a doctrinal ally in Japan, it was Shingon Buddhism, the Tantric-influenced Buddhism that is often glossed in English as "Esoteric Buddhism," a phrase that must have struck Olcott's eye.[56] But the preemi-nence of Honganji was apparent from the moment Olcott reached Kyoto. His first appearance before priests and laypeople occurred at Honganji's Chion-in temple, followed by a cursory call on the chief priest of the Shin-gon sect and another lecture to two thousand people, again at the Chion-in temple. The following day he was given a reception at Western Honganji and a day later at Eastern Honganji. On February 15 he lodged at a Nichiren temple before he gave two lectures at Jodo Shinshu temples on February 16 and held a meeting for unity back at Chion-in.[57] When he spoke in public, in other words, he did so under Honganji auspices, and that connection was

55. *Hochi*, February 10, 1889, 2. The article mentioning Olcott's arrival says nothing of Dharmapala, indicating only that Olcott was met by General Hojo Itoh and a journalist, Suehiro Jukyo, who worked for the newspaper *Asano*.

56. In fact the *Japan Weekly Mail*, March 16, 1889, described him as the "representative of a movement that has made so much stir as Esoteric Buddhism" (250). Christian critics in Japan called him an "evangelist of Esoteric Buddhism," which must have muddled his efforts for sectarian unity. *Japan Weekly Mail*, April 6, 1889, 233.

57. *Old Diary Leaves*, 4:102–5.

natural because Honganji had taken the lead in unifying the Buddhist sects and making contact with Buddhists in other parts of Asia.

As he spoke to audiences of priests in the following days, Olcott struck one chord: Buddhists must reach agreement on some doctrinal fundamentals and find some organizational unity to defend their interests. When he addressed the high priests of the eight sects in the Empress Room at the Chion-in temple, he found them seated "according to age about a long table; each with a brass fire-pot before him for warming his hands." He read salutations from Hikkaduve, the most respected monk in Lanka at the time, and explained his own position:

> I have no special, private word to speak to any of you, but one word for all. My mission is not to propagate the peculiar doctrines of any sect, but to unite you all in one sacred undertaking. Each of you I recognize as a Buddhist and a brother. . . . Listen to the words of the learned Chinese pilgrim and scholar Hiouen Thsang: "The schools of philosophy are always in conflict, and the noise of their passionate discussions rises like the waves of the sea. Heretics of the different sects attach themselves to particular teachers, and by different routes *walk to the same goal*" [emphasis in original].[58]

He argued that reuniting Northern and Southern Buddhists meant coming to know what one another believed; doing so would require scholars comparing the sacred books of each tradition. The results needed to be published in all Buddhist countries, a task that might require "another Great Council at some sacred place, such as Buddha Gaya or Anuradhapura."[59] His words were innocent enough, but both proposed venues must have left his audience feeling that his universalism hid a predisposition toward South Asia and the Southern tradition.[60]

Olcott confronted other obstacles on the path to a united Buddhist world, which were local and organizational. By February 15, he had discovered that the young men of Hanseikai had no money to finance the tour and planned to charge admission to his lectures.[61] Olcott would not have that, and the di-

---

58. "On the President's Japan Tour," *Lucifer* 4 (1893): 243–48, at 245–46.

59. "On the President's Japan Tour," 247.

60. Despite his wanting to established doctrinal agreement between Theravada and Mahayana Buddhism, Olcott regarded *The Buddhist Catechism* as a "perfect compendium of Southern Buddhism." *Old Diary Leaves*, 4:255. Agreement was possible, Olcott assumed, because Theravada was historically prior to, and at the core of, Mahayana Buddhism.

61. *Old Diary Leaves*, 4:111.

rectors of Honganji came forward with an offer to sponsor the tour, provided that the original committee was dismantled and they were put in charge. Instead Olcott suggested establishing a General Committee of Buddhist Affairs, requiring support from each of the eight sects. Without that agreement, he added, he would be taking the next steamer home.[62] A nonsectarian committee was established (*Indo-Busseki-Kofuku-Kai*), and it arranged his tour across Japan, which kept him fully occupied, preaching seventy-six times in the next four months.[63] However often he repeated the message of unity, he found little of it. Toward the end of his visit he established a branch of the Theosophical Society, but the officeholders were Honganji officials, another expression of the "spirit of sectarianism so rife that they [representatives of other sects] could never consent to come into an organization where, of necessity, some must be officers and the others simple members."[64]

When Olcott returned to Japan in 1891, he addressed the unity issue by way of *The Buddhist Catechism*. He intended the questions and answers as a teaching tool for young Buddhists, and it was already serving that purpose in fifteen different languages. To add Japanese to the list, he sent a copy to Ninkai Mizutani, who had the booklet translated and retitled *Buddhism, Questions and Answers*.[65] The subtitle was *A Buddhist Catechism According to the Canon of the Southern Church*, the title page indicating that it had been approved by Hikkaduve. Just before his second trip to Japan, he had organized a meeting of two Japanese, two Burmese, Dharmapala, and another Sinhala at Adyar. When the group had considered "all points of belief in the Northern and Southern Schools of Buddhists . . . [Olcott] drafted a platform, embracing fourteen clauses, upon which all Buddhist sects could agree if disposed to promote brotherly feeling and mutual sympathy between themselves."[66]

In late January Olcott sailed to Burma with the two Burmese he had called to Adyar, and after two nights of heated discussion, he secured "the approval of the leading priests of Burma for [his] compromise platform."[67]

---

62. A Buddhist, "Colonel Olcott in Japan," *Japan Weekly Mail*, March 16, 1889, 262.

63. Prothero, *The White Buddhist*. Prothero says that forming this committee allowed Olcott to resist the financial dominance of any one sect and of the Jodo Shinshu Buddhist sect in particular (125). As it turned out, the eight sects only nominally agreed to support Olcott's project, and the financial backing came from the two Honganjis. See "On the President's Japan Tour," 244.

64. *Old Diary Leaves*, 4:156.

65. Noguchi, "The Way That Dharmapala Came to Japan," 77.

66. *Old Diary Leaves*, 4:276. The "Fundamental Buddhistic Principles" came to be published at the end of *The Buddhist Catechism*, and the careers of the two documents became intertwined.

67. *Old Diary Leaves*, 4:279.

After taking the train north to Mandalay, he met the ranking monks of the *sangha*. During the meeting, he noticed copies of the Burmese translation of *The Buddhist Catechism* in the hands of several of the people present, prompting him to begin with the uses to which *The Buddhist Catechism* was being put elsewhere and to conclude with the work he was contemplating in Japan with the Buddhist sects. He stressed the universalist theme, asking the monks whether they were not obliged to act on "the loving principles of universal human brotherhood and universal loving kindness . . . to make an effort to knit together the Buddhists of all nations and sects in a common relation of reciprocal good-will and tolerance." His translator read directly from the Burmese translation of "Fundamental Buddhistic Ideas." The assembled monks declared each of the fourteen points orthodox, after which the *sangharaja* (chief monk) and the twenty-three other monks affixed their signatures to the document.

To that point the compromise platform had secured the approval of senior Burmese Buddhist monks and six ranking Sinhala monks. The appearance of a special delegate from Chittagong added the support of the Maghs (the Bangla expression for Rakhine people of the Arakan coast).[68] The frenetic Olcott did not reach Japan until late October 1891, having sailed back to Colombo and on to Australia, then back to Colombo and on to Europe, where he carried on propaganda work in England, France, Stockholm, Copenhagen, Kiel, Hamburg, Bremen, and Osnabruck.[69] This time he made his way to Japan by crossing the Atlantic, taking the train across the United States, and sailing from San Francisco. As soon as he reached Yokohama, he discovered that the region had been struck by an earthquake that morning, destroying eighty thousand houses and hundreds of temples.[70] He changed his route but not his objective. With the Kyoto train tracks destroyed by the quake, he sailed to Kobe and made his way overland to Kyoto. His first act was to inform the two Honganjis and the general committee—"which [he] had induced them to form on the occasion of [his] former visit"—of his arrival. Despite the earthquake and what he called "a lot of polite humbugging going on about signing my Platform—idle excuses of all sorts," Olcott won over the priesthood in seven days.[71]

68. *Old Diary Leaves*, 4:277. "The Chittagong Maghs . . . concurred through a special Delegate, acting as proxy for Babu Krishna Chandra Chowdry, the leader of the Maghs, who had requested me by telegraph to appoint one for him." Olcott then asked a Burmese delegate to represent the Maghs. "A Buddhist Council," supplement, *Theosophist* 17 (1891): xxi.

69. Murphet, *Hammer on the Mountain*, 330.

70. Henry Steel Olcott, "An United Buddhist World," *Theosophist* 13 (1892): 239–40, at 40.

71. *Old Diary Leaves*, 4:428 and 433–36.

The Japanese clerics added their agreement to the "Fundamental Buddhistic Principles" already agreed on by the leading monks of Burma, Lanka, and Chittagong:

1. Buddhists are taught to show the same tolerance, forbearance, and brotherly love to all men, without distinction; and an unswerving kindness towards the members of the animal kingdom.
2. The universe was evolved, not created; and it functions according to law, not according to the caprice of any God.
3. The truths upon which Buddhism is founded are natural . . . taught in successive *kalpas* or world periods, by certain illuminated Beings called BUDDHAS . . . .
4. The fourth Teacher of the present *kalpa* was Sakya Muni or Gautama Buddha. . . . He is an historical personage. . . .
5. Sakya Muni taught that ignorance produces desire, unsatisfied desire is the cause of rebirth, and rebirth the cause of sorrow.
6. Ignorance fosters the belief that rebirth is a necessary thing. . . .
7. The dispersion of all this ignorance can be attained by the persevering practice of an all-embracing altruism in conduct, development of intelligence, wisdom in thought, and destruction of desire. . . .
8. The desire to live being the cause of rebirth, when that is extinguished, rebirths cease, and the perfected individual attains by meditation . . . Nirvana.
9. Sakya Muni taught that ignorance can be dispelled and sorrow removed by the knowledge of the four Noble Truths. . . .
10. Right Meditation leads to spiritual enlightenment. . . .
11. The essence of Buddhism, as summed up by the . . . Buddha himself is—
    To cease from all sin,
    To get virtue,
    To purify the heart.
12. The universe is subject to a natural causation known as 'Karma." . . .
13. The obstacles to the attainment of good Karma may be removed by the observance of . . . the moral code of Buddhism, namely, (1) Kill not; (2) Steal not; (3) Indulge in no forbidden sexual pleasure; (4) Lie not; (5) Take no intoxicating or stupefying drug or liquor. . . .
14. Buddhism discourages superstitious credulity. . . . [72]

72. *The Buddhist Catechism* (Adyar: Theosophical Publishing House, 1975), 128–33.

Reduced to propositional form, Olcott's universal Buddhism likely struck the Japanese as alien, if not unrecognizable in parts.

Olcott was thrilled: "I have been able for the first time in history . . . to secure the adhesion of both the Northern and Southern Schools . . . to certain fundamental principles." There were still problems:

> Between what the Chinese and Japanese call Mahayana and Hinayana—distinctions repudiated by Southern Buddhists—there are immense differences. The Northern Buddhism of some of the sects is probably the teaching of Sakya Muni *plus* metaphysical efflorescences, and Southern Buddhism is more or less tainted with nature-worship and a cult of elementals. That is nothing to me; I did not set myself to finding out the points of dispute, but the points of agreement. What I thought the Western world, at least, would profit by was a very plain and succinct compilation of a certain number of general principles of belief universally recognized by the entire Buddhist world.[73]

The last sentence reveals another contradiction in the project. In this context Olcott wanted agreement not to create unity among Buddhists in Asia or to give them a tool to propagate their religion but to present the authentic teachings to a Western audience.

However modest the agreement over a universal Buddhism, it came with qualifications. The signatures of two Japanese Buddhist monks came from students who had been sent to study in Lanka and naturally felt some sympathy for the so-called Southern School. The way the document is organized, not to mention the very idea that distinctions between traditions are inappropriate, reflect the Southern School. The way the text was compiled embodied it more directly. Because he could not give up his belief in a subjective entity that reached nirvana, Olcott wanted to include a note that there is a difference between the Northern and Southern schools in this regard.[74] Conferring with Hikkaduve and his assistant principal, Heyiyantuduve, Olcott found the monks insisting on there being no such entity reaching Nirvana. To make his argument for doctrinal difference con-

---

73. Olcott, "An United Buddhist World," 239. In one of his notebooks, Dharmapala writes of his relationship to Olcott: "In 1889 we were together in Japan. In 1890 Decr. I drafted the fundamental principles of Buddhism, which he approved & then presented as his own compilation!" Sarnath Notebook no. 23. I can find no corroboration for this assertion.

74. *Old Diary Leaves*, 2:300–301.

vincing, Olcott told the them about the beliefs of the Tibetans, Chinese, Japanese, Mongolians, "and even of a Sinhalese school of which the late Polgahawatte was leader."[75] They all entertained the notion of an entity in some form reaching nirvana. Hikkaduve was unpersuaded and threatened to withdraw his endorsement, followed by Olcott's capitulating. Inadvertently he became a spokesperson for more orthodoxy than he wanted.

The orthodoxy compromise met other problems in Japan that derived from the local understanding of Buddhism. The priests had agreed that the fourteen propositions were properly Buddhist but acceptable only as "included within the body of Northern Buddhism."[76] The key word was "within." Those propositions could not capture the breadth and depth of Buddhism in its Japanese form.

> Out of the eight Buddhist sects of Japan, the only one whose adhesion I could not secure is the Shin-shu. It was not that they denied any one of my fourteen propositions . . . but they think these represent so very small a proportion of the whole body of Mahayana, that they did not care to have this platform put forth in so fragmentary a state.[77]

In other words, the sect that provided an overwhelming amount of the support—both financial and human—that Olcott and Dharmapala received on this visit to Japan (and that Dharmapala received on later visits) would not endorse Olcott's platform.[78]

SECTARIANISM AND UNITY

It is easy to overplay Olcott's identity as a Buddhist and underplay his being a Theosophist, whether he was working in Lanka or Japan. Of the "Fourteen Buddhistic Principles" that appear at the end of *The Buddhist Catechism*, he made a claim that must have bewildered Buddhists: "With slight changes of names, this platform may be styled a synthesis of certain fundamental

75. *Old Diary Leaves*, 2:300.

76. Olcott, *The Buddhist Catechism*, 136. By 1975 *The Buddhist Catechism* had gone through forty-six editions, and the "Fundamental Buddhistic Principles" has been included in versions published by the Theosophical Society as an appendix since shortly after Olcott secured common agreement. There are other print versions of the *Catechism* that do not contain the "Principles."

77. Olcott, "An United Buddhist World," 240.

78. Olcott also compiled a Shinshu catechism, "A Shin-shu Catechism," *Theosophist* 10 (1889): 751–6, 11 (1889): 9–13, and 11 (1889): 89–92, and contemplated doing the same for Zoroastrianism and Islam.

Hindu beliefs."[79] His expansiveness aside, the Theosophy he brought to Japan was not so much ideological as administrative. He made establishing Theosophical Society branches a regular part of his lecture tours: he would arrive in a town, give a lecture, and locate some willing Japanese to establish a branch. On later visits, Dharmapala followed the same practice, construing his efforts in Japan as being carried out for the good of the Theosophical Society (Diary, April 18 and May 12, 1889). Olcott's plan, as he described it to his Japanese hosts, was not to spread Theosophy but to use its branch offices to spread Buddhism. Before the gathering of the chief monks of the eight sects, he put it this way:

> Our great Brotherhood [the Theosophical Society, Buddhist Division] comprises already 174 Branches, distributed over the World as follows: India, Ceylon, Burma 129; Europe 13; America 25; Africa 1; Australasia 2; West Indies 2; Japan 1; Singapore 1. Total, 174 Branches of our Society, all under one general management. When I first visited Ceylon (in the year 1880) and formed several Branches, I organized a Buddhist Division of our Society, to include all Buddhist Branches in Ceylon, Burma and Singapore, in the "Buddhist Division"; so that you may all be working together for the common object of promoting the interests of Buddhism. This will be an easy thing to do. You have already many such Societies, each trying to do something, but none able to effect as much as you could by uniting your forces with each other and your sister Societies in foreign countries. It would cost you a great deal of money and years of labour to establish foreign agencies like ours, but I offer you the chance of having these agencies readymade. . . . The people of Ceylon are too poor and too few in number . . . to undertake any such large scheme as I propose, but you and they together could do it successfully.

Asking priests to accept the words of "your ignorant yet sincere American co-religionist," he urged them to "be up and doing." There were many Christian schools and churches in Japan, "but is there a Japanese Buddhist school or temple in London or Paris, or Vienna, or New York?"[80]

Olcott did not mention the Hindu branches of the Theosophical Societies or the fact that a missionary temple in London would not be a strictly Japanese affair preaching a strictly Japanese Buddhism. Nor did he say anything about Theosophy itself, other than that the society would serve as an

79. Olcott, "An United Buddhist World," 240.
80. "On the President's Japan Tour," 247.

honest broker for Buddhism. To that extent, he saw Theosophy as he saw himself, an impartial outsider, able to do for the Japanese what they could not do for themselves. As he was leaving Japan, he mentioned that he had started a local Branch of the Society, admitting that he could hardly say "formed." He had gone through the "ceremony of forming" a local branch, fully aware that all the officers of the Theosophical Society branch were Honganji officials. The branch was a useful fiction, creating a measure of solidarity against the force of sectarianism. "Only a white man," Olcott added, putting modesty behind him, "a foreigner outside all their sects and social groups, could carry on such a Society successfully."[81]

Olcott's interest in unity had a practical motive, enabling Buddhists to stand up to the force of Christian missionary efforts in Japan. But that interest had ideological purposes as well, and it is in this regard that Olcott's being a Theosophist is pertinent. Theosophy was a religion of universal brotherhood and Olcott a man who believed in equality. He looked fondly on his trip aboard the French mail steamer *Djemnah* on his first trip to Japan:

> "Travelling second-class . . . from motives of economy," Olcott remembered, "I found that the whole deck was free to us to occupy day and night; we mixed on terms of equality with the saloon passengers, and were not made to feel as if we were social pariahs, as one is aboard the British liners."[82]

In 1898 Olcott was approached in South India by a delegation of panchamas who wanted to convert to Buddhism (Diary, June 4, 1898). Dharmapala expressed his support, and a month later Olcott brought a panchama delegation to Colombo. Dharmapala described Olcott's attitude to their conversion as "very passionate" (Diary, July 3, 1898).

The thrust of Olcott's work was neither enjoying momentary equality with Europeans who had booked a superior class of travel nor uplifting people at the bottom of the South Asian social hierarchy. Olcott had his gaze fixed on Buddhists—whether ethnic Buddhists or what people nowadays call "practice" Buddhists—and "Asians," whether Buddhist or not. The primary metric of difference and inclusion was nationality, not class or gender. He wanted unity among Buddhists of the various Asian countries. The majority of people he encountered directly were educated and well-

81. *Old Diary Leaves*, 4:156–7.
82. *Old Diary Leaves*, 4:99.

to-do. Many of them were English-speaking, although that was seldom the case in Japan. What linked him to those Asians was the same solidarity that linked a number of Westerners and Asians, brought together by common interests in spiritualism, vegetarianism, animal welfare, or aestheticism, and motivated by a "politics of friendship" with anti-imperial potential.[83] What distinguished him from the majority of those Westerners was his engagement with both a specifically Asian religion and a movement that functioned as a tool for creating brotherhood (as opposed to promoting a practice such as vegetarianism).

The Buddhist flag was one expression of that unity, and it was fully transidiomatic. Constructing a flag for Buddhism—Hikkaduve designed it, and Olcott reset its proportions—produced a flag for all Buddhists, representing Buddhism universalized. Olcott assumed that Buddhists were already familiar with the six-color rainbow emanating from the Buddha.[84] He believed that the human body produced an "aura" and understood those rays of color as the Buddha's aura, encircling his body while in deep meditation. It was that aura that mesmeric healing put to work. Such a flag, he thought, "avoided all possible causes of dispute among Buddhists, as all, without distinction, accept the same tradition as to the Buddha's personal appearance and that of his aura; moreover, the flag would have no political meaning whatever." When he reached Kyoto in 1889, he was received by officials and students of the Western Honganji. The temple was fitted out with the Japanese flag and the Buddhist flag.[85] That same "charming courtesy" he found repeated throughout his tour of Japan, the two flags grouped together at every hotel, railway station, and temple. He said nothing to indicate that he understood that the two flags bespoke the agonistic relationship between universalism and Japanese nationalism that was to grow stronger as the years went by.

Overcoming Japanese sectarianism involved more than amassing numbers and more than a political strategy. It was a suitably Buddhist value as well as a Theosophical one. Olcott had fought against sectarianism in Lanka. When the Kandyan monks resisted meeting with their low country peers in a common space, they did so for reasons of caste, not Buddhist doc-

83. Gandhi, *Affective Communities*, chapter 2.

84. Olcott shared an interest in *budu ras* with Hikkaduve, who wrote of having seen a rainbow over a Buddhist relic mound on a full-moon day. Olcott, "The Buddha Rays at Badulla," ci–cii. Olcott understood budu ras in the kindred and transidiomatic context of human "auras," which in turn guided his efforts at mesmeric healing.

85. Dharmapala writes in his diary that he had sent a rendering of the flag to Kyoto in 1888. Diary, May 31, 1920.

trine. Divisions based on status differences he found even more off-putting than sectarianism. *The Buddhist Catechism*, the "Fundamental Buddhistic Principles," and the Buddhist flag were vehicles for creating equality because solidarity entailed it. Another strategy was haranguing Japanese Buddhists who clung to sectarian interests. Having lectured to crowds of four thousand people at each of the two Honganji temples, Olcott moved on to Gifu, where he repeated his remarks to a group of people who were unwilling to come to the Honganji lecture. He "upbraided them for frivolous quarrels with co-religionists when all ought to be united to promote the interests of our religion" and reminded them that he had come five thousand miles to see them and that they had paid him a poor compliment by compelling him, "ill as [he] was that morning, to give them a special lecture."[86]

Olcott's presumption—an outsider telling the Japanese how to reform their practices, overcome their divisions, and then spread their religion—had sources beyond his self-confidence and managerial competence. One was his own status advantage. He was not simply a Westerner but a Westerner invited to Japan by the Japanese. He was received in Japan with the same acclaim he had received in Lanka as Buddhism's white champion. He told the Japanese that Theosophy was not a sect, merely an organizational tool, "a Brotherhood spread all over the globe, composed of men and women of many races, nationalities and faith."

> The Brotherhood which binds the Society is really a consciousness of a truth that embraces all mankind, nay all lives. The members of the Society do not profess to create this Brotherhood, but only recognize it as a fact in nature.[87]

The one qualification that made him capable of even imagining this higher order of unity was the illusion that he could unite people in ways that transcended not only difference but also politics.[88] His experience in Japan made him recognize that he did not control how his remarks, apolitical or otherwise, were interpreted. The fundamental problem, he knew, was the disparity between what he had said in English and what his audience heard

---

86. *Old Diary Leaves*, 4:148.

87. "The Need of the Times—Creating a Nucleus of Universal Brotherhood," *Ceylon Daily News*, November 18, 1999.

88. Emil Burnouf characterized the society's position in terms borrowed from Olcott: "The Society is foreign to politics. . . . It formally forbids its members to compromise its strict neutrality in these matters." "The Theosophical Society," *Revue des Deux Mondes* (Paris), July 1888, reprinted in *Theosophist* 10 (1888): 1–7, at 3.

translated into Japanese. After one occasion lecturing to a large gathering of priests at the Higashi Honganji temple, he learned from the bilingual Captain Brinckley that his remarks had been translated in a way that gave his words a political meaning, "which, of course, was farthest from [his] thoughts."[89] Olcott remained oblivious to the fact that the Japanese had made his visit political from top to bottom, unaware that the mistranslation of his words was a small part of the backwash created by Japan's encounter with the world.

DHARMAPALA, JAPANESE SECTARIANISM, AND HONGANJI

When Dharmapala returned to Japan in 1893, he was acquainted with the sectarian landscape of Buddhism in Japan. He had participated in the World's Parliament of Religions with the four Japanese monks—Toki Horyu, Yatsubuchi Banryu, Shaku Soen, and Ashitsu Jitsuzen—and their translators, Hirai Kanezo and Noguchi Zenshiro; the priests were less well known to Dharmapala although Shaku Soen had spent three years in Lanka before the parliament.[90] He had heard the various Japanese presentations on that occasion. And over the last months of his first visit—when his health returned—he could not have avoided the conclusion that Japanese Buddhism was hugely different from anything he had seen before. He had witnessed in 1889 "a gorgeous pageant in the Higashi Honganji Temple, the Master, Otani San, typifying Sakya Muni himself," a liberty one would not take with the Buddha in Sri Lanka.[91] Priests of all sects received him at Nagoya, and he hoisted the Buddhist flag (Diary, December 7, 1893). He began to see that the Buddhist sects had ideological as well as sociological differences, and they were not going to cooperate, much less converge, Noguchi's hopes notwithstanding.

After the parliament Dharmapala had traveled by train across the United States before he steamed across the Pacific. The *Oceanic* stopped in Honolulu, where he met Mary Foster, the Theosophist who years later became his chief patron. His ticket home was a gift from the parliament's organizer, J. H. Barrows, who thought that he could profit from visiting his coreligionists in Japan rather than retracing his trip across the Atlantic. When

---

89. *Old Diary Leaves*, 4:132.

90. Konen, *Meiji no Bukkyo-sha*, 212–22. Shaku Soen had been sent to Sri Lanka by Fuzuzawa Yukichi, the founder of Keio University, where Shaku Soen was a student, to study Sanskrit and Southern Buddhism with Hikkaduve (213–4).

91. *Old Diary Leaves*, 4:154. Otani was attended by a group of young people personifying bodhisattvas.

6. Japanese delegation at World's Parliament of Religions, 1893. Standing on right:
Zenshiro Noguchi.

Dharmapala discovered that Noguchi had no money for his return, he asked Barrows to pay for his travel too (Diary, May 1, 1902). The Japanese priests and laypeople returned to Japan together, and Dharmapala sailed on a different ship. Once they returned, Yatsubuchi, Shaku Soen, Noguchi, and Horiuchi (who was a Honganji official and a representative of both the Theosophical and Maha Bodhi societies) began to appear together at Buddhist meetings to discuss the parliament.[92] Plans for making common cause aside, the clerics and Hirai had minimal contact with him in the days that followed, although Noguchi, Horiuchi, and Soen remained longtime associates. Even the practice of referring to the priests after their return from the West as *chanpionra* (champions) suggests that forging a Buddhist world would require accommodating Japan's own interests.

Noguchi was the exception in several ways. At the parliament he described himself as "simply a layman, . . . not belong[ing] to any sect of Buddhism at all. So I present to you four Buddhist sorios [priests]." His humility

92. *Japan Weekly Mail*, November 4, 1893, 549, and November 11, 1893, 553.

duly noted, Noguchi had a vision of Buddhist greatness—sharing Dharmapala's understanding of Buddhism as a missionary religion that could play a role in unifying the people of the world:

> It is to be hoped that the number of religions in the world will be increased by thousands more? No. Why? If such were our hope we ought to finally bring the number of religions to as great a figure as that of the population of the world. . . . In that case [priests of the various religions] should rather say: "Don't believe whatever we preach, get away from the church, and make your own sect as we do." Is it right for the priest to say so? No.
>
> Then, is there hope of decreasing the number of religions? Yes. How far? To one. Why? Because the truth is only one.[93]

If religions were allowed to achieve their full development, he argued, there would be no more distinction among them. He added that such was the end at which they should aim, not mentioning Buddhism at all in this regard, but adding that the Japanese "know the shortest way" to a future where all religious would be one.

Olcott had found himself pulled into the force field that surrounded the two Honganjis. Dharmapala followed behind because he was young, and those gravitational effects weighed on him on every visit that followed. He had corresponded with Honganji students before he reached Japan. They came to his bedside when he was hospitalized in Japan, one spelling another through day and night, seeing to his needs and massaging his rheumatic feet. Honganji paid for his hospital stay and by way of the general committee paid for his travel around Japan when he regained his health (Diary, February 23, 1889). He went with Olcott to the Nishi Honganji temple on April 12, and when they visited the parade grounds, they saw Honganji students performing marching exercises (Diary, April 29, 1889). In early May he visited branch temples of the two Honganjis (Diary, May 7, 1889), returning to Kyoto for the completion of the Higashi Honganji temple (Diary, May 9, 1889). On May 10 he went to see a dramatic performance there. On May 11 he interviewed the chief abbot of Nishi Honganji; on May 12 he visited Honganji colleges; then on May 13 he left for Osaka, where he visited a girls' school of Nishi Honganji and a branch temple of Higashi Honganji. He was accompanied to his steamer by Honganji officials (Diary, May 14, 1889). On the 1893 visit Dharmapala continued to talk about unity, and Honganji

93. "Would Win Converts to Buddhism," 156.

continued to resist any unity it did not itself control. Taking the train to Nagoya, he thought his mission had wide support:

> Auspicious signs met on the way. Received by all Sects at the station. Yamashita Priest, Horiuchi & Ito followed bringing the Image. Lectured at the Honganji about Buddha Gaya Temple. Hoisted the Maha Bodhi Society's Flag for the first time. Great enthusiasm prevailed. (Diary, December 7, 1893)

He was delighted to see a full complement of priests. He could count on the support of the young students of Nishi Honganji who had nursed him on his first visit. They wanted to missionize Buddhism overseas and support the cause by giving up alcohol themselves.[94]

Honganji's preeminence shaped Dharmapala's visits in 1902 and 1913, although he encountered priests and officials from other sects as he moved around Japan. He was especially fond of several priests. But the headquarters of the Maha Bodhi Society was located at Honganji, and the general committee was dominated by its officials. That predominance made getting support from other sects more difficult. One priest made his discomfort explicit:

> Revd: Mokusen Hioki of the Soto Sect, a pleasant noble looking Priest called to see me. He invited me to a place tomorrow. He told me that the Hd: Quarters of the Japanese Maha Bodhi Society are at Higashi Honganji and that the Committee are quarelling, and that therefore it is hard for him to do anything in the interest of the Maha Bodhi Society! Since 1894 I have been doing everything to bring Japan before the Indian public, and that in all his writings in the *Indian Mirror*, Norendro Babu [Norendronath Sen, the paper's editor and Dharmapala's supporter], has helped me to unite the two countries. Japan so far has not done anything for India. The present opportunity on a/c of the Anglo-Japanese alliance is splendid for further work in India. I hope the Japanese will expand their trade in India. (Diary, May 19, 1902)

There were several motivations behind Honganji's interest in Dharmapala's work in Japan. The most basic was its dominant role in Japanese Buddhism relative to other sects. Honganji was prosperous enough to lend

---

94. "To Convert Christendom to Buddhism," *Calcutta National Guardian*, reprinted in *Theosophist* 10 (1889): 244–6, at 246.

money to the state and was the sect to which the Meiji government spoke words of encouragement, reassuring Honganji officials that Buddhism need not fear persecution during the *haibutsu kishaku* movement of 1868 (despite the contrary signs Buddhists were seeing around them). Among the Buddhist sects, Honganji was at least the first among equals; at most, it presumed to represent Buddhism as such. It published its own journal, *Bijou of Asia*, which implicitly made the same claim.[95] Olcott and Dharmapala were distinguished visitors, and Olcott had been invited to Japan at the behest of a Honganji priest, Sano Masamichi.[96] Honganji saw the need to represent Buddhism to the outside world. It did so even in the face of his call for unity and resisted the unity envisioned by the transectarian movement. At the World's Parliament of Religions, Honganji was not represented.[97]

At the time of Olcott and Dharmapala's visit, *Jiji Shimpo*, a newspaper committed to Japan's modernization, looked forward to a time when human beings would have less need for religion. In the face of missionary threat—and the prospect of life without religion relegated to the future—the paper argued that for now Jodo Shinshu should become the state religion:

> Its preachers are skilful; the tact of its propagandists is remarkable; its temples, instead of being hidden away in sequestered spots like the strongholds of feudal barons, are built in populous and accessible places, and despite the license enjoyed by its priests in respect of marriage and flesh-eating, its influence spreads and alone among all the Sects, its prosperity remains unimpaired.[98]

The Christian editors of the *Japan Weekly Mail* reached the opposite conclusion: these qualities made it the least praiseworthy of Buddhist sects.

Honganji also had an interest in reform, and sectarian behavior figured in the way Honganji scholars thought about making Buddhism modern. Faced with the fear that sectarianism was intellectually indefensible, Inoue Enryo rationalized the proliferation of Buddhist sects by arguing that each met the needs of believers in a distinctive way. Although an ordained Shinshu priest, Inoue Enryo gave up that status because of his low opinion of his

---

95. Richard M. Jaffe, "Buddhist Material Culture, 'Indianism,' and the Construction of Pan-Asian Buddhism in Pre-War Japan," *Material Religion* 2 (2006): 266–92. Jaffe says that the journal had a Theosophical flavor as well as a Buddhist orientation, 271.

96. Noguchi, "The Way That Dharmapala . . . Came to Japan," 78.

97. Ketelaar, *Of Heretics and Martyrs*, 159. Noguchi was a lay member of Honganji, whatever his aspirations for unity. Richard Jaffe, personal communication.

98. *Japan Weekly Mail*, April 13, 1889, 347–8.

colleagues and set his mind to remaking Japanese Buddhism. His initiative had a nationalistic motivation: "I want to reform our nation's Buddhism to repay some small part of the tremendous debt I owe my country."[99] The felt need for reform also made Honganji the most outward looking of the sects. Its concern for learning from, and interacting with, the larger world was motivated by an event both poignant and instructive. Traveling in Europe on a tour designed to modernize Japanese institutions, two Honganji priests, Otani Koei and Ishikawa Shundai, came across a Buddhist text they found impenetrable because it was written in Sanskrit. After attempts to learn the language that would decode the text, the pair realized the difficulty of the task and participated in selecting the two Honganji priests, Kasahara Kenju and Nanjo Bun'yu, to be sent to study Sanskrit and Buddhology with Max Muller.[100]

In 1873 Honganji sent a priest to China as part of an effort to demonstrate Buddhism's usefulness to the nation.[101] Later Honganji became involved in more far-flung missionary efforts, sending out priests to establish Honganji communities in Hawaii, Singapore, and Brazil (Diary, August 2, 1897). Like the *Maha Bodhi*, the Honganji journal was published in English and intended for worldwide consumption. These efforts were tied to both the nation and the Japanese people in a way that Dharmapala misunderstood. He thought they were signs of Japanese Buddhism's vitality and assumed they were equivalent to his own efforts to bring the Buddha's teachings to non-Buddhists. Honganji wanted to establish temples in areas where there was a Japanese community not yet gathered into the Honganji fold. Its resources were limited but well used. Headquarters had sent an official, T. Kawakami, to Colombo to study Sanskrit and later to Calcutta (where he fell out with Dharmapala). Later he was posted to Los Angeles, where he managed the Nanka Buddhist Mission (Diary, November 21, 1913).

Honganji had some interest in India, and Horiuchi gave Dharmapala to believe after his first visit to Japan that there was a lot of it. Honganji would be willing to spend lavishly on the propagation of Buddhism in India.[102] If that prospect ever existed, it soon waned, but Dharmapala did everything he could to make a connection to Japan. He flew the Japanese flag next to the Buddhist flag at the international conference he convened at Bodh Gaya,

99. Kathleen M. Staggs, "Defend the Nation and Love the Truth: Inoue Enryo and the Revival of Meiji Buddhism," *Monumenta Nipponica* 38 (1983): 270.

100. Ketelaar, *Of Heretics and Martyrs in Meiji Japan*, 126.

101. Holmes Welch, *The Buddhist Revival in China* (Cambridge, MA: Harvard University Press, 1968), 162.

102. Jayawardana, *Mage Jivita Kathava*, 47.

later noting that he had sent a letter to the lord chamberlain of Japan to bring about a union between Japan and India. "May it have effect for the good of Buddhism," he wrote (Diary, December 30, 1895).[103] He contacted Count Okuma about the upcoming Buddha Jayanti and its importance for all Buddhists (Diary, May 25, 1908). He talked to Sakurai Gicho about establishing a Japanese museum in Colombo (Diary, May 1, 1913) and an Indo-Japanese exhibition in Calcutta (Diary, May 4, 1913). He hoped that he would be reborn in Japan to save India (Diary, July 14, 1913). Japan was on his mind.

Dharmapala looked at uniting Buddhists in Japan and India and doing business in Japan as perfectly compatible. Other members of the Hewavitarne family thought similarly; his brother Edmund visited Japan to establish business connections (Diary, April 15, 1903). Dharmapala looked forward to the family firm's importing matchboxes from Japan, each emblazoned with the Maha Bodhi Society seal (Memorandum of Understanding, 1894 Diary). Traveling in Japan and the United States, he had seen educational institutions that taught practical skills, having encountered in both places an alternative to the British model of classical learning. Some of his economic activities were philanthropic. In 1906 he used family money to send a Sinhala youth to Japan to study weaving, and when the young man returned, Dharmapala established a school at Rajagiriya to educate young men as weavers.[104] He sent a second young man to Japan to learn pottery making. Speaking in Tokyo, he invited Japanese business people to start new businesses in Calcutta (Diary, May 2, 1913). He envisioned the same for Lanka, writing in his diary of the need for a Ceylon Japan Trading Company in Colombo (Diary, June 4, 1913). As he put it elsewhere, the Japanese had gotten rich and now had obligations to the rest of the world: "The Japanese Buddhists should tell the world that the secret of their success is the Dharma of Buddha" (Diary, September 14, 1904).

On one occasion Dharmapala proposed a scheme that followed on his hope that Japanese Buddhists would soon want to make pilgrimage to India. The Maha Bodhi Society in Colombo began to function as a travel agency for local Buddhists wanting to visit the holy sites in North India. In Japan his plans involved his version of a rotating credit association:

103. Interviewed by the *Osaka Mainichi* on his 1913 visit, Dharmapala told the reporter that "the Japanese are heartily welcome in India. They will be worshipped as the saviours of India if they come as permanent residents and apply their energies to the development of the country." *Japan Weekly Mail*, May 3, 1913, 558.

104. U. B. Dolapilla went to Japan as a Hewavitarne scholar to study in Tokyo. After he passed his exams, he returned to Colombo in 1911. "Journal of the Indo-Japanese Association," *Journal of the Maha Bodhi Society* 14 (1911): 123.

His purpose is to arrange for a yearly pilgrimage of 50 Japanese to Buddhagaya in India and the method of procedure is to form a company called
the Buddhagaya Sankei-ko, consisting of 500 members, 50 of whom will
be chosen by lot to make the journey. Membership is not limited to religious folk. Special arrangements as to passage are said to have been made
with the Nippon Yusen Kaisha. It is altogether a novel programme, and
as each member will not have to put up more than 10 *yen* annually, the
thing will probably work well.[105]

The article indicated that he had enlisted the aid of the president of the
Nisshu Seimei Hoken Kaisha (Nichiren Life Insurance Company), noting
that the reader would be surprised by the commercial novelty of the name
of a Buddhist sect attached to an insurance business, although Honganji had
already lent its name to an insurance company established to do business
with its own supporters.

Nichiren (1222–82) had understood Japan as the altar (*kaidan*) from
which the truth of the Lotus Sutra would spread over the world, and subsequent generations of his followers thought that they too lived in times as
degenerate (*mappo*) as the one that drove Nichiren to take desperate measures to reform Buddhism. When Dharmapala visited Tokyo in 1902, he met
the director of the Nichiren Insurance Company, Hojiro Kawai (with whom
he set up the revolving credit association), and Kawai told him that Nichiren had said, "From Japan to India Buddhism will go," a prophesy a man
trying to recover Bodh Gaya could not ignore.[106] Nor was it a prophesy that
a steamship company could ignore. At the end of his two months in Japan,
Sakurai Gicho, the director of the Indo-Busseki and a Honganji official, took
Dharmapala to meet the directors of the Nippon Yusen Kaisha, the steamship company that had paid for his trip to Japan (Sarnath Notebook no. 101).
He convinced the directors to make Calcutta a port of call and give Japanese
pilgrims a 20 percent travel discount (Diary, June 24, 1902). The modern age
was about to fulfill Nichiren's prediction, and he would play a part by ar-
ranging for both a steamship line's calling at Bodh Gaya's nearest port and
a discount for pilgrims.

There were moments when Dharmapala considered joining one of the
Japanese sects. That the reformer who came in the cause of unity would

---

105. " New Pilgrimage," *Japan Weekly Mail*, June 28, 1902, 701.
106. Jacqueline Stone, "Placing Nichiren in the 'Big Picture': Some Ongoing Issues in
Scholarship," *Japanese Journal of Religious Studies* 26, nos. 3–4 (1999): 411–17.

throw off either the advantages of being an outsider or his identity as a Sinhala Buddhist is more than puzzling. His diary indicates his wanting to become a student of Shaku Unsho—although it says nothing about his motives. He simply writes, "Then called upon Vajo. Had a long talk and he will accept me as his pupil" (Diary, November 29, 1893).[107] It is easy enough to find reasons for Dharmapala's affinity for him. He was Kozen's teacher and had instructed him to recover Bodh Gaya for the Buddhists.[108] He was famous for his celibacy and ascetic practice—eating only three rice crackers and tea at 7 a.m. and nothing but vegetables for lunch—and Dharmapala had been put off by Japanese monks having wives, drinking sake, and making merry. Unsho Vajo was renowned for his discipline. One Westerner said there were only two monks in Japan; Shaku Unsho was one, an ascetic monk in Kyushu represented another half, and all other monks made up the remainder.[109]

Dharmapala also contemplated becoming a member of Honganji, and here he was more forthcoming about his thinking. After arriving at Kobe, he took the train to Kyoto to visit the Nishi Honganji "high priest," who was confined to his room and could not meet him; he remarked that a Mr. Maeda also excused himself from talking with him (Diary, May 3, 1902). A day later Dharmapala asked Noguchi to visit him and asked him "whether it was expedient for me to join W. Honganji. He said it was good to get their sympathy; but I should not become a Sectarian." By May 27 he had moved on to Tokyo, where Sakurai called on him, and Dharmapala "made him understand that I should like to work as a Shinshu Missionary." In spite of the high priest and Maeda's avoiding him, officials began to look for a residence for Dharmapala in Japan, and they guided his activities for the rest of the visit. Days before he sailed to the United States, he spoke of wanting to extend his stay in Japan and work for a "purified" Buddhism.

The third visit forced Dharmapala to face several choices—to fight for Buddhist unity or make a sectarian affiliation, to maintain his solitary course or try to arrange for a companion in the person of Miss Otake, to pursue his commercial activities to support his missionary work or stick to the missionary work (and rely on others' philanthropy), and whether to stay in

107. Shaku Unsho's interest in South Asia derived from its association with monastic law and celibacy in particular, the more so in a time when Japanese monks were able to marry legitimately. Konen, *Meiji no Bukkyo-sha*, 84–5. His interest in Vinaya led to the bitter disagreement he was soon to have with Kozen over monastic discipline.

108. Kusunagi Zengi, *Shaku Unsho*, vol. 1 (Tokyo: Tokukyokai, 1913), 126; and Konen, *Meiji no Bukkyo-sha*, 87.

109. Konen, *Meiji no Bukkyo-sha*, 87–91.

Japan or return to India.[110] He negotiated the latter two contradictions but could not advance the cause that Olcott and he had begun in 1889, finding a way to bring Buddhists together. The best he could do was to formulate a rationale for the ideological affinity of various Buddhisms, and again his focus fell on Jodo Shinshu and Nichiren.

> The Shinshu Sect & the Jodo who base their belief in Amida Buddha have the authority of the Pali texts to accentuate their faith. In the Samyutta Nikaya, Devata Samyutta, the gods showed their faith on [sic] Buddha and repeated the gatha "Ye keci Buddham saranam gatase" etc. The Nichiren Sect has their faith based on the Dhamma; and Pali Buddhism concurs with them. Dharma is supreme. I have written to Edmund [his brother] about my plans in Japan and to consult father about opening a branch firm in Tokio. (Diary, May 11, 1902)[111]

After his encounter with Tanaka Chigaku a month later, Dharmapala would have a hard time making the assertion that the Nichiren sect—and certainly not Tanaka's Nichirenist movement—had much in common with his own Buddhism.

DHARMAPALA, TANAKA, AND NICHIRENISM

Dharmapala met Tanaka Chigaku on his 1902 visit. By that point Tanaka had established several Nichrenist lay movements, the final iteration and best-known of which was Kokuchukai.[112] Tanaka's father had told him as a boy that if he wished to serve Buddhism, he should do so by not becoming a monk because "miso that smells like miso is not good miso."[113] Ignoring the advice, Tanaka joined the monkhood, defrocked himself, married, and moved on to a career his father could support, establishing and leading lay Buddhist organizations. His new religion followed a Nichirenist course, pre-

---

110. On the 1913 visit he spoke of wanting to "start Buddhist work in Japan and establish a Buddhist Mission at Tokyo" (Diary, May 12, 1913). He added, "I also have the desire to be a naturalized Japanese," although the rest of the diary entries from that visit make no reference to his having plans to remain in Japan.

111. The branch firm Dharmapala was imagining would sell furniture made by the family business, H. Don Carolis, and generate income for his religious work.

112. Jaffe devotes considerable attention to Kokuchukai, focusing on its innovative approach to clerical marriage. *Neither Monk nor Layman*, 165–88.

113. Lee, "Nichiren and Nationalism," 20.

serving the central place held by both Nichiren Shonin and the Lotus Sutra as the realization of Buddhism, while setting itself in opposition to other Nichiren groups because of their lapsed standards. When he studied for the Nichiren priesthood, Tanaka rejected the Nichiren orthodoxy of the time, which had come to emphasize the accomodationist first half of the Lotus Sutra while ignoring the second half.[114] Nichiren himself had emphasized that second half with its insistence on *shakubuku*—the face-to-face critique of other forms of Buddhism. Kokuchukai followed suit, rejecting all forms of moderation. The Meiji policy of religious freedom made a return to shakubuku practical, for now Buddhists could change their sectarian identities, and aggressive preaching became a tool for Tanaka and his followers both to convert others and act out their commitment to Nichiren and the Lotus Sutra.

Tanaka had equally strong feelings about the emperor. From roughly the 1880s onward he had concentrated on restoring Nichiren's true teachings, but by the time Dharmapala met him in 1902, he was pushing his movement in a political direction, working out a theory of the body politic (*Nihon kokutai gaku*). Jacqueline Stone says that Tanaka "may have been the first Lotus Sutra devotee to formulate a modern reading of the 'this-worldly' Buddha land."[115] When he spoke of the unification of humankind through the Lotus Sutra, he understood unification in terms of both religion and politics. Emperor worship functioned in both contexts, acquiring new motivations in an age of aggressive Western powers. The emperor represented transcendence as well as unity. The Lotus Sutra functioned in this connection as a metonym of the nation: "The nation is the sutra, which is the Buddha, who is incarnated in the emperor, who embodies the nation."[116] For Tanaka, venerating the emperor entailed acting just as aggressively in his cause as one should act in the cause of Nichiren. Little wonder that his followers included Japanese militarists such as Inoue Nissho, who founded a terrorist organization, and Ishiwara Kanji, who led the invasion of northeastern China.

Dharmapala and Tanaka shared several projects—a commitment to

---

114. George J. Tanabe, "Tanaka Chigaku: The Lotus Sutra and the Body Politic," in *The Lotus Sutra in Japanese Culture*, ed. George J. Tanabe and Willa Jane Tanabe (Honolulu: University of Hawaii Press, 1989), 193–4.

115. "Realizing This World as the Buddha Land," in *Readings of the Lotus Sutra*, ed. Stephen F. Teiser and Stone (New York: Columbia University Press, 2009), 225. The universal scope and nondual cosmology of the Lotus Sutra duly noted, by the eighth century the Japanese had begun to link the Lotus Sutra to Japan (217–27).

116. Tanabe, "Tanaka Chigaku," 203.

missionizing, a sense that reform was urgent, and a willingness to criticize others in the process. They both lived on the margins of the monastic tradition—Tanaka, the former monk, leading a lay organization and Dharmapala, the would-be monk, managing another lay organization. Both were reformers with reputations for confronting others aggressively. Both edited Buddhist magazines and wanted to missionize Buddhism. Beyond these similarities it is hard to imagine two figures with less in common. As Jaffe points out, Tanaka denounced world abnegation and laid out a plan for Buddhism to engage the domestic order.[117] Dharmapala understood himself as an *anagarika brahmacarya*, regarding asceticism as the only way by which a man who was not a monk could devote himself to spiritual progress as well as social reform. Tanaka ripped Buddhism out of the hands of the Buddhist monkhood, arguing that there were no monks left in Japan. Dharmapala wanted only to energize the monkhood and engage monks in missionary work. Their meeting left a trail of ironies and misunderstandings. Dharmapala told Tanaka that there was no Buddhism left in India, and Tanaka concurred, already knowing that to be the case. But where Dharmapala was making the general claim that Buddhists had disappeared from India, Tanaka thought Buddhism—whether there were Buddhists in India or not—disappeared from India when the Mahayana tradition moved away from India to reach full realization in Japan.[118] On the Nichiren understanding Buddhism had come to Japan from India, and it was destined to return. But that Buddhism would be Tanaka's interpretation of Nichiren Buddhism, not Dharmapala's or anyone else's.

Tanaka saw one virtue in Dharmapala's variety of Buddhism: he was attracted to the *cakravartin* ideal that played a central role in the formation of early states—usually as much Hindu as Buddhist—in India and Southeast Asia.[119] For well over a millennium the notion served as a template for center-oriented states from Angkhor to Pagan and Sukhothai. The idea that the king was a righteous king of universal power joined Buddhism as doctrine, symbolic formation, and monastic institution to the political process. As the religion spread, cakravartin kingship served to legitimate new states. In the South Asian tradition the first such king was the Buddha himself,

---

117. *Neither Monk nor Layman*, 176.

118. *Neither Monk nor Layman*, 165.

119. For a treatment of *cakravartin/cakkavatti* kingship in its South and Southeast Asian context, see S. J. Tambiah, *World Conqueror and World Renouncer: A Study of Buddhism and Polity in Thailand against a Historical Background* (Cambridge: Cambridge University Press, 1976), 16–8 and 39–53. Tanaka was also interested in what he thought was Dharmapala's facility at street preaching. *Graphic Biography of Tanaka Chigaku*, 114.

able to turn the wheel of power as well as the wheel of righteousness.[120] Asoka was the historical paradigm, the architecture and courtly practices of Asoka's rule replicated by later kings across the region. A successful king commanded the wheel of power but chose to rule by turning the wheel of righteousness. The notion of the wheel-turning universal monarch (as well as the West-East-West trajectory of Buddhism, the absence of dhamma in India, and Japan's peripheral, but synoptic place in Buddhist cosmology) played a part in the Nichiren tradition.[121] In 1904 Tanaka published a pamphlet, "Heavenly Deed of Unifying the World" (sekai toitsu no tengyo), that reiterated the connections between India and Japan, declaring that the emperor's lineage could be traced to India.[122]

Nichiren had preached his doctrine "to the universe and to mankind," and to that extent, proselytizing was entailed. Unlike Honganji's pursuing its missionizing endeavor outside of Japan but largely in Japanese communities, Tanaka had a vision of world unity.[123] He argued that the whole world would become Buddhist fifty years after his 1902 meeting with Dharmapala, with closure achieved when Wellington, New Zealand, accepted his views. His vision was Japan-centric—the world would be converted to a specifically Japanese expression of Buddhism, namely Nichirenism under Tanaka's interpretation, and military expansion would make it happen. When he drew up a list of pilgrimage places, all five were located in Japan and associated with emperors—from Jimmu to Meiji—and Nichiren.[124] His attraction to the cakravartin notion came by way of its resonance with a parallel formulation in a Japanese chronicle that was itself center-oriented and inclusive.[125] The Japanese empire should be extended to embrace all cardinal points and "the eight cords covered to form a roof." That the wheel-turning emperor had an Indian origin supplied another historical narrative, which had to reach Japan to achieve completion.[126] The South Asian refer-

120. Frank E. Reynolds, "The Two Wheels of Dhamma: A Study of Early Buddhism," in The Two Wheels of Dhamma: Essays on the Theravada Tradition in India and Ceylon, ed. Gananath Obeyesekere, Reynolds, and Bardwell L. Smith (Chambersburg, PA: American Academy of Religion, 1972), 6–30.

121. Stone, "Placing Nichiren," 411–7.

122. Kosei, "Dharmapala's Activities in Japan," unpublished paper, 4.

123. Lee, "Nichiren and Nationalism," 27.

124. Graphic Biography of Chigaku Tanaka, chapter 53.

125. See W. G. Aston, trans., Nihongi: Chronicles of Japan from the Earliest Times to A.D. 697 (Oxford: Oxford University Press, 1956), 131.

126. Tambiah uses the Pali expression cakkavatti, while predecessors such as Heine Geldern used the Sanskrit cakravartin. The ambiguity reflects the interdigitation of the two languages and the two religions we now call Hinduism and Buddhism.

ence did not entail Tanaka's having any interest in recovering Bodh Gaya, whatever its place—symbolically, politically, practically—in a Buddhist world.

Dharmapala took the train to Kamakura and spent the day with Tanaka and his supporters. On Tanaka's account, Dharmapala asked for the meeting, and Tanaka responded by renting a banquet room and serving "alcohol and lots of food."[127] Their time together was largely a matter of his lecturing Dharmapala on the virtues of Nichiren Buddhism and Japanese spirit. Throughout the conversation Tanaka's disdain for Dharmapala's simplistic Buddhism was palpable. He called it *yamadashi Bukkyo* (Indian bumpkin Buddhism).[128] His self-confidence outstripped the idea that Japanese Buddhism was Buddhism fully matured or that Nichiren preached real Buddhism, although other Japanese Buddhists claimed the former and Tanaka the latter. When he told Dharmapala that Buddhism is not *myohorengekyo*'s house, but *myohorengekyo* (the chanted phrase at the heart of Nichiren practice) is Buddhism's house, he made a claim about priority and transcendence: that Nichirenism transcends its Buddhist origins.

Tanaka's exchange with Dharmapala is so asymmetrical that it makes one suspect that the transcript is a fiction that used Dharmapala as a foil for Tanaka's views. Dharmapala's diary shows no sign that he thought he was exploited:

> Arrived at Kawakura [*sic*]. Went to see Mr. Chigaku Tanaka, the Editor of the *Sun* was there. Mr. Tanaka's honorific name is Yoshio Minamoto. He took me to the spot where Nichiren first preached. I laid a bouquet of flowers at the spot; and expressed to Mr. Sanaka [*sic*] that I hope the great Dharma will spread all over India. He photographed at the spot. Then he took me to the Kado Sho Hotel, whose proprietor is Mr. Tomita Seizo. Who traces his descent to 58 generations back. His first ancestor was a Shinto. We had a pleasant time. There was European & Jap: food; and there was a geisha girl. She showed her under clothing which was made of silk. Visited the Daibutsu, the great statue of Buddha. Inside the statue is a temple. Mr. Tanaka presented me with several copies of the Photo of the Daibutsu. Rev: Nichika Yaziwara, the Nichiren priest is in charge of the Temple built in honour of Nichiren. (Diary, June 23, 1902)

127. "Dharmapala's Visit to Japan: After I Preached," in *Tanaka Chigaku's Autobiography* (Tokyo: Shishi Obunko, 1977), 251–60, at 252.

128. Jaffe, *Neither Monk nor Layman*, 175.

Given the length and intensity of the conversation, it is hard to believe that Dharmapala did not have more of a reaction to a man who had given him a doctrinal drubbing. Even the title of Tanaka's account refers to the conversation as Tanaka's "preaching" to Dharmapala, a man who also described himself as a "Buddhist preacher." But his representations in Tanaka's text sound very much like Dharmapala, framing his indictment of British imperialism and struggle for Buddhism in terms he used elsewhere. Even his willingness to preach Nichirenism does not seem strange given his contemplating becoming a student of Shaku Unsho or joining Honganji.

Tanaka met Dharmapala at the train station and brought him to the publishing house affiliated with Kokuchukai, where they greeted each other by bowing and drinking green tea. Dr. Takayama and Sejiro Washizuka joined the party for a visit to Kamakura, a place sacred to Nichiren Shonin. The conversation was translated and transcribed by another Tanaka follower, Kuwabara, who was also his biographer. Kuwabara presents the conversation in several parts, marking the pauses when the group ate or visited sites.[129] The encounter is more than a full-bodied example of Dharmapala's works and days in Japan. It represents the meeting of two Buddhists with a common vision of Buddhism's being spread far from their birthplaces at the antipodes of the Buddhist world of the early twentieth century. The occasion lacked the considerable fanfare of Dharmapala's 1893 visit. There are signs in the conversation that Japanese visits to India had revealed to the Japanese public that Dharmapala's operations were less that the grand enterprise it had originally been thought to be. To that extent, Tanaka's aggressiveness was aggravated by the recognition that Dharmapala's star had fallen. The following is a transcript of the encounter as it appears in the published text, omitting passages that are less pertinent to the construction of a united Buddhist world:[130]

DHARMAPALA: I'm so glad to meet Prof. Takayama and Tanaka *sensei* [teacher] who is the head of Rissho Ankokukai.[131] I have deep hopes for

129. Dharmapala's diary entry for the day says little about the meeting, noting the visit to the place where Nichiren Shonin first preached and the Daibutsu in Kamakura, and telling Tanaka "that I hope the great Dharma will spread all over India" (June 23, 1902).

130. Chiou Yamakawa, "Dharmapala's Visit to Japan in Meiji 35," reprinted in Tanaka Kouho, ed., *Recollections of Chigaku Tanaka*, November 13, 1988, 546–67.

131. In 1885 Tanaka changed the name of the *Rengekai* (Lotus Society), which he had founded in 1881, to *Rissho Ankokukai*, a name that brings to the fore his lifelong concerns, *rissho* (the establishment of righteousness) and *ankoku* (the security of the country). Lee, "Nichiren and Nationalism," 21.

Japanese Buddhism. In order to carry this message overseas I need to be careful. And I am eager to hear your opinions, which will be beneficial to Buddhism.

TANAKA: I agree. I hope that too. How many times have you come to Japan?

DHARMAPALA: This is my third time. With each trip to this country, the country's situation improves. I really hope that the Buddhists in this country wake up and work hard and try to teach the Buddha's message to the world in a way that parallels the country's improvement.

TANAKA: I agree. The Japanese Buddhists who have met you before did not talk about our Japanese Buddhism that deeply.

DHARMAPALA: Yes. I unfortunately have never heard the deep story that is necessary for the Buddhist teachings.

TANAKA: Usually when we talk about Japanese Buddhism generally it is under the influence of India and China. In Japan each school has its own teachings, but we Japanese still have the big teaching [dai kyoho]. Westerners have not discovered this yet, and people from India know nothing of it. I guess that Japanese people you have met before did not have any knowledge of these deep teachings. Therefore I will teach you the special doctrine that was invented in Japan, and I would like to talk about Nichiren Shonin who is the great person in the world after the death of the Buddha.

DHARMAPALA: I have great interest in you, but my opinion is that I want to teach the Westerners how to understand Buddhism as a whole.

TANAKA: Buddhism as whole, I think, is too vague, and from my point of view as Nichiren Shonin said, it is not the real Buddhism. As I said before, the special teaching is the one that we should propagate to the world from now on.

DHARMAPALA: Then how are you going to teach this Japanese special Buddhism and how are you going to spread it? I want to know the details.

TANAKA: Okay [daku]. But it is close to noon. I would like to discuss this point some other time such as after lunch. But before then I want to take you to Nichiren Shonin's spiritual place that is the place on the street that Nichiren preached. That teaching is called komachi-tsuji-zeppo [small town, little street preaching]. Nichiren Shonin was exiled and died because he was given punishment by sword, wooden stick, and stone. He was exiled to Izu island [south of Tokyo]. After he returned from exile, he did not change his methods and was exiled to northern Japan on the island of Sado. He returned in 1274 to Kamakura and builds a temple on a mountain named Minobeyama [in Kamakura]. Let's go to that spiritual place and then we will eat lunch.

7. Dharmapala (in white robes) and Chigaku Tanaka (at immediate left) visiting Nichiren shrine, Kamakura, Japan, 1902.

DHARMAPALA: I am more than happy to visit the spiritual place. I would like to have a flower with a good smell and to offer it there.

From this point Chien Nozaki went to the garden and picked one branch of a lily plant and gave it to Dharmapala, who offered it to the marker there. After that he and Tanaka sensei Professor Takayama, Kuwabara, Kudo, Washizuka, and Nozaki visited the spiritual home of *komachi-tsuji-zeppo* by car. The conversation continued:

DHARMAPALA: Today I came to the spiritual place where Nichiren Shonin had a difficult time because of his Buddhist preaching, and I am thinking back to his old-time preaching. I am so glad [pointing at the lily in his left hand] that I can offer a branch of sweet-smelling flowers as a commemoration of Nichiren's life. When I look at this stalk with two blooming lilies, one is opening and the other is still closed. This closed bud is the symbol of Nichiren's Great Doctrine, which is the hope that should bring light to the world. I believe it is so and I am more and more happy.

TANAKA: Exactly. The doctrine of Nichiren Shonin will unite the world in the future. Shonin said "As the moon comes from West to East, the Buddha's teaching came to Japan. As the sun goes East to West, the Japanese teaching goes back to the moon." I don't consider your visit to this spiritual place as the simple visit of you, but I think of you as the representative of the Indian people.[132] I would like to consider this opportunity as the very first time a person who came from India, which is the motherland of Buddhism bowed in front of our great saint [Nichiren].

As Yamakawa walked out, "the gate was opened by Washizuka. Dharmapala offered respectfully, putting the lily in front of the offering stone. Looking at the offering stone, he bowed. Tanaka said, "From the live body to the dead body . . . *nammyohorengekyo*" three times. After he finished he looked at Dharmapala and said, "This sentence comes from the great teaching." All of them took the car and went to Taikaku-kan [Taikaku hall]. . . . There are more than 10,000 old and unique utensils in this hall. At that time the cafeteria was in the hall right next to it, and at the gate there were flags crossed [Japan's and India's] welcoming the guest. In the room there were unique old art objects lined up. . . . Before the meal came from the kitchen, the beneficial conversation began."

TANAKA: I heard you went to Nara, which is the oldest capital in Japan.

DHARMAPALA: I heard Nara has famous big Buddha statues, and I wanted to visit there at least once. I haven't had a chance, and I regret that I haven't been there yet.

TANAKA: The temple that has the big Buddha is called Todai-ji. It was built by Emperor Shomu more than a thousand years ago. When they celebrated the eye-opening ceremony. The Emperor was fond of India, the homeland of Buddhism. He invited the highest monk from India even though it was the time of unimaginably difficult travel. Because of this, we can imagine how deep the Buddhist teaching was.

DHARMAPALA: I would like to hear the beneficial teaching of Nichiren Shonin.

TANAKA: Nichiren Shonin's teaching was completely different from the generality of Buddhists. In his teaching he considered *myohorengekyo* the core of Buddhism. Generally many Buddhists consider this *myohorenge-*

132. Again Dharmapala is identified, if not as an Indian, as a representative of India. His cause was Indian, the Maha Bodhi Society was founded in Calcutta, and his lectures on Bodh Gaya confirmed that association with India.

kyo as just one sutra among many. This is wrong. If there is no *myo-horengekyo* in any Buddhist teaching, the teaching has no spirit. It is the skeleton/core that provides the spirit. Therefore Shonin's doctrine was to unite all Buddhist teachings with *myohorengekyo*. Buddhism is not *myohorengekyo*'s house and *myohorengekyo* is Buddhism's house.

DHARMAPALA: When did Nichiren live and where did he preach his doctrine?

TANAKA: Nichiren was born 681 years ago and he passed away 620 years ago. He preached his doctrine in Kamakura, Sado, and Minobe, and some other places. Among those places, the place he stayed the longest was Kamakura. Therefore the spiritual place where we went and where he preached *komachi-tsuji-zeppo* was the respectable ruins of his preaching career during his 22 years in Kamakura.

DHARMAPALA: What was he preaching at the beginning?

TANAKA: From the beginning he preached *myohorengekyo*. Shonin preached that if we neglect *myohorengekyo* and teach other doctrines, that is the cause of evil ways.

DHARMAPALA: What is the root of the doctrine of *myohorengekyo*?

TANAKA: In order to understand *myohorengekyo* usually other Buddhists think of it in terms of the Buddhist doctrine, however Nichiren's doctrine was based on the Buddha's notion of skillful means or Buddha's thinking.

DHARMAPALA: Nichiren Shonin's teaching is based on Chinese translated version of *myohorengekyo*. Is this Chinese translation of *myohorenge-kyo* also translated into English?

TANAKA: Not yet.

DHARMAPALA: I think that Carus' English translation of *myohorengekyo* is not well translated. Therefore, I strongly hope that the Chinese text will be translated into English and spread to the world immediately.

TANAKA: Nichiren Shonin's interpretation of "skillful means" was Nichiren's own idea, but that study of the Buddha's skillful means was derived from the great Chinese monk Chigi of the Tendai sect. This great Tendai monk had had a Buddhist text called Makashikan, which is the gateway to the Buddhist teachings. For example, at that time Indian scholars heard this teaching of the Tendai school, and they determined that it was just the Buddha's long-cherished plan. Later there was a great monk of Myoraku whose name was Taizen or Tainen. He heard that Indian scholars had agreed, and he said that if we lose Chinese law, there is no need to go back to shii [the four directions—northeast, southwest, northwest, southeast—or the four virtues necessary to preserve the nation, embarrassment, lack of greed and cleanliness, appreciation, and justice. By hearing this, Nichiren Shonin concluded that there is no Buddhist teaching in India. Shonin thought that there was a very interesting idea that in the Tendai teaching which has not been made public. That idea can be released by *myohorengekyo's* skillful means.

DHARMAPALA: Indian Buddhism was destroyed completely more than 700 years ago. The Buddhism that remains in India is just the wreckage of the original.

TANAKA: No, it's not just 700 years. It's more than several thousand years ago. In the time of the great teacher of Tendai there was no true, deep understanding of Buddhism in India. Nichiren Shonin had never been to that place. He knew that Buddhism had vanished in India, and so it comes back to Japanese Buddhist teaching.

DHARMAPALA: It is a noteworthy fact that in Japan Nichiren Shonin [knew without having visited India] that Buddhism would be destroyed in India 700 years ago. Buddhism in India has lost its fruit because of Hinduism. In Japan the seed of Buddhism was transported early enough so that its beautiful flower is now blooming.

TANAKA: The ideal of the students of Nichiren Shonin the saint is to develop the thinking of China and India with the teachings of Nichiren by using *myohorengekyo*, in other words, it is the special doctrine that is developed by Nichiren. After that the Nichiren doctrine should be spread voluntarily to the Western countries in hopes of uniting the world around the preaching.

DHARMAPALA: Shakyamuni preached *myohorengekyo*, and he changed our heart to the lotus flower. Some say the lotus flower of Buddhist tradition is half open, and some others say it is not open at all. Just as the lotus flower opens because of the sunshine, which is the same thing as the people such as us who have lost their way open their minds with the Buddha's tender love and knowledge.

TANAKA: That's right. The great teacher Tendai interpreted the lotus flower metaphorically in six ways. He goes on to say that the lotus flower implies our heart and the material world, in other words the situation of the whole Buddhist world. He called this Buddhist teaching *to-tai renge no ho-mon*, "the Buddhist teaching of the lotus flower." When he explained this, he said that the lotus flower resembles Buddhist teaching. The ideal of hokekyo (*myohorengekyo*) is like the way the lotus blooms because of receiving sunshine; Nichiren Shonin named himself after this notion, sunshine and lotus flower. This is a noteworthy thing.

DHARMAPALA: Who gave him that auspicious name?

TANAKA: He gave it to himself. When he was 32, he advocated the special doctrine of hokekyo, skillful means for the first time. Shonin for the first time proclaimed himself Nichiren Shonin when he first stood as the great Buddhist teacher and at the time he was preaching, the bodhisattva teachings that appeared in hokekyo sutra [that is, the same thing as myohorengekyo].

DHARMAPALA: I know about Nichiren Shonin's teachings by reading Arthur Lloyd's English translation. I highly respect him, and I would like to research Shonin's aims. I think a lot of foreigners still don't know the true value of Shonin. And I came to know that we should research deeply Shonin's teachings from today's conversation. What I strongly hope is to have a complete biography of Shonin in English. I'm looking forward to see this great man introduced to the world.

TANAKA: Not only foreigners, but also Japanese misunderstand Shonin. Some people give him a bad name. People who appreciate him include Mohammed, Savonarola, and Luther.[133] It's surprising. In the future I would like Shonin's actual facts to be revealed in foreign languages.

At this point Dharmapala began speaking directly with Professor Takayama:

TAKAYAMA: The article on Shonin's biography by Mr. Lloyd appeared in a journal in the past. This short article explains Shonin's history briefly. As Mr. Dharmapala said, it is a very honorable project for Japanese to introduce Shonin to the world. In my opinion Shonin is not simply a great man in Japan but also a great mind for the world. By using Luther or Savanarola or Mohammed to compare Shonin loses his value. They should be compared with other Christians.

DHARMAPALA: I think Nichiren Shonin was a man more important than Christ himself. The reason needs no great explanation. Christ was killed by others' hands, even though his preaching spread and became very popular. The person who is killed by others is not the greatest saint. Being killed by others was not holy, sacred or smart. It was not a great achievement. Without looking at Nichiren Shonin's case, we cannot understand the effects of the sword of persecution. With the power and enthusiasm of Nichiren Shonin, it is easier to preach to the world nowadays.

TAKAYAMA: Nichiren Shonin left an order for us to preach to the world with an ideal of Itten-shikai-kaiki-myouhou "one sky, four seas, everyone comes back Buddhist teaching." Therefore there were six great disciples

---

133. Tanaka meant that such figures would have been drawn to Nichiren because they shared revolutionary programs.

of Shonin. One of them is called Himouchi Shonin or Jitsuji Shonin. He crossed the ocean and proceeded to the north when foreign circumstances were not known. That was 600 years ago when transportation was inconvenient. There was evidence that he went to preach from Siberia to northern Asia. By this fact you can see the accomplishment of Nichiren Shonin.

DHARMAPALA: How old was Nichiren Shonin when he passed away?

TANAKA: He was 61 years old.

DHARMAPALA: What kind of religion do the Emperor and Empress practice?

TANAKA: As a religion they don't believe anything. However, the founding spirit of the country comes together in the true Buddhist teaching. It is noteworthy that the Japanese imperial family does not believe in any particular Buddhist sect nowadays. Buddha's true doctrine must be just one thing. There are lots of different sects and groups nowadays, but this is not the Buddha's intention. Therefore there is no doubt that the time when Buddhism will be united will come in the future. The reason why the royal family does not believe in any sect of Buddhism is because they are waiting for the time when Buddhism will be united in the future.

Dharmapala looked impressed with the reference to the imperial family, according to Yamakawa, and he commented several times on the divinity of the Japanese emperor.

TANAKA: I heard that you are furious about British tyranny for people in India, and you attacked this tyranny at the World's Parliament of Religions. I assume it is a very serious racial problem that prompts British cruelty on the Indian people. I heard that the way that English people govern India is truly avaricious and unjust.

TAKAYAMA: Those white people don't think other races are human.

TANAKA: That is because Christian doctrine is narrow-minded. In other words, their love cannot love anyone who is different from them.

TAKAYAMA: Christ himself wasn't that way [i.e., he loved everyone]. Later in history when Jewish taste intersected with Christianity, this change happened.

TANAKA: No. It wasn't just Christ. The basic ideology of Christianity depends on the love for human beings but not animals. His love did not extend to animals. The teaching says that you can kill the lower level animals and use them as the stuff we eat. This is their notion of love. I am furious to hear that they tax all the salt in India. Seventeen or eighteen years ago I gave a lecture with the title "Public Love and Personal Love" at Tokyo Kosei Hall.

DHARMAPALA: I am very upset with the English government's tyranny over the Indian people. Their government does not educate Indian people and leads to their corruption. They don't lead people to civilization but to savagery. In the past 14 years there were more than 34 million people who were cruelly murdered under this tyranny. This number is close to the population of France. To think of this fact makes me grieve, and I cannot express my sadness for the Indian people.

TANAKA: That is because Indian civilization is frail and weak, and it does not have deep ideals, which is like British civilization also.

DHARMAPALA: Exactly. In fact their government [British] is an evil one and cruel.

TANAKA: The way the British govern is despotic, but does not derive from Christian teaching. Christianity is their national religion. And people there do not question the tyranny in India, and this is not because of Christianity. This is because in Christian teaching it says do not question errors.

TAKAYAMA: I think the Christian doctrine is not the basis of European civilization. It is rather Greek and Roman civilization.

YAMAKAWA: There are good politicians such as Gladstone. I heard that he is a faithful Christian. He never advocated tyranny towards India. I think that except for Tolstoy today in general Christianity includes narrow-minded self-regard as its basis. That cannot be denied.

TANAKA: I would like to go to India to unite Indian people by using Buddhist teachings and to drive away the British government and establish an Indian empire.

DHARMAPALA: The British government is lazy and they ill-treat the people, making it their government policy. I think the British are devils. The poor Indian people are under the control of these devils, and their blood and sweat are sucked by those devils.

TANAKA: That's exactly the case. Japanese people are furious over such cruel tyranny, and we are a nation with that characteristic. Nichiren Shonin's teaching shows especially this great national characteristic.

DHARMAPALA: According to teacher Tanaka, I am led to believe Nichiren Shonin's prediction that Japanese Buddhism will return to India does not imply there will be an Indian empire founded on the Buddha's teachings.

TANAKA: Whether it is a big empire or small empire, Shonin's intention was to develop the nation based on *myohorengekyo*. To accomplish this we cannot avoid having a war or fighting. To pursue this policy requires being willing to fight and conquer difficulties. Japanese people have not been aware of this warning voice, and that is unfortunate. Indian people should be made aware of this warning as soon as possible, and [knowledge of the warning] should lead to their revival.

DHARMAPALA: I heard Nichiren Shonin appeared in Japan and *myohorengekyo* is the great law of the universe. He preached that by this doctrine the world should be united. As we mentioned the lotus flower of *myoho* is the reality of our spirit. People's spirit is like the universe. People who don't understand the reality of *myohorengekyo* don't know not to worry about their own smallness [i.e., once you understand "myo" you don't worry about that smallness]. Shonin's warning voice eventually becomes the Buddha's warning voice.

TANAKA: Exactly. Do you know the monk of the Nichiren school, the teacher Asahinae?

DHARMAPALA: In the Nichiren school I only know Mr. Hojiro Kawai.[134] I have seen one old monk who came from Japan. He brought a bronze image and said *nammyohorengekyo,* and he wanted to place it inside Bodh Gaya. I happened to encounter this incident. Kawai is very devoted to the religion. On this trip I'm going to visit him. Tokyo is the center of Japan. Nihonbashi is the center of Tokyo. An insurance company is at the center of Nihonbashi. Nammyoho releases its light and I heard that this light is flourishing.

TANAKA: I heard that there are people who have hostile feelings towards Mr. Dharmapala and who criticize him. I would like to investigate these feelings and work hard on correcting their misunderstandings. If it is true [that Dharmapala is a fraud], I would like to give you a lecture and admonish you.[135] I assume that without understanding the situation [Japanese people] treat the stranger from faraway with coldness. That is not Japanese people's nature.

---

134. In fact he had just met Kawai, the director of the Nichiren Insurance Company with whom Dharmapala organized the rotating credit association for Japanese pilgrims wanting to go to India. Dharmapala heard the assertion about the insurance company's being at the center of Nihonbashi and Nihonbashi being the center of Tokyo from Mr. Kawai two months earlier (Diary, May 26, 1902). A day after the encounter with Tanaka, Dharmapala again met Kawai and went with him to meet the directors of the steamship line regarding subsidized travel for pilgrims (Diary, June 24, 1902).

135. At their most aggressive, Nichiren Buddhists made a practice of "admonishing" Buddhists of other sects, as well as the emperor. In the present context Tanaka politely asks whether Dharmapala would like to be "admonished." See Jacqueline I. Stone, "Rebuking the Enemies of the Lotus: Nichiren Exclusivism in Historical Perspective," *Japanese Journal of Religious Studies* 21 nos. 2–3 (June–September 1994): 231–59.

Kudo Keitatsu jumped into the conversation, confronting Dharmapala with the growing Japanese suspicion that his chances for success in India were negligible.

KUDO: I heard about it [this misunderstanding] from one person. I have had a chance to read general Buddhism [*tsuzoku bukkyo*]. Mr. Tokuno Oda and teacher Asahinae and teacher Koujyun Omiya and Mr. Sasaki are saying that there are misunderstandings. Because Mr. Dharmapala, the head of the Maha Bodhi Society, goes to many countries, Japanese imagine that this is a great thing. And then when the Japanese go to those countries [India or Sri Lanka], they see that his work is unexpectedly small. They see that it [his staff] consists of two Englishmen who rent the second floor. We go to India, thinking Mr. Dharmapala has a great power in that country, but our expectation is not met. Can you deny that you are a fraud?

DHARMAPALA: For a long time in India Hinduism has been dominant and there has been no Buddhism. Whenever I have business in India, I use the head office. Therefore the Maha Bodhi Society office is in Calcutta. However Christianity, Hinduism, and other religions are practiced in Calcutta. The Buddhist community is small. I am trying to revive Bodh Gaya by fighting against our enemies and by bearing up under several persecutions. The sacred place where Buddha broke through and saw the truth [was awakened] is under control of a Hindu who is a heathen. Because of that fact, Buddhists cannot go and worship freely at that sacred place. As a disciple of the Buddha, I am deeply grieved by this fact. I have been fighting over this place for more than ten years, and for a brief time we were able to gain the right to come into the temple and worship freely. In fact people of other religions look at me and hate me. Whenever I'm in Calcutta, I'm a lonely warrior who is surrounded by the enemy. Therefore I cannot provide sufficient hospitality to every visitor. In Colombo Buddhism is flourishing. I can provide adequate accommodations and means for visitors there. Because of this situation in India and because of the language difficulty, there is misunderstanding in both directions, I believe.

TANAKA: The monkly disciples of Nichiren Shonin have the great teaching, which is the basis of the doctrine itself as well as compassion and humility, and they have an attitude of gentleness and patience about things that happen in public. Even if one is treated badly, one should be obsequious and not respond in kind. Japan is a country that will respond with virtue. People who believe in *myoho* have a character that leads to conquering their enemies as well as the capacity of a heart as big as the ocean. I don't have a grudge towards Dharmapala. The reason I say a lot of things to you is as disciples of Nichiren Shonin we want to be courteous to the Indian people who should be reformed by the doctrine of Nichiren Shonin. I have read in a magazine *Myoshu* teacher Asahinae talking about his trip to India. From Nichiren Shonin's point of view there is no Buddhism in India. Therefore there is no need for us ask them for something. If we are not going to India to spread Buddhism, there is no need to go there at all except to visit the sacred places and venerate [the deceased]. It is totally against Nichiren's doctrine when a male or female disciple brings their hair as an offering and goes to a place where there is no Buddhism. This cannot be allowed. There are some monks who are very upset with Dharmapala because he claims Japanese monks are not active, I heard. But I have been speaking publicly about the lethargy of Japanese monks for 20 years. When we hear Dharmapala's criticism coming from a country fallen to ruin [i.e., India, a land without Buddhism], Japanese monks feel shame. Even though the Maha Bodhi Society is small, there is no reason to call you a swindler right off. There are very few people who always act justly. The student who follows the right law is as scarce as the soil on the fingernail. The evil person is as common as the soil that spreads in all directions.

DHARMAPALA: I receive only 65 yen as a salary/month. With that salary I spend 25 yen to rent space. Whenever monks come from Japan or Siam, I would like to give them preferential treatment as much as possible. There was an old monk from Japan who came to my place through Benares but said nothing, and he brought a bronze pagoda that has *nammyohorengekyo* written on it. He wanted to erect it in Bodh Gaya. I agreed with his plan and placed it inside. I don't even know his name.

TANAKA: I think because of the language difficulty, there was miscommunication in both directions. That's where the rumor started. This is a small thing. Not many people are thinking badly of Dharmapala, but I will tell them that you are not a bad person. Buddhists in general consider Amida and Dainichi as the absolute Buddha, but Nichiren Shonin never accepted this understanding. *Myohorengekyo* teaches that these figures are just temporary Buddhas. The true Buddha is Sakyamuni himself who lived in India. Almost 2200 years after Sakyamuni died, nobody has preached this fact [that Sakyamuni is the true Buddha] yet. Shonin's doctrine considers the historical Sakyamuni as the only Buddha. People in India should remember Shonin's doctrine well.

DHARMAPALA: When I first read Nichiren Shonin's biography, I came to know that Shonin said that the true Buddha is Sakyamuni, the true law is *novo*. I was glad that Shonin's teaching captured the true situation of the Buddha. However, Shonin's teaching is buried in one corner of Japan. It hasn't risen and made the jump to the world. Today the Honganji temple is the most active. They have a temple, a magazine, missionaries in America and India and other foreign countries. Therefore disciples of Nichiren Shonin have not achieved the same level as Honganji. Why is that?

TANAKA: My face sweats a lot over this situation. Our disciples have weak minds and actions, fighting among themselves. After the teacher has gone for a while, we lost our ambition/energy, and it's like we have been sleeping until now. We cannot get to the same level as Honganji, our cousin sect. We are in the state of clenching our teeth and crossing our arms and feeling regret over our situation. 300–400 years ago our sect had the power to take possession of half of Japan, but we collided with the government. Heavy restrictions were placed on us, and the monks at the time mistakenly made a makeshift law, and now we are in this state. Like Buddhism was conquered by Hinduism, and like Buddhism collapsed while Hinduism became powerful, we have had our ups and downs, but the problem does not lie in the doctrine itself. The reason for our downfall was human frailty and politics.

DHARMAPALA: I think even though the sect has very sophisticated and deep principles, without the action it is like holding a treasure bowl and not showing it to the world. The first teaching has collapsed, and the second teaching [Honganji] has come into being. In order to replace that first teaching, one acts unjustly. It is pitiful when someone acts improperly in order to overcome the first teaching.[136] The things that Honganji does today is something that a disciple of Nichiren Shonin has to do.

TANAKA: It is true that Nichiren's disciples are inactive nowadays. I deeply regret this, and I have been fighting to change this for 20 years. I wrote a book about that called *Shumon-no-ishin* [The sect and its reformation]; the text is written in Japanese, but please study it.

DHARMAPALA: I am greatly impressed that the ideal of Nichiren Shonin's teachings is to unite the world and that his teaching preaches that Japanese Buddhism which is built by Nichiren Shonin has to go back to

---

136. I cannot do justice to the Japanese, but the sense here is "steal something in order to acquire the first teaching."

India. I would like Shonin's disciples to work for that goal and make it come true as soon as possible.

TANAKA: I agree, however we have to first reform Japanese Buddhism, which has decayed and to purify the Japanese nation. Later on it should influence other countries.

DHARMAPALA: I know that you need to reform modern Buddhism in Japan, but I think the reason why Japan achieved the highest status in the world was because Japan has shown warrior spirit [bu, or bushido]. Especially the rare Nichiren's Buddhism should show this to foreign countries as fast as it can.

TANAKA: Exactly. When we introduce our doctrine, we are not forgetting to teach the pure content.

DHARMAPALA: At that time you both benefit from that. The biography of Shonin and his doctrine, which is pure Buddhism should be shown to foreign countries immediately. They are waiting for it. It is urgent business. I really hope that you Mr. Tanaka work hard.

TANAKA: I understand. I will work on it in the near future. I would like to ask you what is the name of the magazine you publish?

DHARMAPALA: It's called The Maha Bodhi, which is published once a month in hopes uniting the world's Buddhists.

TANAKA: I would like to exchange it with my publication, *Myoshu*. I would like to submit an article. How does that sound?

DHARMAPALA: Yes. That is what I most hope for. My magazine allows writers to submit an article that is less than three pages. But it can run over 6 or 7 issues. My magazine is read by Buddhists all over the world, including America, Burma, Siam. It publishes 700 copies. I have to provide 30 yen each month for publication. Even though I may starve, once I started publishing this magazine I will continue to do so. I would like to submit my article to your magazine *Myoshu*. Please publish it.

TANAKA: It is such a difficult thing to continue publishing a magazine that contains your own doctrine. My magazine *Myoshu* suffers a loss of 150–60 yen every month, but we are still publishing it. I greatly sympathize with your situation. I would like Mr. Takayama to submit an article occasionally for the *Maha Bodhi* magazine.

TAKAYAMA: Sure. I don't mind submitting articles on Nichiren Shonin or other religious matters occasionally.

DHARMAPALA: I would be greatly honored to receive an article from Professor Takayama in my magazine. I would like to hear your sophisticated opinions about things related to Buddhism or Nichiren or religion, philosophy or art.

At this time lunch arrived, and Yamakawa left. While he was gone, Dharmapala, Takayama, and Tanaka continued their discussion. Takayama took over as interpreter.

DHARMAPALA: My country is the island of Sri Lanka. We have a close relationship between Buddhism and the royal family just as in Japan. Both help each other. Our ancestors liked to make war, and we have been fighting against foreign countries. We started a war more than 2000 years ago, and we have been fighting up to the last Sri Lankan king. This royal family descends from a long family line like Japan. The highest and most respected royal family in the world is the Japanese royal family. I think the next one in rank is our royal family, however a lot of people consider Sri Lanka and India as the same country, and take me for an Indian. There are lots of people who think Sri Lanka is part of India, a dependency of India. I really don't like that. It's like the relationship between Japan and China. Sri Lanka and India are similar to that geographically. In Japan people expelled the Ainu people, and my ancestors expelled the natives of India and established an independent country. Sri Lanka is like Japan in having only one island. It has the beautiful scenery of mountains and water, and that is similar to Japan. There is one small location that is surrounded by blue mountains in all four directions like Kamakura. Our king resides there. Our people are all Buddhists.

The group went to see several old Buddhist artifacts displayed in the Taikaku hall. Dharmapala's face was filled with joy as he listened to the explanation of each item, and later that day they left to visit Takiguchi, the spiritual land of the saints of Nichiren Buddhism. After they returned from seeing the big Buddha, rain began to fall. The group arrived at Takiguchi Dera, and first they visited the *Shikikawa-do* (hall). They visited the place where evil Japanese people tried to break the pillar of Japan. Dharmapala looked moved. Then they went to see the headmaster there. He provided tea and sweets. Tanaka pointed to the picture of Seiso-takiguchi-hounan-zu (the scroll picture of the saint ancestor, the Buddha Takiguchi).[137]

DHARMAPALA: After looking at this picture, I think about how much brave Shonin has suffered. I received a boundless lesson and power by looking at this drawing of challenges and obstacles, which says that any servant

137. The Buddha under the appellation "Takeguchi" on the model of the Dainichi Buddha.

of Buddha cannot go wrong. I would like this picture to be copied and
sent to foreign countries.

TANAKA: Later on I would like to send this picture with the complete biography of Nichiren Shonin to you.

DHARMAPALA: I think that the words that came from a great person's mouth
should be realized in real life. I came to know that Nichiren Shonin had
a great ideal of uniting the world by spreading Japanese Buddhism to the
West. However this great ideal, cannot be reached in real life. It is urgent
business for the disciples of Nichiren Shonin to spread the doctrine in
foreign countries.

KUWABARA, here speaking for the first time: Do you believe this mystery
that changes in the weather or the sky as portrayed in the picture known
as Takiguchi honanzu [picture] protected Nichiren Shonin?

DHARMAPALA: I firmly believe in that mysterious fact because of the virtue
of *myoho* and the virtue of Shonin.

FUJIWARA, the headmaster of the temple: In India there is only Hinayana
thinking nowadays.

DHARMAPALA: Exactly. I'm the only one who is familiar with Mahayana.
I have been persecuted by Hinduism, Christianity, other religions, the
Hinayana religion, and the British government. I have been advocating
the arguments of Mahayana Buddhism. The mayor of Calcutta told me
that I should be gentle. So I said to the mayor, Buddha has been always
active. He said that we should preach *myohorengekyo* in any situation.
Whatever happens I follow this idea that I don't change my behavior.
Therefore my nature is to be persecuted, and I think it is funny to find
my god-given job has this characteristic. My father said that I was like
fireworks.

FUJIWARA: Are you an *upasaka* or a *bhikkhu*?

DHARMAPALA: I am neither *bhikkhu* or *upasaka*. I think *bhikkhus* who
have mercy, knowledge, law, and virtue have not vanished even today
after the Buddha the Great has gone. *Upasakas* [lay devotees] have wives
and children. I am not a bhikkhu, but I don't have a wife or children
so I am not an upasaka. I created a category by myself and called myself *Dharma pracharaka* [preacher of *Dharma*]. Therefore Dharma is the
shortened form of *satsudharma*, and the meaning of that phrase is "the
person who preaches and spreads the *myoho* doctrine." Therefore, I have
been practicing the ten *haramitsu* [virtues].

TANAKA: By practicing ten *haramitsu* and claiming that you are practicing
myoho denies Nichiren Shonin's teachings.

DHARMAPALA: Practicing ten *haramitsu* is the practicing of *myoho* in other words; using this I want to get the truth of *myoho*. What do you think?

TANAKA: That's not it. Even though you try to understand the basic teaching of *myoho* and you proceed to practice the three different practices, six *haramitsu*, and ten *haramitsu* and try to bring those practices together with the truth that is like building a palace on sand. Or if you try to understand the basic teachings of *myoho* and practice the ten *haramitsu* alone, that is like building a palace on sand. Therefore we must believe the basics of our teaching of *myoho* and then later on we should discuss the details. That is Nichiren Shonin's argument.

DHARMAPALA: When you practice *myoho* for yourself that is not good. The right method is to follow Nichiren Shonin's practices when we teach *myoho* to disciples. Am I right?

TANAKA: That's it exactly. For both cases—teaching yourself or teaching others—there are two sides of Nichiren Shonin's *myoho* practices. One is "believing and acting." The other is "doctrine and acting." Believing and acting is to believe the truth of *myoho* and to devote your life to the Buddhist teaching by practicing. Doctrine and acting is to practice ten *haramitsu* and others. Nichiren Shonin preached that believing and acting is the basis of the training, doctrine and acting becomes the support of the person who is training.

DHARMAPALA: The chief property of *myoho* is the ten *haramitsu*.[138] For example, as a human has four extremities/limbs and one head and they make up the human body we can reach the truth of *myoho* by practicing the ten *haramitsu* as a single body.

TANAKA: That is the way to discuss the secondary factors. It is Sanjo's teaching, and not the Buddha's teaching, that one tries to prioritize the secondary attributes and leave the doctrine behind. We cannot discuss this argument in one day. It needs a deep understanding of this teaching. I would like to discuss this point further when you become familiar with understanding the Japanese Big Vehicle [Mahayana] teaching. I would like to show you the English translation of Nichiren Shonin later on.

DHARMAPALA: It is like the way science breaks reality into parts in order to observe more clearly and in addition to extract the one set of terms [e.g., neutrons and protons] from the system to interpret reality more

138. Along the side of the Japanese characters for *myoho* in the original appears the expression *satsudharma*, which Dharmapala used earlier to provide an alternative rendering for *myoho*.

generally. *Myoho* likewise becomes the ten *haramitsu* when we break it down. When we synthesize the components, it should become *myoho*.

TANAKA: There are many Buddhists who come to understand that analysis and forget the basis which is *myoho*. The ten *haramitsu* which does not anticipate the *butsujochi* [knowledge of Mahayana]. It is the doctrine of a life buoy. Let me put the ten *haramitsu* into the proper context— Nichiren Shonin devoted his life to preaching and spreading the *butsujochi* or the *myoho*.

DHARMAPALA: It has been almost 700 years since Nichiren Shonin died. It will be nice to have a great person like Nichiren preaching and spreading the teaching now, but at the level of our preaching and spreading we cannot avoid breaking things down. Nichiren Shonin was a mysterious, great person, and even though he did not break down the *myoho* to preach, Shonin's superiority was the explanation. There were a lot of people who recognized the greatness in Shonin himself and they believed everything he said as it was/as he said it. But we are not this now. Therefore there is no way for us to preach and spread with the same height [at the same level of sophistication]. In other words, we should train and replace mysterious greatness by practicing the ten *haramitsu*.

TANAKA: In Nichiren Shonin's teaching to his disciples there are lots of gates/steps along the path to enter Buddhism, but we proceed from the gate of faith. That belief requires devoting one's life to the Buddha. It is like the way Shonin and Sakyamuni subordinated themselves completely to preach and spread the doctrine. This means that from the beginning we disciples did not set ourselves up as a standard/paradigm. We should make *myoho* or Sakyamuni who was a vigorous person or Nichiren Shonin the standard. If we follow this ideal, we can attain *myoho*, Sakyamuni, and Shonin's virtue. Especially today it is obvious that Nichiren Shonin is an example of the one who obtained *myoho* by devoting his life to the Buddha. The gate of the Buddha's teachings of belief and action in *myoho* can be shown vividly in fact. We have to follow the path of our training to attain the *myoho* nowadays.

DHARMAPALA: As you said, it is important that you believe. Of course if I go to America now and suddenly shout "practice the *myohorengekyo*," that is not going to be effective. We have to preach what the *myoho* is by breaking it down. But if we preach what the *myoho* is, they will get it.

TANAKA: Exactly. The thing that I'm saying now is the basis of the doctrine. The things that you say are the methods of preaching *myoho*. When the doctrine is being established and propagated, we need good disciples of

Nichiren Shonin and good disciples have a belief in devoting one's life to Buddhism as the basis and to have the knowledge and the ability to take action, as well as to have body, mouth, and strong mind. The basis of our teaching is the faith that is true and deep in its roots, we shouldn't forget this.

DHARMAPALA: I agree. In Japan there already was a Buddhism before Nichiren Shonin lived, and there was a favorite convenient way of teaching the highest doctrine for both the preachers' side and the listeners' side, but it is hard to approach people in a place like America nowadays who have no background in Buddhism.

TANAKA: That's true, but there is a gate to Buddhist teaching which can be opened in *myohorengekyo*. This Buddhist teaching is the one that blends any kind of ideal with the ideal of *myohorengekyo*. Therefore there is a way to bring people who have other doctrines to *myoho*.

DHARMAPALA: In that case what method of preaching and spreading should we take?

TANAKA: In that case we look at the person's thinking in terms of their personality, their country, and the historical moment with the eye of *hokekyo* [alternate form of *myoho*]. We will break that evil thought [ideals people believed before *myoho*] and suppress it. We will capture their good thoughts by teaching that *myoho* is the highest truth, and we will teach them the truth that is the source of the big, united method.

DHARMAPALA: I have exactly the same opinion as you do. *Myoho* means the true law, and in other words it is the law of truth. I have been acting for this law that is the absolute truth of Buddha. Therefore, I don't have any plans except for preaching and spreading this *myoho*. My pleasure lies here.

TANAKA: *Myohorengekyo* is the big truth for approaching Buddha. Preaching this to the world is a merciful act of bhagavat [blessing].[139] It is our job as children of Buddha to preach this merciful truth completely which is the same as devoting our lives to the Buddha. Nichiren Shonin is the one and only example of this preaching and propagating person of *myoho*, and he is a man of infinite mercy. There is no other way but to follow Shonin's thinking.

DHARMAPALA: I am truly delighted that I could hear so much discussion of Nichiren Shonin. If there is anything translated into English about Shonin, please send it to me. For example, if there is a five-hundred page

139. I am not sure what to make of Tanaka's using the Sanskrit expression for blessing.

publication, I will bring it to America and try to advocate for the contents. After this visit, I'm going to be in America for at least a year, and I'm thinking of moving about all of the states.

TANAKA: Could you give me an address in America where I could reach you? If circumstances permit, I would like to send you the work translated.

DHARMAPALA: The biography of Nichiren by Mr. Lloyd was well-done. That book is very good. Right now so many people are waiting to listen to *myoho*. It should be translated immediately and spread to the world. I am eager to be one of the people who teaches and spreads Nichiren Shonin's doctrine. Japan is in fact the country of great hope for preaching and spreading the *myoho*. I hope the day will come soon that the doctrine of Nichiren Shonin which is the big light of the world and flower of the country will spread across the whole planet together with the culture of Japan.

Yamakawa announced that the conversation had ended. The group urged Dharmapala to have dinner with them, but he said it was raining and he had a prior engagement making it difficult to stay overnight. He said he appreciated the good wishes of his hosts and asked to be excused. At this time the headmaster respectfully gave him money. Everyone moved to Fujisawa and went into the restaurant called Toukatei (Peach Flower restaurant). At the table the group had another conversation.

DHARMAPALA: Today I felt pleasure that I haven't had recently. Not only did we visit the spiritual trace of the great respectful person, but also I was able to hear the gospel of Nichiren. I am delighted. There are no words to express my thankfulness for Tanaka sensei's deep and kind company.

TANAKA: I am satisfied with this deep path that I could respectfully introduce you, a person from the motherland of Buddhism and a representative of the people of your country, to the spiritual marks of the great teacher who lived and preached in the mappo era [the period after the Buddha had died] and I could also tell you about one drop of doctrine. I am satisfied.

DHARMAPALA: I very much love Japan, especially when I recall Nichiren Shonin. My sympathy becomes very deep and more and more I respect his virtue.

TANAKA: Mr. Dharmapala, if you have any chance to come to Japan later, I would like to take you to other spiritual places like Minobu-san [Mount Minobu]. I want to live in Japan until the end of my life. I expect that my hope can be achieved later in life.

Because you are an Indian person, people try to invite you for lunch or to give a lecture as a curiosity or amusement. I don't like that. I would like to introduce foreigners to great or interesting places in this country as much as possible. That is not just for me but it is for them. When we speak of "interesting" places in our country we mean the Emperor's quarters and Nichiren Shonin which cannot be seen in other countries. These two well-known figures have been honored not only by this country alone but also they should provide salvation for the future of the whole world. In other words they are like "the father of a future not yet born." Nichiren Shonin's one tiny sound leaves the whole world in his debt, and those wise philosophers who brought civilization to Europe and America should pay back that debt. The poor Westerners are infatuated with material civilization, while the civilization of the spirit has proceeded to the highest level in Japan but those Westerners don't recognize the true value of Japanese Buddhism.

DHARMAPALA: In fact foreigners are trying to find peace of mind in incomplete religions such as Christianity. Whenever I see them, I can't prevent myself from giving them a punch. In the past days I have visited Miss Pease at the Japanese Women's College. She had an arrogant attitude as if talking to an Indian person in their country. I think that British people are in fact insensitive, stupid people. It's better to hit them with a wooden stick, and give them a surprise. Someone asks. Is there any heaven in Buddhism like in Christianity? I say that is a stupid question. The heaven in Christianity or other religions is in fact the hell in Buddhism. The man who asked the question is surprised and asks, then what is Buddha? I say that question again is silly. If you would like to avoid stupidity, you should study the Buddha, I answered. In order to answer the question from this stupid person, I have to keep providing stupid answers. I really hate these stupid answers.

There is a skillful metaphor to express the moral delusion of the society. In ancient times there was a big group of lions. One of the big lions had so many offspring. There was one lion cub who was raised by a group of dogs, and he thought he was himself a dog. When the parent lion called this lion cub, he didn't come, and he became afraid of the parent lion. The parent lion chased after the cub furiously. The lion cub was surprised and cried out, running away. When he was roared without being aware, he heard a lion's voice [his own]. He came to know that he was a lion in fact after hearing his voice and went back to his parent's group. I think all people understand the Buddha's teaching but don't recognize it, and that this fact is exactly like this story. Surely I

大式長正装の先生　大正十年　六十一歳

8. Chigaku Tanaka in regalia.

think Buddhism is constructive optimism and Christianity is destructive optimism, and the pessimism of brahmana teaching goes astray and is silly, and so on.

Yamakawa provided this account of Dharmapala's departure: We forgot, according to Yamakawa, that time was passing during the conversation. The last train leaves at 10:00 p.m. and it will leave soon. So we promised to see each other again and we parted. Tanaka didn't request anything, he simply took Dharmapala from another line of Buddhism to the spiritual traces [places sacred to Shonin]. Tanaka was able to make a connection between Dharmapala and the law of truth. He corrected Dharmapala's misunderstanding of Buddhism. And he was able to let Dharmapala know that the core of the great Buddha belongs to Nichiren Shonin's doctrine, and he spared no effort—in time and cost—and he was willing to do the trip called "after Shonin passed away, the Indian came to the spiritual place for the first time and prayed." The pure Buddhist event in which the doctrine and the Japanese spirit [*kien*] were taught [literally, the seed was planted, which is the title of the second section of this article] to the visitor came to end. Dharmapala was satisfied/gratified with Tanaka sensei, and he was very impressed with the Japanese people's kindness. Mr. Dharmapala's face was filled with deep emotion because he wanted to make Tanaka sensei his older brother in this teaching. Mr. Dharmapala looked as if he thought Tanaka sensei was "on the left side of things" [thought that Tanaka was the more important person]. The train has come, and they said how sad it was to say goodbye. Dharmapala and Mr. Kudo went into the train together. Dharmapala repeated the promise to exchange pictures. We concluded our meeting of this day with the whistle of the train.

Tanaka's self-confidence derived from more than the idea that Japanese Buddhism was Buddhism fully mature or that Nichiren preached real Buddhism. When he told Dharmapala that Buddhism was not *myohorengekyo*'s house, but *myohorengekyo* Buddhism's house, he made a claim about truths that had grown deeper—Nichirenism outstripped its Indian origins. Under these circumstances, he would hardly want to cast his lot with Dharmapala's campaign for a united Buddhist world. He gave some credence to Dharmapala's exposition of center-oriented and cosmo-magical cakravartin kingship for the way it confirmed a parallel formulation in the *Nihongi*, the ancient source on Japan's mythic origins and early emperors that was equally center-oriented and inclusive.[140] As they were conversing, another long-distance effect occurred in the form of Japanese efforts to make a connection with South Asia. Just before Dharmapala met Tanaka, Okakura Kakuzo had arrived in India to negotiate with the Saivite abbot of Bodh Gaya for a Japanese presence at the place.

140. See Aston, *Nihongi: Chronicles of Japan*, 131.

CHAPTER THREE

Universalists Abroad

We have embarked on this pilgrimage to see signs of the history of India's entry into the universal.
—Rabindranath Tagore, on setting out for Java, 1927

After the annual Theosophical Society meetings in Adyar in 1890, Dharmapala traveled north with two young Japanese—Kozen Gunaratana,
a Shingon monk, and Chiezo Tokuzawa, a layman—who had been studying
in Colombo.[1] Once they reached Bodh Gaya, Dharmapala made a vow at the
platform that marks the spot where the Buddha achieved enlightenment.
The vow set the course for the rest of his life:

> As soon as I touched with my forehead the Vajrasana a sudden impulse
> came to my mind. It prompted me to stop here & take care of this sacred
> spot, so sacred that nothing in the world is equal to this place where
> Prince Sakya Sinha gained enlightenment under the Bodhi tree. . . .
> When the sudden impulse came to me I asked Kozen Priest whether he
> would join me and he joyously assented, and more than this he had been
> thinking the same thing. We both solemnly promised that we would

---

1. As a Shingon monk Kozen had reason for his pursuit of esoteric teachings and secret
doctrines. At Bodh Gaya he cast oracles to determine whether the monks Dharmapala had
summoned from Lanka were coming—he saw three en route (Diary, March 3, 1891)—and
determined by a later consultation that Dharmapala's father was unhappy with him, Olcott
indifferent, and Hikkaduve pleased (Diary, March 5, 1891). Tokuzawa had been sent by his
teacher Bun'yu Nanjio to study Sanskrit with Pandit Batuwantudawe with the idea that both
students would return to Japan and devote themselves to the study of the Northern and Southern canons.

stop here until some Buddhist priests come and take charge of the place.
(Diary, January 22, 1891)

Within two weeks, he had put his own life at issue:

> For six years our Bodhisat underwent his severest trials and subjected
> himself to the most trying penances near about Uruwela [now Bodh
> Gaya]. I have undertaken this work and I mean to carry it through but
> not leave it until I see priests take charge of the temple. If I have no
> means to live starvation would be the end—better to die than to aban-
> don the place. I love Ceylon and the work I was carrying on there, and I
> love this too. If my people don't care to send priests here I shall not see
> them again. (Diary, March 2, 1891)

His vow reinscribes the Buddha's promise that he would remain seated under
the Bodhi tree until he achieved enlightenment or sacrifice his life in trying.

Dharmapala's efforts to recover Bodh Gaya, missionize, and reform Sinhala society duly noted, it is useful to remember that analogy. In all of his
wanderings and projects, he engaged the social world for the sake of his own
spiritual growth. He practiced meditation, he kept to his vow of celibacy—
feeling pangs of self-loathing when he came close to violating it—and he
presented himself as more than a social activist. In Bodh Gaya, the echoes
between the Buddha's life and his own became that much stronger. The
vow he made there is usually interpreted as evidence of his social activism,
returning a Buddhist place to its rightful owners. His words can be read in a
second way, as imitating the vow the Buddha made at the same place—goal
achieved or death.

At first Dharmapala tried to recruit monks from home by mail, and he
got no results (Diary, January 25, 1891). In six weeks he left Bodh Gaya—his
vow notwithstanding—visiting Calcutta and Burma before returning south.
In Colombo he established the Maha Bodhi Society in May 1891 and turned
his mind to recruiting monks in person. To do so he went with his father to
see Hikkaduve (Diary, May 18, 1891), and he appeared to agree to help. Six
weeks later Dharmapala came to realize that Hikkaduve "shilly-shakes"
(Diary, July 3, 1891), leading him to four Ramanna *nikaya* monks who had
their own plans to visit Bodh Gaya. He convinced them not simply to visit
but to stay at the place and escorted them north on a P&O steamer. Once he
had installed the monks—Dunuville Chandrajoti, Matale Sumangala, Anuradhapura Pemananda, and Galle Sudassana—at the Burmese resthouse, he

found lodging in Gaya and began a campaign to establish a Buddhist presence at the place by approaching the Saivite mahant who controlled Bodh
Gaya.[2] "The Lord Buddha conquered the world by love and virtue," he wrote
in his diary. "I shall try to conquer Mahant by the same process" (July 19,
1891). He called on British officials stationed nearby and two days later
hoisted the Maha Bodhi flag.

It looked like love and virtue might do the trick.[3] The mahant offered to
sell land to the Buddhists, even upping his initial offer to two *bighas* (Diary,
July 19, 1891).[4] He was thinking of land west of the inspection bungalow,
but Grierson the collector urged him to sell the Buddhists another parcel
(Diary, July 31, 1891). When Dharmapala visited on July 31, 1891, the mahant had turned cold. When he returned on August 17 with a fellow Theosophist from Gaya, they came to an agreement:

> The land was at last given; but it is only a bigha. After one full month's
> of anxiety am glad that the land had been got. The Voice speaks in soli-
> tude. Happy is the one who listens faithfully. Great works couldn't be
> accomplished without sacrifice. To have obtained this little plot of land
> it took, so many days of parlaying, and the difficulties were indeed great,
> notwithstanding Mr. Grierson's assertion of the Mahant's Geniality
> which was only skin deep. Now we can say that we have got a home in
> the sacred of land [*sic*]. After an exile of nearly seven centuries we have
> again got a foothold. . . . How good if the King of Siam graciously conde-
> scends to build the Monastery. (Diary, August 17, 1891)

Dharmapala's plans were soon confounded—the King of Siam would not be
building a monastery at Bodh Gaya, three of the four monks would quickly

2. Before the end of his first visit (January–February 1891), Dharmapala found that Kozen
wanted to leave. Dharmapala said that his determination had weakened (*hita durvala svabha-
vayaka pä min*). Guruge, *Dharmapala Lipi*, 236.

3. The mahant showed hospitality to important visitors, and the Burmese monks who
came seasonally to Bodh Gaya stayed in his quarters (Diary, January 31,1891). Thus the four Sinhala monks who made their way from Gaya to Bodh Gaya a few days before Dharmapala were
put up in the *baradari* (second story) of the mahant's monastery. Dharmapala made them move
to the Burmese resthouse. The first of many mistakes that undermined Dharmapala's intervention at Bodh Gaya was his dismissing—all the talk of love aside—the mahant's hospitality
(Diary, July 19, 1891).

4. The size of a bigha varied by region across north India. In Bihar and central India, the
bigha amounted to 3,025 square yards, or 5/8 of an acre. Even though 5/8 of an acre is not an
unappreciable plot of land, Dharmapala had estimated that first plot of land at 42,000 square
feet (Diary, July 26, 1891). Had he been able to buy that first parcel, it would have given him a
foothold of approximately one acre.

leave their post, the mahant died, and his successor had less sympathy for Buddhist aspirations. The Giri monks had a deed (*firman*) from a Mughal prince dating to 1729 and, although the first mahant sold him a small plot of land, he had not the slightest interest in parting with the central shrine or its precincts. The new mahant's hostility derived, at least in part, from Dharmapala's own activities, beginning with hoisting the flag.

After the Theosophical convention, the visit to Bodh Gaya, and the trip home via Burma, Dharmapala settled in Calcutta. His motives at Bodh Gaya were both Buddhist and Theosophical, not as independent interests but transidiomatic ones. His diaries of those first days make reference to dhyana meditation (January 9, 1891), occultism (January 15, 1891), Tibet and esoteric Buddhism (January 19, 1891), the practice of yoga (January 30, 1891), and working for humanity [the capital letter H tends to appear in Theosophy talk as a sign of high aspirations] (February 17, 1891), as well as a Bengali brahmacarya who had trekked to Tibet and encountered esoteric Buddhism (February 25, 1891). He took advice from beyond: "I shall listen to the Voice that speaks to me in Silence" (February 26, 1891). Once settled in Calcutta, he encountered "the first Asian social group of any size whose mental world was transformed through its interactions with the West."[5] Theosophists were Bengalis whose lives had been transformed more than most—they were freethinking and cosmopolitan, and they were searching. As Henry Cotton observed,

> Theosophy . . . has lately been exercising a transitory influence. The subtleness of its teaching, and the degree of scope which the supernatural interferences of spiritual, or so-called astral, phenomena afford to the imagination, are features peculiarly congenial to the Hindoo intellect. . . . The Indian mind has also been able to see that in some occult manner, but with a definiteness and force quite unmistakable, the European adherents of the system have been elevated by a kind of moral regeneration from indifferentism, and sometimes positive dislike, into sincere and hearty sympathy with the people of the country.[6]

Whatever effect "astral phenomena" had on the Bengali elite, Theosophical egalitarianism—starting with Olcott, Blavatsky, and Allan Octavian Hume—had as much appeal in Bengal as Lanka.

---

5. Tapan Raychaudhuri, quoted in Dipesh Chakrabarty, *Provincializing Europe: Postcolonial Thought and Historical Difference* (Princeton, NJ: Princeton University Press, 2000), 4.

6. *New India, or India in Transition* (London: Kegan Paul, Trench, Trübner, 1907), 275–6.

Dharmapala stayed first at the home of Neel Kamal Mukherjee, *banian* to a major petroleum company, and a Theosophist, who called his home "Holy House," and took a vow of celibacy at age forty two. Norendronath Sen, editor of a newspaper congenial to Buddhism, became his patron and led him to other "good people" (*bhadralok*).[7] They were Hindus but sympathetic to Buddhism because they were Theosophists as well as Indians with civilizational pride in Buddhism. Their support gave him a place to begin.

> Neel Comul Babu married the Aunt of Gogen Babu. Rabi Babu's [Rabindranath Tagore] sister was married to the brother of Neel Comul and Suprakash Ganguly is the grandson of Rabi Babu's sister. This was in 1907. In his early manhood Rabi Babu lived a bacchanalian life of sensuality. He began Shanti Niketan in 1907 or 1904. I went to see his father the Maharishi with Priya Nath Sastri, when I was living at 2, Creek Row. A few days later a return visit was paid to me by the late Devijendra Babu, the eldest brother of Rabi Babu. I became acquainted with all the Tagores through Neel Comul Babu. I knew Raja Jotindra Mohan Tagore, Kally Kissen Tagore. But for the hospitality shown to me by Neel Comul Babu it wouldn't have been possible for me to start the M.B. work in Calcutta. Norendra Babu & Neel Comul were my best friends. (Diary, June 7, 1926)

In other words, he knew the Bengalis who counted in Calcutta. The people he never came to know were Muslims, Christians, non-elite Bengalis, Chinese Buddhists, and British businesspeople. His relationship with Arakanese Buddhists living in Calcutta had its moments but never came to much.

When Dharmapala introduced the celebration of the Buddha's birthday in 1896, the Bengali elite turned out in large numbers, but they came not so much to venerate the Buddha as to celebrate the virtue of a great man who could be understood as a fellow Indian, a Hindu or simply a civilizational asset.[8] Sen made the *Indian Mirror* a vehicle for propagandizing the Buddhist cause. He believed that the salvation of India depended on the fusion of Hinduism and Buddhism and made daily homage to the Buddha by raising a bronze image of the Buddha above his head and confessing "his allegiance

---

7. St. Nihal Singh, "This Journal," *Journal of the Maha Bodhi Society* 100 (1992): 30–33, reprinted from *Journal of the Maha Bodhi Society* (1910). Dharmapala told Singh that his relationship with Mukherjee was "more fraternal than friendly. In some life Neel Comul and I must have been blood brothers" (31).

8. "The First Great Celebration of Gautama Buddha's Birthday Anniversary in Calcutta," *Journal of the Maha Bodhi Society* 5 (1896): 20–1.

9. Norendronath Sen, Calcutta.

to the great Cause."[9] He pursued other forms of unity and fusion—at the 1882 meeting of Theosophists he called for a press federation of Indian-owned newspapers; in 1884 he proposed a national assembly for India; in 1907 he proposed a union of Buddhist associations in the British Empire.[10] With his guidance Dharmapala gave his first lecture in India, taking pains to emphasize the kinship of Hinduism and Buddhism. The argument for

9. Satyendra Nath Sen, foreword to *The Anagarika Brahmachari Dharmapala*, "Buddhism in Its Relationship to Hinduism," (Calcutta: Maha Bodhi Society, 1918), ii.

10. Anil Seal, *The Emergence of Indian Nationalism: Collaboration and Competition in the Later Nineteenth Century* (London: Cambridge University Press, 1968), 257 and 265.

the unity of the two religions gratified Theosophical sensibilities.[11] Having traced the history of the Maha Bodhi Society, he said that he had pledged his life "to bring[ing] about a reconciliation between the Buddhists and Hindus of India."[12] In May 1892, he established the *Journal of the Maha Bodhi Society and the United Buddhist World* as a vehicle for achieving two goals, returning Buddhism to India and recovering Bodh Gaya for the Buddhists of the world.[13]

The plan to recover Bodh Gaya depended on Dharmapala's also imagining that he could create a pan-Asian community that had never existed—Buddhists now practicing a variety of regional (Burmese, Siamese, Sinhala) and sectarian (Jodo Shinshu, Nichiren, Theravada, Mahayana) Buddhisms. In October 1892 he returned to Bodh Gaya to hold an International Buddhist Conference. As he put it, "After 691 years the Buddhists of all countries met together at the Central Shrine" (Diary, October 30, 1891). The conference was "international" in a local way, drawing a handful of Buddhist participants, virtually all of them living nearby—Kozen Gunaratana and Tokuzawa Chiezo, for instance, represented Japan—or recruited by way of Theosophical connections.[14] The convention agreed to two resolutions—to approach the mahant with a view to purchasing the temple and to collect funds to build a *sangharama* (lodging place for monks) near the Maha Bodhi.[15] The local character of the Japanese delegation aside, Dharmapala flew two flags at the occasion. The Maha Bodhi flag celebrated the inclusiveness of Buddhism by way of the spectrum of colors associated with the

11. That said, Dharmapala's Bengali friends decided it would be best to end the presentation without taking questions "for fear that the lecture would create a discussion" (Diary, October 25, 1891).

12. *London Daily Telegraph*, quoted Rick Fields, *How the Swans Came to the Lake: A Narrative History of Buddhism in America* (Boston: Shambhala, 1992), 115.

13. As early as 1894 Dharmapala began to speak in terms of returning Buddhism to India while explicitly rejecting the idea of converting Indians to Buddhism. "The Present Outlook," *Journal of the Maha Bodhi Society*, 3 (1894): 15–6 at 15. Without conversion, what returning Buddhism to India entailed was simply making the Dhamma available to Indians. Dharmapala's disinterest in conversion derived from his experience with Christian missionizing. But it followed more directly from his putting most of his energy into recovering Bodh Gaya, and it made even more sense in Calcutta by allowing Bengalis to show interest without threatening their own religion or asking too much of them.

14. Alan Trevithick, *The Revival of Buddhist Pilgrimage at Bodh Gaya* (Delhi: Motilal Banarsidass, 2006), 85. Richard Jaffe says that organizing the conference produced considerable correspondence between Dharmapala and Japanese clerics and significant Japanese funding (personal communication).

15. Guruge, *Dharmapala Lipi*, 238.

rays emanating from the Buddha's person. The Japanese flag represented the one industrialized state in Asia, which was also a state not likely to be absorbed in the united Buddhist world. But it was a state simply too captivating for Dharmapala not to treat as first among equals.

The Japanese had a variety of interests in Bodh Gaya before Dharmapala arrived.[16] Kozen Gunaratana was drawn to the place the same way Dharmapala learned of it—by reading an article by Edwin Arnold that described the degradation he had found in

> the spot dear, and divine, and precious beyond every other place on earth, to all the four hundred million Buddhists in China, Japan, Mongolia, Assam, Cambodia, Burma, Arakan, Naupal, Thibet, and Ceylon. . . . If you walked in that spot which all these scores of millions of our race love so well you would observe the shame and grief . . . [of] ancient statues plastered to the walls of an irrigating well . . . [and] stones carved with Buddha's images . . . used as weights in the levers for drawing water. . . . I have seen three feet high statues in an excellent state of preservation, buried under rubbish . . . and the Asokan pillars, the most ancient relics of the site—indeed, "The most antique memorials of all India,"—which graced the temple pavement, are now used as posts of the Mahant's kitchen.[17]

Kozen's teacher shared an interest in Bodh Gaya, and Honganji did as well, if less inspired by Arnold's evocation of a world that had been swept away by events but all the more heartbreaking because it was still visible. For other Japanese Buddhist groups, Bodh Gaya held less appeal, and Dharmapala was never able to get a clear picture of Japanese government policy on its relationship with India or Bodh Gaya in particular. He was no worse off than Bengalis who cared about such things and could make no sense of England's alliance with Japan and the effects of that alliance on India's interests.[18]

16. See Jaffe, "Seeking Sakyamuni."

17. The article appeared in the *London Daily Telegraph*, and parts are reproduced in Fields, *How the Swans Came to the Lake*, 115.

18. Consider this article in the *Bengalee*: "Whilst fire-eaters from the Kaiser down to the 'gentlemen of the pavement' were amusing their leisure hours with the concoction of schemes of offensive and defensive alliances against Japanese aggression, this great nation was steadily pursuing a pacific policy against what must be described as a supremely provocative policy. . . . At one time the Anglo-Japanese policy was attacked as the most inconvenient for England and offensive to America . . . at another subtle insinuations were made against the mother country for maintaining an alliance which went decisively against colonial interest." (February 5, 1909).

Amid complicated and changing circumstances, Dharmapala attempted to cultivate the Japanese while not alienating Indians or the colonial government. At the same time that he was making friendships with Bengalis, he was also trying to separate Bodh Gaya from the mahant. For his part, the mahant made himself an easy man to dislike and party to his own demonization. Dharmapala thought that it would be easy to enlist the unqualified support of all Buddhists, no matter what their local differences. That said, he knew that establishing a Buddhist world as such would be difficult, if not impossible. He knew that even his soft missionizing—not converting people but simply putting the Dhamma on offer—had its own contradictions. Securing control over Bodh Gaya by contrast appeared straightforward. It was the primordial Buddhist place, he assumed, sacred to all Buddhists since a time before sectarian differences began. It was the same kind of thing that the fourteen Buddhist propositions had been for Olcott—something foundational for all Buddhists. Finding that he could not love the mahant into submission, he hoped he could buy Bodh Gaya. Failing that, he moved on to litigating for Buddhist rights at the place. Either course required funds, but he proceeded on the assumption that he could gather financial support from any number of sympathetic people, Buddhist and non-Buddhist alike. Over the years, the Maha Bodhi Society changed and expanded its goals, but one goal endured—making Bodh Gaya Buddhist again—and that struggle, he thought, could lead to a united Buddhist world. All Buddhist societies would recognize the importance of the cause, and he invited the Buddhist countries of Asia to station their own monks at Bodh Gaya. If the prospect of recovering the place was insufficient, having local representatives of one's own Buddhism at the place, standing among monks of other Buddhisms, gave the universal cause a character both national and synoptic.

INTERNATIONALIZING BODH GAYA

The presence of India at Bodh Gaya came with the territory; Japan's presence at the place began with an object, a seven-hundred-year-old statue of the Buddha. Dharmapala received it on his way home from the World's Parliament of Religions. In Japan once again he made contact with many of the people he had met on his earlier visit. This time he had a cause, recovering Bodh Gaya, and he assumed the Japanese would be willing to cast their lot with the Maha Bodhi Society. The support never materialized, but he had a serendipitous meeting with the incumbent of a Buddhist temple in Tokyo.

Dharmapala already had a Buddha image, which he had simply taken from Bodh Gaya:

> This image was made the object of worship at the Temple of the Priest Asahi in Shiba. One day while I was conversing with the Secretary [of the Maha Bodhi Society in Japan] Mr. Horiuchi, he received by post a copy of the M.B.J. [*Journal of the Maha Bodhi Society*]. I opened it and there was an article giving the history of the BudGaya [*sic*] Temple. The writer was Sarat Chandra Das. The article gave the information that the Image which was on the upper floor of the Temple was removed and hidden to save it from the Musulman invaders. The thought came to me to suggest that if a Japanese image could be enshrined in the vacant place it would be meritorious. The idea was taken up by the Revd Asahi, and he got an a [*sic*] historic Image to be placed in the shrine. (Sarnath Notebook no. 6)

On his first trip around the world, Dharmapala carried a token of Bodh Gaya and returned to Bodh Gaya with a token of Japan.

Shuko Asahi had his own reasons for wanting to place another image at Bodh Gaya, telling Dharmapala how sad he was to hear that there was no Buddhism in India, "much less the perfect image of our Lord, the Buddha."[19] He presented Dharmapala with a wooden Buddha. It was the Buddha Amitabha, and Shuko Asahi's understanding of what the image represented must have surprised Dharmapala—"He opened and showed to us the cause of our long, long sufferings from eternity, and made us ready to enter the Infinite Bliss and Eternal Life." Dharmapala by contrast spoke of it as "the historical Buddha image," and being seven hundred years old, it was historical in another sense. The figure was the Savior Buddha of the Western Pure Lands, not Sakyamuni of early Buddhism. But the incongruity reappears in another form in the context of Shinran's teaching about Amitabha: "Beside him there is no Buddha to save one, and accordingly, they should not be worshipped. Not even Sakyamuni . . . is allowed to be worshipped, nor the future Buddha Maitreya, nor any Bodhisatvas, nor gods."[20] The Amitabha image perfected what the Buddha had started at Bodh Gaya. But it also had

19. "The Buddhists and the Hindu Mahant at Buddha-Gaya," *Journal of the Maha Bodhi Society* 3 (1894): 10–11.

20. Junjiro Takakusu, "Buddhism as We Find It in Japan," *Transactions and Proceedings of the Japan Society* 7 (1905–7): 264–79, at 272.

a problematic connection to the man who had achieved enlightenment at Bodh Gaya.[21]

Dharmapala had the image shipped to Colombo, then to Calcutta, and on to Gaya in 1894 (Diary, October 3, 1915). Even before the image was brought to Bodh Gaya, the mahant had begun to resist the presence of the Buddhist monks who had been in and out of the Burmese resthouse since 1891. In January 1893 the mahant's supporters confronted the monks. Thus began a trail of litigation that began with a victory for the Buddhists. However unsettled life at Bodh Gaya must have been after January 1893, events came to a head in February 1895. In his own telling, Dharmapala awoke in the middle of the night in the Theosophical resthouse in Gaya and began to meditate. An idea came to him:

> I thought that the image that I brought from Japan should be brought to the Maha Bodhi. I called for the other monks and induced them to meditate for sometime. Then I decided to bring the image from Gaya to Buddhagaya. I swore seven times that I would offer my life for the sake of the Buddha.[22]

The Maha Bodhi temple already held its own Buddha image, installed by J. D. Beglar—Alexander Cunningham's manager of the restoration—after the British government repaired it in the 1880s.[23] Dharmapala was determined to install his own image of the Buddha as a marker of the Buddhist return to Bodh Gaya, the Maha Bodhi Society's role in administering it, and Japanese support. He wrote that he had received the collector's permission to install the Japanese image as well as the mahant's assent in May 1894. But the mahant changed his mind, and when Dharmapala and his supporters tried to place the image in the temple in 1895, all hell broke loose.

For colonial India the Japanese image was problematic in other ways. One problem was the fear that its installation would legitimate the coming to India of Japanese pilgrims.[24] Newspapers put the incident in the con-

---

21. Amitabha, or Amida, can be seen as an incarnation of the historical Buddha, mitigating the incongruity of his image receiving veneration at the place where the historical Buddha achieved enlightenment (John Strong, personal communication).

22. Jayawardana, *Mage Jivita Kathava*, 53–5.

23. After Francis Buchanan's visit to Bodh Gaya in 1811, the mahant removed the Buddha image that Buchanan reports, installing a Sivalingam in front of the shrine. "The Maha Bodhi Temple at Buddha Gaya," *Journal of the Maha Bodhi Society* 3 (1894): 22-3.

24. Trevithick, *The Revival of Pilgrimage at Bodh Gaya*, 142.

text of religious violence on the upswing in other parts of North India in the 1890s:

> Mr. Dharmapal [*sic*] probably thinks that when the Mahant refused to take back the image and prepared for resistance, the Collector should have interfered and placed the image within the temple with the aid, if necessary, of British soldiers. But every man, with the exception of Mr. Dharmapal and the bigoted editor of the *Indian Mirror*, sees that the cow-slaughter quarrels between Hindus and Musalmans and the Alum riots between the different Musalman sects are enough to occupy the hands of Government. And that it had better not manufacture fresh cause for quarrels. The Editor of the *Indian Mirror* says, with Mr. Dharmapal, that the refusal to take back the image of Buddha into the temple at Buddha Gaya has had the effect of displeasing the people of Japan, China and other Buddhist countries. But suppose the Catholics of Austria, Belgium, France, and other countries want to set up images of Jesus and Mary in a musjid in Turkey and the Mullas object to the proposal.[25]

The editorial was right about Dharmapala's wanting the collector to intervene and place the image in the temple. Doing so offered him a chance to do exactly what the editorial writer feared—reassert the Buddhist presence and internationalize the situation.

When Dharmapala said that he intended the "setting up aforesaid image of LORD BUDDHA . . . presented to the Maha Bodhi Temple by the Japanese nation with befitting rites and ceremonies," he invoked powerful friends. The image, his petition went on, had come from the Japanese nation and not simply the incumbent of a temple in Tokyo. It had been offered by them, not solicited from them, and its proper veneration required

> that the Buddhists' right of perfect freedom of worship in the shape of flowers, scents, &c, and in the suitable embellishment of the temple and its precincts by setting up images, bells, flagstaffs, &c, may be practically enforced.
>
> That the presence of Buddhist priests to officiate at the worship of Buddhist pilgrims being absolutely necessary according to the dictates

---

25. *Dainik-o-Samachar Chandrika*, May 29, 1894. Translations of Indian language newspaper articles come from a colonial government department that began to collect, read, and translate Indian newspapers for official use in 1874. *Report on Native Papers in Bengal*, India Office Records, British Library, IOR/L/6/20. I will henceforth cite Indian newspapers directly.

of the Buddhist religion, their presence in the temple for this purpose
and for the daily worship of LORD BUDDHA which consists in the performance of certain ceremonies, thrice a day as is done in the Buddhist
Temples of Ceylon, Burma, Siam, Japan and China be permitted without
let or hindrance on the part of the Mahant and his people.[26]

Dharmapala had Indian friends too; an article in the *Behar Times* insisted
that he was fighting for a righteous cause and doing so "with the general
sympathy of the Hindu public." The *Indian Mirror* emphasized the international context by arguing that the mahant's resistance would "alienate
the sympathy of Japan, China, and Siam, and political consequences may
ensue."[27]

The mahant was a world renouncer, but he was also one of the richest
men in Bihar, controlling some fifteen thousand acres of land.[28] He was,
in Weberian terms, a "monastic landlord." In local terms, he was a sannyasi whose control of a monastery made him a *zamindar* (landlord) in the
bargain. Having land gave him resources to defend his interests by hiring
the most competent attorneys in Calcutta. He had friends in the British
India Association, most of whom were fellow landowners and politically
influential. The organization was more than a channel for Indian public
opinion. The British India Association created the very possibility of there
being an expressed public opinion in India.[29] Their conservativism was undercut when Norendronath Sen proposed an all-India nationalist association
to take up explicitly political questions.[30] The administrative actions and
litigation that followed Dharmapala's campaign at Bodh Gaya—from W. C.

26. He extracted a lot from the Japan connection: "The image could not be placed in the
temple, and I am at a loss to know what to do with it. If I return it to Japan, it will be an insult
to the nation." "The Buddhists and the Hindu Mahant at Buddha-Gaya," 11. Ven. Asahi was a
Jodo Shinshu priest, but I am uncertain whether his gift had the backing of Honganji. The only
reference that throws any light here is Noguchi's telling Dharmapala that the Japanese government had instructed monks not to interfere at Bodh Gaya (Diary, November 6, 1893).

27. "The Maha Bodhi Temple at Buddha Gaya," quoted in *Journal of the Maha Bodhi Society* 3 (1894) 22–3; *Indian Mirror*, May 25, 1894.

28. Tara Nancy Doyle, "Bodh Gaya: Journey to the Diamond Throne and the Feet of Gayasur" (PhD diss., Harvard University, 1997), 134–5.

29. See Mary Cumpston, "Some Early Indian Nationalists and Their Allies in the British
Parliament, 1851–1906," *English Historical Review* 76, no. 299 (1961): 279–97. The British India Association insisted that the Japanese image's proximity to the central shrine was "deemed
objectionable by a considerable portion of the Hindu Community." "Japanese Image and Buddhist Rest House," *Journal of the Maha Bodhi Society* 18 (1910): 488–92, at 489.

30. Mark Bevir, "Theosophy and the Origins of the Indian National Congress," *International Journal of Hindu Studies* 7 (2003): 109–10.

Macpherson's intervention after the fracas in 1893, Dharmapala's petition to allow the Japanese image to be installed in the Maha Bodhi temple in 1894, the court case that he brought for the return of the Japanese image to the resthouse, administrative actions taken in 1896 after he attempted to lease land in Bodh Gaya, and his efforts between 1897 and 1899 to put up a *dharmasala* for the Buddhists to the mahant's final victory, forcing the removal of the Japanese image from the Burmese resthouse—unfolded against circumstances that drew connections between a local dispute and rising nationalist feeling. Few of these connections worked in Dharmapala's favor.

Nor was he helped by connections between Bodh Gaya and the international context. Japan's success in the Sino-Japanese war in 1894–5 and a more surprising victory in the Russo-Japanese war ten years later forced the British government to reckon with Japan's ambitions across Asia. The country's successes made the Japanese Buddha a symbol of the Japanese nation. When Dharmapala was prevented from leasing land in 1896, *Sanjivani* (March 7, 1896) wrote to this effect:

> One third of the population of the world professes the Buddhist religion. China, Japan, and Siam are Buddhist countries. Budh Gaya, with its temple, is the most sacred spot on earth in the eyes of Buddhists. But they have no right or title to that spot. Hearing that the Budh-Gaya village was going to be sold by public auction, the Buddhists throughout the world felt elated, and began to raise about a lakh of rupees by subscriptions. Prince Damrung of Siam asked his Agent in Calcutta to ascertain whether the property was really on sale. His Agent answered in the negative . . . we cannot believe that the Government has really made up its mind not to allow the Buddhists to acquire land near the Budh Gaya temple.

The article concluded that in blocking the sale the government violated its "praiseworthy neutrality" in religious questions. But whether neutrality was praiseworthy or pernicious depended on whose ox was being gored— *Bangavasi* (April 11, 1903) pointed out that Curzon's Bodh Gaya Commission violated that policy from another direction by merely contemplating whether the place should be made over to the Buddhists.

As the Bodh Gaya Commission was beginning its work, editorial writers played local interests off international ones:

> Attempts are being made on behalf of Buddhists to wrest the Budh Gaya Temple from the hands of the Hindu *Mohant* and give it to Buddhists.

The temple is no doubt of Buddhist origin, but for many centuries Hindus have owned it and offered *pindas* in it. The English Government of India may desire to give it to the Buddhists in order to please the Buddhist Kings and Emperors of Asia, but it ought not to hurt the feelings of its Hindu subjects. Sir Andrew Fraser recently visited the temple and made enquiries about it in the absence of its *Mohant*. If he institutes an impartial enquiry into the matter, he will know that in this temple devout Hindus offer *pindas* to the dead. It is hoped that he will consider every circumstance in connection with the matter before giving his decision in it.[31]

Whatever the extent of Japanese financial support, Dharmapala thought that their charities were insufficient and "the Buddhists Kings and Emperors of Asia" of no help whatsoever. During his visits to Bangkok, he sought out the Thai princes with hopes that one or another of them would put up a monastery at Bodh Gaya or pay him a monthly stipend. On his way home from the World's Parliament of Religions, he met Prince Vajiranana, who suggested that work at home was more important than foreign projects (Diary, January 19, 1894). He seemed to do better with Prince Damrung, who told him that every Thai monk should visit India as part of his education (Diary, January 28, 1894). Prince Devavongsa said that he would bring up the matter of recovering Bodh Gaya with the cabinet, but several ministers responded that the Buddha could be venerated anywhere (Diary, January 26, 1894). When land at Bodh Gaya—variously described as the Tikari Raj land or Maha Bodhi village—became available, Devavongsa inquired about purchasing it (Diary, January 18, 1896). Whatever his intentions, he soon wrote to colonial officials about being importuned by Dharmapala, who was reprimanded by the government.[32]

In the years between his arrival in 1891 and the ultimate court decision in 1910 that the Japanese image could no longer be kept at the Burmese resthouse, Dharmapala found other ways to sustain the Buddhist presence. Having monks stationed permanently at Bodh Gaya created its own problems—they could reside at the Burmese resthouse, but doing so meant lay pilgrims could not use the place. Once three of the original monks left the place, he had to recruit and then support new monks who sporadically made their way to Bodh Gaya from Lanka. In 1901 Lieutenant Governor

31. *Mahima*, November 27, 1903.
32. "The Viceroy's Visit to the City of Gaya and the Maha-Bodhi Temple," *Journal of the Maha Bodhi Society* 4 (1895): 6–7.

Woodburn visited the place and sanctioned the purchase of land on which
Dharmapala built another resthouse for monks.[33] When he next visited
Bodh Gaya, he found the new resthouse completed and the Buddha image
in the shrine covered with turmeric (Diary, May 5, 1904). Inspired by his
travels in the United States, where he had visited Booker T. Washington, he
established an industrial school in Benares (Diary, July 7, 1904). But Bodh
Gaya was considerably more important to him than industrial education or
anything else, merely "extra gains" in his words:

> From January 22, 1891 up to this day with thoughts of perseverance I
> have tried to rescue the Bodhi [shrine]. By that thought good results fol-
> lowed. Building the Calcutta vihara, laying the foundation stone for the
> new Isipatana vihara, starting the *Sinhala Bauddhaya* newspaper, start-
> ing the Maha Bodhi journal, going to the World's Parliament of Religions
> in Chicago, meeting the great upasika Mary Foster. . . . All these are
> extra gains.[34]

Over the years, Dharmapala spent very little time at Bodh Gaya. His mind
was fixed on establishing a Buddhist foothold at the place, and he pursued
that cause all over the world, but he rarely stayed at the place.

On the land he leased from the mahant, Dharmapala had a mud hut
built for the monks he brought to the place, and it served as a kitchen. Conditions were beyond austere because the monks had no toilet facilities, no
steady supply of foodstuffs, and no lay supporters. Once he returned to Calcutta, the monks slipped off one by one: "Three Bhikshus suddenly left BG,
leaving only Chandrajoti. The whole of 1892 he was alone. M. P. Sumangala
returned again" (Sarnath Notebook no. 58). Chandrajoti suddenly left, and
Kozen followed. The only monk who stayed for the long term was Matale Sumangala. He was committed to the cause and one of the Buddhists
involved in the fracas that followed Dharmapala's attempt to install the
Japanese Buddha image. He made Sumangala his representative and gave
him authority to act in his name (Diary, December 4, 1897). Sumangala's
letters kept Dharmapala apprised of the mahant's maneuvers, but Sumangala became involved with a local woman, and the relationship unsettled
Dharmapala. Once Dharmapala had provided money to settle matters with
the woman, Sumangala "remained till the Buddhists were expelled from
BGaya in Feby 1910. He was a very selfish man and very obstinate" (Sarnath

33. Kahawatte Siri Sumedha, *Anagarika Dharmapala: A Glorious Life*, 22.
34. *Sinhala Bauddhaya*, January 27, 1923, reprinted in Guruge, *Dharmapala Lipi*, 242.

Notebook no. 23). Over long stretches of time Sumangala was left to his own devices, representing Buddhist interests usually without other clerics or lay supporters. One time Dharmapala returned to Bodh Gaya and found him nursing an injury to his hand. He explained that he had hurt it doing fencing exercises (Diary, June 10, 1904).

The Japanese Buddha image had its own travails. After the mahant prevented its installation in 1894, the image was kept in a rented house in Gaya for nine months.[35] When Dharmapala tried to place it in the Maha Bodhi temple again in February 1895, the mahant's men removed it to the temple courtyard. The Buddhists apparently returned it to the temple, but when Lord Elgin visited in March, the image had gone missing. The mahant was called to account and had the image moved to the Pancha Pandava temple. Finding that arrangement unacceptable, the Buddhists took the image to the Burmese resthouse, where it remained until 1910. Even with the image removed to the periphery, the mahant was unsatisfied, and he petitioned the commissioner of Patna and the collector of Gaya to have it removed from the resthouse—which meant removing it from Bodh Gaya altogether—on the grounds that he owned the resthouse.[36] The Burmese Buddhists responded by arguing that the resthouse had been built by King Mindon Min in 1880 and intended for Burmese use. There was no doubt that it was the Buddhist place at Bodh Gaya, but exactly what kind of place remained unclear—a monastery for monks who came seasonally, a lodge for lay pilgrims, a storehouse for the valuables that the Burmese king had sent to the place, or a temporary shelter for Burmese workers that was now the de facto possession of the mahant.[37]

35. "The Japanese Image of Buddha," *Journal of the Maha Bodhi Society* 18 (1910): 446–7.

36. In 1907 Dharmapala and his attorneys sailed to Rangoon and took the train to Mandalay to take testimony from King Thibaw's ministers regarding what they remembered of Mindon's intentions (Diary, October 20, 1907).

37. "The History of the Burmese Rest-House at Buddha Gaya," *Journal of the Maha Bodhi Society* 18 (1910): 421–3, at 422. The Calcutta press had been aware of that prospect since the beginning of Dharmapala's campaign to enshrine the Japanese image; *Bangavasi* (June 6, 1896) editorialized that

[we are] sorry to understand that the Lieutenant-Governor has ordered that the image of Buddha in Bodh-Gaya should not be removed from that place but kept where it is at present. The writer had no idea that the Government could be led to commit such a serious mistake. Dharmapal had made matters too hot with any official support. With official support, he will carry things with a high hand. The consequence of the Government's order will be disastrous. It will kindle the fire of religious animosity in peaceful Bodh-Gaya and create an element of disturbance there. Dharmapal is already trying to dissuade pilgrims from visiting the temple. If he can once place an image of Buddha near it, he will get an opportunity to disturb pilgrims. This is certainly cause for ap-

To fortify his position, the mahant got the support of the British India Association, which petitioned the government to have the image removed. The association insisted that Dharmapala was the source of all bad feeling at Bodh Gaya and that Sinhala Buddhist monks, pilgrims, and supporters were more interested in political action than worship.[38] The mahant still would not tolerate the image as close by as the resthouse and brought another case in 1906 against Dharmapala, Sumangala, and the secretary of state for India. He won that case in January 1909. Dharmapala appealed, but the High Court in Calcutta confirmed the lower court's decision in February 1910 when the image was removed to Maha Bodhi headquarters in Calcutta. The *Journal of the Maha Bodhi Society* claimed that the Japanese image had remained for fifteen years in the central shrine at Bodh Gaya, which was clearly not the case.[39] It spent those fifteen years in the Burmese resthouse, where it functioned as a counter to the image in the central shrine and focus of Buddhist veneration.

The image in the central shrine had as many ups and downs as the Japanese Buddha and more ambiguities. Before Dharmapala appeared on the scene, whatever images resided in the central shrine remained undefined and apolitical. Most pilgrims focused on the two Bodhi trees adjacent to the central shrine.[40] After Dharmapala tried to install a proper Buddha image in the shrine, the mahant countered by arguing that even that image was not Sakyamuni but Buddha-dev, that is, the Buddha recast as the ninth incarnation of Visnu. To the extent that the Buddha was a reincarnation of Visnu, Bodh Gaya was a Hindu place. Dharmapala puzzled over exactly why a Saiva renouncer would have such concern for either Buddha-dev or any other incarnation of Visnu:

The Saivite Mahant does not observe the principles of the Vishnu faith in showing compassion to animals. On the contrary he makes bloody

---

prehension. It is to be hoped, however, that the Government will yet see its mistake and rectify it. Otherwise the inauspicious star *Magha* will become ascendant in the *Maghasram*, the Burmese temple in Budh-Gaya.

38. "House of Commons Question on Harassment of the Mahant," India Office Records, British Library, IOR/L/PJ/6/750/file 705, appendixes A and B.

39. "The History of the Burmese Rest-House," 423.

40. There was another binary pair, two Bodhi trees, that were equally venues for political struggle, one tree to the north of the shrine—the Bodhidrum—of particular interest to Hindus offering pindas, and the tree on the west side of the shrine, associated with the vajrasana. In the interest of keeping a complicated narrative as straightforward as possible, I have given minimal attention to a parallel part of the struggle between two communities wanting access to both tree and image.

offerings at Bodh Gaya on the Kali puja day in getting his menials to sacrifice goats in the precincts of the temple.[41]

Construing the image as Buddhist or Vaishnavite, the reasoning went, would
make a claim on whether the place itself was Buddhist or Hindu. For Hindus the image invited second-order acts of appropriation and overcoding,
dressing and marking the image in a way that insisted on its Hindu identity.
For Dharmapala, the strategy was to insist that dressing and marking the
image in any way desecrated it.

The first Sinhala Buddhist pilgrimage of the modern era arrived in Bodh
Gaya in 1895 when Dharmapala escorted his mother's group to the place.
Their joy was sublime, he wrote, when they saw the Maha Bodhi tree, the
place where the Buddha gazed at the tree, the promenade where he walked,
the place where he rested, and the place where he met the two merchants.
The mood changed as soon as they saw "the image of the Divine Teacher
disfigured by Hindu sectarian marks."

> Imagine the face of the Buddha's image disfigured by Vaishnava marks,
> and instead of the orange-colored robe, a Hindu dress put on the image,
> and hungry Brahman priests hired by the Mahant to perform puja to the
> image! Inconsistency could not go any further. In the name of the Bud-
> dhists I raise my voice and protest against this sacrilegious action of the
> Mahant.[42]

The Saivite plan was nothing if not clever, denying the Buddhist character
of the central shrine image by encompassing it in exactly the same way the
Buddha himself had been historically encompassed by the Hindu tradition
and reconstituted as an incarnation of a Hindu god. In 1904 Dharmapala
was back at Bodh Gaya and spoke of seeing the Japanese image at the Burmese resthouse. As for the image in the central shrine, he did not want to
see it, "as . . . the scoundrels are still desecrating the Great statue by rubbing
turmeric on the forehead" (Diary, May 5, 1904).

From 1895 to 1910 two images located at separate venues framed the

---

41. *Oppression and Tyranny at Buddha Gaya*, pamphlet commemorating the visit of the
lieutenant governor of Bengal on December 3, 1909, 19. Dharmapala's willingness to install
the Buddha Amitabha in a spot where the historical Buddha had his enlightenment had its own
complications.

42. "A Historic Pilgrimage," *Journal of the Maha Bodhi Society* 3 (1895): 84–5.

struggle between the Saiva establishment and the Maha Bodhi Society—the Japanese image of the Buddha kept at the Burmese resthouse and the image of the Buddha in the central shrine. In the early days when Dharmapala was still trying to return the Japanese image to the central shrine, his attorney argued that the place had never been Hindu at all on doctrinal grounds, invoking witnesses who said that "a Hindu could not worship there," presuming that the worshipper would be defiled by looking on a Buddha image.[43] Failing to install the Japanese Buddha in the shrine, he settled for keeping it at the Burmese resthouse. Once two images were put in place, new arguments emerged—the image in the shrine could serve only the Hindu community, lest it be polluted by the proximity of Buddhist worshippers and destroy Hindu prospects for rebirth.[44] The Buddhists countered by insisting that the image must remain unsullied lest their religious scruples be violated.[45]

As the years went on, the mahant tried to Hinduize the Buddha in a variety of ways, concentrating on the image in the shrine, while litigating to remove the Japanese image from Bodh Gaya altogether. In 1907 Dharmapala went with a Japanese pilgrim to Bodh Gaya (Diary, February 3, 1907). They stayed the day, and Dharmapala ordered the removal of two butter lamps from the shrine room, which he replaced with two Maha Bodhi lamps.[46] At the temple he found the Buddha image covered with dirty cloths, tore them off, and had Sumangala ascend the platform to remove the marks on the forehead of the Buddha. On some occasions the image was besmeared with turmeric, Vaishanava marks, or Saivite marks on the forehead.[47] Alan Trevithick argues that such adornments violated Dharmapala's "British Buddhism"—that is, his commitment to a primordial Buddhism with a minimum of ritual elaboration. I would say that he was less concerned with

43. "The Buddha Gaya Temple Case," *Journal of the Maha Bodhi Society* 4 (1895): 44–7, at 45.

44. Colonial judges concluded that when the mahant began to adorn the Buddha image in the shrine, he did so to exclude Buddhist worshippers because "Buddhism is a religion to which his own predecessors were literally opposed and that all the ceremonies of Buddhism are completely abhorrent to Hindus." *Buddhist*, December 27, 1897. The mahant's actions had more to do with using religious practice to establish ownership of the shrine than religious scruples.

45. When other compromises failed, the government proposed a temporary solution to the adornment issue, " that clothing should be removed when required by a reasonable number of Buddhist worshippers" and returned to the image after their departure. India Office Records, British Library, IOR/L/PJ/6/760/file 705.

46. Dharmapala insisted that burning ghi was offensive to Buddhists, although British officials pointed out that some varieties of Buddhists, namely Tibetans, did as much themselves.

47. *Oppression and Tyranny at Bodh Gaya*, 20.

proper Buddhist practice—British, Theravada, or otherwise—than waging war with the mahant. Desecration gave him a compelling way to rally Buddhists such as the Burmese to the Bodh Gaya cause. By 1909 he was complaining that the scoundrels had put a Saivite banner on the top branch of the Bodhi tree (Diary, December 2, 1909).

British diplomatic interests were another force at Bodh Gaya. When the colonial government organized a tour across North India for the Panchen lama, they did so trying to advance their interests in Tibet. The mahant had his own interests, providing the hospitality that he and his predecessors showed all distinguished pilgrims. As a British official remembered the event,

> within one mile of Buddh Gaya we were met by the Mohant himself, accompanied by a crowd of followers, and with palanquins and elephants to carry the Lama and his officers to their lodging. We halted and dismounted from our carriages, and after greeting the Mohant, the Lama was conducted to a silver chair, and borne in state to the Mohant's guesthouse. As he moved forward the procession formed up, and we advanced in great state—a Hindu band led the way, followed by the palanquins of the Lama and the Mohant, and the elephants which carried the principal officers and priests; whilst in front and behind and on both sides moved a dense crowd of Hindu priests and miscellaneous natives, carrying flags and garlands, and cheering heartily.[48]

Dharmapala was away from the place at that time but could never have equaled the spectacle. It allowed the mahant to present himself as anything but an enemy to Buddhism and its believers. Dharmapala was excited to learn that the Panchen lama had removed the *tilak* from the image in the central shrine (Diary, December 22, 1905).[49] At last, a slap across the mahant's wrist.

48. Frederick O'Connor, *On the Frontier and Beyond: A Record of Thirty Years' Service* (London: John Murray, 1931), 104.

49. The markings applied to the image in the central shrine have their own complications. When the *Oppression and Tyranny at Buddha Gaya* pamphlet was republished, the Maha Bodhi journal provided a photo of the image with Vaishanava marks on the image's forehead. *Journal of the Maha Bodhi Society* 18 (1910): 339–50, at 343. The article goes on to say that the markings are an attempt to portray the Buddha as Bhairava (Siva's fearsome incarnation) (349). The *Journal of the Maha Bodhi Society* makes reference to the Bhairava marks in other places. "Buddha-Gaya, Jerusalem & Mecca," 15 (1907): 141–3, at 142; and "Buddhists of Asia, Wake Up!" 17 (1909): 286–9, at 289. It is unclear whether different marks appeared at different moments in the struggle or the Buddhist reaction is simply confused.

OTHER UNIVERSALISMS IN OTHER PLACES

In 1891 as he was leaving the steamship in Calcutta harbor on his way back to Bodh Gaya with the four Sinhala monks in tow, Dharmapala ran into a Buddhist monk from Arakan whom he had met the previous February at Bodh Gaya. Kiripasaran took the group back to the place in Calcutta where he was trying to establish a temple for Buddhists who could variously be called Chittagongian, Magh, Arakanese, or Rakhine. "I came in his trap," Dharmapala remembered, "and the priests walked down to a so called Temple in Warris Bagh Lane. Went with the Brother . . . to purchase sundry articles for the priests" (Diary, July 15, 1891). At Bodh Gaya Dharmapala had been taken by his sincerity—he cut his finger, making a vow to the Buddha, and a day later sold his sandals and umbrella in order to purchase oil to light lamps at the shrine (Diary, February 27 and 28, 1891).[50] Kiripasaran was illiterate but charismatic, ascetic but good with laypeople. He recognized that Arakanese Buddhism was corrupt and devoted himself to purifying it.[51] Eventually he would establish the first *vihara* (temple) in Calcutta. He made a natural ally for Dharmapala, sharing his interest in reviving Buddhism in India. In the years that followed, they worked together on and off, but from the start—from the day he came ashore and stumbled upon Kiripasaran—Dharmapala made his way to Mukherjee's house and cast his lot with the Bengali Theosophists.

Dharmapala had his reasons for being drawn to elite Bengalis. The Bengalis he came to know were people like himself—Theosophists, literate in English, and members of prominent families. They were willing to lend their support and prestige to Kiripasaran as much as they supported Dharmapala.[52] Theosophists such as Neel Kamal Mukherjee and Norendron-

50. Kiripasaran was ordained as a bhikkhu in 1885. Standing in front of the bodhi tree at Bodh Gaya, he pledged his life to reviving Buddhism in India and rented space for a temple in Calcutta in 1886. In 1903 he completed the ground floor of the Dharmankur vihara in Calcutta. Hemendu Chowdhury, *Jagajjyoti Kripasaran Mahathera 125th Birth Anniversary Volume* (Calcutta: Bauddha Dharmankur Sabha, 1990), 1–7, at 2–3.

51. An obituary for another Arakanese reformer suggests the practices that Kiripasaran tried to reform: " The Buddhists of Chittagong about 40 years ago . . . were sunk in the darkness of ignorance. They were really neither Buddhists, nor Hindus, nor Muhammedans, nor Christians. . . . Their Bhikkhus mispronounced a few Pali words only and even took meals at night and some of them did not hesitate to slaughter animals for food." Kitish Chandra Barua, "The Late Dr. Sri Rama Chandra Baruya," *Journal of the Maha Bodhi Society* 31 (1923): 108–10, at 108.

52. Sir Asutosh Mukherjee served as the second president of the Maha Bodhi Society in Calcutta. He explained his attraction to Buddhism as a product of his encounter with Kripasaran, who moved to Calcutta in 1886 and eventually built the Dharmankur vihara. Mukherjee

ath Sen were leading participants in interlocking organizations—the Buddhist Text Society, the Royal Asiatic Society, the Maha Bodhi Society, and the Dharmankur Bauddha Sabha, made up of Kiripasaran's lay supporters. Bengalis read *The Light of Asia* and English translations of Buddhist texts. Rabindranath Tagore used Buddhist themes in his plays. What set things in favor of Buddhism was more than its virtues as a religion or a civilizational asset. It was Indian heritage with political potential: "Why should not this unlooked for return of Buddhism in the form of a Buddhist colony at Bodh Gaya bring back with it the hope that the Hindus will recover their place among the great nations of the world?"[53] All that soon changed. As Dharmapala wrote decades later, "It pays to attack Buddhism now, it paid in 1892 to praise Buddhism. In 1892 there was no Mrs. Besant, no Vivekananda, and no awakening of the religious spirit peculiar to India."[54]

Sympathy for Buddhism if not for the Bodh Gaya cause itself provided Dharmapala with friends with whom to drink tea, take evening strolls, and discuss local life. Mukherjee gave him lodging until he found his own quarters at Gangadhar Babu Road in 1892, moving to Creek Row some sixteen months later, where he stayed until he purchased a house on Baniapukur Lane in 1908 not far from where he had first put up with the Mukherjee family.[55] In both Colombo and Calcutta the members of the Maha Bodhi Society "were really Theosophists in another guise," and the Maha Bodhi Society shared the house on Creek Row with the Theosophical Society.[56] During the course of Dharmapala's stay in Calcutta, his friends pursued political interests in a variety of other informal organizations such as the British India Association, campaigning against the partition of Bengal and participating in the noncooperation movement. In that organization they found themselves among other members who aggressively supported the mahant. The *bhadralok* of the day represented a social class at the height

---

and Norendronath Sen also played central roles in the organization that Kripasaran founded, the Bauddha Dharmankur Sabha. Chowdhury, *Jagajjyoti Kripasaran Maha Thera*, 1–7, at 3–4.

53. *Indian Mirror*, November 3, 1891.

54. "The Place of Women in the Buddhist Church," *Journal of the Maha Bodhi Society* 16 (1908): 34.

55. Dharmapala says that the Arakanese Buddhists helped him rent the Creek Row house (Diary, Memorandum for 1916). Elsewhere he says that their help lasted some two years and then abruptly ceased. "The Work of the Maha Bodhi Society," *Journal of the Maha Bodhi Society* 29 (1921): 147–56, at 148.

56. Sarath Amunugama, "A Sinhala Buddhist 'Babu': Anagarika Dharmapala and the Bengal Connection," *Social Science Information* 30, no. 3 (1981): 561. In Calcutta Theosophists shared an interest in the occult and higher religious truth; in Colombo Theosophy served as a vehicle for pursuing Buddhists interests.

of its powers, and their hegemony coincided with Dharmapala's career in Bengal. In Calcutta he entertained no political goals, devoting his time to writing articles for and editing the *Journal of the Maha Bodhi Society*. His most socially engaged act during his time in Bengal was his effort to raise funds for Indian famine relief in 1897 and again in 1900.[57]

The situation required Dharmapala to manage the contradiction between speaking in Calcutta on the affinity of Hinduism and Buddhism (while keeping company with fellow Theosophists who were Hindu) and his hopes at Bodh Gaya for extracting the place from its Hindu owners. Under the control of the Saivite renouncers Bodh Gaya had been a living example of Hindus and Buddhists worshipping side by side, using a common place for disparate purposes. That contradiction grew more blatant as the years passed, but the bhadralok did what they could for Buddhism. They joined the Maha Bodhi Society and celebrated Buddhist holidays. Asutosh Mukherjee was responsible for introducing Pali as a subject at the University of Calcutta. Sen's newspaper, the *Indian Mirror*, publicized the cause and spoke in favor of a Buddhist Bodh Gaya. Dharmapala dwelt on the solidarity he felt with Bengalis: "The same love I have for my own countrymen I have for the Bengalees. Every individual face I see has a strong resemblance to, and is a counterpart of, a Sinhalese" (Diary, September 4, 1891). He sensed a change was coming, believing that in eight to nine years, Bengalis would accept Buddhism (Diary, October 30, 1891). Acceptance in Calcutta clashed with the perception abroad of Hindu intransigence: "I have to work single-handed in this great Empire for the Buddhists have no idea of the tolerant spirit of the Hindus," he worried. "They seem to think that we shall be treated unkindly by them."[58]

In Calcutta Dharmapala did not encounter Swami Vivekananda or his teacher Ramakrishna, the illiterate village Brahman who attracted an urban following in the decade before Dharmapala's arrival. Ramakrishna's appeal to the very literate bhadralok depended on his otherness—his rustic qualities, mad struggle for liberation, and untutored wisdom.[59] Vivekananda inverted many of those practices, transforming bhakti devotion into textual learning and social service. Suavity replaced the rustic and blunt. Vivekananda's worldliness allowed him to negotiate a world that Ramakrishna never understood, capturing otherness for new purposes. He spent the years

---

57. "An Appeal to all the Buddhists," *Journal of the Maha Bodhi Society* 5 (1897): 74–5.
58. "The Budh-Gaya Temple," *Journal of the Maha Bodhi Society* 3 (1894): 16–17, at 16.
59. Sumit Sarkar, "'Kaliyuga,' 'Chakri' and 'Bhakti,'" *Economic and Political Weekly* 27, no. 29 (1992): 1543–59, 1561–6 at 1544–5.

between 1888 and 1893 traveling across India as a wandering monk (*parivra-jaka*). The journey deepened him. But those spiritual effects were produced not by pilgrimage sites and sacred places. Rather, he

> traversed barren country roads and over-crowded bazaars, princely courts and poor quarters. Through his exposure to a wide cross-section of people, he came to appreciate the immense diversity of life. Paradoxically, this also revealed to him the underlying oneness of human problems.[60]

He traveled across North India to Jaipur and Goa in a spirit of universalist self-discovery, studying Muslim, Jain, and Christian theology.[61]

Vivekananda had made a similar journey in 1885 when his teacher was dying of throat cancer. It seems like an odd time to leave one's guru, but at that moment he made the decision to travel to Bodh Gaya with two other disciples. He informed no one and said nothing about when or whether he would return. Hearing about his other disciples' concern for his absence, Ramakrishna asked them,

> Why are you anxious? Where can Naren [Vivekananda] go? How long can he be away? You will see him coming back very soon. Afterwards he said smiling. Even if you go in quest of spirituality all the world over, you will find nothing (no true spirituality) anywhere. Whatever is there, is also here (showing his own body).[62]

The first step to reconciling Vivekananda's making pilgrimage to Bodh Gaya and the values he shared with his teacher about the irrelevance of pilgrimage is to acknowledge that Vivekananda had no tolerance for everyday forms of religious practice. The second is to say that he had an exceptionally strong affinity for the Buddha, and that affinity had consequences for Dharmapala.

Even before Vivekananda returned from that second pilgrimage, he began entertaining the idea of traveling again. He set his sights on the World's Parliament of Religions, itself an exercise in negotiating the one and the many. Both Dharmapala and Vivekananda used the occasion to present universalizing messages in parallel forms. It provided the perfect occasion

60. Amiya P. Sen, *Swami Vivekananda* (Oxford: Oxford University Press, 2000), 28.

61. Narasingha P. Sil, *Swami Vivekananda: A Reassessment* (Selinsgrove, PA: Susquehanna University Press, 1997), 30.

62. Swami Saradananda, *Sri Ramakrishna: The Great Master* (Madras: Sri Ramakrishna Math, 1979), 646.

10. Swami Vivekananda as wandering monk, Jaipur.

for their projecting themselves onto a world stage. Dharmapala remembered
the South Asians:

> In Sept., 1893 at the Parliament of Religions, Chicago, there appeared
> Japanese Buddhists, and myself as delegates to the Parl: Vivekananda rep-
> resented Hinduism, Mozamdar [P. C. Majumdar] represented the Brahmo
> Samaj with Nagarkar of the Piarthana Samaj, Virachand Gandhi repre-
> sented Jainism. Vivekananda and myself were the most cheered.[63] He
> wore the orange coloured coat and I wore white. He drank liquor and ate
> meat. Gandhi and myself were vegetarians. Majumdar returned to Cal-

---

63. Peter Harvey says that Vivekananda made the larger impression. *An Introduction
to Buddhism: Teachings, History, and Practice* (Cambridge: Cambridge University Press,
1990), 307.

cutta and spread the report that V[ivekananda] ate beef and drank wine.
(Diary, March 28, 1926)

He had reason to see himself as Vivekananda's peer, that first generation of
Indian "gurus" to bring the West the wisdom of the East. Both understood
religious reform as fundamental to national reform. In the West they confronted cultural difference on an order they had not seen before. As Dharmapala later put it, he saw differences within differences: "What a strange
people these Britishers are. At home they are philanthropic. Here [in Asia]
they are quite different" (Diary, August 27, 1898).

The campaign for Bodh Gaya was a battle fought in, and from, Calcutta,
where Dharmapala wrote articles and edited the *Journal of the Maha Bodhi
Society*. Publishing the journal led to an invitation to the World's Parliament of Religions in Chicago in 1893 as the representative of "Southern"
Buddhism. The trip took him around the world, and he used it to pursue projects both social and personal. When he reached London, Edwin Arnold took
him to meet the secretary of state for India to plead the Buddhist cause; in
England he carried a meditation manual to Thomas Rhys Davids and asked
him to translate the Pali into English; and on the way home he toured Japan
trying to interest friends old and new in making Bodh Gaya Buddhist. The
parliament was the highlight. Dharmapala delivered a series of addresses
emphasizing not only Buddhist tolerance but also its superior morality.
Photographs of the stage where he sat with the other representatives show
a man of twenty-nine seated among men twice his age. In circumstances
that must have been intimidating, Dharmapala—a young man among gray-
beards, a man of color addressing white men, a layman among clerics, an
Asian far from home—presented himself with extraordinary self-confidence.

Vivekananda was no less confident, especially in view of the fact that
he had not been invited. He simply sailed to America and wrangled an invitation on the strength of the intervention of a Harvard classics professor.
Relative to other speakers—over a thousand addresses were given—both
Vivekananda and Dharmapala were favored with long intervals of time on
stage and their speeches reproduced at length in subsequent publications.
Vivekananda delivered his address on Hinduism on the ninth day of the convention, arguing that the Vedas "are without beginning and without end."
The Vedas can lack both because they are not really a book but the spiri-
tual laws discovered by different persons in different times.[64] That same day

64. Swami Vivekananda, "Hinduism as a Religion," in Houghton, *Neely's History*, 439.

11. Indian delegation at World's Parliament of Religions, Chicago, 1893.

Dharmapala gave his address, "The World's Debt to Buddha." Vivekananda quickly responded with his own address on Buddhism, "Buddhism, the Fulfillment of Hinduism."[65] He began by saying that although not himself a Buddhist, he regarded the Buddha as God incarnate on earth. He could presume to speak of a religion not his own because as the centuries passed, the Buddha had been reabsorbed by Hinduism as an incarnation of Visnu. On that logic, Vivekananda was a Buddhist in a nonsectarian way, a Buddhist who understood the Buddha in his proper place, subservient to the Hindu gods and spiritual laws found in the Vedas. But he was no less a universalist. He gave a talk in New York City with that title, and the universal religion turned out to be Vedanta for non-Hindus.[66]

Positioning himself as a Buddhist without sectarian bias and a Hindu whose Hinduism transcended itself, Vivekananda wanted it both ways. In

65. This address appears in neither of the two dominant histories of the parliament, Barrows's account and *Neely's History* but can be found in *Complete Works of Swami Vivekananda*, 1:21–23. Some addresses were omitted from *Neely's History* for reasons of space, but the criteria for inclusion are unknown.

66. "The Ideal of a Universal Religion," lecture at Hardman Hall, January 12, 1896.

point of fact he wanted it all ways. As his official biographer recalls the "Oriental" delegates—each burdened with sectarian views. They included

> Mazoomdar [P. C. Majumdar] of the Calcutta Brahmo Samaj . . . Dharmapala representing the Ceylon Buddhists; Gandhi representing the Jains. . . . With them sat Vivekananda [who represented] no particular sect, but the Universal Religion of the Vedas, and who spoke . . . for the religious aspiration of all humanity.[67]

In his letters he spoke of plans to work with Dharmapala in India, but he also revealed his contempt for him. He called Dharmapala a "fine boy" (though Dharmapala was less than two years younger than Vivekananda) and observed, "He has not much learning but is very gentle."[68] A more forthcoming characterization appears in a letter he wrote to his brother: "That bloke Dharmapala made himself a representative [of the Buddhist religion], but with his little learning he arranged a lecture. I found him an ignoramus and thus I worked hard to lecture about Buddha to people—after all the Buddha is also one of our *avataras*."[69]

Dharmapala followed the same strategy with regard to the Japanese Buddhists. He brought his brief experience of Japan in 1889 to the parliament, and he had spent two years abroad, largely in Calcutta, but he had just begun a career of religious work. He had received no formal training in Buddhism and, although he wore what must have appeared to be clerical dress—the white robes of a pious Buddhist layman, tied in a distinctive way—he was not a monk and had no monastic education. He lacked knowledge of Pali, and what he knew of the religion he learned largely from English-language texts, mainly Sir Edwin Arnold's *Light of Asia*, Theosophical accounts, and Western scholarship on Buddhism. These deficits did not slow him down:

> Friends, I bring to you the good wishes of 475,000,000 of Buddhists, the blessings and peace of the religious founder of that system which has prevailed so many centuries in Asia, which has made Asia mild, and which is to-day in its twenty-fourth century of its existence, the prevail-

67. Swami Nikhilananda, *Vivekananda: A Biography* (Calcutta: Advaita Ashrama, 1982), 118.

68. Vivekananda to Ramakrishnananda, March 19, 1894, in *Complete Works of Swami Vivekananda*, 6:252.

69. *Londone Swami Vivekananda*, 3 vols. in 2 parts (Calcutta: Mahendra Publishing Committee), 1:16, quoted in Sil, *Swami Vivekananda: A Reassessment*, 159–60.

ing religion of those countries. I have sacrificed the greatest of all work to attend this parliament; I have let the work of . . . consolidating the different Buddhist countries, which is the most important work in the history of modern Buddhism.[70]

Besides making himself the Lord Buddha's ambassador and assuming he was entitled to convey his blessings, he presented himself as the spokesman for all Buddhists, the Japanese monks seated with him on the dais notwithstanding.

Looked at in other terms, he was a young layman. He came from a small multiethnic, multireligious country of some three million people. Barrows's first choice to attend the parliament had been Hikkaduve, and Dharmapala came to the fore only because the distinguished monk was unwilling to travel. Dharmapala spoke English and was already in the business of representing Buddhism to the world. The contrast with the way the Japanese delegation had been introduced just before him reveals his doing to the Japanese what Vivekananda had done to him. After a Japanese Christian minister said a few words, the Protestant organizer introduced four Japanese priests, Yatsubuchi Banryu, Ashitsu Jitsuzen, Shaku Soen, and Toki Horyu. All had been trained as clerics in Japan (although the delegation did not include the two priests who had been sent to Oxford to study with Max Muller). Religious intellectuals and well-placed abbots, they were unsure of their English and had their interpreter—the same Noguchi who had come to Colombo to fetch Olcott—speak for them. Compare his opening remarks to Dharmapala's: "I thank you on behalf of the Japanese Buddhist priests for the welcome you have given us and for the kind invitation to participate in the proceedings of the Congress."[71]

First suppressed after the Meiji restoration for being antimodern and foreign, Japanese Buddhism recovered, and the Meiji Constitution of 1889—the promulgation of which had brought Olcott and Dharmapala to Japan—restored their political rights.[72] The parliament gave the Japanese delegates a chance to respond to these events, above all affirming the close ties between Buddhism and the Meiji state. It gave them a chance to articulate *shin bukkyo*, the philosophical, rationalized, and socially engaged Buddhism that

---

70. "Good Wishes of Ceylon," in Houghton, *Neely's History*, 60.
71. "Speech of the Rt. Rev. Reuchi Shibata," in Barrows, *The World's Parliament of Religions*, 1:92.
72. Martin Collcutt, "Buddhism: The Threat of Eradication," 143–67.

revitalized a religion castigated throughout the first twenty years of Meiji rule.[73] By showing that *shin bukkyo* was modern, they would demonstrate that Japan itself was modern. Jaffe says that the Japanese delegates remained doctrinaire in many ways.[74] Toki recounted the history of Buddhism in Japan and described what the religion had done for Japan. The delegates had a variety of objectives, all shaped by the presence of Christian missionaries in Japan and Western hegemony in Japanese life.[75] That they were representing Buddhism in a setting that was itself hegemonic must not have escaped them.

The celebration of brotherhood duly noted, the parliament was a Christian affair, motivated by Protestant confidence in its superiority and shaped by Western assumptions concerning the nature and function of all religions. Barrows had organized the sessions to address questions of interest to Christians—the divinity of Christ, the nature of man, and the place of science. The Buddhist delegates took as their audience not the delegates in general and only indirectly their fellow Asians—the Hindus, Muslims, Jains, Zoroastrians, Shintoists, and Confucianists in attendance. Their primary audience was the Christians in both the conference hall and society beyond. Dharmapala and the Japanese delegates worked hard to portray Buddhism as a religion compatible with human beings the world over and uniquely suitable for a modern age in which the old gods had been exposed and science ruled. To this extent Buddhism's position as a world religion depended on its modernity. All that was required for Buddhism to realize its potential was for someone to missionize it. Dharmapala was that man.

The Japanese had sent Buddhist monks to the West as early as 1873 when Akamatsu Renjo traveled to England, "preparing the way," as Edward Reed said in his account of Japanese Buddhism in 1880, "for the conversion of the people of Europe to the Shinshu faith."[76] Surviving the effects of Western dominance required more than Japanese Buddhism's becoming a world religion. Universalizing Japanese Buddhism required separating it from Shinto and Confucian practices and expanding charitable institutions.[77] An early step was traveling in the West—from Akamatsu's trip to

73. Judith Snodgrass, *Presenting Japanese Buddhism to the West: Orientalism, Occidentalism, and the Columbian Exposition* (Chapel Hill: University of North Carolina Press, 2003), 115.

74. Personal communication, August 31, 2013.

75. Snodgrass, *Presenting Japanese Buddhism to the West*, 175 and 180.

76. *Japan: Its History, Traditions, and Religions* (London: John Murray, 1880), quoted in Snodgrass, *Presenting Japanese Buddhism to the West*, 113.

77. Grapard, "Japan's Ignored Cultural Revolution."

the students who studied under Max Muller and the Japanese clerics who appeared at the parliament. Reed's account to the contrary, these visits were defensive in nature—study tours meant to strengthen Japanese religion, not to convert non-Japanese.[78] Sending Buddhist priests to Europe and America was an effort to discover how a religion could be remade to fit the contours of the modern, industrial society developing in Japan. Dharmapala was himself impressed by Japanese efforts to missionize their religion in faraway places, but he failed to put two and two together. He praised Buddhist priests and nuns for working in Hawaii, the United States, Korea, Manchuria, and China, oblivious to the fact that those clerics were working with expatriate Japanese. His own definition of missionary work entailed spreading the religion to non-Buddhists (Diary, March 18, 1893).

For the Japanese, there was a second motivation—propagating their own religion and distinguishing it from Southern Buddhism, which they regarded as simplistic. The delegation took pains to prove that Japanese Buddhism was the true teaching of the Lord Buddha, not the corruption of it assumed by Western scholars who knew only the Buddhism of the Pali texts. In the face of Western understandings of Theravada Buddhism as Buddhism simpliciter, the Japanese were confident that their Buddhism was the highest form of Buddhism, its realization. They adopted the expression "Eastern" Buddhism to distance their Buddhism from forms of Mahayana found in China and Tibet, which fell into the category "Northern" at the parliament. Japanese Buddhism, they contended, was the summation of the philosophical sophistication that began in ancient Buddhism even before the religion's movement into East Asia. The parliament gave rise to another Japanese neologism with its own ideological applications. Toki referred to Buddhism as *ekayana*, suggesting at the parliament that Southern and Northern Buddhism could be considered as one Buddhism, the *ekayana*.[79]

78. Akamatsu's visit paid some attention to proselytization. Galen Amstutz, *Interpreting Amida: History and Orientalism in the Study of Pure Land Buddhism* (Albany: State University of New York Press, 1997), 62. Akamatsu's visit suggests "that from the early years of Meiji Japan, Buddhists in Japan became intensely aware of both their past and the potential transnational reach of their faith." James Ketelaar, "Strategic Occidentalism: Meiji Buddhists at the World's Parliament of Religion," *Buddhist-Christian Studies* 11 (1991): 40. Two headquarters temples of Jodo Shinshu Buddhism played the leading role in this transnational project. Akamatsu was sent by Nishi Honganji.

79. "Buddhism in Japan," in Barrows, *World's Parliament of Religions*, 1: 544. There are substantial differences between the way the two accounts—Barrows's two-volume account and *Neely's History*—report the same address. After the *ekayana* assertion, the Barrows's account of Toki's speech says: "This [the unification of the two Buddhisms] is the reason why the Mahabodhi Society [*sic*] was organized in Calcutta, India, and there are in the land of Northern and Southern Buddhism those who want to combine these two systems" (544). Neither this

The terminological emphasis on the unity of Buddhism did not deter the Japanese from understanding the unity of Buddhism in a specifically Japanese way. Japanese Buddhism was the religion's highest expression, taking the truths of the ancient texts and melding them with the more profound ones brought to realization only in Japan. Eastern Buddhism was a vehicle for Japanese feelings of ethnic superiority and longing for the status of a world power.[80] When the Japanese asserted the universality of Buddhism, they argued that it was universal because it was consistent with science and suitable for all people. Toki went further: "Buddha himself called Buddhism 'a round, circulating religion,' which means the truth common to every religion, regardless of the outside garment."[81] In contemplating the expansion of Buddhism, most Japanese gave no consideration to discarding the outer garment, assuming that a Buddhism that was universal was a Buddhism that was Japanese. To that extent, speaking of *ekayana* Buddhism and talking about missionizing it was not an innocent hope for building a Buddhist world united in common belief but an ambition for Japan's managing a program for sharing its own Buddhism with other Asians. It attempted, in other words, to understand Japanese Buddhism as a "world religion" of universal appeal, while also assuming that it could not be separated from its civilizational content. As Toki said elsewhere, "Buddhism is the spirit of Japan; her nationality is Buddhism."[82]

Dharmapala also approached Buddhism as a world religion that could speak to the needs of all human beings. His addresses emphasized that it was universal, scientific, and suitable to modern times in the way Western religions were not because it was "spiritual." Buddhism was especially needed in the West, where it could serve as an antidote to Western materialism. While separating the doctrine from its political and economic realization, he wanted to missionize Buddhism for a variety of reasons. In England, he wanted to missionize it because bringing the Buddha's teachings to the British would humanize them. Once humanized, their newfound compas-

---

reference nor the *ekayana* reference appear in Neely. What does appear there is Toki's conclusion, which may have struck Barrows as too partisan: "It is time to remodel the Japanese Buddhism. . . . We can not but feel rejoiced when we think of the probable result of this new change by which the Buddhism of great Japan will rise and spread its wings under all heaven as the grand Buddhism of the whole world." "History of Buddhism and Its Sects in Japan," 222–26, at 226.

80. Snodgrass, *Presenting Japanese Buddhism to the West*, 201.
81. "What Buddhism Has Done for Japan," in Houghton, *Neely's History*, 2:779.
82. "What Buddhism Has Done for Japan," 780.

sion would cause them to call off the Christian missionaries and reduce the brutality of British colonial rule. In Asia his missionary efforts were tied to recovering the sacred places in North India by the unified efforts of fellow Buddhists. He sought to restore the Buddhist sasana (Buddhism as a historical formation) in India, and that restoration would entail sharing the teachings with Indians now practicing other religions. Restoring Buddhism to India, reforming it in Lanka and Japan, and sharing it with Westerners—all of these purposes were intertwined, but each followed its own logic. Each of these goals depended on recovering Bodh Gaya. It would be the sacred center, memorializing a value all Buddhists held in common—respect for the Buddha's enlightenment.

Indian reformers pursued the universalist project in their own ways. In a letter to Raja Peary Mukerji—after he had chaired a meeting in Calcutta in his honor—Vivekananda traced the degeneration of India to "building a wall of custom round the nation," preventing "the Hindus from coming in contact with the surrounding Buddhistic nations." What lay behind that wall of custom was hatred of others, and its remedy lay in engaging with others and expanding Hinduism's influence:

> Expansion is life; contraction is death. Love is life, hatred is death. We began to die the day we began to contract—to hate other races—and nothing can prevent our death until we come back to life, to expansion.[83]

In the United States Vivekananda preached a religion that he said was universal even though rooted in the Vedas. That universalizing message appealed to Dharmapala because the Hinduism that Vivekananda presented to his American audiences was not sectarian but "pure and undefiled."[84] Speaking to a Bengali audience in Calcutta, Dharmapala urged his audience to send more Hindu missionaries to America. For his part, he would missionize Buddhism because such was its very nature, and it was a way to reform a religion fallen into corruption. This he did not tell the parliament's delegates.

Vivekananda lingered on in the United States until 1897, arguing that it was the Buddha who gave Hinduism its distinctive features, recasting the Buddha as a Hindu teacher, not the *Buddha dev* of Indian tradition, and making the Buddha his own point of access to the fundamental teachings of

83. "Swami Vivekananda," *Journal of the Maha Bodhi Society* 4 (1896): 55.
84. "Buddhists and Hindus," *Indian Mirror*, May 18, 1894.

all religions, not simply the South Asian ones.[85] On that basis he began to preach a universal religion.

> What do I mean by the ideal of universal religion. I do not mean any one universal philosophy, or any one universal mythology, or any one universal ritual, held alike by all; but I mean that this world must go on its wheel within wheel, this intricate mass of complex machinery. . . . What can *we* do then? We may make it run smoothly, we may lessen the friction, we can grease the wheels. . . . By what? By recognizing the natural necessity of variation.[86]

The inclusive spirit that came from his Indian travels notwithstanding, Vivekananda's universalism had a Hindu core: "Vedanta is the bond between the ever conflicting religious differences." He kept Hinduism at the center of his message when he spoke to Americans, while adapting the Vedantic monism, social service, and this-worldly renunciation that marked his message in Calcutta.[87]

Universal religion, he argued, did not rely on any one philosophy, mythology, or ritual. It did not depend on his teacher's exuberant practices. It depended on the idea that God was at the center of all religions, whose practitioners knew him under various descriptions. If it is true, the swami reasoned, that God is at the center of all religions and that each of us is moving toward him,

> greater or less, through high philosophy or low, through the highest or lowest doctrines, through the most refined mythology or the grossest, every sect, every soul, every nation, every religion, consciously or unconsciously, is struggling upward, Godward, and each vision is of Him and of none else.[88]

Vivekananda and Dharmapala both "struggled upward" well enough as long as Vivekananda remained in the West. His condescension toward Dharmapala notwithstanding, the two had joined forces at the Parliament of Religions, and in the lecture of 1894 Dharmapala celebrated Vivekananda's triumphant tour of America, teaching the "deep philosophy of the Upanishad."

85. "Vivekananda in the West," *Amrita Bazar Patrika*, January 20, 1897.
86. *The Ideal of Universal Religion*, (New York: Swami Vivekananda, 1896), 8.
87. Sarkar, "'Kaliyuga,' 'Chakri' and 'Bhakti,'" 1555–9.
88. *The Ideal of Universal Religion*, 8.

In a letter to E. F. Sturdy around the same time, Dharmapala characterized Vivekananda as a "useful and noble-minded Sannyasi [world renouncer]."[89] He sent a token contribution to support Vivekananda's journal and gave a talk in Calcutta defending him from his detractors—Dharmapala thought Majumdar the instigator—who raised the charge that Vivekananda had consumed beef and alcohol in the United States (Diary, March 28, 1926).[90]

What might have developed as a common platform for India's regeneration or even a transreligious universalism—motivated by Vivekananda's confidence that the Buddha was the source of all that was powerful in Hinduism—declined as soon as Vivekananda returned to India. He stopped characterizing the Buddha as the best hope for India's salvation and began to castigate Buddhism as it evolved in the direction of the "left-handed worship" (vamachara). Tantrism repelled both Vivekananda and Dharmapala, who embodied profound anxiety about marriage and sexuality.[91] Physical love was anathema to spiritual progress, and if a serious person were to marry, Vivekananda thought, the heroic course was to avoid sexual contact.[92] When Vivekananda turned against Buddhism, his motives were more tactical than ideological. After Vivekananda's death in 1902, Dharmapala met a sannyasi who had worked with him, and he asked

> why Vivekananda Swami, who had preached Buddhism in America to the Americans, holding up the example of the Buddha as an ideal of the karmayogis, preached against Buddhism with such vehemence in his own home. [He] replied that for policy's sake he had to attack Buddhism in Madras![93]

Unlike his relationship with Japanese Buddhists, which rose and fell before it rose again, Dharmapala had no relationship with Vivekananda after the latter returned to Calcutta in 1897 a few years before his death.

89. Sankari Prasad Basu and Sunil Bihari Ghosh, eds., *Vivekananda in Indian Newspapers, 1893–1902* (Calcutta: Bookland and Modern Book Agency, 1969), 28–9 and 84.

90. Majumdar was the representative of the Calcutta Brahmo Samaj, who spoke at the World's Parliament and had at least hearsay knowledge of Vivekananda's activities in the United States.

91. Sil, *Swami Vivekananda: A Reassessment*, 132–8. Vivekananda's contempt for the household life led him to say, "If Bhagavan (God) incarnates Himself as a householder, I can never believe Him to be sincere. . . . Without renunciation religion can never stand." *Complete Works of Swami Vivekananda*, 5:261.

92. Sil, *Swami Vivekananda: A Reassessment*, 220n55.

93. Anagarika Dharmapala, "Lectures by Swami Vivekananda," *Journal of the Maha Bodhi Society* 18 (1910): 616–20, at 618.

DHARMAPALA'S UNITED BUDDHIST WORLD,
BODH GAYA, AND JAPAN

The "world religion" notion entered the vocabulary of the modern study of religion (*Religionswissenchaft*), emerging from Dutch-German debates regarding the distinction between national religions, tied to a place or a people, and universalistic "world" religions, which had begun in a national context and spread beyond it. Late nineteenth-century scholars argued over the utility of the notion, as well as which candidates—Islam was the favorite case for rejection—deserved to be treated as such. Once unleashed, the notion underwent more changes. Only in the late nineteenth century did Buddhism come to be recognized by practitioners and observers as one religion.

> Until that time, neither European observers nor, for the most part, native "practitioners" of those various devotional, contemplative, divinatory, funereal, and other ordinary and extraordinary cults that are now roundly called Buddhists had thought of these divergent rites and widely scattered institutions as constituting a single religion.[94]

Masuzawa may overstate the case for the nineteenth-century construction of "Buddhism," but it is fair to say that Dharmapala's journals, travels, pamphlets, and struggle at Bodh Gaya gave it a unitary character that it lacked to that point. But the relationship between the local and the global is still more complicated. There are variations across space and time. He preached different Buddhisms in different places, and characterizing the Buddhism he brought to the World's Parliament as Theravada has an anachronistic quality.[95]

What concerns Masuzawa is the object formation by which Buddhism became a "world religion" with a unitary identity. What concerned Dharmapala was a parallel project, "worlding" the religion by constructing the devotional, imaginative, and political forms that could realize what he thought already existed nominally, Buddhists across Asia joined in a single community. All "world religions," Dharmapala assumed, have a sacred center and a pilgrimage tradition that brought coreligionists to that place.

94. Masuzawa, *The Invention of World Religions*, 122.

95. Perriera reviews the sources claiming that Dharmapala introduced Theravada to North America before pointing out that the expression came into use a decade and a half later. "Whence Theravada," 550.

He got that idea from Sir Edwin Arnold's misunderstanding of the Buddhist tradition. Even before it fell into Saivite hands, Bodh Gaya was something less than the "Jerusalem" of the Buddhist world, to use the expression that Dharmapala took from Arnold, and considerably less than its "Mecca."[96] Trevithick characterizes Bodh Gaya as "peripheral" to the lives of most Buddhists before the establishment of the place as a pilgrimage center—sacred, but peripheral.[97] It was one of the eight places associated with the Buddha's life, but these "eight places and the *stupas* at them were never treated in practice by earlier Buddhists as a group or network of eight distinctly related places of pilgrimage," and in the texts these places are treated as objects of memorialization, not objects of direct encounter.[98] When the Thai prince Devavongsa told Dharmapala that his ministers thought the Buddha could be venerated anywhere, he voiced an assumption that must have been widespread in Thai society and beyond (Diary, January 26, 1894). To that extent, Dharmapala's interest in Bodh Gaya as the Buddhist Mecca was as highly imagined as his hopes for a united Buddhist world.

In the centuries before Dharmapala's arrival, pilgrims did indeed visit Bodh Gaya and other sites associated with the life of the Buddha. The number of sites varied—sometimes two or three sites are enumerated, sometimes four, eight, or thirty-two. There is no evidence that any of these groupings was the object of a pilgrimage circuit. The circuit of four places that Faxian made on his visit of 399–414 CE differed from the traditional four mentioned in the Mahaparinibbana Sutta.[99] Buddhists came from various parts of the "great transcontinental sodality" that was premodern Buddhism, but they followed no particular path. If they were guided by Buddhist monks, these monks would have found nothing prescriptive about pilgrimage in the suttas. From 1590 CE to Dharmapala's time, Buddhists found the Maha Bodhi temple controlled by a lineage of Saivite world renouncers, but they did not stop visiting the place. They simply joined the Hindus. From the perspective of the Dasanami renouncers of the Giri lineage who came to reside at Bodh Gaya and the Hindu laypeople who came to perform the death rituals (*sraddha*), Bodh Gaya was the southernmost point of forty-five *sraddha*-performing sites spread around Gaya. Reaching Bodh Gaya, Buddhists found themselves shoulder to shoulder with Hindus per-

96. The analogy comes from Arnold, *India Revisited* (London: Kegan, Paul, Trench, Trübner, 1891), 233.

97. *The Revival of Buddhist Pilgrimage at Bodh Gaya*, 64–6.

98. Toni Huber, *The Holy Land Reborn: Pilgrimage & the Tibetan Reinvention of Buddhist India* (Chicago: University of Chicago Press, 2008), 28.

99. Huber, *The Holy Land Reborn*, 18–9.

forming death rituals at a place associated with the feet of an enormous prone body comprising the length and breadth of the sacred space surrounding Gaya.[100]

Dharmapala's efforts to create a united Buddhist world turned on making Bodh Gaya Buddhist. Early on, no nation was as important to that cause as Japan. In an article he published in a Japanese magazine in 1902, Dharmapala made assertions that put the burden on Japan: "In order to save other friends in Asia from their unfortunate state, isn't that Japan's responsibility?" he asked, and declared, "As the revolutionary movement of the last century was led by the French, the 20th century revolution in Asia is Japan's responsibility."[101] Part of that responsibility involved supplying technical skills to the rest of Asia, and another part involved recovering Bodh Gaya. After his early visits to Japan and the United States, Dharmapala became an advocate for technical education as an alternative to the educational models that the British had brought to Asia, and which he had encountered in a series of missionary schools. First he set up a training program for young Sinhala men to be educated in Japan in crafts such as weaving and pottery making. Then he established a school in the suburbs of Colombo to do the same. He urged Japanese entrepreneurs who had done business in China and Korea to set up shop in India. He contemplated opening a branch of his father's furniture business in Tokyo, and when his brother went into the match business, he did so with Japanese guidance.

In the wake of the Anglo-Japan treaty of 1902, encouraging Japanese economic expansion in India might not have entirely contradicted colonial economic policy, but Dharmapala's overtures to the Japanese must have disturbed the government of India. He put Japan in a position of privilege at the International Buddhist Conference he held at Bodh Gaya in 1892, flying the Japanese flag next to the Maha Bodhi flag.[102] The conference had been sched-

---

100. Doyle, "Bodh Gaya," 217.

101. "Japan and India," *Chuo-Koron* (1902). Dharmapala said much the same in a lecture he delivered in Japan, "The Responsibility of Buddhists towards the World," where he placed emphasis not on Japan or Asia but the world. He brought the same emphasis to a 1927 article entitled "Our Duty to the Peoples of the West," *Journal of the Maha Bodhi Society* 35 (1927): 422–5.

102. Fields, *How the Swans Came to the Lake*, 117. Later Dharmapala held a celebration for the emperor of Japan at the Maha Bodhi Society headquarters at 4A College Square and flew the Japanese flag next to the Buddhist flag (Diary, November 10, 1915). By 1915 the British had become substantially more aware of the effects of Japanese (and German) involvement with Bengali revolutionaries. See Richard Popplewell, *Intelligence and Imperial Defence: British Intelligence and the Defence of the Indian Empire, 1904–1924* (London: Frank Cass, 1995), 200–15.

uled to coincide with the lieutenant governor of Bengal's visit, Dharmapala hoping to bring all the actors together to improve his chances of success at Bodh Gaya. Hearing about the Japanese flag, the lieutenant governor stayed home.[103] In 1895 Dharmapala sent a letter to the lord chamberlain of Japan urging him to bring about a union of Japan and India, hoping that it might have good effects for Buddhism (Diary, December 30, 1895). He had hopes that the Indian princes would follow his example:

> What a good thing if the native Rajahs would visit Japan and see what progress the Japanese have made within the last 30 years. The other thing they should do is send several students to learn Japanese industries. (Diary, June 16, 1898)

By his last trip to Japan in 1913, Dharmapala had drawn so much suspicion from the government that he was put under surveillance as he traveled about Tokyo in a rickshaw, followed by a British agent in his own rickshaw. His friendships with Japanese Buddhists in Calcutta and Tokyo, in other words, led the British to interpret his actions less as building a Buddhist world than undermining a colonial one.

The delegates to the International Buddhist Conference had told Dharmapala that Japanese Buddhists would be willing to raise the funds that would allow him to buy the place from the mahant. When hope for purchase failed, he filed a legal challenge; when the Japanese produced no support, he raised funds in Lanka and Burma. The eventual decision that the mahant was lawfully in control of Bodh Gaya cost him more than his own funds and credibility in his own country. It cost him whatever legitimacy he enjoyed in Japan, however modest local support had been. Looking back thirty years later, he wrote, "For 35 years the Japanese gave no helping hand to the Indian work of the Maha Bodhi Society," adding that he had taken pains to visit Japan four times and donated Rs. 5,000 to earthquake relief efforts in Japan (Diary, October 4, 1926). A year later he noted that Japanese Buddhists had built "many a temple for the use of Japanese only" across the Pacific slope, and he was put off by what he took to be a change in missionary policy (Diary, April 26, 1927). Despite repeated visits to Japan, he drew the

---

103. Although not expressly interested in the political context in which the struggle for Bodh Gaya was fought, Tapati Guha-Thakurta pays attention only to the Hindus and Buddhists, ignoring the influence of imperial concern with Japan's presence in India. *Monuments, Objects, Histories: Institutions of Art in Colonial and Postcolonial India* (New York: Columbia University Press, 2004). There were regular signs of such in the Indian press of the day.

only possible conclusion—a united Buddhist world was not going to receive Japanese support. What he could not foresee was a future in which another Japanese would confront his efforts to recover Bodh Gaya.

When the Japanese aesthete Okakura Kakuzo wrote the three portentous words "Asia is one," the unity he had in mind was dependent on two parts:

> The Himalayas divide . . . [and] accentuate, two mighty civilizations, the Chinese with its communism of Confucius, and the Indian with its individualism of the Vedas. But not even the snowy barriers can interrupt for one moment the broad expanse of love for the Ultimate and universal, which is the common thought-inheritance of every Asiatic race, enabling them to produce all the great religions of the world, and distinguishing them from those maritime peoples of the Mediterranean and the Baltic, who love to dwell on the Particular, and to search out the means, not the end, of life.[104]

China and India were more than states; they were civilizations, united by their "love for the Ultimate and universal," and in a more substantive way, they are held together by Buddhism.[105] But in the fullness of time the unity of Asia depended on yet another country, Okakura's own:

> Buddhism—that great ocean of Idealism, in which merge all the river-systems of Eastern Asiatic thought—is not colored only with the pure water of the Ganges, for the Tartaric nations that joined it made their genius also tributary, bringing new symbolism, new organization, new powers of devotion, to add to the treasures of the faith.
>
> It has been, however, the great privilege of Japan to realize this unity-in-complexity with special clearness. The Indo-Tartaric blood of this race was in itself a heritage, which qualified it to imbibe from the two sources, and so mirror the whole of Asiatic consciousness. The unique blessing of unbroken sovereignty, the proud self-reliance of an unconquered race, and the insular isolation which protected ancestral ideas

---

104. *The Ideals of the East with Special Reference to Japan* (London: John Murray, 1903), 1.

105. Duara argues in "The Discourse of Civilization and Pan-Asianism" that the word *civilization* came to be understood as referring not to a hegemonic and singular Western possession but the core of historically important societies—the culture, let's say, of India and China—only by the First World War. I would put it a little earlier, depending on how we define "recognizable and dominant" (101). Okakura's pan-Asianism is one exercise in formulating the discourse of "civilizations." Duara marks off the intellectual origins of the transformation to Spengler and Toynbee, emphasizing Toynbee's expression "civilizational spirituality" (104).

and instincts at the cost of expansion, made Japan the real repository of the trust of Asiatic thought and culture.[106]

Just as Vivekananda's universalism was a Vedic universalism, Okakura's was a Japanese universalism.

The question was whether the natural affinity Japan enjoyed with India linked it to India's love of the "Ultimate and universal" in general or to a specifically Buddhist commitment to the "Ultimate and universal." Okakura did not attend the Parliament of Religions, but he visited India from November 1901 until October 1902, staying with the Tagore family and traveling in the same circles Dharmapala knew. He became especially friendly with Vivekananda, fast approaching the end of his life. He followed the example of the Japanese pilgrims—Kitabatake and Kurosaki—who reached Bodh Gaya in 1883. Kitabatake left a stele behind, which read, "Since the founding of Japan, I am the first to make a pilgrimage to the tomb of Sakyamuni. Doryu, December 4, Meiji 16 [1883]."[107] His trip was sponsored by Honganji, the primary source of most Japanese clerical travel abroad. Honganji later sponsored the India travel of Rev. T. Kawakami, whom Dharmapala met through their common ties to Olcott and who soon began to write critically about the Maha Bodhi Society (Diary, January 12, 1893). Kawakami remained a presence in Calcutta, studying Sanskrit and Tibetan and participating in the Buddhist Text Society. By 1895 Dharmapala's diaries begin to characterize Kawakami as a traitor, marking the point where his estrangement from the Maha Bodhi Society became obvious to Dharmapala.[108] It seems likely that Kawakami's behavior was shaped less by personal animus than Honganji policy.

Even without the personal alienation between Dharmapala and Vivekananda, there were ideological affinities that drew Okakura to Vivekananda (and away from Dharmapala). Both thought about a universal religion in a highly metaphysical way. For Vivekananda the source was Vedanta, for Okakura, Japanese Buddhism. Making the argument for univer-

---

106. *Ideals of the East*, 1–2.

107. Jaffe, "Seeking Sakyamuni," 76.

108. From the first, Dharmapala writes of Kawakami's hostility (Diary, December 11, 1889) and speaks of Kawakami's attempts to cut a deal with the mahant (Diary, March 7 and 23, April 7 and 10, 1893). Kawakami later told him that the Japanese did not care about Bodh Gaya (Diary, July 30, 1894). When he characterized Kawakami as a traitor, Kawakami had his own dealings with the mahant: "K called on me. . . . He has done immense harm to me in giving the knife to the Mahant to stab me. He has told the Mahant's pleader Motil Lal Das that all this agitation is by me and no Buddhist is concerned and it would be well if the Japanese image is removed to the Museum" (Diary, May 18, 1896).

sality required Vivekananda to formulate a shifting matrix of identities and differences:

> There is very little difference, in essentials, in all the religious systems of the world. Take, for instance, Christianity and Mahomedanism, Buddhism and Baishnavism. They are almost the same in essentials.
>
> It is, however, Buddha who gave distinctive features to Hinduism, as Mahomed gave to his religion. Eliminate Christ, then every Mussulman is a Christian, eliminate Mahomed then every Christian is a Mussulman.
>
> The essentials being the same in every religions [sic]
>
> 1. Christianity is the essentials plus Christ.
> 2. Mahomedanism is the essentials plus Mahomed.
> 3. Buddhism is the essentials plus Buddha.
> 4. Baishnavism is the essentials plus Sri Krishna.
>
> And what is Vedantism? It is the essence of the essentials.[109]

For Vivekananda, the odd man out in this universal religion was the Buddha, indigestible because he denied the reality of the *atman* (soul); for Okakura, the Buddha of the Pali tradition was not so much heterodox as archaic and subsumed by the profundity of Japanese thought.

Over a five-year period after their meeting in Chicago, Vivekananda's international presence began to overshadow Dharmapala's, and once he returned to India, he became more insistent on Hinduism's superiority and universality (Diary, April 3, 1897). Even five years after the swami's death, Dharmapala was still characterizing Vivekananda (and Annie Besant) as the chief obstacle to reviving Buddhism.[110] Under these circumstances— while Dharmapala was away in Colombo and Vivekananda still back in Calcutta—Okakura took the train to Bodh Gaya in the company of Sister Nivedita and Surendranath Tagore. The latter explained what had led Okakura to the place:

> He had originally come, he told me, simply to make his offering of reverence to the Buddha, but far from being rewarded with peace of mind,

---

109. "Vivekananda in the West," *Amrita Bazar Patrika*, January 20, 1897.

110. "Colonel Olcott and the Buddhist Revival Movement," *Journal of the Maha Bodhi Society* 15 (1907): 26–8, at 28.

he had been sorely distressed at the state of the temple and its ill-kept surroundings. Thereupon he had a vision of little colonies of devotees, hailing from all parts of the world, each housed according to the usage of its own land, all clustering round the temple ground, contributing colourful variety of vesture and ceremonial to a common ideal of peace and good-will, inspired by the constant contemplation of the site of the Master's enlightenment.[111]

Having been stirred to action, Okakura met with the mahant to negotiate for a lease. A few months later he had made a formal proposal, apparently under the hand of Tagore.

In return for a grant of land near the Maha Bodhi temple, Okakura gave the mahant proof of his willingness to accept Hindu hegemony at the place and whatever constraints the mahant required. He said nothing of a colonization scheme for Buddhist nations, only a place for the Japanese:

26th April 1902
Paramahansa Acharya Srimat Krishna Dayal Swamiji, Mahant Maharaj of Bodh Gaya
Reverend Sir,
While reminding you of your kind promise of a grant of land in Bodh-Gaya near the Maha Bodhi Temple, I beg to put in writing what I have already submitted to you verbally.

My object is to erect a Rest House for followers of the Mahayana Buddhism of Japan.

I am willing to purchase it from you free of rent at a fair and reasonable price. I intend to acquire it in my own name and make it over to a body of trustees composed of the Mahayana Priesthood of Japan, on such conditions as will effectually prevent them from infringing or interfering in any way with your rights and privileges of whatsoever description concerning the Temple premises. To assure you in this respect I am willing to bind myself or my representative by any terms and conditions, which your legal advisers may think necessary for the purpose.

I may also inform you that I have no connection whatsoever with any of the representatives of the Hinayana Buddhists of Ceylon, Siam or other places some of whom have so sadly abused your kindness. I regret very much to hear that the name of my country has been unwarrantably

---

111. Surendranath Tagore, "Kakuzo Okakura: Some Reminiscences by Surendranath Tagore," in *Okakura Kakuzo: Collected English Writings* (Tokyo: Heibonsha, 1984), 3:236.

used in this connection and I hasten to assure you that the Mahayana priesthood of Japan would emphatically repudiate their having anything to do with that most unfortunate contention.

Our School of Buddhism differs essentially in its tenets from those of Ceylon or Siam, while on the other hand our worship of the Gods and Goddesses many of whom we have in common with you makes our relationship to Hinduism a very close one. . . .

Perhaps you will permit me to point out in this connection that if we had been actuated by feelings antagonistic to your interests, we need not have approached you at all in this matter, but could have easily gained our object by availing ourselves of the opportunity afforded by the erection of the District Board Resthouse for Buddhists or we could have made arrangements with the authorities for the existing Burmese Resthouse.

May I request the favour of your Reverence's favourable consideration of this matter and an early reply. . . . My Calcutta address is c/o Swami Vivekananda, the Math, Belur, Howrah.

I have the honour to be
Your Reverence's most obedient servant,
K. Okakura[112]

Okakura's efforts came some nine years after the first confrontation between Dharmapala's monks and the mahant's men and seven years after Dharmapala's attempt to place the Japanese image in the shrine. Okakura's reference to having no connection "with any of the representatives of the Hinayana Buddhists of Ceylon, Siam or other places some of whom have so sadly abused your kindness" makes it clear that he had knowledge of Dharmapala's struggles with the mahant. His claim that he came to Bodh Gaya merely "to make an offering of reverence" is belied by the richness of his vision for the place—"little colonies of devotees" contemplating the place of enlightenment. Whatever his intentions, by 1902 the mahant had had more than enough of the Maha Bodhi Society and every reason to like Okakura's conciliatory attitude and the commonality that linked the mahant's Hinduism and his Buddhism.

---

112. "Mr. Okakura's Letter That Brought Trouble to the Buddhists," supplement, *Journal of the Maha Bodhi Society* 21 (1923): 35–40. It is unclear how Dharmapala got his hands on the letter.

Okakura left Bodh Gaya and India in quick order, with Dharmapala still
clinging to his hope that the law would provide a foothold for the Maha
Bodhi Society at Bodh Gaya.[113] Whether Okakura wanted simply a place for
Japanese pilgrims—as the proposal indicates—or a Japanese resthouse to be
followed by the cluster of ethnic, sectarian monasteries from across Asia,
as Tagore's reminiscences indicate, remains to be seen. Okakura's vision
of the clustering of local Buddhists was uncanny. Bodh Gaya today has become essentially what Tagore said Okakura envisioned, accommodating an
extraordinary variety of Buddhist places—some twenty-odd temples—each
identified with a "national" or sectarian Buddhism, resthouses, and administrative offices. The effect is wonderful but unnerving, architectural forms
representing many parts of Asia clustered around the Maha Bodhi temple
amid an Indian landscape that prepares the visitor for none of the pan-Asian
spectacle. In either of the two visions, the universalism of Okakura's vision
for Bodh Gaya is clear enough. On the basis of what Okakura told Tagore,
each Asian society brings its own architecture, vesture, and ceremonial
tradition to a place of common importance. Or as his proposal to the mahant suggests, Japanese architecture, vesture, and ceremony offer the essence
of Buddhism compiled in its supreme expression.

PAN-ASIANISM AND THE UNITED BUDDHIST WORLD

An instructive way to situate these three self-fashioned Asian intellectuals
is to start with fashion itself. Each embodied his universalism in local attire.
The telling point is exactly how they understood "local." Dharmapala wore
white robes until 1895, when he adopted the ochre of a world renouncer; Vivekananda moved between the tattered robes of a wandering monk (*parivra-
jaka*) or sannyasin and an ochre *gerrua* and turban. Okakura outdid them
both, appearing in a variety of costumes on different occasions—in the

---

113. Dharmapala's understanding of these events is wrong in several ways, misguided by
ignorance of colonial policy and suspicion of geopolitical forces:

> The secret meetings held at Bodhgaya by Mr. Okakura, Swami Vivekananda, Sister
> Nivedita, to establish a Hindu Japanese Alliance, and the denunciation of Hinayana
> Buddhism showed that Mr. Okakura was actuated by impure motives. The result of
> the private negotiations reacted on the Buddhist monks who were living at Bodhgaya
> in the Burmese resthouse. Lord Curzon appointed a Commission [and] the result of the
> Report was the final decision of the Government of India to eject Buddhists from Bud-
> dhagaya, as they expected the Japanese would come and make it a centre of political
> conspiracy. "Mr. Okakura's Letter," 38.

robes of a Taoist monk, a kimono, *haori-hakama* (two garments worn by a man over a kimono as formal dress), the costume of a Japanese fisherman, and an Indian dhoti.[114] Their sartorial exuberance rivaled Pierre Loti's, but these men were not outsiders pretending to be insiders; these were insiders reinventing the inside and presenting those traditions to people who knew them not at all. What is more striking is that the pan-Asian context brought out these exercises of the imagination as much as the hegemony of Europe in the minds of Asians.

All three spent substantial parts of their adult lives living abroad. In such places they were foreigners and their dress emblematic of their attempts to negotiate a way between the national and the universal. Their costumes were simulacra, signs of a civilization invented for foreign consumption—remembering that many of the foreigners were fellow Asians—not to say signs alien to the region and social class from which each had come.[115] Dharmapala saw dress reform tied directly to social reform, establishing a Dress Reform Society in 1898, and campaigned to move laypeople from Western dress to what has become known in Sri Lanka as "national dress" (*jatika andum*) or "Arya Sinhala" dress (Diary, July 29, 1905).[116] Okakura's dress shifted even within one foreign context—he traveled about India with a supply of cotton kimonos, and he seemed to have presented himself as Japanese when meeting English-speaking, middle-class Indians. But he also affected the costume of a Taoist monk, which he brought out while traveling in village Bengal. The impact of the garb of the Taoist monk produced predictable responses in middle-class settings. When Tagore introduced Okakura to a friend, "weird [was] not the word for its effect." By contrast, when he "glided into the landscape of the remote Bengali village . . . his Taoist robes striking no discordant note in the province of the *aul* and the

114. In India he had a Calcutta tailor make up the Taoist robes from a Chinese image that Okakura provided. See Christine M. E. Guth, "Charles Longfellow and Okakura Kakuzo: Cultural Cross-Dressing in the Colonial Context," *Positions* 8, no. 3 (2000): 622 and 630. To complete the cross-dressing picture, I should add that Okakura had dressed as a Western dandy in early adulthood.

115. Apropos of presenting a foreign, yet Asian identity in an Asian context, Okakura arrived in India in 1901 wearing a kimono; he returned to Japan in 1902 wearing a dhoti. Yasuko Horioka, *The Life of Kakuzo, Author of the Book of Tea* (Tokyo: Hokuseido, 1963), 49.

116. Nira Wickramasinghe, *Dressing the Colonised Body: Politics, Clothing, and Identity in Colonial Sri Lanka* (Hyderabad: Orient Longman, 2003). Wickramasinghe points out that while Dharmapala eschewed the sarong's alien origins, national dress for men is essentially a more elegant version of the sarong (14). She traces its origins to Malays in the island. Dharmapala associated the sarong with *hambankaraya* (Coast Moor, a Muslim from the South Indian coast) and urged Sinhalas not to wear it. See "Gihi Din Chariyava," in Guruge, *Dharmapala Lipi*, 42–4, and chapter 5 of the present volume.

12. Okakura Kakuzo in Taoist robes.

baul.[117] In a village setting Taoist robes must have appeared even more local than whatever effect Okakura had in mind.

The interaction of nationalist and universalist practice was reimagined against the usual sociological variables—class, gender, and region are the relevant ones here—as well as against those egocentric contexts, "home" and "abroad." In Japan Dharmapala spoke as an Indian and for India, and to the extent that he wanted to return Buddhism to its homeland and recover the place of the Buddha's enlightenment, it was hard for people such as the Japanese to imagine that he was not an Indian. In India, he was always a "foreigner," even in the eyes of British officials, themselves far from home. The sessions judge who heard the Bodh Gaya case on appeal in 1895 dismissed his contradictory testimony on the grounds that he was "a foreigner and a student singularly ignorant of the world."[118] The fact that Dharmapala

117. Tagore, "Kakuzo Okakura," 3:238 and 241.
118. Trevithick, *The Revival of Pilgrimage at Bodh Gaya*, 124.

spoke perfectly fluent English did not prevent the judge from dismissing him because of his foreignness. When Japanese Buddhists recognized Sri Lanka's difference at all, they referred to it as "India's Ceylon." And the same kind of encompassment marked his personal relationships. The relationship between Vivekananda and Dharmapala reinscribed the historical relationship between Hinduism and Buddhism, not to mention India and Lanka. The younger man was bound to be encompassed by Vivekananda. He would speak for Buddhism because "Buddha was after all an avatar of Vishnu."

The universalist visions that Okakura and Vivekananda shared were abstract and metaphysical, Okakura having been influenced by Hegel, and Vivekananda by Kant and Hegel.[119] Olcott and Dharmapala had a more sociological and democratic formula for creating universal Buddhism. Having compiled *The Buddhist Catechism* for Sinhala Buddhists, Olcott later submitted it for approval to the leading monks of Burma and Japan. Their approval was grudging, underinformed, and not a little coerced, but the *Catechism* carries their seal of approval. Dharmapala's visits to Japan showed him that Japanese Buddhism was wildly different from his own.[120] Subsequent encounters with other Japanese increased that awareness. Those differences left him all the more invested in securing Bodh Gaya and using relics and pilgrimage as vehicles for Buddhists to come together, even if separately. Having sacred centers and reasons for venerating them worked for other "world religions," and gaining control of Bodh Gaya was an impartial way—and perhaps the only practical way—to create a community of Buddhists with some sense of a common identity. When he said he "took up the larger work of universal Buddhism in January 1891 at the holy spot under the shade of the Bodhi Tree at Buddhagaya," he referenced two unwieldy motivations—his own enlightenment and making Buddhism universal (Diary, February 18, 1930).

Vivekananda's investment in the Buddha brings the relationship between universalism and nationalism full circle. To say that he engaged mightily with the Buddha is to understate the matter. He engaged intellec-

119. Notefelder writes that Okakura's writings reveal two approaches to universalism, adding that he needed a third to realize the universalism he sought. "On Idealism and Realism in the Thought of Okakura Kakuzo," *Journal of Japanese Studies* 16, no. 2 (1990): 354–5.

120. There are different versions of *The Buddhist Catechism*. One instructive difference is whether the agreement of representative monks of Burma, Japan, Sri Lanka, and Chittagong appears at the end of the text, as it does in the Theosophical Society's version (Adyar: Theosophical Society Publishing, 1975), 133–6.

tually with all gods and human beings. That ability to identify with otherness came from Ramakrishna, who was said to eat and drink like the people he wanted to understand, take their initiation, and use their language. "One must learn," he said, "to put oneself in another man's very soul," a prospect that surely outstrips the notion of imagining oneself in another person's shoes.[121] Vivekananda made his teacher's method his own—"no one ever before in India became Christian and Mohammedan and Vaishnava by turns."[122] He engaged the Buddha in the same way. As a college student he had been approached, he said, during meditation by the Buddha, and he had been inspired by both archeological work at Bodh Gaya and Arnold's *The Light of Asia*.[123] He spoke to Sister Nivedita of the perfect rationality of his hero, "the only absolutely sane man" the world had ever seen.[124] But the Buddha alone would not suffice—"The heart of the Buddha and the intellect of Sankaracharya" constituted the "highest possibility of humanity."[125]

His progressive views of caste aside, Vivekananda regularly spoke in a caste idiom, tying together everyday realities with the world-historical patterns he had learned from Hegel. As Sister Nivedita recalled her travels across North India with Vivekananda,

> Sometimes the Swami would deal with the rift between Brahmins and Kshattriyas [*sic*], painting the whole history of India as a struggle between the two, and showing that the latter had always embodied the rising, fetter-destroying impulses of the nation. He would give excellent reason too for the faith that was in him that the Kayasthas of modern Bengal represented the pre-Mauryan Kshattriyas. He would portray the two opposing types of culture, the one classical, intensive, and saturated with an ever-deepening sense of tradition and custom; the other, defiant, impulsive, and liberal in its out-look. It was part of the deep-lying law of historic development that Rama, Krishna, and Buddha had all arisen in the kingly, not the priestly caste.[126]

121. "The Master as I Saw Him," in Sister Nivedita, *The Complete Works of Sister Nivedita: Birth Centenary Publication*, vol. 1 (Calcutta: Sister Nivedita Girls' School, 1967), 150–83, at 160.

122. Sister Nivedita, "The Master as I Saw Him," 160.

123. Arun Kumar Biswas, *Buddha and Bodhisattva: A Hindu View* (New Delhi: Cosmo, 1987), 18.

124. Sister Nivedita, "The Master as I Saw Him," 171.

125. Ibid., 181.

126. Swami Saradananda, ed., *Notes of Some Wanderings with the Swami Vivekananda* (Calcutta: Urbodhan, 1913), 34–5.

Vivekananda was himself a Kayastha who thought his ancestors derived from "pre-Mauryan Kshattriyas." That genealogy meant that he was related to the Buddha (and Rama and Krishna) if not by descent, by virtue of his self-understanding.[127] When as a boy he had a vision of the Buddha entering his room, he saw his future—framed in the same nation-building idiom he used with Nivedita—"embodying the rising fetter-destroying impulses of the nation."[128]

His arguments about Indian history are striking not simply for the reified, not to say substantialist terms in which he constructed his own relationship to that past. His reasoning followed a Whiggish trajectory: Kshatriyas have been the liberating, nationalist forces in the Indian past; Kayasthas are Kshatriyas; Rama, Krishna, Buddha, and Vivekananda are Kshatriyas; he would take it from there. Such ideas are more edifying in the context of the India of his time.[129] He entertained notions about the "world religioning" of Buddhism that did not reify the past. To that extent his characterization resonates with the views of modern scholars of religion:

> There was never a religion in India, "known as Buddhism" with temples and priests of its own order. . . . Sects as a rule unite us with a few, but separate us from the many. And here lies the meaning of the fact that Buddhism in India was no sect. It was the worship of a great personality. It was a monastic order. But it was not a sect.[130]

Real consequences followed from this argument. Vivekananda avoided political entanglements, but his ideas about Bodh Gaya supported his ideas

---

127. Since roughly the eleventh century the Kayastha identity has evolved from occupational descriptor of uncertain status to high-ranking caste group. What complicates Vivekananda's attitude toward his Kayastha origins is the role played by the colonial ethnographers who also figured in the Bodh Gaya case—H. H. Risley, Haraprasad Sastri, Bourdillon, Rajendralala Mitra—in scrutinizing the Kayastha claim to Kshatriya status (at the same time Vivekananda was constructing Indian history in Brahman-Kshatriya terms). Nicholas B. Dirks, *Castes of Mind: Colonialism and the Making of Modern India* (Princeton, NJ: Princeton University Press, 2001), 203–24.

128. Saradananda, *Notes of Some Wanderings*, 34–5.

129. It is hard to find any reference, for instance, to Vivekananda's caste origins. His Advaita Ashrama publications make no mention of it, and other sources are equally silent. My sense is that he could imagine India's history in caste terms, and I think he understood himself in relation to the Brahman-Kshatriya drama but found it inappropriate to talk about his caste in his daily life, especially in encounters with Westerners, except when he spoke of Brahman and Kshatriya as historical tropes.

130. Sister Nivedita, "The Relation between Buddhism and Hinduism," in *Complete Works of Sister Nivedita*, 4:144–6.

about Buddhism, and those ideas, especially his commitment to the unity of India—in its capacity to absorb by subordinating—carried implications as much political as metaphysical.

It was his disciple Sister Nivedita who acted on the political implications of Vivekananda's thought. In the case of Bodh Gaya, she did so in a way that embodied his being a monistic Vedantin, saying, "As Buddha is the glory of Hinduism, even so is Bodh Gaya the glory of India." She made another connection with more direct implications: "and there are few things of which the Indian people have such a right to be proud as the history in relation to [Bodh Gaya] of Sankaracharya and his Giri Monks."[131] The ninth-century teacher of monistic Vedanta started the lineage that culminated in the mahant and the institution he controlled at Bodh Gaya. The mahant inherited a noble tradition of universalism and inclusiveness, she thought, that served Buddhists and other "foreigners" equally well.[132] Her sophisticated views on the reification of Hinduism and Buddhism notwithstanding, Nivedita was less sensitive to the implication of words such as "foreigners." She thought that the Buddhists of her time were "foreign," not future citizens of an Indian state, and "foreign" Buddhists should appreciate that the place of the Buddha's enlightenment had passed into Hindu hands:

> We can easily see the advantage that it has been to Buddhism, to have its central holy place in the hands of a people whose sympathies were commensurate with their own most comprehensive thought, without being identified in any way with their sectarian animosities. To the Hindu . . . few things can be such a source of pride as the hospitality and courtesy shown to foreigners by the Giri monks of Bodh Gaya. There is a royal character in the entertainment offered, for no sooner is the guest identified than the Mohant—strict Hindu ascetic as he is himself—sends to enquire whether he desires meat or wine. . . . And is not the courtesy shown here extended in the person of the Mohant, the friendliness and welcome of the whole of the Indian people to the sister-nations of Asia?[133]

131. "Nivedita to Mr. S. K. Ratcliffe, 1903[?], in Sankara Prasad Basu, ed., *Letters of Sister Nivedita*, vol. 2 (Calcutta: Nababharat, 1982), 601–5, at 604.

132. Trevithick says that the Giri monks of Bodh Gaya have historically been unusually open about accepting ascetics from "any order of Hindus" and that openness to difference has led to their being treated as ritually impure by other sannyasins. *The Revival of Buddhist Pilgrimage at Bodh Gaya*, 21.

133. "Bodh Gaya," in *The Complete Works of Sister Nivedita*, 4:195.

To her, Dharmapala was the mahant's opposite and Bodh Gaya under the mahant's control was "the holy place of Indian nationalism."[134] The "royal" idiom put the mahant in the same position as Vivekananda—openhanded, progressive figures who knew what was best for India. As she wrote to the editor of the *Statesman*,

> All this trouble stirred up by that wretched fanatic Dharmmapala [*sic*] out of misguided idea [*sic*] of glorifying Buddha! At bottom, ignorance of history and limitation of religious ideas. As if "hard-shell Baptists" tried to take exclusive possession of Westminster Abbey.[135]

Sister Nivedita feared that Dharmapala's litigation and the sympathy of Lord Curzon and a host of other British officials for the Buddhist cause at Bodh Gaya could damage the mahant's legitimacy. In response she organized a party to visit the place so that "leaders of public opinion can be brought into personal contact with the Mahunt [*sic*]."[136] The pilgrims were distinguished—Rabindranath Tagore, his wife, and his children, Professor Jagadis Bose, his wife and children, the editor of the Indian *Statesman* and his wife, the son of the Prince of Tripura, Sir Jadunath Sarkar, Indranath Nandi, Professor Chandra Dey, Swami Saddhananda, and three students. They spent almost a month visiting Buddhist sites in North India, an itinerary that did a lot more than lead these notables into contact with the mahant.[137] He "received them like a king" and presented the party with a miniature relic mound in which four Buddhas sat surrounded by hundreds of little Buddhas."[138] Sir Jadunath Sarkar quoted her in a subsequent letter as having said at Bodh Gaya,

> The Hindus who chose Sri Ramakrishna as their guru acted with the same discernment as the Hindus who, in days gone by, followed the

---

134. Lizelle Reymond, *The Dedicated: A Biography of Nivedita* (New York: John Day, 1963), 308.

135. Letter to Mr. S. K. Ratcliffe, 1903[?], in Basu, *Letters of Sister Nivedita*, 2:601–5, at 604.

136. Letter to Miss J. Macleod, September 21, 1904, in Basu, *Letters of Sister Nivedita*, 2:681–2, at 681.

137. Reymond, "Budh-Gaya," in *The Dedicated: A Biography of Nivedita*, 308–16, at 309. Decades later Tagore came to support the Buddhist cause at Bodh Gaya. "The Great Buddhist Temple at Buddha-Gaya and Dr. Rabindranath Tagore," *Journal of the Maha Bodhi Society* 30 (1922): 1–8.

138. Letter to Mrs. Ole Bull, December 1, 1904, in Basu, *Letters of Sister Nivedita*, 2:700–1, at 701.

greatest sadhu of their time, the victorious Buddha. . . . If ever I write the life of Swami Vivekananda, I shall naturally describe him as the greatest sage of all time, and only mention Chaitanya, or the Vaishnava sect to which he belonged, in passing. If, much later, historians, on the authority of my book, affirm that Ramakrishna's followers have seceded from Hindu society to form a caste apart from the Vaishnavas, or that they ousted the followers of Chaitanya, then they will only be making the same mistake as those who teach that Buddhism does not belong to us.[139]

However much universalism Nivedita took from Vivekananda and whatever appreciation she had of the dialectical relationship of Rama, Krishna, and the Buddha, she drew another conclusion from Vivekananda's teachings: Buddhism belongs to the Hindus. Buddha was their *sadhu* (holy man).

The vagaries of future historical accounts duly noted, the situation offers a full share of contradictions and wayward effects. Despite her affection for Okakura and his project, Nivedita chose Indian nationalism over Okakura's pan-Asianism. She had accompanied Okakura on his January 1902 pilgrimage to Bodh Gaya. Her later letters reveal that she had seen him off on his second trip in April, when he made the offer of fealty to the mahant. In July she wrote that he had secured the land and was going to sign a lease.[140] In a subsequent letter, she asked a friend at the *Statesman* to write an article "in your trenchant and seemingly unconscious way," saying,

> Of course there are many amongst the educated classes in India who are doubtless looking for a closer union with Japan—but probably it is not in the view of government that it would be well to give any sect of Buddhists or Buddhist nations as a whole, an independent footing in India. And that in this respect you cannot but think that India's best interests coincide with those of the Govt.[141]

The logic of universalism argued for Okakura's interests at Bodh Gaya only if one ignores his plans for a narrowly Japanese space at Bodh Gaya. To Nivedita, he was a far cry from "that wretched fanatic Dharmmapala." Okakura was a Buddhist who thought that Asia was one and Hinduism and

139. Reymond, "Budh-Gaya," 309–10.

140. Letter to Miss J. Macleod, April 19, 1902, in Basu, *Letters of Sister Nivedita*, 1:458–60, at 458; and Letter to Miss J. Macleod, July 24, 1902 [?], in ibid., 1:482–5, at 485.

141. Letter to S. K. Ratcliffe, in Basu, *Letters of Sister Nivedita*, 2:601–5, at 604.

Buddhism were kindred spirits. But there was a colonial context as well, and in this context, her feelings for Indian national interest trumped metaphysical monism, pan-Asianism, and any other form of universalism.

The editor of Nivedita's letters presents a chronology of her work in India, noting that she became suspicious of Okakura's motives for his revolutionary activities in India and ultimately concluded that he was a Japanese agent.[142] The woman who had written in her introduction to *The Ideals of the East* that it offered the promise of a unified Asia held together by the spirit of a revitalized and inclusive Hinduism now feared that he intended the "abstract idealism" of Asian religiosity as camouflage for Japanese imperialism. The editor of her letters indicates that Nivedita gave a lecture on Bodh Gaya in Calcutta in April 1904 "to counteract Anagarika Dharmapala's communal Bodh Gaya Movement."[143] The word "communal" is anachronistic in several ways, but for Nivedita, Dharmapala was always going to be worse than Okakura—small-minded and sectarian through and through. The man who wanted to create a Buddhist world, joining ethnic Buddhists across Asia with Western Buddhists newly made, was neither a pan-Asianist nor a universalist. He was a "communalist." That he was not an Indian himself and that Indian Buddhists did not count locally as a political force of any consequence did not protect him from the charge. Nivedita accused Dharmapala of communalizing a community that did not yet exist. Even so, the community he had in mind could scarcely compete with the oneness of all beings, living and dead, human and divine, that Vivekananda envisioned.

142. "Sister Nivedita: A Chronology, 1867–1911," in Basu, *Letters of Sister Nivedita*, 1:39.
143. Ibid., 1:41.

CHAPTER FOUR

Dharmapala, the British, and the Bengalis

If there is a Hindu revival in India, there is a Buddhist revival in the world.
—*Indian Mirror*, 1893

Recovering Bodh Gaya gave Dharmapala a way both to imitate the unbreakable resolution of the Buddha and serve the Buddhist world. After his arrival the Saivite renouncers who controlled the place became increasingly hostile to his efforts, and they held an insurmountable advantage in the form of a deed of ownership. Their insistence on their property rights entangled a colonial government in the fray, and the British found themselves caught between their respect for history—they assumed that Bodh Gaya was originally a Buddhist place—and the flowing tide of Hindu identity and nationalist aspirations. When Dharmapala came to Bodh Gaya in 1891, he began to act on possibilities that were a product of both his innocence and the historical moment. He assumed that Bodh Gaya might simply be made over to the Buddhists, a united Buddhist world would naturally take shape around the site of the Buddha's enlightenment, and the return of Buddhism to India in the form of the Maha Bodhi Society would draw widespread Indian support. That brief period in India's history was at least modestly favorable to all of those outcomes, and Dharmapala was inspired by every encouraging sign. By 1910 the Bodh Gaya case had worked its way through the courts, and the universalizing atmosphere had dissipated, swept over by forces still inchoate in 1891.

Before Dharmapala saw Bodh Gaya, he read about it. In Colombo he read *India Revisited*, giving him his first inkling that a place still existed in North

India where the Buddha had achieved enlightenment.[1] Traveling in Japan in 1889, he read *Light of Asia*, and the book gave him a sense of the grandeur of the Buddha's achievement. Arnold called the chapter in *India Revisited* that treats his visit to Bodh Gaya "The Land of the 'Light of Asia,'" emphasizing that his joy at having reached the place was undone by its present condition. The sanctum sanctorum itself had been violated: "The granite floor was . . . desecrated by the Brahmans who have usurped the place, with a stone Lingam [the emblem of Siva]."[2] But Buddhism in India was more than ruined places. Arnold found enduring signs of it in the most Hindu of India's cities:

> It is not Hinduism which—to my mind, at least—chiefly consecrates Benares. The divine memory of the founder of Buddhism broods over all the country hereabouts. . . . Modern Brahmanism is really Buddhism in a Shastri's robes and sacred thread. Shunkuracarya [*sic*] and his priests expelled the brethren of the yellow robe from India, but the spirit of Sakya-Muni's teaching remained unbanished, just as "Greece, overcome, conquered her conquerors." For this reason the country of "The Light of Asia" and the monuments that remain in India of ancient Buddhism ought surely to be esteemed more interesting than the most ornate Brahmanic temples. (222–3)

At Bodh Gaya, the past lingered on in the form of broken sculptures, precious inscriptions lying about, and five or six cartloads of stone fragments piled up in a shed. Lecturing in London, Arnold ticked off artifacts now put to new uses:

> Stones carved with Buddha's images . . . used as weights in the levers for drawing water. . . . I have seen three feet high statues in an excellent state of preservation buried under rubbish . . . and the Asokan pillars . . . are now used as posts for the mahant's kitchen.[3]

When Dharmapala set his own eyes on Bodh Gaya, he saw not things but their absence. He called it a *sunya bhavi* (empty space), the kitchen notwithstanding.[4]

---

1. "The Buddha Sasana in India," talk given in Colombo July 18, 1893, reprinted in Guruge, *Dharmapala Lipi*. Dharmapala writes, "In 1886 . . . I read the chapter on the Maha Bodhi tree in . . . *India Revisited*. At this time it was a wonder even to hear about this place." (235).
2. *India Revisited*, 233–4.
3. *London Daily Telegraph*, quoted in Fields, *How the Swans Came to the Lake*, 115.
4. "Madame Foster of Honolulu," in Guruge, *Dharmapala Lipi*, 321. The same imagery of emptiness appears in other accounts of the arrival scene: "In January 1891 the Anagarika Dhar-

The place was dilapidated, but it was not empty. The British had rebuilt the Maha Bodhi temple itself, following a Burmese attempt to do so in a Burmese way, and the precincts of the temple were anything but desolate. Buddhists did not come in any large numbers, but Hindu pilgrims did, especially during the two pilgrimage seasons of the year. Dharmapala arrived during the cold-season pilgrimage. He saw the pilgrims—"Thousands of Biharees flocked to the shrine, worshipped the statue, Bodhi Tree & the foot print"—but even in the thousands they did not count (Diary, February 9, 1891). The pity was "They worship Him whom they know not."[5] It is not obvious from his aphorism whether the Hindus paid attention to the Buddha image, the Maha Bodhi temple in which it sat, or the eponymous tree located nearby. For him the focus fell on the temple. Wherever Hindus did their devotions, they either ignored the man who attained enlightenment at Bodh Gaya—by not visiting the temple at all—or they worshipped him as the ninth avatar of Visnu or as Siva in heroic form.

At Dharmapala's arrival, the most active part of the landscape was the Saivite *math*, or *mutt* (the most common transliterations deriving from *matam*), where the mahant resided. Almost two hundred years had passed since the Giri renouncers of the Dasanami order had legitimated their control of Bodh Gaya by way of a deed from the Moghul Shah Alam.[6] The deed was dated 1727 CE, but the Giri monks had occupied the site at least since the late sixteenth century. Those first monks gave rise to a lineage of teachers and students. The abbots of the place, the mahants, managed each generation of teachers and students, overseeing about a thousand sannyasins in twenty-odd maths affiliated with Bodh Gaya, itself home to fifty to one hundred sannyasins.[7] Amid the flotsam and jetsam of a Buddhist past stood a thriving Hindu monastic complex, including the site of the Buddha's en-

---

mapala visited the temple and found the place and its precincts abandoned." "Rescue Buddha Gaya," supplement, *Journal of the Maha Bodhi Society* 31 (1923): 1–35, at 28.

5. Dharmapala knew the origins of the phrase from his early education in Christian schools and quoted Saint Paul to the same effect in the first lecture he gave in Calcutta, "Buddhism in Its Relationship with Hinduism," *Journal of the Maha Bodhi Society* 100 (1992): 81–8, at 81.

6. The Dasanamis are students of Sankaracarya, famous for reviving Saivism in South India and establishing the first enduring Hindu monastic order. The Giri monks are one of ten groups (thus *Dasanami*) tracing their ordination to him. The Dasanami order is in turn organized in four monastic seats (*pithas*) associated with Sankaracarya's four chief disciples. The Giri pitha is Badarinath in Uttar Pradesh near the Chinese border. Thus the Bodh Gaya math has both dependent maths and a mother math in a faraway place. See Wade Dazey, "Tradition and Modernization in the Organization of Dasanami Samnyasins," in *Monastic Life in the Christian and Hindu Traditions*, ed. Austin B. Creel and Vasudha Narayanan (Lewiston, NY: Edwin Mellen, 1990), 281–321.

7. Doyle, "Bodh Gaya," 135ff.

lightenment. For Dharmapala to call the site a *sunya bhava*, overlooking
the pilgrims, the Saivites, and their monastic complex, represents an act of
imagination that rivals Arnold's seeing Benares as a Buddhist place.

Monastic standards—at least when Rajendralala Mitra saw the math in
the 1870s—were less than strict:

> The Mahants are pledged to lifelong celibacy, and according to the rule
> of their order the most pious and learned among the disciples (of whom
> there are always from thirty to fifty) is expected to succeed; but as a mat-
> ter of fact I have elsewhere seen that only the youngest, and he who bears
> the strongest personal resemblance to the abbot, generally succeeds to the
> high rank. The monks lead an easy comfortable life; feasting on rich cakes
> (*malpuya*) and puddings (*mohanbhog*), and freely indulging in the exhila-
> rating beverage of *bhanga* [hashish]. Few attempt to learn the sacred books
> of their religion, and most of them are grossly ignorant. Their present Ma-
> hant is an intelligent man, but not particularly well versed in the Sastras.
> He has, however, a fine collection of Sanskrit manuscripts, and employs
> the more intelligent among his disciples to copy manuscripts for him.
> Some of the books of their faith are, however, occasionally expounded to
> the monks by one of their seniors, rarely by the Mahant himself.[8]

Whatever the monks' moral state, their corruption mattered little to Dharmapala; what mattered was the injustice of their not simply yielding to the
Buddhists—how could they not see that they were squatting on land sacred
to another religion?

Resources for supporting these twenty-odd maths and the monks who
lived there came from several sources. The first was land ownership. In
what is now Bihar, where some 90 percent of the land under cultivation
was owned by landlords, the Bodh Gaya mahant was the state's largest zamindar, controlling some fifteen thousand acres of land under cultivation.
Doyle writes that the crops grown by the landless laborers who worked his
fields gave the mahant an annual income upward of Rs. 60,000.[9] The other

8. *Buddha Gaya: The Hermitage of Sakya Muni* (Calcutta: Bengal Secretariat Press, 1878),
5. Mitra follows in a tradition that goes back to Buchanan, exulting the fastidious Vaisnavas of
the Ramanandi order and criticizing the loose conduct of the Dasanamis, who "affect a life of
mortification" but who "are accused of being in private very indulgent to their sensual appe-
tites." Francis Buchanan, *An Account of the Districts of Bihar and Patna in 1811–1812*, vol. 1
(1936; repr., New Delhi: Usha Jain, 1986), 369.

9. Rai Ram Anugraha Narain Singh Bahadur, *A Brief History of the Bodh Gaya Math, District Gaya* (Calcutta: Bengal Secretariat Press, 1893). The "list of immovable Property belonging

source of income came from pilgrims who visited Bodh Gaya to perform *sraddha* (last rites for an ancestor) under the sacred bo tree. In the 1870s Mitra estimated the annual income from pilgrims at Rs. 80,000.[10] The math may have had a third source of wealth, the treasure offered by the Burmese king Mindon to the temple.[11] The math, on any calculation, was rich beyond imagining, and the mahant had no reason to sell the place, whatever Dharmapala was willing to offer.

Other Dasanamis, other economic interests. Dasanami soldier monks controlled both the silk and cotton trade across north India, and other Dasanamis, by controlling maths, were the largest urban property holders in towns along the Ganges and through central India. Bayly is not being facetious when he writes, "It was they who came the nearest of any Indian business community to the emerging bourgeoisie that European theorists from Sleeman to Marx wished to see."[12] With wealth came responsibilities. The Bodh Gaya mahant was expected to redistribute his income in a variety of ways that went beyond feeding and housing his sannyasis. The math served in the same way that Hindu temples function all across South Asia—by redistributing wealth, the place served as an economic nexus inseparable from its role as a symbolic center. Taking contributions was connected seamlessly with giving *darsan* (an audience with a person, place or thing that confers blessings), as was receiving agricultural produce and turning crops into hospitality.[13] Poor pilgrims—as many as three hundred to five hundred on high-traffic days—were fed in the math's almshouse. Sannyasis wishing to die in Benares could spend their last days in a branch math that also functioned as a place where well-to-do laymen and officeholders were lavishly entertained.[14] But the most pertinent form that the mahant's liberality assumed was feeding and sheltering pilgrims—mainly Hindus, but

to the Math of Bodh Gaya," which appears as an appendix, indicates 212 pieces of property belonged to the math in the late nineteenth century. Converted into British pounds of the time, the Rs. 60,000 produced by those lands was worth some £6,000 a year.

10. *Buddha Gaya*, 8.

11. The Burmese king Mindon sent jewel offerings to the mahant with instructions that they were to be "kept in a paribhoga house specially erected at the expense of the King." The Burmese inscription lays out the quantities of those jewels in convincing detail—511 diamonds, 311 emeralds, 3,966 rubies, and 623 pearls. S. Dhammika, *Navel of the Earth: The History and Significance of Bodh-Gaya* (Singapore: Buddha Dhamma Mandala Society, 1996), 31, quoted in Doyle, "Bodh Gaya," 127n53.

12. C. A. Bayly, *Rulers, Townsmen, and Bazaars: North Indian Society in the Age of British Expansion, 1770–1870* (New York: Cambridge University Press, 1983), 241–2.

13. See Arjun Appadurai, *Worship and Conflict under Colonial Rule: A South Indian Case* (New York: Cambridge University Press, 1981).

14. Bahadur, *A Brief History of the Bodh Gaya Math*, 2.

13. Giri sannyasis at Bodh Gaya, 1810.

occasionally Buddhists—at Bodh Gaya itself. Poor pilgrims were not given
accommodation, but the mahant provided shelter and food for wealthy or
distinguished guests. Included in the latter category was a group of Burmese monks who arrived on pilgrimage just days after Dharmapala's arrival
(Diary, February 1, 1891).

The landscape showed signs of the Saivite sannyasis' having made themselves part of Bodh Gaya. Several of the mahant's predecessors—including
the founder of the Giri lineage at Bodh Gaya and a later mahant who built
the math—were buried under *samadhi* (tombs) in the courtyard of the Maha
Bodhi temple. Resembling small Buddhist relic mounds topped off with Siva
lingams (Siva's identifying sign), the *samadhis* testified to the hybridity of
the place. The same is true of the two bo trees under which pilgrims offered
pinda (rice balls). For Buddhists the tree marked the place where the Buddha
achieved enlightenment; for Hindus, the other tree was a place associated
with auspiciousness, a place appropriate for making offerings for parents,
and one of forty-five *vedis* (sacred places) that constitute the pilgrimage

circuit centered on the Visnu temple at Gaya, a few miles to the north. The math stood close to the temple, backed up against the Niranjana River, and that proximity meant that the sannyasis spent time in the temple compound, helping pilgrims, chatting with them, and simply passing the day.

By tradition the temple tower dates back to Asoka and has fallen into ruin and been rebuilt several times.[15] There are architectural traces of influence that art historians identify with present-day Theravada and Mahayana Buddhism as well as Hinduism, and whatever meanings the place carried, those meanings varied with perspective and time. The same could be said for the Hindus. At the time of Xuanzang's visit (630–44 CE), the tree was anathema to Hindus, the emperor Sasanka having dug it up and burned it around 600 CE, "to destroy it utterly and not leave a trace behind." Veneration for a bodhi tree—either the tree that stands in the same place as the tree under which the Buddha had liberation or a second tree on the other side of the temple—was incorporated into Hindu practice by at least the sixteenth century, as attested by the account left by a Hindu pandit in the employ of the zamindar of Patna who reported that Hindus made a practice of "embracing the Bodhi tree." L. S. S. O'Malley saw signs of the place's everyday complexity:

> Pilgrims from places in which the *Tristhalisetu* [the textual rationale for the practice] is held in esteem still offer *pindas* under the Bodhi tree and have done so for more than three centuries, but, on the other hand, such offerings are not made by Bengalis, Oriyas and Maitilis, who do not know the work.[16]

When Francis Buchanan visited in 1811, he found no acts of worship—either Buddhist or Hindu—being conducted in the shrine.[17] Beglar, the British official who oversaw the temple repairs in 1880, found only Hindus at Bodh Gaya, and he observed them both at the bodhi tree and the temple. He encountered "certain men constantly in and about the Temple, whose business it appeared to me to have been to offer daily worship by the recitations of the Shastras, by the ringing of bells and blowing of conch shells, and by the offer of lights and flowers to . . . various Hindu Divinities or their foot-

---

15. Janice Leoshko notes that since Cunningham's time, art-historical interest has focused on the Maha Bodhi temple of the earliest period, namely, Asoka's time, ignoring later sculpture and inscriptions, as well as the site's hybrid character even in the beginning. "On the Construction of a Buddhist Pilgrimage Site," *Art History* 19, no. 4 (1996): 573–97.

16. *Bengal District Gazetteers, Gaya* (Calcutta: Bengal Secretariat Book Depot, 1906), 70.

17. *Account of the Districts of Bihar and Patna*, 1:104–6.

prints, within and about the Temple, to the sacred pipal tree, and to certain sacred spots."[18] It is hard to know what to make of Beglar's testimony. As valuable as it is, it was prompted by the mahant's lawyers after Dharmapala brought suit, and Beglar's description does not specify where the emphasis fell in worship "within and about" the temple. It is possible that it was entirely neglected: the Bodh Gaya temple case commissioners who looked into the matter in 1903 concluded that no Hindu worship had taken place in the temple before 1894.[19] What is indisputable is that after Dharmapala's arrival Hindu worship was either initiated or elaborated.

An image of the Buddha sat in the sanctum at the base of the tower. Hindus regarded that image as a statue of Bhairava, the fearsome form of Siva. During the struggle with Dharmapala, the mahant's attorneys insisted that the image embodied another god altogether—the ninth avatar of Visnu, that is, the Buddha reimagined as a Hindu god (*Buddha dev*) known for his asceticism and association with the bodhi tree. It seems reasonable to suppose that over the centuries when control of the temple was uncontested, the Saivites began to regard the Buddha image as a form of Siva, whether they worshipped the image or not. When British officials began to suggest that the temple had originally been Buddhist, the Saivites saw the advantage of recharacterizing the image as the Buddha, now understood as an avatar of Visnu. Even after Dharmapala's arrival the Saivite lingam on the floor of the sanctum seems to have been overlooked by the Buddhists. The Vaisnavite marks soon to appear on the forehead of the image were the work of the Giri monks, reclaiming their own place, and doubly offensive to Buddhist sensibilities for that reason.

Different pilgrims carried out different forms of worship, and who did what and when they did it depended on political circumstances as much as religious ones. The lingam carved on the floor of the shrine, however anomalous, put the Saivites' claim on the site. What also linked them to the Maha Bodhi temple was a shrine to the goddess Annapurna, whom they regarded as the *istha devi* (patron goddess) of the place.[20] Next to her shrine stood a structure providing further ambiguity. It was called the *pancha pan-*

18. Letter to the Mahant of Buddha-Gaya, quoted in Balindralal Das, *A Hindu Point of View on the Bodh-Gaya Temple Bill* (Delhi: National Journals Press, 1936), 6–8, at 7.

19. W. C. Macpherson, officiating chief secretary to the government of Bengal, to the secretary to the government of India, October 31, 1903, India Office Records, British Library, IOR/L/PJ/6/750/file 705, item 14.

20. Doyle, "Bodh Gaya," 143–4. The Giri tradition has it that the third mahant was able to build the Bodh Gaya math because of benefits received from worshipping the goddess and later built the shrine for her worship.

dav, the six images located there representing the five Pandava brothers and Draupadi. Some people said that the images were representations of the Buddha. And finally there were the engraved footprints of Visnu (which may have been the footprints of the Lord Buddha, now reimagined).

Worship at the central shrine was to become the bone of contention, and that dispute provoked both sides to look back to the state of things before the late nineteenth century. The Buddhist side insinuated at several points that Hindus did not worship the image in the shrine and avoided even its sight. In a paper he read before the Royal Asiatic Society in 1827, Buchanan had explained the construction of a set of stairs leading to the upper terrace where the bo tree stood served not to provide access to the tree so much as to prevent contact with the image—"so that the orthodox may pass up without entering the porch, and thus seeing the hateful image of the Buddha." But he also added that when he visited, this "ancient practice" was no longer followed.[21] At the first trial Dharmapala's attorney called the pandit of a government school. He testified that he had visited the temple three or four times but never entered it "as it is a Buddhist Temple and Hindus are forbidden to enter such." The attorney then elicited testimony that he said was more valuable—Hindus did not worship there, the custodian said, adding that Brahman priests forbade Hindus from entering the temple altogether.[22]

Whatever their attitudes toward the temple in earlier days, at the time of Dharmapala's intervention Hindus were not reluctant to come near the temple to offer pindas at the bodhi tree. Colonial officials made a distinction between the mahant's conducting worship in the Maha Bodhi temple and his right to the offerings pilgrims left there—whether he conducted worship or not. It is possible to dismiss arguments about who worshipped where as "derisive comments of orientalist experts" and thus more of an essentializing effect than a reliable picture of what went on at Maha Bodhi temple.[23] But there is an easier reading that avoids the interpretive questions: the temple itself was on the margins of the practices that counted at

21. C.E.A.W.O. [Charles Oldham], untitled review, *Journal of the Royal Asiatic Society of Great Britain and Ireland*, no. 1 (1928): 169–72, at 171.

22. Macpherson's Judgment in the Court of the District Magistrate of Gaya, *H. Dharmapala v. Jaipal Giri and Others*, July 1895, India Office Records, British Library, IOR/L/PJ/6/404/ file 1545, 1–23, at 9.

23. See Jacob N. Kinnard, "When the Buddha Sued Visnu," in *Constituting Communities: Theravada Buddhism and the Religious Cultures of South and Southeast Asia*, ed. John Clifford Holt, Jacob Kinnard, and Jonathan S. Walters (Albany: State University of New York Press, 2003), 90.

Bodh Gaya during most of the nineteenth century (and perhaps earlier) and became central only when Dharmapala made it so. Before that, whether the image in the temple stood for the Buddha, the ninth avatar of Visnu or Siva in heroic form, was not of much consequence.[24] Hindu pilgrims assumed the image was powerful and auspicious. They had their eyes fixed on the bodhi tree where they made offerings to their ancestors. Not all pilgrims visited Bodh Gaya or all forty-five vedis, but those who had wealth and took orthodoxy seriously tried to visit them all.[25] At Bodh Gaya what was important was the tree, not the temple. For the mahant the tree was important for the "substantial income from the offerings made by Hindu pilgrims at the sacred pipal-tree."[26]

The textual warrant for pilgrimage to Gaya and the sacred sites around Gaya (*Gayakshetra*) derives from the *Gaya-mahatmya*, hymns of praise celebrating sacred places (itself part of the *Vayu purana*).[27] It explains the forty-five vedis as outlining the shape of the giant Gayasur, a demigod (*asura*), the periphery of his fallen body marking the land sacred to Gaya, India's best-known sraddha site. Gayasur, the text says, acquired immense power

24. Although the Vaishnavite marks on the Buddha's forehead dominate accounts of Bodh Gaya, the mahant was the abbot of a Saivite monastery. When the conflict developed, one way the Saivites sought to assert their authority over the place was to daub red paint, "which [gave] it the appearance not of the being Buddha but of dread Bhairav." "Buddhists of Asia, Wake Up!," *Journal of the Maha Bodhi Society* 17 (1909): 286–9, at 289. The unnamed author was uncomfortable with the same ambiguity that troubled Dharmapala: "A Saivite Mahant appointing a Vishnu priest to worship Buddha in the form of Bhairava in a Buddhist Temple is something like the Archbishop of Canterbury appointing a Wesleyan minister to officiate at a chapel in the Vatican wherein is placed the statue of Virgin Mary."

25. Buchanan, *Account of the Districts of Bihar and Patna*, 104–5.

26. Mitra, *Buddha Gaya*, 6. From the time of Mitra's visit in 1887, there have been two bodhi trees of interest. The bo tree under which Hindus offered sraddha, and which Buddhists venerated as the place of enlightenment, blew down before his visit. It was replanted, and pilgrims were urged to offer sraddha at another bo tree on the north side of the Maha Bodhi temple. Macpherson used that substitution as evidence that Hindus had abandoned the appropriate Bodhi tree, and the mahant had acquiesced to it. Judgment in the Court of the District Magistrate of Gaya, *H. Dharmapala v. Jaipal Gir and Others*, India Office Records, British Library, IOR/L/PJ/6/404/file 1545, 10.

27. G. V. Tagare, ed., *Vayu Purana*, part 2, in *Ancient Indian Tradition & Mythology*, ed. G. P. Bhatt, vol. 38 (Delhi: Motilal Banarsidass, 1988). Making a connection between the Hindu tradition and the Buddha appears in a variety of *Puranas*, the *Bhagavad Gita*, the *Mahabharata*, and the *Gitagovinda*. One of Dharmapala's latter-day supporters discovered a pamphlet at Bodh Gaya, quoting from all of those sources, most of which emphasized the Buddha's purity (which I take to mean his celibacy), his rejection of animal sacrifice, and his righteousness. "Quotations from an Anonymous Pamphlet Probably Used by Hindu Mohant of Budhgaya," *Journal of the Maha Bodhi Society* 39 (1931): 79–82.

by way of his asceticism, and coming into contact with his body now has proportionately immense effects. Doing *pinda-dan* at his symbolic navel liberates twenty-one generations of ancestors; doing so at the feet of Gaya-sur liberates seven generations.[28] On reaching Bodh Gaya—the most far-flung vedi of the circuit—the pilgrim is advised to pay homage to the Bo tree with this prayer:

> Obeisance to you, oh King of the *savatthas*! You have taken the form of Brahma, Visnu, and Siv; the tree of enlightenment (*bodhitaru*); and the redeemer of the ancestors (*pitars*); as well as those who perform this *sraddh*.[29]

The *Gaya-mahatmya* is a tradition that has been regularly remade, most pertinently by the rise of Gayawal Brahmans who gained control of Gaya in the late eighteenth century.[30] The tradition served to support the interests of a community of Brahmans just then gaining authority over places celebrated in the tradition.[31]

When Bodh Gaya functioned as a more Buddhist place, it was unlikely to have been exclusively Buddhist. In those times the place may not have been associated with sraddha or Gaya. For that matter Gaya was not included in an eighth-century roster of places where sraddha produces salvation, however many generations were saved.[32] By the nineteenth century doing sraddha was an important motivation for Hindu traffic to Bodh Gaya as part of the Gaya circuit, and thus the reason Vaisnavas came to Bodh Gaya—even though the place was controlled by Saivites. Their motive was

---

28. *Gaya-mahatmya Katha*, (Gaya: Ramayan Pustakalaya, n.d.), 7. Doyle uses this text as an example of the kind of popular translation of the *Gaya-mahatmya* that pilgrims buy on the pavement and thus what pilgrims nowadays learn of the place. "Bodh Gaya," 222–34.

29. Doyle, "Bodh Gaya," 229.

30. Doyle, "Bodh Gaya," 221n17.

31. Mitra argues that the fact that Bodh Gaya, and the bodhi tree in particular, represent the feet of Gayasur is motivated by more than the logic of space. He takes it as an expression of superiority of Gaya over Bodh Gaya, and indirectly of Hinduism over Buddhism, now reduced to the relatively impure position of the foot. *Buddha Gaya*, 16–20. O'Malley, citing Cunningham's work, mentions a parallel practice, the footprints of Visnu, carved into the face of a Buddhist relic mound in the front of the temple, marked with the date 1308 CE. *Bengal District Gazetteer, Gaya*, 48. He makes no comment on the implications of Visnu's footprints appearing on the *stupa*.

32. O'Malley, quoting Haraprasad Sastri on the eighth-century *sloka* (verse), speculates that Gaya did not become an important pilgrimage site until the tenth century. *Bengal District Gazetteers, Gaya*, 61n.

doing right by their ancestors, and what pilgrims understood of the connection to the Buddha and his enlightenment was secondary if not irrelevant. Just as the example of Gayasur suggests, Gaya is associated with asceticism and spiritual development, and the Buddha's presence in a place some six miles south reinscribes that connection. "The tree of enlightenment" provides the symbolic center. Saivites occupying a Vaishavite pilgrimage place, the Giris could not make much of any mythological warrant for their rights. But they could make arguments—of long-term residence and a deed of ownership—the British could appreciate. To clinch the case, they insisted—without evidence—that they had remained loyal during the 1857 mutiny.[33]

A second presence that made Bodh Gaya other than the empty place of Dharmapala's imagination was the British raj itself, understood both narrowly (British civil servants regularly visited Bodh Gaya) and more broadly (the collector resided in Gaya, where he tried legal cases, passing cases that he could not resolve on to appellate courts in Patna and Calcutta). British officials were sometimes a presence at Bodh Gaya, as indicated by Dharmapala's early encounters with officials of the Public Works Division and a police superintendent. When the Burmese king Mindon dispatched a delegation to Bodh Gaya in the 1870s with plans to refurbish the temple, the king's men negotiated with the mahant for permission to begin the work. He allowed them to erect a building nearby, the Burmese resthouse that figured in Dharmapala's struggles. Burmese aspirations notwithstanding, British officials found that the renovation of the temple violated their standards of conservation, and they took over. When Dharmapala arrived and set about to influence events at the place, he was not the first outsider wanting to reshape Bodh Gaya. He brought high aspirations, wanting both to imitate the Buddha and wrest the temple from its owners. He also brought a global following—small but influential—and he would deal with the anomalous position of the Saivites in a confrontational way of which they had no experience.

EFFECTS AT A DISTANCE

Once Dharmapala had arrived in Bodh Gaya, he made the fateful vow:

> Under the shade of the holy Bodhi tree where I bade farewell to all the
> pleasures of the world, to my parents [obscure] I forgot everything at
> the moment when I offered my life to the Lord Buddha: I shall not leave

33. Trevithick, *The Revival of Buddhist Pilgrimage at Bodh Gaya*, 23–4.

the place until I see Bhikkhus come and settle at the place. (Sarnath Notebook no. 53)[34]

Letter of introduction in hand, he sought out the custodian of the temple, who led him to believe that the site was under the control of the govern-ment (and simply managed by the mahant). If he wanted to take custody of the temple, the custodian said, "application should be made to the Govt of Bengal through the Govt of Ceylon" (Diary, January 28, 1891). He also gave him the lay of the land, telling him of the Giri monks' daily routines and diet. He seems to have concluded on his own that the Visnupad (the footprint of Visnu) to which the Saivites offered flowers had once been a Buddha footprint (Diary, January 29, 1891). As Dharmapala wrote in the *Buddhist*,

> The best and most elaborately carved statues and girdlings are now in the Samadh to the east of the temple. The Vajrasana, Sripada [the Bud-dha's footprint] and life-like images are to be seen here in abundance.[35]

Days later four Burmese monks with five attendants arrived at Bodh Gaya, where they found lodging with the mahant. Dharmapala "made them to take up quarters with us" (Diary, January 31, 1891), and thus scarcely a week after his arrival, lines were drawn and notice given that these Bud-dhists would no longer accept the mahant's hospitality.

Acting on his vow not to leave the place until bhikkhus came, Dharma-pala tried to recruit monks by mail. When he failed to receive a response, he concluded that he needed to speak to Hikkaduve in person.[36] By early February he had booked a steamer ticket, although he traveled home by way

34. Later accounts of Dharmapala's first days at Bodh Gaya telescope events for dramatic ef-fect. Karunaratne says that Dharmapala "did not come to Bodh Gaya in a happy mood" because he had witnessed "cruel scenes" on the way—scenes recalling how the Muslim king Moham-mad Gour made his way to Benares and murdered four thousand bhikkhus and how European archeologists had excavated the Dharmacakra stupa at Sarnath and carted off the treasure to Europe. Karunaratne adds that the sadness increased when Dharmapala and Kozen found the Buddha image in the temple topped with a turban and decorated with a tilaka on the forehead. *Anagarika Dharmapala*, 58–9. Dharmapala says nothing in his diaries about seeing any of those signs, and independent accounts suggest that the Hindu adornment came later, in response to Dharmapala's attempt to treat the image as strictly Buddhist.

35. *Buddhist*, June 5, 1891. Dharmapala's first published account of Bodh Gaya was re-printed in *Journal of the Maha Bodhi Society* 33 (1925): 261–71, at 269. The article in the *Bud-dhist* introduced Dharmapala by saying that he "is well-known among the Buddhists of Ceylon as a 'Sanyasi' of the highest order" (261).

36. Guruge, *Dharmapala Lipi*, 237.

of Rangoon, leaving Kozen to watch over Buddhist interests.[37] The prospect of being left alone unsettled Kozen—"The priest is in a state of constant anxiety without a companion Bhikkhu" (Diary, March 7, 1891)—and soon thereafter he wrote to the committee of all Buddhist sects in Japan and his teacher Shaku Unsho, presumably asking for companions to be sent from Japan to Bodh Gaya or support for the project (Diary, March 11, 1891).[38] Before he went off to fetch monks, Dharmapala had an interview with G. A. Grierson, the collector of Gaya, who suggested that he buy the place from the mahant (Diary, March 9, 1891).[39] At first he had the idea that the place was government property and could be transferred to the Buddhists; from Grierson he learned that he was going to have to negotiate with the mahant.[40] The collector left him with hope for the transfer idea, saying that application to the government might be favored (Diary, March 13, 1891). For many years he moved back and forth between both prospects.

In February 1893 Dharmapala and Olcott made an appointment to see the mahant, and they offered to buy the Maha Bodhi temple.[41] On his way to the World's Parliament of Religions later that year, Dharmapala and Sir Edwin Arnold put the transfer idea to Lord Kimberley in London. As late as 1923 Dharmapala published an article in his newspaper in Colombo, insisting that the British had control over the temple.[42] With all of the legal

37. Dharmapala tells the story a little differently in Sarnath Notebook no. 58: "I announced my intention [to stay at Bodh Gaya and protect the place] and asked the Japanese priest to return to Ceylon. He answered and said that he will also stay. And together we remained in the Burmese resthouse."

38. Dharmapala says Kozen lost his determination to stay at Bodh Gaya within a month. Guruge, *Dharmapala Lipi*, 237. The third pilgrim, Chiezo Tokuzawa, came to North India not as a monk but a student. He moved on to study Sanskrit in Calcutta and Varanasi for a time; retraced his steps to Colombo, where he resumed his studies; and returned to Japan after six years in South Asia. "Personal," *Journal of the Maha Bodhi Society* 11 (1896): 88–9. Elsewhere he says Tokuzawa was "fickle-minded" and convinced Kozen to leave Bodh Gaya (Diary, November 20, 1891).

39. The distinguished linguist George Grierson became superintendent of the Linguistic Survey of India in 1898 and pursued a scholarly interest in the inscriptions at Bodh Gaya. As Dharmapala was leaving their first encounter, Grierson asked him to convey his regards to Hikkaduve and Vaskaduve Subhuti, adding that he would send along Hikkaduve's bo saplings.

40. Bhikshu Sangharakshita, "Anagarika Dharmapala: A Biographical Sketch," in *Maha Bodhi Society of India Diamond Jubilee Souvenir, 1891–1951* (Calcutta: Sri Gouranga, 1952), 36.

41. *The Indian Law Reports, Calcutta Series*, vol. 23 (Calcutta: Bengal Secretariat Financial Department Book Depot Branch, 1896), 60–79, at 67.

42. *Sinhala Bauddhaya*, January 23, 1923, reprinted in "The Great Bo Tree at Budh Gaya," in Guruge, *Dharmapala Lipi*, 239. Dharmapala's reasoning went like this: "Why did the government intervene if the vihara [the Maha Bodhi temple] belonged to the mahanta? Ancient ruins not owned by anybody come under the administration of the government. The Maha Bodhi vihara was not permanently given to the mahanta. The government does not allow the mahanta

issues settled against him, renewing the government ownership claim must have seemed the only course left. What he could not avoid seeing as early as 1892 was that whether the British intervened or the mahant would consent to selling the place, there was going to be an issue with food, lodging, and keeping a group of bhikkhus in a place dominated by a large group of Hindu world renouncers and a wealthy abbot. He recognized the difficulty of living at Bodh Gaya, and he was a man who relished deprivation. Almost as therapy for coping with difficult conditions and dim prospects, he repeated what seemed easy and obvious—it was only right that the place where the Buddha achieved enlightenment return to his followers. On that first trip back to Colombo he visited Burma. He spent a considerable amount of time trying to raise support and recruit monks. At the Sule Pagoda he gave his first lecture about his plans to reclaim Bodh Gaya (Diary, June 12, 1926). Once he got home and concluded that Hikkaduve would not provide monks for the scheme, he found his own, a group of Ramanna Nikaya monks.[43] He returned north, bringing the four monks and two boys to attend them. With the monks in place, he assumed the rest of the task would be manageable.[44] He was again given access to the Burmese resthouse and soon acquired land to the west of it from the mahant; Hem Narayana Gir put up an extension to the resthouse to house a kitchen and latrine, but there was still no well.[45]

Once the four monks had been settled, Dharmapala returned to his residence in Calcutta and established a branch of the Maha Bodhi Society as a vehicle for organizing the support of Bengali Hindus. From this point for-

---

to act according to his own wish. To renovate the mahanta has not spent even a rupee. Those expenses have been borne by government. There is an overseer appointed by government to look after the vihara" (240).

43. It is hard to overlook (and equally hard to substantiate) the connection between the Ramanna monks and Bodh Gaya. Ambagahawatte Indrasabhavara, who established the Ramanna Nikaya in 1864 by receiving *upasampada* in Burma, also made a pilgrimage to Bodh Gaya, and Dharmapala wanted to make the journey in 1887 with another Ramanna monk, Ilukwatte Medhankara. "Dharmapala Visits India," in Guruge, *Dharmapala Lipi*, 235. Sarananda, the first modern monk to reside at Sarnath, taking up residence there in 1898, was a Ramanna Nikaya monk. Guruge, *Dharmapala Lipi*, 248.

44. Dharmapala was able to recruit them because they were already intending to visit Bodh Gaya, and Dharmapala had only to get them to commit to a one-year stay. Guruge, *Dharmapala Lipi*, 41, 236. Anne Blackburn suggests that Hikkaduve's reluctance derived from hearing from Kozen how difficult conditions at Bodh Gaya were at the time. *Locations of Buddhism*, 121. One of the early articles Dharmapala wrote for his Sinhala supporters seems to suggest that he wanted conditions to be difficult (assuming that moderate asceticism was the proper course for monks as he took it to be for himself). "News from India," *Sarasavi Sandarasa*, April 4, 1893, reprinted in Guruge, *Dharmapala Lipi*, 208.

45. "The Maha Bodhi Temple at Buddha Gaya," *Journal of the Maha Bodhi Society* 3 (1894): 22. Hem Narayana Gir died in December 1891, succeeded by Krishna Dayal Gir.

ward, he made occasional trips to Bodh Gaya and longer trips to Lanka or beyond. But he spent almost 90 percent of his adult life in Calcutta, where he could not avoid the perturbations of imperial power and growing Bengali opposition to it. There was a Buddhist revival in the world, but he lived in the capital city of the Hindu revival, and he lived there for more than forty years. He established the *Journal of the Maha Bodhi Society and the United Buddhist World* "as a vehicle for the dissemination of [his] views" (Diary, December 31, 1908).[46] The *Buddhist* was his earlier project, but as one of his biographers puts it,

> Years before when he was serving in the Buddhist Theosophical Society, Anagarika Dharmapala had started a magazine, the *Buddhist*, and it was sent all over the world for publicity. That was a magazine that spread the force of Buddhism, but to save Bodh Gaya he started the *Maha Bodhi Journal*.[47]

His move to Calcutta did not indicate his moving on to another project. Rescuing Bodh Gaya was the project, and publishing his journal gave him an instrument by which he could apply considerable leverage.

HINDUS AND BUDDHISTS AT BODH GAYA

Living in Calcutta gave Dharmapala "a habitation in the metropolis of the British Indian Empire."[48] The struggle would be fought on several fronts— soliciting support directly from the Bengali elite, publishing a journal that had worldwide reach, petitioning the colonial government, and corresponding with an extraordinary number of acquaintances. The Maha Bodhi Society attracted elite Bengalis—besides Sen and Mukherjee, Jatindra Nath Tagore, Ananda Mohan Ray, Durga Shankar Bhattacharya, and Parameshwar Lall—because of its affinity to the Theosophical Society and the rationalist humanism both groups shared. Calcutta also gave him access to an efficient postal system and travel by steamer. Correspondence, publications,

46. Dharmapala's father gave him funds for the first visit to Bodh Gaya (Diary, December 13, 1926), and he paid for the monks' travel to Bodh Gaya and maintenance from his son's monthly allowance.

47. Karunaratne, *Anagarika Dharmapala*, 63. The book's introduction says that the account presented therein came from radio broadcasts given in 1944 and that these programs were one of the ways Dharmapala became widely known to the Sinhala public (7).

48. Anagarika Dharmapala, "Our Twenty Years' Work," *Journal of the Maha Bodhi Society* 19 (1911): 6.

The Maha=Bodhi

AND THE

UNITED BUDDHIST WORLD.

The Journal of the Maha-Bodhi Society.

BUDDHA YEAR 2449.

| Vol. XIV. | APRIL, 1906. | No. 4. |

THE MAHA-BODHI TEMPLE AT BUDDHA GAYA.

Please remit your subscription in Advance.

14. *Journal of the Maha Bodhi Society* cover, 1906.

and travel gave him reason to believe that he could produce effects at a distance—one of his motives for later setting up residence in London was to save Sinhalas—and secure benefits for one place while living at another.[49] He thought he could do his best for Bodh Gaya by living in Calcutta.

The four monks did not have those advantages and faced conditions at Bodh Gaya that went beyond austerity. Three of them slipped off in quick order.[50] It is not clear why they left, where they went, or what became of the two attendants. But their living accommodations in the Burmese resthouse—which colonial officials characterized as "leaky and open"— were nothing that they expected, and it was hard for them to get foodstuffs. Coming from a tropical climate, they suffered in the cold weather. The lean-to that Dharmapala built to serve as a kitchen was removed by government order, forcing the monks to cook their meals on the verandah.[51] The underlying issue was that they had received no warning of the hardscrabble conditions they would face. At home they would not have cooked for themselves, but living at Bodh Gaya forced them to do so. Their own plan had been to simply make a pilgrimage. They were staying because Dharmapala had convinced them to commit for a year. Remembering those early days, he put it succinctly:

> Three Bhikshus suddenly left BG, leaving only Chandrajoti. The whole of the year 1892 he was alone, M. P. Sumangala returned again. The old Mahant in the meantime died. Krishna Dayal Gir succeeded. He began to persecute the Bhikkhus. In February 1893 they were assaulted. Col. Olcott went to Bud Gaya and after inquiry removed the Bhikshus to Gaya. The Burmese R.H. [resthouse] was vacated from Feby. 1893, and again reoccupied in Feby. 1895. ("The Maha Bodhi Temple at Buddha Gaya," Sarnath Notebook no. 58)[52]

49. See Christmas Humphreys, *Sixty Years of Buddhism in England, 1907–1967* (London: Buddhist Society, 1968), 22.

50. The *Journal of the Maha Bodhi Society* reported that Sumangala and Devananda were in Gaya, the former learning Bengali, the latter, Hindi. "Personal Items," *Journal of the Maha Bodhi Society* 3 (1894): 30–1, at 31. Much later Dharmapala wrote that only Sumangala was "still alive and living at Bodh Gaya," leaving it unclear whether the other monks had returned home or simply abandoned Bodh Gaya. "The History of the Maha-Bodhi Society," *Journal of the Maha Bodhi Society* 15 (1907): 11–15, at 11.

51. Correspondence, Superintending Engineer, Sone Circle, to the Chief Engineer, Bengal, Judicial and Public Papers, 1898, India Office Records, British Library, IOR/L/PJ/6/493, nos. 22–3.

52. It is hard to determine the severity of the force that the Saivites applied before the 1895 incident when Dharmapala attempted to install the Japanese Buddha image in the company of two bhikkhus, in part because there were no bhikkhus—by Dharmapala's own account—at

In the next paragraph he mentioned the "B. Gaya cause celebre" without indicating either the substance of that cause—his attempt to install in the sanctum of the Maha Bodhi temple a Japanese Buddha image or the court cases—that put the conflict between him and the mahant on a new footing, independent of the presence of Buddhist monks.

Dharmapala returned to Bodh Gaya in 1895 with a Sinhala layman and two monks—the old hand Sumangala and a newcomer, Devananda—and they attempted to enshrine the Japanese Buddha image. Within a few minutes, the Buddhist party was confronted by the Muslim *muktear* (agent) of the mahant and a group of thirty to forty of the mahant's sannyasis. They ordered Dharmapala to take away the image and threatened him: "*Budmash*, we will beat you, there are five hundred of us."[53] The Buddhist party remained in front of the image in seated meditation. Silent resistance forced the mahant's party to retreat to the math, but they quickly returned, took away the Japanese image, and set it in the courtyard in front of the temple. The mahant rushed to Macpherson to ask for help. In due order Dharmapala filed a complaint, and Macpherson himself heard the case. Dharmapala insisted he had both a right to worship freely and an obligation to the Japanese to place the image they had given him in the shrine. The mahant responded that he would not allow it unless the image were entrusted to him and put through a *pranpratisha* (life-giving) ceremony, constituting it as a Hindu deity. He gave no indication of whether he had given the image on the first tier of the temple such a ceremony.

Macpherson bent over backward to support Dharmapala's cause, and his judgment concluded that the "ancient Buddhist shrine . . . ought in justice belong to the Buddhists,"[54] overlooking the mahant's deed of 1727 and the rights that accrued to the Giri monks simply by their longtime possession. By focusing on the temple, he overlooked the bodhi tree and the overwhelming numbers of Hindu worshippers who performed sraddha under it.

Bodh Gaya from February 1893 until February 1895. In an article intended to enumerate the outrages, Dharmapala spoke of one preinstallation incident: "The first act of hostility that was committed by [the mahant's] menials was to murderously assault the Buddhist Monks who were in residence at the Burmese Resthouse since July 1891. This occurred in February 1893." "Oppression and Tyranny at Buddha Gaya," *Journal of the Maha Bodhi Society* 18 (1910): 339–50, at 342. Dharmapala described the events that followed in an article in *Sinhala Bauddhaya*, March 12, 1910: "[The mahant] manhandled the two monks, Chandrajoti and Sumangala. Mr. Olcott came to Bodh Gaya in February 1893, inquired into the incident (*hirihära*) and leased out a house in Gaya for the two monks to stay." Reprinted in Guruge, *Dharmapala Lipi*, 244.

53. Judgment in the Court of the District Magistrate of Gaya, *H. Dharmapala v. Jaipal Gir*, July 30, 1895, India Office Records, British Library, IOR/L/PJ/6/404/file 1545, 1.

54. India Office Records, British Library, IOR/L/PJ/6/750/file 705, 14.

Because the bo tree on the north side of the Maha Bodhi temple had been substituted for the older bodhi tree on the west side blown down in a storm, Macpherson reasoned that Hindus no longer venerated the bodhi tree as such. He pointed out that Hindu worship—offering the light of oil lamps, conch blowing, *tilak* painting on forehead of the image—had begun only after Dharmapala's arrival and only in response to it. Macpherson took testimony from the temple custodian, who said that while those acts of worship were performed by a Kulin Brahman on hire, the mahant and his sannyasis were never seen worshipping at the temple. Macpherson called Durga Shankar Bhattacharya, the Theosophist who had originally escorted Dharmapala to Bodh Gaya, and he testified that no Hindu would ever mistake the Japanese image for a Hindu deity. In June 1894 the judge ruled in Dharmapala's favor, imposing jail time and a fine on the mahant's three sannyasins.[55] To this point his provocation—installing an image in the temple knowing that the mahant would resist—had exactly the effect he intended.

His advantage did not last long. The mahant appealed, and the judgment was overturned on the grounds that the group's meditation in front of the image did not constitute an act of worship. Macpherson had said that the group had "sat down to their devotion in front of the image in the characteristic Buddhist attitude of religious contemplation, the highest form of Buddhist worship,"[56] a view he must have learned from Dharmapala. The appeal of 1895 went against Dharmapala for several reasons, but it is clear that he did not make a convincing witness, because of his inability to make up his mind whether the British controlled the temple or the mahant owned it. In reversing Macpherson's decision, the judge dismissed his reliability:

> Dharmapala was subjected to a very long cross-examination on his denial that the *Mahant* was either the owner or the person in possession of the temple. . . . He certainly came very badly out of it, and furnished the other side with good grounds for questioning his general veracity. It is amply shown from his own writings, and from writings published with his knowledge and under his authority, that he always regarded the *Mahant* . . . as the owner.[57]

55. *India Law Reports*, Calcutta Series, vol. 23, January–December 1896 (Calcutta: Bengal Secretariat Financial Department Book Depot Branch), 60–79, at 60.
56. India Office Records, British Library, IOR/L/PJ/6/750/file 705, 2.
57. *India Law Reports*, 66.

Further questioning led the appellate judges—Macpherson and Banerjee—to conclude that the installation of the image and the "religious contemplation" of it at the temple were not simple acts of worship. The court interpreted Dharmapala's actions as an attempt to "enshrine" the Japanese image on a permanent basis because he "wanted indirectly and in a covert way to do that which he had failed to do directly and openly, namely, to bring the temple under the control of Buddhist priests."[58] Convictions and sentences were set aside and fines refunded.

Dharmapala's loss at the appellate court in 1895 meant the end of his legal campaign to make the Maha Bodhi temple more Buddhist, and it killed public support at home. But it did not stop his efforts to maintain a Buddhist presence at Bodh Gaya. He had learned of the sale of a plot of land near the temple:

> Called on Mr. Macpherson. Had a long interview about the Temple. Mr. Macpherson advises me to put off purchasing the land from the Tikiri Raj and the establishment of the College at Budhgaya! All this has to be done to please the Mahant! (Diary, April 12, 1894)

He had hopes for a larger presence at the temple, and the land would have made a place for a monastery, resthouse for pilgrims, and a Maha Bodhi College. But the government stopped the sale of land, ending his hopes of building a Buddhist complex at Bodh Gaya.[59] After the courts called for removing the image from the Maha Bodhi, and after he had failed to secure the land, the Burmese resthouse became his focus by default. The name of the place—and the Japanese image that came to reside there—gave him the appearance of having friends in faraway places.

The resthouse presented its own ownership issues. Did it belong to the colonial government, Buddhists in general or Burmese in particular (who could make a claim on the now deposed Burmese king who had paid for its construction), or the mahant on whose land it stood? It offered the Buddhists several advantages. Being nearby the shrine, unoccupied, and "Buddhist" made the resthouse a vehicle to sustain a Buddhist presence at Bodh

58. Ibid., 72.

59. H. E. A. Cotton, chief secretary to the Government of Bengal, was destined—along with his son Evan Cotton—to serve as Dharmapala's nemesis, writing to Dharmapala that the government would "undertake no measures for the furtherance of the general objects [that is, taking control of the Maha Bodhi temple] of the Maha Bodhi Society." "The Buddha-Gya [sic] Temple Question," *Journal of the Maha Bodhi Society* 3 (1895): 79.

Gaya. Once Dharmapala had come on the scene, officials felt obliged to apply their policy of "religious neutrality" and provide some relief to the Buddhists, now that that the Maha Bodhi temple itself was to remain in the mahant's hands. Ian Copland writes,

> Secretly, many British officials hoped that the Mahabodhi temple might eventually lose its status as an active place of worship, and become reborn as a secular "monument" to India's classical past.[60]

Dharmapala's project itself made that impossible, and the Buddhist character of the Burmese resthouse—it had been built at the behest of the Burmese king and was intended as a residence for Burmese workmen sent to renovate the temple—gave the Buddhists another reason to see Bodh Gaya as theirs, even under circumstances in which it was clearly not. From the mahant's perspective, the resthouse was simply too close. It gave Dharmapala a place, and the Japanese Buddha provided an object of veneration to which pilgrim traffic could be diverted or from which grander claims could be made.

The mahant's victory on appeal in 1895 left the Japanese image issue unresolved: "No orders were . . . passed regarding the disposal of the image, which continued to remain in the rest-house, where it had been placed by the Magistrate under a police-guard."[61] Even more than the struggle over the temple, the way the colonial government dealt with the Japanese image reveals one concession after another—first the Buddhists got this, later the Hindus got that—that marked British practice at Bodh Gaya, the policy of strict neutrality notwithstanding. Dharmapala believed that the resthouse had "come into our possession," and regarded the Japanese image remaining in the resthouse as small compensation for a large loss (Sarnath Notebook no. 58). In 1896 the mahant petitioned to remove the image from the resthouse, leading the government to resist on the grounds that denying the Buddhists this concession would violate its religious neutrality policy. In July 1896 the lieutenant governor of Bengal, Sir Alexander Mackenzie, visited Gaya, granting interviews to Dharmapala and the mahant. He urged both of them to recognize the need for compromise.[62]

---

60. "Managing Religion in Colonial India: The British Raj and the Bodh Gaya Temple Dispute," *Journal of Church and State* 46 (2004): 527–60, at 533.

61. C. W. Bolton to the Secretary to the Government of India, Darjeeling, June 27, 1896, India Office Records, British Library, IOR/L/PJ/6/493/file 2157.

62. W. C. Macpherson, Officiating Chief Secretary to the Government of Bengal, to Secretary to the Government of India, October 31, 1903, India Office Records, British Library, IOR/L/PJ/6/750/file 705.

Immediately after the interview with Macpherson, Dharmapala left India for a tour of the United States at the invitation of Paul Carus.[63] In his absence other Buddhists petitioned the government in hopes of further privileges at Bodh Gaya, and the mahant offered his own memorial of November 23, 1896, seeking the removal of the Japanese image. The ostensible issue was the proximity of the Burmese resthouse and the Japanese image, which the mahant's memorial characterized in a way as divisive as Dharmapala's project: "Devoted to the worship of a sect that holds views so diametrically opposed to those of the Hindus must be a perpetual source of dispute, perhaps of breaches of the peace."[64] While in Calcutta, Dharmapala received a letter from Matale Sumangala, saying that four constables had arrived at Bodh Gaya to keep watch over the Japanese image (Diary, March 16, 1896).

Amid contradictory arguments for what was traditional at Bodh Gaya, the colonial government recognized the forces working in both camps:

> The ill-advised proceedings of Mr. Dharmapala, far from achieving the objects he had in view, led the Mahant and his disciples to assume in reprisal a more hostile attitude to assert with an insistence hitherto unknown their claim to the Temple as a Hindu shrine, and to give more prominence to the worship carried on there. During the year 1895 and the early part of 1896 the Mahant attempted, but without success, to induce the Government of Bengal to remove the Japanese image from the neighborhood of the temple. In reply to all his applications it was said that while Government would maintain an attitude of strict impartiality on all questions affecting the shrine, it was determined to discourage all attempts from whatever quarter which might lead to a breach of the peace.[65]

63. Dharmapala had a way of leaving India at times when important events were happening at Bodh Gaya: he was abroad in 1903 when Lord Curzon visited Bodh Gaya and in 1905–6, when several things happened: the mahant brought another suit, the Panchen Lama visited Bodh Gaya, and Lord Minto made his visit after being appointed viceroy. In 1896 when the Maha Bodhi temple decision was being reversed, Dharmapala was abroad. The eventual outcome to the contrary, he concluded that he had exerted leverage on government by raising the issue on his travels in the United States: "Brother C. C. Bose writes to say that the Bengal government had come to the conclusion that the temple is a Buddhist one simply because I had agitated in America. Great is the power of Truth. Singlehanded I have done what others thought impossible" (Diary, November 29, 1897). There is no evidence in government correspondence for any such conclusion.

64. Quoted in Trevithick, *The Revival of Buddhist Pilgrimage at Bodh Gaya*, 39.

65. Macpherson, Officiating Chief Secretary to the Government of Bengal, to the Secretary to the Government of India, Calcutta, October 31, 1903, India Office Records, British Library, IOR/L/PJ/6/750/file 705.

Keeping the peace required more than "strict impartiality." It required, and it received, balanced and episodic partiality. In April 1896 the mahant sought to take possession of the Burmese resthouse and to close it to the Buddhists, only to be blocked by the government.[66] His petition denied, the mahant asked the government in May for a smaller concession, removing the Japanese Buddha image from the Burmese resthouse. When the magistrate of Gaya wrote Dharmapala, "instructing him to remove the [Japanese Buddha] image from its present place . . . within one month," the unfolding policy denied the mahant what he really wanted—complete closure—but it still struck the Buddhists as tilting the balance in his favor.[67] Dharmapala replied that removing the image would constitute "an act of profanity" and violate the tenets of his religion.[68] For reasons unclear the government reversed its policy and allowed the image to remain in the resthouse, now under the watch of constables.

Next Dharmapala and the Burmese Buddhists sought permission to rebuild the resthouse and have the local *dak* (inspection) bungalow put at their disposal. On that proposal, the British would build a new bungalow nearby, and the Buddhists would buy the old bungalow and refit it for their purposes, gaining a place for the Japanese image and accommodations for monks or pilgrims.[69] The government recognized the stakes:

> It is clear to the Lieutenant-Governor that the Hindus cannot, with any justification, claim the temple as a shrine intended exclusively for their worship. On the other hand, His Honour cannot approve of the conduct of Mr. Dharmapala and his party. Everything was going on smoothly, the Buddhist pilgrims coming and going and worshipping in the temple unmolested, until the Maha Bodhi Society began their intrusive attempts to annex the shrine as a purely Buddhist sanctuary. First came their attempt to install the Japanese image in the temple, but being unsuccessful in that, they are now stirring up the Buddhists of Mandalay and elsewhere to subscribe for building rest-houses and temples, and asking

66. "Japanese Image and Buddhist Resthouse," *Journal of the Maha Bodhi Society* 18 (1910): 488–92, at 488.

67. C. W. Bolton, Officiating Chief Secretary of the Government of Bengal, to Secretary to the Government of India, June 27, 1896, India Office Records, British Library, IOR/L/PJ/493/2157.

68. "Correspondence," *Journal of the Maha Bodhi Society* 5 (1896): 24.

69. C. W. Bolton, Chief Secretary to the Government of Bengal, to the Secretary to the Government of India, June 11, 1897, India Office Records, British Library, IOR/L/PJ/6/493/no. 41.

Government to procure sites for them. They are also using the shelter afforded to their image in the rest-house to develop a new cult, and deprive the Mohunt of offerings which he has hitherto received.[70]

The plan served two purposes, giving Dharmapala a larger Buddhist presence at Bodh Gaya and a lodging place for monks or laypeople on pilgrimage.

Writing to the government of Bengal in December 1896, Dharmapala offered a new rationale for allowing the Buddhists exclusive use of an inspection bungalow. "The visitors who are not Buddhists," he argued, "during their stay in the Dak Bungalow, often hurt the religious feelings of the Buddhist pilgrims by slaughtering animals for food."[71] Whether pilgrims actually brought animals for slaughter at Bodh Gaya and how often such incidents occurred remain to be seen. But the language of sacrilege and injured sensibilities had come to stay. The commissioner of the Patna district concluded that Dharmapala's rationale "for this request may be passed over in silence," noting a conversation with the mahant, who was convinced that he would never abandon his primary object, the transfer of the Maha Bodhi temple to Buddhist hands. The mahant told the magistrate of Gaya that "he [was] not prepared to put a serpent in his pocket."[72]

When the chief secretary to the government of Bengal relayed an update of events at Bodh Gaya to the government of India in Simla, he emphasized Dharmapala's new strategy—he and his supporters were rallying Burmese Buddhists to subscribe for building resthouses and temples, and asking the government to procure sites for them. He noted that the Buddhists were using the shelter afforded to the image in the resthouse "to develop a new cult" and

deprive the Mohunt of offerings which he has hitherto received. . . . There was recently an altercation regarding a well which a Buddhist pilgrim dedicated to the image in the rest-house, but which one of the

70. India Office Records, British Library, IOR/L/PJ/6/493, no. 41.

71. H. Dharmapala, General Secretary to the Maha Bodhi Society of India and Official Representative of the Buddhists of Asia, to the Private Secretary to Sir Alexander Mackenzie [lieutenant governor of Bengal], December 29, 1896, India Office Records, British Library, IOR/L/PJ/6/493, no. 25. The problem with recasting Asia's Buddhisms as "Buddhism" was that many Buddhists, including Sinhalas, consumed meat as a matter of course.

72. J. A. Bourdillon, Commissioner of the Patna District, to the Chief Secretary to the Government of Bengal, April 5, 1897, India Office Records, British Library, IOR/L/PJ/6/493, nos. 34–5.

Mohunt's servants claimed should have been dedicated to the image in the temple.[73]

Soon the conflict drew the British Indian Association into the fray, rushing to the mahant's defense. Dharmapala was convinced that the commissioner of Patna had directed the mahant to bring a civil suit against the Buddhists to have them ejected from the resthouse (Sarnath Notebook no. 58). Correspondence shows the British more interested in keeping their distance than wanting any particular result—Bolton had suggested that the viceroy inform the mahant that if he objected to the Japanese image residing in the Burmese resthouse, he could bring suit, although the Viceroy's secretary responded by saying that the "government of India are doubtful . . . whether it can divest itself of responsibility for allowing the Japanese image to remain [in the Burmese resthouse] by bidding the Mahant to sue Mr. Dharmapala for removal of the image."[74]

While the mahant lacked supporters beyond Bengal, Dharmapala had a world of them. He turned to the Burmese, his Sinhala supporters having drifted away after he had failed to deliver the temple in 1895. He used the *Journal of the Maha Bodhi Society* to apprize the Buddhist world of the most recent victories and outrages. The journal also encouraged pilgrimage, and Dharmapala's mother soon arrived with a group of Sinhala Buddhists, reestablishing a tradition of pilgrimage, now embodied by laypeople.[75] Even with the Maha Bodhi Society in Colombo functioning as a travel agency, the expense, difficulty, and novelty of long-distance travel meant that Buddhist pilgrimage to Bodh Gaya was unlikely to match the number of Hindu pilgrims. The following numbers came from the mahant at trial, and they are self-serving but useful. He estimated the annual number of pilgrims at more than 100,000 Hindus, 100 Lankans, and 100–200 Buddhists from Burma, Siam, Bhutan, Tibet, and Chittagong, adding that the Chinese of Calcutta "never

73. C. W. Bolton, Chief Secretary to the Government of Bengal, to the Secretary to the Government of India, June 11, 1897, Correspondence, Judicial and Political Papers, 1898, India Office Records, British Library, IOR/L/PJ/6/493, no. 41.

74. J. P. Hewett, Chief Secretary to the Govt of India, to the Chief Secretary to the Government of Bengal, August 30, 1897, India Office Records, British Library, IOR/L/PJ/6/493, no. 42.

75. Hikkaduve had been scheduled to lead a group of pilgrims to Bodh Gaya in December 1894, but he backed out. Blackburn, *Locations of Buddhism*, 24. Mallika Hewavitarne replaced him, leading the first organized pilgrimage of modern times from Colombo to Bodh Gaya, and she returned—usually in the company of other laywomen—in 1900, 1906, 1912, 1915, 1917, and 1920 (Diary, November 18, 1920).

go there."[76] The number of Hindu pilgrims is probably inflated, but my sense is that the mahant is pretty close on the number of Buddhist pilgrims.

TWO CAUSES AND THEIR SUPPORTERS

Discussion of the Bodh Gaya conflict took shape against the vicissitudes of Indian religious life. *Dainik-o-Samachar Chandrika* (May 29, 1904) noted that the temples of Jagannath at Puri and Barga Bhima at Tamluk had once belonged to Buddhists, but this fact would not justify returning either to them. Hindus were not demanding the return of temples now become mosques. When Rajendra Prasad argued in the 1930s that the image in the Jagannath temple in Puri was nothing but a Buddha image, Hindus began to see how things could get out of hand: "We know that there are many Hindu temples in Hindustan where the images worshipped as Hindu Gods, are in reality Buddhist images." Were the bill proposed by Prasad to go forward, it "might result in the future to [*sic*] a forfeiture of many Hindu temples of India and the vesting thereof in Buddhist hands."[77] By the 1920s there was a proposal in newspapers in both India and Lanka for an international exchange. If the Bodh Gaya temple were given back, then the Murugan temple at Kataragama in the southeast of the island—increasingly patronized by Buddhists—should be returned to the Hindus.[78] Once the vicissitudes of Indian history entered public discourse—Buddhist places become Hindu, Hindu places become Muslim—Buddhist cries of injustice at Bodh Gaya lost their distinction and, losing that, their poignancy.

In 1904 Indians watching the political horizon could see, as C. F. Andrews put it, "that great changes were impending in the East." The East in this case was Japan:

> The Musalmans, as one expected, regarded the reverses of Russia chiefly from a territorial standpoint. The reverses seemed to mark the limit of

76. Draft Report of the Commission sent to Bodh Gaya, enclosure B, in J. A. Bourdillon to Curzon, Lord Curzon of Kedleston Correspondence, British Library, April 14, 1903, 1: nos. 104a–104f, at 104e.

77. Das, *A Hindu Point of View on the Bodh-Gaya Temple Bill*, 31.

78. Secondhand accounts appeared in "We'll Give You Kataragama," *Journal of the Maha Bodhi Society* 32 (1924): 124; and "Tamils and Kataragama," *Journal of the Maha Bodhi Society* 43 (1925): 360. Ceylon Tamils internationalized the situation by sending a telegram to *Amrita Bazar Patrika*, asserting their claim on Kataragama. Dharmapala had Devapriya respond, explaining the difference (Diary, April 30, 1925).

the expansion of the Christian nations over the world's surface. The Hindus regarded more the inner significance of the event. The old-time glory and greatness of Asia seemed destined to return. . . . The whole of Buddhaland from Ceylon to Japan might again become one in thought and life. . . . Much had gone before to prepare the way for such a dawn of hope: the Japanese victories made it, for the first time, shining and radiant.[79]

The rhetorical excess implicit in imagining trading Kataragama for Bodh Gaya aside, the looming presence of Japan brought usages such as "Buddhaland" into the public imagination. Just as the colonial other gave force to national feeling in India, so the united Buddhist world gave Indians alternative futures to consider—Buddhism as the source of their own regeneration, complicating factor, or threat to the nation yet to be.

Keeping monks at Bodh Gaya was essential for providing officiants and guides for pilgrims—however small their number—bringing the Buddhist presence alive in a way an image could not. There were never more than four monks at Bodh Gaya in the early period and usually only one or two. For more than a decade only one monk resided there. At intervals all of the monks retreated to Gaya or Calcutta, leaving the place unattended. The monk who endured was Matale Sumangala, and about him Dharmapala had mixed feelings:

Spent the night talking with Sumangala. His life has been contaminated by his behaviour. He has led an ignoble life if the stories are true. He says that the woman with whom he has been associating had nursed him when he was very ill; and that her child is not his issue. He is willing to leave Bodh Gaya; but before leaving the spot he must pay Rs. 50/ for the woman for the services she has rendered him!! When I look at the past history of Sumangala I find that it was one full of devotion to the place. He was assaulted by the Mahant's men in 1893 and he declined to institute proceedings against the assailants. For thirteen years he remained firm and did all he could to help the Buddhists. Considering all this I decided to give him Rs. 40 to pay the woman and to remove him from Bodh Gaya. (Diary, May 4, 1904)[80]

79. *The Renaissance in India* (London: Church Missionary Society, 1912), 5.
80. The mahant had knowledge of Sumangala's misbehavior, asserting that " Sumangala, though attired with yellow robe of a Buddhist Monk, does not live here for the purpose of worship, as he seldom comes over to the temple, but collects money from the pilgrims and

Living in a community, the presence of other monks and laypeople acts as a deterrent to misbehavior, but Sumangala was alone for most of the thirteen years he spent at Bodh Gaya.

The mahant had his own advantages: he had a deed to the place, his order had occupied Bodh Gaya for hundreds of years, and he enjoyed high-priced legal counsel and local support that the Maha Bodhi Society lacked. The British Indian Association gave him the backing of an influential group of well-to-do Bengalis who were major landlords and unabashedly pro-British. *Sanjivani* (August 17, 1895) noted that the association had declined in importance since the time of Kristo Das Pal. The association began to reassert its influence even as Japan was winning military victories and making Indians aware of an Asian nation-state with interest in Indian affairs. Expressing indignation at the actions of "a Society whose *raison d'etre*" as set forth in its prospectus was to "restore the central shrine of Maha-Bodhi" and to "transfer it from the hands of usurping Saivite Mohants to the custody of Buddhist monks," the group urged the government of Bengal to rescind its wavering policy and reminded the government that the High Court had ruled that the Maha Bodhi temple was a Hindu temple.[81] The group's memorial was endorsed by an upstart group of citizens, the Dharma Sabha of the District of Patna, asking that the Japanese Buddha image be removed "to some place beyond the precincts of the Bodh Gaya temple."[82] In subsequent conversation with the mahant, the magistrate of Gaya found him willing to make only one concession. He would give Dharmapala land to build a monastery, provided it was located at a distance of at least two miles from the temple.[83]

In addition to his legal advantages, the mahant made use of extralegal strategies, and they were marvelous to behold. Those tactics provoked Curzon's animus against him for "duplicity and bad faith."[84] He made agree-

---

appropriates the same to the most sinful purposes, quite derogatory to the rank of his order." Srimahat Krishnadayalu Giri to Raja Peary Mohan Mukerji, October 20, 1903, Lord Curzon of Kedleston Correspondence, 2: no. 156.

81. Rai Isser Chunder Mitter Bahadur, Honorary Secretary, British Indian Association, to Chief Secretary to the Government of Bengal, January 29, 1897, India Office Records, British Library, IOR/L/PJ/6/493, no. 24.

82. The Secretary, Dharma Sabha, to the Chief Secretary of the Government of Bengal, February 28, 1897, India Office Records, British Library, IOR/L/PJ/6/493, nos. 29 and 32.

83. H. Savage, Magistrate of Gaya, to the Commissioner of the Patna District, March 8, 1897, India Office Records, British Library, IOR/L/PJ/6/493, nos. 34–5.

84. Curzon to D. C. J. Ibbetson, Member of the Viceroy's Council, September 13, 1903, Lord Curzon of Kedleston Correspondence, 2: no. 67.

ments and then ignored them.[85] He rejected agreements he had made earlier. He avoided meetings, pleading ill health. He invented new practices— applying the mark to the forehead of the Buddha image in the temple—and later agreed to abandon them. He put off negotiations, saying that he was beholden to the sastras and obliged to consult his fellow sannyasis. He co-zied up to the government, again invoking the loyalty of his lineage and telling officials that he would never litigate with the government, for that would make him a "rebel" (baghi), recalling the events of 1857.[86] When Dharmapala invented a new practice, the mahant found an equivalent prac-tice. When Dharmapala made a new accusation, the mahant filed a counter-accusation. All the while, the mahant maintained good relations with other Buddhists, his attorneys insisting that Dharmapala did not speak for the Buddhist world at large.[87]

In the first court case, when charges were brought against three of the mahant's sannyasis for assaulting Dharmapala and his group in 1894, the mahant chose Evan Cotton and Man Mohan Ghose to represent his in-terests in court, and Cotton remained his lead attorney until 1910. It is not clear how the mahant settled on Cotton, but he could not have done better. Evan Cotton (H. E. A. Cotton) and his father, Henry Cotton (H. J. S. Cotton), were British liberals and Anglo-Indians committed to Indian causes. They made Bodh Gaya an Indian cause. The son was an attorney, journalist, and author of several books; Dharmapala first encountered the father as chief secretary to the government of Bengal. Father and son descended from an Anglo-Indian family with an unbroken connection to India from the time of Captain Joseph Cotton's several Indian voyages (1769–82). That connec-tion continued to Indian independence.[88] Man Mohan Ghose was an Indian

85. W. C. Macpherson, Officiating Chief Secretary to the Government of Bengal, to Secretary to the Government of India, in response to House of Commons question on harass-ment of the mahant, October 31, 1903, India Office Records, British Library, IOR/I/PJ/6/750/ file 705.

86. Memo of Interview with the Mahanth of Bodh Gaya, January 19 and 20, 1903, and Feb-ruary 8, 1903, enclosure in C. E. A. Oldham to Walter Lawrence, February 8, 1903, Lord Curzon of Kedleston Correspondence, 1:no. 45.

87. As Evan Cotton pointed out to the Bodh Gaya Case Commission, "As far as relations between the Mahant and the large majority of the Buddhist visitors and pilgrims to the Temple were concerned, the utmost friendliness and good feeling have always existed and . . . the Maha Bodhi Society does not represent the Buddhist community of the world in any sense." W. C. Macpherson, Officiating Chief Secretary to the Government of Bengal, to the Secretary to the Government of India, October 31, 1903, India Office Records, British Library, IOR/L/PJ/6/750/ file 705, no. 14, appendix A.

88. Evan Cotton, East Indiamen: The East India Company's Maritime Service (London: Batchworth, 1949), 8 and 191–2.

nationalist as well as a distinguished attorney.[89] The mahant's choosing two nationalist attorneys could not have been unwitting; Bengal was changing and events at Bodh Gaya would take on new significance in phase with those changes. Curzon took a central role. His public support for reconsidering arrangements at Bodh Gaya automatically put the issue in a larger context by confirming Bengali suspicions of his hostility to them and framing the issue in nationalist terms

Dharmapala had his own suspicions about both Cottons. When he first applied to the government for the transfer of the temple to the Maha Bodhi Society, it was Henry Cotton who responded, saying that the Bengal government was not in a position to give encouragement to the proposal and the lieutenant governor could take no action.[90] When Dharmapala tried to purchase land near the temple for a Buddhist monastery and resthouse, it was Henry Cotton who blocked the sale, telling a Thai prince that there was no possibility of the land being offered for sale.[91] He was aware of Cotton's role, writing in his diary, "Clive the arch forger founded the British Indian Empire, Cotton the arch high priest of bribery will sow the seed for the destruction of the Empire" (April 17, 1896). With government blocking the sale of land to the Buddhists, Dharmapala gained the support of at least one Bengali newspaper (*Hitavadi*, March 6, 1896), which accused the government of "partiality." He encountered Evan Cotton at virtually the same moment, serving as barrister for the sannyasis who had stopped his attempt to install the Japanese image in 1895. Father and son—the father acting as a government servant overseeing the case, the son serving as lead attorney— were working hand in glove against him. Their success, according to Dharmapala, would have a disastrous effect, bringing down the empire.

The substantial correspondence between local officials and their superiors in Calcutta leaves the impression of bureaucrats trying to keep the peace between two difficult actors. But that correspondence also reveals sympathy for Buddhism. Sometimes the language is subtle but telling—letters speak of Buddhist "images" and Hindu "idols." Sometimes the preference for Buddhism came from civil servants (Francis Buchanan and Alexander Mackenzie for example) who earlier had been posted in Burma; sometimes it came from a disposition—however hierarchical their experience of En-

---

89. Henry Cotton described him as "the greatest of Calcutta criminal barristers, than whom no one ever gave his services *gratis* more often to the poor." *Indian and Home Memories* (London: T. Fisher Unwin, 1911), 204.
90. Cited in Das, *A Hindu Point of View on the Bodh-Gaya Temple Bill*, 20.
91. *Sanjivani*, March 7, 1896.

glish society and Anglo-India—toward Buddhist equality over Hindu hierarchy. Buchanan's case is exemplary. Once settled in India, he became bored
with the flora and fauna of Bengal and set himself to become an expert on
local society, attacking orientalists such as William Jones for their "Brahmanical interpretation of Indian society." When he published an essay on
Burmese Buddhism, he contrasted "the egalitarianism of Buddhism against
the oppressive, hierarchical nature of Indian society."[92] Marika Vicziany
concludes: "Buchanan's hatred of the entrenched Brahmin class in India . . .
marked him out as a man ideally equipped to act as the Company's reporter
on native affairs."

Like Dharmapala, British officials acquired sympathy for Buddhism
by reading *Light of Asia*. Some were drawn to the religion's "Protestant"
qualities, which could be set off from Hinduism's "Catholic" ritualism.[93] A
"Protestant" self-understanding characterized British national identity long
before and long after Dharmapala, distinguishing Britain from the French
"Other."[94] Officials such as Curzon were drawn to Buddhism because of
its association with monuments and India's classical past. They were not
drawn to Dharmapala himself. In writing to Curzon's private secretary,
Herbert Holmwood described himself as a "sympathizer of the Buddhists,"
while deploring "Dharmapala's petty and deplorable intrigues."[95] Curzon's
attitude is captured in his saying, "Dharmapala lives in Ceylon; he is an agi-

92. Marika Vicziany, "Imperialism, Botany and Statistics in Early Nineteenth-Century India: The Surveys of Francis Buchanan (1762–1829)," *Modern Asian Studies* 20, no. 4 (1986): 632.

93. Philip C. Almond, *The British Discovery of Buddhism* (Cambridge: Cambridge University Press, 1988). For a treatment of the British experience with Theravada Buddhism in Lanka,
see Elizabeth J. Harris, *Theravada Buddhism and the British Encounter: Religious, Missionary
and Colonial Experience in Nineteenth Century Sri Lanka* (London: Routledge, 2006). The early
works of Robert Spence Hardy, despite their attempt to undermine Buddhism, "stood pretty
much alone as a resource during the first decades of popular enthusiasm for knowledge of Buddhism, and many books and articles written between the 1850s and 1880s obtained information from them," including Arnold's *Light of Asia*. Judith Snodgrass, "Discourse, Authority,
Demand: The Politics of Early English Publications on Buddhism," in *TransBuddhism*, ed.
Nalini Bhushan, Jay L. Garfield, and Abraham Zablocki (Amherst: University of Massachusetts
Press, 2009), 36. In the cause of critiquing Buddhism, Hardy compared the sangha to the Roman
Catholic priesthood and made much of Buddhist ritualism in Sri Lanka in his time, both signs
he took for corruption and decline.

94. See Hugh McLeod, "Protestantism and British National Identity, 1815–1945," in
Nation and Religion: Perspectives on Europe and Asia, ed. Peter van der Veer and Hartmut
Lehmann (Princeton, NJ: Princeton University Press, 1999), 44–70.

95. Lord Curzon's Memo on Bodh Gaya, enclosure to Curzon's letter to C. E. A. Oldham,
Magistrate and Collector, Gaya, Lord Curzon of Kedleston Correspondence, January 17, 1903, 1:
no.12.

tator; and I should think that the less we have to do with him the better."[96] He had equal distaste for both the Cottons and the mahant.

Looking back over the full list, the number of civil servants who supported the Buddhist cause at Bodh Gaya is astonishing—Lord Lansdowne, who was viceroy when Dharmapala arrived at Bodh Gaya; Lord Kimberley, who met Dharmapala on his way to the World's Parliament of Religions; Lord Elgin, who made the customary viceroy visit; Lord Curzon, who visited in 1903; C. W. Bolton, chief secretary to the government of Bengal; J. A. Bourdillon, acting lieutenant governor of Bengal during the Bodh Gaya Case Commission; H. Holmwood, district and sessions judge, Patna; H. Savage, magistrate of Gaya; Frederick O'Connor, the army officer who escorted the Panchen Lama to Bodh Gaya in 1905; Sir Andrew Fraser; Lord Minto; Sir Alexander McKenzie; Sir John Woodburn; Sir Alexander Cunningham; Sir Charles Elliot; Sir John Marshall; and H. H. Risley, not to mention subordinate officials such as Grierson, Macpherson, and Oldham.[97] The figure who counted was Curzon, and his sympathy for the Buddhist cause gave the Bengali public another reason to support the mahant.

At Eton Curzon had heard a lecture by James Fitzjames Stephen celebrating the British Empire as an instrument for the good of humankind, and from that day he confessed that "the fascination and sacredness of India have grown upon me."[98] He visited India as part of a world tour in 1877, and by the time he was appointed to the British cabinet, he was the most well-traveled person ever to serve there and the preeminent authority on Asian affairs. He concluded the India tour with an excursion to the northwest frontier, exposing him to another arena for the imperial imagination, the place where British interests confronted an expanding Russian empire. Appointed viceroy in 1899, he began to pursue his duties with an energy and competence that the office had scarcely known, but concern for Bodh Gaya figures not at all in the early years of his administration. Once engaged, he expended considerable energy on the issue. He visited the place in January 1903 and began to impose order on a situation that had remained unsettled since Dharmapala's arrival.[99] Curzon wanted a particular kind of order. In

96. Lord Curzon to J. A. Bourdillon, March 9, 1903, Lord Curzon of Kedleston Correspondence, 1: no. 34.

97. Critics of Grierson denounced him as "the Buddhaphil magistrate." M.B., "The Temple of Buddha-Gaya," *Statesman*, October 3, 1891.

98. David Dilks, *Curzon in India*, 2vols. (London: Taplinger, 1969), 1:27–8.

99. Dharmapala had left India late in 1901, steaming to Colombo and on to Japan in April 1902 on a world tour that kept him away from India until April 1904. On the day Curzon

a seven-page private memo he recorded after his visit, he cited with approval Bourdillon's "belief that a restoration of the Buddhist shrine to the votaries of that faith was desirable, and perhaps even within the bounds of possibility."[100] He had been greeted at Bodh Gaya by Tibetan, Siamese, Japanese, Burmese, Chittagongian, and Sinhala Buddhists; Dharmapala was away in San Francisco.

Curzon's motivations for involving himself in the Bodh Gaya case ranged from his interest in classical monuments to his sense of what belonged where. As Macpherson noted, "Lord Curzon viewed with vexation and regret the measures which had been taken by the Mahant to convert the ancient Buddhist shrine into a place of Hindu worship."[101] But more, the mahant's behavior made "it impossible for the Bengal Government any longer to acquiesce in the continuance of conditions which constitute a reproach to its administration." Curzon's reasoning here was less than persuasive: the mahant's control of Bodh Gaya (and the ersatz ritualism he invented to counter Dharmapala), he wrote,

[is] repugnant to a large section of the population under [the government of India's] control, and the removal of which with proper limitations would not . . . be seriously objected to by any considerable section of the public.[102]

---

recorded his extensive thoughts from his visit to Bodh Gaya two days previous, Dharmapala wrote in his diary: "Lord Curzon is expected to visit Buddha Gaya this year and I am asked to go there!!" (January 17, 1903). In San Francisco he received a letter from Harischandra Valisinha, saying that "he himself had been deputed to Buddha Gaya with an address to Lord Curzon" (Diary, February 7, 1903).

100. Enclosure to Curzon's letter to C. E. A. Oldham, Magistrate and Collector of Gaya, January 17, 1903, Lord Curzon of Kedleston Correspondence, 1:7–13, at 7.

101. W. C. Macpherson to Secretary to the Government of India, October 31, 1903, India Office Records, British Library, IOR/L/PJ/6/750/file 705.

102. W. C. Macpherson to Secretary to the Government of India, October 31, 1903, India Office Records, British Library, IOR/L/PJ/6/750/file 705. Although there were Buddhist communities in other parts of the British Empire, the percentage of Buddhists living in India was infinitesimal. Dharmapala makes reference to a single monk he had heard of: "There was a hut at Varis Bagan occupied by Bhikkhu Mahavir, a Rajput of Arrah, who had been ordained in Burma or Ceylon. There was a small image of Buddha enshrined in the hut" (Diary, December 13, 1917). There were Buddhist communities living on the borders of Burma, and one charismatic Arakanese monk had moved to Chittagong, where there were communities of Buddhist Baruas as well as Chakmas and Maghs. In Chittagong, this monk, Saramitra Mahasthabir, began as early as 1864 to purify monastic practice and protect Buddhism from the dominance of Hindu and Tantric practices. By Dharmapala's time Saramitra's students had a place in Calcutta, the Dharmankur vihara, led by Kiripasaran. Abdul Mabud Khan, "Bangladesh Indebtedness to Myanmar: A Study of Reformation Movement in the Buddhist Sangha of Bangladesh (1856–1971)," *Arakanese Research Journal* 2 (2003): 25–34.

The fact of the matter is that the people who objected were Dharmapala, his monks, his international supporters, and a small number of sympathetic Hindus.

Colonial officials were determined to find Buddhism living on in India, however unrecognizable it might be. Alexander Cunningham identified the Hindu god Jagannath with the Buddha.[103] His evidence was sketchy. He thought that because caste rules were suspended during festival time at the Puri temple, Jagannath had been venerated as the Buddha at an earlier time, but such is the nature of Hindu festivals. He argued that the Jagannath's trident had a Buddhist reference. H. H. Risley tried to find the Buddha in Hindu places, hoping that signs of Buddhist practice could be found in Bengali folk tradition. In September 1901, he sent local officials a printed circular and an outline of an 1895 account by Haraprasad Shastri of traces of Buddhism in Bengal.[104] They were instructed to make inquiries into whether there might be Buddhist images—such as Dharmaraj Thakur—being worshipped and practices followed that "savour most strongly of Buddhism."[105] A large number of magistrates made inquiries in their districts—many of them painstaking—and they found no evidence of Buddhist practices. How Curzon figured in these inquiries is not clear, but it is hard to ignore the political context in which the search for continuity arose.

Shortly after his visit to Bodh Gaya Lord Curzon seized on the idea of a commission as a way to pressure the mahant to abide by an agreement that he had supported in January 1903 in discussion with Oldham.[106] The

103. *The Bhilsa Topes; or, Buddhist Monuments of Central India* (Varanasi: Indological Book House, 1966), 99 and 232–3.

104. When Sastri was appointed to the Bodh Gaya Commission, he presented Lord Curzon with a copy of his book *Discovery of Living Buddhism in Bengal* (Calcutta: Sanskrit Press Depository, 1897). The 1897 book is the 1895 account in published form. Shastri concludes that volume by arguing, "The diversity of names is infinite. But with a little care a census of the followers of Dhamma may be taken. The population will be considerable, nay, several millions" (31).

105. Reports on Buddhism in Bengal, 1901–2, Risley Collection, India Office Records, British Library, Mss Eur E295/10. Although he does not mention Risley's reports on Buddhism, Frank Korom traces the genealogy of Indian scholars interested in linking Dharmaraj to the Buddha, beginning with Haraprasad Shastri. "'Editing' Dharmaraj: Academic Genealogies of a Bengali Folk Deity," *Western Folklore* 56, no. 1 (1997): 51–77.

106. Srimahat Krishnadayalu Giri to Raja Peary Mohan Mukerji, October 20, 1903, enclosure to Letter from J. A. Bourdillon, Acting Lieutenant Governor of Bengal, to Lord Curzon, October 29, 1903, Lord Curzon of Kedleston Correspondence with Persons in India, July to December 1903, 2: no. 156, Mss Eur F111/208. Krishnadayalu Giri wrote in that letter that Oldham "pressed me to make over the temple in perpetuity to government . . . and to declare that the Hindus had no right to offer *pindas* at the Mahabodhi tree, nor to offer *puja* to the image inside the temple. . . . I was surprised at these novel proposals, and could not but decline to accept them for the interests of the Hindu nation."

Bodh Gaya Commission consisted of two men, chosen specifically to reach the conclusion Curzon favored: S. C. Mitra, judge of the High Court of Calcutta and Shastri, principal of Sanskrit College. They were asked to inspect the place, talk to the mahant, and prepare a report on the matter.[107] Shastri came recommended by Bourdillon, then acting lieutenant governor of Bengal, who described him as

> a Brahman of learning and repute; he is necessarily a strict and orthodox Hindu, and in addition a good Archaeologist and scholar. I judge that the opinion he would give would be to the effect that the existing worship is spurious and impure.[108]

Shastri had written to Bourdillon earlier, telling him that he regarded the transfer of the temple to the Buddhists "a very important work."

Mitra agreed with Shastri that the Hindu worship at the Bodh Gaya shrine was not orthodox and that the mahant ought to surrender authority over the rituals performed there. After their survey of the temple and math, the pair went to Raja Peary Mohan Mukerji, who served as an intermediary between the government and the mahant, to secure his agreement. Their mission was to convince him to persuade the mahant of the wisdom of their position, an unlikely prospect given his role in the British Indian Association, which had already thrown its weight in the opposite direction. To get any agreement, the commission had to make a number of large concessions, and the final agreement was less than officials had hoped. Bourdillon was still optimistic: "We do not get the control of the temple and of the ritual absolutely surrendered, but we get a promise not to clothe or paint the image and the appointment of a Board to control disputes."[109] Curzon was more realistic, saying that very little advantage had been gained by the agreement the commissioners were proposing.

107. Mitra later served as a member of the Buddhist Shrine Restoration Society.

108. J. A. Bourdillon to Lord Curzon, March 9, 1903, Lord Curzon of Kedleston Correspondence, 1: no. 76. Shastri was a Sanskritist, but he was also a government employee, joining the Bureau of Information in 1908. In 1916 he went to Japan to teach Indian philosophy in Tokyo, while working at the same time for British intelligence. He was controlled by Davidson, the official who had Dharmapala followed during his 1913 visit to Japan. Arriving in Japan with another agent, Shastri was astounded to find himself and his companion greeted as Indian nationalists, reporting back to British Intelligence that "the Indian revolutionary movement in Japan was far more important than [C. J. Davidson and Conygnham Greene] had realized." Popplewell, *Intelligence and Imperial Defence*, 278–9.

109. J. A. Bourdillon to Lord Curzon, April 5, 1903, Lord Curzon of Kedleston Correspondence, 1: no. 98a.

If the mahant's estimate of the numbers of pilgrims who came to Bodh Gaya each year was instructive, his account of what pilgrims actually did at there was still more so:

> The Buddhists of Tibet and Nepal anoint the forehead of the image with a paste.
> The Ceylonese Buddhists sprinkle eau-de-cologne upon the forehead of the image, but do not anoint the forehead.
> The Burmese and Siamese Buddhists clothe the image.
> It is not the Mohant who clothed the image, but the pilgrims who do so. Only a month ago a Siamese priest clothed the image at a cost of Rs. 2500 or more.[110]

After Dharmapala's arrival, the mahant had reason to pay attention to everyday routines at the shrine, giving him ethnographic knowledge sufficient to deny the distinction that identified Buddhists and Hindus with a set of ritual practices: that the Buddhists venerated the image without adornment, and the Hindus were inclined to anoint and clothe it. By confounding those differences, the mahant vexed British authorities and reduced Dharmapala's case to rubble. He could have included Dharmapala's own treatment of the Japanese image: As he recorded in his diary, he "spent the afternoon in setting up the Burmese [that is, the Japanese image now in the Burmese resthouse] image in the big hall. . . . There was a gold umbrella and two parasols, and a cloth decorated with tinsel, and another silk canopy. It looks grand now" (November 21, 1904).

Evan Cotton took the case on without fee. He compared his position to Mukerji's: he was the mahant's supporter, now acting in the role of attorney.[111] The mahant would not act without his advice: "[the mahant] suggested he should send for Mr. Cotton, barrister-at-law, and that he would do as he approved."[112] Curzon felt no more affection for the son than his father:

> I learned that on March 30th the Raja had been introduced on to the scene; and with still greater regret that at a yet later stage I heard that

110. Draft Report of the Commission sent to Bodh Gaya, enclosure B, in J. A. Bourdillon to Curzon, April 14, 1903, Lord Curzon of Kedleston Correspondence, 1: no. 104a.

111. H. E. A. Cotton to J. A. Bourdillon, June 17, 1903, enclosure to J. A. Bourdillon to Lord Curzon, June 20, 1903, Lord Curzon of Kedleston Correspondence, 1: no. 157.

112. Memo of interviews with the Mahant of Bodh Gaya, enclosure to C. E. A. Oldham to Walter Lawrence, Lord Curzon of Kedleston Correspondence, February 8, 1903, 1: no. 30a.

15. Buddha image with Vaisnavite marks, Bodh Gaya.

Mr. Cotton had been admitted into counsel. I distrust the former
gentleman. I have every reason for knowing that the latter is a bitter op-
ponent, and would gladly wreck any scheme in which I am concerned.[113]

He put together the commission to give the Buddhists relief, and his involvement in the negotiations that followed raised the stakes—as his colleagues kept reminding him—and Cotton's involvement raised them again,
casting the Anglo-Indian as defender of the Indian people.

When the mahant continued to resist settlement after protracted negotiations, Bourdillon invited Mukerji to the lieutenant governor's residence

---

113. Lord Curzon to J. A. Bourdillon, May 26, 1903, Lord Curzon of Kedleston Correspondence, 1: no. 78b.

in Calcutta, warning him that the government had grown weary of negotiations and wanted the matter brought to a conclusion, if not by agreement,
then by government action.[114] That invitation was the carrot; the threat of
government action to take over the shrine was the stick. As it turned out,
that threat had no visible effect on the mahant. The deadline passed with
only trivial concessions proposed by Cotton, forcing Curzon to consider
publishing a government of India resolution in the *Calcutta Gazette* laying
out the mahant's malfeasance and the unsatisfactory conclusion to their negotiations. D. C. J. Ibbetson of the Viceroy's Council told Curzon that doing
so could prompt nationalist "agitation . . . among the orthodox Hindu community . . . fomented by disloyal sections of the native press."[115] Bourdillon
saw a different result, with international significance: "Your Excellency has
no doubt considered the effect which a spontaneous concession [giving over
the Maha Bodhi temple] to the Buddhists would have at a time when our relations with China and Tibet are so strained."[116] In the end, Ibbetson talked
Curzon down from going public with his grievances, and his silence left the
mahant's authority intact.

Once again, the mahant had succeeded in thwarting colonial India's
most competent viceroy and his Buddhist adversary. Curzon remained viceroy for another two years but never returned to the matter. Copland argues
that Curzon did not even brief his successor, Lord Minto, on the matter
before the latter made his own visit to Bodh Gaya in 1906. Minto too was
put off by the Hindu marks on the forehead of the Buddha image and impressed by the "very reasonable claims of the followers of Budha [*sic*]."[117] In
a letter to Mukerji, the mahant had argued that he "could not but decline to
accept [the proposal] for the interests of the Hindu nation," suggesting the
mahant's recognition of a new source of leverage. Absent a national community for the Buddhists to invoke, Dharmapala used his journal to bemoan
the outcome. He gained a number of distinguished Indian sympathizers,
including Gandhi, Chittaranjan Das, Rabindranath Tagore, and Rajendra
Prasad, but their support was nominal.[118]

---

114. J. A. Bourdillon to Lord Curzon, August 11, 1903, Lord Curzon of Kedleston Correspondence, 2: no. 36.

115. D. C. J. Ibbetson, Member of the Viceroy's Council, to Lord Curzon, September 16,
1903, Lord Curzon of Kedleston Correspondence, 2: no. 88e.

116. J. A. Bourdillon to Lord Curzon, October 9, 1903, Lord Curzon of Kedleston Correspondence, 2: no. 120.

117. Copland, "Managing Religion in Colonial India," 561.

118. There are several helpful sources on Bodh Gaya between 1910 and the present. One of
the more accessible sources is Copland, "Managing Religion in Colonial India," 556–9; one of
the more thorough is Doyle, "Bodh Gaya," 173–216 and 387–422. The Maha Bodhi temple is

Following the commission's report, the mahant pressed his advantage and litigated again to have both the Japanese image and resident monks removed from the Burmese resthouse. Dharmapala blamed the suit on the government's anxiety about Okakura's attempt to lease a plot of land at Bodh Gaya for Japanese pilgrims and monks, telling his readers that Levinge, the commissioner of Patna, had counseled the mahant to bring suit if he wanted to have the monks removed.[119] In December 1908 Dharmapala attempted to present a petition to the visiting lieutenant governor, Sir Edward Baker, but his staff prevented him from doing so.[120] In January 1909, the court in Calcutta ruled in the mahant's favor, and Dharmapala's failed appeal of February 1910 finally settled things. From that point both the Japanese image and the Bodh Gaya monks moved to Maha Bodhi Society headquarters in Calcutta. In the years that followed the commission's work, Dharmapala saw prejudice against the Buddhists behind every government policy and practice. A more reliable explanation for talking to the mahant about his options and rejecting Dharmapala's memorial pivots on discretion: better not to further rile up Indians at the time when the Partition of Bengal was being proposed and allow the Indian National Congress to straighten out things over the long term.

Tapati Guha-Thakurta concludes that through the 1890s the British wanted simply to maintain the status quo at Bodh Gaya and only later came

---

now controlled by a committee of Hindus and Buddhists, and its politics remain as contentious they were in Dharmapala's time. Doyle also mentions that the mahant's ownership of land and control of thousands of landless laborers was successfully challenged by J. P. Narayan's campaign to redistribute land in 1978. She writes that the mahant of Bodh Gaya now controls one hundred acres of land (213n6). An account of how Bodh Gaya now functions as a World Heritage Site, pilgrimage center, and center of numerous transnational activities can be found in David Geary, "Destination Enlightenment: Buddhism and the Global Bazaar in Bodh Gaya, Bihar" (PhD diss., University of British Columbia, 2009).

119. "The History of the Burmese Rest-House," 422. Dharmapala misread both the mahant's motives and his financial interests:

Since July 1894 he has prevented the Buddhists from accumulating good karma by his dog in the manger policy. What has he gained after all? There is no regular income from the Temple, the Buddhists do not pay him anything. His predecessor absolutely ignored the temple. For nearly five years the Temple was abandoned by the Buddhists and the Mahant as well as by the Govt. In Decr 1890 the PWD of Bengal for the first time, urged by the Collector of Gaya, Dr. G. A. Grierson, had a custodian appointed. But for the vindictive policy adopted by the Govt. in 1905 the Mahant would not have cared to bring a suit against the Buddhists. In the two cases he lost a good deal of money and the good will of the Buddhists. He is now an old man. The turbulent boisterous spirit I believe is now on the decline. (Sarnath Notebook no. 58)

120. Trevithick, The Revival of Buddhist Pilgrimage at Bodh Gaya, 173.

to show increasing support for the Buddhists.[121] Scrutinizing their representations to Dharmapala, their correspondence, and many of their actions reveals an extraordinary sympathy for the Buddhist cause from the beginning of this struggle until its end—from Macpherson's giving Dharmapala the key to the resthouse in 1891 to Lord Curzon's time—overlain by the official policy of religious neutrality. Despite that sympathy, Dharmapala misread all signs of it, interpreting any act of partiality to the mahant or any constraint posed by law on what could be done for the Buddhists as evidence of the government's favoring the mahant. In his diary and publications he avoided mentioning the mahant's having a deed to Bodh Gaya or the legal weight of the Giri sannyasins having occupied the place for several hundred years. Behind every legal reversal he saw British complicity: "I never expected that in the future strife would arise over this issue between the Saivites and the Indian government on one side and Buddhists on the other side."[122]

He laid out a step-by-step account of how events had spun out of control, beginning with the argument that Okakura had intended

to establish a centre of Japanese activity at Bodhgaya. Okakura . . . [had] selfish designs and [acted] in collusion with Vivekananda against the Buddhists of the so called Southern Church. His idea was to provoke the religious emotions of the mahant by showing there was [obscure] between Buddhism and Hinduism, but there was a clear hostility between Japanese [Buddhism?] and the so called Hinayana of Ceylon & Burma. The Japanese therefore wished to [have] a separate establishment at Bodhgaya with the idea of forming a Hindu Japanese alliance. The negociation ended in a fiasco. Mr. Okakura had to leave India, Vivekananda and the Government came to know of the transaction which [unclear] Mr Levinge Commissioner of Patna to advise the Mahant [unclear] suit against the ["Buddhists," crossed out in pencil] MBS and have the Buddhist [obscure] from the Burmese Rest House at Bodhgaya. Hari Prasad Sastri is a strict Hindu, and very inimical [obscure] and the Govt. instructed him to write the Report against Buddhists. In 1916 I met Mr. Sastri in his [obscure] at Calcutta and I asked him why he had written agst the Buddhists. The answer was that he was privately asked by the Govt to do so! The work [obscure] that I began in January 1891 ended in

---

121. Guha-Thakurta, *Monuments, Objects, Histories,* 292–98, at 293.

122. "How the Buddhist Flag Was Hoisted at Buddha Gaya," in Jayawardana, *Mage Jivita Kathava,* 57.

the expulsion [words bleached out] most holy shrine in 1910 by order of government. (Sarnath Notebook no. 6)

Long before the resolution of the Japanese Buddha case in 1910, Dharmapala's efforts to construct Buddhism as ancient, Indian, and at one with Hinduism cut in one direction; events cut in another, making it foreign and other. Bengali newspapers such as *Bangavasi* saw what they took to be a change in policy under Curzon and attacked the government's favoritism toward Buddhism (April 11, 1903). It explained the mahant's reluctance to respond to a proposal because he needed to consider the implications of his agreement "being the representative of the Hindu community." The idea that the abbot of a math represented a community and that the community was "Hindu" came to the foreground in the process.

BUDDHISM AND THE BENGALI PUBLIC SPHERE

Dharmapala appeared in Calcutta at a time of turmoil and transition, and religion was involved in both. As Henry Cotton observed,

> Absolute Nihilism, Brahmoism, Theosophy, Theism which conforms to Hindooism, and lastly, Christianity, these generally are the varying creeds which among Hindus survive the wreck of their early faith. . . . Wandering hither and thither like sheep without a shepherd, they beat the air in the vain pursuit after religious truth.[123]

In much the same way as he had found the Japanese negotiating a similar landscape during his 1889 visit, Dharmapala settled in Calcutta at a propitious moment. How likely was it that a leading Bengali religious intellectual would have made an earlier tour of Lanka and praised Buddhist rationalism, as did Keshab Chandra Sen in 1859, producing a book published just before Dharmapala's arrival?[124] How likely was it that at that moment a solitary Buddhist arriving in North India would find Bengalis entertaining a newfound interest in a religion that had been absent from North India for a thousand years? That interest was more than casual, although it is instructive that Cotton did not include Buddhism in his list of movements

123. Henry Cotton, *New India, or India in Transition*, 278.
124. *Diary in Ceylon, from 27th September to 5th November 1859* (Calcutta: Brahmo Tract Society, 1888).

by which Bengalis addressed "the wreck of their early faith." More than a decade before Dharmapala's arrival, the Brahmo Samaj had established the Shakya Samagam as a vehicle for Indians interested in Buddhism. Bengalis were coming to understand something of Buddhism by reading *Light of Asia* (1879), followed by Bengali translations of the *Buddhacarita* and *Asoka Carita* (1892). They also encountered a religion long neglected until articles on Buddhism began to appear in periodicals such as *Prabasi, Vasumati, Bharatavarsa, Modern Review,* and the *Indian Mirror.*[125]

Scholars, usually with training in Sanskrit, turned toward Buddhism, their research interests motivated by the same humanistic values that made the religion appealing to Bengalis more generally. Sarat Chandra Das was a distinguished student of Sanskrit and Tibetan (and a British intelligence agent) who made two trips to the Tashilurpo monastery and returned with hundreds of Buddhist manuscripts. Das founded the Buddhist Text Society in Calcutta with Dharmapala, and when he engaged 2 Creek Row, it served as headquarters for the Maha Bodhi Society, the Theosophical Society, and the Buddhist Text Society (Diary, June 30, 1904). Other Bengali scholars— Charu Chandra Bose and Satis Chandra Vidyabhushan—shared an interest in Buddhism and became members of the Maha Bodhi Society. Leaving Calcutta for his trip to the Parliament of Religions, Dharmapala left the place "in the hands of Sarat babu and Charu babu" (Diary, February 14, 1893).

Affection for Buddhism gathered Westerners and Indians in one of the few contexts where both groups interacted socially. As president of the Asiatic Society of Bengal, C. W. Bolton (the same Bolton who had tried to manage the Japanese Buddha issue as chief secretary to the government of Bengal) addressed the annual meeting by singing the praises of a long list of Indianists, beginning with Jones, Wilson, Prinsep, and Cunningham. The emphasis on Buddhism was just as striking when he surveyed the work ahead, even as the future was darkening:

The era of great discoveries in India itself may have passed. No undiscovered Asoka pillar, Buddhist Topes and Buddhist caves, no undeciphered inscriptions and coins of an unknown language and an unknown epoch, and no great unpublished work in the Sanskritic and Semitic classics may remain.[126]

125. S. K. Pathak, "The Maha Bodhi Society in Calcutta—Culture," *Journal of the Maha Bodhi Society* 100, no. 4 (1992): 13–4.

126. "The Presidential Address," *Englishman*, February 6, 1903, 6.

He went on to say that there was still important work to be done, point-
ing to scholars pursuing those projects—Grierson, Das, Vidyabhushan, the
Reverend Graham Sandberg, and Reverend A. Heyde—who were focused on
Buddhism and especially Tibetan Buddhism.[127]

When Dharmapala came to live in Calcutta, he was helped by his affiliation with Olcott, who had made a considerable stir in India over the previous decade.[128] He found Theosophists virtually everywhere he went; even
at Bodh Gaya he found Theosophists six miles away. Looking back over his
career, he put it thus:

> I came to India first because I was a Theosophist, and I came to Buddha
> Gaya as a Buddhist, but I was warmly welcomed by the Theosophists.
> Upendra Nath Bose, Govinda Dasa in Benares, and Durga Sh: Bhatta-
> carya of Gaya. (Diary, Memorandum for 1919, 4)[129]

The *Indian Mirror* became the voice of the Buddhist revival, and because it
was the only daily newspaper in Bengal at that time under Indian control,
that voice carried.[130] Sen was the source of the epigraph to this chapter: "If
there is a Hindu revival in India, there is a Buddhist revival in the world."
From the day of Dharmapala's arrival in Calcutta, Sen made readers aware
of his doings, despairing over his reversals at Bodh Gaya, noting his travels
across India and the world, and celebrating his accomplishments. Most pertinently, he insisted on Buddhism's being a world religion, portraying Dhar-

127. Bolton leaves out the name of T. Kawakami, who had worked with Dharmapala during
his earlier visits to Japan and began living in Calcutta and studying Tibetan in 1894. "Personal
Items," *Journal of the Maha Bodhi Society* 3 (1894): 30.

128. *Amrita Bazar Patrika*, September 11, 1890, gushed over Olcott: " We could never repay the services of Colonel Olcott to India. . . . His love of India cannot be measured by the love
which a Hindu feels for his country—it is much higher and nobler." The *Indian Mirror* followed
Olcott's travels across India, reporting on his lectures in India and abroad. "Trying to Explain
Theosophy: Colonel Olcott's Lecture," October 26, 1889. The *Mirror* summed up the challenges
the society faced in India: "Madame Blavatsky and Colonel Olcott, who had come to India to
learn and acquire the wisdom of the East at the feet of Indian sages, found that sages were at
a discount in the country of their birth, that the educated Indians . . . worshipped Huxley and
Herbert Spencer." "Accomplishments of the Mission of the Theosophical Society," November 21, 1889.

129. Durga Shankar Bhattacharya had accompanied Dharmapala, Kozen, and Chiezo
Takazawa to Bodh Gaya on that first visit, procuring the key to the Burmese resthouse for them
(Sarnath Notebook no. 58). Blackburn says that Dharmapala's entry to Bengali society was
facilitated by Hikkaduve Sumangala. Blackburn, *Locations of Buddhism*, 120.

130. Surendranath Banerjea, *A Nation in Making: Being the Reminiscences of Fifty Years of
Public Life* (1925; repr., Calcutta: Paschimbanga Bangla Akademi, 1998), 188.

mapala's campaign as a matter of interest to the many Buddhist countries of Asia. He saw the larger scene in a more material way: looking around Asia, Sen noticed that Buddhist countries were better off than India, an argument Vivekananda had made (Diary, November 7, 1908). He concluded that India's decline began with Buddhism's disappearance; restoring it would lead to India's "national salvation," bringing both moral and economic revival.[131] When Dharmapala arrived in 1891, Sen told him that he had "come as a saviour to India" (Diary, August 15, 1898). They eventually fell out, but Dharmapala became a public figure in Calcutta because of Sen's efforts.

Dharmapala approached the Hindu elite in a fraternal way. Having made himself known to several rajas, he solicited support for the Bodh Gaya project:

I was introduced to the Durans [sic] of the Rajahs of Dumron and Hatwa. Got another Memorial to be signed by the Hindus printed. Wrote to Hara Prasad Sastu [sic], Mohesh Chandra Nyasatna, Bhandarkar, K. T. Telang, N. N. Sen, Govinda Das, asking them to give their opinion whether the Hindus have any objection to put the Bud. Gaya Temple under Buddhist guardianship. (Diary, October 29, 1891)

In a letter to the *Behar Times*, he wrote of the natural affinity between Hindus and Buddhists:

I have to work single-handed in this great Empire, for the Buddhists have no idea of the tolerant spirit of the Hindus. They seem to think that we shall be treated unkindly. We solicit the sympathy of your people. . . . We want to get back our Central Shrine in Budh-Gaya; but the Government fears that the Hindus will raise objections if the temple is transferred to us. The King of Siam does and the King of Burma did support the Brahmans; and in Siam, the Buddhists get the Brahman priests to perform all Vedic ceremonies. The Brahmans have always been supported by the Buddhists and so there could be no hostility between the two great families.[132]

131. "The Vaisakha Festival," *Journal of the Maha Bodhi Society* 17 (1909): 88–100, at 98–9. Dharmapala responded with arguments that Buddhism would empower India's economic development. "The Principles of National Prosperity as Enunciated by Lord Buddha," *Indian Mirror*, June 13, 1907.

132. Quoted in "The Budh-Gaya Temple," *Journal of the Maha Bodhi Society* 3 (1894): 16–17.

Dismissing the distinction between Hindu India and Buddhist Asia, he found common ground: Buddhists in Burma and Siam are also Hindus, at least to the extent that they rely on Brahmanical ritual services.

Shortly after his arrival in Calcutta he gave his first lecture at the Albert Hall. He recounted the law of cause and effect and the Eightfold Path. The challenge was situating that doctrine in an Indian context.[133] Buddhism was "the highest form of philosophic thought," and the antidote to India's not having progressed for centuries. In the years before his arrival in Calcutta, Bengali newspapers had begun to rail about the "sadhu" problem and the practice of greedy mahants extracting fees from innocent pilgrims all over India.[134] Buddhism was free of supernatural agency, realistic and scientific, and it was free of anthropomorphism. Its world renouncers were well mannered and not interested in collecting fees. The Buddhism described in *The Light of Asia* was more evolved than the crude theology of the Upanishads. When Dharmapala quoted Western scholars on Buddhism's virtues, he did not stress its universalism, emphasizing instead that it was an Indian solution to Indian problems. Without missing a beat, he announced that four Buddhist monks were now resident at Bodh Gaya, and Buddhism had returned to its homeland. After many centuries India was on the move again.

Bengalis had been hearing about the package of virtues that Dharmapala stressed in Buddhism—antiritualism, rationality, self-development coupled with social development—before he reached their shores. To Bengali ears, Buddhism resonated with the kind of reform Hinduism that the Brahmo Samaj had envisioned since 1830. Another source of affinity was visceral. They "all say that I look quite one of them," Dharmapala noted, adding that they love the Buddha, "only they call him Buddha dev" (Diary, January 21, 1891). The facial similarity was not limited to Dharmapala alone— "The same love I have for my own countrymen I have for the Bengalees. Every individual face I see has a strong resemblance to, and is a counterpart of, a Sinhalese"(Diary, September 4, 1891). He confessed he was "more at home in the company of Bengalees. . . . The Sinhalese are a little behind" (Diary, August 6, 1891). The diaries provide no example of his converting a

133. "Buddhism in Its Relationship with Hinduism," *Indian Mirror*, October 29, 1891. The lecture can also be found in *Journal of the Maha Bodhi Society* 100 (1992): 81–88.

134. The following captures the complaints: "The days of irresponsible and reckless Mohunts are numbered. The heavy hand of retribution is upon them. You have your Mohant [*sic*] of Tarkeswar, and we have our Mohunt of Tiramalai or Tirupati. . . . You do not love your Mohunt, and you would have him out of Bengal. . . . But that is something better than what we wish to our Mohunt." "Mohunts, from our Madras Correspondent," *Indian Mirror*, October 15, 1889. Also see *Hitavadi*, January 24, 1896.

Bengali. He came merely to make Buddhism present again in India.[135] His dilemma was doing so while denouncing Saivite hegemony as having turned Bodh Gaya into a *jatila tirthaka* (misbelievers' place).[136]

A surprising number of Hindus responded, finding Buddhism attractive for a variety of reasons. Sometimes their reasoning fixed on the Buddhist understanding of the nature of human beings and their potential for individual development; more often they were drawn to Buddhism as a language that aptly described India's decline and subjection by a colonial power:

> There was a strong feeling among pro-Buddhist Hindus that Buddhism with its emphasis on self-reliance, sacrifice and endurance could be a source of inspiration to Indian nationalism. Pro-Buddhist Hindus also believed that some at any rate of the problems which faced Indians could be best explained in terms of Buddhism. . . . Just as the wellbeing of individuals was governed by their *karma* or actions, "national karma" too was determined by the activities of the mass of people in a country. In India misguided Hindus had subjected Buddhism to harassment and persecution.[137]

Decline and colonial domination, the argument went, were the payback for driving a noble Indian religion from the land.[138] Sen blamed the persecution and disappearance of Buddhism on the Muslim invasions, an argument that Dharmapala seems not to have heard before then. It was especially convenient because it allowed him to invoke the solidarity of Hindus and Buddhists by putting the burden on a community with which he had no connection.[139] Blaming Islam did not preempt the more persuasive argument that India's decline and Buddhism's disappearance were linked.

135. "Duties of Buddhists to the People of India," *Journal of the Maha Bodhi Society* 15 (1907): 2–5.

136. *Sarasavi Sandarasa*, April 4, 1893, reprinted as "News from India," in Guruge, *Dharmapala Lipi*, 207–8, at 207.

137. L. Ananda Wickremeratne, *The Genesis of an Orientalist: Thomas William Rhys Davids in Sri Lanka* (New Delhi: South Asia Books, 1985), 212–3.

138. For a later expression of the position, see Sameer Chander Mookerjee, *The Decline and Fall of the Hindus, the Book of India's Regeneration* (Calcutta: Indian Rationalistic Society, 1919).

139. Dharmapala also told his Hindu audience that historians, namely Bengal's own Rajendralala Mitra, had exonerated Sankaracarya, the traditional culprit, of the disappearance of Buddhism. Hindus had not persecuted Buddhism, Dharmapala argued; Muslims had. "Buddhism in Its Relationship to Hinduism," 83–4. Laying the blame on Muslims had no cost for him because he had no interactions with Muslims in Calcutta except for an unpleasant relationship with a neighbor with whom he had a boundary dispute.

Vivekananda had similar views of Buddhism's role in Indian history, although he was not a model of consistency. He traced the downfall of India
to a provincialism that kept his ancestors from coming into contact with
Buddhists from nearby countries.[140] India's decline derived from Buddhism's
focus on liberation at the cost of not providing a social ethics.[141] In other
places he blamed Buddhism for causing India's decline by its abhorrence of
animal sacrifice and meat eating, causing Indians to become less manly.[142]
If there is a pattern in his comments, it is that early on he was more positive about what the two religions might contribute to India's reformation by
their interaction. When he said that Buddhism was the fulfillment of Hinduism, he did not mean that it superseded Vedantic Hinduism. There could
be no higher thinking than Vedantic Hinduism. The problem, he said at the
World's Parliament of Religions, was that the Buddha "was not understood
properly by his disciples," for he preached nothing new. They did not see
that what the Buddha preached was simply the logical development of the
religion of the Hindus.[143] If he was no doctrinal innovator, he brought social innovation. The Buddha had sympathy for ordinary people and charity
for everyone, and those qualities, according to Vivekananda, were revolutionary. The Buddha gave India humanism. India had to learn from Buddhist
humanism: "We cannot live without [Buddhism]. . . . [Buddhism] cannot
stand without the brain and the philosophy of the Brahmin."[144]

Reducing Buddhism to "the wonderful humanizing power of the Great
Master" was an act of considerable intellectual bravado, itself central to
Vivekananda's charisma. Behavior that charmed Americans looked like sacrilege in India. Once returned to Calcutta, Dharmapala had the stage to
himself because Vivekananda did not come home for almost four years. In
his absence rumors of misbehavior abroad made their way to Calcutta, and
Dharmapala came to his defense, giving a lecture at the Minerva theater,
which he claimed saved Vivekananda's reputation.[145] He had his own rea-

---

140. "Swami Vivekananda," *Journal of the Maha Bodhi Society* 4 (1895): 7.

141. "Lectures by Swami Vivekananda," *Journal of the Maha Bodhi Society* 18 (1910): 616–
20, at 616–7.

142. "Reawakening of Hinduism on a National Basis," *Prabuddha Bharata*, September
1898, reprinted in *Complete Works of Swami Vivekananda*, 5:225–8, at 225–6.

143. "Buddhism, the Fulfillment of Hinduism," in *Complete Works of Swami Vivekananda*, 1:21–3 at 21.

144. Swami Vivekananda, *Indian Mirror*, June 29, 1895. The article recounts remarks
Vivekananda made at the World's Parliament, characterizing Buddhism as the fulfillment of
Hinduism.

145. It is not clear from Vivekananda's own account whether he took meat and wine in
America or simply ate *mlechcha* (impure) food of other sorts in the company of *mlechchas*. He

sons to defend Vivekananda—he had been told that only Vivekananda's intervention would make the mahant give Bodh Gaya to the Buddhists (Diary,
August 13, 1894). When Vivekananda returned to India in 1897, he was
greeted in Chennai as a hero. But in Calcutta the bravado that worked well
abroad did not mesh with his Kayastha origins. Raja Peary Mukerji refused
to address him as "Swami"; other Bengalis discounted his claims to being
a legitimate sannyasi, much less a spokesperson for Hinduism; and he was
refused admission to the Dakshineswar temple, which Ramakrishna frequented.[146] Years later when Indians began speaking of the Bodh Gaya mahant's as a representative of Hinduism, they found a more serviceable figure,
lacking Vivekananda's physical presence, but also his flair for controversy.
Vivekananda's return to India changed everything:

> In the USA & England he found only praise for Buddhism. On the lad-
> der of Buddhism he climbed up. When he got fame he returned to India
> and began his vicious and baseless criticisms on Buddhism. (Diary,
> March 18, 1921)[147]

What Vivekananda loved about Buddhism was the Buddha, not the present "degraded" condition of Buddhism. He acquired his views about the
religion's present-day condition by traveling, and Lanka played a central
role: "My trip to Ceylon has entirely disillusioned me . . . the only living
people there are Hindus."[148] In the same letter, he spoke of Dharmapala's
anger after having learned of his "remarks about degraded Buddhism." After

---

readily admitted the latter (*Complete Works of Swami Vivekananda*, 5:171), worrying in a letter
that on his return to India he might not be allowed into certain Hindu temples. But he also says
in an article that the distinguishing feature of his movement was "aggression" (225) and that
Buddhism had destroyed India by teaching Indians to be overly fastidious about "cow-killing"
(226), suggesting that he saw the familiar connection between India's weakness and vegetarianism. An independent account from the time of the World's Parliament comes from a Dr. Bowers,
who accompanied Vivekananda to dinner in a restaurant at the Art Institute. He asked Vivekananda what he wanted to eat and was told: "Give me beef!" *Outlook*, July 17, 1897.

146. Sen, *Swami Vivekananda*, 39–41.

147. Dharmapala recalled in his diary decades later: "When I returned to Calcutta in April,
1894 Vivekananda's relations called to see me and requested me to save the reputation of Vivekananda. . . . I spoke of Vivekananda and the great good he had done for Hinduism. Norendra
Nath Sen at first was against Vivekananda, but after my lecture he was converted. Vivekananda
in 1896 treacherously attacked the Buddhists" (March 28, 1926). If Dharmapala is correct
about the 1896 date, he must have discovered—contrary to his saying that Vivekananda never
attacked Buddhism while in the West—Vivekananda attacking Buddhism before his return to
India in January 1897.

148. Letter to Mrs. Ole Bull," in *Complete Works of Swami Vivekananda*, 7:505–6.

writing that Dharmapala "is a good man, and I love him," he dismissed his "very wroth" reaction because it is "entirely wrong for him to go into fits over things Indian," seeing no contradiction in his own intervention in Dharmapala's native place. On his second trip to the West in June 1899, he again toured the island, giving an open-air lecture in Anuradhapura. Having heard that "Buddhists were very quiet people and equally tolerant of all religions," the occasion gave him reason to believe that they did not live up to their values. He was surprised when his lecture was interrupted—the more so because his audience was largely Hindu—"when a whole host of Buddhist monks and laymen, men and women, came out beating drums and cymbals and set up an awful uproar."[149] In this case, he found himself on the receiving end of the pressure to reclaim Anuradhapura as an exclusively Buddhist place by the hands of Dharmapala and his acolyte Harischandra.

Even before the emergence of nationalist politics, Indian prospects for a universal brotherhood of the kind that Dharmapala envisioned (a united world of Buddhists) or that Vivekananda propagated (a universalism organized around his highly imaginative understanding of Vedantic Hinduism) were equally unlikely.[150] When Olcott and Blavatsky arrived in Bombay in 1879, for instance, the *Indian Mirror* captured the dilemma neatly: "They did not find half a dozen Indians ready to receive their ideas of an Universal Brotherhood, and not even of an Indian Brotherhood."[151] Over the decades that followed, Olcott found Indians ready to consider the "ancient wisdom," and Dharmapala found his own constituency. On paper the numbers were impressive. Olcott claimed to have established 145 branches of the Theosophical Society by 1892 but admitted that many branches had only nominal existence.[152] Vivekananda recognized how overextended the movement was. Once returned to India, he wrote to Mrs. Ole Bull, "You must remember first that in India Theosophists and Buddhists are nonen-

149. "Memoirs of European Travel," in *Complete Works of Swami Vivekananda*, 7:297–404, at 337.

150. If Dharmapala had a discernible and stable strategy for building that world, it was to start with Asia's Buddhists, unifying them, and then turning to the West. For instance: "When our Lord passed away entrusting the Body of the Law to the Bhikkhu Sangha, He lay down facing the West. Followers of the Tathagata of Buddhist Asia unite, working harmoniously cooperate with loving hearts for the good of the larger World of life." "Buddhist Unity," *Journal of the Maha Bodhi Society* 19 (1911): 181–4, at 184.

151. "Accomplishments of the Mission of the Theosophical Society," November 21, 1879.

152. Olcott classified those branches in four categories, indicating that his class IV branches were "entirely dormant." "Indian Section Report," *Theosophist* 13 (1892): 20–33, at 22.

tities. They publish a few papers and make a lot of splash and try to catch Occidental ears."[153]

If the appeal of Buddhism for Indians derived from its being politically potent, the appeal of Vivekananda's reformation was tied to its being innovative, recognizably Hindu, and engaged.

> [Vivekananda] was immensely proud, in his own physiognomy, of what he called his "Mongolian Jaw," regarding it as a sign of "bull-dog tenacity of purpose" and referring to this particular race-element, which he believed to be behind every Aryan people, he one day exclaimed, "Don't you see? the Tartar is the wine of the race! He gives energy and power to every blood!"[154]

The key to reforming India was making Hinduism aggressive. His notion that making Hinduism more masculine would lead to India's salvation was inspired by the Buddha: "How calm! How masculine! Verily was he the bull in the herd and a moon amongst men!"[155] The Buddha's manliness had made Buddhism a missionary religion, and to this extent, the Buddha provided a paradigm for his own missionizing. Sister Nivedita characterized Vivekananda's project by saying that he had two purposes in life—one of world moving and another of nation making—and the world-moving imagery suggests the affinity between the Buddha's activism and his own.

EMPIRE AND NATION

Curzon regarded imperialism "or the lack of it, the test by which the claims of the two parties to represent the nation should be judged." He would stand by imperialism because "his extended travels had taught him

> at an earlier age than some of his contemporaries to think Imperially and had imbued him with a burning faith in the Imperial destiny of Great Britain—a faith that burned all the more brightly because it was founded

153. *Complete Works of Swami Vivekananda*, 7:506. Vivekananda was thinking of Dharmapala's need for recognition in European contexts near and far. Later Dharmapala provided evidence for Vivekananda's contention: "Seven years ago, the Maha-Bodhi Society announced its object of propaganda, which has become historical in having been quoted by Sir W. W. Hunter in his 'Indian Empire.'" "Buddhism in India," *Journal of the Maha Bodhi Society* 7 (1899): 93.

154. Quoted in Nivedita, "The Master as I Saw Him," 153.

155. Sister Nivedita, *The Complete Works of Sister Nivedita*1, 1:171.

not merely on a recognition of the necessity of developing new lands for a surplus population or of acquiring new markets for an expanding trade, but upon the unbounded belief and pride in the moral qualities of the British race.[156]

Thinking imperially was Curzon's universalism fitted to historical circumstances. His critics were unmoved by his idealism and found his aloofness hard to distinguish from superciliousness. Englishmen and Bengalis alike were put off by Curzon's condescension, stiffness, and habit of correcting other people's English usage.

Curzon said in a speech after his appointment as viceroy, "I love India, its people, its history, its government, the complexities of its civilization and life."[157] He looked at governing with a kind of double vision that brought England and India together in the same field of view. He shared that double vision with elite Asians and Africans across the British imperium, but he had personal reasons for seeing double. Appointed undersecretary for India in 1891, he went to see Government House in Calcutta and remarked: "When I next see this, I shall see it as Viceroy; and I shall bring Walter Lawrence as my Secretary."[158] Presumption aside, he looked at the place with more than his everyday enthusiasm for monuments, historic buildings, and landscapes. Government House was already his home. It had been modeled on the Curzon country seat, Kedleston, on land that his family had occupied since their arrival with William the Conqueror. The Curzons had lived at Kedleston as long as Hindus had occupied Bodh Gaya. The double vision had other motivations. During its construction in the middle of the eighteenth century, money to complete Kedleston had run out, and two of the four wings had to be forgotten. Looking at Government House, he saw home as fully realized, and looking at India and its governance, he saw the same blending of India and home, past, present, and future. For Curzon, Calcutta was a "great European city placed in Asia."[159] He would construct England in India, giving Indians the advantages of rationalized policies joined to their own conditions.

The contrast between Curzon and the Cottons—father and son—embodies the forces against which the Bodh Gaya case came into public

---

156. Earl of Ronaldshay, *The Life of Lord Curzon* (London: Boni and Liveright, 1928), 237.

157. Banerjea put Curzon's comment in context: "He loved the people of India after a fashion they did not appreciate." *A Nation in Making*, 149.

158. Dilks, *Curzon in India*, 1:66.

159. Ronaldshay, *The Life of Lord Curzon*, 127.

view. H. J. S. Cotton and H. E. A. Cotton were socially familiar with Calcutta's Indian elite.[160] Surendranath Banerjea counted Henry Cotton as a friend for forty years; he never met Curzon.[161] The Cottons were "country-born" which put them at a social disadvantage in dealing with the highest reaches of British society in India, despite their education at British schools and universities. They had lived in Calcutta—sometimes in official capacities, sometimes as private citizens—for generations, and Henry Cotton sat on the Calcutta Corporation along with Banerjea, serving as chair in 1887 and advocating for the rights of ratepayers. In that context he acted the part of a private citizen despite the fact that he was at the same time chief secretary to the government of Bengal. He also worked as a private citizen, writing articles for the *Pioneer* and *Englishman* on a freelance basis. "From both of these sources," he noted, "I received many a liberal cheque which helped me to eke out my means of subsistence."[162] His son's account of Calcutta stresses his father's work as a public servant: "His direct connection with the Government of Bengal covered a period of thirty years: and during the whole of that time his interest in the civic life of Calcutta was of the closest and keenest description."[163] He and Banerjea disagreed on a number of issues, but it is easy to see their respect for one another.[164] Henry Cotton described himself as a mediocre linguist, although he spoke Bengali fluently and Hindustani colloquially.[165] Curzon knew other languages; the one that slipped into his correspondence most often was Latin.

Evan Cotton made his living as a barrister and worked as the Calcutta correspondent for the *Daily News*.[166] The job gave him more than a way to keep abreast of local affairs—it gave him a tool for shaping public opinion. His father wrote an account of India's political situation intended to inspire policy, and that book endeared him to the Indian elite because it spoke of

---

160. At receptions Lord Dufferin employed Cotton as the aide who stood behind him, feeding him the names of Indians he was about to meet. Henry Cotton, *Indian and Home Memories*, 198.

161. He came close on two occasions. At a memorial for Queen Victoria, Curzon presided and Banerjea spoke. Afterward Curzon's private secretary congratulated Banerjea and said in parting, "I hope we shall meet often." Banerjea's comment was to the point: "We . . . never met at all." *A Nation in Making*, 150.

162. *Indian and Home Memories*, 108.

163. Evan Cotton, *Calcutta, Old and New: A Historical and Descriptive Handbook to the City* (Calcutta: W. Newman and Co, 1907), 741.

164. *Indian Mirror*, December 3, 1889.

165. *Indian and Home Memories*, 71.

166. Chandrika Kaul, "A New Angle of Vision: The London Press, Governmental Information Management and the Indian Empire, 1900–22," *Contemporary British History* 8, no. 2 (1994): 214.

India's destiny as a self-governing state.[167] In the 1890s he used his son as his deputy, and they held political views similar enough that when the father retired and moved to England, the son took over the Cotton legacy. Even retired in England, the elder Cotton did not abandon India, serving as the president of the Indian National Congress and later entering Parliament, where he set himself to regularly interpellating government on Indian affairs. Despite having no evidence of collusion, Dharmapala was sure that the Cottons had corrupted one another:

> Well, the Bodh Gaya temple made me a prominent character in India. The Hindu Mahant with his myrmidons by all sorts of nefarious means failed to drive me out of India. Leading criminal lawyers were engaged by him, the son of the Chief Secretary was paid over Rs. 10,000 to influence his father, the papers presided over by English editors were bribed, the lawyer, Mr. Jackson, who was retained by me was taken over to their side and their attempt to make the Bud:Gaya temple a Hindu temple proved futile. The two Judges of the High Court, one a notorious gambler and the other an orthodox Hindu gave judgment saying that the Temple was not Hindu but Buddhistic, and impugned me [sic] my "general veracity." I did not stop the battle until I won it, and the Bengal Govt had to accede to my wishes and placed the Japanese image in the monastery and gave us room to live permanently. (Diary, May 24, 1897)

The bribery allegation seems even less credible in light of Evan Cotton's representing the mahant without remuneration.

Curzon and Henry Cotton shared a common sense of revulsion at the behavior of British citizens and soldiers with regard to Indians. In 1899 Curzon learned of a notorious case—the rape of an elderly Burmese woman by twenty British soldiers in Rangoon. The case fit a common pattern of atrocious behavior—the battering to death of a punkah-wallah by soldiers, the killing of two Indians by soldiers out hunting and shooting carelessly— each followed by minor punishments. Curzon was offended, and he made enemies in both the army and the War Office by trying to impose a heavier punishment for these offenses.[168] Stationed in Assam as chief commissioner, Cotton had similar experiences with the tea planters who dominated the local economic and political landscape, men who regarded the death of Indian laborers—some five hundred thousand died in those years—as "de-

---

167. Henry Cotton, *New India, or India in Transition*.
168. Dilks, *Curzon in India*, 1:199.

preciation en bloque."[169] He became the defender of Indian workers sorely used on North Indian tea and indigo plantations:

One Mihir Das was going on horseback from one tea-garden to another in search of employment. Mr. Black, the Manager of a tea-garden, had him summoned by a chaukidar. Mihir instantly left his horse at a distance and coming up to Mr. Black saluted him respectfully. But the *Saheb* had seen Mihir ride, and Mihir had besides come to him with his shoes on. The *Saheb* became all fire and flame at Mihir's presumption. Mihir was at once assailed with cuffs on his face, with whip-strokes on his back, and with kicks on his breast. . . . Mr. Black was prosecuted and confessed his guilt. The Magistrate commented on Mr. Black's conduct, but let him off with a fine of Rs. 60. Lord Curzon, now think of the noble-minded Mr. Cotton, and you will see that it is impossible for him to feel any sympathy for these demons. From what class of the English community do the tea and indigo-planters come?[170]

Curzon railed against soldier's crimes because such actions could weaken the Raj; Cotton acted against the exploitations of tea planters because their behavior violated his sense of humanity.[171]

They were linked in other ways. Curzon was viceroy, and Cotton the man who served as undersecretary or secretary to the government of Bengal under seven lieutenant governors. His long civic experience aside, he was excluded from several boards because of his intimacy with Indians.[172] Like Allan Octavian Hume's, his chances for the viceroyalty were undermined by his "radical" politics.[173] The Indian public saw the two as a binary pair. Several Calcutta newspapers made the contrast; *Hitavarta* (Calcutta, Janu-

169. Rana P. Behal and Prabhu P. Mohapatra, "'Tea and Money versus Human Life': The Rise and Fall of the Indenture System in the Assam Tea Plantations 1840–1908," *Journal of Peasant Studies* 19, nos. 3–4 (1992): 171. Cotton was involved in the controversy of 1899–1900 that followed his inquiry into wages in Assam. Cotton "showed that throughout the whole period of indenture to 1900 . . . the average wage . . . remained well below the statutory minimum" (157). While wages stagnated from 1865 to 1900, the price of food grains doubled.

170. *Prativasi*, June 1, 1901. The article concludes, "It is hard to believe that any human being can take delight in tormenting another human being in this way. We are of the opinion that some English *savant* converts wild beasts into men by some magical process and then lets them loose in the wilds of Assam and other places."

171. Dilks, *Curzon in India*, 1:199.

172. Mrinalini Sinha, *Colonial Masculinity: The "Manly Englishman" and the "Effeminate Bengali" in the Late Nineteenth Century* (Manchester: Manchester University Press, 1995), 109 and 121.

173. On Hume, see Bevir, "Theosophy and the Origins of the Indian National Congress," 102.

ary 1, 1905) described in glowing terms the reception accorded to Cotton on landing at Bombay, distinguishing it from that accorded to Curzon when he landed two weeks later. "The real ruler is one whom the people elect. A robber obtains his ends by inspiring awe and fear, but can he become a king for all that?" "What a difference there was," wrote the *Bengalee*, "between the reception accorded to Lord Curzon, the great proconsul, and Sir Henry Cotton, the President-Elect of the Indian National Congress, whose arrivals took place within 15 days of one another" (December 25, 1904).

Of all of Curzon's initiatives the one that most antagonized the Bengali public was the Partition of Bengal. It is hard to overstate the hostility that it provoked. Curzon justified creating two states where there had been one by emphasizing that Bengal was too large to administer efficiently. No Bengali could mistake the political advantage the policy offered Curzon. Two provinces—the first Bengal and the second Eastern Bengal and Assam—would give Biharis and Oriyas the majority voice in Bengal and Muslims the advantage in Eastern Bengal. In turn, the bhadralok would lose its ability to influence events. In Broomfield's words,

> For bhadralok intellectuals the partition of Bengal and the agitation against it was a seminal experience that influenced their political thinking for forty years. It gave them a new pride in their country, and a pantheon of nationalist heroes and martyrs which could be invoked for inspiration or justification. It revealed to them the potentialities of radical political agitation, and it left them with an uneasy awareness of its dangers. It provoked an open clash between liberal secular and Hindu revivalist ideals, but it left that crucial conflict unresolved.[174]

Banerjea endorsed the resistance movement—a campaign to withdraw Indians from government service, replacing British goods with *svadesi* goods, and establishing "national" education—but he and other members of the Indian Association were overtaken by younger men more comfortable with extraconstitutional agitation. Changing times brought figures such as Bipin Chandra Pal, Aswini Kumar Dutt, and Aurobindo Ghose to the fore, although the list of characters who resisted the Partition of Bengal would also include Banerjea (who refused to return to the Calcutta Corporation which he had dominated for decades until Partition was revoked in 1911) and Anglo-Indians such as C. J. O'Donnell and Henry Cotton.

174. *Elite Conflict in a Plural Society: Twentieth-Century Bengal* (Berkeley: University of California Press, 1968), 29.

At the extremist end of resistance to Curzon's partition were Para-
mathanath Mitra, Sarala Devi Ghosal, Sister Nivedita, Jatindra Nath Banerjee, Satish Chandra Bose, and Aurobindo Ghose. They understood resistance
in terms of physical culture, *lathi* (bamboo stick) training, and more revolutionary tactics. Some of the group had been present in the audience when
Okakura gave a talk in Calcutta in late 1901. He urged the audience to take
action: "Why do you let a handful of Englishmen tread you down? Do everything you can to achieve freedom, openly as well as secretly. Japan will assist you."[175] Satish Chandra Bose heard his call and responded by calling on
Mitra and proposing a physical culture group. Named in honor of the band
of fighting sannyasis who led resistance to British rule in *Anandamath*, the
Anushilan Samiti (self-culture association) provided the Bodh Gaya mahant
with a paradigm for his own struggle. More moderate Bengalis and liberal
Anglo-Indians stuck to constitutional measures.[176] To the extent that both
Cotton, because of his being "country-born," and O'Donnell, because of his
Catholic religion and Irish ethnicity, were marginal figures in the Raj, their
sympathy for Indians and social justice had origins close to home. To the
extent that Ireland, Buddhism, and Japanese interventions shaped Indian
events, their actions resonated with influences far from India.

Cotton warned Curzon of the dangers associated with partition. After
the 1904 session of the Indian National Congress, he corresponded with
Curzon in hopes of presenting him with the resolutions reached at the annual meetings. Curzon refused to receive him or read the list of resolutions,
reacting to his dislike of Cotton, his critique of tea planters in Assam and
sympathy for the political aspirations of the bhadralok class.[177] When he retired from India in 1902 and moved to England, serving as president of the
Indian National Congress and winning a seat in Parliament, his influence

175. Sri Aurobindo, *On Himself* (Pondicherry: Sri Aurobindo Ashram, 1989), 3.

176. O'Donnell was an Irish Catholic, and his ability to sympathize with Indians and their
mistreatment under British rule derived from his own position. See Scott B. Cook, "The Irish
Raj: Social Origins and Careers of Irishmen in the Indian Civil Service, 1855–1914," *Journal of
Social History* 20, no. 3 (1987): 507–29; and Michael Silvestri, "'The Sinn Fein of India': Irish
Nationalism and the Policing of Revolutionary Bengal," *Journal of British Studies* 39, no. 4
(2000): 454–86.

177. Henry Cotton, *New India, or India in Transition*, 290. The pair had a complicated
relationship, Cotton praising Curzon's virtues as a viceroy: " His abilities, his restless energy,
his masterful character—a personal magnetism which all who have come into contact with
him feel—mark him out among the run of ordinary public men with uncommon distinction."
Indian and Home Memories, 309. Curzon may have blocked Cotton's way to the lieutenant
governorship of Bengal (see *Rangalaya*, April 26, 1902). By the same token, Curzon was responsible for Cotton's being awarded the Knight Commander of the Star of India. *Indian and Home
Memories*, 280.

lived on in India itself because Curzon's partition proposal lingered until 1911. Curzon himself soon left India, but the pair's mutual antipathy embodied the rise of Bengali nationalism. Later editions of *New India* end with an appendix, taking up the proposal for partition, which Cotton called "a most arbitrary and unsympathetic evidence of irresponsible and autocratic statesmanship."

Cotton recognized the vanguard role Bengalis played, knowing that their aspirations were becoming Indian aspirations:

> The Baboos of Bengal . . . now rule public opinion from Peshawar to Chittagong; and although the natives of North-Western India are immeasurably behind those of Bengal in education and in their sense of political independence, they are gradually becoming as amenable as their brethren of the lower provinces to intellectual control and guidance. A few short years ago and there was no trace of this; the idea of any Bengalee influence in Punjab would have been a conception incredible to Lord Lawrence. . . . At the present moment the name of Surendra Nath Banerjea excites as much enthusiasm among the rising generation of Mooltan as in Dacca.[178]

His reference to "political independence" notwithstanding, Cotton did not imagine Indian independence happening in short order and shared Curzon's confidence in British rule. He considered his own freedom to argue against the government's proposals as evidence of imperial virtue.[179] Moderating a public meeting at town hall, he guided a discussion that produced a resolution opposing Curzon's attempt to partition Bengal.[180] He defended a local world of which he could claim a part because the resolution drew the line not between the British and Indians but between the people of India and the government of Bengal on one side and Curzon and the government of India on the other.

The two Cottons had their own motives for acting in the Bodh Gaya case. Henry Cotton did not act on his own in blocking the sale of the Tikari Raj land. As liberal Anglo-Indians, father and son were committed to the people of India, supporting their political independence and regarding Indians as friends and associates. Dharmapala once observed to himself

---

178. *New India, or India in Transition*, 28.
179. *Indian and Home Memories*, 108.
180. Harish P. Kaushik, *Indian National Movement: The Role of British Liberals* (New Delhi: Criterion, 1986), 157–8.

that it was a great loss that colonial officials in Lanka lacked sympathy for the people, with which he credited at least some colonial officials in India (Diary, December 24, 1913). His dilemma was encountering the Cottons, who were fully sympathetic to the people of India but looked on him—his long residence in India and insistence on Buddhism as an "Indian" religion notwithstanding—as an outsider and less Indian than they were themselves. Dharmapala faced another dilemma equally beyond his control—he found his cause supported by an extremely unpopular viceroy. Curzon did not hide his feelings toward the Indian National Congress, dismissing it as "a small, noisy, middle-class movement," ultimately hostile to the government. The worst of the lot were the Bengalis, unrepresentative of the "real" India, an India better served by native princes and the British.[181] And the worst of the worst were the Bengali bhadralok.

The partition struggle was an issue more central to the politics of colonial Bengal than the fate of Bodh Gaya, but the latter got caught up in the wake of the former. The struggle between Dharmapala and the mahant resonated with the struggle between Curzon and the two Cottons in a way that went beyond Curzon's support for the Buddhists, Henry Cotton's role in preventing the sale of the Tikari Raj land to the Maha Bodhi Society, and Evan Cotton's role as the mahant's attorney. Curzon favored the Buddhists for many reasons, but the fundamental one was the notion that Bodh Gaya had been originally Buddhist, and it ought to return to Buddhist control. The Cottons had their reasons for taking the mahant's side, including their sympathy for Indians and friendship with Calcutta's bhadralok. Evan Cotton's legal practice was tied to the interests of Bengali zamindars by way of the British Indian Association, and those zamindars favored the mahant. From the time of Curzon's appointment, Calcutta became a battlefield between an activist viceroy and the Bengali bhadralok, led by Banerjea. Henry Cotton provided a sympathetic government connection for the bhadralok, and Evan Cotton provided legal counsel.

The Indian National Congress had been an entirely secular organization at its founding, and it remained secular roughly until Curzon's proposal to partition Bengal.[182] The secular character of Bengali life itself changed; the Theosophical Society saw it happening even faster: "The atheistical Bengal of 1881 is gradually becoming an orthodox Bengal in 1892."[183] Partition pre-

181. David Gilmour, *Curzon: Imperial Statesman* (New York: Farrar, Strauss, and Giroux, 1994), 169.
182. See *Indian Mirror*, October 11, 1889.
183. *Theosophist* 13 (1892): 9.

sented Bengalis with a proposal that would have undone their own political influence. They fought back with religious associations such as the Anush-ilan Samiti, which celebrated the heroism of the fighting sannyasis.[184] In the process national interests became one with the interests of the nation's largest religious community. There had been political violence of a religious nature in western India, but in Bengal, Michael Edwardes observes,

> where the middle classes had benefited most from British rule, Indians still seemed to place their faith in legislative reform, and considerations of race and religion played a small part in political activity. When, for ex-ample, Barindra Kumar Ghosh—who had been educated at Cambridge, had passed the Indian Civil Service examinations and then been rejected because he could not ride a horse—arrived in Calcutta in 1902 to arouse anti-British feelings amongst the educated classes, he received so little support that he decided the only way to stir up political enthusiasm was to give politics a religious bias. What was needed, he decided was the stimulus of some great event which would tap the springs of religious pa-triotism. Curzon provided the stimulus by deciding to partition Bengal.[185]

The Hinduization of political resistance, in turn, replaced whatever sympa-thy the Bengali elite felt for Buddhism and Bodh Gaya.

Newspapers noticed an upturn in feelings of identity and difference. Hav-ing labored since the mutiny to keep their distance from Indians, the British now complained that they were increasingly being taken as "foreigners":

> The natives of India—at least the English-speaking portion of them—are beginning to speak and think of the British in this country as "foreign-ers," adopting the parlance of the Japanese and Chinese treaty ports. It was hinted that the usage might be the result of the increasing inter-course between the English-speaking natives of India and Japan. "On the contrary," says one native Indian newspaper in effect, "we did not require to go to Japan for a term which we were perfectly capable of em-ploying for ourselves. Europeans are foreigners in India, their interests are foreign."[186]

184. William R. Pinch, "Soldier Monks and Militant Sadhus," in *Contesting the Nation: Religion, Community, and the Politics of Democracy in India*, ed. David Ludden (Philadelphia: University of Pennsylvania Press, 1996), 140–61, at 147.

185. *High Noon of Empire: India under Curzon* (London: Eyre and Spottiswoode, 1965), 210.

186. *Englishman*, February 25, 1903.

The role of Japanese students and merchants in Calcutta and Okakura's efforts to buy land in Bodh Gaya added another complication due not so much to the new vocabulary—because the Indian newspaper recognized the Bengali tendency to see the British as foreign—but the presence of new actors who were foreign in an unprecedented way.

Copland writes that after the 1906 decision in the Burmese resthouse case Dharmapala courted public opinion, pursuing newspaper editors and writing pamphlets. But his efforts were swamped "by the outpourings of the Bengali vernacular newspapers which continued in the main to back the Hindu cause."[187] He pursued a second strategy, now proposing that the government take over the Maha Bodhi temple and manage it. When word got out in 1905, the *Indian Mirror* itself abandoned its support for the Buddhist cause, reacting strongly to the prospect of a "foreign" government controlling the place:

> It might be imagined that we ourselves would jump at the proposal but it is not so. We have strenuously advocated the Buddhist right over the Temple, but we cannot entertain the idea of a foreign government practically assuming Mahantoship over it. Our private information is . . . that the Mahanto was in negotiation with some Japanese gentlemen for the sale of some lands at Bodh Gaya and the Government getting scent of it vetoed the proposal on political grounds. Well whether that be the truth of the matter or not the fact remains that neither the Government nor the Hindu Mahanto can shut out Buddhist pilgrims from Bodh Gaya. . . . We are not in alliance with the foremost Asiatic power and the Japanese are mostly Buddhists by religion. We trust Lord Curzon will not take a leap in the dark.[188]

From the first, its support of the Buddhist cause had put the *Indian Mirror* in a contradictory position. Even absent the language of "foreignness," advocating the interests of Buddhists left the newspaper open to critique. The *Dainik-o-Samachar Chandrika* saw the presumption of the Buddhist cause. It insisted that the *Mirror* could not really believe that there was any force in the argument that the mahant's resistance to accepting the Japanese Buddha image in the temple would displease the Chinese, Japanese, and any Buddhist country (May 25, 1894). By that logic, the *Dainik-o-Samachar* rea-

187. "Managing Religion in Colonial India," 553–4.
188. *Indian Mirror*, July 16, 1905, quoted in Dipak K. Barua, *Buddha Gaya Temple: Its History* (Buddha Gaya: Budha Gaya Temple Management Committee, 1981), 101–2.

soned, Catholics of Austria, Belgium, and France would be entitled to set up images of Jesus and Mary in a *musjid* in Turkey. No one would accept that arrangement in Turkey, so why should the government accept it in India? A government already dealing with cow-slaughter quarrels between Hindus and Muslims and disputes about the *muksh* and *dir* processions between Sunnis and Shias—which had led to riots in Alum—was not a government that should cause itself more trouble by favoring the Buddhists (*Bangavasi*, August 31, 1895).

By the time Curzon made his inspection tour of Bodh Gaya, public opinion was changing in other ways, the dispute between two men having become a dispute between religious communities and the charges made by each having become extreme and exaggerated. The *Prativasi* (July 15, 1903) spoke of the fear of orthodox Hindus that the government was contemplating taking control of the Maha Bodhi temple, but what is more striking is the reified and expansive form these arguments ultimately began to assume. *Mahima* insisted that however much the English government of India might want to please the Buddhist emperors of Asia, "it ought not to hurt the feelings of its Hindu subjects" (November 27, 1903). The *Bangavasi* of December 5, 1903, referenced Oldham's visit to the mahant when he proposed a new arrangement at the temple. The paper complained that Oldham gave the mahant only a few hours to consider the matter: "He rejected the proposal, and how could he, who is the representative of the entire Hindu community, do otherwise?" Two weeks later, the *Bangavasi* (December 19, 1903) made the ultimate claim:

> We learn from history that the founder of the temple was not a Buddhist, but a Brahman of the Saiva sect, and that it was dedicated to the god Maheswara. . . . The claims of Dharmapal will certainly not find favor with Government, inasmuch as the question involves the religious faith of millions of Hindus by whom Budh-Gaya is regarded as a sacred place.

Reaching Calcutta in 1891, Dharmapala had thought that when he looked in the eyes of Bengalis he saw his own people, but by the early twentieth century when Bengalis looked at him, they saw a foreigner without a local constituency. After his appearance at the Parliament of Religions he acquired a battery of distinguished supporters around the world, but they could not give him any decisive support at Bodh Gaya. Long after the Japanese Buddha was removed to Calcutta and the Burmese resthouse abandoned in 1910, he continued to win supporters and fight on. Over the years he won expressions of support from an extraordinary list of Indians—

Rabindranath Tagore, Chittaranjan Das, Lala Rajpat Rai, Rajendra Prasad, and Mahatma Gandhi, who told him that he would solve the Bodh Gaya problem ten minutes after independence. Their support was in many ways nominal, even if sincere. What Dharmapala could not do was gather broad support behind his cause—not in 1891 and less so as the twentieth century began.

It is easy to see where things were headed. When he was appointed viceroy in 1899, Curzon arrived in India and found that arrangements had been made to hand over a collection of recently excavated Buddha relics to the king of Siam.[189] Once in Bangkok, the Piprahwa tranche was divided and shares given to the leading Buddhist monks of Burma and Lanka. Curzon used later discoveries of Buddha relics once again to felicitate Buddhist communities, and whether relics were to leave India became a lightning rod for unprecedented concerns. Curzon believed that relics—and artworks—should be conserved in the country of origin, not entirely because they were Indian and therefore immovable, but because they were, to modify Trevithick's phrase, "Imperial British Indian Buddhist Relic[s]."[190] Dharmapala himself was a beneficiary of relics that he installed at the Dharmarajika vihara he established in Calcutta in 1920 and the Mulagandhakuti vihara in Sarnath in 1931. In the politics of relic redistribution Dharmapala had one advantage. He was a Buddhist and thus an outsider, but an outsider who wanted to keep those relics in India. By 1910 the distribution of relics had become a nationalist issue. The *Indian Mirror* (February 26, 1910) expressed disappointment at the prospect that a newly found tranche of relics was going to be given over to the Burmese. Surely those relics belonged at Varanasi, a place sacred to both Hindus and Buddhists. The one newspaper that consistently supported Dharmapala's cause ignored the possibility that the relics might be installed at Bodh Gaya itself. In *India Revisited* Arnold had imagined that the spirit of Buddhism brooded over Benares. Now the *Indian Mirror* wanted to place relics in Varanasi not to embody the spirit of Buddhism but to imagine the Indian nation.

189. Charles Allen, *The Buddha and Dr. Führer: An Archeological Scandal* (London: Haus, 2008), 212. Curzon also had a geopolitical motive in keeping relics in India. He feared that a relic gifted to the palace in Bangkok would quickly end up in the Louvre.

190. *The Revival of Pilgrimage at Bodh Gaya*, 144.

CHAPTER FIVE

Dharmapala and the British Empire

I had a dream, the King of England [and I] together walking and talking.
I showed incomparable affection.
—Diary, September 3, 1921

D harmapala constructed his life amid two universalisms, each a transcontinental community—one organized around the Asian Buddhisms
and the other created by the growth of the Theosophical Society. From Olcott he inherited notions of a global community of Buddhists with some
level of doctrinal agreement, but he had only instrumental interest in building it and no visible interest in doctrinal agreement. He worked instead for
recovering Bodh Gaya, returning the sasana to India, reforming and reinvigorating the Sinhala people, and spreading the Dhamma to the West. What
he took from Theosophy was affection for the mahatmas as a model for
ascetic discipline, meditation, esoteric knowledge, and service to humanity. Having reached Bodh Gaya on that first visit, he applied for initiation in
the Esoteric Section of the Theosophical Society, and the comments of the
days following make clear the association he drew between the place and a
life that favored withdrawal: "A new life has begun. All bad thoughts, deeds
& words should be destroyed. Henceforth it must be done. . . . Meditation
must be practiced" (Diary, January 4, 1891).

Another universalism was just as important, the British Empire. In most
accounts of Dharmapala's career, it appears as either empty space about
which he moved from project to project or an object of scorn and constraint
on his actions. It makes more sense to approach the empire as a thing in itself with which he had a relationship as active and productive as the other
two universalisms. Otherwise, a central force in his life is reduced to in-
dexical status—"in 1926 Dharmapala took up residence in London"—and

the possibility of making sense of his volatile relationship with both Britain and Lanka is forfeited. However contrarian and contentious his relationship with both, those relationships provide fundamental sources for understanding Dharmapala and his life's work. I think that his connections to England were a lot stronger than usually noted and his ties to Lanka a lot weaker.

Paying attention to Dharmapala's relationship to the British Empire has one immediate benefit. It reinserts the mythologized Dharmapala—of newspaper, radio, and television, everyday talk in Sri Lanka today, and some academic accounts—into the historical record. Consider, for instance, the popular association of his fiery speechifying with the rise of militant and politicized monks.[1] One monk sometimes taken as a link between him and the emergence of monks affiliated with political parties and other forms of social activism was Udakendawala Saranakara. In the 1920s Udakendawala was one of the students Dharmapala brought to India and educated at Tagore's school, Shanti Niketan. Through the 1930s and 1940s, he organized for the Communist party and fought for independence.[2] According to Wiswa Warnapala, monks such as Udakendawala, Kotahena Pannakitti, Walpola Rahula, Kalalelle Ananda Sagara, and Natandiya Pannakara answered Dharmapala's call for monks to become politically active.[3]

The fact was that Dharmapala did not call monks to political action; he urged them to be more engaged in the spiritual life, more learned, and committed to a new task with little nationalist content, carrying the Dhamma overseas to non-Buddhist places. He wanted Sinhala monks to energize themselves and direct that energy at reconstructing Sinhala society, not toward playing a political role of any kind. He died before the heyday of Udakendawala and other political monks, but the worldliness of the monks of his day horrified him. He associated it with the materialism and indo-

1. The essential sources are S. J. Tambiah, *Buddhism Betrayed: Religion, Politics, and Violence in Sri Lanka* (Chicago: University of Chicago Press, 1992); and Seneviratne, *The Work of Kings.*

2. W. A. Wiswa Warnapala, "Sangha and Politics in Sri Lanka: Nature of the Continuing Controversy," *Indian Journal of Politics* 12, nos. 1–2 (1978): 66–76. Wiswa Warnapala writes that the *Sinhala Bauddhaya Wesak Annual* of 1937 argued for the sangha becoming active in politics. Such was not what Dharmapala intended. Udakendawala's own account of his anti-imperialist struggle as a Marxist can be found in *Satanaka Satahan* (Colombo: Janata Lekhaka Peramuna, n.d.).

3. Udakendawala's effort to justify his activism by inventing a politicized Dharmapala led him to devote a special edition of *Navalokaya* to setting the record straight on Dharmapala: "He wanted to arouse [Buddhist monks] with a view to getting them to play a militant role in the campaign against imperialism." W. A. Wiswa Warnapala, *Udakendawala Siri Saranakara: An Assessment of His Role in the Anti-imperialist Struggle in Sri Lanka* (Colombo: Godage, 2002), 12–3.

lence for which he attacked the generality of monks. He wanted monks to play their traditional roles under increased state control:

> The State should be the guardian of the Bhikkhu Sangha. The endowments made in favour of the Bhikkhu Sangha should be managed by the State. They should be given the four requisites according to the Vinaya Rules. They should study the Dhamma, Vinaya and the Abhidhamma and preach to the people to become good upasakas. They should be taught foreign languages, especially the Indian vernaculars. India must be made to listen to the Dhamma. (Sarnath Notebook no. 23)

He had views, in other words, that would scarcely gain support from the monks of his later years or the present. His views on politics were fixed on the person—"Buddhism is spiritual self-government"—not the political order. He had a vision of social reform, to be sure, but that reform began with the individual. He summed up his views in a lecture at the Dharmarajika temple: "The Buddha did not interfere with the politics of Governments. He taught the way to Nirvana and also concord & unity" (Diary, June 8, 1924). Seneviratne has it right, writing that Dharmapala viewed government as a "perfunctory epiphenomenon," provided we add his wanting monks to have no part in that epiphenomenon.[4]

Every year Dharmapala's birthday, September 17, brings forth newspaper accounts celebrating his life. In 1992 the *Island* ran a headline on that day making another claim—"Anagarika Dharmapala was an anti-imperialist freedom fighter"—for which the article gives no evidence.[5] As the present chapter suggests, that article cannot live up to its headline because Dharmapala had conservative feelings about empire and modest interest in Sri Lankan independence. It is fair enough to call him an "anti-imperialist" if imperialism refers to the cultural and economic domination of colonized countries. As for his interest in fighting for freedom, when he spoke of freedom, he thought of it as personal and spiritual, not collective and political. His views on politics paralleled those of Annie Besant, who wanted Commonwealth status for India. It was Besant's considerable insight to recognize that the genius of imperialism was its offer of membership in a larger community, coupled with the promise of brotherhood.[6] To that extent, the

---

4. *The Work of Kings*, 32n10.
5. Basil de Silva, *Island*, September 17, 1992.
6. Gauri Visvanathan, *Outside the Fold: Conversion, Modernity, and Belief* (Princeton, NJ: Princeton University Press, 1998), 186–7.

British Empire competed with the Theosophical Society, another vehicle for creating brotherhood. Middle-class South Asians of Victorian times did not see the world separated into England and India or England and Lanka. They saw it as metropole and periphery. When many elite Sinhalas found Dharmapala's project preposterous or irrelevant, he tried to justify his plans to build a vihara in London by speaking in a traditional idiom, saying that London was the *rajadhani* (capital or king's place) of the empire (Diary, November 30, 1926). The empire looked one way when viewed from London, quite another viewed from the periphery. But it was one world, and for South Asians such as Dharmapala, what made applying the traditional expression to new circumstances plausible was the prospect of brotherhood and respect or at least mutual recognition.

Dharmapala was infuriated by the structural exploitation of the colonies as well as regular incidents where South Asians were treated not as brothers in the empire but objects of indifference or contempt. What endured in public memory was the strong language he used in both the articles he wrote for his column Danagatayutu Karanu (Things that should be known) for the *Sinhala Bauddhaya* and talks he gave at home and abroad. He meant the speeches to be inflammatory: "Lectured to the Sinhalese race. Attacked the Roman Catholics and stirred up the young men for greater activity. I shall do my duty" (Diary, August 25, 1909). As he traveled about India and Lanka, confrontations with English men and women were, by contrast, visceral and spontaneous. He was typically provoked by a British clerk or traveler who treated him with disrespect. Those occasions meant enough to him to cause him to make a summary record in his diaries, listing each occasion when he had a run-in.[7] He regarded himself as a subject of the empire and the eldest son of a well-to-do family who would not tolerate anything less than respect. Treating him as a "brown Englishman" captures that part of his life, but it misses everything else.

There is a considerable body of scholarship on the British imperium as a single social system.[8] It is complemented by work on the reciprocal interaction between religion and nationalism in the mother country and the colo-

---

7. Compiling lists—the chronology of his life, his achievements, his enemies, and his confrontations—was a regular part of his note keeping, and he rewrote those lists time and again over the thirty-five years he kept diaries and notebooks.

8. See, for instance, P. J. Marshall, *"A Free Though Conquering People": Eighteenth-Century Britain and Its Empire* (London: Ashgate, 2003); C. A. Bayly, *Imperial Meridian: The British Empire and the World, 1780–1830* (London: Longman, 1989); and David Cannadine, *Ornamentalism: How the British Saw Their Empire* (New York: Oxford University Press, 2001).

nies.[9] Dharmapala's travels in India, England, and Sinhala villages afford a distinctive perspective on these interactions, his peripatetic life leading him to change his subject position on a regular basis. One of the changes is more thoroughgoing than simply encountering another way of doing things. In Japan and the West he often presented himself as an Indian. In Japan he was regularly taken for such—after all he came to Japan from India, practiced an Indian religion, and represented an Indian cause, recovering Bodh Gaya—and he sometimes spoke to Japanese audiences as someone who could represent an Indian perspective. Given the peopling of the island from India, he could claim he was an Indian by descent. But he also believed that he was an Indian for reasons of karma and rebirth: "In my last rebirth I believe I was born in India," he wrote, "and as there was no Buddhist family where I could take birth I had my birth in the foremost Buddhist family in Colombo" (Diary, November 2, 1927). Small wonder that his final wish was to be reborn in an Indian Brahman family. The next Buddha, it was believed in his time, would be born in Benares as the son of a Brahman family.

Dharmapala was observant enough to see a difference between the behavior of civil servants in India and Lanka, concluding that there were more British civil servants with sympathies for the people of the place in India than his own country. Colonial officials such as Curzon were sympathetic to Buddhism but constrained by circumstances.[10] The two Cottons were sympathetic to local people, but the local people were Indians, not Sinhalas, and the one place where Dharmapala could not be an Indian was in India. The awakening potential of moving about the world did not make him cosmopolitan. But it gave him a sense of the vagaries of people and places. He recognized the blandishments of badge and sash. Before he became a world renouncer, he served the colonial government as a clerk. In several accounts of giving up his job in the Department of Public Instruction, Dharmapala says he had been motivated by his desire to "serve Humanity." In an account he intended for publication, he put it differently, saying that he resigned from government service to avoid being offered a mudaliyarship,

9. Partha Chatterjee, *The Nation and Its Fragments: Colonial and Postcolonial Histories* (Princeton, NJ: Princeton University Press, 1993); Gauri Visvanathan, *Outside the Fold*; and Peter van der Veer, *Imperial Encounters: Religion and Modernity in India and Britain* (Princeton, NJ: Princeton University Press, 2001).

10. Dharmapala had a chronic inability to distinguish friend from foe: long after the Bodh Gaya Commission he continued to believe that Curzon had thwarted his campaign to gain control of Bodh Gaya: "Marquis Curzon is dead. He was Viceroy of India. He was an enemy of the Buddhists. He did not want the Temple to go to Buddhists" (Diary, March 22, 1925).

the native office to which many middle-class Lankans aspired.[11] Renouncing the world was also renouncing those seductions.[12] Renunciation gave him a path to personal freedom: "To be a Servant of another Servant meant degradation" (Sarnath Notebook no. 50). "Slavery" recurs in the diaries, and the way he freed himself from subordination to others was by keeping his distance. In his reckoning slavery's binary opposite was not political independence but renunciation.

What tied together Dharmapala's experiences wherever he went—and what gave him his own reasons for assuming that the British imperium was a single system—was class and civilization. Those tropes held together the imperium. "The adventurous class of British hooligans who go to India & the Colonies bring shame on the good people of England," he wrote (Diary, October 9, 1926). He had only one run-in in America and no such encounters in England, although by the 1920s—when he spent his longest sojourn there—he was frail and his health declining. The violent confrontations often took place in India and usually while traveling. They were all the more bitter because he had hopes for respect and recognition. What made those incidents sting was his sense of himself as well born and civilized. He visited the school he had established in Rajagiriya and asked the children whether they thought the British were kind to them. "Unanimously they declared—NO. How can you love a person who is always hating you and treating you with scorn" (Diary, March 3, 1911). The message was to resist the British not because they were the colonial masters but because the British had misused them.

In the eyes of the public, Dharmapala was Goivanse or Goyigama (farmer caste, the dominant group in number and rank in the Sinhala caste system), and while that status gave him advantage in local society, that claim was undercut in two ways. He was not Radala, which is to say, Goyigama of highest rank by the logic of the Kandyan state, which put him at a disadvantage relative to Kandyan laymen and monks he encountered in religious contexts, and his mother was not Goyigama at all.[13] He never spoke of either issue in his diaries, but he regularly indicated other people's caste identities, identifying this person as Goyigama and that as Karava (fisher

---

11. "I Became an Anagarika," in Jayawardana, *Mage Jivita Kathava*, 97–8.

12. On one occasion he wrote of his decision as more evenly balanced than the fateful decision to abandon the world: "I rejected that job saying that I could reap better results by working for the country and the religion than working under the British." Guruge, *Dharmapala Lipi*, 67.

13. Roberts, "Himself and Project," 116.

caste), for example. More often he used the language of caste metaphorically, vilifying others for being Christian or uncivilized by calling them Chandala or Rodiya (low-caste) when they were not. He identified other enemies by their caste (in an unmetaphorical way) and glossed his hostility to them in those terms. One of the monks he supported in Calcutta was Polwatte Dhammadhara. He believed that Dhammadhara told the mahant that the "temple should be given over to 'Kauravansa' people!" (Diary, March 10, 1925). More often caste functions in his diaries as a measure of high and low as such, much like figures such as class and civilization.

Civilization was the trope that organized many of his representations, and civilization and class are tropes regularly forgotten in most accounts of his being a nationalist. The British were the most civilized people in the world, but they were not so in the colonies. British civilization was undone by class in the colonies, which attracted either low-class Englishmen or caused the well-born ones to discard their manners—at one point he condemned Curzon of all people for "upstartism" (Diary, August 11, 1904).[14] The British looked down on Sinhalas because, he said, they thought that they were not civilized. He knew better, regarding all Asians as civilized in a variety of ways—vegetarian, temperate in drink and behavior, kind to animals, and compassionate in a way made possible by believing in one of the world's religions of compassion, Hinduism, Buddhism, and Jainism (Sarnath Notebook no. 4). Against this background, his sojourn in London was as much a civilizing mission as anything Europeans had offered their African and Asian colonies. Its public face was religious, but its motivations included a civilizational component. By sojourning in London he put Buddhism on offer, but he put himself on offer too, a civilized person among other civilized people. Those virtues were not separate. He assumed there was a connection between being Buddhist and being civilized: "To do good karma man has to be civilized" (Diary, August 10, 1927).

Dharmapala felt connected to the empire because he felt connected to other civilized people in the empire, and he felt that solidarity with similar people in Japan, America, and Europe. The great majority of these people were well-to-do, and some had aristocratic origins. With such people he felt a sense of common identity. Had he not been the son of one of Colombo's

---

14. I'd like to think that Dharmapala was speaking of the larger historical context, putting an English aristocrat whose ancestors distinguished themselves during the Norman Conquest in his proper place. Harking back to the civilizations of Asoka's reign in India and early Anuradhapura in Sri Lanka was a rhetorical convention in South Asia from Dharmapala's life onward. It gave South Asians the advantage and made Curzon an "upstart."

leading families, he would have acquired those same social connections by virtue of his membership in the Theosophical Society. Telling a newspaper reporter that he had come to the United States to raise funds from the Rockefellers and the Carnegies, he had doubly good reason to seek out such people.[15] He took them to be his peers, and he needed them to finance his many projects. As it happened, he had no contact with either Rockefeller or Carnegie, but he gained the support of one woman, namely Mary Foster, who was enormously generous with him, and to a lesser extent he sought and found support from the maharajahs of Baroda, Benares, and Bhinga and a variety of well-to-do women.[16] He felt at ease with such people and far less so in villages, where he found altogether too much nakedness, alcohol use, and "inanition." When Olcott traveled to villages by bullock cart, he wanted to get close to the people; Dharmapala traveled in a camping car that kept him at a remove from them. A monk who knew him wrote that he felt more comfortable with Europeans than with his own people.[17]

Having no direct knowledge of rural England, he discovered a source that provided him with knowledge comparable to what he learned by touring Sinhala villages:

Yesterday I had written to my brother in London suggesting him [*sic*] to study the English country life. Two years ago I had the desire to know about the morality of the rural people in England. There is a vulgar animality in the village people. I was delightfully astonished to read "Juicy Joe" by Blyth—anticipating what I had thought on the subject. It is a good book to be given to English upstarts who boast of their civilization. (Diary, March 19, 1904)[18]

15. *Boston Globe*, May 5, 1903.

16. Even after her substantial contributions to Dharmapala and a variety of Hindu gurus, Foster left an estate of over $3,000,000. Patricia Masters, "Mary Foster: The First Hawaiian Buddhist," in *Innovative Buddhist Women: Swimming against the Stream*, ed. Karma Lekshe Tsomo (London: Curzon, 2000), 243. Her wealth came from her family's shipping company. In 1913 she sold water rights on the wet side of Oahu, allowing its diversion to the dry side of the island at a rent of $40,000 each year. "Another Great Tunnel Project Is Now Possible—Oahu Plantation Leases the Foster Water Rights on Windward Side," *Pacific Commercial Advertiser*, May 24, 1913, 1.

17. Ven. H. Dhammananda, "Remembering the Anagarika," *Island*, September 18, 1987.

18. James Blyth, *Juicy Joe: A Romance of the Norfolk Marshlands* (London: Grant Richards, 1903). When one reads Blyth's preface, it is not hard to see what drew Dharmapala to this account of village life in the mother country: "The motto of the marsh village is a mutilated one. It is 'Everyone for himself, and the devil take the hindmost.' In these remote remnants of the old colonies established more than twelve hundred years ago . . . modernity, and even civilization are as yet unknown factors in the scheme of life. . . . Christianity is used solely as a cloak for vice. The more regular the church or chapel goer the greater the hypocrite" (vii).

He was reassured to discover that the villagers of the Norfolk marshlands were no more civilized than Sinhala villagers. On one occasion he drew a distinction between the British planters and Sinhala villagers that cuts in a surprising direction:

> At Avissawella. Finlay Muir & Co. own the largest tea estates. Thousands of acres have been purchased at nominal prices. The same land in the hands of the Natives were not yielding more than a rupee per acre; in the hands of the Englishman the same acre produces more than a thousand rupees! Herein consists the greatness of wisdom. Both have the same sense organs but in brain power the Englishman excels the native in as much as the former develops his brain. (Diary, July 24, 1905)

His problem in advocating for Buddhist civilization was that its local representatives were empty categories. Middle-class Sinhalas had traded Buddhism for trousers, frocks, ballroom dancing, beef eating, and alcohol, and villagers had forgotten their ancient ideals.

THE IMPERIAL CONTEXT

The imperial system enabled Dharmapala's frequent movements between India and Lanka and on to England and the rest of the world. Knowing English gave him the symbolic capital of elite origins, and Theosophical connections and the financial backing of others made it possible for him to travel abroad regularly. Once he had bought a house in Ealing, he began to lay out his plans:

> We shall buy the plot of land at Clapham Park, Clarence road and build the Temple. . . . It will be my gift to the English nation in gratitude for the intellectual benefits I received from the English language. Whatever good thing I have done since my youth is due to the benefits I have received from my knowledge of English. Queen Mab was the first poem I read in my boyish days. My early association were all Christian and yet I was never influenced by their vicious adominations [sic]. (Diary, July 14, 1927)

In addition to reducing the travails of travel, speaking English made other things possible. It allowed him to establish and edit the *Journal of the Maha Bodhi Society*, which in turn put him "in touch with Oriental scholars throughout the world and [led to] the invitation to attend the Congress of

Religions in 1893 at Chicago and brought [him] to the notice of Mrs. Foster" (Sarnath Notebook no. 23). It allowed him to preach the Dhamma, not only in English-speaking countries, but also in places where local elites knew English, namely Germany, India, Burma, and Lanka.

For the sake of simplicity, he usually traveled second class, but he had no intention of being treated in a second-class way. The yellow robes drew people's attention; when he was taking a seaside vacation at Bournemouth, a little girl asked the man and woman he was traveling with, "Does he belong to you?" (Diary, May 20, 1926). The attention made him uneasy, but he knew that Indian dress was essential to missionary allure, writing that bringing samaneras (novice monks) to London in their robes would make a "fine sight" (Diary, December 19, 1926). Unable to rent a suitable place, he envisioned traveling across Europe in a camping car similar to the one he had used to tour Sinhala villages: "I need not hire a house. It will be a grand spectacle and the people when they see the caravan will be attracted" (Diary, September 19, 1925). The anomaly of an English-speaking South Asian traveling by train and steamship in places far from home and dressed in the yellow toga, socks, and shoes must have puzzled people, prompting some of the disrespectful treatment he received from clerks and fellow travelers:

> Arrived in Paris at 11 P.M. The yellow robe I wear draws the attention of both men and women. When a woman sees me she will give a push by her arm to her companion; vice versa. Several think that I am a woman. (Diary, August 10, 1926)

He needed the robes to ground his project's legitimacy and display his otherness; the price was scrutiny and occasional abuse. An account of his visit to Washington, DC, conveys another form of otherness, beginning with the assumption he was a Hindu:

> For a few days past there has been seen about Washington a strange-looking figure in a flowing yellow robe and wearing a white turban. The man's swarthy face and peculiar waddling manner of locomotion added to the striking garb have attracted much attention to him.[19]

To Western eyes, the robes, turban, and "swarthy face" made him a Hindu. As widely as Dharmapala traveled, his asceticism made cosmopolitanism irrelevant to his life's work. He smoked cigarettes on and off through-

---

19. "Washington Stares at Hindu," *New York Times*, June 29, 1903.

out his life but not in public and not as an affectation. At one point, he felt
beholden to a nurse who showed him "great love" during his convalescence
in a Swiss sanatorium. She demurred when he mentioned wanting to give
her a present, but he pressed her to accept the silk dhoti and uttari (upper
garment) that he had worn for twelve years (Diary, August 5, 1925); he never
indicated her reaction, but one can imagine. He was not always suave, but
he learned from his travels. Living in Calcutta among Bengalis who dressed
in local styles, not borrowed ones, he learned that there was an alternative
to Western-style dress for urban elites. In Burma he again saw the local elite
wearing local attire. When he convalesced in Switzerland, he learned that
there were higher levels of social unity and patriotism in other parts of the
world (and reason to criticize the absence of both in Calcutta).[20] He saw
himself as a man who knew the world and acted on that knowledge:

> Foster House . . . The Collection up to date for the London Vihara is Rs.
> 18126.11.0. There is hardly any one who is taking an intelligent interest
> in the London Buddhist Mission. The so-called wealthy Buddhists are
> indifferent. There is no unity among the educated. The Sinhalese Bud-
> dhists who do not know English are dull headed. The Theros are lack-
> ing in insight. They do not travel, do not care to see the world. They sit
> chewing betel and gossip. (Diary, August 23, 1927)

Part of his estrangement is a product of his people's indifference to his overseas projects, which was actively opposed by important Buddhists in Colombo. But it also derived from his own wandering, creating a world for
himself both solitary and rootless. His universalism needs to be seen in this
context—he undertook his work for the good of humanity, and doing so
kept him at a remove from other human beings.

Dharmapala's travels also left him more aware of the might of the imperial system. In 1897 he had a dream that he recorded without comment that
is hard to reconcile with talk about him as a freedom fighter: "Dream . . . Saw
the Queen of England and I stroked her hand and sat like a son would near a
mother" (Diary, March 22, 1897).[21] He had waking regard for the queen too,
writing that Buddhism had prospered during the reign of Queen Victoria, and

20. "Patriots of the Swiss type are not born in India. Brotherhood is an illusion to the
Indian." Dharmapala, "My European Tour," *Journal of the Maha Bodhi Society* 35 (1926): 70–6,
at 72.

21. Whatever significance lies in the content of the dream, I think it is instructive that he
did not add a comment about having such a dream. No "Isn't this odd" or "I am repelled by this
dream"—he simply mentions the dream and moves on.

that warranted his bringing monks from all Buddhist countries to London to bless her before she died (Diary, November 6, 1893). It could hardly be said that Lankan Buddhism had prospered under her rule, at least not until the Buddhist revival of the 1880s, and his gratitude to her seems as unlikely as his docility in the dream. Whatever status he held in the imperial system— citizen, subject, or denizen—he entertained patriotic feelings without irony or self-consciousness. He petitioned the Crown directly on several occasions, writing the Prince of Wales regarding his plans to felicitate Queen Victoria with an assemblage of monks, and urging Edward VII to make Bodh Gaya an exclusively Buddhist place of worship for the Buddhists of Japan, China, Tibet, Korea, Siam, Lanka, and Burma (Sarnath Notebook no. 19). Usually his petitions were rewarded with a note from a private secretary saying that "the King has not been pleased to give any directions in this matter."

Entangled in the British Empire though he was, he was capable of opposing it, writing in a letter that "nothing should be done to support the British government."[22] On one occasion, he urged Sinhalas to construct effigies of white men (*para suddhas*), hanging them in places where children could see their fathers beating a white man with a stick.[23] The former amounts to an act of resistance by constitutional means, and the latter served as a practicum in resistance and self-strengthening. The epigraph to Guruge's compilation of Dharmapala's writings—"I have to be active and activity means agitation according to constitutional means"—sums up the temperate character of his position on empire, and even what he called agitation was not Gandhian confrontation or self-suffering but petition, litigation, letter writing, and intemperate speech.[24] The moderation has several sources. His eyes were fixed on his own salvation, making his worldly activities, however ambitious, come second—and he saw himself as a critic, but a loyal one. In formal encounters with the colonial establishment, he insisted on his loyalty.[25] When he was interned in Calcutta following the 1915 riots in Ceylon, he made frequent entries in his diaries about that loyalty, writing, for example, "I am not seditious, but everyone opposed because I am critical.

22. "News from India," in Guruge, *Dharmapala Lipi*, 254.

23. "Anagarika Dharmapala Was an Anti-imperialist Freedom Fighter," *Island*, September 17, 1992.

24. *Return to Righteousness*, 753.

25. "Vihara Report," *Journal of the Maha Bodhi Society* 30 (1922): 445–52. At the foundation stone laying at the Buddhist vihara at Sarnath, Dharmapala welcomed Sir Spencer Harcourt Butler and a suite of local officials by recounting the history of the place. When he came to his difficult relations with the Archaeological Department, he praised Butler's peacemaking gesture, concluding that "the Maha Bodhi Society, ever loyal to the British Government, whose enlightened tolerance, has made their activities possible in India, accepted this wise decision" (450).

Like the Bodhisattva . . . the Buddha preached unity but you cannot preach unity under the British" (Sarnath Notebook no. 23). He repeated the idea elsewhere in the same notebook, insisting "I was never seditious" and "I have never been disloyal," not only to make a record of his intentions, but also to fret over how he had gotten himself into such a fix.

His attacks on British rule came in public contexts, and they do not jibe with his less well-known statements of loyalty to the Crown. But he was not alone in playing two games at once. The generosity of the Archeological Department in offering him relics came at the same time as the Political and Intelligence Department was trying to sort out whether he was a seditionist or a nuisance. At the same time his supporters argued for his being allowed to return home after his internment in 1919, he wrote to the Crown, restating his loyalty. The colonial secretary resisted but dismissed any threat he posed:

> Dharmapala is absolutely impossible, which you can see from the letter here, which breaks off into abuse just when he is endeavouring to make a good impression. I doubt whether he could really do much harm. . . . Mrs. Besant and he might stir up some trouble among the young heads here which it would be better to avoid. I do not advise allowing him to return.[26]

From 1905 on, colonial governments monitored his activities, the British consulate putting him under surveillance during his 1913 trip to Japan, where the Political Office had him followed as he made his way around Tokyo.

There was an array of associations that made Dharmapala look like more of a revolutionary than he was—his brothers were centrally involved in the temperance movement (which the colonial government thought was seditious). He had long-term relationships with German and Japanese Buddhists. He met more than once with Indian nationalist leaders including Lala Lajpat Rai, Mahatma Gandhi, the Maharajah of Baroda, and Mohammed Barakatullah. In Europe he met Prince Kropotkin. He made few references in the diaries of his actions drawing suspicion or his trying to avoid surveillance. In Japan he was unaware that he was being followed in 1913. After the 1915 riots, his internment allowed him to move about Calcutta, but he knew his house was watched and his mail censored. When a Criminal

26. Vimal Weerasinghe, "British Attitude towards Anagarika Dharmapala,' *Sunday Observer*, September 11, 1983.

Investigation Department official characterized him as a "seditionist of the worst sort," he reacted with considerable self-control. "The British government is persecuting me and as a Buddhist I wish the more to help them," he noted, and that response characterized many of his representations during the 1926–8 period he spent in London (Sarnath Notebook no. 27). His moderation increased late in life for reasons besides age and declining health— interned during World War I, he was sobered by the experience.

His harshness toward the British was of a piece with his harshness toward the monkhood, Sinhala villagers, and the Colombo elite, not to mention his own family. Listing the groups he criticized, he included the gods themselves, saying that they had forgiven him. He had criticized British government and its bureaucracy long before World War I and his internment, but his statements of loyalty also began before those events. When he gave a speech at the opening of the Kadugannawa Buddhist School, a "shabbily-dressed European without a collar or tie" in the audience began to look dismayed and soon walked out. Later, as Dharmapala waited for the train to Colombo, the man came up and told him that he should not criticize the British. He responded:

"Look here you may have read the speeches of Lloyd George to his countrymen. What Lloyd George is trying to do for his own people I am trying to do for my people." The man at once changed his hostility, and showing a friendly feeling, said "Shake hands, I am a Welsh man, I'm an Engine Driver, and my name is Jones, and Lloyd George is my Cousin." (Sarnath Notebook no. 4)

From that point on, when Jones saw Dharmapala at Kadugannawa, he said hello and asked about his health. The torrent of vituperation duly noted, his criticism fixed not so much on British rule as on economic exploitation and the cultural corruption it brought.

Finding his mail opened during his internment, Dharmapala made an entry that comes as close to summarizing his views as anything he wrote:

The letter addressed to me by the Colombo Branch of Hong Kong & Shanghai Bank had been opened by the Censor, Colombo. What distrust, what humiliation. In my dream I had never entertained any idea of disloyalty. I have criticized the British bureaucracy of Ceylon on economic grounds; and always cherished the desire that Ceylon should have Home Rule under British Protection. I sent the cover to the Col: Secy: Colombo with a letter. Higher patriotism is based on Universal Righteousness not on Racial Arrogance. The Buddha is my example. (Diary, January 10, 1916)

The passage speaks to the experiential logic of colonial unease—British arrogance married to South Asian humiliation—coupled with his distinctive views on a higher patriotism that overrides the distinction between the colonized and the colonizers as much as between self and other. Its foundation is righteousness with "universal" application, skillfully distinguished from the racial arrogance that he found in many encounters as he moved about the empire. But he acted on an unspoken assumption: his asceticism had earned him the right to look back at the world and criticize it.

Annie Besant grounded the prospect for a better future on the possibility of human brotherhood; Dharmapala grounded his on universal righteousness and the notion that Asians were just as civilized as Europeans. To both aspirations, the British offered a single response—"Not yet," not till you become more civilized can you expect self-government.[27] He shared that gradualist vision:

> I had asked the people to educate the children, so that forty years after when the present generation leaves the world, our children might enjoy the happiness of self-government under the British Crown similar to the Government of New Zealand.[28]

Even though he wrote those words in a petition to the secretary of state for the colonies in July 1916 when he was being placed under an internment order, his moderation and protests of loyalty are no different from what he had said long before, down to the example of New Zealand. The notion of "forty years" is instructive in a second way because 1956 had in those years come to be fixed as the twenty-five hundredth anniversary of the Buddha's life, the Buddha Jayanti, which Dharmapala understood as a time of social renewal.[29] The momentousness of the event meant one thing for the Bud-

27. Chakrabarty, *Provincializing Europe*, 8–11.

28. Ananda W. P. Guruge, *The Unforgettable Dharmapala: A Miscellany on the Life and Achievements of Anagarika Dharmapala (1864–1933) of Sri Lanka* (Huntington Beach, CA: Ananda W. P. Guruge, 2002), 86.

29. In his notebooks Dharmapala calculates the number of lifetimes that would unfold, starting with various dates for his putative death, before his incarnation as a young man in 1956 at the Buddha Jayanti. Even without a doctrinal warrant, he shared the prospect of social renewal with other Sinhalas. I suspect that he came by this notion from his association with U Ohn Ghine, with whom he stayed when he visited Burma. Ghine's son was one of Sarkisyanz's informants, telling him in 1952 that "there is some belief even here that the 2500th anni-

dhists of Burma and Lanka. For Dharmapala once reborn, the event would be momentous for another reason—he would see the future Buddha in the same way Sumedha had met the Dipamkara Buddha many lifetimes before his life as Gautama. The meeting would legitimate his hopes and initiate his struggle for liberation in earnest.

He was wrongheaded about many things, taking friends for enemies, misreading events, and drawing far-fetched conclusions.[30] But his understanding of colonialism was clear sighted. The brutality of the colonial system was hard for the British to recognize, he thought, but no less painful to colonized people:

> British bureaucracy in India is like the fishwife who, when asked whether the eels that are flayed alive don't suffer pains, answered "Oh they are used to it." The European tourist who visits India is naturally glad to see this vast country under the rule of the British Civil Service. He extols the work done by the British Civilian, but he never consults the desires of the people whether they would wish to have a continuance of this slavery. (Sarnath Notebook no. 23)

Envisioning the perspective of a European tourist seems an odd choice for him, but he had been a tourist himself, especially during his travels in the United States. On several trips he had evidence of the way Americans thought about colonial rule. In one instance, he noted,

> From San Francisco to Washington I have not met as yet one man who did not express his views favourably about England. England has hoodwinked the whole world about her charities in India. The world does not know the truth of her tyrannical administration in India. (Diary, June 26, 1903)

The tyranny was obvious to him, but he had to acknowledge "there is something wonderful in the British people that the world admires. For another 100 years they are sure of their position. They stand supreme" (Sarnath Notebook no. 23).

---

versary of the Mahaparinibbana of the Buddha will mark a great Revival of Buddhism and there is some feeling that the 'Golden Age' for which all men long, may dawn with this." E. Sarkisyanz, *Buddhist Backgrounds of the Burmese Revolution* (The Hague: Nijhoff, 1965), 207.

30. As he was beginning his two-year stay in England, he wrote in his diary, "The British are known for their snobbery. They have learned all this from the Indian people." (September 28, 1925).

Sometimes he revealed extravagant admiration for the West. British domination was the "best of foreign rule." The British were, he said, "the most enlightened, the most philanthropic, the most cultured of European races."[31] He even thought that English aristocrats were better-looking than their French and Italian counterparts, attributing their good looks to living their lives outdoors (Sarnath Notebook no. 4). Elsewhere he made an invidious distinction between the British and their Indian subjects: "India has lost its place on account of the immorality of her children. The British are holding India by virtue of their superior morality" (Sarnath Notebook no. 23). That morality was tied to the mother country, and what recommended England to him was that it was a society where people knew their place. All he encountered interacting with the British in South Asia was misbehavior and unwarranted class presumption:

> The British adventurers in their own country are nobodies, but when they come over to Asia they adopt an attitude of foolish arrogance which they can only maintain for a time. Why this arrogance? In their own land their compatriots are willing to remove the chamber pot and clean the commode of every "damned nigger." It is the arrogance of the bounder. (Diary, September 9, 1913)

He spoke from standing outside the affairs of the world as a homeless wanderer, ever observant of the local scheme of things yet sufficiently in touch with everyday English to call a bounder a bounder.

The long voyage out to South Asia set off a transformation of manners, turning Anglo-Indians into what Dharmapala called "sea-wolves." As he put it, "What a strange people these Britishers are. At home they are philanthropic. Here they are different" (Diary, August 27, 1896). This sea change was not the only example of his looking at the empire as a social system in which no one is improved by moving from his or her native place—not civil servants, not missionaries, not civilians, not even South Asian students who study in England and later return home:

> In England a party sit and begin drinking and the contents of the bottle are proportionately divided. Therefore there is no occasion to get intoxi-

---

31. Ananda Guruge, "Anagarika Dharmapala! Thou Shouldst be Living at this Hour," in *An Agenda for the International Buddhist Community* (Colombo: Karunaratne and Sons, 1993), 258. The first statement comes from 1892, the second from 1909.

cated. When the Indian or the Sinhalese comes over to England he learns to drink in company; and when he returns he gets no company, so he keeps company with the bottle, and he falls a victim of alcohol. (Diary, May 1, 1927)

Just as in his argument that only low-class Britons went out to the colonies, Dharmapala saw class figuring in the experiences of South Asians spending time in England. "They learn the vicious habits," he wrote, "of low-class English people."[32] Alcohol was the worst of it, but the sensual diversions of Western life were unending—casual relations among men and women, social dancing, horse racing, movies, and theater.[33] Having seen a Jackie Coogan movie while traveling through France, he wrote, "So long as I live amidst sensual surroundings it is not possible to get rid of *Kamachanda nivarana* [nighttime aberrations]" (Diary, December 25, 1927).

There are two places in the diaries where he found something positive in movement around the empire. He wrote that well-to-do Sinhalas should travel to England so that their wives could deliver their babies abroad, making their children "natives of England" (Diary, April 30, 1926). The other thing that could travel with advantage was the Dhamma. Adapted to local circumstances, it would give the British what they needed.

The Dhamma in its perfected form can't be accepted by the European people. A modified form leading to heaven & Brahmaloka may be preached to the English people. They are an arrogant race, but their ancestors were pagan savages. They have a record of black deeds which they have done, and unless they become morally good they will degenerate. For their future good I have come to give them the warning. (Diary, July 24, 1926)[34]

32. "Buddhism in England," *Journal of the Maha Bodhi Society* 34 (1926): 547–52, at 551.

33. On the drinking issue, Dharmapala recognized the disjuncture inherent in traveling across the empire—a well-to-do Lankan student returning from England to the island with a taste for alcohol at the beginning of the twentieth century would likely be forced to hide his new habit, drinking in anonymous places uncongenial to the measured use of alcohol.

34. Characterizing Buddhism as a religion without a concept of hell and without mendicancy, Dharmapala reframed his Buddhism to fit his British audience. Contrary to what he suggested, that "modified form" of Buddhist practice leading to heaven, not nirvana, is precisely the goal of most Buddhists in Theravada Asia nowadays. See S. J. Tambiah, "The Ideology of Merit and the Social Correlates of Buddhism in a Thai Village," in *Dialectic in Practical Religion*, ed. E. R. Leach (Cambridge: Cambridge University Press, 1968), 41–5. In approaching the British, Dharmapala drew the contrast between his vision of "pure" Buddhism and a Buddhism of lower aspirations (which happened to coincide with the practices of ordinary Theravada Buddhists).

His own travels notwithstanding, he found little value in cosmopolitanism, cultural exchange, or hybridity. What he learned from traveling the world was the inequity of the imperial system, the might of the metropole on the one side and the destitution of people in the colonial periphery on the other. Japan and the United States served as examples of societies that had prospered by fending off colonial domination. England exemplified who profited from colonialism, and South Asia, who paid. He saw need for forms of reciprocity between mother country and the colonies. Asking for funds for the vihara he wanted to build in London, he envisioned an advertisement for the *Journal*, saying "The selfish policy of British exploitation must be stopped to avoid the destruction of the weaker races of Asia & Africa" (Diary, August 9, 1926). Buddhism would humanize the British, and they would educate the peoples under their rule. Asked by two South Indian Christians how they could free India from British rule, he gave an answer that they must not have expected: teach the young generation morals and technical industries (Diary, December 18, 1925).

If Dharmapala saw himself as part of the British Empire, the question is what part. During the First World War, he wrote in his diary of "our losses in the Dardanelles . . . 87,650 up to August 21, 1915" (Sarnath Notebook no. 53). On the next page of that notebook, he returned to his conventional complaint, quoting a passage from the *Times*: "No nation deals as violently with the rights of other people, international treaties or with neutrality." But his loyalties are clear. In 1892 he spoke of British rule as the best form of foreign domination.[35] In 1911 he wrote articles for the *Sinhala Bauddhaya* with titles such as "Our Noble and Great King."[36] In November of that year the lead article in the *Journal of the Maha Bodhi Society* celebrated India's place in the imperial system.[37] It quoted the Aga Khan to the effect that England's investing in Indian education would strengthen both the empire and India. Education would also allow Indians to "form opinions . . . on public questions" by suppressing ignorant anticolonial prejudices. The venues that produced most of the imperial interactions in his life were the sacred sites of India and Lanka, followed by the temple he built in Calcutta. The British gave him relics, and he gave them respect. The Raj used him to legitimate its rule; he

---

35. Guruge, "Anagarika Dharmapala!," 258.

36. Guruge, *Dharmapala Lipi*, 289.

37. "India's Education and Her Future Position in the Empire," *Journal of the Maha Bodhi Society* 19 (1911): 321–2. The article is unsigned, but I believe it was written by Dharmapala. Even if it was not, I have found little in the journal that does not reflect his views as expressed elsewhere.

16. Lord Ronaldshay presents relic to Sir Asutosh Mukherjee, Calcutta, 1920.

used it to legitimate his projects. When he opened a temple, he invited the most distinguished officials he could wrangle. When he built a resthouse for pilgrims in Gaya, he called it the Victoria Memorial Dharmasala.[38]

After the government of Lanka had him interned in Calcutta in 1916–7, he saw no connection between his actions and the sedition of which the British suspected him. He thought he had offended them by writing an article criticizing the morality of British women (Sarnath Notebook no. 23). He put the blame entirely on a piece he published in *Sinhala Bauddhaya* that related what a British officer had told him—that as long as his wife satisfies him, the Englishman does not care about her chastity (Sarnath Notebook no. 4). He cared about such things, and caring about proper behavior was a motive for bringing the Dhamma to the British. Doing so assumed that the empire was a unified whole. He wrote in his diary that "Ceylon & England can never again be disunited" (September 4, 1925), repeating that same line in the *Journal* a year later.[39] When an associate argued against

38. Copland, "Managing Religion in Colonial India," 542.
39. "Buddhism in England," *Journal of the Maha Bodhi Society* 34 (1926): 550.

building a vihara in London, he was unpersuaded, observing, "He has no idea of the tie that binds the British & the Buddhists" (Diary, February 1, 1927). Two days later he saw that project extending into the next life and legitimated by royal birth: "The thought came to me that I should be born in the British royal family in my next birth and work for the establishment of the Sasana in England" (Diary, February 3, 1927).

CIVILIZATION

When Dharmapala made the contrast between East and West, he did so by moving between a religious idiom and a civilizational one. In the first case, Buddhism and Christianity furnished the binary opposition, and in the second, England exemplified Western civilization and either Lanka, Aryan Sinhalas, or Aryan India stood for Eastern civilization.[40] He located the golden age of his own civilization almost two millennia earlier in the time of the Buddhist king who drove off the usurper Elara:

> As if by the waving of a magic wand, temples, tanks, parks, gardens, public baths, resting-houses for man and beast, hospitals—also for man and beast—free almonries, schools, colleges for Bhikkhus and nuns, gymnasiums, and public halls were erected throughout the land. Free from foreign influence, untainted by alien customs, with the word of the Buddha as their guiding light, the Sinhalese people lived a joyously cheerful life in these bygone times. . . . There was dazzling magnificence within the sacred city [Anuradhapura], which contained nine-storeyed houses; and the streets were crowded day and night by throngs of pilgrims and also traders from all parts of the then known world. The atmosphere was saturated with the fragrance of sweet-smelling flowers and delicate perfumes.[41]

Those assertions come from an account Dharmapala made to an early twentieth-century survey of people, commerce, and resources, arguing that Buddhist civilization was the work of Buddhist monks. That civilization

---

40. When Dharmapala used India as Europe's binary opposite, Asoka served as the paradigmatic righteous king. He adverted to Asoka because he was a missionizing king by tradition and provided a paradigm for his own project.

41. Anagarika Dharmapala, "Buddhism, Past and Present," in *Twentieth Century Impressions of Ceylon*, by Arnold Wright (London: Lloyd's Greater Britain, 1907), 286.

was national and more, for an "ancient national religion" united the sub-continent from the Himalayas to Lanka.[42]

The civilization that Buddhism brought with it was more civilized than others by virtue of what it lacked: "no slaughter houses, no pawnshops, no brothels, no prisons and law Courts and no arrack taverns and opium dens."

> For seventeen centuries this fair Lanka had only one form of pure religion—Buddhism. It taught pity to animals, charity, purity of life, truth, and temperance, and daily the temples were crowded with devo-tees who repeated the TUN SARANA and the PANCHA SILA . . . . The people were mild and gentle and they loved to do good deeds.[43]

The "ancient national religion" lived on until the coming of foreign invaders—first Muslims and later Europeans—and created what Dharma-pala called a "spiritualized Aryanism," perfectly suited to the "gentle spirit of the Aryan race."[44] He was hardly alone in invoking the Aryan idea in late colonial India.[45] Aryanism functioned as a racialized discourse in places as diverse as Argentina, Ireland, Nigeria, Australia, and New Zealand.[46] That discourse functioned to give colonized people pride of place among the very people who had colonized them. It allowed both unspoken equality with the British and the distinction between his own gentle Aryan origins and local immigrant communities such as Muslims.

Once the "brutal races" of Western Asia and Europe arrived, "UnAryan practices" brought down Buddhism and its ennobling qualities. With this transition—roughly at the same moment that Bodh Gaya ceased to serve as a functioning Buddhist site—Dharmapala left behind his Eisenstadtian ac-count of Asian civilization and spoke of civilization in Eliasian terms.[47] In

---

42. "How a Nation Prospers or Declines According to Lord Buddha," *Journal of the Maha Bodhi Society* 15 (1907): 131–7, at 136.

43. "Ceylon, Past and Present," *Journal of the Maha Bodhi Society* 14 (1906): 37–38, at 38.

44. "Buddhism, Science and Christianity," *Journal of the Maha Bodhi Society* 34 (1924): 158–62.

45. Romila Thapar, "The Theory of Aryan Race and India: History and Politics," *Social Scientist* 24 (1996): 3–29; Thomas R. Trautmann, *Aryans and British India* (Berkeley: University of California Press, 1997).

46. Tony Ballantyne, "Race and the Webs of Empire: Aryanism from India to the Pacific," *Journal of Colonialism and Colonial History* 2, no. 3 (2001).

47. The definitive source for Eisenstadt's comparative treatment of civilization is *The Origins and Diversity of Axial Age Civilization* (Albany: State University of New York Press, 1986). For Norbert Elias, see *The Civilizing Process* (New York: Urizen Books, 1978) and *The History of Manners* (New York: Pantheon, 1982), both translated by Edmund Jephcott.

India, these "unAryan practices" included "child marriage, enforced widow-hood of virgin girls, the tyrannical caste distinctions, confinement of women within the four walls of the Zenana, the prohibition of foreign travel."[48] In Lanka the coming of those "brutal races" had worse consequences:

> thousands of kine and other dumb animals daily slaughtered, dishonesty and burglary rampant, brothels in the principal towns where hundreds of maidens are kidnapped from villages and brought and imprisoned in these hells, arrack taverns and opium dens opened in every inhabited locality. . . . A hundred years of British Rule the country has had, and yet the Sinhalese are today the most backward of all Asiatic peoples. There is neither a weaving School nor a polytechnic institute for teach-ing practical methods of economic industrialism. The higher grade of the Civil Service is closed to the Sinhalese; he is given an education that will make him seek only a clerical appointment which enslaves him for life. . . . There are no Architects, Engineers, Electricians nor Artists among the Sinhalese.[49]

Sinhala suffered twice, first by having its ancient religion suppressed, then by having its people denied access to the benefits of British rule.

The collapse of Aryan civilization had one effect in urban Lanka and another in village settings. In Colombo and other major cities Portuguese, Dutch, and British rule had produced what Dharmapala thought was a de-racinated class, the local elite portrayed in Arnold Wright's *Twentieth Cen-tury Impressions of Ceylon* (1907). Sinhalas lost more than other Lankans because they had more at stake—a civilization reaching back over two mil-lennia. They were the natives of the island, and as "sons of the soil" they had special rights to the place. The Sinhala elite had traded that civilization for a mess of pottage (including the Victorian furniture Dharmapala's father produced for civil servants, planters, and the local elite). Life in villages and small towns had been less influenced by British rule but was still corrupted by its collateral effects. Beginning with lecturing tours he made with Ol-cott, Dharmapala had experience of a world that had been as alien to him as England, and this encounter with village lethargy and dissipation left him thoroughly shaken. Whatever influence opium and arrack had in urban set-

---

48. "How a Nation Prospers or Declines According to Lord Buddha," 137.
49. "Ceylon, Past and Present," 38. Gombrich and Obeyesekere write that beef—the para-digm for all meat eating—"has been the meat most widely available to the Sinhala population and very widely consumed." *Buddhism Transformed*, 233.

tings, he argued, they had even more tragic results in villages, and when he spoke of the Sinhala people dying "slowly from inanition," he had Sinhala villagers in mind.[50]

Dharmapala insisted that villages had suffered the blunt force of the outside world twice over—first from Europeans carving space for plantations from village lands and then with rapacious trading communities such as Muslims who came from the coast of India for trade in the nineteenth century:

> Every village industry is now being killed by articles made in Germany. . . . In the wilds of Hiniduma . . . the illiterate villagers complained to me that their only source of livelihood depended upon chena cultivation, and fields they have very few or none. Aliens are taking away the wealth of the country and the sons of the soil where are they to go?[51]

The disorienting effects of foreign influence duly noted, the cities were not indolent, and urban dwellers were not uncivilized. They had simply traded their own civilization for an alien one. The villages were left without civilization of any kind. Dharmapala's tone was sympathetic, patronizing, and as critical of villagers for their lack of civilization as he was of middle-class Sinhalas for their Western affectations.

When he spoke of Sinhalas as such, the referent was usually village life and its failings. He held villagers responsible for provoking British contempt for all Sinhalas:

> The Sinhalese people are treated with contempt by the British people on account of the dirty habits of the former. The Bhikshus form a separate class on account of their Vinaya. The social roles & Society etiquette preclude the civilized English from associating with them. We can't blame the English. We have to rise to their standard. (Diary, November 7, 1897)

Aside from the notion of rising to English standards, this passage carries several implications. Dharmapala was not thinking of his own family in

---

50. Steven Kemper, "Dharmapala's Dharmadutha and the Buddhist Ethnoscape," in *Buddhist Missionaries in the Era of Globalization*, ed. Linda Learman (Honolulu: University of Hawaii Press, 2005), 27–32.

51. "The Fate of Sinhalese Villagers," in *Return to Righteousness*, 527–8, at 528. Dharmapala was either oblivious to the long-term presence of Muslim farmers and merchants in various parts of the island or willing to give them a pass, training his scorn on recently arrived traders from South India.

speaking of "dirty habits," and he was certainly not thinking of himself, because early on he acquired a commitment to cleanliness and hygiene that he pursued all his life.[52] Nor was he thinking of urban Lanka or the Buddhist monkhood, centered in village settings but set apart by Vinaya rules regarding cleanliness. The British might look down on the local brown English men and women, but they had no reason to think that their personal habits were dirty.

Village Lanka was Dharmapala's other, at least with regard to cleanliness and other Eliasian forms of civilization. He had learned the virtues of hygiene from one of his elementary school teachers:

> I was greatly influenced by my Sinhalese teacher, a man of immaculate habits and a strict disciplinarian. He was a bachelor. I learned lessons of cleanliness from him. He was known as Harmanis Gurunnanse [teacher]. ("My Early Associations," Sarnath Notebook no. 4)

Uncleanliness, even savagery, began at the outskirts of Colombo.

> Started in the evening for Sedawatte. Everywhere it is the same picture. Savage barbarism, dirt, drink & the devil. At 6 PM addressed the "Savages" at the Grand Pass Municipal Market. (Diary, February 21, 1898)

After his several trips abroad, his forays into village settings by bullock cart shocked him to the point of disgust:

> The Sinhalese of the present day are ignorant. There is no sense of thoughtful honesty in the people. Unintentionally they do things. At Attanagalla I spoke to the people. All are like little children. (Diary, March 8, 1898)

> At 2PM started for Minuwangoda. Saw a few women without any covering for their breasts! Oh, this strange race of Sinhalese. Large crows at Minuwangoda. Lectured agst: the Hambayas [Muslims]. (August 16, 1898)

---

52. Dharmapala's cleanliness had effects on his uneasy relationship with his mother: "Every day almost I tell mother to keep things in the room occupied by father [who was then very ill] clean. She will not do; and as to him nothing is so essential as cleanliness. 6 pieces of cloth are all that are wanted. It causes provocation when there is a persistent desire to pooh pooh what I say. I should have left home had I not a duty to perform. What am I to do?" (Diary, June 21, 1905).

What a degraded people the present Sinhalese are. All the low conditions of the savages are to be found in these villages. For every 3 miles there is an arrack shop. The children are made to drink. They apply the principle, "Do unto others." Worse than the animals they are. The animal takes care of the young; but not these people. Oh, the inhumanity of the administration. I promised help. (September 1, 1898)

His dismay was not limited to cleanliness. On later trips he lectured against beef eating, cattle stealing, selfishness, disunity, arrack drinking, backbiting and quarreling. But the lack of cleanliness and clothing troubled him disproportionately, reflecting his Victorian upbringing and his own predispositions:

[The] Sinhalese villager is half civilized. He is half naked, the women are ignorant, the children are neglected. He should be taught to wear clothes at all times, to keep his garden clean, to plant useful trees, to give his children education. Where there is no Govt: School there should be a temple School; the women should be taught home Industries, gardening, the children can till the ground. (Diary, June 19, 1913)

Elsewhere he made statements regarding sanitation that are so anomalous that they suggest the central place cleanliness occupied in both civilization and salvation. In Calcutta, he wrote:[53]

Something prompted me to let the dirty water of the tank near the kitchen off, and I found an indescribable accumulation of filth. It was horrible, disgusting. I rebuked the inmates. Bhikkhu Siddhartha, the Doctor of Vinaya is here; but he has no idea of cleanliness. I had attempted to reform the Buddhists of Ceylon, the result was that I lost my beloved Brother. The foolish bureaucrats misunderstood my efforts, and misconstrued them as political. Mine was moral and economical. It was spiritual economics that I preached to the people. . . . Sanitation is the highest science leading to spiritual aesthetics. (Diary, January 25, 1916)[54]

53. Dharmapala explained the connection between cleanliness and salvation in these terms: "Robes, body, nails, hair, surroundings should be kept scrupulously clean. The odors of perspiration, the smell of soiled robes, long nails, unkempt hair are obstacles in the path of psychological progress" ("What a Bhikkhu Is Expected To Do," Sarnath Notebook no. 4).

54. Rambukwella Siddhartha came to Calcutta to study and passed the entrance examination of the Calcutta University, followed by a difficult relationship with Dharmapala (Sarnath Notebook no. 58).

Even with the ellipsis near the end of this passage, it is hard to follow Dharmapala's reasoning here as it cascades forward. But his feeling of revulsion
at seeing dirty water, his understanding of his life as apolitical, his brother's
death in prison following the 1915 riots, and the connection between sanitation and spiritual growth suggest hygiene lurking behind an array of other
concerns.

In laying out his expectations for good behavior, his emphasis on cleanliness provides context for his argument that "sanitation is the highest
science leading to spiritual aesthetics":

> The Bhikkhu life is a thorough going discipline of mind and body. . . . He
> has strictly to observe the duties of sweeping, cleaning, removing refuse
> from the bodhiyangana [area around the bo tree] and chetiyangana [area
> around the relic mound]. Cleanliness has been extolled by the Blessed One
> as godliness. To keep the temple ground cleanly swept, to keep the seats,
> robes clean etc. is essential to progress. The Blessed one declared that the
> Bhikkhu who attends to the duties of sweeping and keeping the place
> clean fulfills the duties of religion (Sammajjana vattam karontena satthu
> sasanam katam hoti). The meritoriousness of sweeping the monastery
> grounds is shown in the life of Nagasena Thero and King Milinda. The life
> of Sariputta Thero given in the Samantapasadika wherein he neglected
> to have the place swept before he entered into the Nirodha samopatti
> wherein for seven days breathing, feelings, and perceptions are suspended.
> The Thero by iddhi power went aerially to the Himalayas, and sat in a
> suitable place and entered into the jhanas with the resolute will to not to
> [sic] get up for seven days. . . . The Blessed One found that Sariputta Thero
> had sat and entered into the Nirodha Samapatti without first having swept
> the place . . . and seeing that he was in trance, left the impression of His
> sacred feet to be seen when he comes [sic] back to consciousness, and re-
> turned to the Vihara. At the expiration of the seventh day Sariputta Thero
> came back to consciousness and observed the impression of the Sacred
> Feet left by the Blessed One, and looking to the cause found out that he
> had failed to sweep the place before he sat down. Instantaneously [unclear]
> Sariputta came through space and bowed down before the Lord and asked
> for forgiveness. Whereupon the Blessed One declared that the Bhikkhu
> who sweeps the ground and keeps things clean, fulfills the greater duties
> of religion. The Blessed One explained that the Bhikkhu who fails to
> observe the minor duties of abhisama carika vattam [lower duties] shall
> never fulfill the larger duties of adibrahma cariyam [higher renunciation].
> ("What a Bhikkhu Is Expected to Do," Sarnath Notebook no. 4)

If this passage exists in the *Samantapasadika*—a text mainly concerned with Sariputta's conversion, his receiving instruction from the Buddha, his mastery of *Abhidhamma*, and return home to comfort his mother before he died—I have not been able to find it. Other commentaries on Sariputta are intended to celebrate his virtues, not expose his flaws.[55] Whether the story is commentarial or not, Dharmapala's telling of it puts a monastic example of cleanliness to work, reiterating the importance of cleanliness for spiritual development. When he first bought a house in London, he had it cleaned and painted: "The painting work of the Foster House . . . cost £35. The house will look better after the cleaning. I do this for the sake of cleanliness, which is emphasized by our Lord" (Diary, September 28, 1927).

Dharmapala's attitude toward the body reflected a Victorian prudishness, but he had characteristically Buddhist reasons for his anxiety. He was a celibate, and the female body threatened his resolve. The sight of women affected him with a Tolstoyan frisson of desire and revulsion. Feelings of remorse left Tolstoy loathing himself. Dharmapala had only one occasion to feel remorse because he had made a vow and kept it—the incident in the Japanese hotel was an exception about which he felt quite a lot of guilt. But he was troubled by the very sensation of desire, which he countered by seeking the protection of the Buddha's teaching on the emptiness of the self (Diary, September 25, 1913). Especially on his birthday he tried to enact the teaching on no-self, addressing the event that celebrates the individual by deconstructing his own self. He describes the day as "the birthday of the five skandas [elements that create the illusion of self] of Anagarika Dharmapala" (Diary, September 17, 1915).

During his early days in Calcutta he visited the Theosophical Society and observed, "The room is badly situated, all around you are confronted with sights. . . . My mind was deeply agitated and I used every effort to cure

---

55. The latter part of the *Visuddhimagga* includes instructions for a bhikkhu seeking salvation. He must finish his meal, wash his hands and feet, sit down on a well-prepared seat in a secluded place (23: 32). He must make sure any property that is not his—robe and bowl, bed and chair, or a living room or any kind of requisite—will not be damaged during the seven-day trance by "fire, water, wind, thieves, rats, and so on" (23: 35). He must make his mind ready to return to consciousness before the end of the seven days should the community want to enact a resolution before that time (23: 38). Likewise if the master should want to examine a case or teach the Dhamma (23: 40). And he must make sure that his life will continue for seven days because sudden death would prevent him from declaring final knowledge, advising the bhikkhus, and testifying to the Dispensation's power (23: 42 and 42n17). Bhadantacariya Buddhaghosa, *The Path of Purification: Visuddhimagga*, vol. 2, trans. Bhikkhu Nyanamoli (Berkeley, CA: Shambhala, 1976), 828–31. The *Visuddhimagga* says nothing of sweeping. John Strong, personal communication.

it. To things I desired—to see every woman as my mother—and no evil thought to come at the sight of a female" (Diary, May 8, 1896). Traveling in either Japan or the West was a special challenge; the presence of women and their openness affected him in ways daily life in Lanka and India did not:

> Pain, pain, pain is the result of sensual excitement. Daily bathing also has a tendency to evil thoughts. Alone in the bathroom, undressed, bathing naked and applying soap daily on the various parts of the body has a bad effect. Sensual thoughts spring up momentarily and before there is time to think of the *Adhinavas* the work of Mara is done. Why did the Buddha prevent disciples from daily bathing. Self contact brings on sensation etc. After the bath the thought came to me *not to bathe daily*. The painful experience taught me an important lesson. Blessed Buddha, glory be to Him. (Diary, July 8, 1904; emphasis in original)

Even in old age he struggled: "Foster House . . . There were some of Ravivarma's nude oleographs in the kitchen. I tore them to bits and threw them into the stove" (Diary, June 17, 1927).

More was at stake here than either prudery or celibacy. Clothing represents civilization, and nakedness, savagery. The English are fully dressed. In Lanka and India they are overdressed, and middle-class South Asians followed their foolish practices. "Savages" wear no clothes, and for Dharmapala's taste, villagers fall between these extremes. In his terms, to be half naked is to be half civilized. Dharmapala's name is associated with Arya Sinhala dress for men—a white lower garment topped by long, kurta-like overshirt—but his own diaries focused on women's dress, namely the Kandyan sari (*osariya*), which he thought suited to tropical weather even while fully covering the body.[56] His motives were reformative: "I feel for the poor Sinhalese women who go about half naked. I wish to present each woman with a sari" (Diary, April, 28 1921).[57] But clothing was bound up with other issues—his feelings about Hinduism, India, and what the Indian press of the

---

56. When Dharmapala's mother led her pilgrimage group to Bodh Gaya in early 1895, the ladies in the party wore the Kandyan sari (Diary, November 18, 1920). What made the pilgrimage doubly consequential was providing the first occasion in their lives for the women to wear the sari. Noel Wijenaike, "The Answer to a Mother's Prayer," *Sunday Observer*, September 17, 1989. The sight of low-country women wearing the Kandyan sari must have struck Kandyans as an act of cross-dressing.

57. What he had in mind, I suspect, was the Portuguese-style jacket that women of the low country then wore with an unstitched, ankle-covering cloth. The jacket covered the arms but left the midriff bare. In speaking to a crowd at Beruwela, he urged women to replace the "short jacket" with the sari (Diary, January 31, 1925).

day called "the *sadhu* problem"—themselves tied to his hopes for remaking an Asian civilization able to stand up to Western hegemony.

His first sight of Hindu ascetics in Benares, Calcutta, Hardwar, and Gaya left him repulsed: "Saw a stark naked ascetic and it was disgusting in the extreme" (Diary, August 18, 1891). In an 1899 newspaper interview, he made an argument that echoed Vivekananda's views on diet and reform:

> Mr. Dharmapala spoke strongly against asceticism. He said that asceticism had been one cause from which the people of India suffered. "A half starved, withered mummy can never reform a people or nation, and if all people become mummies they will be fit only for the museum for people to gaze at. They cannot do the work elevating the people. But my asceticism has also a philosophical side in the way of confining yourself to a moderate diet and a temperate life."[58]

In the years that followed, he set his reformative zeal against the indolence and self-absorption of the sadhu:

> The Householder must follow the Middle Way and be neither sensual nor ascetic. Above all he must practise charity and love. . . . Active charity must be practised money being freely spent for the good of the public What Indian Householders want today, said the Anagarika Dharmapala, is more public spirit. "Let me be sacrificed, let others enjoy life"—that is the lesson taught to children in Japan.[59]

The argument turned on a set of binaries—egotism and public spirit, the unlikely combination of sensuality and asceticism (he accused sadhus of both) against moderation—that distinguish the two social roles, the sadhu contrasted with the bhikkhu or the brahmacarya.[60]

The Buddhist monk dresses in a manner appropriate to a tropical climate, yet he is clothed (as was Dharmapala, the single example in India

58. *Madras Standard*, September 28, 1899.

59. *Bengalee*, August 5, 1910, reprinted as "A Buddhist Missionary," *Journal of the Maha Bodhi Society* 18 (1910): 580–83, at 582.

60. His distaste for exposed body parts extended to the subtle distinctions of monkly attire as well. Siyam Nikaya monks usually follow the Thai tradition, wearing the robe over only one shoulder. Following the Burmese tradition, Amarapura and Ramanna monks cover both shoulders (at least in formal settings). Dharmapala dismissed a monk who came to Colombo to invite him to his village with these words: " He is of the [betel] chewing type, one shoulder bare" (Diary, December 11, 1926).

of the anagarika); the sadhu is naked or half-naked.⁶¹ Dharmapala told the
Bangkok Times,

> During the three years that I have spent in India since 1891 I have seen
> the religious life of the people and it is indeed startling to find today the
> successive followers of some of the contemporary ascetics of Buddha.
> Today you see the naked Achelakas, the Ajivakas, the Nigantas, the Kap-
> ilas, the Aghoris, the Jatilas—whose predecessors were subdued by the
> powerful wand of Buddha's love. You love Buddha the more after having
> once seen these ignorant fanatics who in hope of gaining salvation in a
> future life practise the most revolting asceticism, for it was Buddha that
> showed the uselessness of giving pain to the body to gain salvation.⁶²

He found reason to admire some qualities of other South Asian religions,
writing that the "religions that preach mercy are Buddhagama, Vishnua-
gama, and Jainism" ("Vegetarianism and Meat Diet," Sarnath Notebook
no. 4). He characterized Jainism elsewhere as a religion of vitality, "full
of power" (Diary, March 24, 1923).⁶³ The affinities between Jainism and
Buddhism—beginning with the commitment to *ahimsa* (nonviolence)—
should have made it an easy religion for him to like. It was hard to distinguish from Buddhism. When he first got to Sarnath in 1891, he and his colleagues "were admitted into the local Jain temple. We thought that we were
inside a Buddhist temple. We worshipped the Jain image of their Saviour
Tirthankara" (Sarnath Notebook no. 4). Yet in another notebook, he wrote
down an invidious verse, characterizing Jains in a different tone: Christians
are donkey drivers, Hindus are bullock drivers, Muslims are camel drivers, Jains are savages. The reduction of Jainism to savagery is so abrupt and
inconsistent with his positive evaluation of the religion generally that the
prejudice is hard to place. I can only imagine that it derived from his encounter with "sky-clad" (*digambara*) Jain ascetics who wear no clothes.

---

61. Dharmapala wore white robes of his own devising to the Parliament of Religions. In
October 1895, he began wearing ochre robes, appropriate to his status as a world renouncer.
Jayawardana, *Mage Jivita Kathava*, 96. Before that transition he had tried out both white and
ochre robes. As he writes, "Had breakfast at Dr. H. C. Chatterjee's. He advised me to wear the
orange coloured dress and to give up using lavender. He said I must be above criticism" (Diary,
April 15, 1894).

62. Reprinted in *Buddhist* 6 (1894).

63. Dharmapala had minimal contact with Jains, although the Jaina monastery at Sarnath
made them his next-door neighbors, and as he notes, he got his ideas about vitality and power
from reading Mrs. Sinclair Stevenson's *Heart of Jainism* and Puran Chand Nahar's *An Epitome
of Jainism* (Diary, August 18, 1920).

The project to restore "civilization" fixed on both Eisenstadtian and Eliasian elements, but his practical program fell on more personal forms of the Eliasian kind—cleanliness, clothing, diet, drink, and etiquette—and the program was aimed at village life.[64] His interest derived from his own temperament:

> I was always active in doing domestic acts. I was very fond of nursing babies, keeping everything clean, sweeping places neglected by others, lighting lamps, learning to cook, learning to sew, and to arrange things artistically, indifferent to things, listening, but doing what I think best. . . . My mind aspired to reach transcendental space, to float in the upper regions. I put no value on worldly things. I was fond of humour, and used to commit practical jokes on elderly people. They were annoyed but I did not mind. I was in a way iconoclastic and made fun of my unAryan gods. I had no faith in astrology, palmistry, [and so on]. (Sarnath Notebook no. 4)

When he joined Olcott on his preaching tours, he encountered village life for the first time. His weekly Danagatayutu Karanu column in the *Sinhala Bauddhaya* gave him a vehicle to speak to a rural audience. He established the paper in 1906 with the idea of promoting "pure Buddhism," which is to say he intended to use it as a vehicle to distinguish his ideas from the Theosophical interpretation of Buddhism found in the *Sarasavi Sandarasa*, which he had edited previously (Diary, June 6–7, 1916). He financed the new paper himself—unlike most of his projects, which were also Maha Bodhi Society projects—and he wrote a variety of pieces. His main focus fell on the Danagatayutu Karanu column, to which he contributed an article every Wednesday.[65] They covered a range of topics—from "Reading Erotic Novels will not lead you to Wisdom" and "Our Noble King," praising King George's contributions to Indian education, to "Mahatma Gandhi and Buddhism," relating Gandhi's talk at the Vesak celebration at the Dharmarajika vihara

64. Hikkaduve was also interested in civilization (*silacaratvaya*), using the word to mean both "culture" and "practical morality." Blackburn, *Locations of Buddhism*, 43. He was involved in Dharmapala's project, writing him to suggest certain changes in the *Gihi Dina Chariyava* (Diary, August 23, 1898). He replied, "nothing should be changed."

65. By 1911 Dharmapala had started the *Ceylon Nation* in Colombo, as an English-language counterpart to the *Bauddhaya*, which spoke to a Sinhala-reading audience (Diary, February 9, 1926). As he said of an article on the London Buddhist mission he published in the *Bauddhaya*, "Only the poor people read this article which is written with so much labour" (Diary, October 19, 1927).

in Calcutta.[66] Most of the articles were written abroad—relaying his experiences in places of which his readers had no experience—and posted to Colombo. The tone moved from the informational to the critical to the hortatory. Sometimes he used the articles to raise accusations against fellow Buddhists who were obstructing his progress—as in the case of a Karava-caste monk, Polwatte Dhammadhara, whom he accused of interceding with the mahant in order to deny Bodh Gaya to the Goyigama, by which I assume he meant the Maha Bodhi Society.[67] Taken as a whole, the material he published in Danagatayutu Karanu resonated with material he took up in his village lectures, cycling from politics or spiritual reform to civilizational issues. The articles made him a presence in Lanka whether he was living in Calcutta, traveling on a steamship, or sojourning in the West. He received copies of the *Bauddhaya* when abroad, and thus it served as his window on Buddhist reform in the island.

The avuncular role entailed more than criticism: Dharmapala also furnished guidance to redress the problems he observed. He urged his readers not to follow advice of "interested leaders," presumably D. B. Jayatilaka (Diary, January 23, 1924). He noticed that there was no place for students to venerate the Buddha at Ananda College and asked readers to build a Buddhist chapel (Diary, February 27, 1925). Concluding that the financial support of British civilians in Lanka would help the cause of building a vihara in London, he suggested the formation of a "Buddhist Mission to Ceylon Planters" (Diary, January 19, 1926). The most sustained attempt to provide advice came in 1898 in a Sinhala pamphlet he published almost a decade before he took up his weekly advice column.[68] The pamphlet related his advice regarding to "How meals should be taken," "Chewing Betel," "Wearing Clean Clothes," "What you should do walking along a Public Road," "How to Behave at Public Meetings," "What Women Should Do," "What Children Should Do," "What Lay Supporters Should do for Monks," "What You Should do while traveling on a bus or train," "What Village Protection Societies Should Do," "Visiting a Patient in the Hospital," "Conducting

66. October 14 and December 23, 1911, and May 23, 1925. In his Vesak talk Gandhi praised the Buddha as an incomparably great human being but provoked Dharmapala by saying that Hindus were more devoted to the Buddha than the Buddhists of Lanka, Burma, Japan, and China because Hindus did not eat beef.

67. "Bodh Gaya and the Great Meeting of the Hindu Sabha," *Sinhala Bauddhaya*, April 25, 1925.

68. *Gihi Din Chariyava* (Daily schedule for laypeople), in Guruge, *Dharmapala Lipi*, 31–46. It went through nineteen editions between 1898 and 1958. Dharmapala sometimes referred to the text as the "Gihi Vinaya" in his diaries (August 12 and 14, 1918), but he also used the title *Gihi Din Chariyava*.

a Funeral House," "Rules for Bullock Drivers," "Sinhala Dress," "Sinhala Names," "What teachers Should Do," "What Servants Should do," "Conducting Festivals," "What Upasakas and Upasikas [lay devotees, male and female] should do at Temples," "How Children should behave towards Parents," and "Life Cycle Practices."

The following is a summary of Dharmapala's advice on cleanliness and clothing. Both were key elements in his campaign to reconstruct Aryan conduct and allow Sinhalas to deal with the British from a position of equality.[69] I have added categorical headings in brackets. Over 40 percent of the two hundred rules relate to cleanliness and clothing:

1. [How meals are to be taken] Wash face and hands and sit properly before eating. [p. 32]
2. When you are eating with others, don't stick your hand in the serving plate.
3. Mix rice with curry and carefully move the food into your mouth.
4. Don't open your mouth before the ball of rice reaches your mouth.
5. Once the rice is in your mouth, chew it without noise.
6. Don't talk with rice in your mouth.
7. Don't swallow rice without masticating.
8. Don't wash your hand with the plate you have eaten from. If there is no other vessel to clean your hand, take permission from others and go outside to wash your hand.
9. When you are taking your meal, keep a small towel or handkerchief on your lap.
10. When you are taking your meal, don't exhale loudly.
11. With that small towel or handkerchief you can wipe your lips and hands, but not your nose and face.
12. If someone else has cleaned their face or lips with a towel, don't use it yourself.
13. Use forks and spoons without noise.
14 In your left hand take the fork and spoon in your right hand.[70]
15. After taking your meal, don't smack your lips or lick your fingers.
16. Don't bite your nails.

69. I have renumbered the items consecutively, but I indicate the page breaks as they fall in *Dharmapala Lipi.*

70. Eating with the hand was the traditional practice, but Dharmapala preferred Western cutlery for the reconstruction of Asian culture, and cleanliness and Western propriety may have recommended fork and spoon to Dharmapala, their foreignness duly noted.

17. Rinse your mouth after eating.

18. Don't take food while standing or walking.

19. When you are drinking water, don't make the sound "buzz, buzz" and don't drink water left by someone else.

20. When drinking water, you must be seated.

21. When taking meals, you must be dressed suitably. Don't come to the table in an *amude* [loincloth]. [p. 33]

22. Aryans made betel packets out of areca nut, cinnamon, *ingurupiyali* [a tasty root], *velmi* [a vine that produces a sweet liquid], lime, and *kasturi* [musk]. You should not include tobacco.

23. Don't spit betel juice near your doorway or on the highway and don't chew betel on the train or in the vihara.

24. It is not good to chew betel more than three times a day. Don't chew when working or writing correspondence or hearing a discourse on Dhamma.

25. Students should not chew betel. Don't spit betel juice in front of people.

26. Don't take lime and apply it to your mouth. Apply it to the betel leaf.

27. Don't apply the lime remaining on your finger to your chair or to a doorframe.

28. However poor, you should not wear dirty clothes.

29. Underwear should be 2½ yards long. If the cloth is sweaty, don't wear it. You can have five yards of cloth, so you can make two cloths and wear them alternately. The banian you wear, the shirt, handkerchief to wipe your face, towel, the pillowcase where you rest your head while sleeping, the towel you use as a napkin, and bedspread should be washed after two days' use. This you can do in your home. You can bathe wearing your underwear. Aryans never bathe exposing half the leg, nor exposing legs and genitals [*rahas pradesha*]. After cleaning your body, don't wear dirty clothes. [p. 34]

30. [Lavatory] The body should be washed daily.

31. Face, hands, legs, armpits [*kesili*], chest, back, and private parts should be kept clean.

32. Don't allow fingernails to grow and hairs to grow in your nose.

33. Don't talk when you go to the lavatory. Don't inhale the air in the lavatory. When you go to the toilet, don't allow urine to be mixed with feces.

34. When feces are mixed with urine, the air becomes poisonous. After using the toilet, wash well.

35. After using the toilet, wash your hands with soap or clay.

36. You should not urinate in public places or in front of other people.

37. When walking on the road, don't chew betel and tobacco.

38. Don't expose the body completely when walking on the road. [p. 35]

39. [Public meetings] At a public meeting or when a Dhamma sermon is made, don't approach with unclean clothes or exposing the body.

40. You should attend a meeting wearing clean clothes, covering your whole body by wearing a coat or an *uturu saluva* [a scarf of two yards of cloth worn around the neck with national dress]. If you don't have those items, cover your body with a *lensuva* [large handkerchief] or towel.

41. Smoking, chewing tobacco or betel, spitting, and clearing your throat should not be done in public meetings.

42. A speaker should not chew betel and spit or wash with water after using betel or clear the throat when delivering a speech. [p. 36]

43. In meetings you should not scratch private parts and arm pits. Take your handkerchief and clean face, eyes, nose, and lips.

44. [Wives] When your husband is at home, ask him how he is [*suvaduk*]. Keep water for ablutions to wash face and hands and offer a clean towel to wash his face and then offer food.

45. Keep the house clean, furniture, glasswear on a daily basis. Clean the cobwebs. Remove leaves and roots from the garden. When the garden is like a forest, sweep and clean it. Everything should be kept clean. Keep the bathroom clean always. A vessel must be kept in the bathroom filled with water. Polish brass lamps, other lamps, brass boxes, and spittoon daily. You should act like a mother towards your servants. Ask about their health. They must be convinced to clean their own clothes. The housewife should see to all of these tasks.

46. You should rise before your husband. Make your ablutions and instruct servants to clean themselves, allowing them to do the work assigned to them. Make preparations necessary for your husband and have your meal after his meal. Rest for a while and think of the virtues of the Buddha.

47. Don't raise swine or poultry in your house. They are dirty animals. [p. 37]

48. The [woman's] jacket/blouse should cover your body completely—breasts, stomach, and back.

49. You must wear a sari or an *osariya* [Kandyan sari], having a length of five yards.

50. When what you wear becomes unclean, you must wash it.

51. Don't comb your hair in front of others or pick lice from your hair or comb.

52. Don't expose your mats, pillows, and clothes in the sunlight where people on the road can see them.

53. When addressing children, don't call them "*yakkha*" [demon] or "*yodaya*" [giant] or "*pretaya*" [spirit who eats dirty things] or say "*nodakin*"—"I hate to see you." Talk to them in loving language.

54. Don't spend time chewing betel.

55. The husband's torn clothes or sarongs should be stitched during the day. [p. 38]

56. Induce your daughters to wear the Kandyan sari which is good-looking.

57. Straw hats should not be worn or Portuguese frocks and short blouses [for sari tops].

58. [Children] Before the sun rises, get up and do ablutions. Put on clean clothes and do anapana meditation [breathing meditation] in seated position [like Lord Buddha]. That gives a brain wash and things will remain in your mind well.

59. In the school house, you should not spit.

60. Tobacco, cigars, and betel should not be used. You should not use bad words and dirty language.

61. [Lay supporters] The dana offered to monks should be clean and tasty. Chillies, dried fish, salt, fish, spoiled meat, and beef should not be given to monks. [p. 39]

62. [Travelers] You must be careful to spit betel juice while traveling on a train. [p. 40]

63. Don't spit in the train.

64. Don't expose your body like Veddas while traveling.[71]

65. Don't chew betel and spit in train stations.

66. Don't dirty the benches in the stations.

67. [Village protection societies] These societies should look to cleaning the house of the villagers, cleaning compounds, and encourage villagers to unite against communal enemies [*anya jatika saturu senaga*]. [Our] lost culture should be brought to life again. [p. 41]

68. [Funeral houses] The cloth suitable for a funeral is not black but white, consistent with Sinhala culture.

71. Veddas are the aboriginal people of the island.

69. The air blowing at the funeral place is toxic to the body. Once you return from that place you must wash your body and wear clean clothes.

70. It's not good to take food in a funeral house.

71. [Bullock cart drivers] Clean the manger and give necessary food to your oxen. [p. 42]

72. [Sinhala dress] The clothing worn by Devanampiyatissa, Dutugemunu, and great Parakramabahu was a cloth worn over the legs, the upper body covered with another cloth. All used a turban for the head. During the time of Dutugemunu, Sinhalas had cut their hair short and wore a turban. They did not wear the sarong, trousers and combs worn by people at present. They wore a white cloth and covered the upper body with an *uturu saluva,* and wore their hair short.

73. Don't expose the body like Veddahs wearing a loin cloth.

74. Don't wear only a sarong like Coast Moors [*hambaya*].[72]

75. Don't wear trousers like the Portuguese.

76. Don't wear the head comb like the Javanese in Batavia.

77. Don't wear a hat made of rolled cloth, a comb, a colored tie, an undershirt or vest banian [*mes banian*] or a shirt.[73] Don't collect all of these things and wear.

78. [Teachers] Wear clean clothes, avoid tobacco, cigars, alcohol, and eating beef and the meat of dirty animals that eat excreta [pigs and chickens].

72. It is not clear here whether Dharmapala is hostile to sarongs themselves or wearing one without a shirt. A diary entry is helpful: "At Kelaniya before upasakas/upasikas I addressed on the observance of ancient Sinhalese Customs and wearing Sinhalese costumes. It was unanimously decided to discard the Cambay & Sarong. Down with the Hambankarayas [Coast Moors]" (March 7, 1898). The Coast Moors were expatriate Muslim traders from the coast of South India who appeared in Lanka in the nineteenth century. Dennis McGilvray, "Arabs, Moors, and Muslims: Sri Lankan Muslim Ethnicity in Regional Perspective," *Contributions to Indian Sociology* 32 (1998): 433–83.

73. An exchange between Dharmapala and a second Buddhist leader suggests another reason beyond their Western origins why he disliked hats. They are unclean. At a Colombo reception following his return following his internment, Dharmapala skipped the expected words of thanks and immediately began to quiz the audience on their knowledge of Dhamma. He reminded the monks to discipline their senses and excoriated the laypeople for their ignorance of the Buddha's teachings. He then turned to the president of a Buddhist society, asking him to lend him his hat. "It was an old pigsticker, a popular headgear of the time. [Dharmapala] would open the rim and demonstrate to the audience a thick layer of dirt that had accumulated there. How can a Buddhist leader think clearly if he carried so much dirt on his head, he asked amidst roars of laughter." Senator A. Ratnayake, "My Personal Recollections," *Ceylon Daily News,* September 17, 1965.

79. Children should be taught to wear clothes completely covering the body when in school.
80. [Servants] The clothes you wear should be cleaned by you or someone else. [p. 44]
81. In the place where you work, keep the house and furnishings clean.
82. [Conducting festivals] During festival days related to ancient Sinhala culture, wear clean clothes and leave aside foreign culture.
83. Poor travelers and beggars should be treated with food and clothes.
84. [Buddhist laypeople] In temple compounds you should not spit, smoke, chew betel, wear shoes or hats. [p. 45]

Summarizing Dharmapala's list, Obeyesekere fixes on the minute regulation of everyday life, characterizing the list as a code of conduct for an "emerging Sinhalese elite."[74] He interprets that code as "an aspect of the larger process. . . . Protestant and Western norms have been cathected and assimilated as pure or ideal Sinhalese norms."[75] Some of the Western norms are recognizable, but they could just as well be called upper-class Sinhala norms, and some—such as the instructions for chewing betel and bathing in one's underwear—speak to entirely local practices, not Western ones. I would link those rules—as well as the remaining 60 percent—not to Protestantism, its Weberian interpretation, or rationalization as such, but to a civilization model of the Eliasian sort. Looking over the 116 rules I have not enumerated, I cannot find any that has a specifically Protestant reference. "Don't walk on the road swinging your arms" surely does not have much to do with Protestantism, and it has no relation to rational behavior other than the act of rule giving itself being a form of rationalization. If this is Buddhism being Protestantized, the list should be made of sterner stuff.

Calling these rules Protestant or rationalizing attaches a descriptor to recommendations of diffuse origins and motivations. For all the talk of Protestant rationality, Catholicism has been much more committed to rule giving and not usually seen as a vehicle for rationality (and Dharmapala's education was largely in the hands of Catholic teachers, not Protestant ones). For that matter, the key to Protestant rationality was not as much the production of rules as the reduction of life to a single rationale, such as "live your whole life as if a prayer." I would characterize the list as a product of

---

74. "Religious Symbolism and Political Change in Ceylon," 72.
75. Decades later, Gombrich and Obeyesekere argued that Dharmapala did more than speak to an inchoate village elite. He "created" that elite. *Buddhism Transformed*, 211.

his lifelong concerns with cleanliness and bodily modesty, Victorian ideas about health, desire to impose the rule-bound discipline of Buddhist monasticism on laypeople, and hopes for an Asian civilization revitalized through self-discipline. The goal was not rationalization on the Protestant model; the goal was showing Sinhalas how to be more civilized (so that in "forty years" they could win the benefits of self-rule in both senses of the word).[76]

BRITISH BUREAUCRACY

In 1905 Dharmapala learned that the colonial secretary had spoken ill of him to Solomon Obeyesekera, passing along gossip regarding his efforts to block the construction of an Anglican church near the Buddhist sites at Anuradhapura. Unwilling to leave the rumor unaddressed, he wrote the colonial secretary, offering a brief report of his life and characterizing his actions in defense of his religion and ethnic community. He added a phrase that is now emblematic: "I have to be active and activity means agitation according to constitutional means."[77] The government of Bengal likely learned of his political views in 1904 when he wrote a letter to a Calcutta newspaper, followed by an article.[78] He soon broke from the Buddhist Theosophical Society and established the *Sinhala Bauddhaya*. In October 1906 he made a preaching tour of villages in the Southern Province in the company of Harischandra Valisinha, attacking the evils of arrack and advocating temperance.[79] In Hiniduma—where his father was born and the Hewavitarne family owned a rubber estate—he stayed for a longer time, making plans for a school and a Buddhist temple; as the *Journal* noted, "The Jesuit Padre will find henceforth a Buddhist centre working to counteract his pernicious influence."[80] The following month he returned to Calcutta, where he spent two and a half years before returning home to make a pilgrimage to Anuradhapura, give lectures, retrace his steps to Hiniduma, and then returned to Calcutta again six months later. He lectured frequently on those trips back

76. Stephen Prothero has argued that Dharmapala's code was not an attempt at laicization and was inspired not by Calvin and the sixteenth-century reform tradition but by Olcott. "Henry Steel Olcott and 'Protestant Buddhism,'" *Journal of the American Academy of Religion* 63, no. 2 (1995): 297. I think he is right on the first count, although I see no evidence of Olcott's direct influence.

77. *Return to Righteousness*, liii–lvi, at liv.

78. *Indian Mirror*, September 24–25, 1904.

79. Abhayasundere, *Brahmachari Walisinghe Harischandra*, 146–200;"The Society's Educational Work," *Journal of the Maha Bodhi Society* 3 (1913): 73–74.

80. "Anagarika Dharmapala," *Journal of the Maha Bodhi Society* 14 (1906): 159.

home, but the occasions were arranged virtually on the spot, so attendance could be uneven. His regular articles in the *Bauddhaya* gave him more of a presence than his physical presence.

Absent an event comparable to the Indian Mutiny of 1857, the colonial government did not see the need to translate Sinhala or Tamil newspapers. But officials kept their eyes on events, and the government agent in the Southern Province took steps to derail Dharmapala's plans in Hiniduma:

> Heard that the Govt: Agent is come. He has frightened the poor villagers not to bring the procession to Hiniduma, and if they do come not to have toms-toms beaten when nearing the R.C chapel. He has referred to me being present and has called me a "fire brand." I told the people that I am willing to die, that I am prepared to go to jail and that I am prepared to spend money if anything happens to the procession. (Diary, October 17, 1906)

If any of his *Danagatayutu Karanu* articles received government attention, it should have been the piece entitled "The Country of the Sinhalese Should Be Governed by the Sinhalese."[81] The problem was that the chief representative of the Crown and his chief legal advisor did not know exactly what to make of him or his pronouncements. The governor took Dharmapala for an extremist but a negligible one until he wrote another article attacking the English people. Reacting to the article in the *Bauddhaya*, the attorney general concluded, "This seems to me the language of religious fanaticism and not of sedition." The governor thought otherwise: "Is the A.G. aware of who Anagarika Dharmapala is and his antecedents. He is stirring up sedition under the veil of religion?"[82]

Dharmapala knew he was under scrutiny but continued to write articles for the *Bauddhaya* with his customary intensity. He wrote from Calcutta, so when the government of Lanka brought libel charges against the newspaper, it could not lay hands on him. When a judgment in favor of the prosecution forced the paper's closure, he traced official displeasure to neither religion nor politics. He thought the attorney general had brought charges because of a single word:

---

81. *Sinhala Bauddhaya*, September 1911.

82. *Return to Righteousness*, lvii. Where Curzon dismissed the Indian nationalist movement because its leaders spoke in a religious idiom (which was thus not political by his definition), Curzon's colleagues in Lanka could not make up their minds whether Dharmapala's agitation was religious or political.

In June 1914 an event occurred that necessitated my staying away from Ceylon. The Govt of Ceylon had brought a libel suit against the Printer of the Sinhala Bauddhaya, my own organ, based on one word I had used in my weekly article to the paper. The Sinhalese word . . . waeda connotes business and this word I used in writing about the social ethics of the European. My enemies in Colombo gave a forced interpretation to the word and urged the Ceylon Govt to institute legal proceedings. (Sarnath Notebook no. 4)[83]

He telegraphed the Lankan government of his willingness to return to stand trial. He was not called, and the printer was convicted. Dharmapala's mother wrote him to keep away from the island for at least two years because the European community was "up in arms agst [him]." When World War I broke out, followed by Buddhist rioting against Muslims in the island, the government had additional reasons to question his loyalty. Internment followed, restricting his movements to Calcutta from June 1916 until December 1917.[84]

From that point on, Dharmapala was characterized by the government of Lanka as a seditionist and looked upon "with the greatest disfavour and suspicion."[85] Against the backdrop of World War I, his ties to Buddhists in Germany and Japan acquired geopolitical significance. The government of Bengal wrote to the Lankan government that

he was the instigator of a scheme for sending young Sinhalese to Japan for technical education in the belief that the students would return with

83. As he wrote elsewhere in Sarnath Notebook no. 4, "Had I not gone to Chittagong in June 1914 I would not have written the article in the 'Sinhala Bauddhaya' which had only one word that offended the European Community. The word was 'business.' It was an English noncommissioned officer who told me that so long as the wife satisfies her husband he does not care anything about her chastity. Seven years after this came to my mind and I wrote about it in the article." His concern with British sexuality reflects both the concerns of a renouncer and his obliviousness to the political climate in which he lived.

84. Dharmapala often described his internment as lasting five years, calling it "imprisonment." He was never imprisoned, traveling around town in an automobile he owned during the period. The five-year figure refers to the period when the government of Lanka prevented him from returning home. His letters to Louis Conductor, who worked at the Hewavitarne estate, are his most forthcoming statement on being interned: "August 23, 1919, The government tried to destroy me . . . having imprisoned me for five years. Due to the power of Dhamma I did not die. Nothing came of my writing the King. They do not deliver my letters. Therefore I suffer continuously. . . . I have never done anything wrong to anyone any day. My mind does not allow me to beg for help. Asking for such a favor is a disgrace to Dhamma." Quoted in Ganegama Saranamkara, *Jatiya Piya ha Anagarika Dharmapala* (n.p., n.d.), 99–102, at 99.

85. "Sedition in Ceylon," June 7, 1916, British National Archives, FO/371/1220/111070.

anti-British views. . . . It would appear that the German Indian Party
contemplate working through the Japanese and that the Party relies on
Dharmapala to play an important part in the scheme.[86]

By January 1917 the agent who ran the Criminal Investigation Division at
the British consulate in Japan produced a fanciful account of Dharmapala's
part in that scheme.

Dharmapala Buddhinour was, I believe, in Japan in 1914. . . . He is said
to be well acquainted with a number of influential Japanese in Tokio
and elsewhere and is credited with being the head of a movement directed against British rule in Ceylon. He is said to be receiving supplies
of arms and ammunition from Japan and elsewhere and to have secreted
a large quantity on the Island. . . . The only information regarding Dharmapala in my possession is that he is a person whose arrest is urgently
required.[87]

The government of India soon put him at the center of a global conspiracy of Indian nationalists linked to Germany and Japan:

In Japan Dharmapala a Buddhist Priest who placed golden statue in
Gaya temple and who has already been to Japan is expected to make
another journey and visit the Mikado and Okuma and confer with Buddhist bishops/stop/ He is asked to take Lajpat Rai as his helper in Japan/
stop/ As soon as Dharmapala arrives in Japan money and fuller propaganda being sent there/stop/ Dharmapala will communicate with Berlin by following addresses S. Brahmachari care of Swami Bodhananda
Vedanta Society New York/stop/ Bhupendra Nath Datta will also communicate messages to him/stop/ In Siam Prince Chandradatta a brother
of late King and collegue [sic] of Dharmapala to be used to influence
King/stop/ In Ceylon Priest Sumangala should be persuaded to join in

86. *Return to Righteousness*, lx. Don Carolis established a fund of Rs. 30,000 shortly before
his death to send Buddhist youths to Japan for technical training. Wright, *Twentieth Century
Impressions of Ceylon*, 478. Having seen a number of technical schools in Japan, Europe, and
America, Dharmapala began to send students to Japan to acquire industrial skills as early as
1906, using his father's money to support U. B. Dolapilla's studies of textile manufacturing
from 1906 to 1911. When Dolapilla returned to the island, he taught at Dharmapala's Rajagiriya
School, and Dharmapala sent four more students to study in Tokyo in 1914. "Notes and News,"
Journal of the Maha Bodhi Society 22 (1914): 209–10.

87. "Dharmapala Buddhinour," March 31, 1917, British National Archives,
CO/54/809/16998, Foreign Office correspondence.

with Dharmapala/stop/ Arms/stop/ These to be bought not in Japan but from Chinese revolutionaries who get them from Japan/stop/ Only Chinese agents to be used in transmitting messages to German Minister Pekin/stop/ Efforts are also being made from Persian Afghan side/stop/ Important that too drastic executive action be not taken on this information owing to risk of my informant's identity being found out/stop/ It is likely that instructions and letters to German agents in India and elsewhere will be conveyed to them in thin glass tubes fused at both ends tubes are about two inches long and may be very secretly carried or sent/ends/[88]

The errors here are legion. Dharmapala made no trips to Japan after 1913, he never met the Mikado, Hikkaduve Sumangala had died in 1911, and Lala Lajpat Rai was not his "helper" or collaborator. However much of the intelligence is preposterous, his internment began one month after the telegram was sent.

After the 1915 riots Dharmapala's brother Edmund was imprisoned for inciting violence against Muslim traders, dying in prison before it was discovered that allegations against him were likely untrue for reasons of chronology. Dharmapala believed that he was being interned on equally flimsy grounds, writing that "when I was young the British officials did not suspect me, and now in my old age that I should be interned and suspected and watched is rather shocking."[89] "When the war broke out and there was a temporary run on the Savings Bank," the government blamed him for sins of omission: the *Sinhala Bauddhaya* (and the *Sinhala Jatiya*) failed to publish the government's "reassuring note," even though he was neither the editor of the paper nor present in the island. It characterized the typical agitator as "very frequently a disciple of Dharmapala's, who undoubtedly is principally responsible for starting and first preaching the doctrine of 'removal of the foreigner.'"[90] The "foreigners" Dharmapala wanted removed were Muslim merchants, recently arrived from the coast of India. Even when he attacked British officials, he insisted on his innocence:

88. May 16, 1916, British National Archives, CO/54/807/ 23266. The register prefaces this telegram from the government of India to the government of Lanka with a cover letter that characterizes the information as "interesting and concrete" and "of especial interest to Ceylon," confirming its reliability by quoting Dharmapala himself, who in a previous letter to the government of India had volunteered that he was "engaged in an important work in India."

89. Dharmapala to the attorney general, August 21, 1914, quoted in *Return to Righteousness*, lxi.

90. British National Archives, FO/371/1220/ 37091.

True that I criticize in my articles the officials; but my loyalty to the British Throne is as solid as a rock and I have invariably expressed sentiments of loyalty to the King. But I love my religion, and Sinhalese Race, and my happiness depends on their welfare.[91]

He criticized British bureaucracy and expressed his loyalty as a subject, attributing official disdain for him to bureaucrats' not understanding his love for Buddhism and the Sinhala people.[92]

Dharmapala wrote to the king in 1913 from China, introducing himself as a Buddhist missionary, working for Buddhists in Asia, especially Lanka, and fixing his complaints on British bureaucrats. The handwritten letter emphasized the indifference of those bureaucrats to his people: "The Government ignoring the wishes of the people for industrial education, only pass laws to repress crime, but they do not care to investigate into the causes."[93] "Discontent is everywhere to be seen in the island," he added. "The English officials rule with a rod of iron, the revenue collected from the people is not spent for the people's welfare." He offered his views of the British dilemma in Lanka in a tone that was informative and helpful, a Danagatayutu Karanu from a citizen to His Majesty. He assured His Majesty that his people were

> a loyal people, and they are absolutely loyal to your Majesty. But it is not to be expected that the Sinhalese will see in every Englishman in Ceylon the personality of the King, and this is what every white man that hails from a British colony or from Great Britain expects from the native Sinhalese.

He concluded with a tangle of figures and a proposition: take Lanka under your gracious protection lest the "historic race" die out or be converted into a race of coolies to work as slaves on British tea and rubber plantations.

Seeking royal favor required moderation, but even after his brother died

91. *Return to Righteousness*, lix.

92. British law of the time spoke only of "subjects, naturalized subjects, and denizens," the idea of "citizenship" not developing until the coming of the British Commonwealth of Nations. Despite the absence of the "citizen" idea from British common law, Indians of Dharmapala's time were worrying over the logic of citizenship and spoke of their being citizens before the emergence of any notion of an autonomous nation-state. Banerjee, *Becoming Imperial Citizens*, 5.

93. "Complaint against Administration," September 24, 1913, British National Archives, CO/54/768/33250.

in prison, Dharmapala continued to write temperately to British officials, Governor Chalmers, the government of Bengal, and the censor in Colombo. "Sent letter to the Governor of Ceylon," he noted in his diary on July 9, 1916. "I have done all I could to show that I have no malice agst the British, but the bureaucrats are not satisfied." He purchased war bonds and sent the governor a thousand-rupee contribution for the poor after his internment had ended (Diary, July 7, 1919).[94] He sought royal sanction for the temple he was building in Calcutta, hoping that "all controversies will be stopped" (Diary, February 24, 1920). When Maharajah Tagore asked him to provide bhikkhus to bless the Prince of Wales, he did so and earned the abuse of radical Bengalis (Diary, November 21 and December 23, 1921). Even when he spoke of self-government, he understood it in moderate form: "The Ceylon republic. The Sinhalese Commonwealth to be self governing like New Zealand" (Diary, October 30, 1919).[95] When his brother relayed the governor's insistence that he not participate in public affairs, he said what he always said: "Foolish Governor. He does not know that the mind is free, that even gods cannot stop its operation" (Diary, December 10, 1919), framing his compliance in terms that were both doctrinal and imperial:

I wrote to my brother "Hence forth my tongue will not utter one harsh word against the British. By love I shall conquer the British heart. You may tell the Governor that the MBS will henceforth be an ally of the British through Good & Evil. We cannot exist without their help, and our duty is to give them the Good Law. I hope the MBS will be reorganized under the patronage of the governor." (Diary, December 11, 1919)

Assuming that the first sentence was intended, at least in part, facetiously, the shifting tone—sarcasm yielding to his speaking forthrightly in

94. "The 2461st Anniversary Celebration of the Parinirvana of the Tathagata-Buddha at Calcutta," *Journal of the Maha Bodhi Society* 25 (1917): 97–107. "The Anagarika Dharmapala as Trustee of the Mrs. T. R. Foster Fund has invested Rs. 18000/- in War Bonds, and requested the Dewan of His Highness the Maharajah of Baroda to buy War Bonds for the sum of Rs. 5000/- and the Dewan has written to say that the Maha Rajah Saheb has agreed to do so. The Anagarika has also further invested Rs. 9000 in War Bonds of the Vihara Fund. Last year on behalf of the Maha Bodhi Society he contributed Rs. 1000 to the Carmichael War Fund" (102).

95. He said the same thing in a letter to the secretary of state for the colonies in a letter of July 1916: "I had asked the people to educate their children, so that forty years after when the present government leaves the world, the children might enjoy the happiness of self-government under the British Crown, similar to the government of New Zealand." British National Archives, CO/54/801/36713/1916. Dharmapala's forty-year projection was fixed not by independence, which came in the late 1940s, but the Buddha Jayanti, the twenty-five-hundred-year anniversary of the Buddha's life in 1956.

the following sentences—captures Dharmapala's ambivalence. It was exacerbated by moving in and out of the island, subject to the will of one colonial government and then another. India and Lanka were ruled by distinctive colonial systems, and those governments treated him in distinctive ways. After the 1915 riots the government of Lanka asked Bengal for his internment, and Bengal complied. But the British imperium moved forward unevenly. During his internment he had congenial interviews with administrators in Calcutta.[96] Two days before he was interned, the Archaeological Department added another complication. In March he had visited Sir John Marshall at his quarters at Saraikala near where he was excavating Taxila. The government of India informed him the following June that it was prepared to present a Buddha relic to the society if a suitable building for it could be built at Sarnath.[97] In other words, the government of Bengal sent him two messages in the space of a few days that would leave anyone confused, the first relaying a message from the government of India offering him a relic, the second interning him at the request of the government of Lanka.

Even the incidents that look revolutionary have their nuances. At the Widiyawatte temple in Lanka, he spoke to a crowded audience and promised them svaraj in five years (Diary, May 9, 1921). But achieving self-rule required Sinhalas to reform themselves, not to take political action—"The unity of the Sinhalese Race. The low country Sinhalese to dispose of the comb."[98] A decade later he spoke of independence twenty-six years in the future, tying it to a millenarian moment:

> May the people of England accept the Dhamma. May the Dhamma spread throughout the world. May my death take place at Isipatana. May the MBS become a useful body to spread the Dhamma throughout the world. May the Sinhalese become righteous. May they get their independence in the year 2500 of the Buddha's parinirvana. (Diary, April 19, 1930)[99]

96. Whatever suspicions the government of Bengal held about Dharmapala, he had no record as an agitator in India, and the government had its hands full with Bengali agitators.

97. Letter no. 1022, Gen. Dept., Miscell Branch, cited in Kahawatte Siri Sumedha, *Anagarika Dharmapala: A Glorious Life*, 17.

98. High-ranking low-country headmen of the time wore the tortoise-shell comb in their hair, having gathered and tied it at the back of their heads.

99. Dharmapala made frequent references in his diaries of the 1920s to his imminent death, estimating how old he would be at the Buddha Jayanti in his next life. His object was to meet the Buddha Maitreya and receive his *vivarana* (permission) to advance on the path to nirvana, following the same exchange the historical Buddha had with the Buddha Dipamkara when he took permission from his predecessor.

The Buddha Jayanti was the propitious time for independence. But even then he saw independence as part of a continuing connection between England and India:

> We don't wish to sever our connection with the People & King of England; but we do desire that we shall be allowed to live according to the traditions of our race governing according to our immemorial law under the leadership of our own Council paying tribute to the Crown of England, whose representative will be an English man fresh from England without colonial and India experience. (Diary, November 10, 1919)

Two distinctions are key—first, between the actual Englishmen who rule the colonies and "the People & King of England, " and second, between those bureaucrats he detested and the ones he hoped for, newly arrived and unprejudiced.

This web of distinctions is just one of the narrative conventions that make reading Dharmapala's intentions difficult. He believed that he had a right to criticize the empire's administration, excusing his ferocity by repeating that he was loyal to the Crown and loved the British people. In an entry dated shortly after the 1915 riots, he recognized the ripeness of the moment:

> For 24 years in India I did nothing evil to anybody except good. Started all good work in the name of the Lord Buddha after 700 years of oblivion. Now an evil time has come for the Buddhists. When all Sinhalese Buddhists are being punished it is foolish to expect immunity in my case. I am prepared to face death fearlessly. A powerful Govt like the British, when it is spending 3 to 4 millions daily to kill people, how easy it is to destroy a worm. I have never engendered disloyal or treacherous thoughts against the British Throne. I have found fault with the administrators for passing such laws as are injurious [word obscure] the Sinhalese people. If the officials resent honest criticism they are at liberty to crush me. (Sarnath Notebook no. 53, September 4, 1915)

Elsewhere in that notebook, he reviewed his life in a more comprehensive way:

> Gave up worldly life & took up the life of the Bodhisat. 34 years I spent in India. First the Buddhists were against me because I began to criticize them. The bhikkhus were against me. Wherever I went I have worked for the public good. I have spent my father's wealth in opening schools,

in going on missionary work, in visiting Buddhist Countries, in building rest houses for Buddhist pilgrims, and so on. I have spent Rs. 3 lakhs
of rupees for Buddhist public work. I have been a critic of all kinds of
shams. I have criticized the British bureaucrats and the British settlers
for their arrogance. I have held up the Ceylon Moor as an example of industry & thrift [sentence obscure]. But I was never seditious.

Besides saying that he had criticized everyone—it is the job of the public
worker—he preempted a charge of sedition, and when he praised Coast
Moors for their industry and thrift, he failed to add that those Weberian
qualities allowed them to exploit his own people.

Another characteristic that makes his public statements problematic is
their moving back and forth between a religious register and a political one.
He regularly used the figure of "slavery" to capture the degraded condition
of South Asia. In some contexts "slavery" is tied to being a political subject,
as when he told the Welshman that his criticism of British administration
was not any different from Lloyd George's Limehouse speech.[100] On a train
in the American South, a man tried to strike up a conversation by asking
whether Dharmapala was a subject of King George. Dharmapala wanted
nothing of it, and made no reply. The man asked again, and eventually he
wrote a sentence in his notebook for the man to read: "I am the subject of
nobody." He used the same imagery in public addresses and clarified what
he meant in his diary:

> England the dumping ground of the continental refuse. The Jew, the
> Welsh, the Pole, Russian, Swede, German becomes a naturalized En-
> glishman and he becomes a tyrant later on. . . . The English Jew Mr.
> Henry who met me in New York . . . said that he is an Englishman, and
> when I asserted my individuality said he is a Jew! The New York Acad-
> emy of Political Science when I said in my lecture on English Rule in
> India that I am a subject of nobody, cheered and applauded. Ah, for the
> noble freedom I have gained by my studies of Pali. (March 13, 1904)

From Mr. Henry's perspective, his reply to Dharmapala's insistence on his
own individuality is symptomatic of the historical moment and the process

---

100. Lloyd George gave the 1909 political speech in what had been London's original China-
town, giving rise to the expression "limehousing" for incendiary political speech and abusive
language. Dharmapala had discovered incendiary speech before 1909, but the analogy with
Lloyd George is dead on.

that separated citizenship from religious identity.[101] Dharmapala's views are harder to rationalize, but his speaking in a religious register is clear. From his perspective, Henry could not be both a Englishman—that is, a full-fledged citizen of England—and a Jew (which was precisely what the emancipation of religious minorities entailed, beginning with Macauley and realized in 1845 under Peel's Tory government). Dharmapala's conclusion does not follow logically, but it follows Dharmapala's logic, moving from the political to the religious. Freedom and individuality, he thought, depend on a higher form of liberation, "my studies of Pali."

"Slavery" is what happens to a person who submits to the authority of another person. It can happen in setting up a household, as in Dharmapala's efforts to find quarters in London:

> In the evening G. A. de Soysa called. He had been to Wales where he had given lectures on Buddhism. I told him about the house which we are going to occupy not as tenants independently but as subtenants of another man, and after consideration that I do not think it is proper to be under somebody. We must have perfect freedom and individuality of our own. Soysa concurs. (Diary, January 10, 1926)

He used the expression "slavery" in a religious context, saying that Christianity was a religion of slaves, because of its ritualism and the hegemony of the clergy.[102] In castigating the lethargy of Asian nations, he spoke in a political idiom—"slaves they were content to remain under diabolical Albion"—but he glosses that situation with a Buddhist referent: the law of change has begun to operate, and Sinhalas will awaken from their slumber (Sarnath Notebook no. 4). He repeated the "slavery" figure in a *Sinhala Bauddhaya* article urging readers to contribute to the London vihara. If they did not contribute, they were slaves, oblivious to how valuable is the happiness of liberation (*sukkaya vimukti*). In other words, liberation references a religious condition, and happiness comes from seeking liberation in ways that counteract compliance or inactivity.

The blurring of meanings had unintended consequences, enabling the British to discipline Dharmapala and latter-day commentators to see him

---

101. Visvanathan, *Outside the Fold*, 6–8. As Visvanathan has it, "That the Anglicization of Indians was crafted from the same political philosophy that advocated the emancipation of religious minorities in England establishes Macauley's colonizing mission of humanistic education as the international counterpart in his domestic revision of criteria for citizenship" (6).

102. "My Impressions in England and America," *Journal of the Maha Bodhi Society* 34 (1926): 268–78, at 268.

as a forefather of political independence. Guruge takes the same figures—
slavery, individuality—I have discussed and uses in a purely political way:

> The Anagarika was convinced that no nation could be great unless it
> was politically independent. "When a nation is politically dependent on
> another nation the weaker nation loses its individuality. A subject race
> could not produce heroes" (p. 396). "As slaves no social or economic pro-
> gress is possible. . . . If a nation that is able to supply their own wants
> finds themselves handicapped by the obstacles that are set forth by a
> superior race, no progress is possible" (p. 400).[103]

I would read that passage against the background of Dharmapala's approaching politics in interpersonal terms—in this case, master and slave—while
emphasizing that Guruge's interpretation is widely accepted. The "slavery"
Dharmapala references resonates with its opposite. In most contexts that
opposite is not political independence but self-discipline.

Dharmapala did not eschew Sri Lankan independence altogether, and he
made public speeches that were more provocative. He regularly stretched
his views to fit his audience—in Japan, encouraging Japanese ambitions in
other parts of Asia, while understanding those ambitions as economic, not
military—and his views changed over time. But they certainly did not become more revolutionary as he aged.[104] To make the case for his embedded-
ness in the British imperium is not to deny his anti-British speeches and
writings. It seems fair to call him a "fiery nationalist" and acknowledge
the torrent of vituperation that he unleashed on the British. The "fire" goes
without question. The "nationalism" is harder to weigh out, but I would
say that he was a nationalist to the extent that he wanted to recuperate
the Sinhala nation, less of one in the sense of being committed to independence, and certainly not a nationalist who could imagine armed struggle.

---

103. *Return to Righteousness*, lxxi.

104. Wickremeratne, "Annie Besant." Wickremeratne characterizes Dharmapala's politics
as consistent with the Lankan elite of his time—inspired by nationalist agitation in India, but
anxious that Indian nationalists were moving too fast, and thus more comfortable with Gokhale
than Tilak—and concludes that his politics became more radical after 1914 (71). I would say just
the opposite. Government officials in the island did not know what to make of him. The inspec-
tor general of police argued for denying Dharmapala's right to address public meetings after he
returned home in 1920. The governor thought otherwise: "He is a man of no account now. He
has no influence. . . . Prior to 1915 he was a mob leader and a man to be watched closely." Vimal
Weerasinghe, "British Attitude to Anagarika Dharmapala," *Sunday Observer*, September 17,
1983.

His internment in 1916–7 gave him practical reason to moderate his tone, and declining health in the 1920s made it hard to be as impassioned as he had been as a younger man. When he delivered his first address in London in 1926, the chair introduced him by saying that Dharmapala would speak sitting down. But recounting his education at the hands of missionaries caused him to stand and brandish his walking stick.[105]

When he spoke of self-rule, he saw it as a challenge requiring religious as much as political reform. He never contemplated policies for an independent Sri Lanka, never thinking through, for instance, the future position of Tamils and Muslims relative to the Sinhala majority. His thinking was shaped by specifically South Asian concerns often obscured by the hybrid elements in his life. Where Gandhi saw his own self-disciplining as the foundation of the political struggle, Dharmapala wanted the Sinhala people to reform themselves as a prelude to political self-rule. He had already disciplined himself. He was not headed where he wanted his people headed. He was a brahmacarya; they were not. Without recognizing his understanding of the empire as an interactive system, the invocation of his desire to "serve Humanity," and the otherworldliness of his own goals, it becomes that much harder to understand why a Sinhala nationalist in the last years of his life would have moved to the capital of the empire. His decision to spend that decade not at home but in England and India opens up another question—how to balance his nationalism with his alienation from other human beings. The contrast with Dharmapala's fellow South Asian ascetic and reformer makes a start. Imagine Gandhi spending his last years in England or wanting his remains kept in Sri Lanka.

BRINGING BUDDHISM TO THE BRITISH

In 1926 Dharmapala moved to London with the intention of spending two years establishing the sasana and building a vihara. Always a hypochondriac, by the 1920s he had reason to worry about his health. His behavior changed in London too, angry confrontations with arrogant and presumptuous Anglo-Indians replaced by moderation and references to the "Buddha of Love" (Sarnath Notebook no. 4). Almost four decades earlier, while assisting Leadbeater, he noted that the older man had said to him that the climax of Vesak (the Buddha's birthday) would be reached when a vihara was built

---

105. F. Yeats-Brown, "A Buddhist in Bayswater," *Journal of the Maha Bodhi Society* 34, nos. 4–5 (1926): 221.

in London (Diary, July 18, 1925). Listening to another Theosophical worker in Colombo, he got the idea of training five monks for missionary work (Diary, August 7, 1889).[106] He repeated that hope regularly, writing of his plan to missionize Europe and America (Diary, May 8, 1891). When he visited Burma in 1900, he told the Burmese of his desire to establish a Buddhist center in London (Sarnath Notebook no. 53). In soliciting support for the London vihara, he pointed out that "Moslems have a Mosque in Paris and at Woking," praising their initiative. Those mosques—the one in Woking and an Ahmadiya mosque built later in Wimbledon—were meant to serve diasporic Muslims. He would give Buddhism to the British themselves. They had brought their civilizing mission to Asia; he would reciprocate by placing a vihara among the mosques, making Buddhism and the civilization it epitomized visible to the British.

World War I had cut his European plans short—he wrote in his diary that "in 1914 I thought of going to England to preach the Dhamma there. War came and the Indian Mirror wrote against me. I was interned" (June 20, 1924). His diary jottings from that period pick up the persecution theme. All the same, what he called persecution did not deter him. It furnished another motivation for spreading the Dhamma in England:

> For five years I was not allowed to return to Ceylon and during the period of my internment I had to go through various kinds of physical suffering. Want of exercise, and proper diet broke down my health, and after five years I found that I was the victim of sciatica, beriberi, palpitation of the heart and anaemia. For no cause I was punished, and yet I made up my mind to send thoughts of love to the British bureaucrats who were responsible for my internment. Instead of hatred, compassion sprang up in my heart to the British people. . . . I decided to come over to England and work for the establishment of Buddhism there. In my Diary, of 4th August I have made the following entry. "Ceylon and England can never again be divided. I shall therefore work for the welfare of the British people. England should not treat India like a wife-beating husband."[107]

While he was interned, he wrote a similar note in the upper left-hand corner of Sarnath Notebook no. 58: "Love those who injure you." He foresaw a series of projects.

---

106. Five is the number of monks required to robe a young boy as a novice or to confer higher ordination.

107. "Buddhism in England," 549–50.

The future work that I wish to do I note down here. The building of a Vihara at Sarnath, Benares, the printing of the Pali texts in Devanagari, building a Vihara in Madras, preaching to the people in England, and erecting a Vihara near Stone henge. (Sarnath Notebook no. 23)

Nothing more was heard of Stonehenge, but he sailed from Calcutta in 1925, spending the summer in a Swiss sanitarium. He then toured Europe, crossed the Atlantic, and took a train across the United States, where he fell ill in San Francisco and was hospitalized with hemorrhaging, before he retraced his steps to England.

He was not the first Buddhist missionary in England. That title goes to R. J. Jackson, who announced that he was a practicing Buddhist in 1906 and began to preach the Dhamma on a soapbox in Hyde Park.[108] A British soldier who had served in Burma and gone on to establish a Buddhist bookstore in Bloomsbury helped Jackson in establishing a Buddhist Society. They were joined by Allan Bennett, ordained in Burma as Ananda Metteyya.[109] When Bennett returned to England in 1908, he began to preach and convert people (although he was a native returning home to missionize), and he admitted a handful of Britons as Buddhists.[110] In a few years the number of converts and interested persons reached 150, and the group devoted itself to public and private meetings and publishing the *Buddhist Review*. The society languished during World War I and was revived in the years that followed with financial support from Dharmapala and his brother Charles.[111] Membership was composed of both scholars and practicing Buddhists—Captain J. E. Ellam, Francis Payne, Caroline Rhys Davids, W. A. de Silva, and D. B. Jayatilaka.[112] Many of the leading lights of the Buddhist Society died in the early

108. William Pieris, *The Western Contribution to Buddhism* (Delhi: Motilal Banarsidass, 1973), 6.

109. Bennett had moved to Lanka initially to practice Buddhism. Christmas Humphreys writes that Bennett would have been ordained there but for the fact that "ordination into one of the principal sects would automatically exclude him from free intercourse with those of other sects." *The Development of Buddhism in England* (London: Buddhist Lodge, 1937), 14. The same sectarianism characterized the Burmese monkhood absent caste prejudices.

110. Olcott learned in 1890 that a Committee of Burmese Buddhists had raised Rs. 20,000, asking him to lead a preaching mission to Europe. He declined on the grounds that the delegation would lack English. *Old Diary Leaves*, 4:272. Murphet, however, says that Olcott discouraged the delegation for another reason, thinking that Buddhists should unify themselves and agree to a common platform before spreading their religion. *Hammer on the Mountain*, 143.

111. Humphreys, *The Development of Buddhism in England*, 40. Charles Hewavitarne later provided the money to buy a cemetery plot and gravestone for Ananda Metteyya (45).

112. Humphreys, *Sixty Years of Buddhism in England*, 10–12. Dharmapala's diary suggests his continuing Theosophical interests and intention to utilize his Theosophical connections

1920s, and the group was supplanted by the Christmas Humphreys's Buddhist Lodge of the Theosophical Society, which maintained a shrine room for Buddhists in Hyde Park.

During his European tour, Dharmapala telegraphed Humphreys of his interest in joining forces. The institutional home of the Buddhist community in England having Theosophical interests did not put him off. For good reason—Dharmapala was himself still a Theosophist. During his convalescence in Switzerland, he told Humphreys that "he was a member of the Blavatsky Association and was quite sure that there would be many English Theosophists willing to receive the Buddha Dhamma at his hands." In July 1926 he founded the British Maha Bodhi Society, saying that the society would work with Humphreys's group in complementary ways—the society providing public lectures and eventually the services of several bhikkhus, while confining itself to the Buddhism of Lanka; the lodge "paid an equal attention to the Mahayana and even studied other religions in the light of Buddhism."[113] By the time of Dharmapala's arrival late in 1925, the Buddhist Lodge of the Theosophical Society was near death, soon to be reborn as the Buddhist Lodge.[114]

"October 11th. Crawled to Lodge from bed of flu to find three members and five others—no quorum. Position desperate. We have eleven members, three in Portsmouth, three duds, and the remaining five all needed for a quorum." The remedy was at hand. "I then proposed that we leave the T.S. Agreed with cheers." . . . Thus was born the BUDDHIST LODGE, LONDON.[115]

---

to spread the Dhamma: "I have only one idea now in mind, i.e., to spend 2 years in England in carrying the Message of the Lord Buddha to the European people. The Mahatmas through HPB have paved the way. There is a Buddhist Society and the HPB Association and there are English Buddhist Theosophists. May I live a few years to sow the seed of the Dhamma. If we could erect the Arama [retreat] somewhere near Hampstead Heath it would serve our purposes. . . . I shall try to visit the different Theosophical branches in Great Britain & Ireland and also in Spain, Holland & Germany etc." (Diary, October 12, 1925).

113. Christmas Humphreys, "History of Buddhism in the West," *Journal of the Maha Bodhi Society*, 54 (1946): 76.

114. Humphreys, *Sixty Years of Buddhism in England*, 27.

115. When the lodge got back on its feet, it practiced an eclectic Buddhism, elsewhere referred to as *navayana* (new Buddhism). In a book explaining Buddhism to Westerners, Humphreys characterized the book's authorship and content as similar to the Buddhist Lodge itself: "The whole book is a in fact a compromise. Compiled by a group composed of many minds, of either sex, both Schools of Buddhism and a dozen nationalities, it is the 'common denominator' of many, often conflicting, points of view. Based though it is upon the Thera Vada [*sic*] point of view, it borrows from the Mahayana sufficient of its principles to make once more of the whole

Dharmapala thought that Humphreys was an unreconstructed Theosophist (Diary, December 5, 1926), and Humphreys assumed the same of Dharmapala on the basis of his having told him that he was coming to England as a member of the Blavatsky Association "to see through it the spread of such teachings as were given by H.P.B. as she received them from the Masters."[116]

In an earlier letter Dharmapala characterized Buddhism in a way Humphreys would not recognize, as both ethnic and imperial:

> It is too bad that although Ceylon Buddhists have been friends of England yet no attempt has been made to enlighten the English regarding the Dhamma. If Ceylon Buddhism dies it would be a calamity. I think the danger could be averted with the help of British Buddhists. During the time of H.P.B. British Theosophists went to Ceylon and worked with the Buddhists. Since her death the bond has been loosened.[117]

Humphreys stuck with Theosophy: "It is clear that the Anagarika came as a Buddhist Theosophist." Humphreys wrote in his diary, "Wanted: a personality," thinking that Dharmapala would play that role and assuming that he would be willing to work under the auspices of the Buddhist Lodge.[118] Dharmapala's motives were nationalist in an indirect way, and they were equally imperial and universalizing. The British needed to strengthen their ties to Lanka for everyone's benefit, Britons and Buddhists, the metropole and the periphery. "If Ceylonese Buddhism dies, it would be a calamity" for the world at large.

Humphreys had quite a lot in common with Dharmapala. Both were committed to Madame Blavatsky and her two favorite mahatmas.[119] Both

---

the complete philosophy for daily needs which the Buddha gave the world." *What Is Buddhism?* (London: Buddhist Lodge, 1928), x. In his last years, Dharmapala proposed other expressions for the Buddhism he had in mind: "We now have to preach the Sambodhiyana Doctrine to Buddhists and non-Buddhists. It is called the Maha Bodhi Yana in the *Cariya Pitaka*" (Diary, May 12, 1930).

116. Humphreys, *Sixty Years of Buddhism in England*, 22.

117. Quoted in Humphreys, *The Development of Buddhism in England*, 57.

118. Humphreys, *The Development of Buddhism in England*, 57. Humphreys writes that he had been interested in Buddhism since he was seventeen, joining the Adyar Theosophical Society in 1920, and continuing his "studies of Buddhism on the wider basis of its all-embracing platform." But he felt compelled to include details of his own religious evolution because "the part I have played in the Buddhist movement in this country can never be divorced from the Theosophical background against which I stand." *Sixty Years of Buddhism in England*, 18.

119. Christmas Humphreys, *Zen Comes West* (Richmond, UK: Curzon 1977), 75. By 1927 D. T. Suzuki's *Essay in Zen Buddhism* had brought Zen to Western attention, and Humphreys became increasingly interested in Zen practice.

were committed to bearing the sufferings of the world, having read and been moved by Shelley's *Queen Mab.*[120] Both wanted a British Buddhism. They joined forces on a few occasions, sharing the same podium in 1927 when their organizations celebrated Vesak together. Humphreys drifted from religious eclecticism to a steady focus on Zen, and by 1927 he wanted to propagate one form of Buddhism and Dharmapala another.[121] If ideological differences were not enough, there were temperamental forces pulling them in opposite directions. Dharmapala had no stomach for working under Humphreys (or anyone else)—that would represent another "slavish" relationship, and Humphreys did not like Dharmapala's bringing out the eight-page journal he called the *British Buddhist* (Diary, October 23, 1926). Dharmapala assured him that it was meant not to compete but to serve as a vehicle of communication for Asian students living in London. The truth was that it was meant to compete.

In July Dharmapala purchased a house in Ealing to serve as Maha Bodhi Society headquarters, drawing on his money and his brother's, and by October 1926 he left for Colombo to raise money for the London vihara. Soon he was caught up in a scandal produced by Humphreys's correspondence with an American, Ernest Power, whom Dharmapala had sent to Lanka to learn Pali (Diary, June 21, 1926). When Dharmapala cut off his stipend, Power wrote to the *Ceylon Daily News*, quoting Humphreys's "unBuddhistic" letter to him, relaying unflattering references to Dharmapala (Diary, December 31, 1926). Later Humphreys offended him by taking away one-half of the property—three Buddha images and piles of publications—left behind by the Buddhist Society (Diary, May 7, 1927). Two days later Humphreys called on Dharmapala, who told him, "I will not have anything to do with people like you" (Diary, May 9, 1927). In an account celebrating the cooperation between the Buddhist Lodge and the Maha Bodhi Society, Humphreys put it kindly: "From his first arrival . . . [Dharmapala] made it clear that he had his own way of working."[122]

---

120. Humphreys, *What Is Buddhism?*, x.

121. Admitting his views were purely his own, Humphreys had a Theosophical understanding of Buddhist metaphysics, derived from Mahayana: "I am of the Mahayana, which has never been troubled with this pother of choice between Rebirth and Anatta. I pity my friends of the Theravada as they vainly mutter, 'No self, no self.' I prefer the freedom and joy of the universal process, its living unity with the Unborn whence it came." *A Western Approach to Zen* (Wheaton, IL: Theosophical Publishing House, 1971), 48.

122. *The Development of Buddhism in England*, 62. Humphreys says that Dharmapala's buying a house in Ealing was useless to the members of the lodge, who wanted a more central location, but there was advantage even there—the faraway location kept the Theravada character of Dharmapala's Buddhism at a distance.

17. Foster House, Ealing, London.

Dharmapala's nephew Daya was studying in London during his 1926–7 stay. As Daya's letter to the editor of the *British Buddhist* makes clear, Humphreys was dead set against the project:

> The Buddhist Lodge makes the following strange statement with regards to the Vihara proposition in London:—"But we have grave doubts as to the advisability of making any attempt at the moment to raise thousands of precious pounds to be spent of a heap of bricks while the only active Buddhist organization in London cannot even afford to pay for one room to be kept for purely Buddhist purposes." . . . If in the opinion of the writer a Vihara is only a "heap of bricks," I am sorry for him.[123]

During the winters of 1927 and 1928 Dharmapala made his own case for the vihara, returning to Colombo to raise support. At a meeting at Vidyodaya he argued,

123. H. Dayananda, "The Vihara Proposition in London," *British Buddhist* 1 (1927): 3–4.

The Buddha had said that "dharma dhana" [*sic*] was the greatest of gifts, but in Ceylon they did not realize that. They gave "dhana" in other ways. For instance, when an umbrella was to be presented to a bhikku [*sic*] the person who was making the presentation asked a number of others to touch the umbrella in order to participate in the merit. This was their idea of "dhana."

Not settling for one invidious distinction, Dharmapala went on to lay out what he took to be the moral failings of his own people:

> Mr. Dharmapala next referred in humorous vein to what he called the lethargy of the Sinhalese . . . [and] their readiness to ape everything that came from the West while they were dependent on other countries for everything even their food. . . . A Bombay merchant in Colombo who had made some study of the Sinhalese had remarked to him that they were like apes without originality or effort. (Voice "Give us his name!"). He could not understand why they would not exert themselves to do something in the world. Continuing Mr. Dharmapala said that the more intellectual people of the world today were found in the West and he thought that if Buddhism were preached to them it would have a special appeal because they would be able to appreciate its truths more keenly.[124]

The treasurer of the London Vihara Committee announced that Rs. 26,224 had been collected and another Rs. 9,000 promised, but Dharmapala needed more. He had just purchased a Georgian mansion at 41 Gloucester Road for Rs. 75,000, and he was paying for the passage of three monks to London. He asked the Buddhist public to see that they received their *dana* during their stay in London.

Dharmapala had other problems with members of the Blavatsky Association in London. Mrs. A. J. Davey told him that the members of the association would support him individually but the association would not support him officially (Diary, January 13, 1926). Later she advised him that England was not ready for a vihara. He complained in his dairy that she was more than ready for other gifts from Asia—"tea, coffee, polo, tennis, Chinese art works, Kashmere [*sic*] shawls, Jodhpur trousers, and even Arabian Christianity" (May 28, 1927). Davey was offended by his fraternizing with Annie Besant:

124. "Buddhism in England," *British Buddhist* 2 (1928): 1–3, at 2-3.

Mrs. Davey called at 11 AM. She showed rather an unpleasant attitude because at the City Temple I sat on the platform with Annie Besant and expressed my gratitude to her. Blavatsky Assn: Members are angry. I know that Annie Besant harbours anger agst: me; but I thought of her personality as it appeared in 1893. I said I shall send a letter to the Assn: that I did not prejudice the Cause of HPB. I told Mrs. Davey that the black magicians are in favour of Annie Besant. They are active while we are inactive. (Diary, October 7, 1927)

Even with minimal support from local Buddhists and Theosophists, he assumed he could still rely on Mary Foster—she had after all underwritten the vihara in Calcutta. In 1925 she had paid the medical bills for his convalescence in Switzerland and San Francisco, but her attorney prevented her from supplying the $150,000 he had asked of her soon after he arrived in London, telling Dharmapala, "Mrs Foster feels that she has reached the limit of her ability to give," and thus ending their relationship (Diary, January 4 and February 22, 1926).[125]

As soon as Dharmapala arrived in London, Professor Don Martino De Zilva Wickremasinghe approached him and told him that his young English wife would "be at [his] service," saying

that she will take care of me, and do my typing work and edit my Autobiography. I then thought it was rather strange of him to say all that about his wife. On the 2nd day of my arrival at his house the first thing he did was to get from me a loan of £300. . . . I am now disgusted with him. Think of the man taking his wife to a Cabaret in the company of a West Indian Negro. Poor girl, through fear she had to go. (Diary, August 13, 1926)[126]

125. When he arrived in San Francisco in 1925 to pay his respects to Mary Foster, Dharmapala found that his patron had been giving large sums of money to Indian gurus—Prakasananda, $35,000; Yogananda, $20,000; and Abhedananda, amount unknown—and to a Bengali named Chatterjee, $18,000. The uncertain reliability of these figures duly noted, there was good reason for Foster's attorney to protect her from solicitations. She was then in her eighties, living under the care of relatives in San Francisco. Dharmapala had another confrontation with Abhedananda—presumably because of his connection to Mary Foster—when Abhedananda attempted to gain control of the Calcutta vihara. One guru gave lectures on "Sex force and spiritual marriage," and Dharmapala found them all distasteful, observing, "These scoundrels do nothing but eat, sleep and cheat women by telling them how to develop their sensual nature. I starve to do good for others" (Diary, October 31, 1925).

126. Wickremasinghe was the author of *The Catalogue of the Sinhalese Manuscripts in the British Museum* (London: British Museum, 1900). Wickremasinghe was Dharmapala's age and four decades older than Vera, whom he married at seventeen, four years before Dharmapala's arrival.

He discovered that some landlords were unwilling to rent to a South Asian, and in March he suffered another attack of hemorrhaging, which put him in a convalescent home. Now he had two more reasons to join forces with the Wickremasinghes, moving in with them and receiving Vera's attention as a nurse. Hospitality was soon replaced by melodrama. Living in the Wickremasinghes' study, he found himself in circumstances not conducive to renunciation. The professor had a problem with alcohol and was on the brink of bankruptcy; Vera was flirtatious with the young Sinhalas who boarded at the professor's house, and who played the piano and danced with Vera. She told Dharmapala

> that since she first saw me she felt attracted to me; but she was afraid to approach me. She says she loves Indians & Sinhalese more than the English. She tells me that she would take care of me. By next October I shall have about £2268 in the Bank in London which I shall offer to establish the Buddhasasana in England. . . . Vera is most anxious to visit Ceylon. She brushed my hair and expressed her desire to be born in India in a Brahman family. (Diary, May 1, 1926)

The next day "Vera won [my heart] by showing great kindness" (Diary, May 2, 1926). He began to hope that she would become his "spiritual companion" (Diary, May 19, 1926).

Dharmapala was hardly blameless in these events, but the Wickremasinghes took advantage of him. As soon as he reached London, the two older men—Wickremasinghe had been born in 1865—and the younger woman made plans to purchase a house together, and money began to pass from Dharmapala's hand to Wickremasinghe's, who found convenient reasons to put off repaying the considerable amounts of money he had borrowed. He urged Dharmapala to buy a house in Ealing, making himself the coproprietor of a place that would provide their lodging, a Buddhist hostel, shrine room, and meeting space. Dharmapala noted that Wickremasinghe told him, "If I agree with his views he would join me, otherwise not" (Diary, January 18, 1926). Dharmapala thought he was more interested in solving his financial problems by taking in boarders than he was in spreading the Dhamma (Diary, April 16, 1926). Wickremasinghe refused to stop drinking and then agreed to do so; he wanted to be the coproprietor of the Foster House, then begged off, saying that propagandizing Buddhism would taint his reputation and deny him a looming government appointment (Diary, May 26, 1926). Dharmapala thought of Vera "like a little sister," gave her a pearl brooch, wrote of being besieged by *kamachanda* (lustful thoughts), while holding onto his hopes for Vera's becoming his "co-worker" (Diary, April 3; May 17, October 2, 1926).[127] Whether the Wickremasinghes' separation was unplanned or a scheme to manipulate a renouncer with huge assets, the elements of a scandal had fallen into place.

Back at home Dharmapala had problems with Buddhists that had started thirty years earlier when he raised financial support for the Bodh Gaya case. When the court's judgment went against him in 1895, they raised questions about where their substantial contributions had gone. Despite published accounts at the end of each year's run of the *Journal of the Maha Bodhi Society*, it is also clear that he commingled his own funds, Hewavitarne funds, and society funds. He had founded the Maha Bodhi Society, and in many ways he was the Maha Bodhi Society—how many charismatic leaders have not commingled funds? Even in 1926 when Wickremasinghe asked him for a loan, he contemplated drawing on Maha Bodhi Society money but remembered that he had already given a mortgage to the principal of Ananda College and changed his mind (Diary, March 16, 1926). One of his supporters had a clearer notion of the dangers of casual accounting than he did:

Here is McKechnie full of prejudice agst me. I gave him every help, but in his heart he shows no sympathy. He believes what other evil minded people say against me. This evening I told him that he could help me by going through the accounts. He then asked me in whose name is Mrs. Foster's donation is [sic] deposited in the Bank. I told in my name. He became furious. He said "This is why people blame you"! I said there is none else in London except myself and Mrs. Foster gave the money to me to carry on the work. I said the Calcutta & Colombo moneys are in the name of those who do the work. He has a very low heart and nobody supports him. He says that I abuse people. I replied that when anyone attacks our Lord I condemn. (Diary, September 3, 1927)[128]

His Colombo enemies opposed him for reasons other than his bookkeeping. People found his abrasive personality too much to tolerate, and still others were simply opposed to the notion that the British needed a Buddhist mission or that Sinhalas should provide it. Articles had already appeared in

127. Dharmapala's attitude toward Vera repeated his attitude toward Gudrun Holm, the American woman he envisioned as his "spiritual companion" during his 1903 trip to the United States—he called them both "Amara" and hoped that each would become his "co-worker" (Diary, October 2, 1926).

128. McKechnie had been ordained in Burma as Ven. Silacara, later defrocking himself and working with Dharmapala as an editor and propagandist.

local newspapers, raising all of these issues. When he learned of Wickremasinghe's plans to call Dharmapala as corespondent in divorce proceedings
against Vera, his brother called him home to avoid more scandal (Diary, December 6, 1926). A brahmacarya brought to trial for alienation of affection?

IMPERIAL RECIPROCITY

For all of his talk about wanting to work alone, Dharmapala also wanted
financial help from other Buddhists. For the sake of establishing the sasana
in England, he appealed once again to the Buddhist world. This disjunc-
tion defined his self-understanding and his problems with supporters—he
sought support from the limits of the Buddhist world while imagining that
he worked alone:

> To hold a Conference composed of all the Nikayas to adopt methods, to
> propagate the Dhamma in European countries and to establish the Sam-
> buddha Sasana in England, and America. To send a Dispatch signed by
> the Chief Priests of all the Nikayas to the Kings of Siam and Cambodia
> & to the Chief Priests of the principal Sects of Japan and to the Presi-
> dent of the Chinese republic to co-operate with the Ceylon Buddhists
> to establish the Sasana in England. To invite the leading Buddhists of
> Ceylon to attend the Conference to co-operate with the Maha Bodhi So-
> ciety to establish the Sasana in England, Europe & America. Every year
> a day should be set apart throughout Ceylon to collect subscriptions for
> the erection of the Vihara in London. The best artists to be taken from
> Ceylon to paint frescoes when the Vihara is completed. London is the
> rajadhani of the British Empire & it is proper that an imposing Vihara
> should be erected in that great city. (Diary, November 30, 1926)

Buddhist help was sporadic and small, leading him to complain time and
again that he received no help from his coreligionists. He purchased the
house in Ealing that he named Foster House from his own funds—money
from his family allowance and his brother.[129] Not getting broad financial
support had its compensations. It allowed him to embellish a central part of

---

129. Dharmapala, "Buddhism in England," 550–1. He kept the $50,000 Mary Foster gave
him in 1923 in a permanent fund. Kahawatte Siri Sumedha, *Anagarika Dharmapala: A Glorious Life*, 19. Why he did not use the Foster Fund to purchase the house is unclear, although
he wrote Devapriya in Calcutta that he was reluctant to draw on anything but the interest of
the fund.

his self-understanding; he had returned the sasana to India and spread it to England, and he had done so by his solitary efforts. "Buddha has no friends in India, neither do I," he told himself (Sarnath Notebook no. 27).

One motive for bringing Buddhism to the British was to serve the British people: "I think of the future greatness of the English people and I therefore wish to make them learn the Dhamma" (Diary, September 27, 1927). Even as he saved the British from themselves, he stressed that he was not expecting converts:

> The Buddhist religion is austere. It demands sacrifice. I doubt that many Englishmen would give up drink to become Buddhists. But we shall accomplish much if we manage to teach them what our religion is.[130]

The plan not to convert had disparate sources. The most fundamental was not wanting to re-create those missionary practices of his youth that he found so offensive. The second motivation was more instructive. He came to England with intentions more educational than religious, to teach the British about the Buddhist religion in its imperial context, not to convert them. For a Western audience, his message must have been confusing—he called himself a missionary, he preached, but he had an even more distant relationship to English people than he had with Bengalis.

Buddhism was fully suited to the British, he insisted, drink notwithstanding:

> Mr. Dharmapala said that the more intellectual people of the world to-day were found in the West and he thought that if Buddhism was preached to them it would have special appeal because they would be able to appreciate its truths more keenly.[131]

He emphasized the freedom that the renouncer seeks, sometimes shifting to the adjoining register and speaking of political freedom. He had other reasons for thinking that Buddhism matched the British temperament:

> The future of Buddhism in England ought to be a very favourable one because Englishmen are practical men and desire above all what is prac-

---

130. "First Buddhist Mission in England," *Daily Chronicle*, reprinted in *Journal of the Maha Bodhi Society* 34 (1926): 555–6. His authority to convert people aside, there are no signs of his having converted anyone after Strauss and Canavarro.

131. "Buddhism in England," 2–3.

tical; and Buddhism is a practical religion. . . . Not only is a man told
to abstain from killing and stealing and illicit lustful actions and evil
speech; but also from the taking of intoxicating liquors which predispose
a man to commit all these offences almost more than any other cause
that may be mentioned.[132]

The disposition toward drinking alcohol that Dharmapala saw in British
people brought practical consequences—all of the crimes associated with
alcohol abuse—and those consequences argued more strongly for the adoption of Buddhism. Buddhism, moreover, was as much a religion of rationality as practicality and freedom, and it was usefully distinguished from
religions that tell believers to do something because "God says they must
do so, or he will be angry with them and punish them." Buddhism offered,
he went on, a rational alternative. It was suited to the temperament of free
people.

In addressing a meeting of the British Maha Bodhi Society in the Ealing
house, Dharmapala began by invoking his Theosophical connections:

> [On] his first visit to England in 1893 . . . he was welcomed by and stayed
> in the house of Sir Edwin Arnold, and addressed Theosophical gatherings
> at the request of Mrs. Annie Besant. He added that he was also a friend
> of the late Madam Blavatsky, who first persuaded him to devote his life
> for the service of humanity.[133]

He cited a fourth rationale for his religion—"Buddhism was the religion
of love; there was no doctrine of hell in its teachings, and mendicancy"—
concluding by taking the seed of the banyan tree as a metaphor for his
project in England:

> I hope this tiny seed of the truth of the religion of love which I plant
> today among you British people will grow into a big banyan tree, of bless-
> ing not only to yourselves but to the world.[134]

---

132. "The Future of Buddhism in England," *British Buddhist*, reprinted in *Journal of the Maha Bodhi Society* 34 (1926): 601–5, at 601. A year later Dharmapala wrote in his diary, "I wish to build a Vihara which will be a kind of School of Practical Psychology" (May 16, 1927).

133. "Buddhism in Britain: Formation of British Maha Bodhi Society," *Journal of the Maha Bodhi Society* 34 (1926): 587–90, at 589.

134. In Dharmapala's time Sinhala monks did not collect food on alms rounds, and the disappearance of mendicancy is usually taken as a sign of decline. In this case I suspect that he felt mendicancy was inappropriate in London or off-putting to the British.

At the celebration of the anniversary of the Buddha's first sermon, he spoke of Buddhism as a religion of love and wisdom that "teaches us to conquer hatred by love."[135] The Buddha taught us to seek wisdom and love, and "we will enjoy all the heavenly pleasures here." A surprising strategy for reaching a Christian audience was his saying that the Buddha was no atheist—Buddha taught that we are surrounded by gods.[136]

Stressing happiness in this world and the idea that Buddhism was a religion of love, Dharmapala envisioned other uses of love as a global phenomenon. When he wrote in his diary that the London vihara would be a "conclave of the gods," including the British gods, he moved quickly to a network of connections: by allowing the British gods to take a share in the holy work, he said, "The Natives of England will come to know of the religious conditions existing in India" (Diary, February 23, 1927). Half a year later, he was still contemplating the advantages of reciprocity:

[At Foster House] I satirized the gods of different religions for their foolishness, albeit they have helped me because they know I do not mean any ill to them. Now I am asking the British god to help me to erect a Vihara for the Lord Buddha and I am sure he will help me. . . . May the British people become compassionate & help the starving millions in India. (Diary, July 15, 1927)

It is hard to make sense of the man who spent his career at home castigating the foolishness of Christianity now invoking the British god, or even what he meant by that expression. However implausible the notion that incorporating the Christian god in the vihara would make the British help the people of India, it furnishes an example of his several Buddhisms as well as his hybridity and imperial reciprocity.[137]

135. "The Dhamma Cakka Celebration in London," *Journal of the Maha Bodhi Society* 35 (1927): 577–85, at 580.

136. A curious effect of Dharmapala's Buddhism in a Western setting was melding the gods of the South Asian tradition with the Christian god. "When the vihara is completed in London I shall have a small room set apart for each of the Devatas, viz., Vishnu, Siva, Surya, Brahma etc., attached to the vihara. A follower of Vishnu will then be able to commune with him. . . . It will be a conclave of the gods. I shall invite the British gods to take a share in the holy work" (Diary, February 23, 1927). In the years after his internment he acted on his commitment to the Hindu gods, especially Visnu, whom he regarded as the protector of the Buddhasasana. His sharing merit with a myriad of gods sits uncomfortably with the idea that Dharmapala was a Protestant Buddhist. See Gombrich and Obeyesekere, *Buddhism Transformed*, 432.

137. That same year Dharmapala gave an address at the City Temple in London, praising Christianity, at least in its New Testament form. "An Appreciation of Christianity," *Journal of the Maha Bodhi Society* 35 (1927): 593–97.

What motivated the emphasis on love and Christianity was another imperial calculation because his efforts in London had as much to do with South Asia as England. During his first month in London, he wrote Devapriya, who was administering the Maha Bodhi Society in Calcutta, with instructions and news:

> Don't spend the money for the Foster Fund to construct the Dharmasala at Gaya. It is not wrong to spend the interest. It is very useful to purchase land in London. If the English people join us our country and India would receive kindness.[138]

As his two years in London went on, he fleshed out the argument about "receiving kindness," writing home to explain what he was doing in England:

> There are 5,500,000 Englishmen in this country. Not 200 of them are aware of the greatness of the Buddha. Ceylon is known for tea and rubber only. . . . Meritorious indeed to teach these Englishmen Buddhism. That would transform them to teach them in kindness.[139]

The benefits would not culminate in England. He did not want the British to be kinder to one another—after all, they were already polite, philanthropic, and civilized. He wanted them to be kinder to his own people in Lanka and India. He wanted to change the hearts of people in the metropole to benefit people in the colonies. Even when he wrote that he was doing missionary work in England "for the welfare of the sasana," he made the same point. He had envisioned reciprocity from the moment of his arrival in London; as he wrote then, "I hope my stay in England will be of service to England, India, and Ceylon" (Diary, January 14, 1926).

Sometimes he focused on British bureaucrats—by which he meant simply colonial administrators—in India and Lanka as the focus of his plans for transforming people in one place so that there might be positive effects far away; at other times, he concentrated on missionaries. Bureaucracy was the vehicle for the economic ruin of South Asian traditions and economies; missionaries were the vehicle for the destruction of Buddhism. In his first month in London setting up for missionary work, he told a young woman who showed an interest in Buddhism, "I am not come to convert the Christians to Buddhism, but to ask them to listen to the teachings of the religion

---

138. January 19, 1926, in Guruge, *Dharmapala Lipi*, 432.
139. Letter to Louis Conductor, September 6, 1926, in Guruge, *Dharmapala Lipi*, 108.

which . . . missionaries sent by them exert to destroy" (Diary, January 12, 1926). His diction is awkward for a reason—his intentions were awkward. From the first, he breathed fire on his audiences, and his harshness surely played a part in his lack of success. His harsh words for Christian missionaries had their effect on English listeners whether they sympathized with the missionary enterprise or not, but he felt that an ancient and noble civilization was at stake and his listeners obliged to stop that destruction.

> Miss Balls told me yesterday that those who come to hear me resent my criticisms. Well that it is good. 13000 British Missionaries are in Asia attacking Buddhism and destroying Buddhist ideals. There is no protest raised by the Buddhists because they are dead. The British 200 years ago were half savages. Their civilization began since the "conquest" of India. (Diary, October 29, 1926)[140]

The justice implicit in the empire striking back duly noted, his global ambitions were more than a little unrealistic, and his British audiences not likely to draw the connection between their spiritual development in England and social reform in the colonies.

Dharmapala made the argument so often—"I shall work for the welfare of the British people and when they learn to become compassionate they will help the poor people of India" (Diary, November 2, 1925)—that creating a kind of imperial mutuality was more than a sidebar to his missionary activities. It derived from the way he thought about the empire. He saw a future in which the British would become missionaries to themselves, but only after he and his followers brought Buddhism to them:

> A number of the best English educated youngmen and youngwomen from Ceylon should be selected to become preachers of the Dhamma to the people of England. They will have to follow the Sotapatti Precepts. The youngmen to marry English Buddhist young ladies, & the youngwomen to marry English Buddhist youngmen, thus to found a Buddhist Colony in England to perpetuate the work there. England has become a neighbour by means of aeroplanes. In 5 days the journey can be made by aeroplane from India to England. Sadhu! Sadhu! (Diary, November 30, 1926)

---

140. The *Mahavamsa* says that the sasana would be established in Lanka when Sinhala men got themselves ordained as Buddhist monks, but at this point in his two-year ministry, he had not brought Buddhist monks to staff the proposed vihara, nor had he converted anyone.

The "Sadhu! Sadhu!" that ends the passage is an expression of approbation made when a Buddhist participates in a meritorious act. Whether the expression here refers to air travel or the entire passage is hard to determine. The world was growing smaller in 1926, and he imagined a kind of internal colonialism by which Buddhists from England and Lanka intermarried and spread the faith in the world beyond.

During the two years he spent in London, the binary logic that dominated his thinking stretched between the British at home and the bureaucrats and civilians he knew in South Asia. It is difficult to imagine him proposing a future in which local Buddhists and British Buddhists in India would intermarry and harder still to contemplate that proposal at home, where he saw absolutely no hope for local Englishmen:

> The adventurous class of British hooligans who go to India & the Colonies bring shame on the good people of England. On account of the few bad Britishers the name of England is besmeared with dung. The British MBS will protect the people from the hooligan class. The Americans are the only people who could control the British hooligans. (Diary, October 9, 1926)

At home the British were philanthropic and polite; in South Asia, they were rapacious and cruel. His confrontations followed a long trajectory: "I have rebuked English men, first in 1887 and since then I have had to rebuke them in Lanka, Benares, Calcutta, Gaya, Tokio, Boro Bodur, USA" (Diary, June 13, 1926). But he had no such encounters in England, not during his short, early visits and not on the 1926–7 sojourn.

The assessment of one of his students, Hapugoda Dhammananda, suggests the virtues of self-assertion in a world where the British exercised control over Buddhists but seldom the reverse. He told the story of one of Dharmapala's confrontations: An Englishman approached him at a railway station, asking him, "Where are you from, Sir?" Dharmapala replied "Ceylon," and the man said, "Where is that?" leading Dharmapala to answer, "Go back to school."[141] The encounter ran its usual course, absent any sign of presumption or arrogance from his fellow traveler. In another celebratory piece Dhammananda returned to the same theme, saying that whereas Vivekananda was more comfortable in the United States than England, Dharmapala "found a more congenial atmosphere" in England than

---

141. Ven. Hapugoda Dhammananda, "Remembering the Anagarika," *Island*, September 17, 1987.

18. British Maha Bodhi Society, London, 1929. Back row, far left, Devapriya Valisinha. Front row, center: the two novices Devapriya escorted to London, Matara Pannasara and Hagoda Nandasara.

at home. Dhammananda attributed that comfort to the presence of the Pali Text Society, Rhys Davids, and Sir Edwin Arnold, and then added another explanation:

> Nationalism however important it may be is yet a prejudice and a barrier against free thinking and it was predominant in [the] Anagarika at home while in countries abroad he was naturally free from such sentiments. He was in an international atmosphere, with an audience more educated and more enthusiastic. He was much more at ease to deliver his message.[142]

By the mid-1920s, Arnold and Rhys Davids were dead and the Pali Text Society in the hands of Caroline Rhys Davids, whose relationship with Dharmapala had turned sour—these connections were broken and did not recommend England to him. But Dhammananda may be right for other reasons—Dharmapala got on better with foreigners and in foreign places.

However congenial London might have been, Dharmapala knew he was

142. "The Flame in the Darkness," *Weekend,* September 11, 1988.

alone. He could not believe that other Sinhalas did not share his commit-
ment to spreading Buddhism in the West: "One day in London is better that
100 years in a land of slaves. It is a pity that Buddhists do not appreciate the
work of giving the Dhamma to Westerns [sic]" (Diary, September 23, 1926).
During his stay in London, his isolation from his own people increased:
"Over a hundred Sinhalese students are in London. Only one or two visit"
(Diary, June 26, 1927). Leading Buddhists passed through London—G. P.
Malalasekera, W. A. de Silva, and D. B. Jayatilaka—and they avoided him.
Then again, he did not feel any more solidarity with Buddhists in England
or Lanka. When he wrote, "It is not possible to work with Budhists [sic].
They are agst Buddhists and the Hinayana," he was thinking, I suspect, of
Humphreys as a Buddhist who, he thought, was against Buddhism. Caroline
Rhys Davids might also qualify—someone in principle favorable to Bud-
dhism (Diary, May 10, 1927).[143] She was convinced that the Buddhist texts
came not from the mouth of the Buddha but from scholarly monks. Equally
bad, she was wrong about the nature of *anatta* (no-soul).[144]

A year and a half after his arrival in England, Dharmapala saw how
things were going to turn out:

> The London Buddhist Mission is going to be a failure. The Vihara can't
> be built without my money. Burmese Buddhists are not giving to help us.
> The poor Sinhalese Buddhists are willing but they are unable to raise the
> required amount. Mrs. Foster has gone to live with her relations. I don't
> know what help she would give our work in the near future. The Sarnath
> Vihara must be built. . . . I shall keep my promise even at the risk of my
> life; but after July 1928 I am free. If by that time I am still alive I shall
> return to Sarnath and till death I shall work in India & Ceylon. I should
> like to visit Ireland & Scotland. (Diary, June 13, 1927)

Before he left London, he purchased a house on Gloucester Road, and Devapriya brought Palane Vajiranana and two samaneras from Colombo, install-

143. By the 1920s Dharmapala had moved beyond "Southern" Buddhism, but he still was
not calling the Buddhism he professed Theravada.

144. In a diary entry of February 24, 1926, Dharmapala laid out the deterioration of his relationship with Caroline Rhys Davids: "Until 1922 she showed her great sympathy for Buddhism.
After the death of her husband the true personality of Mrs. R.D. came out. She then became an
open foe of our Lord." He used the *Journal of the Maha Bodhi Society* to attack her, beginning
in 1924 with "Buddhist Philosophy," 32 (1924): 101–4; "Notes and News," 33 (1925): 357–8;
"My European Tour," 34 (1926): 70–76, at 75; "The Unknown Co-Founders of Buddhism," 36
(1928): 67–71.

ing them in the new vihara. He returned to Colombo in fragile condition, and his health deteriorated with major downturns in June 1929 and early 1930. Bad health did not prevent him from making a final move, however, as he left Colombo for India in March 1931, carried in a chair to the steamer. He had already sent eight samaneras north to Bengal to be trained up as missionary monks by Ven. Dhammalokatissa at Bolpur (Diary, March 31, 1930). His pessimism regarding the London vihara was not entirely fair. He had not won the support of many English people or changed the conditions of life in India and Lanka. But he established a place for the first missionary monks to reside in the West, and they continue to serve Westerners.

CHAPTER SIX

World Wanderer Returns Home

Backbiting is the religion of the Sinhalese.
—Anagarika Dharmapala, Diary, March 10, 1930

Olcott's universalism depended on a commitment to equality, and what he preached of equality, he practiced. In Japan he resisted the hegemony of the Honganji establishment, insisting that he would not proceed until all eight Buddhist sects agreed to sponsor his visit. When monks favored a seating arrangement that would place them according to the founding date of their sects, Olcott's knowledge of monastic rules led him to an alternative. He asked the monks to seat themselves relative to the year of their ordinations.[1] Rank remained visible, but sectarian division did not. In Lanka he found that Kandyan monks would not cooperate with low-country monks for a different reason, caste prejudice. Hoping to convince monks of various monastic communities to hear his plans for pan-Asian Buddhist unity, Olcott knew he first had to address disunity in the monkhood. He made the best of it, seating each group in adjoining rooms, asking the monks to communicate through a wide doorway.[2] Before a crowd of Buddhists, he ceremoniously drank a glass of water served to him by a low-caste headman.[3] His example did not spread, and it had no effect on Dharmapala, whose interest in Theosophy was epitomized by his joining the Esoteric Section, Olcott's commitment to brotherhood aside (Diary, January 4, 1891).

1. *Old Diary Leaves*, 4:114–5. The Theravada Vinaya pays no attention to the seniority of monastic communities and ranks monks by the date of their ordination. Whatever the Japanese practice, Olcott's approach may have appeared to Japanese monks as less the imposition of a South Asian practice than an example of Olcott's imperiousness.

2. *Old Diary Leaves*, 2:200–03.

3. *Old Diary Leaves*, 6:185.

When Olcott wrangled government recognition of the Buddha's birthday as a holiday in 1884, Sinhalas began to carry the celebration into the public sphere. Vesak brought forth the display of the new Buddhist flag and the singing of carols. In Panadura, a caroling procession enacted Olcott's universalism in the form of "a faithful and true representation of the various Buddhistic nations":

> The singers comprised 12 choristers, walking two and two, each couple dressed in special costume, and representing an adult and a boy, of the Indian, Burmese, Siamese, Chinese, Japanese, American, and the British people respectively. The leader who helped and led the singing, was appropriately dressed in the costume of an up-country Nilame (gentleman).[4]
>
> The leader of the party, the up-country Nilame, chanted a song in praise of Lord Buddha, which was taken up by the foremost line. . . . The chant was concluded with a song to a Hindustani melody, the last verse of which purports thus:—"Let us worship the holy feet of the chief sage (Muni) who has taught and declared the great 32 blessings; and may long life, health and happiness, be unto Colonel Olcott for helping to make the Full Moon day of the month of Wesak a Government holiday, wherein to exalt and spread the glory and virtues of Omniscient Buddha."
>
> Then the party divided into two opposite lines, facing each other, with the space of a few yards between them. Then both ranks with the first line of each verse faced sidewise to right and left; with the second line of the song, advancing till they met each other in the centre, shaking hands each with another of a different race to shew the Buddhistic unity in faith.[5]

Global unity choreographed in the low country was practicable; getting Kandyan aristocrats and Siyam Nikaya monks to support the call for monastic unity was another thing.

Olcott put two projects at the center of his program: reforming Bud-

---

4. The leader's Kandyan dress is as interesting as the celebration itself. Whether the man dressed as a Nilame was a Kandyan who happened to be living in the low country—with a traditional right to wear the costume—is unclear. In the case of his being a low-country Buddhist, this procession was one of the first occasions where low-country Sinhalas appropriated the highly charged forms of Kandyan culture, surely to the dismay of Kandyan Buddhists. Over the next decades low-country Buddhists were to insert themselves into affairs that Kandyans felt was their prerogative. Blackburn draws on an 1868 diary kept by a low-country official. It mentions Hikkaduve Sumangala being greeted by laymen, "some dressed after the Kandyan style." *Locations of Buddhism*, 80.

5. Two Buddhists, "Buddha's Birthday in Ceylon," *Theosophist* 9 (1888): 622–6, at 624–6.

dhism and consolidating Buddhists. Those were goals that Dharmapala took seriously, but he had little interest in fostering equality among Buddhists and even less in carrying on Olcott's interests in creating a common platform of Buddhist belief. His experiences in Japan may have convinced him of the impossibility of finding common ground—certainly his encounter with Chigaku Tanaka had that effect. Having grown up in Lanka, he was more realistic than Olcott regarding the prospects for reorganizing the monkhood and reducing caste hierarchy. His family's close relationship to Hikkaduve made it impossible to ignore the contention between low-country Goyigama (farmer caste) monks and Kandyan monks, which entailed contention between low-country Goyigama laypeople—such as the Hewavitarnes—and the Kandyan aristocracy.[6] How to bring Kandyan monks into harmony with the monks of the newly assertive low-country caste groups complicated matters. This is a problem he did not tackle. Instead he railed against the lethargy of the monks and their lack of discipline and learning: "It is difficult to find even five monks from Ceylon who are pious and learned. The sasana is declining due to impious monks."[7]

It is also true that Dharmapala established the Maha Bodhi Society as caste-free and nonsectarian. But he took no interest in addressing the arrogance of birth that lay behind the distinction between the Siyam Nikaya and the low-country Nikayas. His concern for the monks' misbehavior overrode concern for the corruption enabled by British legislation that dissociated colonial rule from Buddhist affairs:

> Today in Lanka there are monks who cover one shoulder, both shoulders, and neither; who shave and do not shave their eyebrows; who wear belts; who carry silk umbrellas; who have short hair and shave their beards; barrister monks who carry leather bags; who eat from plates; who eat from bowls; immoral monks who hang around restaurants and courthouses; immoral monks who practice medicine and astrology; immoral monks who teach science like medicine to young laymen; immoral monks who have taken to socializing; immoral monks who associate people unworthy of doing so; monks who pompously use the letter "sri" (before their names) and who practice "sri" more than adhere to

6. For Hikkaduve's dilemmas in dealing with fellow monks of various caste origins, see Blackburn, *Locations of Buddhism*. The predominance of the Hewavitarne family and Hikkaduve must have given the Maha Bodhi Society a Goyigama character, the more so because of Hikkaduve's involvement in the Goyigama-Karava caste controversy of the 1860s and 1870s, (78–90).

7. Guruge, *Dharmapala Lipi*, 22.

morality (*sila*); monks who do editorships of magazines for the sake of money with a layman as the frontman; and monks who deposit Rs. 4000 in the bank account of their acolytes.[8]

The mismanagement of Buddhist temporalities was the issue of the day. Other lay groups—the Ceylon National Congress, the Buddhist Congress, and the International Buddhist Brotherhood—pursued monastic reform throughout Dharmapala's later life.[9] Kandyan aristocrats and monks reacted to this intervention as presumptuous—the more so because low-country Buddhists were behind it—and began to speak of Kandyan home rule once the British went home.[10]

If ever there was one overbearing low-country layman who took up one reformative cause after another, it was Dharmapala, but reforming the monastic system was one battle he never joined. One goal outweighed all others—regaining Bodh Gaya. His lesser goals came and went. The projects that attracted what remained of his attention—building Buddhist temples in Calcutta, Sarnath, and London—took his focus away from his own country. At first he regarded his Indian projects as more important than his Lankan work, writing in his diary, "Mazumdar thinks I should give my time to the Ceylon work. He thinks India work less important!!!" (July 19, 1893). A decade later, stymied by difficulties moving his project forward at Sarnath, he felt different.

> As soon as . . . the land is purchased from Raghu Vir Singh I shall entrust the work of the school to Viggars and go to the thrice sacred land where my ancestors worked for the good of the Great Religion. Ceylon is the *agga khetta* [great field]. (Diary, August 21, 1904)

Behind that change lay his fickle temperament and habit of coping with disappointment by moving immediately to the next project, shuttling back and forth between India and Lanka.

---

8. Guruge, *Dharmapala Lipi*, 114, quoted in Seneviratne, *The Work of Kings*, 38–9.

9. See "Welcome to Congressmen," *Ceylon Daily News*, December 19, 1925; "Buddhist Protest," *Ceylon Daily News*, December 24, 1925; and "Seventh Buddhist Congress," *Ceylon Daily News*, December 29, 1925.

10. "Kandyans Want Home Rule," *Ceylon Daily News*, January 31,1927. The previous year Kandyan chiefs had sent a secret memorial to the government, claiming that only signatories to the 1815 convention, which is to say, only Kandyan aristocrats, had any rights to negotiate with the government regarding Buddhist interests. "Kandyans and Temporalities," *Ceylon Daily News*, November 26, 1926.

What most of his plans had in common was bricks and mortar. The building focus can be seen in a list of projects he contemplated while interned in Calcutta:

1. Building a hostel
2. Building a Vihara
3. Gaya Town School
4. Infant School
5. Start Printing Press & Paper
6. A Pali Class
7. To erect the Isipatana Mausoleum[11]
8. To purchase land at Sarnath for a garden
9. The employment of a Preacher (Diary, January 1, 1916)

The man who wanted to leave the world built or owned an extraordinary number of buildings in this world, and the projects that succeeded were usually ones that involved putting up a building.

The projects he thought were important included both material initiatives and more abstract ones. Another list speaks of "ventures":

I ventured to obtain knowledge when I was 20 years old. HPB stood by me in 1884. In 1889 Jany: the 2nd venture, I made the 3rd venture at B. Gaya. In 1892 the 4th venture in starting the MBJ, in 1893 the 5th venture in going to USA in 1895 the 6th, the BG Case; in 1896 again started to USA, in 1898 made the 8th century in the Rajagiri Psychological College; in 1902 the industrial venture the Weaving School, the 11th venture the "Bauddhaya"; 12th venture in 1908 purchased the Baniapuker lane house; the 13th Home Rule venture in 1911, in 1913 the 14th venture, the Foster Memorial Hospital, the Vihara in 1915. (Diary, February 20, 1920)[12]

What he meant by "venture" produced a list different from his other lists of accomplishments, all of them evidence of the power of diary keeping to enable a conversation between the "I who writes" and the "I that gets

---

11. I presume that he intended the mausoleum as his own. If so, the mausoleum provides an early example of his intention to have his ashes interred in India.

12. What Dharmapala means by the "Home Rule" venture of 1911 was his speaking for Lanka's achieving semi-independent status. See Chapter 5.

written."[13] Seeking knowledge by renouncing the world, he acted in a South
Asian way. By keeping a diary, he sought knowledge in a more Western form.

DHARMAPALA AND THE MAHA BODHI SOCIETY

Dharmapala established the Maha Bodhi Society in 1891 with an international board. It was not a board of Sinhala Buddhists interested in either
converting India or uniting Asian Buddhists.[14] The board was composed of
distinguished Asians—people he had met on his travels—called together to
help him. Hikkaduve Sumangala was appointed president, Olcott the director, and Dharmapala served as general secretary, the same office he held in
the Theosophical Society. The balance of the board was made up of Buddhists such as a prince of Siam and people he had met elsewhere in Asia:
Shaku Unsho, the Oxford-educated Japanese monk, and S. Horiuchi, the
secretary of the Indo-Busseki Kofuku Society, the temperance society that
served as Dharmapala's first contact with Japanese Buddhists. There were
representatives of branches of the Maha Bodhi Society in Rangoon and Calcutta, which he had already established, and one other Sinhala, G. P. Weerasekera. The original members of the Maha Bodhi Society, by contrast with
the board, were all Sinhala Buddhists: "Dullewa Adigar, D. C. Hevavitha-
rana, Jeremias Dias, Pandit Batuwantudawe, M. Dharmaratna, Richard Silva,
Wlm de Abrew, Don Carolis, P. Weeragama, CPG [C. P. Gunawardana], JR de
Silva, RA Mirando were elected members" (Diary, May 31, 1904)—family,
family friends, and fellow Theosophists predominating.

Among the interests he took from Theosophy was the notion of humankind itself, a Kantian community of all people. He said as much early and
late—"Charu Babu wrote that I should sell Rajgir and come to Calcutta!!!
To me all the world is the same" (Diary, August 29, 1898) and "The world
was my home" (Diary, April 10, 1926). Elsewhere: "Under a tree or a roof
of a house, is all the same. Just a place to lay my head is all that is wanted"
(Diary, October 7, 1891). "I was a world-wanderer for forty years with no
place to call my own," residences at Aloe Avenue in Colombo; 2 Creek
Road, Baniapukur Lane, and 4A College Square in Calcutta; a meditation
retreat in Colombo; a house in Ealing on the west side of London; a house-

---

13. Roberts, "Himself and Project," 128–9.
14. Nalinaksha Dutt, "The Maha Bodhi Society, Its History and Influence," in *Maha Bodhi
Society of India: Diamond Jubilee Souvenir, 1891–1951*, ed. Suniti Kumar Chatterjee (Calcutta:
Maha Bodhi Society, 1951), 66–133, at 68–9.

become-seminary in Kandy; and Maha Bodhi headquarters at Sarnath not-withstanding.[15] In both diaries and other writings, he wrote of "saving Humanity," and his choice to live his life away from his native place itself suggests that same orientation. Even at home, he sometimes spoke not of serving Sinhalas but "saving the world" (Diary, August 29, 1898); in San Francisco he wrote, "To me the whole world is like my own country. I work for Humanity" (Diary, April 13, 1903). My sense is that his self-understanding as a world renouncer and his homelessness were driven more by his desire for solitude and independence than a focus on humanity. As a boy, he spent his most precious moments alone in his father's garden (Sarnath Notebook no. 53). Because his father moved him from one school to the next—he was enrolled at eight schools—he made few friends and had little chance to keep them. But he says nothing of having friends, losing them, or wanting to have them.

Diary keeping gave Dharmapala a tool to shape and reshape his experiences. He writes about painful incidents, later returning to each indignity and his response to them, and those incidents are hard to ignore. One is his investment in the idea of freedom, and that idea is synoptic as well as long running. He was committed to his own freedom, and the life of renunciation followed logically. Here freedom carries two senses: he wanted to be independent of others who might control him, such as an employer, but he also wanted freedom from samsara, which begins with breaking the cycle of desire. Freedom's opposite is slavery. Dharmapala wanted to be independent of all others, and by independent he sometimes meant spiritual independence and other times meant political independence. Visiting the British Museum, he was approached by a stranger, who introduced himself as a professor of jurisprudence. After they had exchanged a few words, the professor "said that all other natives of India were serious and I was different. He asked me whether I was a British subject. I told him I am not a subject of anyone" (Diary, February 8, 1904).

In that case Dharmapala referred to freedom as a political notion, but more often he used "freedom" in a spiritual sense, as when he wrote, "I have no attachment to anything and I leave Ceylon with a freedom that gives me power. No one is attached to me and I am attached to no person" (Diary, April 20, 1898). He often employed a cook, but he dwelt on his self-sufficiency: "I am my own barber, laundryman, typist, clerk, messenger, ac-

---

15. Anagarika Dharmapala, "Message of the Buddha," *Journal of the Maha Bodhi Society* 34 (1926): 116–31, at 125.

countant, despatcher, darner, cleaner, cook, bookseller, Asst. Secy., Librarian" (Sarnath Notebook no. 58). Part of his father's motivation for moving him from school to school was the hope that a new school might spark an interest in his son to take his lessons more seriously. What he took seriously was "general knowledge," and once out of school he spent considerable amounts of time reading at the Pettah library. It was schoolwork that he could not abide: "The desire to study was not in me. I was fond of freedom and religion" ("My Autobiography," Sarnath Notebook no. 53). The word "freedom" here refers not so much to a person's political condition as the clarity of mind that accompanied ascetic renunciation; those who lack such clarity are "slaves": "My article in the Bulletin of the IR Assn. has been criticized. Slaves cannot like it" (Diary, January 17, 1921).

Freedom was tied to the solitude provided by his father's garden and the act of renunciation. But he sought solitude in the world—"I may pass away at any time. I tried to do my best for the lokasasana. I could have done better but Buddhists were bitterly hostile to me. The world was my home. I wished to spread Buddhism in non-Buddhist lands" (Diary, April 10, 1926). He believed the British were also hostile to him, and when he was interned in Calcutta, he had another form of solitude thrust on him. After the 1895 Bodh Gaya decision went against him, Sinhalas who had made contributions for legal expenses discovered that he could not deliver the temple. When he reallocated funds that remained after the decision and made no public accounting of so doing, he lost credibility with both Burmese and Sinhala contributors.[16] Those misgivings led to declining Burmese interest in the Maha Bodhi Society, but the drop-off in Sinhala support was naturally more important. These events were not the source of his sense of aggravation and isolation—they simply provided new material for a man who in childhood had come to an agonistic sense of himself operating in a world of change and disappointment.

From his youth he had a sense of his confronting overwhelming forces by himself. His favorite text as a boy was Shelley's *Queen Mab*, which he loved not for its republicanism but Queen Mab's rectitude and willingness to confront authority. A passage is worth reproducing as it appears in his 1892 diary:[17]

16. H. S. Olcott, "The 'Wail' of Dharmapala," supplement, *Theosophist* 20, no. 7 (1899): xxix.

17. Elsewhere he writes that Shelley's poem "showed Jehovah to me as a fiend" (Diary, September 28, 1925).

There is a nobler glory which survives
Until our being fades, and solacing
All human care, accompanies its change;
. . . .
The consciousness of good, which neither gold
Nor sordid fame, nor hope of heavenly bliss,
Can purchase; but a life of resolute good,
Unalterable will, quenchless desire
Of Universal happiness, the heart
That beats with it in unison, the brain,
Whose ever-wakeful wisdom toild [sic] to change
Reason's rich stores for its eternal weal
That "commerce" of sincerest virtue needs
No meditative signs of selfishness,
No jealous intercourse of wretched gain,
No balancing of prudence, cold and long;
In just and equal measure all is weighed;
One scale contains the sum of human weal
And one, the good man's heart.

The poem was more than a childhood enthusiasm, it was a call to action.

His diaries quote William Lloyd Garrison to similar effect, Garrison speaking directly to Dharmapala's sense of himself: "I will be harsh as truth and as uncompromising as justice—I will not equivocate—I will not excuse—I will not retreat a single inch—and I will be heard" (December 30, 1895). Finding a parody of Kipling's poem "Naulakha" in the *Theosophist*, he was amused enough to transcribe it (Diary, November 2, 1892).

And the end of the flight is a tombstone white, with the name of the
    late deceased.
And the epitaph drew [obscure]: a fool lies here who wanted to serve
    the east.

The notion of service in the parody is hard to overlook, but so is the undertone that the odds were against him even at the start of his public career. Three years before his disappointment over the first Bodh Gaya decision, and long before the court's ultimate decision in 1910, he set off with a sense of the unavailing character of a life lived under samsaric conditions.

The generosity of his parents made it possible for him to "give his life to the cause of Humanity" (Diary, June 16, 1897). The complication goes back to the life of the Buddha—he pursued his spiritual goals in the form of projects that required action in the world, and most of that action was collective. To make matters worse, although he wanted to achieve nirvana, "this experience I do not want to realize alone, and I want to save others" (Diary, September 29, 1896). That commitment led him to become a spiritual preacher, yet the goal of his teaching was salvation, and reaching it in the Theravada tradition requires doing so alone. He was interested in dreams and their interpretation, an interest motivated by Theosophy and travels in the West. In 1897 he had a dream—"a warning to keep my independence and to express my sentiments. The spiritual teacher must be absolutely independent" (Diary, July 19, 1897). Because he had a picture of what a spiritual teacher looked like, he avoided being seen in public with either eyeglasses or smoking material. His meager diet kept his weight down, especially in those periods when he limited himself to one meal a day. On one occasion when he ate meat, he chided himself, saying "an ascetic should not look robust" (Diary, January 9, 1907). He was anything but robust, weighing 105 pounds (Diary, September 4, 1893). Forgoing an evening meal, following a largely vegetarian diet, and smoking cigarettes kept his weight down.

As a young man he thought of himself as an old man and soon to die. Just entering his thirties, he began to long for the Himalayas:

> My system requires rest. Under the loving care of my dear mother, I will get the rest for the last time. For eleven years I have had no rest. In 1886 March I began the Buddhist work, and ever since I have not known what it is to rest. Comforts of home, loving kindness of parents, I gave up spontaneously and took up the life of the student. Day and night I worked in Ceylon for several years for the welfare of my people. India the motherland became a home to me from 1891 to 1896. To build up the MBS I had to work hard. And I made sacrifices as no man has done. From 1896 August I gave my services to the American people and in that land of luxury and plenty I lived the same sacrificing life. Eating the simplest food, wearing the Yellow garb, caring for no comforts I wandered from place to place preaching. . . . I have seen enough. . . . My mind now yearns for the Grand Lama, the only visible embodiment of living Truth. May I see him? If there is truth in me I will see his blessed face. May I get the strength and the power of the Bodhisat. (Diary, September 5, 1897)

The passage is notable for its self-dramatizing, the world-weariness as much a practicum in feelings he wanted to cultivate as a product of his own experience.

The commitment to solitude and independence was only one problem confronting his public career. He came from a family committed to public work:

Colombo had no Buddhism until the establishment of the Dharma Deepti Society. Soon after was established the Vidyodaya Pirivena. My father & my uncle & WHW Perera's father went to Galle to bring the High Priest Sumangala down to Colombo. My grandfather presented the garden at Maligakanda to establish the Parivena. Not one from outside the town came forward to help the Pirivena. Epa Appuhamy or Veda Appuhamy was the eldest of the members. (Diary, January 15, 1927)

Just as his father and uncle had established the Vidyodaya pirivena on their own, Dharmapala established the Maha Bodhi Society. It is hard to argue with his own conclusion: "The Maha Bodhi Society is my child" (Diary, September 21, 1926). Treating the society as his own "child" led to problems with both his supporters and his opponents, but it follows from his family's thinking of Maligakanda as being as much of a family affair as H. Don Carolis and Company.

The Hewavitarne and Dharmagunawardene families had kept their attention fixed on the Vidyodaya pirivena. They had donated the land, recruited Hikkaduve to take up residence, and run the Buddhist College there, remaining major benefactors of new projects long after Dharmapala's death.[18] Dharmapala had other inclinations. Just as he kept moving from place to place, he kept moving from project to project. His father, mother, and three brothers assumed roles in the operations of the Maha Bodhi Society. The men predominated, but Mallika Hewavitarne led the first organized pilgrimage of Buddhist women to Bodh Gaya, asking the women to join her in wearing the Kandyan sari. She made seven trips to North India, visiting her son in Calcutta and then traveling on to the sacred sites, and the Maha Bodhi Society became a travel agency, organizing the logistics of the pilgrimage for the Buddhist public. On one of those trips north she monitored the construction of the Dharmarajika temple in Calcutta. The brothers played leadership roles in the organization, representing it in Dharmapala's absence, and by the First World War C. A. Hewavitarne—home from

---

18. "Vidyodaya Pirivena," *Ceylon Daily News*, November 27, 1926. When a new *dharmasala* was constructed in 1927, the Hewavitarne family donated Rs. 30,000. The other major donors—Helena Wijewardene (mother of D. R. Wijewardene, Dharmapala's nemesis), A. E. de Silva, and D. C. Senanayake—each contributed Rs. 100.

London with a medical degree—became a spokesman for, and defender of, his brother and his plans to build a Buddhist temple in London.

There is nothing unique about a family playing a dominant role in an informal organization. Elite families take on similar responsibilities in many societies. But Dharmapala's accomplishments outstrip the life of a reformer running a family charity. Whether those accomplishments depended on "charisma" is a question I will not address, except to say that if the ability to recruit followers—following Weber's characterization of charismatic authority—he was hardly charismatic.[19] He was no Vivekananda. To the extent that charismatic leadership lives "outside everyday social organization," it is easy to make a case for him. He ran the Maha Bodhi Society with the nonchalance and impetuosity of a charismatic leader. He had gained administrative experience in his role as secretary of the Theosophical Society, and he included lists of subscriptions and cash flows in his notebooks and in the *Journal of the Maha Bodhi Society* on the model of the *Theosophist*. The Maha Bodhi Society was the institutional vehicle for his reformative projects, and when he left Colombo for Calcutta, soon after its establishment, the organization went with him.

Dharmapala's leadership faced other problems, often brought on by his habit of ignoring the distinction between public and private, melding Maha Bodhi Society funds with his own money as well as the financial resources of the Hewavitarne family business. Even with the highly personalistic way he managed the society, he could have skirted public criticism by keeping private funds separate from public. When Mary Foster diverted her annual contribution to the Maha Bodhi Society to support the building of the Dharmarajika vihara in Calcutta, he paid the society's expenses from his own pocket (Diary, January 2, 1919). When a bhikkhu was recruited to take up residence in India, Dharmapala offered to have the family firm pay for his travel (Sarnath Notebook no. 23). In the next breath, he indicated that his mother would oversee the construction of the vihara when she sojourned in Calcutta (Sarnath Notebook no. 23, dated December 18, 1918). The problem was that these projects required subscriptions, and the Buddhist public wanted to know who was spending their money and how.

On some occasions he could have financed a project without public help, and when Mary Foster began to make enormous contributions to him—in addition to her regular contributions, she gave him $50,000 in 1919 and $100,000 in 1923—he could have afforded to go it alone even more easily.

---

19. Talcott Parsons, ed., *Max Weber: The Theory of Social and Economic Organization* (New York: Free Press, 1947), 367.

The magnitude of Foster's gifts had effects good and bad, allowing him his independence, but also raising public suspicion. The problem was that he wanted public support but was insensitive to public opinion. Sometimes a project was completed or well under way when he made a call for support. His own substantial contributions to his causes made him more insensitive to what others thought. When his critics began to gather force in the 1920s, he held a public meeting at Dharmaraja College, making the case for public support for the London Buddhist vihara and pointing out that he had received only Rs. 8,000 for his projects "over the last so many years," while he had distributed Rs. 52,000 in Lanka.[20] Besides his own willingness to sacrifice everything for the cause, another source of his insensitivity was his conception of himself as living in a world to which he had no ties. Years before his father's death (and several decades before his mother's and brothers'), he wrote, "Today here I am without father, mother, brothers, leaving my share go to the devil; with one supreme idea in my mind to be pure and righteous and to spread the Dhamma" (Diary, August 16, 1902).

His difficulties with the Sinhala public were not helped by his living most of the time abroad, and his flying visits to the island and abrupt departures did not help either. Colleagues wanted him to direct his efforts to Lanka exclusively (and others wanted him to leave it alone). Harischandra once threatened to resign if he did not return to the island (Diary, January 30, 1907). His flightiness was not limited to Lanka, because he was as much on wing abroad as at home, and even when his health was failing. In the midst of projects in Lanka he had thoughts of returning to India, trekking into the Himalayas, or going to Sagaing and living the ascetic life in Burma (Diary, December 15, 1909). His longing for other places was known to his supporters; as he once wrote, for example, "I am receiving letters from certain good people asking me not to leave Ceylon" (Diary, December 27, 1911). In the background he was overcome by a feeling of being repelled by this world:

> There is so much to be done that it makes me anxious. The thought comes to me to leave all and go (Diary, December 11, 1911).

> The feeling of disgust comes to me strongly to abandon all things and go to Benares (Diary, December 21, 1911).

20. "Buddhist Work in England," *Ceylon Daily News*, December 20, 1926.

Sometimes he responded to such feelings by working harder or sending off a petition to the king. Other times he simply left the place and whatever project he was pursuing.

A sense of his own suffering runs through the diaries, but it comes to the fore during the 1915–6 period when a government order forbade his leaving Calcutta—"Bishtoo [his cook] brought the vegetable curry after I had finished eating. What torture I undergo on account of the Sinhalese Buddhists, at the hand of the Government" (March 22, 1917). The curry being brought late was the least of it:

> A month after I shall be a man on the threshold of death. 1914 was the cessation of my activities. 1914–1918 under a dark cloud. Persecutions, oppressions, raids, espionage, destruction of records, exile and internment accentuated by physical illnesses—piles, hydrocele, neuralgia and final collapse by the sprain of my ligaments of my left knee which kept me confined to my room for 2 months & 21 days. (Diary, August 17, 1918)

Internment came down to his movements being monitored, Maha Bodhi Society documents confiscated, and his being told not to leave Calcutta. The period lasted 18 months—in the passage above he pegs it at four years; elsewhere he says five years.[21] The vocabulary he uses for his internment— "misery," "torture," "prison"—overstates the situation, but he had used similar language before the internment began: "Since 17 inst: food that we eat is cold rice and cold vegetable. More misery than this no man can undergo. No proper diet, no friend, no companion, life is that of a prisoner. With death persecution shall cease" (Diary, December 1, 1915). During the internment period he was shut off from the monthly stipend he received from his family. But he had Mary Foster's monthly contribution. Months before, she had sent him a draft for £1,046 (Diary, December 1, 1915). He could have drawn on those funds to avoid hunger. Instead he sustained the notion that he was poor by drawing lines that did not exist—setting Mary Foster's money aside when he was genuinely hungry, just as he did by saying that he had no possessions while acquiring properties in three countries and owning several motor vehicles.[22]

21. Once released from internment, Dharmapala was denied permission to return home until the early 1920s, and to that extent his movements were controlled for longer than eighteen months.

22. E. S. Jayasinha, "Letters to the Editor: Maha Bodhi Society," *Ceylon Daily News*, December 24, 1926. According to Jayasinha, who served as chief clerk to both Don Carolis Hewavitarne and the Maha Bodhi Society, Mary Foster directed all of her contributions to Dharmapala,

His first experience of ascetic practice came when his father had him try out the brahmacarya vow for a day as a nine-year-old boy. He spoke of renunciation again when he gave up his job in the Department of Public Instruction in 1885 and when he took on the ochre robes for good in 1895, looking for forms of self-abnegation wherever he could find them. As a volunteer for the Theosophical Society, he would eat dinner at home and walk to the headquarters to assist the secretary, C. P. Gunawardana. Instead of returning home, he slept at the Theosophical Society office "on a hard bench," making a pillow from "an unused coir mat with a very rough surface" ("My Autobiography," Sarnath Notebook no. 53). He lost a pair of eyeglasses and decided simply not to replace them (Diary, June 1–2, 1893). For him renunciation was a product of temperament: "From my 10th year the ethic of 'otherworldliness' and the beauty of saintliness became impregnated in my mind" (Sarnath Notebook no. 4). To that extent his "otherworldliness" predated his encounter with Theosophical spirituality.

He saw a lot of death in his family. In 1880 and 1885 two of his brothers died. Around 1882 his infant sister died.[23] In 1902 an elder sister died, followed by his father in 1906; his brother Simon died young in 1913, and his brother Edmund in 1915. His deceased brothers had been major supporters of the Maha Bodhi Society, and Edmund had died while incarcerated in Jaffna Fort on charges arising from the 1915 riots. As Dharmapala put it, "Since 51 years Death is with me" (Diary, January 18, 1919).[24] He was not especially close with any of his siblings, and although his diaries make reference regularly to his love for his mother and father, he resented both of them—his mother for fostering him out to her brother's family when he was a young child and his father for being cold and distant. On one occasion he toyed with the idea that his mother's indifference had forced him into the homeless life:

My mother's attitude towards me was strange. I prayed for her happiness many thousand times in 1901. I went to her with great expectations; but

---

not the Maha Bodhi Society. In 1923 she wrote him, "I am grateful for all you have done for me. Please grant me this one wish. Do take care of yourself and take enjoyment . . . by being with your mother more often. Live for your work, that is by taking good care of your health and give yourself more comforts." Dutt, "The Maha Bodhi Society, Its History and Influence," 133.

23. This death led him to the conclusion that because his parents' intercourse had given rise to the child (and the child's early death to his mother's inconsolable grief), practicing celibacy was the one way to avoid inflicting pain on other women (Sarnath Notebook no. 4).

24. Even his last surviving brother, Charles, predeceased Dharmapala, dying in an automobile accident in 1929 (Diary, February 22, 1930).

I found a cold heart; and she forced me by her expressions to leave her home. Why should this have happened. Miss Holmes thinks it was the work of the angels of light; they did not want that I should be tied down to a home life; and nobody could have forced me out except mother and she was influenced to make me get out!! (Diary, August 16, 1902)

He interpreted the tragic events of his life—his physical ailments, his internment, his parents' coldness, and the death of family members—as evidence of the very nature of samsara. He had chosen solitude early on, and events unfolded in ways that gave him evidence of the logic of change and the inevitability of suffering. "Great indeed have been the sufferings I have had for the cause of Humanity," he said, long before the suffering of his later years (Diary, January 14, 1904).

Dharmapala's renunciation worked against his activism. In some ways, he got on better with members of the Calcutta Maha Bodhi Society than with the Maha Bodhi Society in Colombo. The Bengalis had the enthusiasm of non-Buddhists for a religion of humanistic appeal, and he did not ask much of them. But he was still alone. As he put it in one of his notebooks, "Buddha has no friends in India. Neither do I" (Sarnath Notebook no. 27, dated March 28, 1918). He expected more support from Sinhala Buddhists, and he received it at least until he lost the Bodh Gaya case. The Burmese had given him more support than Sinhalas, and his Calcutta supporters had given far less, but he spent little time celebrating the Burmese or bemoaning Indian shortcomings. Sinhalas were the ones who were ungrateful and the ones who should have appreciated what he was attempting. They were the people he was trying to improve. When he returned to Colombo from his trip to visit Mary Foster, he wrote:

The Hirano Maru arrived at 3.30 PM and anchored outside Colombo harbour. Paid waiters, lemonade etc—Rs 17.60. Dolapihilla and the Ruwanwela Youngman came on board. Not one in my family cared to come and receive me. Not one Buddhist was there to meet me! After a triumphant tour in the Far East here I am returning to Ceylon after an absence of six months and not one to welcome me. What does this indicate? The utter degradation of the Sinhalese Buddhists. Not that I care for applause; but the absence of the sense of gratitude in the people's mind is what is unhealthy. You can't expect gratitude from children and the Sinhalese are like that. They are utterly ignorant and as a mother to her children I shall love them. (Diary, October 22, 1913)

However his wanting to love his people "as a mother to her children" strikes the ear, the resonance with the mother who did not love him enough to keep him at home is hard to overlook.

I would not claim he tried to create the conditions for his own independence or solitude by treating others so harshly that they avoided him, but his behavior had that effect. He shows no signs in his diary entries of being aware of the effect of his words on other people. His sense of his own spiritual goals—achieving enlightenment, saving humanity, and doing so on his own—surely lay beneath his difficult relationships with others. He may well have been wrong about his motivations for criticizing any and all, but he kept telling himself that he was doing it for them (Diary, April 25, 1911). It was always for them:

> Gave up worldly pleasures & took up the life of the Bodhisat. First the Buddhists were against me because I began to criticize them. The Bhikkhus were against me. Where I went I worked for the public good. (Sarnath Notebook no. 53)

Once he wrote: "I can roar and yet be gentle. When I do get the opportunity I show what sort of stuff the Buddhist has. In Burma, Ceylon, Siam, Japan, America, England & India I have roared" (Diary, March 19, 1904), attributing that "roaring" to a Buddhist source.[25] His supporters were not so sure. As he laid out plans for living with others—"only to use harsh words to be forgiving, always exerting to lead the brahmachari life and to live in solitude—these I want" (Diary, March 11, 1907). The contradictory logic—"to use harsh words to be forgiving"—captures the problem.

His attacks on the colonial government derived from his feeling responsible to point out and criticize uncivilized behavior. Sinhalas responded to his critiques in various ways, but the British responded by raising doubts concerning his political loyalty. He took those charges in stride: "I was never seditious but everyone opposed me because I was critical" (Sarnath Notebook no. 53). When he criticized his people, he was acting in the cause of national regeneration and religious reform. When he attacked the British,

---

25. Roaring like a lion functions in the Anguttara Nikaya as a "declaration of Enlightenment," as in the case of the monk Pindola, "the last man of the golden age of miracles." John Strong, "The Legend of the Lion-Roarer: A Study of the Buddhist Arhat Pindola Bharadvaja," *Numen* 26 (1979): 68–71 and 75. Pindola was also distinguished by being an arhat who remained in the monkhood after gaining arhatship.

he did so as an imperial citizen with reason to expect better of government. He also acted in this connection as a universalist. He owed his capacity to stand alone to meditation because the jhanic states they produce fostered human will (Diary, November 7, 1926). His knowledge of the problems of human life, by contrast, he gained by understanding Buddhism and submitting himself to suffering. Because he cared about the whole world, he had to put people straight—Sinhalas, Buddhists, British, family, fellow passengers on trains—he met an Indian attorney on a train and told him to stop spending so much on cigars and give the money to the poor (Diary, April 24, 1911). He knew he was alone: "In 1902 when I was in Ceylon, I felt the want of association and made myself think as if I was not worth even a dog; but this time I feel glad that am able to stand alone and above all" (Diary, March 21, 1905).

Standing alone and above was expressed in the condescension and "aristocratic hauteur" to which he confessed (Sarnath Notebook no. 4). It showed itself in structural ways such as the organizations he established. He was a member of the Theosophical Society from an early age, he established the Maha Bodhi Society in due course, and he envisioned a number of organizations that never came to pass, died out, or in which he played no part. In 1896 he sent a proposal to Norendronath Sen to found a group to prevent the slaughter of animals (Diary, May 11, 1896). Later he established the Mitrivardhana Samagama (Diary, October 1, 1898) and participated in the formation of the Sinhalese National Reform Association (Diary, October 23, 1898). In 1913 W. A. de Silva, D. B. Jayatilaka, Dharmapala, and his two brothers established the Buddhist Educational Society (Diary, November 17, 1913). He chaired a meeting of the Sinhala Taruna Samagama (Diary, November 19, 1913). Organizations bursting into life all around, he had no role in them once established. These groups had overlapping memberships, and members of the Colombo elite took up leadership positions in more than one group. His brother Charles led the Maha Bodhi Society in Dharmapala's absence, but he was also a member of the Buddhist Theosophical Society, the International Dharmadutha Society, and the Congress of Buddhist Associations.[26] Aside from his on-again, off-again relationship to the Theosophical Society, Dharmapala was active in only one organization, his own.

---

26. W. D. Jayatunga pointed out that four members of the Hewavitarne family continued as members of the Buddhist Theosophical Society after Dharmapala left the group, a circumstance that provides a small example of his isolation from his family. "Mr. D. Hewawitarana and the Buddhists of Ceylon," letter to the editor, *Ceylon Independent*, April 26, 1906.

Despite his lack of a social network, he had financial relationships with other Buddhist reformers. He made gifts to other people for their projects, he took mortgages from Buddhist groups, and he lent money much more freely than one would expect of a thrifty person. He saw a number of people during the day and expected people to call on him, taking offense when they did not come to visit him in London or Colombo. But he did not cultivate friendships and did not have an inner circle, even in the Maha Bodhi Society. In that regard, his offering money to other Buddhist reformers is instructive. Sinhala, Burmese, and Japanese Buddhists sent him contributions to pay attorneys' fees during the Bodh Gaya case.[27] All evidence to the contrary, he did not think of himself as receiving support from others:

> I have no friend who knows me, no Buddhist has given me the least help, and I don't go to solicit help, but I help all. Senanayaka came to me asking for a loan, W. A. de Silva's wife came and I gave her Rs. 2000/, Musaeus School people came & I gave Rs. 1000 from the Foster fund. (Diary, December 16, 1926)

As with his sense of himself as homeless, without possessions, and alone, Dharmapala cultivated the idea that Buddhists had not helped him, however much he had helped them.

He was right about his having given loans and gifts to others. He wrote Lady Blake offering Rs. 1,000 for a school she was trying to build (Diary, January 16, 1907). When leaders of the Dharmaraja College called on him for support, he gave them Rs. 1,000 (Diary, December 23, 1913). He lent £500 to a German Buddhist (Diary, November 15, 1926). He lent money to Annie Besant. He gave money to a destitute British woman in Calcutta (Diary, August 12, 1917). He supported bhikkhus—including Polwatte Dhammadhara—who arrived in Calcutta without funds. He supported other people's charities because it was good for the Buddhist cause. With loans he expected repayment. With charity he expected reciprocity, and that he did not always receive. His motives went beyond reform:

> I gave 1000/- rupees to the War Ambulance fund, a 1000/- to the Visuddhi Magga fund, a 1000/- to the Pali research Gold Medal and now I give 1000/- to the Ceylon Relief fund. I gave Rs. 500/- to Mrs. Besant for her Home Rule fund; 10,000 to the Vihara fund. I have since 1915 spent about Rs. 7000/- to keep up the MBS in Calcutta. May I get the Sabban-

27. Guruge, *Dharmapala Lipi*, 75.

nutanana by the power of this dana to save suffering Humanity. (Diary, July 3, 1919)[28]

The Maha Bodhi Society was his vehicle for social change, and he chose to maintain his solitary life by not serving on the boards of other organizations. His economic activities—giving money to groups and governments, lending money to individuals—followed the same logic. Behind his charities lay an otherworldly goal, his own salvation, which he pursued alone.

THE MAHA BODHI SOCIETY AND ITS WORK

Dharmapala established the Maha Bodhi Society in Colombo, even though "the principal center of the Society is in India, the birth-place of the Buddha and his sublime teachings."[29] The Maha Bodhi Society in Calcutta came later, and the two groups were one single body until 1915.[30] When Dharmapala was interned in Calcutta, not to return home until 1920, the Colombo Maha Bodhi Society disappeared for a time. At that moment the government of India offered him a Buddha relic that had been excavated at the Brattiprolu stupa in South India, and to facilitate its transfer to Buddhist hands, the Maha Bodhi Society of India was registered under the Societies Act. He served as general secretary, supported by a substantial number of Bengalis who were also members of the Theosophical Society. By way of the society he introduced the celebration of Vesak to India, moved the headquarters to a series of more substantial houses in Calcutta, and campaigned for Bodh Gaya. What the Calcutta Maha Bodhi Society did not do—with the exception of raising funds for famine relief in the 1890s—was launch reformative projects in India at large.[31]

The contrast with Lanka is striking because there Dharmapala pursued one project after another. Those projects have an opportunistic quality. A critical evaluation of his public work might accuse him of being impulsive; a sympathetic one would stress that reform required his acting on many fronts. In 1918 he made another list summing up his life's work. The list makes no distinction between what he accomplished in India and Lanka and represents what he understood to be his most important work:

28. In Dharmapala's notebooks and diaries "sabbannutanana" functions as the transidiomatic equivalent to nirvana.

29. "The Mission of the Maha Bodhi Society," *Journal of the Maha Bodhi Society* 6 (1898): 66–7, at 67.

30. Amunugama, "A Sinhalese Buddhist 'Babu,'" 569.

31. Dutt, "The Maha Bodhi Society, Its History and Influence," 88.

The works accomplished by Anagarika Dharmapala, since 1896. Converted the weekly Sandaresa into biweekly. Started the *Buddhist*. Enlarged the Buddhist Press. Conversion of Christian names into Aryan,
introduced the *ohariya* [the Kandyan sari] among the low country ladies.
Organized pilgrimage to Buddha Gaya. Illustrated lectures, the first to
go to America to preach Buddhism, the first to introduce Buddhism to
India, the first Sinhalese to travel around the world. Started the MB Journal in 1892; built the Dharmasala at Buddha Gaya; founded the Hewavitarna [obscure] scholarship. First vihara in Calcutta; started school at Rajagiriya. Started the *Sinhala Bauddhaya* and Maha Bodhi Press, Started
the first Sinhalese hospital; Started the Santhaghara. Started the M.B.
Library. Started the Hiniduma Estate for Buddhist propaganda. (Sarnath
Notebook no. 23)

There are some noticeable absences, such as the Maha Bodhi Society itself.
His great success putting up buildings depended on family contributions and
Mary Foster's philanthropy. When the Colombo Society determined to apply
resources for work in the island, he insisted on using those funds for work
in India. He prevailed, saying that "if they [his supporters] want to appropriate 15000/- for Ceylon work, I told them I shall leave the island" (Diary,
January 9, 1898).[32] Without his presence, there would not be any public
work, and he believed that the society was his child. In the 1920s, faced
with local opposition to his campaign to raise funds for the London Buddhist vihara, he raised the stakes, insisting that if the funds were not forthcoming, he would not only leave for England but also die there. The threat
was undercut by many people knowing he would leave soon in any case.

The Ethico-Psychological College, which he established at Rajagiriya
in 1898, represents another case of his wanting to go it alone. It was his
first substantial project in Lanka, and he brought great enthusiasm to it.
He had extravagant plans to inaugurate the place: "thinking of proposed
grand Procession consisting of 1000 Bhikshus, 1000 Upasakas, 1000 Upasikas, 100 horses, 10 elephants, Volunteers, regiment etc which I want to
take on the Full Moon Day of Wesak to Rajgir, the new Arama" (Diary,
January 1, 1898). He wanted to ride on horseback in the procession (Diary,
April 1, 1898). He had equally grandiose plans for the place itself, hoping to
make it look like the Jetavanarama in Anuradhapura. He imagined build-

---

32. The period that begins in 1904 was one of his most productive intervals in the island.
On this occasion he was in India, and the Maha Bodhi Society discouraged him from returning
to Lanka (Diary, September 1 and 20, 1904). He returned nonetheless.

ing a one-hundred-foot image of the Buddha as part of the complex (Diary, February 12 and April 21, 1898). By March his father had insisted on calling off the procession (Diary, March 19, 1898). But Don Carolis also invested Rs. 25,000 in purchasing forty acres of land on the outskirts of Colombo for the college, so the Rajagiriya project went forward, and Dharmapala had his procession too.

Dharmapala modeled the Ethico-Psychological College on Western higher education, complemented by Buddhist practices that would develop the mind "beyond the realm of the phenomenal stage."[33] Some of the vocabulary derived from his visit to the United States in 1896, when he was exposed to American higher education and the discipline of psychology in inchoate form. It also reflected his interest in dhyana meditation and the mental states that he hoped it would produce in meditators, allowing them to penetrate the "phenomenal stage." Earlier he had announced his plans for a community of *"anagarika brahmacharis"* (Diary, July 26, 1896). Soon he had another plan—he wanted monks, brahmacaryas, and interested laypeople to take up residence at the college to pursue a course of mental and physical training:

> The student who wishes to realize Truth . . . should abstain from all evil actions and regulate his life according to the rules laid down in the Noble Eightfold Path. . . . Diet, hygienic clothing, gentle exercise, sleep, etc., are the requirements necessary for the building of character. . . . The curriculum will embrace Eastern and Western Psychology, Natural Philosophy, English, and Pali.[34]

Admission was open to all, "without distinction of colour or creed" and he insisted that the school was congenial to the study of "Brahminism, Christianity, Zoroastrianism, Confucianism, Taoism, and Islamism." All expenses including clothing were to be provided by the Maha Bodhi Society, but there was a stipulation: having completed the four-month course of study, students would agree "to give their services free for the welfare of humanity." He included laypeople in his first formulation but later indicated that he intended the training for "young Buddhist Bhikkhus to be sent abroad to preach the immortal doctrines of our Lord Buddha."[35]

33. "The Ceylon Ethico-Psychological College," *Journal of the Maha Bodhi Society* 6 (1898): 85–6, at 85.

34. "The Ceylon Ethico-Psychological College," 85.

35. "Our Seventh Year," *Journal of the Maha Bodhi Society* 7 (1898): 5–6, at 6.

The procession that opened the college in April 1898 was as grand as he had hoped, although he could not come up with the elephants:

> To the sweet strains of the Band—and the chanting of 1000 boys—came first in line, our beloved High Priest Sumangala—in his carriage, drawn by eight strong and sturdy men, dressed in white, then following, two by two, 780 yellow-robed Priests with canopies held over their heads to protect them from the sun's rays. Next, three by three Upasaka numbering 1,000, in pure white, carrying banners and offerings, and then most charming of all was the 1,000 Virgins, wearing the Singhalese ancient costume—the o'horiya. . . . Next in line 1,000 Upasikas then the multitude.[36]
>
> N.B.—The most notable feature of the Procession was the Anagarika Dharmapala, tall and commanding, in his peculiar orange red robes.

A month later, the journal announced that he would start a pan-Asian campaign to raise funds for an International Buddhist Monastery and Missionary College in Calcutta, at which he wanted to train young monks as missionaries to Lanka, Burma, Siam, Japan, Europe, and America.[37] He had already raised Rs. 23,000 for the Bodh Gaya case and Rs. 15,000 to buy a house for the Society in Calcutta. Now he hoped that the Burmese would do their part by giving him Rs. 12,000.

Despite its splendid beginning, the Ethico-Psychological College failed almost immediately. Neither monks nor laymen were interested in taking the training, and Dharmapala blamed T. G. Harrison, his Theosophical colleague, and the Kandyan monk Rambukpota for working against him (Diary, January 14, 1926). He concluded that the moment was not right for the project, and he also found himself confronted by local forces: he had fallen out with the Colombo Theosophists over his desire to separate Buddhism from Theosophy institutionally. He had to manage the turbulent emotions of Marie de Souza Canavarro, who had come to Colombo to revive the order of Buddhist nuns under his guidance; he had lost the Bodh Gaya case; the Sinhala public was disaffected; and his father still held the purse strings.[38]

---

36. "Opening of the Rajgiri Ethico-Psychological College, Colombo," *Journal of the Maha Bodhi Society* 7 (1898): 6–7.

37. N. Saddhananda, "Revival of Buddhism in India," *Journal of the Maha Bodhi Society* 7, no. 3 (1898): 20. Saddhananda reported that Sinhala Buddhists contributed Rs. 15,000 to the cause.

38. Dharmapala had converted Canavarro in New York City on his second visit to the United States, and once in Lanka she had accompanied him on a tour of the Southern Province.

Don Carolis soon sold part of the property (Diary, January 13, 1898). When he wrote that he accepted advice from the Buddha, not other people, he revealed as much about his temperament as his policy.[39]

Serious opposition came from Olcott, and Dharmapala's relationship with him was broken by 1898. He had opposed Dharmapala's attending the World's Parliament of Religions, and he went; when Olcott advised him against litigating for Bodh Gaya, he went ahead. Olcott's opposition to the Ethico-Psychological College ran so deep that he decided to go public on the subject in the *Theosophist*. His attack in those pages reveals not just what he found unrealistic about the project to teach meditation and prepare missionaries for overseas work. The piece also lays out Dharmapala's failings in a more general way, which many of his critics would have shared. Dharmapala, according to Olcott, had criticized Sinhalas for not supporting Buddhist causes, calling their indifference to Canavarro's attempt to bring about "all manner of reforms" evidence of the decline of Buddhism. Olcott's response gave him a chance to defend both Sinhala Buddhists and the revival of Buddhism that he had initiated decades earlier.

He focused on Dharmapala's criticizing Buddhists for ignoring his attempt to educate monks to missionize overseas, arguing that the problem lay in the project, not other Buddhists:

I do not want to say a harsh word [of] Dharmapala, but I am duty bound to defend the Sinhalese from his unjust aspersions and tell the truth. Dharmapala has been in intimate relations with me from the time when, as a very young man, he threw up his clerkship in a Government office, at Colombo to devote his life to Buddhistic propaganda, and for many years he followed my advice. But since his visit to America, to attend the Exposition, he has not seemed willing to listen to the advice of his elders, but has put forth various schemes which they were obliged to regard as impracticable, if not utopian. Among them, was his "Ethico-Psychological College"—a title bad enough to strangle it at its birth. This embryonic college was opened without pupils or teaching staff, with a big and showy procession, a great tom-toming and trumpet-blowing, a

---

Accounts of Canavarro's career can be found in Thomas A. Tweed, "Inclusivism and the Spiritual Journey of Marie de Souza Canavarro (1849–1933)," *Religion* 24, no. 1 (1994): 43–58; and Tessa Bartholomeusz, "Real Life and Romance: The Life of Miranda de Souza Canavarro," *Journal of Feminist Studies in Religion* 10 (1994): 27–47. Bartholomeusz mentions Canavarro's attempt to seduce Dharmapala and her later "companionate marriage" with a fellow Buddhist, Myron Phelps, whom she met in New Jersey.

39. Guruge, *Dharmapala Lipi*, 55.

sensational telegraphing to the papers, and after that came reaction and silence.[40]

He went on to reveal more of Dharmapala's self-injuring behavior, citing the Bodh Gaya case as an example. He had promised to deliver the place to Buddhist hands, and he had not. The court's decision produced a minor victory, declaring the Maha Bodhi shrine Buddhist but leaving control of it with the mahant. The case had cost the Buddhists almost Rs. 40,000, and the outcome did not satisfy his donors. Olcott observed that "On the witness stand Dharmapala made almost as bad a figure as was possible, becoming utterly confused and losing his memory of facts, and alienating sympathies that he ought to have secured."[41] He added that "a stronger man would have come out of the ordeal much better."

Olcott raised another charge that would live on, writing that Dharmapala had not taken subscribers to the Maha Bodhi Fund into his confidence by providing detailed accounts of where their money had gone. Nor did he have those accounts audited. No one, Olcott said, had reason to question the young man's honesty or his selflessness. The problem was accountability. But there was another issue lying behind the public's wanting more information about his handling of funds. He moved money from place to place as he liked, taking money in one case raised to support four monks residing at Bodh Gaya and reallocating it to underwrite the first issues of the *Journal of the Maha Bodhi Society*. He did not consult with anyone, including his supporters at home and abroad. Even when he provided accounts at the end of journal's annual run, the accounts were his unaudited work, and they failed to reveal more than an overview of cash flows and obligations. For him, that was enough.

The diaries provide evidence of his refusing to yield control of the projects he launched to the Maha Bodhi Society. One motivation is clear in a comment he wrote late in life about his relationship to the Maha Bodhi Society:

> People who have not paid a rupee for the Maha Bodhi Society wish to control the affairs thereof. I have worked for 39 years & contributed nearly 2 lacs to the Society, and my duty is to protect the interest thereof. (Diary, April 28, 1930)

---

40. "The 'Wail' of Dharmapala," supplement, *Theosophist* 20 (April 1899), pp. xxvii–xxx, xxviii–xxix.

41. "The 'Wail' of Dharmapala," xxix–xxx.

He opposed the incorporation of the Maha Bodhi Society from the first moment his supporters brought it up. When the principal of the Maha Bodhi College broached the idea, he argued that incorporation could lead to the Foster Fund being absorbed by the Buddhist Theosophical Society in Colombo (Diary, April 11, 1930). As Dharmapala approached death, he reacted to the opposite fear, foreseeing that "any one of my relatives can take possession of the property that is in my name" (Diary, September 28, 1930). He was especially concerned that the Foster money and the inheritance he received from his father be put to Buddhist work. When the Dharmapala Trust was formed for that purpose, it had accounts worth 7.5 lakhs of rupees. J. R. Jayewardene served as one of the first trustees and found "the Trust a very wealthy one."[42]

If there is any surprise here it is that Dharmapala produced annual accounts at all. He must have followed the practice of doing so from his experience as secretary of the Theosophical Society, because the *Theosophist* included an annual accounting. At the end of his life, he continued to fight the bureaucratization of the Maha Bodhi Society. He chose the name, put together the founding capital, and made contributions to it throughout his life (Diary, September 21, 1926).[43] He saw scant distinction between his personal philanthropy and the society's. The Maha Bodhi Society borrowed money from HDC & Sons when needed and without security, as with a tranche of Rs. 10,000 in 1909 (Diary, June 21, 1927). As the diary has it,

> The MBS owes the firm Rs. 20,000. This amount was lent to the Society during a period of several years. It is impossible for the Society to pay this amount at once. It will be necessary to hold a fancy bazaar to raise money. The money was lent to carry on the work of the MBS. (May 29, 1927)

In other words, he wanted subscribers to donate money to pay off the society's debts to his family's firm. But money also passed from his hand to the society: "Wrote to HDC & S[ons] asking for details of the debt due to them by the MBS. Had I been told of the debt I would have paid it by instalments [sic]. The MBS owes me Rs. 10,000/- & the firm Rs. 22,442" (Diary, May 31, 1927). Because he set up the Foster Fund as an independent account under

---

42. "The Dharmapala Trust and the London Vihara Trust," *Ceylon Daily News*, September 17, 1933.

43. Dharmapala said that he donated nearly two lakhs of rupees to the society over his life (Diary, April 28, 1930). I'm unsure whether that means money contributed to the society, given in the name of the society or given personally as charity, or whether he saw the difference.

his control, things became still more convoluted, funds moving among his personal accounts, the Maha Bodhi Society's accounts, the Foster Fund, and Don Carolis Hewavitarne and Company.[44]

Dharmapala's casual attitude to commingling funds upset donors even when the stakes were lower. When he was trying to establish a convent for a new order of Buddhist nuns with Canavarro, he was more than cavalier about raising public money and moving it about. As Olcott laid it out,

> [Dharmapala] borrowed Rs.15,000 of Maha Bodhi Society money to partly
> pay for a property that he bought for the Convent in Colombo at a cost of
> Rs. 25,000, and he put a mortgage on it as security for the unpaid remain-
> der of Rs. 10,000; then, as no individual would give that money, he and
> the Countess went on tour to try and raise it by popular subscription.[45]

There was a charismatic innocence about all of his enterprises, and that innocence resonates with his father's thinking that he was not cut out for a career in business. From Dharmapala's perspective, it must have seemed that if the cause was urgent and just, the management of finances did not matter. The Lord Buddha never published his account books.

LEAVING PLACES

Probably only a few Sinhala Buddhists saw Olcott's 1899 critique of Dharmapala, describing him as "willful, impractical, juvenile critical capacity," but it was read by subscribers to the *Theosophist*. The leadership of the Buddhist Theosophical Society—people such as D. B. Jayatilaka, W. A. de Silva, F. R. Senanayaka, and E. W. Perera—would have known about it, and gossip was sure to spread beyond them. There were other criticisms both before Dharmapala left the island in 1914 and after his return in 1920. He used his diaries to keep track of criticisms that appeared in the local press.[46]

---

44. With Hewavitarne D. C. & Sons becoming a limited company, Dharmapala says, the firm would cease operating the Foster Fund—which belonged to Dharmapala and not the Maha Bodhi Society—and Julius of the law firm Julius Creasy brought in to manage finances, charging 2.5 percent on the money collected by the fund (Diary, February 8, 1927). These arrangements were Dharmapala's response to growing public criticism in late 1926 of his management of Maha Bodhi monies.

45. "The 'Wail' of Dharmapala," xxix.

46. These critiques appeared in both the Sinhala-language press and English newspapers. They include *Sandarasa*, May 3, 1897, October 1, November 21 and 28, 1911; *Samaya*, October 14, and November 4, 1905; *Ceylon Independent*, September 26, 1911, June 15 and 30, 1925; *Ceylon Observer*, March 22, 1905; *Lakminipahana*, December 25 and 30, 1911; *Times of Ceylon*,

Well-to-do Sinhalas criticized him for being financially irresponsible.[47] The rest of the critiques tended to focus on either the problems that Olcott highlighted or the argument that missionizing Buddhism overseas was less important than revitalizing it at home. Even his supporters were sometimes more comfortable with him at a distance:

MBS suggests that I should not return to Colombo !!! but work in India. (Diary, August 31, 1904)

Why should the MBS take steps to prevent my returning to Ceylon? I have almost decided to return home to see my father. (Diary, September 1, 1904)

Mr. P. Wimalasuriya writes that I should remain in India and not return to Ceylon for 2 years. (Diary, September 20, 1904)

It is hard to escape the conclusion that there were both psychological and external forces motivating his working alone and his frequent travels between Sri Lanka and India.

Between the critique that Olcott launched in 1898 and the spate of criticisms that followed his return to Colombo in 1926, Dharmapala lived out his most productive years. I lay out his accomplishments in tabular form for the sake of revealing his movements in and out of Lanka as well as the way he rushed from one project to another:

January and August–September 1898: made bullock-cart tours around Lanka
1900: established branch of the Maha Bodhi Society at Madras
February 1901: purchased three bighas of land at Sarnath
October 1901: received permission to make use of Burmese resthouse at Bodh Gaya, housing monks and placing the Japanese Buddha image there
1902: third visit to Japan
September 1902: Mary Foster became Dharmapala's chief supporter

May 4, 1921; *Dinamina*, August 14, 1930; *Saraswati*, September 12 and December 25, 1930; and *Sinhala Jatiya*, August 19 and September 17, 1930. The most substantial body of criticism appeared in the *Ceylon Daily News* in the mid-1920s, and an ongoing series of articles in the leading English-language paper of the day had its effect on Dharmapala. I discovered these articles and their dates because he makes note of them in his diaries.
47. Amunugama, "A Sinhalese Buddhist 'Babu,'" 583.

July 1904: started industrial school at Sarnath with Foster funds

1905: established plantation industry at Hiniduma, southern Lanka

May 1905: made plans to celebrate the anniversary of the Lord Buddha's birth in Calcutta

1906: father died, leaving inheritance for his four sons and daughter

May 1906: began to publish the *Sinhala Bauddhaya* and established schools at Rajagiriya and Hiniduma

July–September 1906: lecture tour in Southern Province

July 1908: purchased Baniapukur house in Calcutta as headquarters of the Maha Bodhi Society in Indian

1909: another lecture tour in southern Lanka

1910: court ordered the removal of the Japanese Buddha image from Bodh Gaya

1911: campaign to raise funds for Buddhist mission in London

1911–13: July 10, 1911–April 21, 1912, and May 6, 1912–February 19, 1913: period of sustained propaganda work in Lanka and criticism of indolent monks

1912: established the *Ceylonese Nation*, a weekly newspaper in commemoration of the coronation of George V to give Buddhists as a vehicle to express grievances in English to British authorities

1912: purchased motor car in Colombo to conduct temperance campaign

April 1912: returned to Calcutta

April 1913: tour of Japan, on way to visit Mary Foster in Hawaii and return via China and Korea

1914: established the Foster-Robinson Free Hospital with Mary Foster's funds on land given by father

May 1914: returned to Calcutta

May 1915: riots in Lanka

July 1915: purchased 4 College Square as future site of Dharmarajika vihara

March 1916: made trip to Rawalpindi to talk with John Marshall regarding Taxila relic

June 1916: began internment in Calcutta, ending December 1917

July 1918: started work on the College Square vihara

November 1919: received $50,000 worth of war bonds from Foster

March–April 1920: made first return to Ceylon after internment

November 1920: Lord Ronaldshay, governor of Bengal, inaugurated Dharmarajika vihara

1921: recruited Buddhist missionaries in Colombo and returned to Calcutta

1922: restarted *Sinhala Bauddhaya*

1923: established Mary Foster Permanent Fund

August 1923: attended Hindu Maha Sabha in North India

1924: returned to Colombo to raise funds for Sarnath project

1925: received $100,000 from Mary Foster

February–March 1925: lecture tour in southern Lanka

1925: established the Foster Buddhist Seminary in Kandy

July–August 1925: convalescence in Swiss sanatorium

September–October 1925: visited Munich and London en route to pay
   thanks to Mary Foster in San Francisco

January 1926: arrived in London for prospective two-year visit to establish London Buddhist vihara

December 1926: returned to Colombo to raise funds for London vihara

April 1927: returned to London via Calcutta, installing monks at the
   London Buddhist vihara

January 1928: fell ill at Marseilles en route home, reaching Colombo in
   February

June 1929: fell ill again, convalescing at Maligakanda

1930: returned to India

1931: final trip to Colombo to establish the Dharmapala Trust

March 1931: returned to India, spending most of his remaining years at
   Sarnath

Dharmapala's internment in Calcutta ended in December 1917, but the
British prevented his return to Lanka until 1920. Without his regular articles in the *Sinhala Bauddhaya*, he also lost his presence in local life until
he restarted the newspaper in 1922. By that time, elite politics had turned
on its axis. When he began his public career in the 1890s, the politics of
the colony centered on elite Lankans jostling with one another to win British favor. By the 1920s the British mattered far less, and politics turned to
local leaders competing with one another.[48] Politics had moved on, and he
had not. His views remained stuck on what he believed in the 1890s, and
he kept his gaze on the colonial state, not his fellow Lankans. For their
part, the British had come to believe that he was a spent force. Given the
unreliability of British intelligence, I am reluctant to accept their evaluation of the trajectory of his life, but his long absence from the island had
consequences. The man who regularly visited his family in Colombo, met
with Maha Bodhi supporters, gave public lectures, and made village tours

48. I owe this characterization to John Rogers.

disappeared from the public sphere.[49] He speaks of the paltry readership of the *Sinhala Bauddhaya* after he restarted it in 1922. Another effect of his absence was exacerbating the widespread sentiment that his overseas focus was irrelevant to Lankan interests. When he returned in 1924, he purchased a house in Kandy for a seminary to train young monks to missionize overseas; even when he came home, in other words, he came to set up another project with no focus on the island. He renewed his campaign to raise funds for the London vihara, and what seems to have rankled Buddhists was a reiteration of Olcott's grievances; the public knew of the great wealth that Mary Foster had given him, yet he continued to ask Buddhists to finance a project in London from their own pockets. To make matters worse, he made those demands petulantly to a public unsure of his good faith.

From some people he received extraordinary respect. In 1905 he preached at a temple in Nugegoda, and the incumbent monk offered him his own seat (which no layman properly occupies) (Diary, September 25, 1905). He described the monk's gesture as a *dharma garu* (expression of moral respect). Amid scandal and controversy in the decades that followed, he received similar gestures. In 1930 he visited a Buddhist temple in Colombo:

> I went to the Pirivena in my bath chair and remained for a few minutes facing the Dagoba. The old Upasaka came & bowed down and all the Upasikas followed him. Both old & young. It is all the result of the Bodhi sat life [*sic*]. . . . Allis gave me a cup of tea at 3 and vanished. For 2 hours I had none to attend to my wants. I warned him that if he does not attend on me he will have to go. (Diary, May 11, 1930)

Later he heard that there had been *pahan pujavas* (the ritual lighting of oil lamps) celebrated in his honor in a local prison (Diary, May 27, 1930). When the *Sinhala Bauddhaya* took a survey in 1927 of readers' rankings of the most popular national leaders, he came first in a list of ten.[50] Because the newspaper was his own operation (and readers were centered in villages and small towns), the sample has its limits, but the list is still instructive. Ranked in order of popularity, Dharmapala was followed by D. B. Jayatilaka, D. S. Senanayaka, E. W. Perera, C. A. Hewavitarne, Arthur Dias, Sir James

---

49. Dharmapala was aware that he was slipping from public view, writing in his diary, "Why not get arrested and create a sensation? The world does not know my sufferings" (February 6, 1919).

50. *Sinhala Bauddhaya*, August 6, 1927. Dharmapala mentions the list in a diary entry of August 28, 1927.

Pieris, W. A. de Silva, D. C. Senanayaka, and C. W. Kannangara. His problem consisted in the fact that virtually all of these men—the central figures in the Buddhist revival of the time—opposed his work overseas.[51] The exception was his brother Charles.

There were signs of public suspicion about his financial affairs as early as 1895.[52] He had spent enormous amounts of money, and he had spent it outside the island, and some of the funds came from Sinhala Buddhists. Those suspicions turned into a flood in the 1920s when a series of newspaper articles took Dharmapala to task for a variety of sins. The account that struck dead center was a letter to the editor of the *Ceylon Daily News* from "A Sincere Buddhist." Dharmapala could not uncover the writer's identity but suspected Arthur Dias (Diary, January 6, 1927).[53] He knew that the Wijewardene family was hostile to him, and that meant that the stinging rebuke in the *Ceylon Daily News* was also seen in their other papers, *Dinamina* and the *Times of Ceylon*.[54] Dias or not, the letter writer was someone who knew him well:[55]

To the Editor, Ceylon Daily News,

Sir—Mr. Dharmapala has earned a great reputation for starting new movements; but unfortunately, his habit of jumping from one thing to another, has detracted much from the value of his services to the cause

51. These other leaders were not opposed to taking a loan from Dharmapala, nor he to giving one: "Jayatilaka & Senanayaka called and gave me a letter asking for a loan of Rs. 40,000. They will purchase Kanatta House and mortgage it to me. I gave a letter to Senanayaka to be delivered to W. A. de Silva to pay the loan of Rs. 10,000/- to Senanayaka. Senanayaka said that the trust money should never be lent on pro notes" (Diary, March 25, 1924).

52. They begin with the disposition of Sinhala contributions in the first Bodh Gaya case. One critic later accused him of having "practically thrown away nearly fifty thousand rupees contributed by the 'poor Buddhists' for his big schemes in India and Ceylon." W. D. Jayatunga, "Mr D. Hewawitarana and the Buddhists of Ceylon," *Ceylon Independent*, April 26, 1906.

53. Dias had served as secretary of the Buddhist Theosophical Society, a position—given the financial woes of that organization—that must have left him sensitive to financial issues. "Mass Meeting of Buddhists," *Ceylon Daily News*, March 23, 1920.

54. "The conspiracy was hatched," Dharmapala thought, "in the Daily News office" (Diary, February 9, 1927). Dharmapala's most influential critic was D. R. Wijewardene, who both owned and edited the *Ceylon Daily News*. Wijewardene regarded the press as a tool for political action and used his newspapers to pursue the nationalist cause. His interest in politics began at Cambridge, where he was exposed to Indian nationalists. Henry Cotton figured in his life too: Wijewardene persuaded him to raise the issue of representative government for Ceylon in Parliament. H. A. J. Hulugalle, *The Life and Times of Don Richard Wijewardene* (Colombo: Associated Newspapers of Ceylon, 1960), 11–4.

55. A Sincere Buddhist, "Mr. Dharmapala and his Work," *Ceylon Daily News*, December 9, 1926.

of Buddhism. Ever since he took to public work, Mr. Dharmapala, with
the generous financial support from the Buddhist public, and, in later
years, from that philanthropic lady of Honolulu, has launched numerous ventures entailing the expenditure of thousands and thousands of
rupees. How many of these works have been completed? It is perhaps the
temple in Calcutta only, that stands to his credit in this respect. From
the Ethico-Psychological Institute in Rajagiriya downwards, he started
many a scheme, e.g., the restoration of the Maha-Bodhi to the Buddhists,
building a bungalow at Gaya City, a Buddhist Seminary at Kandy, a great
temple at Saranath and a number of other things of minor importance.
Leaving all these behind Mr. Dharmapala now wants to erect a Vihare
in London. If the Buddhists of Ceylon did not help him to get this up, he
said in the course of his speech at Maligakanda, that he would not return
home after going back to England, where he actually threatens to lay
his bones. But why all this sudden enthusiasm and hurry about it? And
what, in the name of commonsense, is the urgent necessity of building
a Vihare in London? Why does he, at this moment, choose to postpone
or abandon the erection of the proposed temple at Saranath, over which
at one time, he made so much fuss, and for which, according to the report in Maha-Bodhi Journal, a sum of Rs. 42,710 has been collected up to
the end of October last, to which sum must be added a further amount
of Rs. 10,000, the compensation paid by the Government of India for
the piece of land taken over for the use of the Archaeological Department. After making all the fuss and parade, of which the country is well
aware, the work of the Saranath temple is totally neglected and apparently given up, and why, nobody knows. Now the opposition arises as to
what has been done with the money collected for this work. Who has got
the Rs. 52,700 at present, and what is being done with it?

Even if a Vihare is supposed to be necessary at this juncture in London, what organization has Mr. Dharmapala prepared to manage it and
carry on the propaganda work, for which alone such an institution can
be justified. If proper arrangements are not made, the Temple or the Vihare, without such organization, is bound to prove a "white elephant."
Moreover, before starting his new venture, Mr. Dharmapala has to attend to many other things here; it is his bounden duty to give a faithful
account of his previous ventures before venturing on new enterprises. He
has collected lakhs for public purposes, but up to now, so far as I know,
he has rendered no full and satisfactory accounts of these funds. It was
recently stated in a Colombo newspaper that Mrs. T. R. Foster of Hono-

lulu has entrusted to Mr. Dharmapala a sum of Rs. 450,000 for Buddhist purposes. If this statement is correct—and there is no reason to doubt its correctness—to what use is Mr. Dharmapala putting this vast sum of money? Has he invested it? If so, how and where?

Maha-Bodhi Society, too, is a public concern. It owns extensive landed property, such as the Hiniduma Rubber Estate, in extent several hundred acres, yielding a large income. Will Mr. Dharmapala tell the public in whose name these properties are held and what is their income? When was the last general meeting of the Maha-Bodhi Society held? And were properly audited accounts submitted? In asking these questions I must not be understood as in any way impugning the good faith and sincerity of Mr. Dharmapala. But, I have reason to think that the affairs of the Maha-Bodhi Society and various other ventures of Mr. Dharmapala are not conducted in a proper business-like manner and there is the grave risk that all these institutions may one day collapse owing to the lack of proper organization. They all form a one man's show, that one man being Mr. Dharmapala. He is now getting on in years, and had been recently very seriously ill. Therefore, it behoves [sic] him, before he launches another large undertaking, to take the public into his confidence and state exactly what he has already done and what he is now doing in connection with the ventures he has launched and also of the future of the Maha-Bodhi Society. The Buddhist public too must regard it as due to themselves and Mr. Dharmapala to call upon him to perform this very important duty before they help him to send up another sky-rocket for the astonishment of the world—Yours, etc.

A Sincere Buddhist
Colombo, December 7

Anyone who had known Olcott's characterization of Dharmapala's inclinations thirty years earlier would have recognized the young man in the old. It had always been a "one man show."

His brother saw the article and rushed to defend him.[56] His letter dismissed Dharmapala's missteps by saying that his "ideas were always in advance of his contemporaries." Insisting that his other initiatives were simply ventures that had not been completed, he ticked off Dharmapala's

56. C. A. Hewavitarne, "The Anagarika Dharmapala," letter to the editor, *Ceylon Daily News*, December 11, 1926.

successes—the *Journal of the Maha Bodhi Society*, the society itself, the Foster-Robinson Hospital and Dispensary providing free Ayurvedic treatment to twenty-four thousand patients each year, the free school and pilgrim's resthouse at Sarnath, the Foster free school in Madras, and the Maha Bodhi resthouse at Bodh Gaya. The resthouse at Gaya and the Sarnath vihara were still under construction. He assured readers: "The Anagarika's work in India has been almost entirely carried out with his own money and generous support from . . . Mrs. Foster." He said that the figure of Rs. 52,700 was really Rs. 42,700 and that the Hiniduma estate was managed by the trustees of the Maha Bodhi Society and profits used to support the society's educational work. As for the Buddhist public, it was not "generously supporting" his brother's work. Profits from the rubber estate were doing that. The society always acknowledged contributions, he added, without providing fresh statements of account. He closed by assuring readers that in the matter of the London vihara, the Anagarika "has a clearer view than his contemporaries and sees the future possibilities." He had made up his mind to build the vihara before his death "and we may be sure that he will do it."

Public perceptions continued to be shaped by the bad feelings left by Dharmapala's inability to recover Bodh Gaya and suspicion over exactly where the subscriptions he had raised for that cause had gone—some Rs. 40,000 had been raised from Burma and Lanka, yet only Rs. 23,000 had been spent (Diary, August 24, 1920). The stunning size of Mary Foster's gifts to him increased suspicion about him but not confidence in him. Subscriptions for the Bodh Gaya case had been run through the Maha Bodhi Society, the public thought, and the assumption was that Foster's money was likewise controlled by the society. As it happened, she had given the money to him directly, and he played his cards close to his chest, keeping the Foster Fund in his name, as opposed to most of his funds, which were kept in Maha Bodhi Society accounts. When members suggested registering the society as a legal entity, he balked. His resistance had a nearby source—his family's firm was incorporated only in 1927 (Diary, February 8, 1927). The firm lent its clerk's services to the society to manage accounts, and neither organizations suffered.

Following the first "Sincere Buddhist" letter, a series of questions and answers appeared in the *Ceylon Daily News*—first a short letter to the editor, suggesting that C. A. Hewavitarne's defense was "not complete," and then another letter from the "Sincere Buddhist" arguing that his explanation sang the praises of Dharmapala but skimmed over the financial details. The "Buddhist" did not care whether Charles Hewavitarne thought his brother was a hero:

> I don't mind agreeing with him that Mr. Dharmapala is far in advance of his contemporaries, but all this is no excuse whatever for his being behind-hand with his various ambitious schemes, which he has from time to time launched at public expense. My complaint is that neither the Maha Bodhi Society nor the various institutions which Mr. Dharmapala has started both in Ceylon and abroad are managed in a business-like manner.[57]

He then raised more questions in numbered order: was the Foster Fund given to him as a personal gift or for Buddhist work, who were the Trustees of the Hiniduma Estate, what had been accomplished at Sarnath with the public funds collected for this project, when was the last general meeting of the Maha Bodhi Society, and were audited accounts submitted at that time?

Charles asked his brother whether he had read his rebuttal of the "Sincere Buddhist's" charges. He said he had read both. He recognized that he had both a perception problem and an objective one, writing in his diary on the day of that first attack, "It is a pity that the Ceylon MBS has not issued a report for a number of years" (Diary, December 9, 1926). After another critical letter appeared in the newspapers, he confessed that the society

> has miserably failed to do its duty. Money has been spent lavishly but no accounts have been published in a business like way. No anniversary meeting had been held, no balance sheet submitted since the reorganization of the MBS in 1922. (Diary, December 13, 1926)

He knew that the activities of the Foster Seminary, the Anuradhapura school, the Calcutta vihara, the Sarnath construction, the Calcutta Maha Bodhi Society, and the journal were supported by the Foster Fund, but he had no idea of the extent of those transfers, noting in one diary entry, "The total interest received during the period between July 1915 & December 1926 I should like to know" (December 15, 1926).

Instead of trying to address what he knew privately were problems, he threatened his followers on December 16 with leaving the island altogether. On December 20 Dharmapala spoke at a reception for him at Dharmaraja

57. *Ceylon Daily News*, December 16, 1926.

College, addressing a large meeting of Kandyan monks and laypeople. He
began with his struggles:

> In his old age he required assistance. Even Lord Buddha when he was
> 55 years old required the services of someone to assist him, and he (the
> speaker) was only human.
>
> He had travelled about 20,000 miles during his last mission to for-
> eign countries. He was not advanced in age and his feebleness was due
> to the fact that he was interned in a small room during the 1915 riots by
> the Government.[58] Though he was feeble in health, he was not going to
> stop his work for the spread of Buddha Dharma . . .
>
> Referring to his recent visit to New York, the Anagarika said that he
> was greatly helped by Mr. Kira, a Ceylonese living there, in his propa-
> ganda work. He was a Sinhalese who kept a hotel where rice and curry
> were sold to the Americans. To engage a hall for Mr. Dharmapala to ad-
> dress an American audience, Mr. Kira had to pay Rs. 750 for an hour and
> on advertisements another Rs. 2000. He wished that other Ceylon Bud-
> dhists were as good as Mr. Kira . . .
>
> England was now clamouring for a new religion. There were 76 mil-
> lion people in England. It was for them, the Buddhists, to take their re-
> ligion to the people in England. He was the first Buddhist Missionary
> in England and it was his intention to go back again in March. But yet
> people called him a rogue and a fraud.
>
> Proceeding, the Anagarika Dharmapala referred to a correspondence
> in "The Daily News" and "The Dinamina" regarding his work, and
> read out a statement of expenditures of Mrs. Foster Robinson's Fund in
> Ceylon. Out of other money he had distributed Rs. 52,000 in Ceylon.
> But what, he asked, had the Sinhalese given him for propaganda. Only
> Rs. 8,000 for the last so many years.[59]

The article concluded, "After the meeting, some contributions were made."

Days later Dharmapala addressed the charges brought by the "Sincere
Buddhist," beginning by saying that he was replying to that letter "with
diffidence." He summarized his career, harking back to his arrival at Bodh

---

58. Dharmapala saw himself as old from an early age, often indicating that he was soon to
die three decades before the fact. Here he put aside the weight of his advanced age in favor of
dramatizing his belief that he had been victimized by the British government.

59. "Buddhist Work in England," *Ceylon Daily News*, December 20, 1926.

Gaya in 1891. Moving on to his hopes for the Ethico-Psychological College—the "Sincere Buddhist's" first point of attack—he said it was

> established by me in 1898 with the object of reviving the forgotten science of Dhyana Yoga, but the Bhikkhus thought that in the Kali-yuga it is not possible to practise the sacred science of "uttari manussa dharma." After a year of trial the College was closed, the property sold and with the money my father purchased the present Mallika Santhagara and presented it to me. The property was offered a lac of rupees, but thought it would be better if it is dedicated to Buddhist work, and since 1924 it has been used by the Maha Bodhi College.[60]

The free Ayurvedic hospital he established was prompted by a gift from Mary Foster when he visited her in 1913, and if he had paid for the building outright, there would not have been sufficient funds to operate the dispensary. He concluded that the hospital treated patients without fee and served "Moslems, Sinhalese, Tamils [and] Burghers alike."

He moved on to more recent accomplishments—the Maha Bodhi College, other Buddhist schools, the Hiniduma estate, the vihara in Calcutta, the latter "built without the help of Buddhists." He regularly informed Mary Foster of expenditures from the interest of the Foster Fund and itemized his other charitable donations, reminding readers that

> since 1894 no Ceylon Buddhist had the kindness to help the Indian Maha Bodhi Society. The Riots of 1915 played havoc on the activities of the Maha Bodhi Society. Everything was crushed to atoms. And in 1922 I revived the Society without Buddhist help.

He closed on the same note: for forty-one years he "had worked in the interest of Buddhism without the help of [his] Sinhalese Buddhist brothers," even though in a previous paragraph he mentioned that he had received Rs. 8,607 from Sinhalas toward the construction of the Sarnath vihara. He actually wrote that the contribution was "only Rs. 8607," and it is true that local contributions paled in comparison to Mary Foster's donations, but his saying that he received no help just after he had presented evidence to the contrary had other sources. He nursed real bitterness toward his own

---

60. "The Maha Bodhi Society, Statement by Mr. Dharmapala," *Ceylon Daily News*, December 29, 1926.

people, feeling both financially abandoned and unappreciated by them.[61] He reflected on returning home, "Any good thoughts vanish when one arrives" (Diary, April 18, 1921). He had made contributions to the charities of other Buddhist leaders, but they would not support him, and he did not like being disrespected with paltry donations and abuse.

E. S. Jayasinha, "at one time Hony. Secretary of the Maha Bodhi Society," followed with a letter, responding to the charges by assuring readers that financial statements for the Maha Bodhi Society had been published in the *Sinhala Bauddhaya*. Whether Sinhalas supported the London project, the vihara remained a noble idea.[62] Before the dust could settle came an attack from another direction. Erle Power, an American volunteer for the Maha Bodhi Society in the island, produced an indictment of Dharmapala and his family for treating him shabbily; he was given a shared room at the Maha Bodhi College and then moved to a small room with no bedsheets before being asked by Charles Hewavitarne to take over management of the Maha Bodhi Press.[63] He found the Foster-Robinson hospital "filthily dirty," and the Foster Seminary in Kandy both dirty and badly managed. He had met a Hungarian Buddhist volunteer at the seminary, Dr. Arpad Ferenczy, and he too was being treated badly. To make matters worse, Power concluded by producing the contents of a letter he had received from Christmas Humphreys:

Dear Erle . . . If you by any streak of fate have any hand in influencing his (the Anagarika's) future movements, use it against his wasting his time in this country. . . . The old man sent for money from Ceylon and bought a house in Ealing which is so far out no one will come out so far to see him more than once or twice, and sits there high and dry with an incompetent crowd of well-meaning idiots round him who advise him this way and that according to the weather, but all with equal disregard for common-sense! But no money or advice will avail. The Anagarika is played out. As a means of propaganda he does more harm than good. His idea of a lecture on Buddhism is to tell funny stories on Christian-

61. In a diary entry of August 23, 1927, Dharmapala noted that contributions for the London Buddhist vihara had reached Rs. 18,126. In other words, he managed to raise another Rs. 10,000 in the eight months that followed the public critique by the "Sincere Buddhist."

62. "The Maha Bodhi Society," *Ceylon Daily News*, December 24, 1926.

63. Ernest Erle Power, "The Maha Bodhi Society: American Convert Contradicts Mr. Dharmapala," *Ceylon Daily News*, December 31, 1926. The death of Dr. Arpad Ferenczy was announced on page 1 of the *Ceylon Daily News* that day, and it was revealed in the January 5, 1927, edition that he had died of an overdose of opium.

ity, so undoing our work rather than helping it. A true Buddhist builds up rather than everlastingly pulling down. Yours aye, Toby Humphreys[64]

Politics had left him behind, the British had come to regard him as irrelevant, and now a distinguished Buddhist and ostensible collaborator was revealed in the island's leading newspaper as believing that Dharmapala was "played out."

Amid all of these accusations, Dharmapala knew that rumors of another scandal—the threat of a lawsuit from Don Martino de Zilva Wickremasinghe for alienation of affection—could reach Colombo at any time, and that was a rumor with immeasurably greater public impact, not to mention one that threatened his self-esteem. Whatever his worries over the Wickremasinghe scandal reaching Colombo, he would not trim his sails. Instead he gave a talk at a pirivena in Mount Lavinia. A monk introduced him to the gathering, saying that Dharmapala was breaking new ground for Buddhism in all parts of the world and

> building a new Jetavanarama in the hub of the universe. He was soon to leave for London and would probably return by aeroplane (Laughter). There was however a great failing in the Anagarika and that was his strong language (Laughter) . . . not even [monks] were immune from that (Continued laughter).

Dharmapala did not disappoint. Having characterized the society of his times—"nowadays people here are not in a position to invoke the Gods because they were wicked, drank too much, and behaved like pigs (Laughter)"—he turned to the British in particular:

> Europe was decadent, the clothes of the women there were indecorous in the extreme. The women there were always dabbing their faces with pomades and pastes and looking in small hand-mirrors all the time! The speaker here imitated how this was done to the merriment of the house.

He turned his attention to local women, and they did not profit from comparison.

> The English house maid and her Ceylon prototype were at two extremes. In Ceylon, women, especially servants, bathed rarely. They chewed betel

64. Ibid.

and squirted the saliva all over the place. The lamp posts and telegraph standards were standing evidence to the indiscriminate use of chunam [the lime chewed with betel leaf] (loud laughter). They use too much salt in their curries (Laughter). When poor women meet in Ceylon they invariably began picking lice from each other's heads (Loud laughter). English pillow cases were neat and clean, but never could that be said of Ceylonese pillow-cases. In England, children were fed at certain times of the day and nothing more. In Ceylon they were fed at all times and the result was bad digestion (Loud laughter).[65]

Sinhalas were always litigating, he argued, they were "denationalized," and they were slothful. Having explained the London vihara project, he made another appeal for funds. The talk was diverting but scarcely a helpful way to respond to charges about his financial dealings and the disarray at his schools.

He gave three other talks before he left the island, beginning with a conference of monks at his family's home on Aloe Avenue.[66] On that occasion he said that the English were trying to convert Lankans to Christianity and English Buddhists trying to prevent him from returning to London. He urged the monks to help him spread Buddhism in England. Two days later he addressed the public in Kandy at a meeting called to pass a vote of confidence in his work.[67] After asking the gathering to observe *maitreya bhavana* (meditation on compassion) for half a minute, he made jokes about the Bible, discussed the problem of intoxicating drinks, and attacked the British. He saved his most caustic remarks for Power, the *Ceylon Daily News*, and *Dinamina*. His final public presentation came at the annual meeting of the Maha Bodhi Society. On this occasion he addressed financial issues, insisting that "most of the work of the Society had been done with money that [Foster] had given him from time to time." Her contributions came to seven lakhs of rupees, all given without his asking. The contrast with local Buddhists was unmistakable:

One day he was very very sad and wanted money very very badly and meditated about it. Two months afterwards he received Rs. 150,000 from

65. "Anagarika Bitter, A Generation of Vipers," *Ceylon Daily News*, January 11, 1927.

66. "A London Vihare, Anagarika's Whip of Scorpions," *Ceylon Daily News*, January 24, 1927.

67. "Anagarika in Typical Vein, Orgy of Personal Vituperation," *Ceylon Daily News*, January 26, 1927.

Mrs. Foster. Sometime afterwards he was again in need of money and made an entry in his diary to that effect and two months later he received three lakhs from her. Strangely enough the date of sending that money corresponded with the entry in the diary and he thought that even the devas were helping the Society. "A Sincere Buddhist" had derided and disgraced him. He had never asked for money from anyone but if it was given to him he took it.

Ignoring the contradiction between his saying he never asked for money and the fact that he often did just that, Dharmapala concluded with a statement that captured his life work:

> Long years ago he had passed the Government Clerical Service and had he accepted his appointment he would have been like a "wild elephant" not known to anyone. He was now glad that he had not joined the Government Service. Mudaliyar D. D. Wirasinha, who was seated there, was one of those who sat for that examination with him and for the past 30 years he had been living in constant fear. The coloured man lived in constant fear of the white man. The Mahabodhi Society to which he had devoted his services was now known throughout the world. That Society was purely the work of Sinhalese.[68]

That address was his last public presentation in Lanka. The man who had established a universalist organization for the sake of creating a Buddhist world ended up characterizing the Maha Bodhi Society as the "work of Sinhalese."[69]

EXIT, VOICE, AND LOYALTY

Dharmapala couched his sense of estrangement from other human beings in doctrinal terms, but it was constitutional. When he sojourned in London, his alienation fixed on those Sinhalas who lived there or passed through and did not visit him. Feeling neglected and alone was a product of his tempera-

68. "Maha Bodhi Society, Colombo," *Ceylon Daily News*, February 15, 1927.
69. He added that in three more years he would complete forty-five years of service—the length of the Buddha's ministry—and then retire. He reached that iconic figure, if we overlook his diminished health after 1928, assuming his ministry continued to 1930. Leaving the island shortly after the talk, he returned to London, falling sick there, and returned home again in the spring of 1928. He convalesced in Colombo, made no public appearances, and in March 1931 was carried in a chair to the steamer that took him to Calcutta.

ment, not being a Sinhala in a faraway place. He expected more of his own countrymen, but other Buddhists had failed him in their own way:

> AC March [a leading member of the Buddhist Lodge] writes a long letter about the difference between East & West. It is rubbish. The difference is in the skin. In the temperament the non-conformists act differently from the Established Chruchman [sic]. In politics the Tories act differently. No two men act alike. The Westerner eats sugar, rice etc which his ancestor did not get. . . . March wishes to work in harmony with us. It is not possible to work with *Budhists* [sic]. They are agst: *Buddhists* and the Hinayana. (Diary, May 10, 1927)

Dismissing differences between East and West, he made the argument for the universality of Buddhism. The problem was that wherever he pursued that cause, people could not understand the nature of Buddhism, his projects, or his methods of working.

In an inadvertent way Dharmapala's life follows Louis Dumont's schematic interpretation of the Indian life cycle—a person becomes an individual in Indian society only by casting family aside and leading the life of a world renouncer.[70] Only by doing so can he escape caste; only by escaping caste can he become an individual and experience freedom. Calling himself a "brahmacharya," an anagarika—and early on a chela—Dharmapala cut himself off from the householder's life before he entered it. What is more instructive is the Buddhist turn that followed. Having left the social world—as the Buddha had done—he returned to that world and engaged with issues that were distinctly modern, global in their reach, and motivated by the disastrous effects of colonial domination. His inventing the anagarika role is sometimes attributed to his wanting to lead a life of both renunciation and "serving Humanity." He invented the role, the argument goes, because he wanted to be more active in social causes than the monk's role allowed.

The fact of the matter is that the anagarika role had other sources. The first was Theosophical—he got the chela notion from the example of Damodar Mavalankar, and he got the idea to devote himself to social work from an elderly American Theosophist who passed through the island on a social welfare mission as well as from the example of Charles Leadbeater. He

---

70. Louis Dumont, "World Renunciation in Indian Religions," in *Religion, Politics, and History in India: Collected Papers in Indian Sociology*, ed. Dumont (Paris: Mouton, 1970), 48–60.

took a role appropriated by the Theosophical Society and reinvented it in a way for which there was no precedent. The second reason was shaped by the nature of Buddhist renunciation. As his diaries reveal, he would have joined the sangha at an early age if he had not suffered from a disability. To that extent, becoming an anagarika was a response to the constraints on renunciation he found in the Buddhist tradition. At age four, his right leg was disabled by a "paralytic stroke" (Diary, September 17, 1926). The robes, in other words, were more than a way to step outside the householder's life. They reflected his intentions to live a life as renunciatory as his disability would allow, and the yellow robes promised celibacy.

The tension that dominated his adult career was a product of his pursuing the renunciatory life in a public context. He was not the political activist that Gandhi was and imagined no political benefit to be achieved by his own suffering. He was not the global unifier that Olcott tried to be. But he called his periodical the *Journal of the Maha Bodhi Society and the United Buddhist World* for a reason. He wanted to gather support from across the Buddhist world for recovering Bodh Gaya. That support never materialized, and as the years went on, many of his supporters opposed him. In the privacy of his diaries he looked on a distinguished set of Sinhalas as enemies: D. B. Jayatilaka, F. R. Senanayake, G. P. Malalasekera, D. M. de Z. Wickremasinghe, Cassius Perera (Diary, April 13, 1926), and Piyadasa Sirisena (Diary, February 16, 1926). A smaller number of Britons ended up on his enemies list—Humphreys, Caroline Rhys Davids, and Silacara Bhikkhu. Dharmapala fell out with Olcott and Besant, and his relationship with Blavatsky remained intact because of her leaving India early in his career and never returning. He treated his two closest associates—Harischandra Valisinha and Devapriya—with periodic contempt, calling Devapriya a "veritable idiot" (Diary, November 26, 1930). In Calcutta, many of his friendships turned sour, and others were ended when colonial officials advised his Bengali friends to keep away from him during his internment. His relationship with the generality of Sinhala monks was full of suspicion and recrimination, especially the monks who volunteered for missionary work in India. With his own family, his feelings ran cold and hot; he praised his brothers for their support on some occasions and later vilified them for not treating him more generously. When he justified his criticism of British colonialism by saying he had criticized everyone, he spoke the truth, leaving aside what motivated his harshness to family and friends.[71]

---

71. It might be said that his diaries give an unbalanced view of his feelings toward other people, and it is certainly the case that diary keeping allows the writer to exorcise deep emo-

All of these contradictions came together in a talk he gave to Ananda College students. He told the boys how he had traveled on a train in Burma just a month earlier. He had a first-class ticket and settled himself in a first-class compartment, only to be informed by the stationmaster that he had to give his seat to another passenger. He protested that he had a first-class ticket and was told that it was a European bigwig who wanted his place. Dharmapala caught the neck of the stationmaster and pushed him out of the train directly onto the European stepping up into the compartment. He demonstrated how he had gained leverage over the situation by grabbing the *uturusaluva* (scarf) draped around the neck of Principal Kularatne, and throwing him aside. A thousand boys broke into laughter, as he held their attentions as tightly as he held Kularatne's scarf. He then delivered his moral:

> Api sinhalayo. Apata kisi karanayak naha suddhekuTa bayavenTa. Anandayo umbalat sinhala collo. Eka amataka caragatTa cavamadavat epa. (We are Sinhalas. There is no reason why we should be afraid of any white man. You Anandians are Sinhala lads. Always remember that.)[72]

The article concludes that Dharmapala addressed everyone with the pejorative second-person pronoun—"Umba Jayatilaka, umba Arthur Silva, umba Senanayake, moo mage malli Hewavitarana." He added that he used disrespectful words for his attacks on Lanka's greatest men (in the reporter's words) "whenever he wanted to put them or others wise about their failings." As for the Ananda College students, the writer concluded that they were thrilled to be called *umbala* and told of their worth as Sinhalas and Buddhists. I suspect they were less thrilled than confused by the exhortation to greater things couched in a vocabulary of contempt.

Dharmapala's criticism emerged from a need to criticize, and in that regard, he was a critic first and a social reformer second. He acted on his predisposition to criticize others over a lifetime spent persuading others to join him in projects that required collective effort—from recovering Bodh Gaya to reforming Sinhala society and the Buddhist religion. What justified

---

tions. But the pattern is overwhelming, and it is exemplified in the trajectory—initial warmth followed by hostility and anger—of most of his relationships. I have provided only a small fraction of all the hostile feelings—best exemplified by his keeping lists of enemies—he lays out in the diaries.

72. B. A. Pathiratne, "A Lion's Roar against 'Sudda'-Aping Sinhalayas," *Sunday Times of Ceylon*, September 27, 1964.

his harshness were two values that acted as one, his asceticism and his idealism. If he could devote his life to recovering Bodh Gaya, Buddhists could contribute a little to the cause; for the sake of the Buddha's teachings he was celibate, vegetarian, and living at a remove from life; Sinhala Buddhists, his reasoning went, should be willing to become better Buddhists. Because his daily life was more ascetic than the lives of most Sinhala monks, he felt free to criticize them. His asceticism justified his harshness, and his harshness guaranteed his solitude. As against the Dumontian renouncer becoming a pure individual by leaving caste and dharma behind, he gained the renouncer's freedom by virtue of his enormous idealism and splenetic personality.

In the context of a life lived in such an expansive way, those personal qualities had distinctive effects. Just before he was robed as a novice monk in 1931, Dharmapala wrote out a last will, indicating that he wished to be "born again in India in some noble Brahman family and learn the Dhamma in Pali and become a Bhikkhu to preach the Dhamma to India's millions."[73] He told Karandana Jinaratana that Sinhalas could take care of the sasana in Lanka; there was need for workers in India.[74] He saw himself as one of those workers, his last words expressing the hope to keep at the job, being reborn twenty-five times into the future to spread the Dhamma in India. As death approached, he left instructions for the disposition of his remains:

> I am old and feeble and not expected to live and as I am suffering from heart disease, death may occur at any moment.
>
> In the event of my sudden death, I authorize Revd. U. Ottama and Brahmachari Devapriya to take charge of the dead body and have it removed to Holy Isipatana, Sarnath, Benares and there cremated according to Buddhist rites, and the ashes buried in the middle of the Mulagandhakuti Vihara and a small chunar stone Stupa 3 feet high be erected over the ashes.[75]

After news of his failing health reached Colombo, high-ranking monks and the Hewavitarne family ignored his wishes, reclaiming the man who wanted

---

73. Kahawatte Siri Sumedha, *Anagarika Dharmapala: A Glorious Life,* 2 and 37. When his last words were telegraphed from Benares to Sri Lankan newspapers, the reference to his wanting to be reborn in India was not mentioned. " "The Ven. Sri Devamitta Dharmapala, 'Let Me Be Reborn,' Last Words," *Ceylon Daily News,* May 1, 1933.

74. "Ven. Devamitta Dhammapala," *Ceylon Daily News,* May 2, 1933.

75. "Monument over Ashes, Letter by Late Buddhist Leader," *Ceylon Independent,* May 18, 1933.

his ashes kept in India and hoped for future lives there.[76] Raja Hewavitarne took the train north to have his uncle's body embalmed for the sake of accompanying it back to the island for cremation. He reached Sarnath in time but could not find a competent embalmer, and Dharmapala had to be cremated on the spot.[77] The nephew arranged for half of his remains to be interred at Sarnath and carried the other half to Colombo, where his ashes were enshrined at the Maligakanda vihara.[78]

76. An earlier reference to his intentions has him envisioning his ashes being divided, with shares going to London, Calcutta, Sarnath, the Foster-Robinson hospital in Colombo, Maha Bodhi land in Anuradhapura, and Bodh Gaya (Diary, April 30, 1926).

77. "Ven. Devamitta Dhammapala," *Times* [Ceylon], May 2, 1933.

78. "The Ven. Dhammapala's Ashes," *Journal of the Maha Bodhi Society* 61 (1933): 288.

AFTERWORD

On the alter shelf above my desk stands a brass Buddha, looking down
at me . . . my Master's own picture, to the right, is so like . . . this image,
which represents the centuries-long adoration of an Indian man, by foreign people. Nor is the likeness a matter purely of my imagination.
—Sister Nivedita, "The Master as I Saw Him," 271

I want to conclude by saying a few things about the historical moment in
which Dharmapala lived his extraordinary life. It would be wrongheaded
to overstate either the structural forces of his time or his own agency and
self-invention or to speak of sorting out these forces, assigning weight or
priority to one or the other. Instead I have presumed only to characterize
the man and a set of contexts that span a colonial port city, Sinhala villages,
Japanese temples, Western drawing rooms, a camping car before its time, a
colonial legal system, as well as emergent forms of global communication—
newspaper, journals, letters, colonial petitions, and astral messages from the
Himalayas. The moment brought ideological forces to the fore: on the one
side, universalisms that ran from Marxism to Theosophy; on the other, the
full array of nationalisms, the most pertinent one, of course, the rising sense
of Sinhala identity and privilege in his own country. He lived at a moment
when colonialism reached its fullest expression, but that same time saw
broadening signs of anticolonial resistance, burning white-hot in Calcutta,
where he spent most of his days.

It is tempting to say that globalization gained escape velocity during
Dharmapala's lifetime. That is true in a way, but globalization has been
a long-term historical process, and the world has always been becoming
more globalized. Over the long and even the medium term, there are always
more interactions—economic, political, social—between different parts of

the globe and more interactions within any one region, nation-state, empire, and so on. Approaching the present, the spread of what might be called global practices—Theosophy, Western biomedicine, Islam, Christianity, public hygiene, photography—reached faraway places. Those practices produced hybridity, countermovements, and local friction.

A more structural process that characterizes globalization is the rising presence of what C. A. Bayly calls "uniformities."[1] He traces the birth of the modern world to the rise of "uniformities" in the state, religion, political ideologies, economic life, and bodily practices as they developed through the nineteenth century. Those uniformities enabled the widening of the scale of group identity that marked the "long" nineteenth century. Uniformity does not mean homogeneity. It simply means "adjusting practice to create similarities on a larger scale" and "formal similarity and mutual translatability" between forms adopted across the world and filled with local meaning. National flags and postage stamps are good examples—recognizable and perfectly useable absent any knowledge of their local referents. To the extent that these institutions have a modular form and spread from one part of the globe to others, the societies of the world themselves become more uniform, even allowing for hybridity.

Bayly gives considerable attention to the role of religion in the rise of the modern. The "world" religions came to resemble one another: "Islam and Hinduism were more like Christianity in 1914 than they had been in 1780," Bayly writes. By extracting them from the political and economic contexts, they could be more easily distinguished as "faiths." The World's Parliament of Religions played its own part in that process. As Bayly puts it, what the delegates said to one another was less important

> than the fact that the traditions which had once been bundles of rights, shamanistic practices, rituals and antique verities could now be formally ranked as "religions," with their own spheres of interest and supposedly uniform characteristics.[2]

The process—before the World's Parliament and after—had implications for both doctrine and practice because what scholars said of various religions had its influence on what practitioners made of any religion. Dharmapala's advantage as a Buddhist missionary was his knowledge of English, but his

1. *The Birth of the Modern World 1780–1914: Global Connections and Comparisons* (Malden, MA: Blackwell, 2004).

2. *The Birth of the Modern World*, 20.

Pali was acquired late and self-taught. As a consequence most of his knowledge of Buddhism came from English-language translations and explications of Buddhism. Reading Western authors such as Edwin Arnold, he acquired Western assumptions about Buddhism as a world religion.

Making religions "uniform" was only one part of the process that marked Buddhism's engagement with modernity. Conventional wisdom stresses that the rise of science, industrialization, the spread of education, and Marxism contributed to the nineteenth-century decline of religion. Bayly says the opposite:

> More even than a period when liberalism or the concept of class rose to power, the nineteenth century saw the triumphal reemergence and expansion of "religion" in the sense in which we now use the term.[3]

In other words, religion, once reified, institutionalized, and made uniform, became a central part of modern life. It also contributed to the new identities of individuals and societies alike. The claims of each world religion became much better known and acted on in the period Bayly takes on.[4] In a religion such as Buddhism, one of those claims was its very generality—what the religion asserted was good not for an ethnic group or the original community of believers alone. The message was good for humankind. Buddhists can rightfully claim that the Dhamma carried a universal message from the beginning. Even so, Buddhism was transformed in the 1780–1914 period from a birth religion to one that welcomed new practitioners and from an Asian religion to a global one.

Preaching Buddhism as a doctrine addressed to the human condition has a history of several thousand years. What changed in the late nineteenth century was the circumstances of the moment—a colonial subject preaching to his masters, a brown man instructing white men and women, a layman addressing clerics about their own religion. Dharmapala played all of those roles. When he greeted the delegates at the World's Parliament of Religions by saying that he brought the good wishes of 475 million Buddhists, he reiterated the logic of the occasion, world religions encountering one another in embodied form. He put on offer a religion that Westerners would have had a hard time identifying with a century earlier. By publishing a journal that transcended ethnic and sectarian difference, he did more than create a channel of communication among Buddhists. He addressed an

---

3. *The Birth of the Modern World*, 325.
4. *The Birth of the Modern World*, 364–5.

imagined community of Buddhists. He assumed that Buddhism was a world religion with the same formal qualities as other religions.

Bodh Gaya's significance derived not simply from its role in the Buddha's awakening. It became a pilgrimage site commensurate with the holy places of other religions. The tragedy, Dharmapala thought, was that pilgrims' access to the place was jeopardized by its being controlled by people of another religion, a religion that had been historically hostile to his own. To that extent his struggle at Bodh Gaya played a part in the social construction of two world religions, each with competing interests and emergent identities. The struggle had a second interactive consequence, for putting a Buddhist claim on the place led to popularizing and routinizing the practice of pilgrimage itself.[5] All world religions have one; Buddhism had one organized around a sacred site held by another religion, and that was simply wrong.

In other ways Dharmapala did not play much of a role in the nineteenth-century standardizing of Buddhism. His role in establishing correct belief was modest. Hikkaduve Sumangala tried to do so for Theravada, as did Olcott acting in the cause of establishing Buddhist beliefs all Buddhists could endorse.[6] Dharmapala wrote that he translated *The Buddhist Catechism* into Sinhala and insisted on doctrinal corrections being inserted into later editions (Diary, September 16, 1908). His efforts at reforming Buddhism by returning it to ancient practice followed Olcott's logic, constructing it as a world religion with an ancient history and modern appeal to non-Buddhists. His articles in the *Journal of the Maha Bodhi Society* explained the key points of the Buddha's teachings, compared Buddhism to other world religions, and made the argument for the compatibility of Buddhism and science. Most of the pieces explain the Buddhism of Lanka, Burma, and Thailand, and when Japan appears, the articles concentrate on her industrial might and consequent obligations. A stream of articles in the journal give a running account of Dharmapala's own Buddhism with its emphasis on missionizing, celibacy, cleanliness, the uttari manussa dhamma, and the bodhisat life.[7]

---

5. Huber, *The Holy Land Reborn.*

6. Blackburn's *Locations of Buddhism* provides a good account of Hikkaduve's role in doing so.

7. "Wanted Buddhist Missionaries and Brahmacharis," *Journal of the Maha Bodhi Society* 20 (1912): 222–3 and 226–7; "Precepts to Be Observed by Brahmachari (Celibate)," *Journal of the Maha Bodhi Society* 22 (1914): 237–9; "The Duty of the Bhikkhus and Laymen," *Journal of the Maha Bodhi Society* 27 (1919): 115–7; "Why Not Establish an Anagarika Order of Brothers?,"

As he made his way around the world, the Buddhism he preached changed from place to place, marked by what Blackburn calls "locative pluralism."[8] As he moved about, he strategized relative to groups and interests that shifted. In Lanka, the Buddhism that concerned him was less a world religion than a social and political formation, now corrupted by British rule. In India, his Buddhism turned out to be perfectly compatible with Hinduism, just as his British Buddhism was comfortable with Christianity, emphasizing love and a place for both the Hindu gods and British god. And that religion was Theravada Buddhism, preached by Theravada monks, not Buddhism in generic form. Even without including the uttari manussa dhamma that he himself pursued, it is better in Dharmapala's case to speak of Buddhisms than a standardized world religion. In some ways he was neither a traditionalist nor a modernizer. Preaching different Buddhisms around the world was hardly an example of making the religion uniform, and on this count it is hard to call him either a standardizer or modernizer. Against this background, his conception of the brahmacarya life—celibacy, cleanliness, regulating sleep to produce a union of sleep and wakefulness—becomes the still point of the turning world.[9]

In the matter of demystifying belief, he sought to reform standards of monkly behavior, less so to change their practices. His own sermonizing influenced Sinhala monks to transform Buddhist preaching from reciting and chanting Pali to demotic Sinhala. He had little use for astrology, but his own Buddhism contained its share of mystical elements. The popularity of lay meditation in Sri Lanka has sources more important than Dharmapala, and neither the journal nor his written work says much about it, his own practice notwithstanding. Meditation is scarcely a rational practice.[10] But it has become a major source of Buddhism's appeal to non-Buddhists and Western Buddhists, however uncomfortably it fits the model of Buddhism as a rationalistic religion. Nor are the elements that he took from Theosophy—adepts living in the Himalayas, communications received from them in ways that physics did not understand, and the very idea of the otherworld—a model of rationality. The elements of Buddhism that interested him most centered

---

Journal of the Maha Bodhi Society 33 (1925): 181–2. These articles were followed by a proposal for the organization of the anagarika order in Europe. George Grimm, "Draft of Rules for a Buddhist Order Colony," *Journal of the Maha Bodhi Society* 35 (1927): 168–78.

8. *Locations of Buddhism*, 209–10.

9. "Precepts to Be Observed by the Brahmachari (Celibate), " 237–9.

10. Arthur Danto, *Mysticism and Morality: Oriental Thought and Moral Philosophy* (New York: Harper and Row, 1972).

on entering "into the penetralia of Paramartha Dharma wherein is to be found the secrets of mystic development." One of his last articles laid out what he understood to be the place of mysticism in Buddhism.[11]

He had real influence on the construction of modern Buddhism, but much of that influence derived from the ways in which others appropriated his example and applied it to the social and political sphere. His heart was in another place. The key to understanding all of his representations is to begin from his own self-conception. He described himself as "brahmacharya Anagarika Dharmapala," and the language is as instructive as the ochre robes. Had his leg not been injured, he would have sought ordination as a monk. Even without it, he identified himself with the Buddha, himself a world renouncer who invested forty-five years in advising and interacting with society. He tried to sleep just four hours a night as the Buddha had. He wanted to meet the future Buddha at the Buddha Jayanti so he could begin his search for salvation in earnest. Whatever claim we might make for his being a social reformer and a modernizer needs to begin from his foundational commitment to world renunciation. However modern and rational his campaign to recover Bodh Gaya by way of litigation, his campaign had ascetic motivations. He would make Bodh Gaya Buddhist or die trying.

The most instructive formula I have found for making sense of Dharmapala's self-understanding is to think about his life in three stages—layman, brahmacarya, and bhikkhu—that produced a liminal middle stage in which he spent most of his days. I owe the schema to Tessa Bartholomeusz, who suggested the Van Gennepian paradigm for understanding Dharmapala's life chronologically.[12] The analogy is helpful, but Bartholomeusz locates Dharmapala for most of his adult life at the front side of the limen, the interface of being a layman and being a brahmacarya. We can get closer to the way he lived his life by locating him at the far side of the limen. In my interpretation he remains a liminal figure, but renunciation comes to the fore and social reform moves to the side. I suggest thinking about him as a would-be bhikkhu or a brahmacarya, not a lay reformer who practiced asceticism on an incidental basis. In China he gave a talk entitled "The Social Gospel of the Buddha" to a audience of Christians, but the social part of the Dhamma turned out to be the Buddha's telling his monks to preach for the good of the many.[13]

11. "The Mystic Element in the Buddha Dhamma," *Journal of the Maha Bodhi Society* 33 (1925): 641–4.

12. *Women under the Bo Tree*, pp. 55–6.

13. *Journal of the Maha Bodhi Society* 21 (1913): 221–4.

Theosophy played a central role in his life, and when we ignore that fact, he returns to his narrative status as a white-robed Buddhist layman who spent his life trying to reclaim sacred places, missionize, and reform Sinhala society. He did all of those things, but his goal was to set out on the long march to his own enlightenment. Theosophy did not inspire the ochre robes, but it gave him the examples of adepts with advanced spiritual status he could emulate. It gave him the model of selfless service to all "Humanity" as both the natural consequence of his spiritual status and tool for further progress. As he writes in his diaries, Theosophy gave him a way to be a Buddhist with higher aspirations than the local monkhood, and it motivated practices such as meditation and asceticism. Those were of course Buddhist practices, but he came to them overcoded with Theosophical referents. He railed against the low standards of the monks and their disinterest in meditation. The mahatmas had high standards, and they practiced meditation. Living as a brahmacarya allowed him to identify his work with the mahatmas without disparaging the religion to which he was born.

Characterizing the place of Theosophy and Buddhism in Dharmapala's life can seldom escape the transidiomatic environment in which he lived. As he lived his life, he moved among subject positions that were Buddhist, Theosophical, and both. I have tried to avoid reifying these forces because it would be foolish to parcel out his life that way. He lived a life of one piece, but it was also a life subject to frequent changes of location and attendant changes in his subject position. Theosophy is a good example. No one underplays the Buddhist elements—that is just the problem. No one underplays the reformative projects he initiated, and my goal has been only to complete the picture. His being a brahmacarya organized his life, and we can characterize his commitment to it as both Buddhist and Theosophical. His efforts to return Buddhism to India were as much Theosophical as Buddhist because the mahatmas themselves were working toward that end. Both of those cultural forms were fluid at any one historical moment and changing over time. I have tried to understand both forms not as things but as adjectives, avoiding the substantialism of the noun *culture* and recognizing the ongoing and pervasive effects of difference and disjuncture.[14]

Dharmapala lived his life as a brahmacarya at the interface of being a celibate ascetic and a member of the monastic order. His renunciation outstripped the lives of the Buddhist monkhood, to be sure, and he aspired

14. I have been reminded of this point by Gananath Obeyesekere. See Arjun Appadurai, "Here and Now," in *Modernity at Large: Cultural Dimensions of Globalization* (Minneapolis: University of Minnesota Press, 1996), 1–23.

to the example of the mahatmas living high in the Himalayas who kept a watchful eye over humankind. He sought to join their company, pursuing the uttari manussa dhamma, which he called "the divine science of Mind," taking parts of the expression from Blavatsky. That expression was joined to the parama vijnana, because he was committed to the highest wisdom, just as he chose membership in the Esoteric Section of the Theosophical Society. This was not a man interested in Protestant Buddhism or laicization but a man interested in the highest wisdom. Only celibates—brahmacaryas and bhikkhus—could aspire to insight into the Dhamma, and only they were entitled to reform the sasana. He had difficult relations with D. B. Jayatilaka, aggravated by the worldliness of his fellow Buddhist and made worse by his choosing to enter the "political field" (Diary, September 28, 1930).

Against the backdrop of Bayly's interest in "uniformities" in the structural evolution of modern religion, the brahmacarya role is an anomaly. Its origins lay in the South Asian tradition, but the notion of celibate restraint came to Dharmapala in several forms. His father likely thought about it in a specifically Buddhist way, but Dharmapala was equally influenced by the chela role and the example of Damodar Mavalankar. The brahmacarya notion was overdetermined as much as it was overcoded. His father had him try it out at age nine, and Dharmapala became a full-time brahmacarya in stages. Obeyesekere and Gombrich point out how Theosophical discourse represented an overcoding of Buddhist doctrine. What they overlook in Dharmapala's own life was that his own self-conception was both overcoded and overdetermined—he was motivated by Theosophical as well as Buddhist meanings. Being a brahmacarya served the peculiarities of his own temperament—he happened to live in a place and a time where a life of renunciation and solitude carried its own legitimacy. But how many Buddhists of his time or any other time dreamed of the solitude of the Himalayas, rose at two in the morning to practice meditation, or wanted to meet the grand lama?

Dharmapala sought solitude at an early age, and the brahmacarya role gave him a vehicle to have it. The practice also gave him a way to play a renunciatory role in a social context where his disability prevented his becoming a monk. He was a monastic up to his limits, and he took full ordination at the end of his life. It was his celibacy above all else that justified his presumption to criticize others, and his inclination to criticism was constitutional.[15] When he was a teenager, his mother lost a daughter in infancy

---

15. The parenthetical descriptor at the end of his title "Precepts to Be Observed by the Brahmachari (Celibate)" suggests he wanted no mistake about it—the religious life requires celibacy.

and became deeply depressed. He scolded her and told her to snap out of it. Dharmapala's account of the incident emphasizes the role it played in justifying his celibacy, lest he inflict similar pain on another woman by way of the death of a child he had fathered. An equally important conclusion is the transgressive quality of a young boy presuming to criticize his mother, the more so in a South Asian context.

He knew he was critical of others, but his renunciation justified his criticism in the same way it allowed him access to the deepest truths of the Dhamma unavailable to Western scholars and anyone who did not practice celibacy. My view is that he would have been hypercritical had he become an executive of his father's furniture company. His renunciation had another virtue. It allowed him to play the same role abroad as at home. He was not cosmopolitan abroad and a nationalist at home. He was a renouncer, critic, missionary, and reformer wherever he went, but he was especially uneasy in Sinhala villages. The camping car gave him an instrument to keep his distance, interacting with people without becoming dependent on them.

Being a brahmacarya also enabled his life of social reform. Seeking salvation did not prevent social reform and service to humanity—it required it. Dharmapala's paradigm was the Lord Buddha himself. The ultimacy of his spiritual aspirations makes his social achievements—establishing the Maha Bodhi Society, founding a journal, initiating the struggle for control of Bodh Gaya, building a temple in Calcutta and installing monks in London, restoring Sarnath, and urging Sinhalas to higher standards—no less important. He had his share of failures—the Bodh Gaya case, the Ethico-Psychological College at Rajagiriya, the industrial school at Sarnath—always moving on to the next challenge, never lingering to administer his successes or reflect on failure. A telling expression he used to refer to himself was "pilgrim Dharmapala," and movement is appropriate to the renouncer seeking to leave samsara (Diary, October 21, 1926).

The binary quality of his life was a product of the Lord Buddha's example. Its hybrid character derived from the historical moment, his far-ranging travels, and his engagement with Theosophy. Koot Hoomi's injunction that "the Buddha alone is the way to true perfection" reinscribes that hybridity perfectly, and the mahatmas may have been distant paradigms of spiritual excellence and service to Humanity, but they were also instruments that he could use to reflect on the monkhood of his day. The mahatmas were untiring in their efforts to serve others, selfless, and incapable of corruption. They provided Dharmapala with exemplars of what could be done in a world that transcended the enervating effects of colonial rule. His affection for Blavatsky owed to her mythopoetic genius, but it also came from her willingness to put him in touch with Koot Hoomi. To that extent the pristine Buddhism often associated with his life had Theosophical motivations.

It is harder to know what to say about his encounter with "spiritual marriage." It seems altogether alien to his commitment to celibacy, even allowing for the role Theosophy played in his life. His contemplating having a "spiritual companion" could be attributed to any number of sources—the openness of all human lives, his inconstancy, his hybridity, or his exposure to Theosophists and other Westerners. It could be justified by interpreting the practice as a higher form of self-denial—the proximity of a woman is nothing that the Himalayan adepts contended with—and thus suitably South Asian. Beyond making the connection to Theosophy and the historical moment, I can add only one point: the way he approached "spiritual marriage" furnishes another example of his considerable inventiveness. In a Theosophical context spiritual marriage developed in the context of marriage itself, as in the case of Neel Kamal Mukherjee, and it represented a retreat from the householder way of life. For Dharmapala, the prospect was reimagined. The celibacy came first, as opposed to the conventional withdrawal from sexuality in marriage. But it was characteristic of a life of regular invention—taking on the ochre robes and preaching while not entering the monkhood, traveling across India, Japan, and the West to carry the Buddha's message, reforming his own community while not living in it or wanting to be a part of it—all acts that entail presumption as much as imagination.

The hybrid character of his life went beyond his transidiomatic passage between Theosophy and Buddhism. It included his engagement with the British imperium. He lacked the rights of citizenship, but he was fully aware of his role in the imperial system. The regular petitions are an apt example. I take his being embedded in the imperial system as typical of his times and his social class, and social class, I think, played a central part in his regarding himself as a part of the empire. That relationship was full of contradictions, but most accounts pick up on only his nationalism. If we want to understand the man, we need to begin with his being a brahmacarya and then add that he was a British imperial brahmacarya, sending petitions to the king, feting colonial officials, and buying war bonds during the First World War. When a South Asian man takes the path of renunciation, he gives up not only his family but also his class identity. It is a single package. But Dharmapala's invention was being both in the world and out of it, and his diaries reveal his class identity on a regular basis.

His being a son of a well-to-do and urban family led to many things. He was reputedly more comfortable with Westerners than with his own people, but I believe a more accurate way to put it is that he was comfortable with the kinds of Westerners he met, English-speaking, well-to-do, and cultured members of the Theosophical society, not the generality of Westerners. To that extent he was comfortable with similar sorts of Sri Lankans and Bengalis. Discomfort began at the city limits of Colombo, and his *Gihi Dina Chariyava* was his attempt to bring civilized manners to village life. If that assertion makes Dharmapala sound condescending, the condescension was a product of his class origins, his privilege as a renouncer to criticize, and his assumption that the empire had responsibilities to its people. But they must do their part. Only by behaving by his standards would Sinhalas win colonial sympathy for the benefit of the people of the island. Without Sinhala self-reform, the British were not going to think about their colonies with any measure of fellow feeling.

He may have wanted to become a monk, but the liminal qualities of the brahmacarya role fitted him perfectly. He could act on social issues in a way that a monk could not because the limen has its advantages. He could travel by himself and live independently of others, and his autonomy was not an issue in the way it would have been for a monk. He did not have to worry about the 227 monastic rules. Being a brahmacarya allowed him to contemplate what a monk could not, "spiritual marriage." As for the ways monks should conduct themselves, he had largely traditional ideas. I quote his most comprehensive account of the monkly role at length because what he wanted was wildly different from what he got:

> The duty of a good Bhikkhu is to study the Dhamma, to attend to the daily duties in connection with the worship of Buddha, to keep the arama (temple premises) clean, to get his food by begging, to practice kammatthana for the development of his psychic faculties, and for the attenuation of passions. He has to observe the disciplinary rules of perfect conduct; has to control his sense organs in walking, standing, sitting lying down, moving from place to place, and to cultivate attentiveness coupled with wisdom in every act he does. He has to observe the rules of perfect livelihood in order to get his food . . . and make strenuous effort to prevent sinful thoughts arising, to create good thoughts and to fertilise them; he has to resolve that either he shall die in the battle field of psychic progress or conquer and avoid all passionate and sensual longings; cast off angry thoughts and hatred; not let his mind become indolent and slothful, and his perceptions weak; nor let restlessness and scepticism have control over him. . . . His mind must not dwell on any

other subject outside his special psychical field of activity. He should practice wakefulness by sleeping only four hours during night, that is from ten o'clock to two o'clock in the morning, and from two o'clock he should live the awakened life. A cloister to promenade daily is a necessity for the Bhikkhu, and he is enjoined to walk to and fro before going to sleep, and the first thing after he gets up from sleep at two o'clock in the cloister to use the cloister. Cleanliness is absolutely necessary for the psychical student. The Lord Buddha emphasizing cleanliness declared that the observance of cleanliness is the fulfillment of the law of the Buddha. Physical cleanliness is a corollary to mental purity. . . . The object of the Bhikkhu life is to preserve the perfect life of Brahmachariyam. Renunciation is the law of the Bhikkhu's life. He must not touch gold or silver, nor be attached to his residence, his patrons, his clan, and he must not hesitate to impart knowledge to others. . . . He must be content with whatever food he gets and be ready to share it with other Bhikkhus. He must not covet anything. He must be ready to leave his residence just as the bird readily leaves one tree to another. He should love solitude, and not be fond of society. Gossip he has to avoid, and where he could not be engaged in spiritual talk, he should observe the principles of jhana. He must keep the mind in a state of perpetual activity with perceptions of light and cultivate serenity of mind. . . . These are the essentials of the perfect life of a Bhikkhu.[16]

We can argue about where to draw the line between the traditional understanding of the bhikkhu's life and Dharmapala's own interpretation of "the perfect life of Brahmachariyam." What we cannot do is imagine that he wanted Buddhist monks to pursue social reform, salaried employment, or political activities.

In a long piece he laid out in Sarnath Notebook no. 4 and signed— usually an indication that he intended the piece for publication—he summarized his views in these words:

The object of wearing the yellow Robe is to put an end to the recurrence of the sorrows of disease, old age, death and to realize the infinite happiness of Nibbana, if not in this life, in some subsequent life not exceeding seven lives.

16. "The Duty of the Bhikkhus and Laymen," *Journal of the Maha Bodhi Society* 27 (1919): 115–7, at 115–6. I have shortened the passage by eliminating Pali expressions and repetitions, while trying to be faithful to the whole.

I know of no other place where he says that enlightenment lies within seven lifetimes, as opposed to the more common "countless lifetimes away" imagery. But the relatively proximate goal makes concentrating on meditation and retreat all the more pressing.

Nor can we imagine that he wanted to laicize Buddhism. His views on the duties of laypeople have their idiosyncrasies—he draws a distinction between "independent" householders who are fitted for the holy life and "menials" who are not—but he clearly did not intend to reduce the authority of the monkhood, enhance the role of the laity, or blur the distinction between them:

> Now the duties of a layman are to take refuge in the Buddha, Dhamma, and Sangha . . . Upasaka [layman] has to observe, most scrupulously, the five observances of non-destruction, non-stealing, non-sensuality, no-lying, and non-intoxication. He must get rid of superstitions, avoid worship of false gods; take care of holy Bhikkhus by helping them with robes, food, residences, and medicines. He should visit the Bhikkhus and listen to the Dhamma. He must not engage in unrighteous occupations, viz. trading in flesh, intoxicants, living beings, murderous weapons, and poisons. He has to contribute to the welfare of his relations, show hospitality to strangers, give thanks to the guardian angels, and departed spirits and pay taxes to the king. He should visit the temple and pay worship to the Bodhi tree and the Relic Sthupa [sic], and on sabbath days observe the eight precepts.[17]

His interpretation of lay responsibilities follows from what he took to be primordial Buddhism. It serves as a parallel world to the actual behavior of monks and householders of his time and occupies a place of hybridity where one "pays taxes to the king" and observes the Buddhist Sabbath.

In the next paragraph he moves in a direction that seems to blur the line he has just drawn, saying that the Buddha made no distinction among bhikkhus and bhikkhunis, upasakas and upasikas.

> They were all to learn the Pali Dhamma and study it and proclaim it for the welfare of others. The consummation of the Brahmachariya life was not only for the Bhikkhus and Bhikkhunis, but also for upasikas and upasikas. The door to Nibbanam is open to all. The highest Arhatship was not the monopoly of the male species of human beings. It was the appanage of both men and women.

17. "The Duty of the Bhikkhus and Laymen," 116.

> To the Bhikkhus the Blessed One gave the Higher Doctrine, the ut-
> tari manussa dhamma, for the realization of Nibbana and fruits of holi-
> ness. . . . To the lay people he taught the Doctrine of Domestic Ethics
> ending in the happiness of heaven.
>
> The householder who is following the profession of trade or agricul-
> ture is best fitted for the holy calling. The menial engaged in servitude
> is unfit for the high calling. But the independent householder, engaged
> in either trade or agriculture, . . . after he has heard the Dhamma from
> either the Blessed One or one of His disciples, begins to think of the en-
> cumbrances of the family life, and wishing to realize the holy life joins
> the Order of Bhikkhus, and strives for Arhatship.

In his view, renouncers and laypeople are not equivalent in status or similar
in responsibilities. What makes them similar is one exceptional thing: their
potential to aspire to enlightenment. The key is the "the consummation of
the Brahmacharya life," and here he is referencing his own life, the layman
following the uttari manussa dhamma, taking advantage of his independence, and entering the monkhood in his final years. For his part, joining
the monkhood at the end of his life did not contradict his earlier assumption
that he was unqualified. It was the consummation of the spiritual progress
he had made since that time.

Dharmapala held largely traditional and conventional views about the
role of monks and laypeople, however distinctive his emphases on cleanliness, independence, solitude, and everyone's acting on the prospect of enlightenment. The question is why he has been seen to have invented new
and modern practices for both roles. Why is he the inspiration for monkly
activism and laicization? I can only repeat the point with which I began
and add a second one. The narrative compulsions of the story of an old society becoming a new nation are subtle but powerful. So is the power of
seeing him as a modernizing and rationalizing figure. There is no denying
that laypeople are increasingly involved in the public life of Buddhism and
monks increasingly involved in political affairs, social reform, and secular
employment. His life was central to the process by which Buddhism was
dragged into the public sphere. He played a part in demanding monks become more active and laypeople more concerned with acting on their religious responsibilities. But his instructions to renouncers and householders
were calls to pursue traditional roles more aggressively, not take on new
ones. As Buddhists of both categories threw themselves into new activities,
harking back to Dharmapala became a way to talk of the emergence of a national subjectivity—Sinhala, Buddhist, righteous, and activist.

I have a second suggestion that moves beyond the logic of *post hoc ergo propter hoc* and narrative compulsion. Abroad Dharmapala was an anomalous if not bewildering figure: in Japan he was taken for an Indian; in England, for a woman and on another occasion a child; and in America, for a Hindu. His liminal identity must have confused Sinhala Buddhists, even if their threshold of confusion was higher than that of foreigners. His own people knew he was not a bhikkhu. Lithographs of the Buddha aside, they had no referent for the robes tied in a way that the monks did not, and he did not preface his public presentations by explaining his dress, his celibacy, or his spiritual aspirations. Early on in his public career he wore a beard, and neither monks nor laymen of his time did that. Until he took ordination, he did not shave his head, and while he kept his hair neat, he usually wore it longer than a layman of his social class. In the 1880s he wore his hair shoulder length. The public knew he was not a Hindu sannyasin. No one could ignore the fact that he was a Hewavitarne and the eldest son of parents known for their piety. His travels abroad, residence in India, list of achievements, and presumption to criticize must have confirmed his being a pious Buddhist of uncertain status.

He hectored Sinhalas with their failures and urged them to reform. His list of two hundred rules made what he had in mind absolutely clear to the most inattentive. He insisted on recovering the high aspirations of the distinguished ancestors who built the irrigation systems and great cities of ancient Lanka. He wanted ordinary people to energize themselves—just as he had done, traveling constantly, sleeping little—in order to rebuild a way of life that could be traced back two millennia. The Maha Bodhi Society was a society of laymen, but he left its management to Devapriya, and he was a fellow celibate. Doing sasana work required celibacy above all other forms of renunciation. If Sinhalas drew a moral from Dharmapala's life, they drew it from an energetic Buddhist who appeared more a layman than a renouncer, even if he thought of himself in the opposite way. He may not have wanted to elevate the status of Buddhist laypeople, but his ambiguous example was compelling. Self-invention has its privileges, but it leaves in its wake its own excitements and provocations.

The Diaries and Notebooks Explained

In their present form the Dharmapala diaries cover a forty-year period in thirty-six foolscap-size, hardbound volumes. They provide a real-time description of his life from the point when he caught the diary-keeping habit in 1889 until 1930, when the diary ceases without explanation (although Dharmapala's deteriorating health over the last three years of his life seems like a sufficient explanation). The diaries were written by hand, although he acquired a typewriter when his patron Mary Foster sent him one in 1907 (Diary, August 23, 1907). He was enthusiastic about using the typewriter but seems to have saved it for correspondence with English-speakers and petitions to colonial officials. Even after the arrival of the typewriter, he kept to making handwritten entries in the diary. The diary-keeping practice invited it, and his world wandering would have made traveling with a typewriter difficult.

The daily entries were written in English, although occasionally Sinhala phrases and less often passages in Pali appear. Dharmapala usually made entries on a daily basis, writing in Colombo, Kandy, on his tours by camping car across Sri Lanka, and on ocean voyages and train trips. The magnitude of his daily recollections grew as he approached the end of his diary keeping in 1930. The earlier entries run a paragraph or two; in the 1926–30 interval he often produced several pages of material for a day. Sometimes he fell behind in recording his works and days and then related the events of several days after the fact.

The diaries took their present form in the 1960s when the board of management of the Dharmapala Trust in Colombo decided to launch the typing project. Typing began in 1961, and the last numbered volume for 1927 was transcribed in April and May of 1962. One volume was not put in typed form until 1977, suggesting that it must have been lost for a time. I have not been able to discover what became of the original handwritten diaries. The typescript diaries now reside at the Sri Lankan National Archives and the Maha Bodhi Society library in Colombo.

Dharmapala made an earlier attempt to have the diaries typed in 1926 after he had arranged to have the original diaries shipped from Calcutta to London. He was contemplating writing his autobiography at the time, and Don Martino de Zilva Wickremasinghe told him that his wife, Vera, would do the typing (Diary, September 26, 1926). Dharmapala had no hand in producing the 1965 transcript, but the transcript he envisioned in 1926 was his idea. He was aware of the historical significance of his life, and the text takes a middle course between private reminiscences and laying down the day-by-day incidents, thoughts, and historical markers that would give him an aide-mémoire from which to write an autobiography.

Dharmapala was a list maker—of friends, enemies, accomplishments. Some lists appear repeatedly, and listing things seems to be less a matter of record keeping than internal conversation. In the Sarnath notebooks, there appear talks and papers that seem written for publication. In the diaries a "memorandum" occupies either the first or last pages of each annual volume and typically includes addresses of friends and supporters, records of funds transferred from one account to another, doctrinal taxonomies, quotations from his reading, and random intelligence such as the population of Sri Lanka broken down by religion and ethnicity. The annual financial accounts of the Maha Bodhi Society appear at the end of many diaries. Michael Roberts calls the diaries a "serialized autobiography," stressing that they are "more than a prosaic corpus of daily appointments."[1] They are both more and less than an autobiography narrowly defined. Dharmapala writes most often of everyday events, his diet, the flow of money between himself and others, his correspondence and his reading, the weather, and servant problems. The notebooks were not written on a daily basis and have fewer references to Dharmapala's life. They contain sermons, long stretches of text copied from books he had read, jottings, doodles, lists, and reflections on the British, various monks, and world affairs.

Most of the material is entirely prosaic. Consider what Dharmapala says on the first day of the diary:

> Went to see the Peoples' Park & Museum in Madras. Bought stationery etc. for office use in Colombo. Paper etc from the Theosophist. Bid farewell to Mr. Johnson & the Barones [sic] & Mr. Harte. Conferred with Col: Olcott about the Jap: trip. Got Rs. 20 from the Theosophist Manager for expenses. Made nam to the G, K.H. and M. (January 1, 1889)

1. "Himself and Project," 117.

The writing is straightforward and without rhetorical effects, whatever one makes of the veneration of the Theosophical adepts, Koot Hoomi and Master Moriya. I would characterize the diaries by emphasizing their uneven, eclectic quality. Some entries are a record of people seen and places visited, but others are more reflective and generalizing. If there is a thematic focus in the text, it is Dharmapala's spiritual development, but much of the text simply marks daily incidents and his response to them.

Dharmapala learned the diary-keeping habit from Olcott.[2] He explained his diaries in an article that appeared in his column in the *Sinhala Bauddhaya*. The diaries begin with an invocation of the god Sakra out one day in his chariot. His charioteer noticed that the Sakra was raising his hands in worship to certain people as they passed them in the chariot and asked him why he was doing that. Sakra replied that good people—people who take care of their families and observe *sil* (Buddhist precepts)—deserve the worship of the gods.[3] Sakra intended to write their names in a golden book. Elsewhere Dharmapala explained his motives in similar terms:

> Earlier Buddhists had pinpot [merit books] where they wrote their good deeds. . . . From the age of nineteen, I have been keeping a diary. From morning til I go to sleep, what I did that day I note in the diary. Diaries are useful to [sic] include both bad and good actions, journeys, the books I read, joy and woes, friends and relatives, the ideas I am thinking, the time I arise, the time I go to bed.[4]

The diaries are considerably more than merit books. Dharmapala was not hugely introspective, but neither was he a proper Victorian. He was forthcoming on matters one might not expect, such as his struggles with his own sexual urges, and he regularly indicated practices that have no connection to merit making— his smoking cigarettes, the times when he ate meat, and anxiety about his numerous physical ailments.

The bound volumes give the diaries an illusion of uniformity. I have no way of knowing whether the typists took everything from Dharmapala's handwritten original without editing or deletion. Some years are missing. "Wrote to Devapriya about the missing Diary of 1926," he noted. "No one cares to take the least interest in the work I am doing" (Diary, August 31, 1930). Either a new typist takes up the task of transcribing entries for October 1930, or the incumbent

2. Karunaratne, *Anagarika Dharmapala*, 56.
3. Guruge, *Dharmapala Lipi*, 108.
4. Karunaratne, *Anagarika Dharmapala*, 57.

becomes slipshod in transcribing Dharmapala's words. There is a huge increase in the number of typographical errors. One passage suggests both the quality of the typing and the certainty of missing pages:

> After I had written the letters to *Vajiranana, Kanti, Devapriya & Payne* the mind became active and the body was made to go I [*sic*] the book case wherein my old diaries are placed. They were arranged by Manamperi and he had them to arranged [*sic*] that it was easy to solict [*sic*] the one required. There was one Diary with out [*sic*] the year and the cover was of black colour. I pulled it out and to my astonishiment [*sic*] I found it was the missing one. But on going over the pages I discovered that in certain months several pages have been removed each month. . . . The number of pages missing from my Diary of 1926 is 44, [*sic*] Very likely they have been removed by some one who is in touch with DMDZ Wickramasinha. (Diary, October 1930)

Dharmapala then enumerates the pages he cannot find—"4 pp in May, June 3pp. July 17pp, Aug. 10pp, Sept. 8pp total 42 pages missing." Those are pages referring to incidents that he feared might be exploited were Wickremasinghe to bring suit in a divorce case.

I have not been able to find any explanation of the absence of diaries for 1910, 1912, 1914, 1922, 1923, 1928, 1929 and for the critical years Dharmapala spent interned in Calcutta (1916–7). It is likely that those diaries were confiscated by colonial officials and never returned. What remains of 1915, 1916, and part of 1917 is an account so brief that they have been bound in a single volume. There is also text for those missing years found in Sarnath Notebook no. 27 labeled "Diary for 1915–19" and "Diary for 1918." The diaries end three years before Dharmapala's death because of his extremely frail condition.[5] The last three years for which we have diaries (1926, 1927, 1930) have entries many times longer than those he made in previous years, testimony to his having more time on his hands despite his deteriorating health.

There are other complications. Volume 23 in bound form includes stretches from 1911, 1912, 1915, 1916, and parts of 1917. The 1911 text takes a new direction. Instead of accounting for Dharmapala's encounters with people, his rising early for meditation, and his battles with sexual urges, the diary becomes an office register, in which teachers and employees of the Maha Bodhi Society are obliged to note when they arrived at work and when they left. Nothing in this

---

5. Sarnath Notebook no. MBS 2475 begins with Dharmapala's attempt to restart his diary on January 1, 1932, but it is likely he was too feeble by 1932 to carry on.

stretch of entries—which starts in April 1911 and comes to an abrupt halt on October 29, 1911—suggests Dharmapala's presence.[6] These entries follow this form: "I attended School at 10.35 A.M. I have worked according to the routine of the classes and left School at 4.05 P.M. M.N. Chatterjee, Teacher." I have no way of knowing who decided to include this register as part of the thirty-six volumes or what motivated the change from diary keeping to personnel management and back to diary keeping.

Dharmapala's hand is not apparent in any of these deviations from form. The entry for October 29, 1911, says that "The Anagarika Dharmapala returned from Ceylon after an absence of nearly 9 months. He came especially to celebrate the Wesakha Festival," and the writer is not Dharmapala speaking of himself in the third person. By the end of that page, which skips over many days, there is an entry indicating that he left Calcutta on May 6, 1912, on the Madras Mail for Colombo, catching a steamer there for a final trip to Japan and on to Hawaii to visit Mary Foster. Matters get messier on the following page (June 13, 1912) when the writer speaks in the first person while also making reference to Dharmapala: "I wanted keys from Nagahawatta [who was then running the Calcutta vihara], who gave me the keys of [the] Almirah only with the remark 'Mr. Dharmapala has told me to keep the keys with me and to give to you when required and to get back them from you when you have done with them.' 'Very well' I replied. He gave me not the keys of Mr. Dharmapala's room." It is unclear who is speaking, here, but it is not Dharmapala.

This anomalous stretch continues for two pages in the bound diary up to June 13, 1912, where there is a reference to Maha Bodhi furniture being sent from 46 Baniapukker Lane to 4A College Square, but those events are indicated as having occurred on September 6, 7, 8, and 9, 1915. In other words, because of the vagaries of collecting, typing, and binding the original diaries, Dharmapala disappears from his own diary from June 13, 1912, until the page following the anachronism just described. From this point (June 2, 1916) he seems to be doing the writing. The passage sounds like him: "Car gone out of order. Driver utterly unfit." The entry that follows—and the entries that continue for the rest of the diaries—return to Dharmapala's life, indicating that the writer went on a motor drive with Naranath Mukherjee, who had been Dharmapala's friend since he took up residence at the Mukherjee house in 1891. The upshot is this: in addition to the several years where there is no diary accounting for his daily life, there is a composite volume (no. 23) that compiles material from 1911, 1912, 1915, 1916, and 1917. Entries from June 1912 until June 1916 are few and discon-

6. Dharmapala spent large blocks of time in Lanka in 1911, but he had managed previously to keep up with his diary wherever he found himself.

tinuous, but more important, whoever is speaking about daily life at the Maha Bodhi Society in Calcutta, the voice is not Dharmapala's.

The most perplexing stretch of diary entries begins in 1917, becoming yet more confusing in December of that year. Some of the 1917 entries seem to have been written several years after the fact and inserted into the diary post facto. Given the long stretches of missing entries just before and during the years Dharmapala was interned, the interval between 1913 and 1918 is generally suspect. Two parallel accounts of Dharmapala's daily life appear in different parts of the diary. The events discussed are represented in similar ways but do not represent two transcripts of one handwritten original. There is an account of December 1917 in one stretch saying one thing and in another place there appears a different treatment of those same days. It is unclear whether one or both accounts is Dharmapala's post facto chronology (from memory?) or an artifact of the typing process of the 1960s. But the 1917–8 interval in the diaries seems to have been written after the fact or transcribed from some source—perhaps a notebook—and added to the diary proper.

Toward the end of Dharmapala's life the diary begins to function in new ways. The diary for 1927 is two to three times as long as earlier volumes, and the "serial autobiography" notion applies much more to the diaries of the final years. He pours himself into accounting for his activities, making a record, and remembering. He was hospitalized during his stay in San Francisco and not well when he got back to London in 1926, and it may be his illness that allowed him to spend so much time on the diary. By 1930 the pattern changed. He was seriously ill—his physician Frank Gunasekera took to praying for his survival—and the diary ceases for almost two months, roughly January 26–March 21. Yet those pages are filled in subsequently, and the focus of the narrative is not Dharmapala's doings (because he is not doing much, although people come to visit him). He focuses on Christianity and critiques it on a running basis through long stretches of the text, all presumably composed long after their dates with large stretches composed at one sitting and inserted in a daily format even though they were not written on that basis.

Another source of information on Dharmapala's life—and more evidence of the uneven quality of the text—comes at the beginning or end of many volumes. The memorandum that appears at the end of the 1889 diary includes a copy of the letter that Japanese Buddhists sent to Hikkaduve Sumangala in response to the letter of welcome that Olcott had carried from Hikkaduve to Japan. The following page includes a guide to the Japanese figures seen in a group photograph taken in Kyoto, followed by a quick accounting of money that Olcott had lent Dharmapala and his minor expenses in Japan, concluding with a list of Japanese priests who served on Olcott's committee and their sects.

Dharmapala calls the material that appears at the end of 1891 "Memoranda. of Reference . . . Addresses, Quotations, and other Matter of Interest." Memoranda in other years are exactly that—addresses of people he has met, inventories of his clothing, lists of texts such as the books that make up the Pali canon, and sayings from the Bible.[7]

Dharmapala's notebooks—of various sizes, bindings, and orientations—are preserved at the Dharmapala Museum in Sarnath, India, and they represent another underutilized source of Dharmapala's representation of his life. They focus on the final stretch of his life. The museum holds fifty-four notebooks and four pocket diaries. Most are dated, and one notebook that carries the title "Tit-Bits 1932" represents material from the years after the diaries themselves cease. The notebooks are readable, but they suffer from wormholes, and the paper in some volumes is decrepit. These notebooks do not follow the chronological form of the diaries proper. They range from Dharmapala's ad hoc thoughts on random topics to his commentaries on texts he has recently read or contemplated. These notebooks are in handwritten form, largely in English, but marked by larger sections in Sinhala or Pali than the diaries. (Dharmapala's correspondence kept on microfilm at the Sri Lankan National Archives reverses this proportion. It is almost entirely in Sinhala with a few letters in English). Some pages contain Dharmapala's doodles and sketches of renovations he envisioned for Sarnath. Focusing on the second half of Dharmapala's life, many notebooks speak of his big projects of that time, completing the Dharmarajika vihara in Calcutta and the Mulagandhakuti vihara in Sarnath.

Making sense of the Sarnath notebooks presents another set of challenges. Some passages are incidental and mundane; some are as revealing as the diaries. There are Dharmapala's sporadic attempts to write a history of his life and reference to a plan for a full-scale autobiography as well as his laying out his views on whatever crosses his mind. Sarnath Notebook no. 4 is entitled "Notes on Muslim Period" but contains his account of vegetarianism, praise for Annie Besant, and "sermons delivered within the hearing of the Gods" and "sermons delivered to the Ghosts of Monotheistic, Polytheistic, and Pantheistic Religions." I have been able to find my way through these notebooks because of the work of Professor Noel Salmond of the University of Ottawa, who put together a guide to the notebooks in March 2003, which remains at the Dharmapala Museum in Sarnath.

As valuable as the diaries are for understanding Dharmapala's life and times, the notebooks have their own virtues as a repository of Dharmapala's comments

---

7. The biblical aphorisms appear in the middle of Dharmapala's entries for April 1892, deviating from the diary form in the middle of the year.

on topics ranging from the Muslim period in India to the life of Dhammananda Kosambi, the Bible, and Kipling's *Kim*. Notebook no. 23 follows the jumbled quality of many of the notebooks but includes a wide range of Dharmapala's views on life, his reading, and accounts of people he encounters in Calcutta. It is entitled "1918, The postponement of the laying of the foundation of the vihara, notes on Christian propaganda, nations, opium trade, booksellers in London, autobiography, Statements of Receipts." Notebook no. 50 includes wonderful material, a substantial commentary dated October 1919 and "To the Beloved Mahatmas who loved our Lord," signed by Dharmapala as if for publication. Number 4 contains Dharmapala's views on astrology, relics, and the "expansion of political Christianity."

The diaries and the notebooks may have served as no more than a place where he could vent his feelings, record his reactions to readings and encounters, and save material for future publication. He prepared a biographical account of his life in Sarnath Notebook no. 4, and the diaries contain occasional summaries of his life and accomplishments, as well as memoranda—often fixed on financial issues—at the end of most volumes. He loved to write down passages from books and newspapers that he found noteworthy. The diaries have a confessional tone, which goes along with the writer's sense of his historical importance. He wanted to have his notebooks published:

> I pasted labels on to my Note Books. Now they are handy. All these were written during the period of my internment at Calcutta. If I had the assistance of an Oriental Scholar all these could be arranged for publication. They are there for future use. I am now feeble to do the work. (Diary, July 5, 1927)

My view is that he regarded diaries and notebooks alike as vehicles for clarifying his own experiences and setting the record straight.

A Chronology of the Life of
Anagarika Dharmapala

1864   September 17, 1864. Dharmapala born Don David Hewavitarne.

1865–70   Dharmapala's education begins at Colombo Girls' Infant School; he then studies under Harmanis gurunanse in a Sinhala-language school.

1868   At age four he is fostered out to his mother Mallika's brother (S. P. D. Gunawardana) and his wife and remains there for some two years. In the same year, his right leg is permanently injured, preventing him from later joining the Buddhist monkhood.

1870–2   Attends Pettah Catholic School, later named St. Mary's.

1872–4   Attends Baptist Sinhala School.

1873   Dharmapala's father has him try out the brahmacarya role at temple for one day and advises him to be content with whatever he gets to eat and to sleep very little.

1874   Hewavitarne family moves from Pettah to Kotahena.

1874–6   Dharmapala attends St. Benedict's College.

1875   November 1875. Theosophical Society established in New York City.

1876   July 9, 1876. Harischandra Valisinha born in Hunupitiya, Negombo.

1876–8   Dharmapala attends and boards at CMS Boys' English School in Kotte.

1878   Migettuvatte Gunananda tells Dharmapala that a Russian lady and an American gentleman have established the Theosophical Society in New York City.

            Dharmapala reads first number of the *Theosophist*.

1878–83   Dharmapala attends St. Thomas Collegiate Institute, North Colombo. Removed by father after Catholic attack on Buddhists at St. Lucia and remains out of school for nine months, attending meetings of the Liberal Association and Salvation Army.

Attends Royal College.

Returns as a student to St. Thomas Collegiate Institute.

1879   September 1879. Olcott and Blavatsky move to Bombay and establish the Theosophical Society in India.

1880   May 1880. Olcott and Blavatsky make first trip to Lanka. In Colombo Dharmapala walks to lecture and stays after with father and uncle to meet the visitors.

May 22, 1880. Ceylon Theosophical Society established.

June 17, 1880. Colombo Theosophical Society established, later renamed the Buddhist Theosophical Society.

1882   After leaving school, Dharmapala spends some eight months borrowing books from the Pettah library. In November 1882 he reads an article in the *Theosophist*, "Chelas and Lay Chelas," and Sinnett's *Occult World* and resolves to join the Himalayan School of Adepts, hoping to gain admission as a chela of Koot Hoomi.

Dharmapala reads passage in *Light of Asia* that convinces him to take up life of renunciation.

1883   Kotahena riots: Christians attack Buddhists.

Dharmapala reads an English-language vegetarian cookbook and becomes a vegetarian, and sends a letter via Blavatsky to Koot Hoomi.

1884   January 1884. Olcott returns to Colombo to file suit against the Christians for their attack on the Buddhist procession.

February 1884. Dharmapala joins Theosophical Society, "accepting the principles of Chelaship."

December 1884. Dharmapala makes first foreign trip to South India, traveling with Blavatsky, Hartman, Abrew, Leadbeater, and the Cooper-Oakleys to the annual convention of the Theosophical Society.

1884–6   Dharmapala works at the Department of Public Instruction.

April 1885. When Blavatsky is forced to leave India because of scandal, her ship docks at Colombo, and Dharmapala visits her on board, seeing her for the last time.

1885   November 1885. Dharmapala leaves home to take up a life of renunciation.

December 1885. Sir Edwin Arnold visits Bodh Gaya.

1886   February 1886. Olcott and Leadbeater arrive in Colombo to collect funds for the Buddhist Educational Fund. Dharmapala publishes article in the *Ceylon Observer*, relating Edwin Arnold's reception in Colombo. Arnold takes up the Bodh Gaya question with Valigama Sri

Sumangala, urging Buddhists to petition the Indian government for the restoration of Bodh Gaya to the control of Buddhist monks.

March 1886. Government Gazette publishes news that Dharmapala has passed the public administration exam.

March 1886. Dharmapala decides to make renunciation, living at the Theosophical Society headquarters. Dharmapala spends time with Olcott, translating for him on village tours and living in the "travelling cart."

November 1, 1886. Ananda College established under the aegis of the Buddhist Theosophical Society.

December 1886. Dharmapala takes Theosophical training in Colombo and attends convention at Adyar with Abrew and bhikkhu Medhankara.

1886–90   Dharmapala serves as general manager and assistant secretary of Buddhist Theosophical Society and manager of *Sarasavi Sandarasa*. From March 1886 until December 1890, he also serves as assistant secretary of the Buddhist Defense Committee.

Assumes the name Dharmapala, for a period of years identifying himself as Hewavitarne Dharmapala.

1887   Dharmapala reads article about Japan in *Fortnightly Review* and resolves to visit. He soon begins corresponding with the young students of Hasshi Zansei and submits articles to their periodical.

Dharmapala conceives plan to visit Bodh Gaya in the company of the bhikkhu Medhankara, but Olcott convinces the monk that the trip is too difficult. Medhankara decides against going and soon dies.

March 8, 1887. Japanese monk Shaku Soen leaves Japan for Colombo, arriving three weeks later.

Olcott tours Bengal to strengthen Theosophical Society branches. By this time Norendronath Sen has become its major supporter.

December 1887. Dharmapala attends annual Theosophical convention in Adyar.

1888   Japanese students come to Colombo, and Dharmapala assists them.

Japanese Buddhists send Noguchi Zenshiro to Sri Lanka to invite Olcott to Japan, but he must make two trips because on the first, Olcott is abroad. Dharmapala provides him lodging.

December 1888. Noguchi travels to Adyar for the Theosophical Society annual convention, giving a speech deploring the miserable condition of Buddhism in Japan. Dharmapala travels to the conference with Leadbeater and likely makes the acquaintance of Norendronath Sen, editor of the *Indian Mirror* in Calcutta.

Leadbeater and Dharmapala establish the *Buddhist.*

1889   January 4, 1889. Dharmapala returns to Colombo.

January 8, 1889. Dharmapala writes article on India for *Sandarasa.*

January 18, 1889. Noguchi invites Dharmapala to accompany Olcott on trip to Japan, and the party sails from Colombo soon thereafter.

February 9, 1889. The party reaches Kobe and is received by representatives of the seven leading Buddhist sects. Sumangala's message is read and the six-colored Buddhist flag is raised for the first time in Japan. The group is taken to a Tendai temple in Kobe, then to Kyoto for a celebration of the promulgation of the Japanese constitution.

February 10, 1889. Olcott and Dharmapala reach Kyoto, where they meet a convention of chief monks at Chion-in temple.

February 23, 1889. Dharmapala falls ill and is moved to the general hospital, convalescing for two months.

April 27, 1889. Olcott and Dharmapala address 1,500 Japanese monks at Chion-in temple.

April 29, 1889. Olcott and Dharmapala are invited to witness military parade of Honganji cadets. They also meet the Japanese prime minister, General Count Kuroda; cabinet ministers; the imperial chamberlain, Viscount Sannomiya; and the governor of Tokyo.

May 12, 1889. Dharmapala gives final lecture in Osaka and sails home.

June 5, 1889. Dharmapala reaches Colombo, suffering from diarrhea.

June 18, 1889. Olcott returns to Colombo, bringing three Japanese monks, Riotayi Koisumi, Joshojee, and Tohijin Sabaya, who intend to study in Sri Lanka.

June 19, 1889. Dharmapala travels by bullock cart with Olcott to Anuradhapura.

August 6, 1889. Dharmapala sends first deposit to savings bank for Buddhist Printing Press Fund.

August 7, 1889. Along with others in Theosophical Society, Dharmapala begins contemplating the idea of sending five Buddhist missionary monks abroad.

Late August 1889. Dharmapala tours Eastern Province with C. F. Powell, an American Theosophist.

Dharmapala says he began the practice of rising at 2:00 a.m. in 1889, although early morning meditation started years later.

1890   December 7, 1890. Dharmapala, accompanied by Kozen Gunaratana
         and Tokuzawa, two Japanese, attends Theosophical convention at
         Adyar. Afterward the three travel north to Bodh Gaya. Dharmapala
         finances the trip with money from his father.

1891   January 12, 1891. Dharmapala and party leave Adyar for Bombay and
         onward to Sarnath.

         January 18, 1891. Dharmapala and party reach Bodh Gaya.

         January 22, 1891. Dharmapala pledges his life to the cause of the Maha
         Bodhi movement.

         February 27, 1891. Dharmapala pledges to work for humanity in all of
         his future incarnations.

         March 6, 1891. Dharmapala begins practice of early morning medi-
         tation.

         March 12, 1891. Dharmapala leaves Bodh Gaya for Calcutta, where he
         resides with family of Neel Kamal Mukherjee. Kozen and Tokuzawa
         remain at Bodh Gaya.

         Dharmapala travels home via Burma, lodging first with a Sinhala gold-
         smith and moving eventually to house of Moung Hpo Mhyin, where
         he spends a month.

         April 1891. Dharmapala delivers first lecture on Bodh Gaya at Sule
         Pagoda, Rangoon.

         May 8, 1891. Blavatsky dies in London.

         May 1891. Sailing from Rangoon, Dharmapala stops at Adyar and
         encounters Kozen Gunaratana, who has left Bodh Gaya. Once in
         Colombo, he establishes the Maha Bodhi Society (May 31). He writes
         that the objectives of the society are "to revive Buddhism in India,
         to disseminate Pali Buddhist Literature, to publish Buddhist tracts
         in the Indian vernaculars, to educate the illiterate millions of Indian
         people in scientific industrialism, to maintain teachers and bhikkhus
         at Buddha-Gaya, Benares, Kusinara, Savatthi, Madras, Calcutta, &c . . .
         to build Schools, Dharmasalas [almshalls] at these places, and to send
         Buddhist missionaries abroad." *Journal of the Maha Bodhi Society* 15
         (1907).

         July 1891. Dharmapala returns to India, characterizing his settling in
         Calcutta as establishing the Buddhist sasana in Bengal. He resides at
         Holy House with the Mukherjee family from July 1891 to 1892.

         July 21, 1891. Dharmapala returns to Sri Lanka, recruits monks to
         replace Kozen, and escorts four bhikkhus back to Bodh Gaya.

         August 31, 1891. Dharmapala leaves Bodh Gaya for Calcutta.

September 1891. Dharmapala establishes a branch of the Maha Bodhi Society in Calcutta. He continues to live with the Mukherjee family on Baniapukur Lane and becomes friendly with Neel Kamal, his son, Nirodanath, and grandson Naranath. Their home serves as temporary headquarters of the Maha Bodhi Society until Dharmapala relocates to 2 Creek Row in October 1892, sharing space with the Theosophical Society.

October 1891. Dharmapala returns to Bodh Gaya and begins small building project to provide kitchen for resident monks.

October 25, 1891. Dharmapala gives his first lecture in India, on the kinship of Hinduism and Buddhism, at Albert Hall, Calcutta, under the chairmanship of Norendronath Sen.

November 1, 1891. Sir Charles Eliot, lieutenant governor of Bengal, visits Bodh Gaya.

November 11, 1891. Dharmapala takes train to Calcutta.

December 1, 1891. Dharmapala sails to Colombo, arriving December 6.

December 8, 1891. Dharmapala approaches bhikkhu Heyiyantuduve Devamitta to get his copy of *Gihi Vinaya* translated.

December 22, 1891. Dharmapala sails to Adyar for annual Theosophical convention.

December 1891. The Bodh Gaya mahant dies.

1892   June 14, 1892. Dharmapala travels to Darjeeling, where he meets with Tibetan lamas.

October 1892. Dharmapala visits Akyab with Olcott and establishes the Akyab Maha Bodhi Society.

October 31, 1892. International Buddhist conference at Bodh Gaya unanimously passes resolution that Bodh Gaya should be handed over to Buddhists.

November 1892. Dharmapala launches the *Journal of the Maha Bodhi Society and the United Buddhist World*. He has five hundred copies printed for English-speaking Buddhists and Europeans.

Sir Edwin Arnold in Tokyo addresses some 250 Buddhist monks at one of the principal Buddhist temples, telling them of the need to recover sacred Buddhist places in India.

With Sarat Chandra Das, Dharmapala establishes Buddhist Text Society.

1893   January 12, 1893. Olcott arrives in Calcutta with Japanese representative of Honganji, T. Kawakami, who intends to study Sanskrit.

February 1893. Dharmapala visits Sarnath with Olcott and enters into negotiations with commissioner of Benares to restore site. He also negotiates to buy three *bighas* of land. Olcott advises him to quit Bodh Gaya and concentrate on Sarnath.

February 1893. The new mahant's men set upon monks at Bodh Gaya.

June 1893. J. H. Barrows invites Dharmapala to the World's Parliament of Religions as representative of Theravada Buddhism.

June 1893. Dharmapala visits Rangoon.

July 1893. Dharmapala leaves Colombo in July, spends week with Sir Edwin Arnold in London, moving to headquarters of Theosophical Society at suggestion of Annie Besant, and then sails to New York City with her. While in England Dharmapala gives Rhys-Davids a copy of the manual on dhyana meditation he found in Teldeniya, and Rhys-Davids translates it as *Manual of a Mystic*.

August 26, 1893. Dharmapala departs Southampton on *City of Paris*, arriving in New York City on September 2, 1893.

September 11–27, 1893. Dharmapala participates in World's Parliament of Religions, Chicago.

September 24, 1893. In Chicago Dharmapala makes his first Buddhist convert, admitting C. T. Strauss as an upasaka by administering pansil to him.

October 1, 1893. Dharmapala begins trip home, traveling by train to San Francisco.

October 6, 1893. In California Dharmapala takes train to Santa Cruz to meet Philangi Dasa, an early convert to Buddhism.

October 10, 1893. Dharmapala sails to Japan from San Francisco.

October 18, 1893. In Honolulu harbor Dharmapala meets local party of Theosophists, including Mary Foster and possibly Countess Canavarro, who come on shipboard.

October 31, 1893. Dharmapala arrives at Yokohama and gives first lecture on Buddhism.

November 1893. Dharmapala's second visit to Japan. Received by secretary of the Indo-Busseki-Kofuku-Kai.

November 15, 1893. Dharmapala delivers lecture to "Tokio public," at Shiba park in Tokyo on the similarities between Northern and Southern Buddhism and urging the restoration of Bodh Gaya and soliciting support.

November 15 or 16, 1893. Dharmapala gives lecture on the water damage and rescue project for Okayama and eight other prefectures, Kinkikan Hall, and Jiseikan Hall in Shiba.

November 24, 1893. Dharmapala receives Buddha image from Asahi San en route to Bodh Gaya.

December 4, 1893. Dharmapala begins tour of Japan by taking train to Kanogawa.

November 15, 1893–December 15, 1893. Dharmapala lectures widely in Japan on Buddhist sacred places but fails to raise appreciable support.

December 15, 1893. Dharmapala leaves Japan on *Yokohama Maru*.

December 19, 1893. Dharmapala arrives at Shanghai, delivering lecture translated by Rev. Eakins and Dr. Franks. He again fails to raise the monetary support he expected.

1894   January 2, 1894. Dharmapala arrives at Hong Kong and departs on January 4.

January 9, 1894. Dharmapala arrives at Singapore and departs on January 13 for Bangkok.

February 1894. While a guest of Prince Rajsaki in Bangkok, Dharmapala establishes a branch of the Maha Bodhi Society with help of Prince Vivit and other princes, again failing to raise funds for Bodh Gaya project.

February 12, 1894. Dharmapala leaves for Singapore via SS *Gorgon*, sailing from Singapore on February 21, arriving in Colombo on February 27. In Colombo he is greeted by elephants, drums, and a procession and begins to receive pledges from wealthy Buddhists toward the purchase of the Maha Bodhi village at Bodh Gaya.

March 14, 1894. Dharmapala establishes offices of Maha Bodhi Society in Colombo at 61 Maliban Street.

March 26, 1894. Dharmapala returns to India, escorting bhikkhu Saddhananda to Bodh Gaya, stopping at Adyar en route.

August 8, 1894. Dharmapala returns to Colombo with Nirodanath Mukherjee, arriving August 13.

Late August–September 1894. Dharmapala lectures along south coast, trying to raise subscriptions for Bodh Gaya projects.

September 1894. Dharmapala establishes the Bodh Gaya Fund.

September or October 1894. Dharmapala convenes senior monks and laymen and lectures them about the deplorable state to which Bodh Gaya has fallen.

October 1894. Accompanied by G. P. Weerasekera, Dharmapala goes on lecture tour to Kalutara, Kosgoda, Welitara, Balapitiya, Ambalangoda, and several other places. He lectures in villages between Galle and Weligama, returning to Colombo, leaving for Kurunegala on the October 9, and lecturing at Malagomuwa on October 11, at Balalla on October 15, at Variapola on October 17, at Naramwala on October 19, and at Giriula on October 21.

1895   Dharmapala's father advises him by letter to follow the bodhisattva path.

February 1895. Dharmapala installs Japanese Buddha at Bodh Gaya in Maha Bodhi temple, and confrontation with mahant's supporters follows. Government removes image, and litigation begins. The Burmese resthouse is placed at the disposal of the Maha Bodhi Society, and the Japanese image moves there.

February 1895. Dharmapala files case against mahant's men for disturbing worship.

May 1895. The Calcutta High Court upholds the mahant's appeal against a sentence imposed by a lower court for interfering with Buddhist worship at Bodh Gaya.

December 1895. Mallika Hewavitarne leads first group pilgrimage to Bodh Gaya of modern times. The party of Sinhala Buddhists comes ashore at Chennai and meets Olcott.

1896   Olcott and Annie Besant advise Dharmapala not to purchase land at Bodh Gaya. Dharmapala begins to act independently of Olcott, leading him to resign from the Maha Bodhi Society. Dharmapala says that Olcott deserted him in May 1896.

May 1896. Dharmapala initiates first Vesak celebration in Calcutta.

June 6, 1896. Dharmapala gives lecture "Life of Buddha" at Albert Hall, followed by another a week later, "The Fundamental Teachings of the Buddha."

June 1896. Dharmapala receives invitation from Paul Carus to visit the United States; Carus also provides small stipend to purchase steamer ticket.

July 21, 1896. Dharmapala returns to Colombo en route to United States.

July 26, 1896. Dharmapala gives lecture to 1,800 people at Ananda College.

July 28, 1896. In Heneratgoda Dharmapala announces his plans for establishing a group of anagarika brahmacarya, having entertained the idea since 1891.

July 31, 1896. Olcott resigns from Maha Bodhi Society at meeting in Maligakanda.

August 4, 1896. Dharmapala makes second visit to America to preach Buddhism, planning to spend 1896–8 abroad. Between September and December, he makes trips from Chicago to Grand Rapids, Freeport, Indianapolis, Guelph, Canada, Cincinnati, Duluth, St. Cloud, Fargo, Minneapolis, and New Ulm.

August 20, 1896. Dharmapala reaches London, visiting Sir Edwin Arnold.

September 8, 1896. Dharmapala sails from Southampton and arrives in New York City on September 15.

September 19, 1896. Dharmapala takes train to Chicago. On September 24, he meets the founding president of the University of Chicago, William Rainey Harper, and visits the university's scientific laboratories.

1897   January 26, 1897. Dharmapala makes second midwestern tour, visiting Toledo, Dayton, Columbus, Geneseo, Davenport, Iowa City, and Des Moines.

February 20, 1897. Dharmapala departs Chicago, arriving in San Francisco by train on February 24.

March 6, 1897. Dharmapala meets Countess Canavarro, and she begins plans for a upasikarama (nunnery or training school) for Buddhist women in Colombo.

March 22, 1897. Dharmapala gives lecture to a large number of students at Stanford.

March 29, 1897. Dharmapala returns by train to Boston and moves on to New York City on April 24.

May 1897. In San Francisco Dharmapala officiates at the first Vesak celebration in the United States.

June–August 1897. Dharmapala takes up residence at a variety of chautauquas across the Northeast, including Lake Hopatcong, Lake Pleasant, and Green Acre. A local paper writes that he "has postponed a contemplated journey to Tibet to participate in the work of the Monsalvat School, thus affording a rare opportunity for the study of Buddhism."

July 1897. Maha Bodhi Society in Calcutta establishes relief fund for Bengal famine and appeals to Buddhist countries for donations.

Late August 1897. At New Century Hall in New York City Dharmapala admits Countess Canavarro as a Buddhist upasika (lay devotee). She is his second and last convert.

September 1, 1897. Dharmapala leaves New York City for Europe.

September 8, 1897. Dharmapala arrives in Paris for Congress of Orientalists at invitation of Rhys Davids and announces his intention to go to Tibet. His father dissuades him, providing him a place to practice dhyana in Welikada, Colombo.

September 12, 1897. Following Orientalist conference, Dharmapala travels from Paris to Belgium, Berlin, Switzerland, and Rome and sails from Naples to Colombo.

September 1897. Countess Canavarro arrives in Colombo for Buddhist work. Greeted by Buddhist women and Dharmapala's mother on arrival, Canavarro manages the Sanghamitta convent for Buddhist nuns and abandons that post in 1901, leaving for Calcutta.

November 6, 1897. Harischandra Valisinha accompanies Dharmapala on a preaching tour of villages near Negombo, including Harischandra's own, Hunupitiya.

1898   January 1, 1898. Harischandra Valisinha becomes a brahmacarya at a meeting of the Maha Bodhi Society at Vidyodaya pirivena. The meeting is chaired by Hikkaduve Sumangala, and the consent of all members of the Maha Bodhi Society is given.

January 1898. Dharmapala resumes village tours.

April 6, 1898. Dharmapala holds festival at Rajagiriya, and Harischandra assists. That night Harischandra returns to his village and gives his first public lecture, excoriating the evils of liquor.

April 20, 1898. Dharmapala sails to Calcutta, arriving April 25 and returning to Colombo June 22 via coastal steamer to Cuttack, where he visits former Buddhist sites in South India.

April 1898. Dharmapala establishes Ethico-Psychological College in Rajagiriya, but the bhikkhus are skeptical, and the project fails. Some Rajagiriya land sold, but the name survives in Rajagiriya Industrial School.

June 30, 1898. Harischandra tells Dharmapala of his hopes to join him in his work.

August–September 1898. Dharmapala makes village tour in Sri Lanka.

November 1, 1898. Dharmapala introduces Harischandra to Maha Bodhi Society as his chief follower, and by December Harischandra begins serving as assistant secretary.

Dharmapala establishes a dress reform society. He also says his relationship with Olcott began to deteriorate further in 1898 because Olcott became "selfish."

1899   January 2, 1899. Harischandra and four other men enter Dharmapala's
        order of brahmacarya.

        January 6, 1899. Harischandra accompanies Countess Canavarro
        and Upasika Dhammadinna to Nupe, Matara, where at the house of
        J. Moonasingha, Dharmapala's brother-in-law, he gives sermon.

        February 5, 1899. Harischandra gives a lecture at Mirissa and makes
        arrangements to start a girls' school there, giving some twenty lec-
        tures that month.

        March–May 1899. Dharmapala makes fact-finding tour of North India,
        traveling "as a pilgrim, not caring at all for comforts. Mixing with
        sanyasins . . . Hindu pilgrims and with passengers in the third and
        intermediate classes eating at times the poorest food."

        March 2, 1899. Harischandra departs for Calcutta on mission for the
        Maha Bodhi Society accompanied by Countess Canavarro and Upasika
        Dhammadinna, spending four days in Calcutta before departing for
        Bodh Gaya.

        September 1899. Dharmapala leaves Calcutta for Chennai, where he
        reestablishes a branch of the Maha Bodhi society.

        October 1899. Dharmapala gives lecture in Chennai.

        October 28, 1899. Harischandra appointed secretary of the Maha Bodhi
        Society.

        Dharmapala establishes Maha Bodhi Society branch at Chennai.

1900   At Hikkaduve's request Dharmapala travels to Bangkok to receive the
        Lankan share of relics given to Thais by the Indian government.

1901   February 1901. Don Carolis gives Dharmapala Rs. 600 to buy three
        bighas of land at Sarnath in his mother's name. Maharajah of Benares
        gives Rs. 2,000 for ten bighas.

        October 1901. Lieutenant Governor Woodburn visits Bodh Gaya,
        where presentations are made by Maha Bodhi Society to have a *dhar-
        masala* (resthouse) built. The governor sanctions the land acquisition,
        financed by Burmese and Lankan Maha Bodhi Societies. The resthouse
        becomes an alternative venue for Buddhist interests at Bodh Gaya,
        sheltering pilgrims and monks.

        October–November 1901. Dharmapala leaves Calcutta, traveling via
        Punjab Mail to Hardwar and Rishikesh and returning to Benares No-
        vember 2.

        Norendronath Sen advises Dharmapala to return to Lanka because
        Olcott is working against him. Dharmapala remains in Colombo for

several months, until Sen advises him to leave for Japan, which he does in 1902.

December 1901. Dharmapala leaves Calcutta and lays over in Colombo in preparation for East Asian trip.

1902   January 1902. Count Okakura and party travel to Bodh Gaya, Nalanda, and Sarnath. In Dharmapala's absence Okakura began to negotiate with mahant for land on which to build a resthouse for Japanese pilgrims.

April 9, 1902. Dharmapala sails to Japan en route to the United States and meets Chigaku Tanaka.

April 30, 1902. Dharmapala arrives in Kobe.

May 1902. Dharmapala leaves Japan, sailing across the Pacific to California. By September Mary Foster has become his chief supporter.

June 1902. Dharmapala's sister dies at Aloe Avenue, Colombo.

August 1902. Dharmapala spends first month of his third trip to the United States in Los Angeles.

1903   January 1903. Dharmapala spends month in San Francisco and pursues his new project, raising money for educational work in India.

January 15, 1903. Lord Curzon, returning from Delhi Durbar, visits Bodh Gaya while Dharmapala tours the United States.

March 14, 1903. Dharmapala represents Buddhism at Congress of Religions at Stanford.

April 27, 1903. Dharmapala departs San Francisco by train for Chicago.

June 22, 1903. Dharmapala leaves Chicago for Tuskegee Institute, where he meets Booker T. Washington and studies industrial education.

June 25, 1903. Dharmapala takes train north to Washington, DC.

June 28, 1903. Dharmapala talks to boys at Indian school in Carlisle, Pennsylvania, traveling on to East Aurora, New York, and Niagara Falls.

July 7, 1903. Dharmapala arrives in Boston and travels to Green Acre in Eliot, Maine, a week later.

August 1903. Dharmapala and Gudrun Holm pledge to be eternal companions.

October 1903. Dharmasala at Bodh Gaya completed.

1904   January 1904. With money from Mary Foster Dharmapala establishes industrial school fund in San Francisco with Rs. 10,000.

January 20, 1904. Dharmapala departs New York City, arriving at London and visiting industrial schools in Europe.

February 10, 1904. Devapriya Valisinha born.

February17, 1904. Dharmapala visits the Netherlands.

March 4, 1904. Dharmapala departs London for Paris.

March 9, 1904. Dharmapala sails from Naples.

March 26, 1904. Dharmapala arrives at Colombo.

April 19, 1904. Dharmapala sails on to Calcutta.

May 4, 1904. Dharmapala returns to Bodh Gaya and finds dharmasala completed and Buddha image covered with turmeric.

June–July. 1904. Dharmapala establishes industrial school in Sarnath and starts to plan for the Abhisambodhi anniversary of Lord Buddha. The 2,500th anniversary will occur in 1911, and he intends a huge celebration in Calcutta.

July 7, 1904. Dharmapala opens Benares School.

September 1904. Benares School fails.

September 19, 1904. Negotiations completed to buy remainder of land at Sarnath.

October 1904. Dharmapala leaves Benares for Colombo, visiting Olcott in Adyar. They have an altercation over relics.

November 1904. Dharmapala travels from Isipatana to Bodh Gaya and returns to Sarnath.

December 7, 1904. Dharmapala returns to Colombo to visit ailing father.

1906   January 1906. Captain W. F. O'Connell and the Panchen Lama establish the Buddhist Shrine Restoration Society to recover Bodh Gaya for the Buddhists independent of the activities of the Maha Bodhi Society.

January 1906. Lord Minto visits Bodh Gaya.

February 17, 1906. Don Carolis Hewavitarne dies in Kollupitiya, having stipulated in his will that Dharmapala should spend his bequest on Buddhism. Olcott dies exactly one year later. "When I lost my beloved father in January 1906 [sic]," Dharmapala writes, "I wrote to her [Mary Foster] of the great loss I had sustained as he had been my best supporter since the day I left home in October 1885. The reply I received from Mrs. Foster was that she would help me to carry on the work and that she would be a foster parent to me." Foster says she will show motherly affection and sends Rs. 3,000.

March 1906. Dharmapala resigns from Theosophical Society, later saying that he had been at loggerheads with Annie Besant since 1905. He reconciles with her in 1911 and rejoins the Theosophical Society in 1913. Thereafter he describes himself as "active and in sympathy with Mrs Besant" and lends her Rs. 500 in 1916.

March 1906. Dharmapala begins campaign against Theosophical Society in Colombo.

May 1906. Dharmapala establishes *Sinhala Bauddhaya* in Colombo as well as Maha Bodhi Press and weaving school in Rajagiriya with Mary Foster's support.

July 29, 1906. Dharmapala makes lecture tour by cart to Southern Province and buys land in Hiniduma with an eye to establishing an industrial arts school. "The Anagarika left Colombo on a preaching tour. He will proceed on to the extreme limits of the Southern Province and thence to Badulla, enroute to Kandy. Thence he shall go to Kegalle district, returning to Colombo via Ratnapure. He has lectured since at Bambalapitiya, Wellawatta, Dehiwela, Desastara Kalutara, Kalutara South, Kalamulla, Payagala, Maggona, Alutgama, Bentota. He travels in a cart drawn by a pair of bulls, which is useful in manifold ways. The former he uses to exhibit views of the sacred places in India, Burma, Ceylon and Japan. He expounds the Doctrine of the Buddha, talks about his travels to Europe, American, Japan, Burma, and ends by an appeal which stirs the hearts of the audience for greater activity." *Journal of the Maha Bodhi Society* (1906): 126.

September 1906. "The Anagarika is still touring in the Southern Province. On the 19th instant he was at Baddegama, the strong hold of the Church Missionary Society." *Journal of the Maha Bodhi Society* (1906): 126.

October 20, 1906. Dharmapala visits Hiniduma with Harischandra and makes plans to return to Calcutta with his mother on pilgrimage to Bodh Gaya.

October 1906. Governor Woodburne visits Bodh Gaya, sanctioning the dharmasala.

November 1906. Dharmapala condemns Olcott at Kandy meeting for insulting the Tooth Relic and then sails to Tuticorin, and on to Calcutta. His mother accompanies him, making another pilgrimage to Bodh Gaya.

1907   February 17, 1907. Olcott dies at Adyar.

May 1907. Mahant files the Burmese resthouse case, seeking removal of the Japanese image.

August 1907. "The Anagarika Dharmapala: 'This gentleman is still in India, busily engaged in matters concerning the case about the Burmese Monastery at Buddha Gaya. His present address is No. 2, Creek Row, Calcutta." *Journal of the Maha Bodhi Society* (1907): 124.

October 15–18, 1907. Dharmapala sails to Burma with Nanda Kishore Lall, his attorney, to gather evidence at Burmese court in Mandalay for Bodh Gaya resthouse case. They take train north to Mandalay on October 19.

October 1907. Neel Kamal Mukherjee, original treasurer of the Maha Bodhi Society in Calcutta and Dharmapala's host in Calcutta, dies.

1908   January 1908. Dharmapala returns to residence in Calcutta.

July 1908. With funds provided by Mary Foster, Dharmapala purchases a house on Baniapukker Street, Calcutta, for Rs. 15,000, as well as a printing press.

1909   May 14, 1909. Dharmapala leaves Calcutta by train for Tuticorin, arriving in Colombo on May 21, 1909, after two and a half years in India.

June 4, 1909. Dharmapala makes pilgrimage to Anuradhapura.

June 15, 1909. Dharmapala delivers three lectures at Saraswati Hall, Colombo.

October 13–24, 1909. Dharmapala makes village tour in south, concentrating on area around Hiniduma.

November 1909. Dharmapala leaves Colombo for Calcutta on the *Purnaa*, traveling first class.

1910   Dharmapala resides in Calcutta from 1910 to early 1911 and gives regular Sunday addresses at Maha Bodhi Society.

February 1910. Japanese image ordered removed from Bodh Gaya, and Buddhists install it at Maha Bodhi headquarters in Calcutta.

Having lost foothold at Bodh Gaya, Dharmapala decides to turn his attention homeward, where he hopes to "wake up" the Sinhala people.

1911   Dharmapala travels to Colombo, going by train to Tuticorin and thence by steamer, arriving February 18, 1911.

March 15, 1911. Dharmapala takes train to Anuradhapura.

April 18, 1911. Dharmapala returns to India via Tuticorin.

April 1911. Hikkaduve Sumangala dies in Colombo.

June 29, 1911. Dharmapala takes train to Chennai from Calcutta.

July 10, 1911. Dharmapala arrives in Colombo and soon begins writing weekly article for the *Sinhala Bauddhaya*. He criticizes indolent monks, leading to controversy with D. J. Subasinghe in the pages of the *Sandarasa*.

December 2, 1911. Dharmapala delivers sermon in Udugama, traveling in a cart drawn by two bulls, and speaking with a gramophone. Where there are no motorable roads, he walks or travels by catamaran.

December 12, 1911. Partition of Bengal modified via announcement made by the king at Delhi.

December 1911. Norendronath Sen dies.

1912   January 1912. In Colombo, Dharmapala begins writing "Things that one should know" column in *Sinhala Bauddhaya* and criticizes indolent bhikkhus, resulting in controversy with D. J. Subasinghe writing in *Sandarasa*.

January 1912. Dharmapala establishes the *Ceylonese Nation*, a weekly newspaper in commemoration of the Delhi coronation of George V, providing Buddhists with a vehicle to express grievances to British authorities in English.

April 21, 1912. Dharmapala returns to Calcutta from Colombo.

May 6, 1912. Dharmapala returns to Colombo via Madras Mail from Calcutta.

May 1912–February 1913. Dharmapala works in Lanka.

June 1912. Dharmapala purchases a lorry to conduct temperance and anti–meat eating campaign in island.

1913   January 17, 1913. Simon Hewavitarne dies in Kollupitiya.

February 19, 1913. Dharmapala makes quick visit to Calcutta.

March 18, 1913. Dharmapala returns by train from Calcutta to Tuticorin.

April 9, 1913. Dharmapala departs Colombo for Japan.

April 29, 1913. Dharmapala arrives at Kobe. Japanese papers, including the *Japan Chronicle*, credit him with the following statement: "Indian resources are being fully developed under the British administration. The British profit in India can never be smaller than two million. So Indian wealth brings happiness to Englishmen but not to the Indians. Most of the Indians are poor and ignorant. In short, they are miserable both spiritually and materially."

While in Japan Dharmapala is rebuffed by Count Otani, meets Sakurai Yoshikazu, and receives treatment for ear trouble.

May 5, 1913. Dharmapala is interviewed by *Hochi*, *Yamato Maiyu*, *Jiji*, and *Asahi* newspapers.

May 7, 1913. Dharmapala attends party thrown by Indian revolutionary A. H. Mohammad Barakatullah.

May 9, 1913. Dharmapala is interviewed by *Ikkatsu* magazine.

May 10, 1913. Dharmapala departs for Hawaii on *Shinzo Maru*, meeting Mary Foster in June. She makes a donation of Rs. 50,000 for the maintenance of a hospital and convalescent home in Colombo named in honor of Dharmapala's mother.

May 24, 1913. Mary Foster sells water rights to Oahu Sugar Company for $40,000 a year.

June 10, 1913. Dharmapala sails back from Honolulu, reaching Yokohama on June 21.

July 9, 1913. Dharmapala visits girls' high school in Japan.

August 1913. Dharmapala visits Korea, arriving in Pusan on August 18, giving lecture in Seoul, and presenting relic to Korean sangha. "A letter has been received by us dated 25th August from Mukden, in which the Anagarika says that he spent three days at Seoul . . . where he addressed a distinguished assembly including the Ex-Empress. He has presented a Buddha relic, which he had with him to the Korean Sangha who has promised to build a new temple to enshrine it. From Mukden he will visit Port Arthur and Dairen and will visit Peking, Nangking, and Shanghai and will reach Singapore about the end of September. Unless the news of the death of the Brahmacari alters his plans he will visit the Buddhist ruins of Boro Budoor in Java and reach Ceylon about the end of October." *Journal of the Maha Bodhi Society* (1913): 199.

September 5, 1913. Dharmapala gives lecture in China, "The Danger of 'White Peril,'" drawing interest of British intelligence.

September 13, 1913. Harischandra Valisinha dies, which Dharmapala learns only when he reaches Singapore on return trip home.

September 18, 1913. Dharmapala gives lecture in Shanghai, "The Social Gospel of the Buddha."

September 20, 1913. Dharmapala departs Shanghai on *Iyo Maru*, visiting Singapore and Borobudur before returning to Colombo in October.

1914   January 1914. Dharmapala establishes Mallika Santhagaraya, or the Foster Free Dispensary and Hospital, in house on Darley Lane donated by his father.

April or May 1914. Dharmapala departs Colombo for Calcutta, celebrating Vesak in on May 8 and traveling on to Chittagong on May 15.

June 1914. Dharmapala's mother warns him not to return to Colombo, and he remains in Calcutta through internment.

1915   Dharmapala lectures at Bengal Social Service League and invites Kalidas Nag to stand in for the retiring F. L. Woodward at Mahinda College.

Dharmapala registers the Maha Bodhi Society in Calcutta in order to distance it from its Colombo headquarters.

May 1915. Riots in Lanka. Buddhists assault Muslims.

Dharmapala moves Maha Bodhi College to the Foster Hospital.

June 9, 1915. Police raid Dharmapala's quarters at Baniapukker Lane.

July 1915. Dharmapala purchases property at 4 College Square, Calcutta, to build a vihara, saying this is a dream he had first had in 1909. He also receives word from the government of India of its willingness to present a Buddha relic for the temple.

August 1915. Dharmapala vacates Baniapukker Lane and moves to College Square.

November 19, 1915. Imprisoned after the Lankan riots, Dharmapala's brother Edmund dies in Jaffna prison.

1916   March 28–early April 1916. Dharmapala travels to Rawalpindi and Saraikala, where he discusses disposition of Taxila relics with Sir John Marshall.

June 28, 1916. Government of Bengal, acting on instructions from government of Lanka, interns Dharmapala in Calcutta. Internment lasts until December 1917.

November 16, 1916. Naranath Mukherjee dies in Calcutta.

1917   January 1917. Dharmapala's mother and her party make pilgrimage to Bodh Gaya. While in Calcutta she visits Dharmapala and leaves Devapriya as his ward and assistant.

February 1917. Dharmapala writes to governor of Lanka offering his services.

December 13, 1917. Dharmapala is officially released from internment.

1918   January 1918. Dharmapala's mother visits him in Calcutta again on pilgrimage.

April 1, 1918. Dharmapala returns to Baniapukker Lane residence, having lived in College Square residence two years, eight months.

November 28, 1918. Nanda Kishore Lall, Dharmapala's attorney, dies in Patna.

July 1918. Dharmapala starts work on vihara at College Square. Foundation stone laid December 6, 1918.

1919   November 1919. Dharmapala receives $50,000 bond from Mary Foster, using the interest from that contribution to cover expenses for the Maha Bodhi Society.

1920   March 16, 1920. Dharmapala takes train from Calcutta to Tuticorin and continues by ferry to Colombo.

April 6, 1920. Dharmapala takes ferry to Talaimannar on way back to Calcutta.

November 1920. Dharmarajika caitya opens with visit of Lord Ronaldshay, governor of Bengal. Asutosh Mukherjee and Annie Besant walk with Dharmapala to Government House, followed by procession of Burmese, Sinhala, Chinese, Japanese, and Indian Buddhist monks and a concourse of some two thousand people. Ronaldshay hands over relics in a crystal casket to Mukherjee and Dharmapala.

1921   April 1921. Dharmapala takes train from Calcutta to Colombo to recruit ten Buddhist missionaries.

May 8, 1921. Dharmapala departs Colombo with one monk, two samaneras, and two boys.

1922   July 1922. Dharmapala restarts *Sinhala Bauddhaya*, which had been suspended by order of the government of Lanka in 1915.

September 1922. Dharmapala completes Dharmarajika vihara residence for monks.

November 1922. Foundation stone for vihara at Sarnath laid by the governor of Uttar Pradesh, Sir Harcourt Butler.

December 5, 1922. Dharmapala returns to Lanka, leaving Calcutta via train. Six days later he returns to India.

1923   January 15, 1923. Dharmapala visits Madurai en route to Calcutta.

April 1923. Having returned to India, Dharmapala sojourns at Sarnath.

July–September 1923. Dharmapala makes extended tour of Patna, Benares, Punjab, and Kashmir.

July 1923. Dharmapala establishes the Mary Foster Permanent Fund with capital of $150,000.

August 18, 1923. Dharmapala attends the Hindu Maha Sabha at Benares by request of the president, Pandit Madan Mohan Malaviya.

November 1923. Dharmapala leaves Calcutta for Chennai and Lanka, returning February 1924.

1924   January 18, 1924. Dharmapala purchases property in Kandy, which he intends to use as the Foster seminary for training monks for missionary work.

April 9, 1924. Dharmapala travels to Sarnath with Alma Senda.

August 30, 1924. Dharmapala leaves Calcutta for Lanka to recover his health.

November–December 1924. Dharmapala returns to Kandy to work on plans for seminary.

December 1924. Dharmapala is injured in auto accident at Kospillewa, en route to Colombo. He remains bedridden for a fortnight.

1925   January 1925. Dharmapala says he will offer Foster seminary to the Tooth Relic.

February–early March 1925. Dharmapala makes lecture tour of Southern Province.

March 4, 1925. Dharmapala departs Colombo via train for Calcutta.

March. 26, 1925. Dharmapala in Sarnath.

April 3, 1925. Dharmapala in Patna.

May 20, 1925. Dharmapala takes train from Calcutta to Bombay and thence to Madras. "The Anagarika Dharmapala left from Calcutta on the 20th of last month [May] for Colombo and on the 4th instant he is expected to leave Colombo for Europe. He hopes to spend two months in some German sanitarium and return to India to carry on the work of building the Vihara and the College, so dear to his heart at the holy spot, where the Lord Buddha promulgated the universal religion of Love and Truth." *Journal of the Maha Bodhi Society* 33 (1925): 228.

June 18, 1925. Dharmapala leaves Colombo for Marseilles on Japanese steamer, traveling with Raja Hewavitarne.

July 1925. Steamer arrives in Marseilles. Dharmapala and Raja take train to Zurich. In sanitarium at Kuranstadt near Lucerne, Dharmapala has operation and spends seven weeks convalescing.

July 1925. While in Switzerland, Dharmapala makes resolution to take up work in England, hoping to establish a Buddhist mission.

July 1925. In Switzerland Dharmapala sends letter to Christmas Humphreys, pointing out that "he was a member of the Blavatsky Assn and was quite sure that there would be many English Theosophists willing to receive the Buddha Dhamma at his hands." *Journal of the Maha Bodhi Society* (1946): 76.

September 1925. Dharmapala takes train to Berlin and stays at Buddhisches Haus in Frohnau.

September 27, 1925. Dharmapala arrives in England and makes first appearance at Buddhist Lodge of the Theosophical Society in Bedford Square. He tells a *Morning Post* representative before the proceedings that he intends to devote two years of his life to spreading the doctrines of Buddha in England and teaching his gospel of love. He wears a long orange-colored robe with sandals of the same color. Some forty members and friends gather at 23 Bedford Square to hear his talk.

October 4, 1925. Dharmapala leaves London for San Francisco to felicitate Mary Foster. He reaches New York City on October 13 and travels by train to San Francisco to meet Foster, who has taken up residence with her sister.

October 16, 1925. Dharmapala arrives in Chicago, gives two lectures, travels west, giving talks at Theosophical lodges in Salt Lake City (twice), Reno, and Sacramento. Dharmapala says that he was misused by Dr. Velar van Hook, who accompanied him and forced him to give lectures.

November 1925. Dharmapala is hospitalized at St. Luke's Hospital in San Francisco, where he writes letter to Sir John Marshall regarding his complaints against the Archeological Department's handling of restoration at Sarnath.

November 6, 1925. Dharmapala lectures in San Francisco.

November 20, 1925. Mary Foster accompanies Dharmapala to Oakland, where he catches a train eastward.

Late November 1925. In New York City Dharmapala gives lecture on Buddhism at Town Hall, supported by local Sinhala restaurateur K. Y. Kira.

November 29, 1925. Dharmapala departs New York City, arriving in London on December 10.

1926   The Archeological Department stops construction on Sarnath vihara. Dr. Hewavitarne, Raja Hewavitarne, and Devapriya Valisinha go to Taxila to petition Sir John Marshall. The dispute is resolved when the government agrees to bear the cost of foundation construction and provide suitable land for the vihara that Dharmapala intends to build.

March 9, 1926. Dharmapala makes trip with Daya Hewavitarne and others to unmarked grave of Allen Bennett (Ven. Ananda Metteyya) in London cemetery.

March 22, 1926. Dharmapala has hemorrhage and is cared for by Professor D. M. Z. Wickremasinghe and his wife, Vera. Because of sickness, he cancels plans to sail to Colombo in May.

May 1926. Dharmapala establishes the London Buddhist vihara, first at Ealing in a house he buys with £2,000 received from the firm of Don Carolis and a personal gift from Mary Foster. He initiates the work on Vesak, the 2,470th anniversary of the Maha parinirvana and establishes the English branch of the Maha Bodhi Society in July.

August 1926. Dharmapala travels to Switzerland to visit Basil Guirkowsky.

August 1926. Dharmapala starts monthly journal the *British Buddhist*, writing the first number by himself.

October 20, 1926. Humphreys holds farewell meeting for Dharmapala at Ealing.

November 1, 1926. Dharmapala leaves England for Lausanne and sails home from Marseilles on November 13.

December 2, 1926. Dharmapala arrives in Colombo to raise funds for the British Buddhist mission and attends to family business regarding the disposition of Aloe Avenue property.

December 1926. A series of letters to the editor criticizing Dharmapala's plans for the London Buddhist vihara appears in the *Ceylon Daily News*. Dharmapala publishes a statement defending himself in late December.

1927   January 10, 1927. Dharmapala delivers a bitter attack on his detractors at a public meeting in Mount Lavinia.

January 22, 1927. Dharmapala hosts a meeting of monks at his family home in Kollupitiya, attacking present-day Theosophists in England and urging support of the London mission.

January 24, 1927. *Ceylon Daily News* publishes an editorial defending itself against charges that it has published unfounded attacks on Dharmapala and insisting that the public has every right to know more about Dharmapala's management of funds given to him by the Buddhist public.

January 26, 1927. Dharmapala holds meeting in Kandy and attacks Ceylon *Daily News* for publishing charges against him.

February 14, 1927. Dharmapala addresses the annual meeting of the Maha Bodhi Society, recounting his career in India and his dealings with Mary Foster, noting that in three more years he would complete forty-five years of service. Until then he was determined to work toward building a vihara in London.

February 20, 1927. Dharmapala departs Colombo for Calcutta.

April 13, 1927. Having traveled by train from Calcutta to Bombay, Dharmapala sails for Venice.

Vesak 1927. Gandhi participates in celebrations at Dharmarajika vihara in Calcutta at invitation of Devapriya. Dharmapala meanwhile holds another celebration in London.

July 15, 1927. Dharmapala speaks at Dharmacakra celebration in London.

August 1, 1927. Dharmapala publishes article in *Sinhala Bauddhaya* saying he will open London vihara and appoint three monks— Paravahera Vajiranana, Hagoda Nandasara, and Matara Pannasara—to reside there.

October 3, 1927. Dharmapala returns to London and gives talk "An Appreciation of Christianity" at the City Temple.

November 13–25, 1927. Gandhi makes lecture tour of Lanka, visiting Jaffna, Kandy, and Galle.

December 7, 1927. Dharmapala leaves London to restore health in Vichy.

1928   January 1928. Dharmapala falls ill at Marseilles. He cancels plans to return to India straightaway to pursue plans for the Mulagandhakuti vihara at Sarnath and ends up in Colombo convalescing.

February 1928. Dharmapala returns to England and sells Ealing house. He collects enough money to buy house at 41 Gloucester Road. Devapriya escorts three bhikkhus to London, and they take up residence in June.

March 1928. Dharmapala falls ill with heart trouble and returns to Colombo, while the work of the London Buddhist vihara is carried on by his nephew Daya Hewavitarne.

June 1928. Dharmapala has a serious relapse in Colombo.

Late 1928. Now confined to a wheelchair, Dharmapala plans trip to Burma but cancels because of health problems.

1929   April 3, 1929. Dr. Charles Hewavitarne dies in an auto collision at a railway crossing.

June 1929. Dharmapala's health deteriorates further, and by August he is on the verge of death.

October 1929. Dharmapala convalesces at Maha Bodhi headquarters in Maligakanda, having spent four weeks in Colombo General Hospital. By late 1929 he is able to take a drive along the Colombo beach.

November 1929. Dharmapala sends two bhikkhus and eight samaneras to be educated as missionary monks at Shantiniketan, Bolpur.

1930   January 1, 1930. Dharmapala reports that doctors want him to remain
        in bed for six months, but he is able to take automobile rides.

        January 26–March 21, 1930. Dharmapala remains very ill, convalesc-
        ing at Maligakanda seminary, writing he has been continuously sick
        for two years.

        May–June 1930. Having moved to Sarnath, Dharmapala writes to the
        Maha Bodhi Society that for the first time since his illness began in
        February 1928 he is slowly improving, although he cannot move freely
        because his legs are still weak.

        Mulagandhakuti vihara nears completion. Dharmapala gives the name
        Mulagandhakuti to the vihara after the monastery in which the Lord
        Buddha first resided.

        Dharmapala suggests celebrating the parinirvana of Sariputta and
        Moggallana by Maha Bodhi Society in Lanka and India.

        December 19, 1930. Mary Foster dies.

1931   Dharmapala returns to Colombo for the last time and establishes the
        Anagarika Dharmapala Trust.

        March 10, 1931. Borne in a chair to the steamer, Dharmapala returns
        to Calcutta and leaves for Sarnath two weeks later.

        May 1931. Dharmapala makes plans to establish an International Bud-
        dhist Institute to train students from all parts of the Buddhist world.

        July 13, 1931. Ven. Boruggamuve Rewatha robes Dharmapala as a
        samanera. Dharmapala takes the name Sri Devamitta Dhammapala.

        August 1931. Dharmapala takes train to Calcutta to oversee the ac-
        tivities of the Maha Bodhi Society, gives three speeches, and returns to
        Sarnath on September 2.

        November 11, 1931. Inauguration of the Mulagandhakuti vihara.
        Tagore speaks. Director general of the Archeological Department,
        Rai Bahadur Dayaram Sahini, representing Lord Willingdon, presents
        relics to Maha Bodhi Society. In evening Dharmapala addresses public
        meeting of a thousand, and on following day three bo tree saplings are
        planted.

        Representing the British Maha Bodhi Society, B. L. Boughton offers
        Rs. 10,000 as a personal donation to bring Japanese artist to paint fres-
        coes on the walls of the vihara.

1932   March 11, 1932. Dharmapala visits Bodh Gaya for first time in many
        years.

        May–June 1932. Dharmapala falls ill with a chill leading to bronchitis.
        His condition improves in June.

December 1932. Dharmapala falls ill again, living on orange juice and three cups of Nestlé's milk food a day.

1933   January 16, 1933. M. Siddharta, Anunayake of Malwatte, two principals of Vidyodaya and Vidyalankara, and ten other monks give Dharmapala higher ordination.

Near death, Dharmapala survives on liquid diet.

April 26, 1933. Raja Hewavitarne arrives from Colombo and summons bhikkhus to chant pirit during night until Dharmapala dies gazing at Isipatana on April 29.

Two weeks after his death, Dharmapala's ashes are taken by train to South India, by steamship to Talaimannar, by train to Colombo, and conveyed in a procession to Maligakanda.

BIBLIOGRAPHY

Abhayasundere, Praneeth. *Brahmachari Walisinghe Harischandra*. Colombo: Department of Cultural Affairs, 2000.

Agarwal, C. V. *The Buddhist and Theosophical Movements, 1873–2001*. Calcutta: Maha Bodhi Society of India, 2001.

Allen, Charles. *The Buddha and Dr. Führer: An Archaeological Scandal*. London: Haus, 2008.

Almond, Philip. *The British Discovery of Buddhism*. Cambridge: Cambridge University Press, 1988.

Amerasekera, Gunadasa. *Dharmapala Marksvadida?* [Was Dharmapala a Marxist?]. Colombo: M. D. Gunasena, 1980.

Amstutz, Galen. *Interpreting Amida: History and Orientalism in the Study of Pure Land Buddhism*. Albany: State University of New York Press, 1997.

Amunugama, Sarath. "Anagarika Dharmapala (1864–1933) and the Transformation of Sinhalese Buddhist Organization in a Colonial State." *Social Science Information* 24, no. 4 (1985): 697–730.

———. "A Sinhalese Buddhist 'Babu': Anagarika Dharmapala (1864–1933) and the Bengal Connection." *Social Science Information* 30, no. 3 (1991): 555–91.

Anderson, Benedict. *Imagined Communities: Reflections on the Origin and Spread of Nationalism*. London: Verso, 1987.

Andrews, C. F. *The Renaissance in India*. London: Church Missionary Society, 1912.

Appadurai, Arjun. "Here and Now." In *Modernity at Large: Cultural Dimensions of Globalization*, 1–23. Minneapolis: University of Minnesota Press, 1996.

———. *Worship and Conflict under Colonial Rule: A South Indian Case*. New York: Cambridge University Press, 1981.

Aravamudan, Srinivas. *Guru English: South Asian Religion in a Cosmopolitan Language*. Princeton, NJ: Princeton University Press, 2006.

Arnold, Edwin. *India Revisited*. London: Kegan, Paul, Trench, Trübner, 1886.

———. *The Light of Asia; or, The Great Renunciation: The Life and Teaching of Gautama, Prince of India and Founder of Buddhism*. New York: A. L. Burt, 1879.

473

Aston, W. G., trans. *Nihongi: Chronicles of Japan from the Earliest Times to A.D. 697.* 1896. Reprint, Oxford: Oxford University Press, 1956.

Aurobindo, Sri. *On Himself.* Pondicherry: Aurobindo Ashram, 1989.

Ballantyne, Tony. "Race and the Webs of Empire: Aryanism from India to the Pacific." *Journal of Colonialism and Colonial History* 2 (2001): 31.

Banerjea, Surendranath. *A Nation in Making: Being the Reminiscences of Fifty Years of Public Life.* 1925. Reprint, Calcutta: Paschimbanga Bangla Akademi, 1998.

Banerjee, Sukanya. *Becoming Imperial Citizens: Indians in Late-Victorian Empire.* Durham, NC: Duke University, 2010.

A. T. Barker, trans. and ed. *The Mahatma Letters to A. P. Sinnett from the Mahatmas M. & K.H.* (Pasadena, CA: Theosophical University Press, 1926).

Barnett, Yukiko Sumi. "Indian in Asia: Okawa Shumei's Pan-Asian Thought and His Idea of India in Early Twentieth-Century Japan." *Journal of the Oxford University History Society* 1 (2004): 1–23.

Bartholomeusz, Tessa. "Real Life and Romance: The Life of Miranda de Souza Canavarro." *Journal of Feminist Studies in Religion* 10, no. 2 (1994): 27–47.

———. *Women under the Bo Tree: Buddhist Nuns in Sri Lanka.* Cambridge: Cambridge University Press, 1997.

Barua, Dipak Kumar. *Buddha Gaya Temple: Its History.* Buddha Gaya: Buddha Gaya Temple Management Committee, 1981.

Barua, Kitish Chandra. "The Late Dr. Sri Rama Chandra Baruya." *Journal of the Maha Bodhi Society* 31 (1923): 108–10.

Basu, Sankara Prasad, ed. *Letters of Sister Nivedita.* 2 vols. Calcutta: Nababharat, 1982.

Basu, Shankara Prasad, and Sunil Bihari Ghosh, eds. *Vivekananda in Indian Newspapers, 1893–1902.* Calcutta: Bookland and Modern Book Agency, 1969.

Bayly, C. A. *The Birth of the Modern World: 1780–1914.* Malden, MA: Blackwell, 2004.

———. *Imperial Meridian: The British Empire and the World, 1780–1830.* London: Longman, 1989.

———. *Rulers, Townsmen, and Bazaars: North Indian Society in the Age of British Expansion, 1770–1870.* New York: Cambridge University Press, 1983.

Bechert, Heinz, and Richard Gombrich. "The Buddhist Way." In *The World of Buddhism: Buddhist Monks and Nuns in Society and Culture,* edited by Heinz Bechert and Richard Gombrich, 9–14. London: Thames and Hudson, 1984.

Behal, Rana P., and Prabhu P. Mohapatra. "'Tea and Money versus Human Life': The Rise and Fall of the Indenture System in the Assam Tea Plantations, 1840–1908." *Journal of Peasant Studies* 19, nos. 3–4 (1992): 142–72.

Bevir, Mark. "Theosophy and the Origins of the Indian National Congress." *International Journal of Hindu Studies* 7, nos. 1–3 (2003): 99–115.

Bharucha, Rustom. *Another Asia: Rabindranath Tagore and Okakura Tenshin.* Oxford: Oxford University Press, 2006.

Biswas, Arun Kumar. *Buddha and Bodhisattva: A Hindu View.* New Delhi: Cosmo, 1987.

Blackburn, Anne. *Locations of Buddhism: Colonialism and Modernity in Sri Lanka.* Chicago: University of Chicago Press, 2010.

Blavatsky, H. P. *The Secret Doctrine: The Synthesis of Science, Religion, and Philosophy.* 6 vols. London: Theosophical Publishers, 1971.

———. *Isis Unveiled: Collected Writings, 1877*. Rev. and corr. ed. Wheaton, IL.: Theosophical Publishing House, 1972.

Blyth, James. *Juicy Joe: A Romance of the Norfolk Marshlands*. London: Grant Richards, 1903.

Bose, Arun Coomer. *Indian Revolutionaries Abroad, 1905–1922, in the Background of International Developments*. Patna: Bharati Bhawan, 1971.

Brekke, Torkel. *Makers of Modern Indian Religion in the Late Nineteenth Century*. Oxford: Oxford University Press, 2002.

Bromfield, John. *Elite Conflict in a Plural Society: Twentieth-Century Bengal*. Berkeley: University of California Press, 1968.

Buchanan, Francis. *An Account of the Districts of Bihar and Patna in 1811–1812*. 2 vols. 1936. Reprint, New Delhi: Usha Jain, 1986.

Buddhaghosa, Bhadantacariya. *The Path of Purification: Visuddhimagga*. Translated by Bhikkhu Nyanamoli. Berkeley, CA: Shambhala, 1976.

Cannadine, David. *Ornamentalism: How the British Saw Their Empire*. New York: Oxford University Press, 2001.

Chakrabarty, Dipesh. *Provincializing Europe: Postcolonial Thought and Historical Difference*. Princeton, NJ: Princeton University Press, 2000.

Chakravarti, G. N. "Hindu Marriage." *Theosophist* 10 (1888): 53–8.

Chandraprema, C. A. "The J.V.P. and Gunadasa Amerasekera: Two Sinhala Buddhist Tendencies." *Lanka Guardian* 11, no. 8 (August 15, 1988): 15, 24.

Chatterjee, Partha. *The Nation and Its Fragments: Colonial and Postcolonial Histories*. Princeton, NJ: Princeton University Press, 1993.

Chigaku Kouho, ed. *Graphic Biography of Chigaku Tanaka*. Tokyo: Kokuchukai, 1961.

Chiou Yamakawa. "Dharmapala's Visit to Japan in 1902." In *Recollections of Chigaku Tanaka*, edited by Kouho Tanaka, 546–63. Tokyo: Shin-Sekai sha, 1988.

Chowdhury, Hemendu B. *Jagajjyoti Kripasaran Mahathera 125 Birth Anniversary Volume*. Calcutta: Bauddha Dharmankur Sabha, 1990.

Collcutt, Martin. "Buddhism: The Threat of Eradication." In *Japan in Transition: From Tokugawa to Meiji*, edited by Marius B. Jensen and Gilbert Rozman, 143–67. Princeton, NJ: Princeton University Press, 1986.

"Congress of Theosophists." In Houghton, *Neely's History*, 926–28.

Cook, Scott B. "The Irish Raj: Social Origins and Careers of Irishmen in the Indian Civil Service, 1855–1914." *Journal of Social History* 20, no. 3 (1987): 507–29.

Copland, Ian. "Managing Religion in Colonial India: The British Raj and the Bodh Gaya Temple Dispute." *Journal of Church and State* 46, no. 3 (2004): 527–60.

Cotton, Evan. *Calcutta, Old and New: A Historical and Descriptive Handbook to the City*. Calcutta: W. Newman, 1907.

———. *East Indiamen: The East India Company's Maritime Service*. London: Batchworth, 1949.

Cotton, Henry. *Indian and Home Memories*. London: T. Fisher Unwin, 1911.

———. *New India, or India in Transition*. London: Kegan Paul, Trench, Trübner, 1909.

Courtright, Paul, B. "Sati, Sacrifice, and Marriage: The Modernity of Tradition." In *From the Margins of Hindu Marriage: Essays on Gender, Religion, and Culture*, edited by Lindsey Harlan and Paul B. Courtright, 184–203. Oxford: Oxford University Press, 1995.

Cousins, L. S. "Aspects of Esoteric Southern Buddhism." In *Indian Insights: Buddhism, Brahmanism and Bhakti: Papers from the Annual Spalding Symposium on Indian Religion*, edited by Peter Connolly and Sue Hamilton, 185–207. London: Luzac Oriental, 1997.

Crump, Basil. "A Theosophical Criticism of Mrs. Cleather's Books." *Journal of the Maha Bodhi Society* 31, no.12 (1923): 474–81.

Cumpston, Mary. "Some Early Indian Nationalists and Their Allies in the British Parliament, 1851–1906." *English Historical Review* 76, no. 299 (1961): 279–97.

Cunningham, Alexander. *The Bhilsa Topes; or, Buddhist Monuments of Central India.* Varanasi: Indological Book House, 1966.

Danto, Arthur. *Mysticism and Morality: Oriental Thought and Moral Philosophy.* New York: Harper and Row, 1972.

Das, Balindralal. *A Hindu Point of View on the Bodh-Gaya Temple Bill.* Delhi: National Journals Press, 1936.

Davids, Thomas Rhys. *Manual of a Mystic.* London: Pali Text Society, 1916.

Dayananda, H. "The Vihara Proposition in London." *British Buddhist* 1, no. 4 (1927): 3–4.

Dazey, Wade. "Tradition and Modernization in the Organization of Dasanami Samnyasins." In *Monastic Life in the Christian and Hindu Traditions*, edited by Austin B. Creel and Vasudha Narayanan, 281–321. Lewiston, NY: Edwin Mellen, 1990.

De Silva, K. M. *A History of Sri Lanka.* Delhi: Oxford University Press, 1973.

———. "The Reform and Nationalist Movements in the Early Twentieth Century." In *University of Ceylon History of Ceylon*, vol. 3, edited by de Silva, 381–407. Colombo: Colombo Apothecaries, 1973.

De Zirkoff, Boris, ed. *H. P. Blavatsky: Collected Writings, 1883.* Los Angeles: Theosophical Research Society, 1950.

Dhammananda, Ven. Hapugoda. "The Flame in the Darkness." *Weekend*, September 11, 1988.

Dhammapala, Devamitta. "Reminiscences of My Early Life." *Journal of the Maha Bodhi Society* 41, nos. 5–6 (1933): 151–62.

Dharmapala, Anagarika. "Buddhism and Christianity." In Houghton, *Neely's History*, 803–6.

———. "Buddhism in England." *Journal of the Maha Bodhi Society* 34 (1926): 547–52.

———. "Buddhism, Past and Present." In Wright, *Twentieth Century Impressions of Ceylon*, 284–90.

———. The Diaries of Anagarika Dharmapala. Typescript. 36 vols. Maha Bodhi Society, Colombo, Sri Lanka.

———. "European Explorers of Tibet." *Journal of the Maha Bodhi Society* 7 (1899): 115–6.

———. "Good Wishes of Ceylon." In Houghton, *Neely's History*, 60–1.

———. "Is There More Than One Buddhism?" *Open Court*, February 11, 1897.

———. "Japan and India." *Chuo Koron*, June 1902.

———. The Notebooks of Anagarika Dharmapala. Manuscript. 58 vols. Dharmapala Museum, Sarnath, India.

———. "Our Twenty Years' Work." *Journal of the Maha Bodhi Society* 19 (1911): 1–9.

———. "The Place of Women in the Buddhist Church." *Journal of the Maha Bodhi Society* 16 (1908): 32–5.

Dilks, David. *Curzon in India*. 2 vols. London: Taplinger, 1969.

Dirks, Nicholas B. *Castes of Mind: Colonialism and the Making of Modern India*. Princeton, NJ: Princeton University Press, 2001.

Dixon, Joy. "Sexology and the Occult: Sexuality and Subjectivity in Theosophy's New Age." *Journal of the History of Sexuality* 7, no. 3 (1997): 409–33.

Doyle, Tara Nancy. "Bodh Gaya: Journey to the Diamond Throne and the Feet of Gayasur." PhD diss., Harvard University, 1997.

Duara, Prasenjit. "The Discourse of Civilization and Decolonization." *Journal of World History* 15, no. 1 (2004): 1–5.

———. *Rescuing History from the Nation: Questioning Narratives of Modern China*. Chicago: University of Chicago Press, 1995.

Dumont, Louis. "World Renunciation in Indian Religions." In *Religion, Politics, and History in India: Collected Papers in Indian Sociology*, edited by Louis Dumont, 48–60. Paris: Mouton, 1971.

Dutt, Nalinaksha. "The Maha Bodhi Society, Its History and Influence." In *Maha Bodhi Society of India: Diamond Jubilee Souvenir, 1891–1951*, edited by Suniti Kumar Chatterjee, 66–133. Calcutta: Maha Bodhi Society, 1951.

Edwardes, Michael. *The High Noon of Empire: India under Curzon*. London: Eyre and Spottiswoode, 1965.

Eisenstadt, S. N. *The Origins and Diversity of Axial Age Civilizations*. Albany: State University of New York Press, 1986.

Eitel, Ernest. *Buddhism: Its Historical, Theoretical and Popular Aspects*. London: Trübner, 1873.

Elias, Norbert. *The Civilizing Process*. Translated by Edmund Jephcott. New York: Urizen Books, 1978.

———. *The History of Manners*. Translated by Edmund Jephcott. New York: Pantheon, 1982.

Fields, Rick. *How the Swans Came to the Lake: A Narrative History of Buddhism in America*. Boston: Shambhala, 1992.

Frost, Mark. "'Wider Opportunities': Religious Revival, Nationalist Awakening and the Global Dimension in Colombo, 1870–1920." *Modern Asian Studies* 36, no. 4 (2002): 937–67.

Gandhi, Leela. *Affective Communities: Anticolonial Thought, Fin-de-Siècle Radicalism, and the Politics of Friendship*. Durham, NC: Duke University Press, 2006.

Gaya-mahatmya Katha. Gaya: Ramayan Pustakalaya, n.d.

Geary, David. "Destination Enlightenment: Buddhism and the Global Bazaar in Bodh Gaya, Bihar." PhD diss., University of British Columbia, 2009.

Gilmour, David. *Curzon: Imperial Statesmen*. New York: Farrar, Strauss, and Giroux, 1994.

Gombrich, Richard. "The Buddhist Way." In *The World of Buddhism*, edited by Heinz Bechert and Richard Gombrich, 9–14. London: Thames and Hudson, 1984.

———. *Theravada Buddhism: A Social History from Ancient Benares to Modern Colombo*. London: Routledge, 1988.

Gombrich, Richard, and Gananath Obeyesekere. *Buddhism Transformed: Religious Change in Sri Lanka*. Princeton, NJ: Princeton University Press, 1988.

Goodman, Grant. "Dharmapala in Japan, 1913." *Japan Forum* 5, no. 2 (1993): 195–202.

Graf, Susan Johnston. *W. B. Yeats, Twentieth-Century Magus*. York Beach, ME: Samuel Weiser, 2000.

Grapard, Allan G. "Japan's Ignored Cultural Revolution: The Separation of Shinto and Buddhist Divinities in Meiji (*shimbutsu bunri*) and a Case Study, Tonomine." *History of Religions* 23, no. 3 (1984): 240–65.

Graphic Biography of Tanaka Chigaku. Tokyo: Kokuchukai, 1961.

Greene, Jack P., ed. *Exclusionary Empire: English Liberty Overseas, 1600–1900*. Cambridge: Cambridge University Press, 2010.

Guha-Thakurta, Tapati. *Monuments, Objects, Histories: Institutions of Art in Colonial and Postcolonial India*. New York: Columbia University Press, 2004.

Guruge, Ananda W. P. "Anagarika Dharmapala! Thou Shouldst be Living at This Hour." In *An Agenda for the International Buddhist Community*, 244–70. Colombo: Karunaratne and Sons, 1993.

———, ed. *Dharmapala Lipi (Anagarika Dharmapala ge Sinhala Lipi Sangrahayaki)*. Colombo: Government Press, 1965.

———. *From the Living Fountains of Buddhism: Sri Lankan Support to Pioneering Western Orientalists*. Colombo: Ministry of Cultural Affairs, 1984.

———. *Return to Righteousness: A Collection of Speeches, Essays and Letters of the Anagarika Dharmapala*. 1965. Reprint, Colombo: Ministry of Cultural Affairs, 1991.

———. *The Unforgettable Dharmapala: A Miscellany on the Life and Achievements of Anagarika Dharmapala (1864–1933) of Sri Lanka*. Huntington Beach, CA: Ananda W. P. Guruge, 2002.

Guth, Christine M. E. "Charles Longfellow and Okakura Kakuzo: Cultural Cross-Dressing in the Colonial Context." *Positions* 8, no. 3 (2000): 605–36.

Harris, Elizabeth J. *Theravada Buddhism and the British Encounter: Religious, Missionary and Colonial Experience in Nineteenth Century Sri Lanka*. London: Routledge, 2006.

Harvey, Peter. *An Introduction to Buddhism: Teachings, History, and Practice*. Cambridge: Cambridge University Press, 1990.

Holt, John. "Protestant Buddhism?" *Religious Studies Review* 17, no. 4 (1991): 307–12.

Horioka, Yasuko. *The Life of Kakuzo, Author of the Book of Tea*. Tokyo: Hokuseido, 1963.

Horner, I. B. *Buddhavamsa*. London: Pali Text Society, 1975.

Houghton, Walter R. *Neely's History of the Parliament of Religions and Religious Congresses at the World's Columbian Exposition*. Chicago: E. T. Neely, 1893.

Huber, Toni. *The Holy Land Reborn: Pilgrimage & the Tibetan Reinvention of Buddhist India*. Chicago: University of Chicago Press, 2008.

Humphreys, Christmas. *The Development of Buddhism in England*. London: Buddhist Lodge, 1937.

———. "History of Buddhism in the West." *Journal of the Maha Bodhi Society* 54 (1946): 73–83.

———. *Sixty Years of Buddhism in England (1907–1967)*. London: Buddhist Society, 1968.

———. *A Western Approach to Zen*. Wheaton, IL: Theosophical Publishing House, 1971.

————. *What Is Buddhism?* London: Buddhist Lodge, 1928.

————. *Zen Comes West*. Richmond, UK: Curzon, 1977.

Hulugalle, H. A. I. *The Life and Times of Don Richard Wijewardene*. Colombo: Associated Newspapers of Ceylon, 1960.

Hutton, Christopher M., and John E. Joseph. "Back to Blavatsky: The Impact of Theosophy on Modern Linguistics." *Language and Communication* 18 (1998): 181–204.

Jaffe, Richard M. "Buddhist Material Culture, 'Indianism,' and the Construction of Pan-Asian Buddhism in Pre-War Japan." *Material Religion* 2, no. 3 (2006): 266–92.

————. *Neither Monk nor Layman: Clerical Marriage in Modern Japanese Buddhism*. Princeton, NJ: Princeton University Press, 2001.

————. "Seeking Sakyamuni: Travel and the Reconstruction of Japanese Buddhism." *Journal of Japanese Studies* 30, no. 1 (2004): 65–96.

Jayawardana, Lakshman, ed. *Mage Jivita Kathava*. Colombo: Dayawansa Jayakody, 2000.

Jinarajadasa, Curuppumullage, ed. *The Golden Book of the Theosophical Society: A Brief History of the Society's Growth from 1875–1925*. Adyar: Theosophical Publishing House, 1925.

Kahawatte Siri Sumedha, Thero. *Anagarika Dharmapala: A Glorious Life Dedicated to the Cause of Buddhism*. Varanasi: Maha Bodhi Society of India, 1999.

Kant, Immanuel. "The Metaphysics of Morals." In *Kant's Political Writings*, edited by Hans Siegbert Reiss, translated by Hans Reiss, 131–75. Cambridge: Cambridge University Press, 1970.

————. "Towards Perpetual Peace." In *Kant's Political Writings*, edited by Hans Siegbert Reiss, translated by Hans Reiss, 93–130, Cambridge: Cambridge University Press, 1970.

Karpiel, Frank J. "Theosophy, Culture, and Politics in Honolulu, 1890–1920." *Hawaiian Journal of History* 30 (1996): 169–94.

Karunaratne, David. *Anagarika Dharmapala*. Colombo: M. D. Gunasena, 1965.

Kaul, Chandrika. "A New Angle of Vision: The London Press, Governmental Information Management and the Indian Empire, 1900–22." *Contemporary British History* 8, no. 2 (1994): 213–41.

Kaushik, Harish P. *Indian National Movement: The Role of British Liberals*. New Delhi: Criterion, 1986.

Kawanami, Hiroko. "Japanese Nationalism and the Universal *Dharma*." In *Buddhism and Politics in Twentieth-Century Asia*, edited by Ian Harris, 105–26. London: Pinter, 1999.

Kemper, Steven. "Buddhism without Bhikkhus: The Sri Lanka Vinaya Vardana Society." In *Religion and the Legitimation of Power in Sri Lanka*, edited by Bardwell Smith, 212–35. Chambersburg, PA: Anima, 1974.

————. "Dharmapala's Dharmadutha and the Buddhist Ethnoscape." In *Buddhist Missionaries in the Era of Globalization*, edited by Linda Learman, 22–50. Honolulu: University of Hawaii Press, 2005.

————. *The Presence of the Past: Chronicles, Politics, and Culture in Sinhala Life*. Ithaca, NY: Cornell University Press, 1991.

Ketelaar, James. *Of Heretics and Martyrs in Meiji Japan: Buddhism and Its Persecution*. Princeton, NJ: Princeton University Press, 1990.

————. "Strategic Occidentalism: Meiji Buddhists at the World's Parliament of Religion." *Buddhist-Christian Studies* 11 (1911): 37–57.

Khan, Abdul Mabud. "Bangladesh Indebtedness to Myanmar: A Study of Reformation Movement in the Buddhist Sangha of Bangladesh (1856–1971)." *Arakanese Research Journal* 2 (2003): 25–34.

Kinnard, Jacob N. "When the Buddha Sued Visnu." In *Constituting Communities: Theravada Buddhism and the Religious Cultures of South and Southeast Asia*, edited by John Clifford Holt, Jacob Kinnard, and Jonathan S. Walters, 85–106. Albany: State University of New York Press, 2003.

Kloppenberg, Ria. "A Buddhist-Christian Encounter in Sri Lanka: The Panadura Vada." In *Religion: Empirical Studies*, edited by Steven. J. Sutcliffe, 179–91. Aldershot: Ashgate, 2004.

Konen, Tsunemitsu. *Meiji no Bukkyo-sha* (Buddhists in the Meiji Period). Tokyo: Shunjusha, 1968.

Korom, Frank. "'Editing' Dharmaraj: Academic Genealogies of a Bengali Folk Deity." *Western Folklore* 56, no. 1 (1997): 51–77.

Kosei, Ishii. "Dharmapala's Activities in Japan." Unpublished paper.

Laclau, Ernesto. "Universalism, Particularism, and the Question of Identity." *October* 61 (1992): 83–90.

Laroui, Abdullah. *The Crisis of the Arab Intellectual: Traditionalism or Historicism?* Translated by Diarmid Cammel. Berkeley: University of California Press, 1976.

Lee, Edwin. "Nichiren and Nationalism: The Religious Patriotism of Tanaka Chigaku." *Monumenta Nipponica* 30, no. 1 (1975): 19–35.

Leoshko, Janet. "On the Construction of a Buddhist Pilgrimage Site." *Art History* 19, no. 4 (1996): 573–97.

Lessing, Doris. *Walking in the Shade: Volume Two of My Autobiography, 1949–1962.* London: HarperCollins, 1997.

Li Rongxi. *The Life of Hsuan-Tseng: The Tripitaka-Master of the Great Tzu En Monastery.* Beijing: Chinese Buddhist Association, 1993.

Malalgoda, Kitsiri. *Buddhism in Sinhalese Society, 1750–1900.* Berkeley: University of California Press, 1976.

Marshall, P. J. *"A Free Though Conquering People": Eighteenth-Century Britain and Its Empire.* London: Ashgate, 2003.

Masefield, Peter. *Divine Revelation in Pali Buddhism.* London: Allen and Unwin, 1986.

Masters, Patricia. "Mary Foster: The First Hawaiian Buddhist." In *Innovative Buddhist Women: Swimming against the Stream*, edited by Karma Lekshe Tsomo, 25–48. London: Curzon, 2000.

Masuzawa, Tomoko. *The Invention of World Religions; or, How European Universalism Was Preserved in the Language of Pluralism.* Chicago: University of Chicago Press, 2005.

McGilvray, Dennis. "Arabs, Moors, and Muslims: Sri Lankan Muslim Ethnicity in Regional Perspective." *Contributions to Indian Sociology* 32 (1998): 433–83.

McLeod, Hugh. "Protestantism and British National Identity, 1815–1945." In *Nation and Religion: Perspectives on Europe and Asia*, edited by Peter van der Veer and Hartmut Lehmann, 44–70. Princeton, NJ: Princeton University Press, 1999.

Mitra, Rajendralala. *Buddha Gaya: The Hermitage of Sakya Muni.* Calcutta: Bengal
    Secretariat Press, 1878.
Mookerjee, Sameer Chander. *The Decline and Fall of the Hindus: The Book of India's
    Regeneration.* Calcutta: Indian Rationalistic Society, 1919.
Muller, F. H. "Meeting at Darjeeling." Supplement, *Theosophist* 13 (1892): lxxxvii–
    lxxxviii.
Mullin, Katherine. "Typhoid Turnips and Crooked Cucumber." *Modernism/Modernity* 8,
    no. 1 (2001): 77–97.
Murphet, Howard. *Hammer on the Mountain: The Life of Henry Steel Olcott (1832–
    1907).* Wheaton, IL: Theosophical Publishing House, 1972.
———. *When Daylight Comes: A Biography of Helena Petrovna Blavatsky.* Wheaton, IL:
    Theosophical Publishing House, 1975.
Nahar, Pramod Chand, and Krishnachandra Ghosh. *An Epitome of Jainism, Being a
    Critical Study of Its Metaphysics, Ethics, and History, & c. in Relation to Modern
    Thought.* Calcutta: H. Duby, 1917.
Nandiswara, Ellawala. "The Life & Times of a National Hero." *Ceylon Daily News,*
    September 17, 1965.
Nattier, Jan. "The Meanings of the Maitreya Myth: A Typological Analysis." In *Maitreya,
    the Future Buddha,* edited by Alan Sponberg and Helen Hardacre, 23–47. Cambridge:
    Cambridge University Press, 1988.
Nikhilananda, Swami. *Vivekananda: A Biography.* Calcutta: Advaita Ashrama, 1982.
Nivedita, Sister. "Bodh Gaya." In *Complete Works of Sister Nivedita,* 4:193–8.
———. *The Complete Works of Sister Nivedita: Birth Centenary Publication.* 5 vols.
    Calcutta: Sister Nivedita Girls' School, 1967–90.
———. "The Master as I Saw Him." In *Complete Works of Sister Nivedita,* 1:15–272.
———. "The Relation between Buddhism and Hinduism." In *Complete Works of Sister
    Nivedita,* 4: 144–53.
Noguchi Zenshiro. "The Way That Dharmapala, Who Has Passed Away Recently, Came
    to Japan." *Contemporary Buddhism* 106 (1933): 77–82.
———. "Would Win Converts to Buddhism." In Houghton, *Neely's History,* edited by
    Walter Houghton, 156–7. Chicago: F. T. Neely, 1893.
Notefelder, F. G. "On Idealism and Realism in the Thought of Okakura Tenshin." *Journal
    of Japanese Studies* 16, no. 2 (1990): 309–55.
Nussbaum, Martha. "Kant and Cosmopolitanism." In *Perpetual Peace: Essays on Kant's
    Cosmopolitan Ideal,* edited by James Bohman and Matthias Lutz-Bachmann, 25–57.
    Cambridge, MA: MIT Press, 1997.
Obeyesekere, Gananath. "On Buddhist Identity in Sri Lanka." In *Ethnic Identity: Crea-
    tion, Conflict, and Accommodation,* 3rd ed., edited by Lola Romanucci-Ross and
    George A. De Vos, 222–47. Walnut Creek, CA: Altamira, 1995.
———. "Personal Identity and Cultural Crisis: The Case of Anagarika Dharmapala of Sri
    Lanka." In *The Biographical Process: Studies in the History and Psychology of Reli-
    gion,* edited by Frank E. Reynolds and Donald Capps, 221–52. The Hague: Mouton,
    1976.
———. "Religious Symbolism and Political Change in Ceylon." In *The Two Wheels of
    Dhamma: Essays on the Theravada Tradition in India and Ceylon,* edited by Obeye-

sekere, Frank Reynolds, and Bardwell L. Smith, 58–78. Chambersburg, PA: American Academy of Religion, 1972.

O'Connor, Frederick. *On the Frontier and Beyond: A Record of Thirty Years' Service*. London: John Murray, 1931.

O'Donnell, C. J. *The Causes of the Present Discontents in India*. London: T. Fisher Unwin, 1908.

Okakura Kakuzo. *The Ideals of the East with Special Reference to Japan*. London: John Murray, 1903.

———. *Okakura Kakuzo: Collected English Writings*. Edited by Koshiro Okakura, Sunao Nakamura, et al. Tokyo: Heibonsha, 1984.

Olcott, Henry Steel. "The Buddha Rays at Badulla." *Theosophist* 11, no. 125 (1890): ci–cii.

———. *The Buddhist Catechism*. Adyar: Theosophical Publishing House, 1975.

———. "The Buddhist Revival." *Theosophist* 13 (1892): 576–7.

———. "Indian Section Report." *Theosophist* 13 (1892): 20–33.

———. *Old Diary Leaves: The True Story of the Theosophical Society*. 6 vols. Adyar: Theosophical Publishing House, 1895–1935.

———. "A Recent Conversation with the Mahatmas." *Theosophist* 18 (1907): 388.

———. "A Shin-shu Catechism." *Theosophist* 10, no. 120 (1889): 751–3; no. 121 (1889): 9–13; and no. 122 (1889): 89–92.

———. "The Theosophical Society and Its Aims." In *A Collection of Lectures on Theosophy and Archaic Religions*, 1–17. Madras: Theyaga Rajier, 1883.

———. "Theosophy and Buddhism." In *A Collection of Lectures on Theosophy and Archaic Religions, Delivered in India and Ceylon*, edited by Olcott, 26–38. Madras: A. Theyaga Rajier, 1883.

———. "An United Buddhist World." *Theosophist* 13 (1892): 239–43.

———. "The 'Wail' of Dharmapala." Supplement, *Theosophist* 20, no. 7 (1899): xxviii–xxx.

Oldham, Charles E. A. W. Untitled review. *Journal of the Royal Asiatic Society of Great Britain and Ireland* 1 (1928): 169–72.

O'Malley, L. S. S. *Bengal District Gazetteers, Gaya*. Calcutta: Bengal Secretariat Book Depot, 1906.

Parsons, Talcott, ed. *Max Weber: The Theory of Social and Economic Organization*. New York: Free Press, 1947.

Pathak, S. K. "The Maha Bodhi Society in Calcutta—Culture." *Journal of the Maha Bodhi Society* 100, no. 4 (1992): 12–14.

Perriera, Todd Leroy. "Whence Theravada: The Modern Genealogy of an Ancient Term." In *How Theravada Is Theravada? Exploring Buddhist Identities*, edited by Peter Skilling, Jason A. Carbine, Claudio Cicuzza, Santi Pakdeekham, 443–571. Chiang Mai, Thailand: Silkworm Books, 2012.

Perry, Anne Gordon, et al. *Green Acre on the Piscataquis*. Wilmette, IL: Bahai Publishing Trust, 2005.

Pieris, William. *The Western Contribution to Buddhism*. Delhi: Motilal Banarsidass, 1973.

Pinch, William R. "Soldier Monks and Militant Sadhus." In *Contesting the Nation: Religion, Community, and the Politics of Democracy in India*, edited by David Ludden, 140–61. Philadelphia: University of Pennsylvania Press, 1996.

Pollock, Sheldon. "Ramayana and Political Imagination in India." *Journal of Asian Studies* 52, no. 2 (1993): 261–97.

Popplewell, Richard. *Intelligence and Imperial Defence: British Intelligence and the Defence of the Indian Empire, 1904–1924.* London: Frank Cass, 1995.

Prothero, Stephen. "Henry Steel Olcott and 'Protestant Buddhism.'" *Journal of the American Academy of Religion* 63, no. 2 (1995): 281–302.

———. *The White Buddhist: The Asian Odyssey of Henry Steel Olcott.* Bloomington: Indiana University Press, 1996.

Ratnatunga, Sinha. *They Turned the Tide: The 100 Year History of the Maha Bodhi Society of Sri Lanka.* Colombo: Government Press, 1991.

Reed, Edward. *Japan: Its History, Traditions, and Religions.* London: John Murray, 1880.

Reymond, Lizelle. *The Dedicated: A Biography of Nivedita.* New York: John Day, 1953.

Reynolds, Frank E. "The Two Wheels of Dhamma: A Study of Early Buddhism." In *The Two Wheels of Dhamma: Essays on the Theravada Tradition in India and Ceylon,* ed. Gananath Obeyesekere, Reynolds, and Bardwell L. Smith, 6–30. Chambersburg, PA: American Academy of Religion, 1972.

Reynolds, Frank E., and Charles Hallisey. "Buddhism." In *Encyclopedia of Religion,* 2nd ed., edited by Lindsay Jones, 1087–1101. Detroit: Thomson/Gale, 2005.

Roberts, Michael. "Himself and Project. A Serial Autobiography. Our Journey with a Zealot, Anagarika Dharmapala." *Social Analysis* 44, no. 1 (2000): 113–41.

Rogers, Minor L., and Ann T. Rogers. "The Honganji: Guardian of the State (1868–1945)." *Japanese Journal of Religious Studies* 17, no. 1 (1990): 3–28.

Ronaldshay, Earl of. *The Life of Lord Curzon.* New York: Boni and Liveright, 1928.

Saddhananda, N. "Revival of Buddhism in India." *Journal of the Maha Bodhi Society* 7, no. 3 (1898): 20.

Sangharakshita, Bhikshu. "Anagarika Dharmapala: A Biographical Sketch." In *Maha Bodhi Society of India Diamond Jubilee Souvenir, 1891–1951,* 9–65. Calcutta: Sri Gouranga, 1952.

Saradananda, Swami. *Notes of Some Wanderings with the Swami Vivekananda.* Calcutta: Urbodhan, 1913.

———. *Sri Ramakrishna: The Great Master.* Madras: Sri Ramakrishna Math, 1979.

Saranamkara, Ganegama. *Jatiya Piya ha Anagarika Dharmapala* [The father of the nation or Anagarika Dharmapala]. N.p., n.d.

Sarkar, Sumit. "'Kaliyuga,' 'Chakri' and 'Bhakti.'" *Economic and Political Weekly* 27, no. 29 (1992): 1543–59, 1561–6.

Sarkisyanz, E. *Buddhist Backgrounds of the Burmese Revolution.* The Hague: Nijhoff, 1965.

Schor, Naomi. "The Crisis of French Universalism." *Yale French Studies* 100 (2001): 43–64.

Seal, Anil. *The Emergence of Indian Nationalism: Competition and Collaboration in the Later Nineteenth Century.* London: Cambridge University Press, 1968.

Sears, Laurie J. "Intellectuals, Theosophy, and Failed Narratives of the Nation in Late Colonial Java." In *A Companion to Postcolonial Studies,* edited by Henry Schwartz and Sangeeta Ray, 333–57. London: Blackwell, 2000.

Sen, Amiya P. *Swami Vivekananda.* Oxford: Oxford University Press, 2000.

Sen, Keshab Chandra. *Diary in Ceylon from 27th September to 5th November 1859.* Calcutta: Brahmo Tract Society, 1888.

Sen, Satyendra Nath. "Buddhism in Its Relationship to Hinduism." Foreword to *The Anagarika Brahmachari Dharmapala*. Calcutta: Maha Bodhi Society, 1918.

Sen, Sri Chandra. "The Ven'ble Sri Devamitta Dhammapala." *Journal of the Maha Bodhi Society* 41, (1933): 326–57.

Seneviratne, H. L. *The Work of Kings: The New Buddhism in Sri Lanka*. Chicago: University of Chicago Press, 1999.

Sharf, Robert. "The Zen of Japanese Nationalism." In *Curators of the Buddha: The Study of Buddhism under Colonialism*, edited by Donald S. Lopez, 107–60. Chicago: University of Chicago Press, 1995.

Shastri, Haraprasad. *Discovery of Living Buddhism in Bengal*. Calcutta: Sanskrit Press Depository, 1897.

Shibata, Reuchi. "Speech of the Rt. Rev. Reuchi Shibata." In *The World's Parliament of Religions*, edited by John Henry Burrows, 1:90–2. Chicago: Parliament, 1893.

Sil, Narasingha P. *Swami Vivekananda: A Reassessment*. Selinsgrove, PA: Susquehanna University Press, 1997.

Silvestri, Michael. "'The Sinn Fein of India': Irish Nationalism and the Policing of Revolutionary Bengal." *Journal of British Studies* 39, no. 4 (2000): 454–86.

Singh Bahadur, Rai Ram Anugraha Narain. *A Brief History of the Bodh Gaya Math, District Gaya*. Calcutta: Bengal Secretariat Press, 1893.

Singh, St. Nihal. "This Journal." *Journal of the Maha Bodhi Society* 100, no. 4 (1992): 30–33.

Sinha, Mrinalini. *Colonial Masculinity: The "Manly Englishman" and the "Effeminate Bengali" in the Late Nineteenth Century*. Manchester: Manchester University Press, 1995.

Sinnett, A. P. *Occult World*. London: Theosophical Publishing House, 1984.

———. *The Mahatma Letters to A. P. Sinnett from the Mahatmas M. & K. H.* Transcribed by A. T. Barker. Pasadena: Theosophical University Press, 1926.

Snodgrass, Judith. "Discourse, Authority, Demand: The Politics of Early English Publications on Buddhism." In *TransBuddhism: Transmission, Translation, Transformation*, edited by Nalini Bhushan, Jay L. Garfield, and Abraham Zablocki, 21–41. Amherst: University of Massachusetts Press, 2009.

———. "Performing Modernity: The Lumbini Project, Tokyo 1925." *Journal of Religious History* 33, no. 2 (2009): 133–48.

———. *Presenting Japanese Buddhism to the West: Orientalism, Occidentalism, and the Columbian Exposition*. Chapel Hill: University of North Carolina Press, 2003.

Staggs, Kathleen M. "Defend the Nation and Love the Truth: Inoue Enryo and the Revival of Meiji Buddhism." *Monumenta Nipponica* 38, no. 3 (1983): 251–281.

Stevenson. Mrs. Sinclair. *Heart of Jainism*. London: Humphrey Milford, Oxford University Press, 1915.

Stone, Jacqueline I. "Placing Nichiren in the 'Big Picture': Some Ongoing Issues in Scholarship." *Japanese Journal of Religious Studies* 26, nos. 3–4 (1999): 383–421.

———. "Realizing This World as the Buddha Land." In *Readings of the Lotus Sutra*, edited by Stephen F. Teiser and Stone, 209–36. New York: Columbia University Press, 2009.

———. "Rebuking the Enemies of the Lotus: Nichiren Exclusivism in Historical Perspective." *Japanese Journal of Religious Studies* 21, nos. 2–3 (June–September 1994): 231–59.

Strong, John. "The Legend of the Lion-Roarer: A Study of the Buddhist Arhat Pindola Bharadvaja." *Numen* 26 (1979): 50–88.

Suzuki, D. T. *Essays in Zen Buddhism*. London: Luzac, 1927.

Tagare, G. V., ed., *Vayu Purana*, part 2, in *Ancient Indian Tradition & Mythology*, vol. 38, edited by G. P. Bhatt. Delhi: Motilal Banarsidass, 1988.

Tagore, Surendranath. "Kakuzo Okakura: Some Reminiscences by Surendranath Tagore." In *Okakura Kakuzo: Collected English Writings*, edited by Okakura Kakuzo et al., 3:233–42. Tokyo: Heibonsha, 1984.

Takakusu, Junjiro. "Buddhism as We Find It in Japan." *Transactions and Proceedings of the Japan Society* 7 (1905–7): 264–79.

Tambiah, S. J. *Buddhism Betrayed: Religion, Politics, and Violence in Sri Lanka*. Chicago: University of Chicago Press, 1992.

———. "The Ideology of Merit and the Social Correlates of Buddhism in a Thai Village." In *Dialectic in Practical Religion*, edited by E. R. Leach, 41–121. Cambridge: Cambridge University Press, 1968.

———. *World Conqueror and World Renouncer: A Study of Buddhism and Polity in Thailand against a Historical Background*. Cambridge: Cambridge University Press, 1976.

Tanabe, George J. "Tanaka Chigaku: The Lotus Sutra and the Body Politic." In *The Lotus Sutra in Japanese Culture*, edited by George J. Tanabe and Willa Jane Tanabe, 191–208. Honolulu: University of Hawaii Press, 1989.

Tanaka Chigaku. "Dharmapala's Visit to Japan: After I Preached." In *Tanaka Chigaku's Autobiography*, 251–60. Tokyo: Shishi Obunko, 1977.

———. "Texts about Budh Gaya and Buddha." *National Magazine*, 131–2, 1904.

Thapar, Romila. "The Theory of Aryan Race and India: History and Politics." *Social Scientist* 24 (1996): 3–29.

Thelle, Notto. *Buddhism and Christianity in Japan: From Conflict to Dialogue, 1854–1899*. Honolulu: University of Hawaii Press, 1987.

Thornton, E. L. R. "God Save the King." *Hindu*. Reprinted in *Journal of the Maha Society* 20, no. 1 (1912): 22.

Toki Horin [Toki Horyu]. "Buddhism in Japan." In *The World's Parliament of Religions: An Illustrated and Popular Story of the World's First Parliament of Religions*, 2 vols., edited by John Henry Barrows, 1:543–52. Chicago: Parliament, 1893.

———. "What Buddhism Has Done for Japan." In Houghton, *Neely's History*, 779–81.

Trautmann, Thomas. R. *Aryans and British India*. Berkeley: University of California Press, 1997.

Trevithick, Alan. *The Revival of Buddhist Pilgrimage at Bodh Gaya*. Delhi: Motilal Banarsidass, 2006.

———. "The Theosophical Society and Its Subaltern Acolytes (1880–1986)." *Marburg Journal of Religion* 13, no. 1 (May 2008). http://archiv.ub.uni-marburg.de/mjr/art_trevithick_2008.html.

Tweed, Thomas A. "Inclusivism and the Spiritual Journey of Marie de Souza Canavarro (1849–1933)." *Religion* 24, no. 1 (1994): 43–58.

Van der Veer, Peter. *Imperial Encounters: Religion and Modernity in India and Britain.* Princeton, NJ: Princeton University Press, 2001.

Vicziany, Marika. "Imperialism, Botany and Statistics in Early Nineteenth-Century India: The Surveys of Francis Buchanan (1762–1829)." *Modern Asian Studies* 20, no. 4 (1986): 625–60.

Visvanathan, Gauri. *Outside the Fold: Conversion, Modernity, and Belief.* Princeton, NJ: Princeton University Press, 1998.

Vivekananda, Swami. *The Complete Works of Swami Vivekananda.* 8 vols. Calcutta: Advaita Ashrama, 1977.

———. "Hinduism as a Religion." In Houghton, *Neely's History,* 438–45.

———. *The Ideal of Universal Religion.* New York: n.p., 1896.

Washington, Peter. *Madame Blavatsky's Baboon: A History of the Mystics, Mediums, and Misfits Who Brought Spiritualism to America.* New York: Schocken Books, 1995.

Welch, Holmes. *The Buddhist Revival in China.* Cambridge, MA: Harvard University Press, 1968.

Wickramasinghe, Nira. *Dressing the Colonised Body: Politics, Clothing, and Identity in Colonial Sri Lanka.* New Delhi: Orient Longman, 2003.

Wickremasinghe, D. M. de Z. *The Catalogue of the Sinhalese Manuscripts in the British Museum.* London: British Museum, 1900.

Wickremeratne, L. Ananda. "Annie Besant, Theosophism and Buddhist Nationalism in Sri Lanka." *Ceylon Journal of the Historical and Social Sciences* 6 (1976): 62–79.

———. *The Genesis of an Orientalist: Thomas William Rhys Davids in Sri Lanka.* New Delhi: South Asia Books, 1985.

Wijesekera, Nandadeva. *Sir D. B. Jayatilaka.* Colombo: n.p., 1973.

Wipulasara, Mapalagama, ed. *The Maha Bodhi Centenary Volume, 1891–1991.* Calcutta: Maha Bodhi Society, 1991.

Wiswa Warnapala, W. A. "Sangha and Politics in Sri Lanka: Nature of the Continuing Controversy." *Indian Journal of Politics* 12, nos. 1–2 (1978): 66–76.

———. *Udakendawala Siri Saranankara: An Assessment of His Role in the Anti-Imperialist Struggle in Sri Lanka.* Colombo: Godage, 2002.

Wright, Arnold. *Twentieth Century Impressions of Ceylon: Its History, People, Commerce, Industries, and Resources,* London: Lloyd's Greater Britain, 1907.

Yamakawa, Kazushige. "Dharmapala and Japan: His First and Second Visits." *Journal of Pali and Buddhist Studies* 14 (2000): 43–52.

Yeats-Brown, F. "A Buddhist in Bayswater." *Journal of the Maha Bodhi Society* 34, nos. 4–5 (1926): 221–4.

Yoshino Kosaku. *Cultural Nationalism in Contemporary Japan: A Sociological Enquiry.* London: Routledge, 1992.

Young, R. F., and G. P. V. Somaratna. *Vain Debates: The Buddhist-Christian Controversies of Nineteenth-Century Ceylon.* Vienna: Sammlung De Nobili, 1996.

Zengi Kusunagi. *Shaku Unsho.* Vol. 1. Tokyo: Tokukyokai, 1913.

Page numbers followed by an *f* indicate a figure.